The Definitive Guide to SUSE Linux Enterprise Server 12

Sander van Vugt

Apress®

The Definitive Guide to SUSE Linux Enterprise Server 12

ISBN-13 (pbk): 978-1-4302-6821-5

ISBN-13 (electronic): 978-1-4302-6820-8

Managing Director: Welmoed Spahr
Lead Editor: Michelle Lowman
Production Editor: Douglas Pundick
Technical Reviewer: Stewart Watkiss
Editorial Board: Steve Anglin, Mark Beckner, Ewan Buckingham, Gary Cornell, Louise Corrigan,
    Jim DeWolf, Jonathan Gennick, Robert Hutchinson, Michelle Lowman, James Markham, Matthew Moodie,
    Jeff Olson, Jeffrey Pepper, Douglas Pundick, Ben Renow-Clarke, Dominic Shakeshaft, Gwenan Spearing,
    Matt Wade, Steve Weiss
Coordinating Editor: Kevin Walter
Copy Editor: Michael G. Laraque
Compositor: SPi Global
Indexer: SPi Global
Artist: SPi Global
Cover Designer: Anna Ishchenko

Distributed to the book trade worldwide by Springer Science+Business Media New York, 233 Spring Street, 6th Floor, New York, NY 10013. Phone 1-800-SPRINGER, fax (201) 348-4505, e-mail orders-ny@springer-sbm.com, or visit www.springeronline.com. Apress Media, LLC is a California LLC and the sole member (owner) is Springer Science + Business Media Finance Inc (SSBM Finance Inc). SSBM Finance Inc is a Delaware corporation.

For information on translations, please e-mail rights@apress.com, or visit www.apress.com.

Apress and friends of ED books may be purchased in bulk for academic, corporate, or promotional use. eBook versions and licenses are also available for most titles. For more information, reference our Special Bulk Sales–eBook Licensing web page at www.apress.com/bulk-sales.

Any source code or other supplementary material referenced by the author in this text is available to readers at www.apress.com. For detailed information about how to locate your book's source code, go to www.apress.com/source-code.

This book is dedicated to Alex. It's the joy in your eyes that inspires me to do great things in my life.

Contents at a Glance

Contents

About the Author

Sander van Vugt is a Linux expert working from the Netherlands as an author, technical trainer, and consultant for clients around the world. Sander has published several books about different Linux distributions and is a regular contributor to major international Linux-related web sites. As a consultant, he is specialized in Linux high availability and performance optimization. As a technical trainer, Sander is an authorized trainer for SUSE Linux Enterprise Server and Red Hat Enterprise Linux. More information about the author can be found at his web site at www.sandervanvugt.com.

About the Technical Reviewer

Stewart Watkiss graduated from the University of Hull, UK, with a master's degree in electronic engineering. He has been a Linux user since first installing it on a home computer during the late 1990s. Stewart has worked in the IT industry for 18 years, including positions in computer networking, IT security, and as a Linux system administrator.

While working as a Linux system administrator, he was awarded Advanced Linux Certification (LPIC 2) in 2006 and Novell Certified Linux Administrator for SUSE Linux Enterprise 11 in 2010. He created the PenguinTutor web site to help others learning Linux and working toward Linux certification (www.penguintutor.com).

Stewart also volunteers as a STEM ambassador, going into local schools to help support the teachers and to teach programming to teachers and children.

About the Technical Reviewer

Acknowledgments

First, I want to thank Dominic Shakeshaft and Michelle Lowman, for their willingness to publish this book. I also want to thank Kevin Walter, who has helped me throughout the long road that has lead to the realization of the first draft of all chapters being ready, even before the final software was realized. This is the 59th book I have written and the very first time that the rough version of the book was ready before the software! Kevin, if you had not pushed me at the right moments, this would never have happened! I also want to thank technical editor Stewart Watkiss and Michael G. Laraque for their excellent work, which has helped improve the quality of this book.

Apart from the people at Apress, I'd like to thank those at SUSE who have helped me get the software and information I needed to realize the book. A special thanks to Matthias Eckermann, product manager of SLES, who has played an important role in this process, and to Gábor Nyers, who provided me with excellent information that has lead to the chapter about SELinux.

I also want to thank the people at Kiabi in Lille, France. It was while instructing them in early 2014 that I got the inspiration to start writing the chapter about high availability, which motivated me to add 17 other chapters as well, which has lead to the book in front of you.

Finally, I want to thank my son Franck for helping with the line art in this book. Keep on doing that, and I'm sure you'll be a great graphic artist!

Introduction

This book is about SUSE Linux Enterprise Server 12. It is intended for readers who already have basic Linux skills, so you won't find information on how to perform really basic tasks. Some elementary skills are briefly explained, after which, in a total of 18 chapters, the specifics of working with SUSE Linux Enterprise Server are touched upon.

While writing this book, I have decided it should not be just any generic Linux book that happens by accident to be about SUSE Linux Enterprise Server. Instead, I have focused on those tasks that are essential for Linux professionals who need to know how specific tasks are performed in an SUSE environment. That is why the SUSE administration tool YaST plays an important role in this book. YaST was developed to make administering SUSE Linux easy. In previous versions of SUSE Linux, YaST had a bad reputation, as on some occasions, it had overwritten configurations that the administrator had carefully built manually. On SUSE Linux Enterprise Server (SLES) 12 that doesn't happen anymore, and that is why YaST provides an excellent tool to build the basic configurations that are needed to do whatever you want to do on your Linux server. That is why many chapters begin with an explanation of how tasks are accomplished through YaST.

I am also aware, however, that using YaST alone is not sufficient to build a fully functional SLES server. That is why after explaining how to accomplish tasks with YaST, you'll learn which processes and configuration files are used behind them, which allows you to manually create the exact configuration you require to accomplish whatever you need to accomplish on your server.

As I am a technical trainer myself, I have also included exercises throughout this book. These exercises help readers apply newly acquired skills in SLES and also help those who are preparing for the SUSE CLA and CLP exams. I have not written this book as a complete course manual for these exams, however, although it will serve as an excellent guide to preparing for these exams.

This book is organized in four different parts. The first parts briefly touch on basic skills. In Chapter 1, you'll learn how SUSE relates to other Linux distributions, and Chapter 2 covers the SUSE Linux Management basics. In this chapter, you'll learn how YaST is organized and what you can do to make the best possible use of it.

The second part is about Linux administration basics. You'll first learn about file systems, including the new Btrfs file system and its features, in Chapter 3. Following that, you'll learn how to create users, configure permissions, apply common tasks, and harden SLES. The last two chapters in this section are about virtualization and management of hardware, the kernel, and the boot procedure, which includes the new systems process that takes care of everything that happens while booting.

The third part is about networking SLES. You'll learn how to use the new wicked tool to configure networking and how to set up essential services that are used in a network context, including firewalling, SSL managing, DNS, DHCP, LDAP, LAMP, NFS, and FTP. This section should help you get going, no matter which network services you want to configure.

The fourth and final part of this book is about advanced administration tasks. You'll learn how to write and read shell scripts, how to optimize performance, how to build a high-availability cluster, how to configure an installation server, and how to manage SUSE Linux using SUSE Manager.

PART I

Basic Skills

CHAPTER 1

■ ■ ■

Introduction and Installation

In this chapter, you'll learn about SUSE Linux Enterprise 12 and how to install it. You'll read how it relates to other versions of SUSE Linux and how modules are used to deliver functionality in a flexible way.

Understanding SUSE Linux Enterprise

Linux is an open source operating system. That means that the programs are available for free and that anyone can install Linux without having to pay for it. It also means that the source code for all software in Linux is freely available. There are no secrets in open source. Because of this freedom, Linux features can be used by anyone and implemented in a specific way by anyone, as long as the source code remains open.

To work with Linux, users can gather software themselves and install all programs for themselves. That is a lot of work and is why, since the earliest days of Linux, distributions have been offered. A distribution is a collection of Linux packages that is offered with an installation program, to make working with the distribution easy. One of these distributions is SUSE. Other distributions that currently are often used include Ubuntu and Red Hat.

SUSE (which stands for *Software und System Entwicklung*—Software and Systems Development) was founded in Germany in September 1992 and, as such, is one of the oldest Linux distributions available. When it was purchased by Novell in 2004, SUSE rapidly became one of the leading enterprise Linux distributions.

Versions of SUSE

Currently, there are two branches of SUSE Linux. openSUSE is the pure open source version of SUSE. It is available for free and is released on a regular basis. In openSUSE, new features and programs are tested before they find their way to SUSE Linux Enterprise.

openSUSE provides a very decent operating system, but it was never meant to be an enterprise operating system. One of the reasons is that a version of openSUSE is not maintained very long, meaning that openSUSE users have to upgrade to a newer version of the operating system after a relatively short period. openSUSE, however, is an excellent operating system for professionals who are working with Linux. It allows them to explore new features before they are brought to market in a new version of SUSE Linux Enterprise.

SUSE also provides a branch of the operating system for enterprise use. This branch is known as SUSE Linux Enterprise. Two main versions of SUSE Linux Enterprise are available: SUSE Linux Enterprise Server (SLES) and SUSE Linux Enterprise Desktop (SLED).

In the past, some serious attempts have been made to make Linux into a desktop operating system. That, however, never became a large-scale success. On the server, however, SUSE Linux has become an important player, being used by small and large companies all over the world.

About Supported Linux

An important difference between SUSE Linux Enterprise and openSUSE is that SUSE Linux Enterprise is supported. That is also why customers are paying for SUSE Linux Enterprise, even if it can be downloaded and installed for free. The support of SUSE Linux Enterprise includes a few important features that are essential for corporate IT.

- SUSE is certified for specific hardware. That means that hardware vendors certify their platform for SUSE Linux Enterprise. So, if a customer gets in trouble on specific hardware, he or she will receive help, even if the hardware runs SUSE Linux Enterprise. Also, hardware vendors are knowledgeable about SUSE Linux Enterprise, so customers can get assistance from that side, in case of problems.

- Specific applications are certified for use on SUSE Linux Enterprise. If a company wants to run business applications on Linux, it is important that the business application is well integrated with Linux. That is what running a supported application means. More than 5,000 applications are certified for SUSE Linux Enterprise, which means that if a user has problems with the application, the application vendor will be able to offer support, because it is used on a known and supported platform.

- Updates are verified and guaranteed. On a new version of SUSE Linux Enterprise, updates will be provided for a period of seven years, after which an additional five years of extended support is available. That means that SUSE Linux Enterprise can be used for twelve years, thus guaranteeing that business customers don't have to perform any upgrade of the software in the meantime.

- Support also means that SUSE offers direct help to customers who are having trouble. Different levels of support are available, from e-mail support, which is available for a relatively low price, up to premium support from engineers who will contact clients within a few hours.

Working with SUSE Linux Enterprise 12 Modules

In SLE 12, SUSE has introduced modules. Modules consist of specific software solutions, but with a custom life cycle. By working with modules, SUSE makes it easier to provide updates on specific software. A module is not a new way of selling solutions. Software that was included in earlier versions of SLE is still included in SLE 12. A module, however, is a collection of software packages with a common-use case, a common support status, and a common life cycle. This makes sense, because for some modules, a support life cycle of ten years is too much. Public cloud management software, for example, is developing very fast, as is the case for solutions such as web and scripting. By putting these in modules, SUSE makes it possible to provide updates on versions that are providing new functionality, without breaking the generic support status of SUSE Linux Enterprise.

Currently, SUSE is providing modules for different solutions, including the following:

- Scripting languages, such as PHP, Python, and Ruby on Rails

- UNIX legacy, such as sendmail, old IMAP, and old Java

- Public cloud integration tools

- Advanced systems management

While installing SLE, these modules can be selected in the Extension Selection option. At the time of writing, modules were provided not as an ISO image but via online repositories only, although this policy might change.

Aside from the modules that are provided as an integrated part, there are extensions as well. The most common extension is the High Availability Extension (see Chapter 18), but other extensions may be provided too.

Apart from these, SUSE is also selling different products. An example of these is SUSE Manager, which is discussed in Chapter 18.

Installing SUSE Linux Enterprise Server 12

To perform a basic installation of SUSE Linux Enterprise Server 12, you need an ISO or an installation disk. Advanced installation solutions are available also, such as an installation by using PXE boot and an installation server. These are discussed in Chapter 17. To install SLES, your server needs to meet some minimal system requirements. These depend on the kind of installation you want to perform. A text-only installation has requirements other than a full graphical installation. Table 1-1 provides an overview of recommended minimal specifications.

Table 1-1. Installation Requirements

	text-based	graphical
CPU	i5 or better	i5 or better
RAM	512MB	1GB
Available disk space	2GB	4GB
Network	100Mbit	100Mbit

The SLES software is available on www.suse.com. Even if SLES is a paid product, you can download an ISO image for free. You will find it classed as "trial" on the web site. If you're using a free version, you won't be able to get support or updates, but you can install a fully functional version of SLES without paying anything. Don't worry about the "trial" classification; the software is fully functional.

Performing a Basic Installation

After starting the installation from the installation media, you'll see the welcome screen (see Figure 1-1). On this screen, you see different options, of which Boot from Hard Disk is selected by default. Select Installation to start the installation procedure. Other options are

- *Upgrade*: Use this to upgrade a previous version of SUSE Linux Enterprise Server.

- *Rescue System*: This option provides access to a rescue system that you can use to repair a server that doesn't start normally anymore.

- *Check Installation Media*: Use this option to verify that your installation disk has no physical problems before starting the installation. Note that, in general, this option takes a lot of time.

- *Firmware Test*: This option verifies the compatibility of firmware that is used.

- *Memory Test*: This option checks the integrity of system RAM and can mark segments of a RAM chip as unusable, so that it will not be used upon installation.

In the lower part of the screen, you'll also see several function keys that allow you to change settings, such as installation language, video mode, and installation source. Also, by using these options, you can specify additional drivers to be loaded. If you're using a non-US keyboard, it makes sense to select the installation language and choose the correct keyboard settings before continuing. This option allows you to change the language as well as the keyboard. If you want to install in English but have to select a different keyboard, you'll need the option that is presented in the next screen.

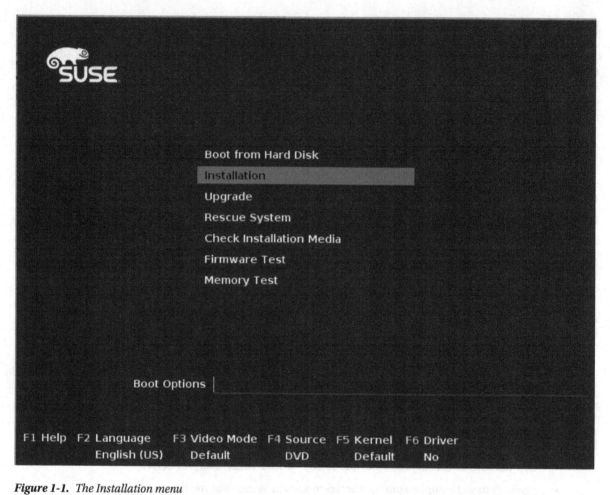

Figure 1-1. *The Installation menu*

After selecting the Installation option, a Linux kernel and the corresponding installation program is loaded. While this happens, the hardware in your server is detected. This can take some time. After hardware detection has occurred, you'll see the screen shown in Figure 1-2, from which you can select the Language and Keyboard and agree to the License Agreement.

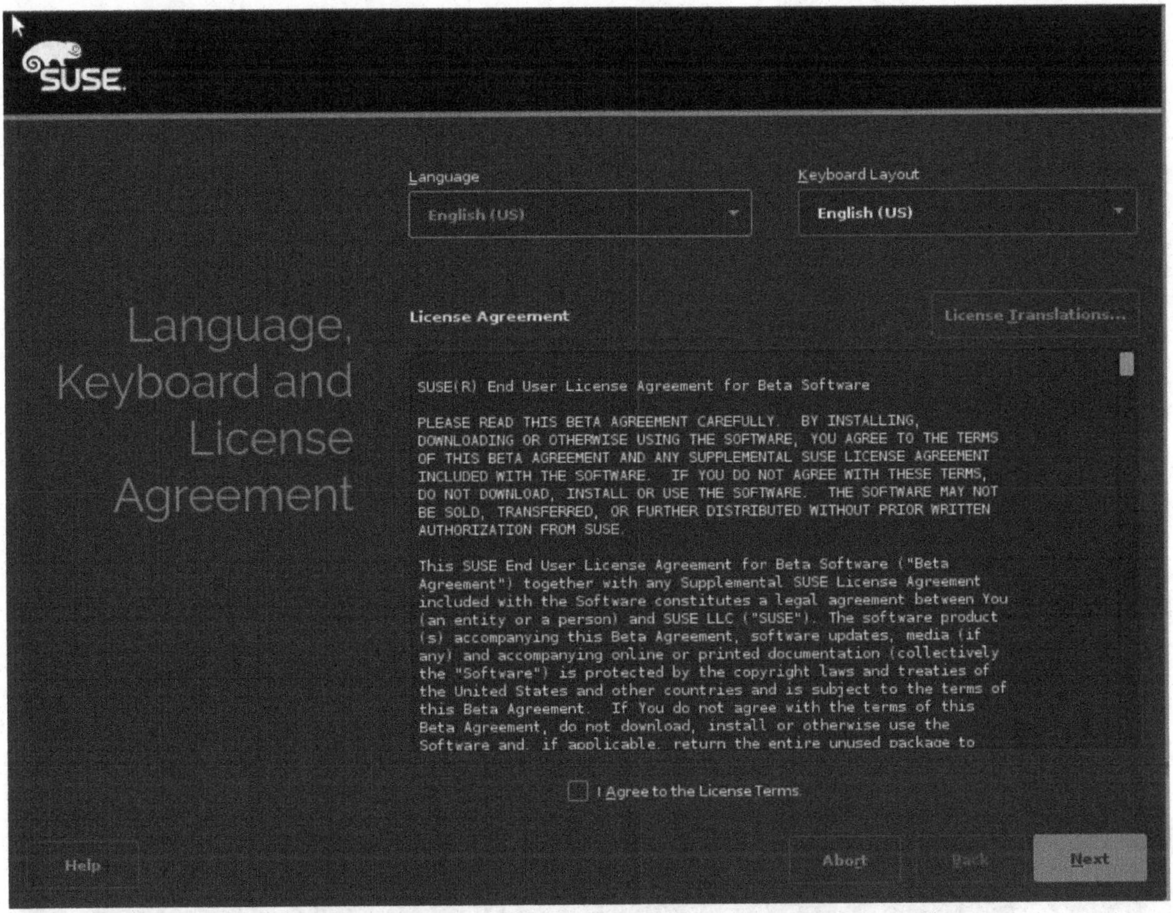

Figure 1-2. *Selecting the installation language*

To access patches and updates, you must provide an e-mail address and associated registration code at this point (see Figure 1-3). If you don't, you can still continue the installation and continue this part later. So, if you have a valid e-mail address and registration code, enter it now. If you don't, or if you want to perform an offline installation, click Skip Registration. If you're using a local registration server, such as a SUSE Manager server or an SMT server, click Local Registration Server and enter the relevant credentials.

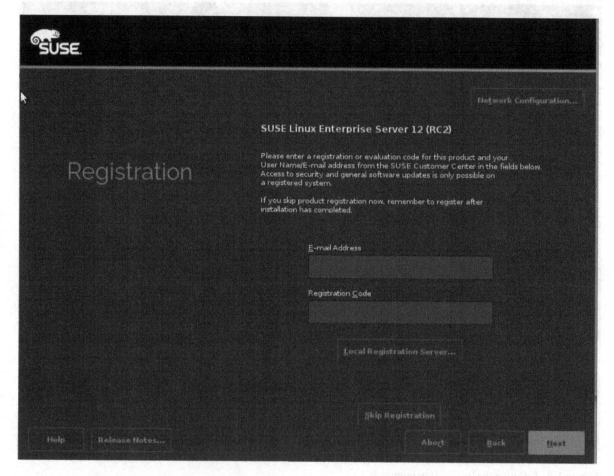

Figure 1-3. *Entering your registration details*

After entering your registration details, you can select optional Add On Products (see Figure 1-4). These are additional SUSE solutions, such as the High Availability Extension, which is not included in SUSE Linux Enterprise. To tell the installation program where to find the installation files, select the installation source from this screen. You can install add-on products from any installation source, including local directories, hard disks, or installation servers. If you don't have any additional products to install, just select nothing and click Next.

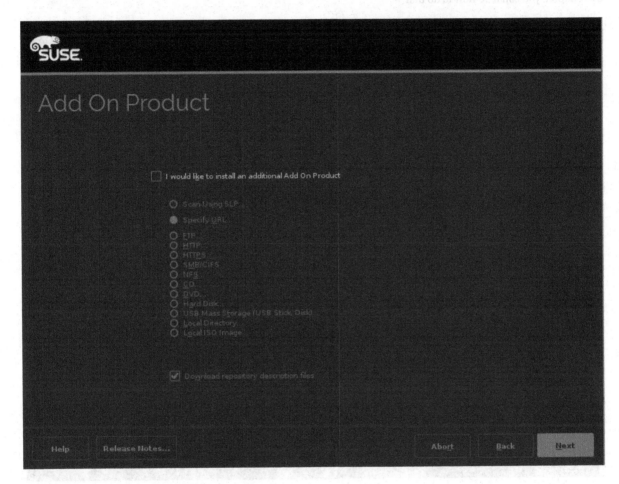

Figure 1-4. Selecting an optional add-on product

On the screen that you see in Figure 1-5, you can select the partitioning for your server. By default, two partitions are created: one containing a swap volume, and the other containing a Btrfs file system. If you want to use Btrfs on SLES 12, it doesn't make much sense to create several partitions, as every directory can be mounted as a subvolume, with its own mount properties (see Chapter 3 for more details on this). If you don't want to use Btrfs, you can use the Expert Partitioner, to create your own partitioning. In the section "Installing with a Custom Partition Scheme," later in this chapter, you can read how to do that.

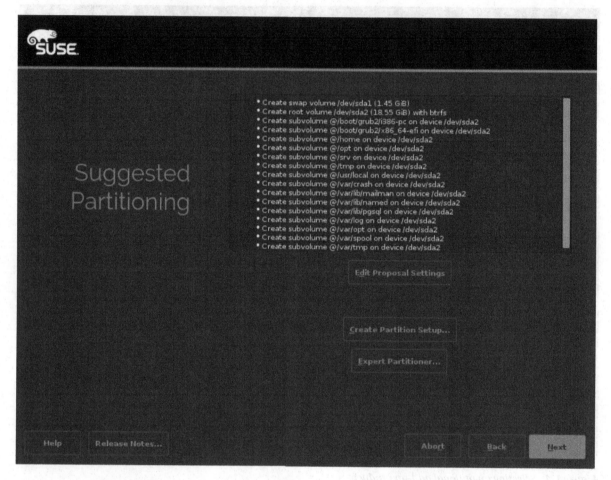

Figure 1-5. *Specifying hard disk layout*

Many services such as databases rely on correct time configuration. In the Clock and Time Zone window that you see in Figure 1-6, you can specify your locale settings. Normally, you first click on the map, to set the right settings. Next, you specify if the hardware clock on your computer is set to Universal Time Coordinated (UTC). UTC more or less corresponds to Greenwich Mean Time (GMT), and it allows all of your servers to communicate at the same time. UTC is often used for Linux servers. If your server is using local time, you can set it here. If you're not sure, just look at the current time that is shown. If it's wrong, it is likely that you're using the wrong setting here. You can also manually adjust the time settings, by clicking the Other Settings button. This allows you to manually set time and specify which NTP time servers you want to use. (Read Chapter 11 for more details about working with NTP.)

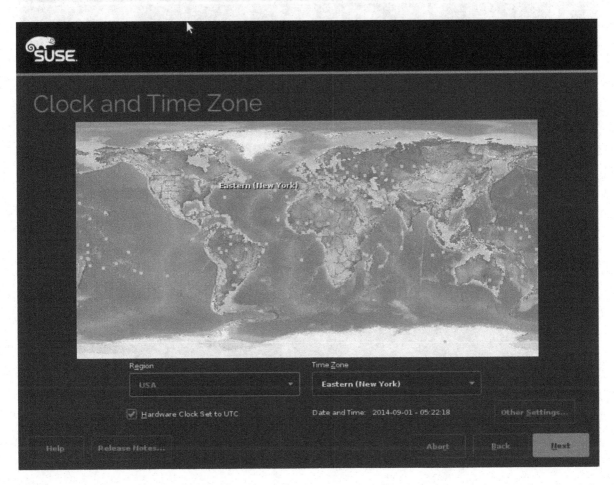

Figure 1-6. *Specifying clock and time zone settings*

On the screen shown in Figure 1-7, you can create a new user account and set properties for this user. It's a good idea to create at least one local user account, so that you don't have to work as root if that's not necessary. If you don't want to create a local user account, you can just click Next, to proceed to the next step.

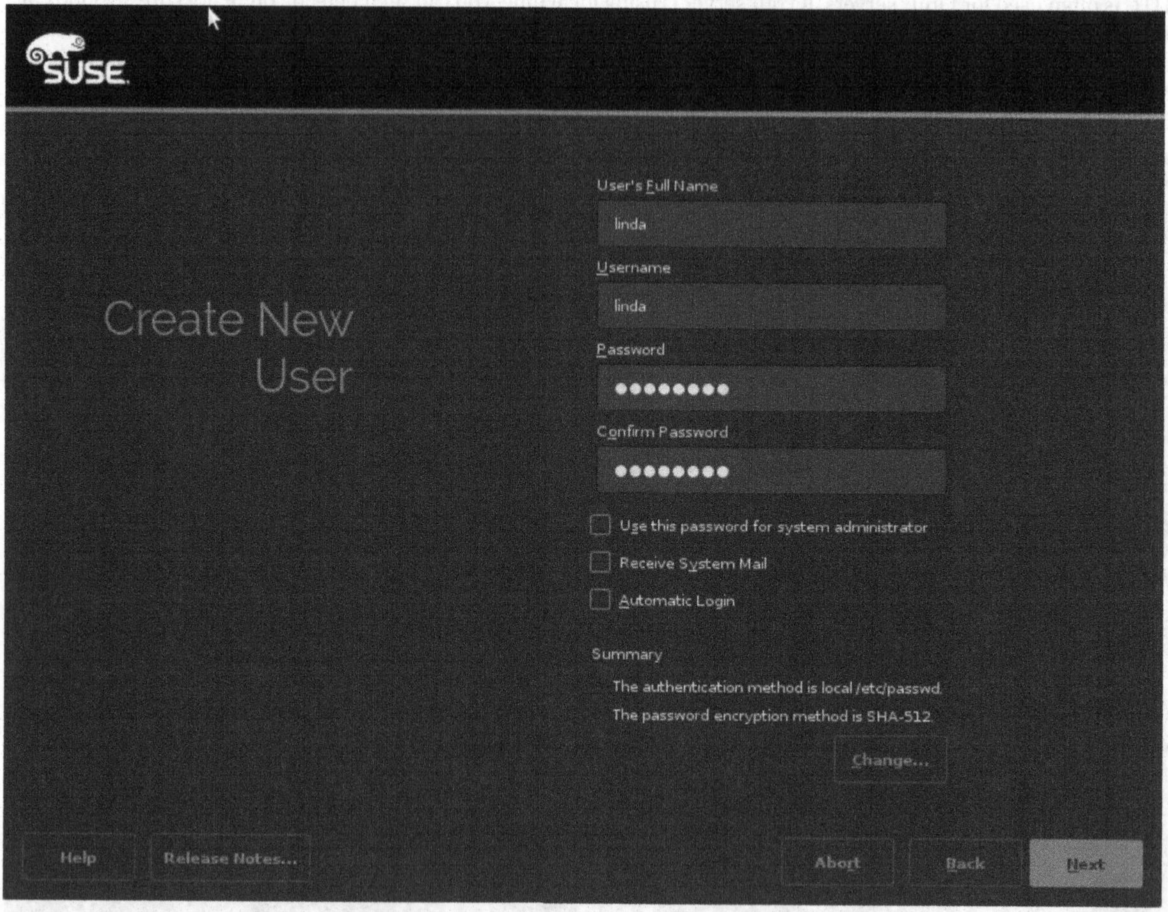

Figure 1-7. *Creating a local user account*

At this point, you'll have to enter a password for the user root (see Figure 1-8). Make sure to set a password that is complicated enough to be secure. To make sure that you don't enter a wrong password because of keyboard incompatibility, you can use the Test Keyboard Layout option, to verify the current keyboard settings.

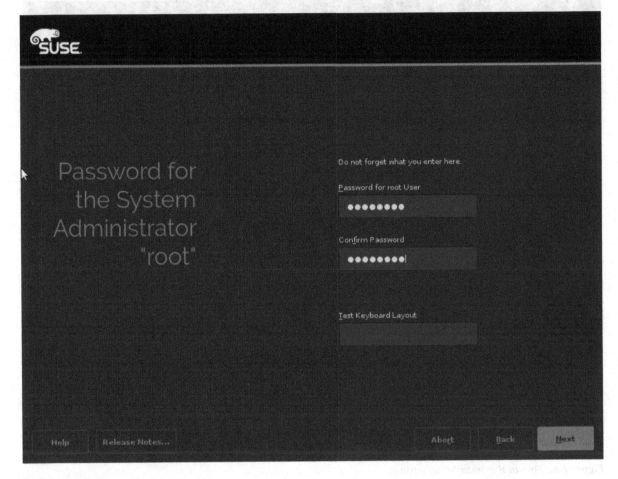

Figure 1-8. Setting the root password

You'll now access the Installation Settings window, which you can see in Figure 1-9. In this window, you'll find many options to further fine-tune your installation settings.

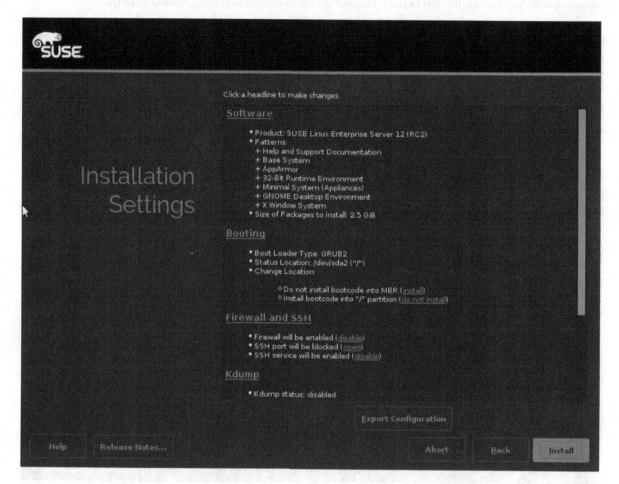

Figure 1-9. *Fine-tuning installation settings*

The Software option, allows you to choose from different package categories, to make an entire class of software and all of its dependencies available. If you require more detail, click the Details button, which still shows all of the different categories of software but also allows you to select or de-select individual packages (see Figure 1-10). After selecting this option, you can select one of the software patterns on the left, to show all the individual packages in that category. If you're looking for specific packages, you can use the Search option (see Figure 1-11). Enter a keyword and click Search, to start your search operation. This shows a list of packages found to the left, from which you can select everything you need. From any of the four tabs in the Software Selection utility, click Accept, once you're done. You may now see a window about dependencies, telling you that in order to install the packages you've selected, some other packages must be installed as well. Confirm, to get back to the main settings window, from which you can continue configuring the next part of your environment.

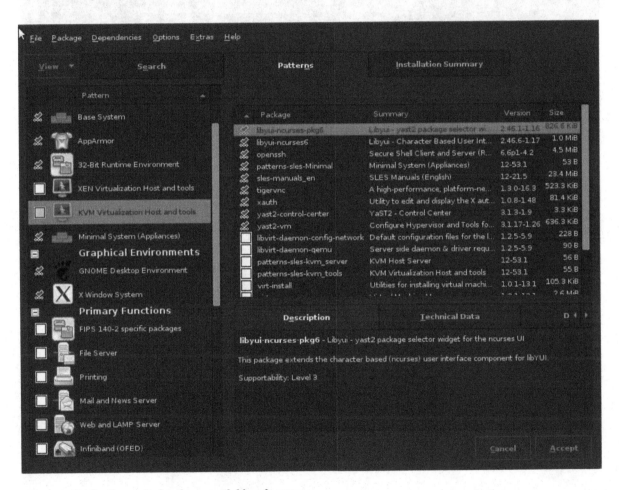

Figure 1-10. *Getting more details on available software*

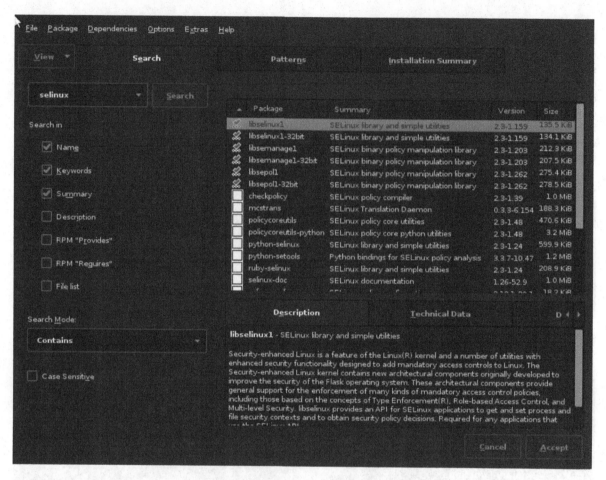

Figure 1-11. *Use the Search option, if you're looking for something specific*

The next part of the configuration settings is about the boot loader (see Figure 1-12). SLES 12 uses GRUB 2 as its default boot loader. The correct version is automatically selected, depending on the hardware you're using, you might need either GRUB2 or GRUB2-EFI. You can also select where to install the boot loader. By default, SLES installs to the boot sector of the partition that contains the root file system (which is also set as the active partition in the partition table). In the MBR, some generic boot code is written, which allows the boot loader to find the code you've written to the active partition. If you prefer to write the boot code directly to the MBR, you can select Boot from Master Boot Record instead.

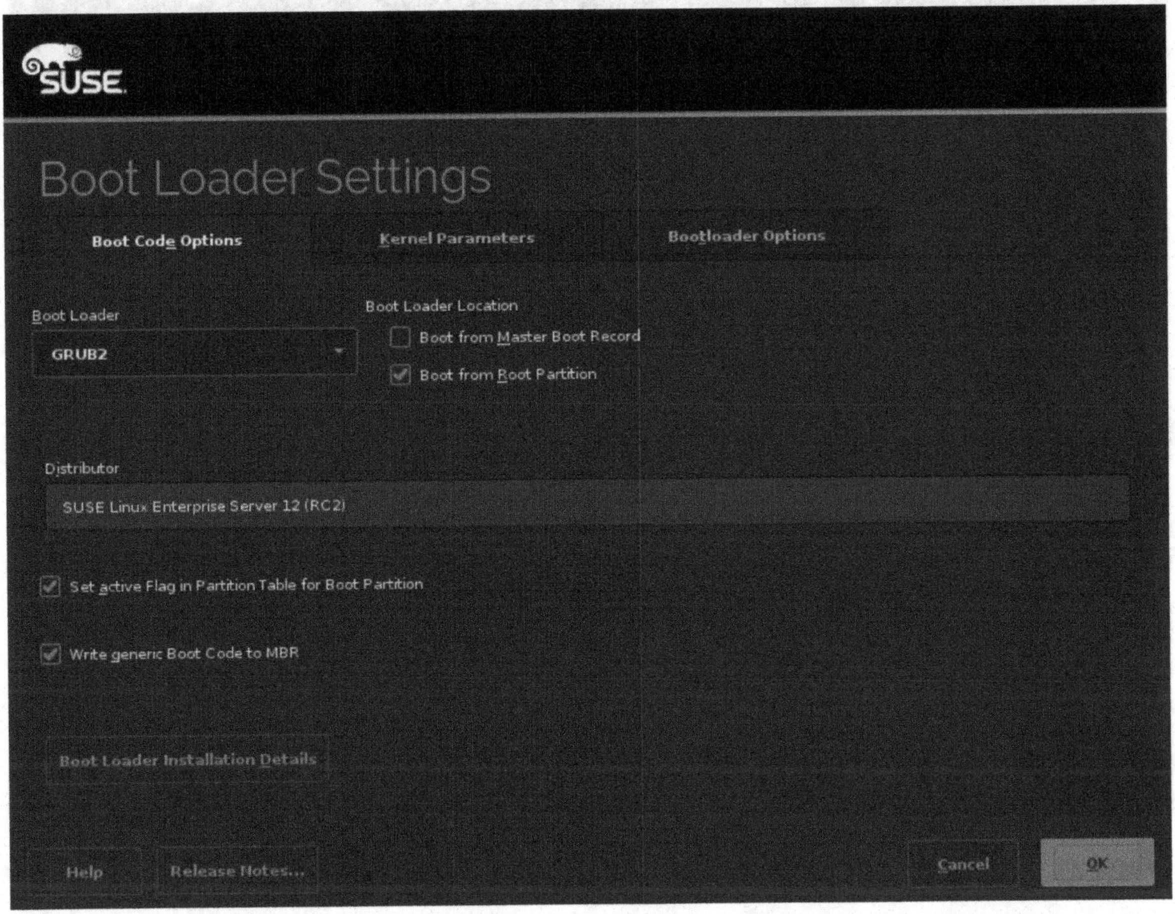

Figure 1-12. Selecting a boot loader

While booting, you can pass kernel parameters to the kernel from the boot loader (see Figure 1-13). This allows you to further fine-tune the behavior of the kernel and to include or exclude specific drivers, which is sometimes required for compatibility reasons. From this window, you can also specify which type of console you want to use (graphical or something else) and specify a console resolution.

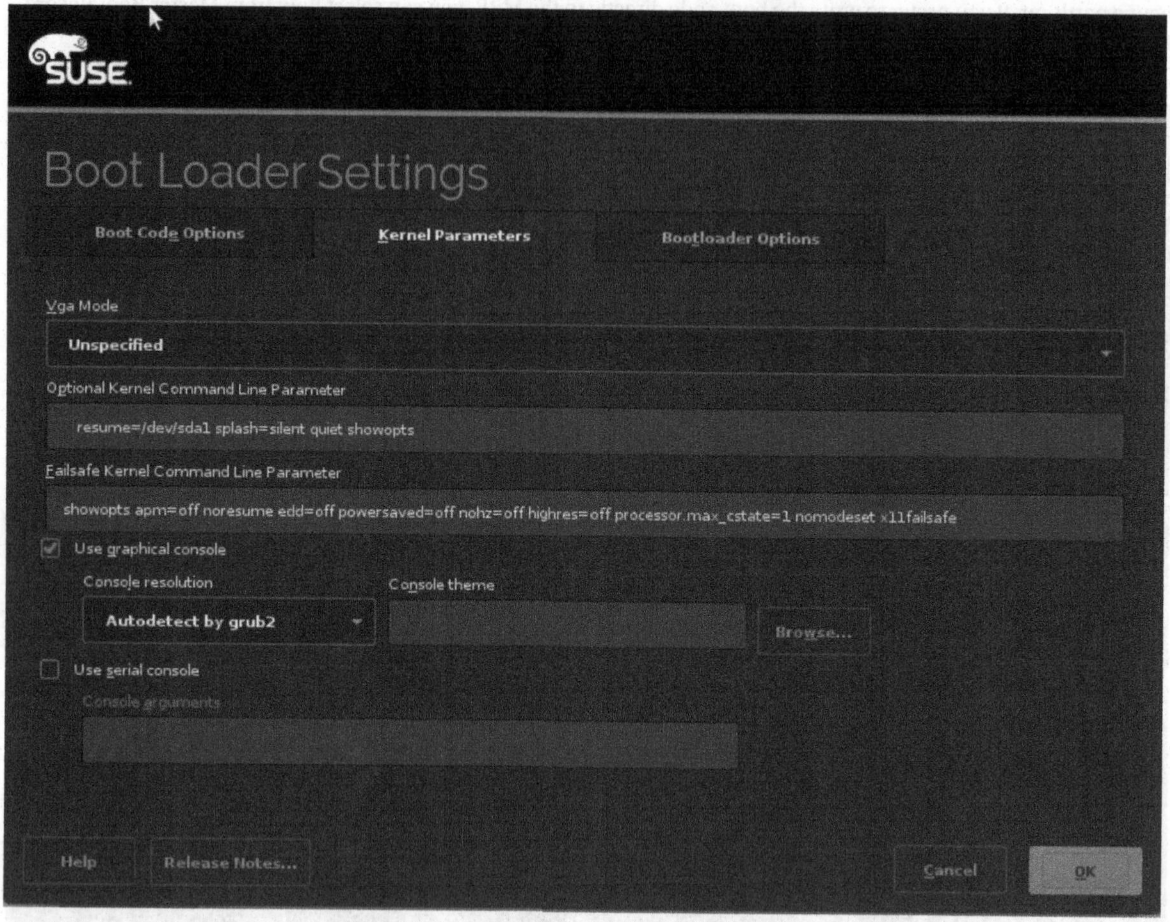

Figure 1-13. Specifying kernel boot parameters

The third tab of the boot loader configuration menu allows you to set a time out, the default section you want to boot, and a boot loader password. You should consider setting a boot loader password, as without such a password, anyone can access the GRUB boot menu and pass specific options to the boot loader. This is a security risk for environments in which the console can be physically accessed. If you protect the boot loader with a password, such options can only be entered after providing the correct password.

After indicating how you want the boot loader to work, you can configure the firewall and Secure Shell (SSH). By default, the firewall is enabled, as is the SSH service, but the SSH port is blocked. To change this configuration, select Firewall and SSH and make appropriate selections (see Figure 1-14). There is no advanced interface for firewall configuration available at this point, but you probably want to open at least the SSH port.

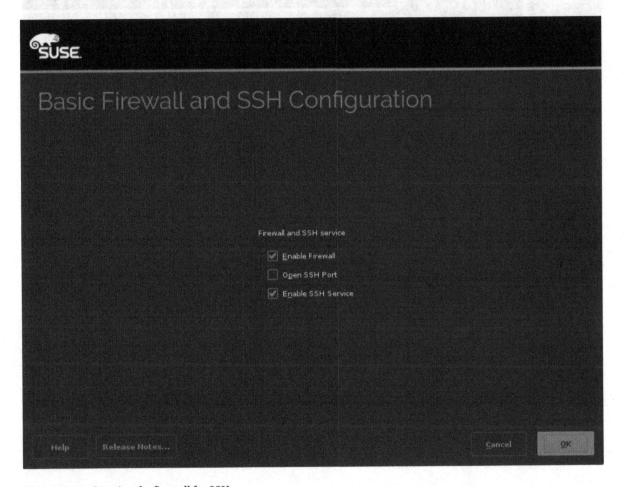

Figure 1-14. *Opening the firewall for SSH*

Next, you can specify if you want to use Kdump. Kdump is a core dump kernel that can be loaded with your default kernel. If the kernel crashes, the core dump kernel can write a memory core dump to a specified partition, to make it easier to analyze what was going wrong when your server crashed. If you want to enable Kdump, you must specify settings for available memory, as well as the Dump target, which is the default location to which the core dump will be written (see Figure 1-15).

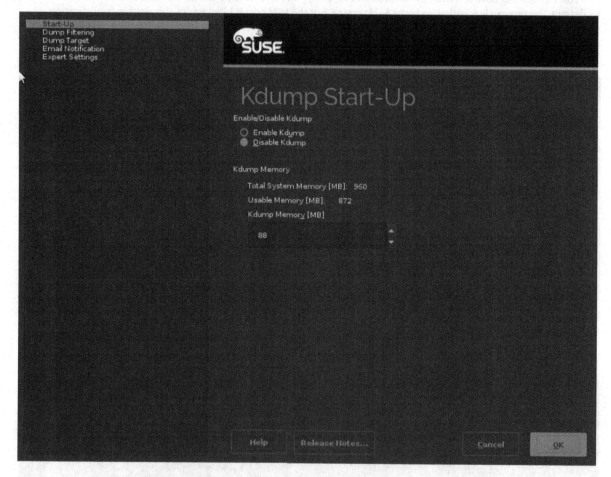

Figure 1-15. Specifying Kdump settings

After selecting Kdump settings, you can choose a default `systemd` target. This determines the mode your server is started in. By default, it will be started in a graphical mode, if graphical packages have been installed. From this menu interface, you can choose Text mode as an alternative start-up mode (see Figure 1-16).

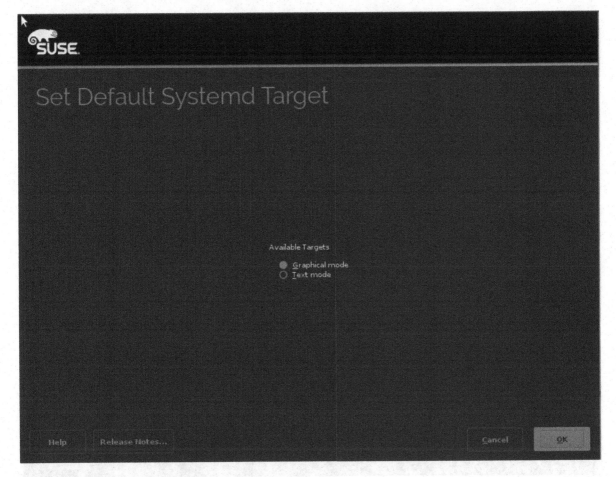

Figure 1-16. *Selecting the startup mode*

Next, you'll encounter the system option. This is a very interesting option that probes for available hardware in your server and allows you to easily change settings for that hardware. These are advanced hardware settings that change the performance profile of your server (see Figure 1-17). Don't change them from here, if you don't know what you're doing, but read Chapter 15 instead. It explains the results of the modifications that you can apply here in detail.

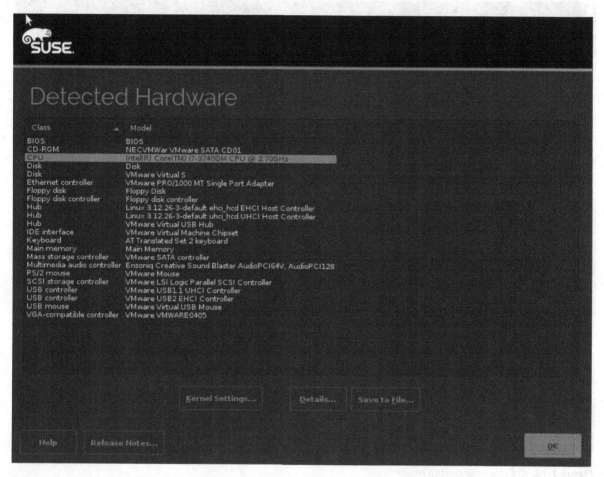

Figure 1-17. During installation, you can easily change advanced performance parameters

The last setting allows you to clone configuration setting to the file /root/autoinst.xml. This is default behavior that makes it easy to install another server using the same settings. If you don't want to do that, click Do not write it. After selecting appropriate settings, click Install, to start the actual installation procedure. Once the file copy has completed, the system is started with the new settings, and you can start working.

Installing with a Custom Partition Scheme

By default, the SLES installer proposes a partition scheme in which two partitions are created. The first partition is configured as swap space, while the second partition is configured as the root file system, using a Btrfs file system. In some cases, you might want to select a different partitioning scheme, for example, if you're using applications that haven't been certified for Btrfs yet, or if you want to separate different data types. If that's the case, you have to use the custom partitioning interface. In this section, you'll learn how to use it.

When the installer prompts the Suggested partitioning window, click Expert Partitioner, to open the custom partitioning interface. This opens the window shown in Figure 1-18. On this window, you see a System View tree on the left, with, under the Linux item, an overview of the storage on your server. By default, the installer shows the detected hard disk(s), as well as the default partitioning that is proposed for the detected storage.

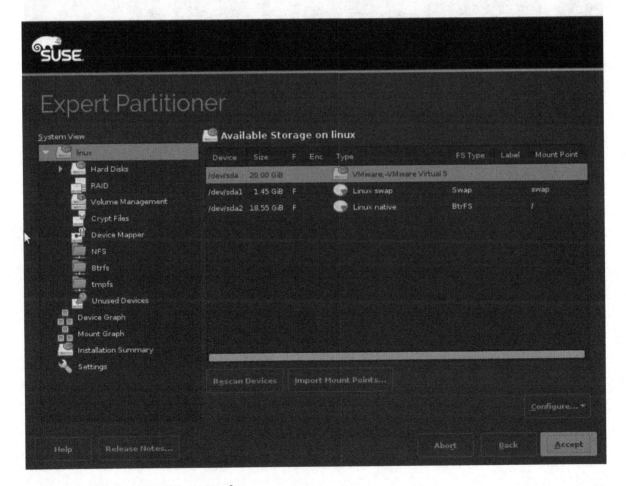

Figure 1-18. The Expert Partitioner interface

To make changes to a disk, you first have to active the Linux ➤ Hard Disks ➤ sda item. This brings you to the Partitions window, which you can see in Figure 1-19. From this window, you can use different operations on the partitions. To start with, you probably want to delete the existing partitions, so that you can create new partitions. Select the partitions one by one, and next, click Delete, to remove them from your system. This gives you a starting point from which your hard disk is completely empty.

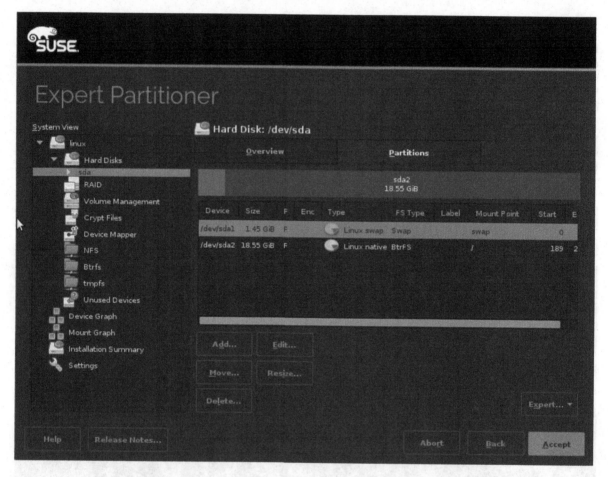

Figure 1-19. *The Partitions interface*

On modern configurations, you might want to start creating your custom disk layout by setting a partition table. Default partitioning is based on the MSDOS partition table, which allows you to address partitions with a maximum size of 2TiB. If you want to use the modern GPT (GUID Partition Table) disk layout, select Expert ➤ Create new partition table. After selecting the GPT partition table type, you'll work in an environment that is a bit different. For example, there are no extended partitions in GPT. Read Chapter 3 for more details about these differences.

To create a new partition, from the Partitions menu on your selected hard disk, click Add. This opens the window shown in Figure 1-20. In this window, you can select the size of the partition you want to use. When specifying a custom size, enter a size in GiB (1,024 × 1,024 × 1,024) and not GB. You should note that many hardware vendors work with GB (1,000 × 1,000 × 1,000) as the default unit, so you may find that you don't have as many GiB available as the amount of GB that was sold to you by your hardware vendor.

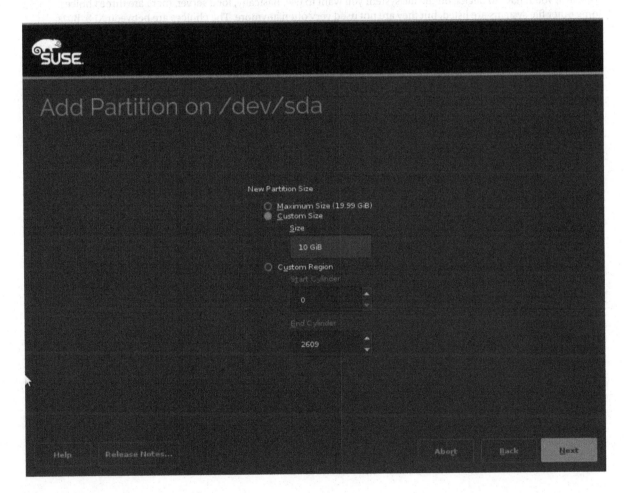

Figure 1-20. *Creating a new partition*

After specifying the size of the partition, in the next screen, you can select a role for the partition. That is the type of use you intend for the new partition. Based on the selection you make here, you'll get a default selection for the file system to use as well. It doesn't really matter much what you select here, as you can change the selection in the next screen anyway.

In the following step, you'll have to specify formatting options. There are two important choices to be made here: which file system you are going to use and whether or not you are going to use Logical Volume Manager (LVM).

If you're planning on using any file system other than Btrfs, it might be interesting to use LVM. When using LVM, disk devices can be joined in a volume group (VG), and from the VG, Logical Volumes can be created as the base allocation unit for all your storage. Using LVM allows you to easily resize your storage volumes and offers some other benefits as well, which is why this is a relatively frequently used solution for storage layout.

Next, you'll have to decide on the file system you want to use. Basically, for a server, there are three choices. Some other file systems are listed, but they are not used very often anymore. The choices are between XFS, Btrfs, and Ext4. Use Btrfs, if you want the latest and greatest file system for Linux. In Chapter 3, you'll learn about all the features Btrfs has to offer. If you want a very stable and reliable file system, you're better off using XFS, a flexible, fast, and well-proven file system that has been around for a long time. If you need backward compatibility, you can select the Ext4 file system. This file system doesn't offer the speed and scaling options that you might need on a modern server, which is why Ext4 should not be your first choice. But it's still around, and it's a very stable file system, so if your applications require you to use Ext4, it's there for you.

To show you as many options as possible, in the following procedure, you'll learn how to configure a server that uses the following disk layout:

- A small boot partition, using Ext4

- All remaining disk space in another partition that is configured for use of LVM

- A root logical volume, using XFS

- A swap logical volume

- A dedicated logical volume for /var, using Btrfs

To offer the best possible booting support, it's a good idea to use a small boot partition. To do this, first create the partition with a size of 500MiB. Next, set the mount point to /boot, and select the Ext4 file system. As the boot partition contains only a small number of files, there's no need to use an advanced file system, such as XFS or Btrfs, on this partition. After selecting these features, you can click Finish, to write the changes to disk and continue (see Figure 1-21).

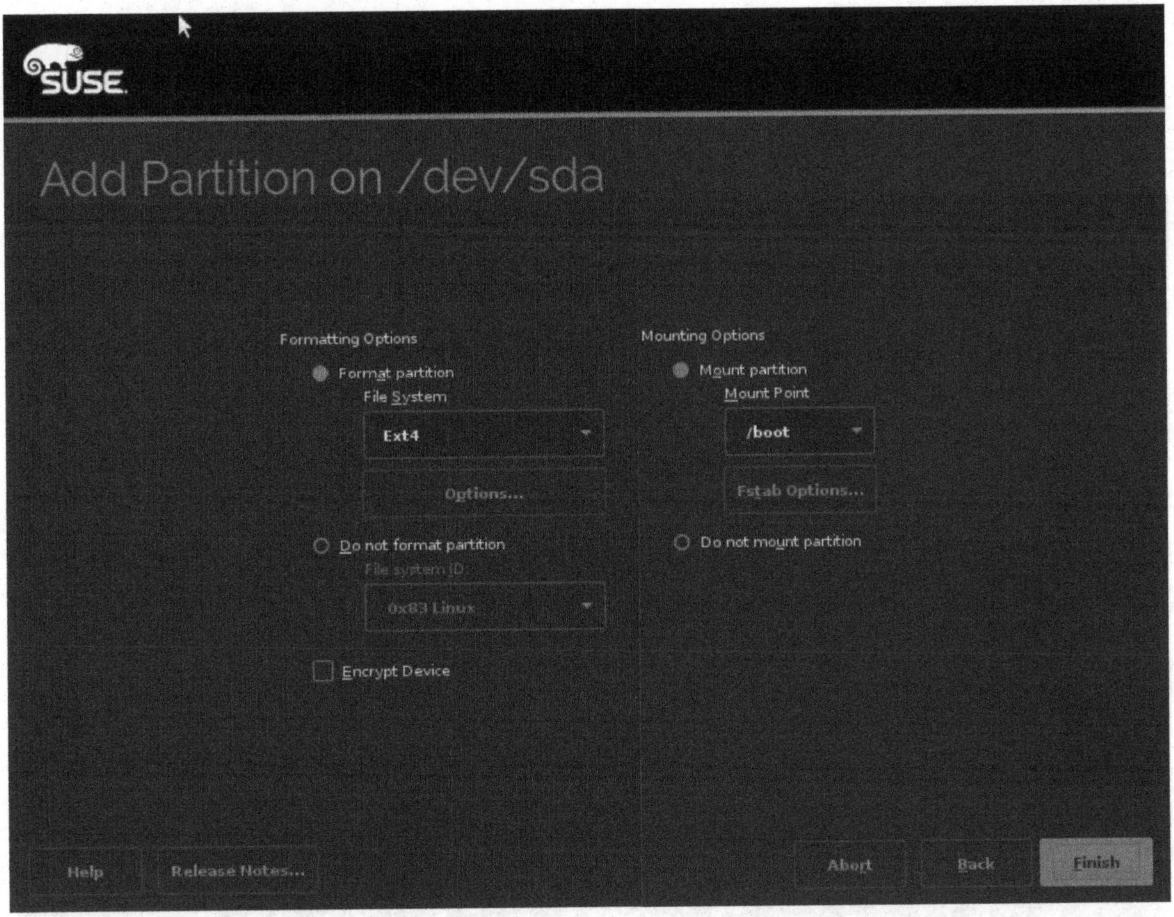

Figure 1-21. *Creating a /boot partition*

Back in the main Partitions overview, you can now add all remaining disk space in a partition that you're going to use for LVM. To do this, when asked for the New Partition Size, you can select the option Maximum Size, which allocates all remaining disk space. Then click Next and select the Raw Volume Role. This will automatically select the Do not format partition option in the next screen and select the file system type 0x8E Linux LVM. You can now click Finish, to complete this part of the configuration.

After creating the partitions, from the Expert Partitioner main window, you'll have to select the Volume Management option. From this interface, click Add and select Volume Group. This opens the Add Volume Group interface, which you can see in Figure 1-22. The Volume Group is the collection of all available storage. You'll have to give it a name and assign storage devices to it. It's a good idea to use a volume group name that is easy to recognize. For example, use *vgdata* as its name.

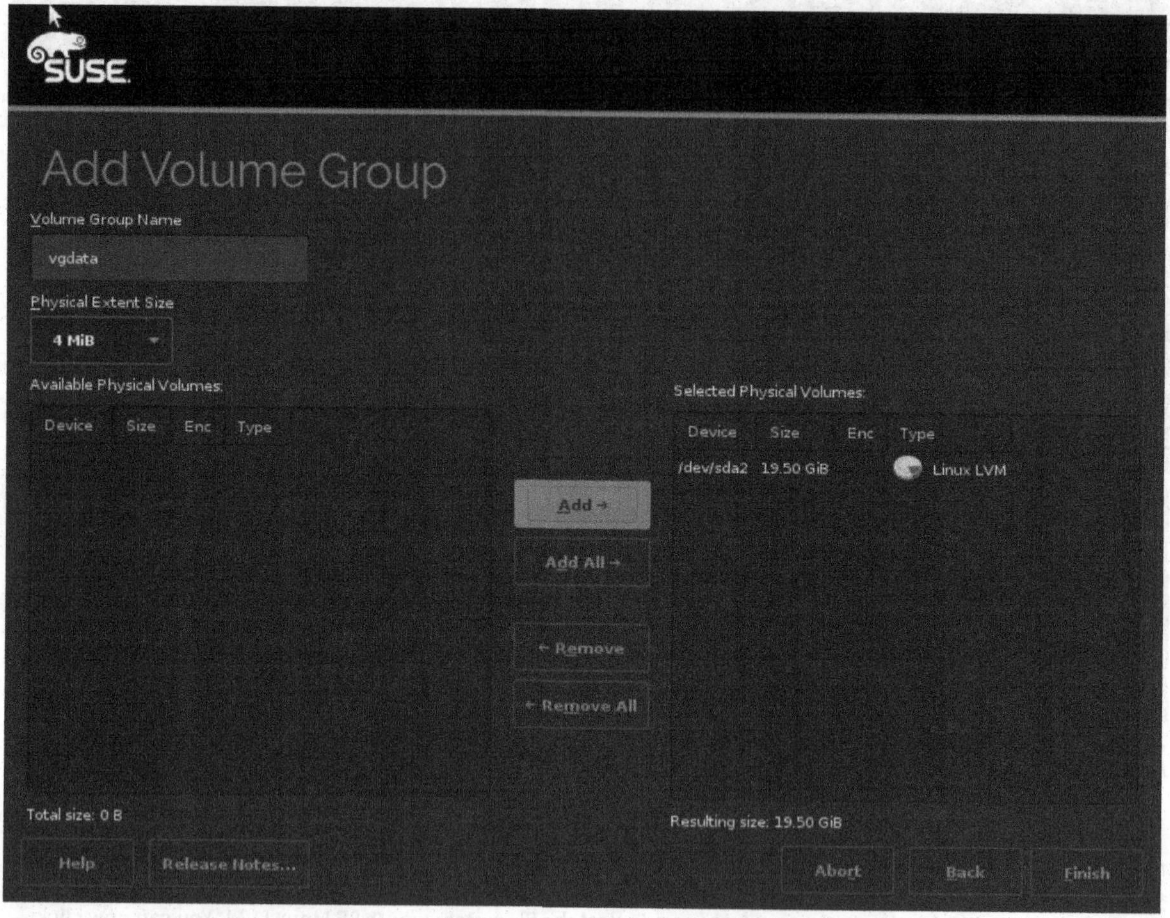

Figure 1-22. *Creating a volume group*

Next, you can set the Physical Extent Size. A physical extent is the base building block from creating logical volumes. All logical volumes will always have the size of a multiple of physical extents. For many cases, an extent of 4MiB works well, but if you want to use large logical volumes, you're better off using bigger physical extents.

The last step to create volume groups is to assign physical volumes to the volume group. You'll find all partitions that have been set up with the partition type 0x8E in the list of available physical volumes. Select them and click Add, to add to the volume group. Next, click Finish, to proceed to the next step.

After creating the volume group, the installer brings you back to the Expert Partitioner window. From here, click Add ➤ Logical Volume, to add a logical volume. This opens the window shown in Figure 1-23, from which you can specify a name and type for the logical volume. For normal use, you would use the Normal Volume type. Use Thin Pool / Thin Volume for environments in which you want to do thin provisioning, which makes sense, for example, in an environment in which desktop virtualization is used. In addition, all logical volumes require a unique name. You're free in choosing whatever name you like, but it might make sense to select a name that makes it easy to identify the purpose of the volume.

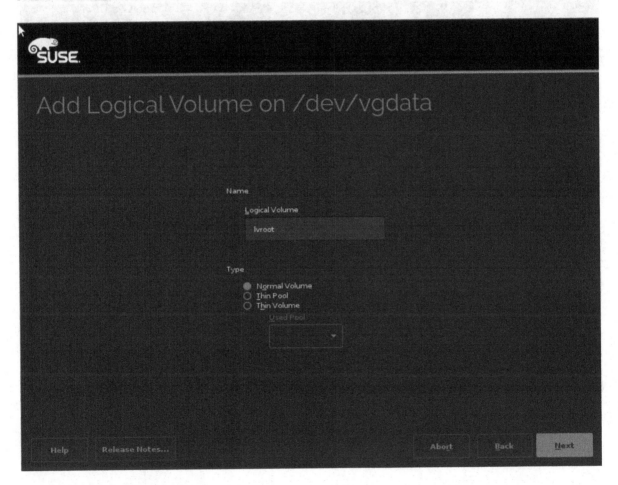

Figure 1-23. *Creating logical volumes*

After specifying the properties of the logical volumes, you must specify a size as well (see Figure 1-24). If you plan on using more than one logical volume, don't leave the Maximum Size option selected. It will take all available disk space, and you cannot create any additional volumes anymore. Logical volumes support resizing. You can grow the size of any file system; you cannot shrink all file systems. As a volume is easy to grow, it's a good idea to keep the volumes relatively small and some disk space unallocated, to accommodate for future growth. Once the volume has been created, you'll get to the same interface that is used for creation of partitions. From this interface, you can select the file system to use, as well as the mount point. Note that when configuring an LVM volume for swap, you don't have to set a directory as a mount point. The system interface swap is set as the mount point, and that cannot be changed.

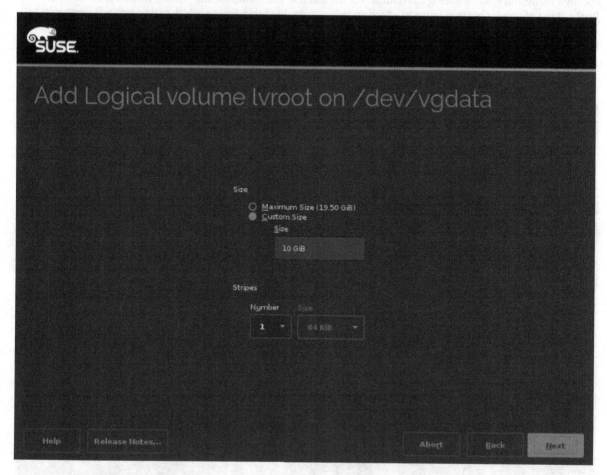

Figure 1-24. *Specifying volume size*

After finalizing your custom disk layout, you can write it to disk. The installer will now bring you back to the main installation procedure, which has been explained in the previous section.

Summary

In this chapter, you've learned about the SUSE product portfolio, focusing on SUSE Linux Enterprise Server, in particular. You have also learned about the different choices you have to make while performing an installation. A basic installation has been explained, as has the creation of an advanced disk layout. In the next chapter, you'll learn about some of the essentials required to get you going with SUSE Linux Enterprise Server.

CHAPTER 2

■ ■ ■

Basic Skills

Now that you have SUSE Linux Enterprise Server (SLES) installed, in this chapter, I'll cover some basic skills to help you in getting started. I won't cover Linux basics in much detail here. If you have never worked with Linux before, I suggest you read my *Beginning the Linux Command Line* (Apress, 2009). What you will learn in this chapter is how an SLES is organized and where you can find important components of the operating system. You'll receive an introduction to working from the GNOME graphical environment as well. You'll also get an introduction to working with YaST, the integrated management utility on SUSE Linux Enterprise Server.

In this chapter, the following topics are discussed:

- Exploring SLES Interfaces
- Working with YaST

Exploring SLES Interfaces

After installing SLES, there are two interfaces that you can work from: the graphical interface and the console interface. When working from the console interface, you can use SLES just like any other Linux distribution. You'll notice it has some minor differences, related to some of the utilities that are used and locations of files and directories, but it's still a bash shell, and if you have previous experience with any other Linux distribution, it should not be difficult to work with it.

Graphical or Not?

In the past, the graphical interface was considered an interface for novice Linux administrators. "Real administrators work from the shell," is what many people stated. Also, servers in the past had a good reason not to run a graphical interface by default. Only a few utilities needed a graphical interface; most were written to be used in a text-only environment. In addition, servers had limited resources, and it was considered a waste to install a server with a graphical interface, especially if it wasn't going to be used.

Nowadays, servers tend to have many more resources, so the waste of resources is not that significant anymore. Also, there are quite a few good graphical utilities available, which makes it more tempting to use a graphical interface. And last but not least, on a graphical interface, administrators can open more than one shell window at the same time, which may make it easier to work on complex tasks.

All this doesn't take away the fact that servers are also frequently configured to run in "headless" mode, without even a terminal connected to it, and administrators only connect to it using Secure Shell (SSH). If that is the case, it still doesn't make sense to run a complete graphical environment. In the end, you'll have to decide how you want to run your servers yourself anyway. Pick what's best. SUSE has developed SLES to fully support both environments.

GNOME or KDE?

SUSE has a long history of rivalry between GNOME and KDE users. While in OpenSUSE, you can choose which graphical interface to use, on SUSE Linux Enterprise, GNOME is used as the default graphical interface. SUSE does not want to dedicate any resources on development and maintenance of another graphical interface, which is why KDE packages are not included.

Exploring GNOME

If you've selected a default installation, and the hardware configuration of your server has allowed for it, you'll have a GNOME 3 graphical interface. Figure 2-1 shows what this interface looks like after logging in to it.

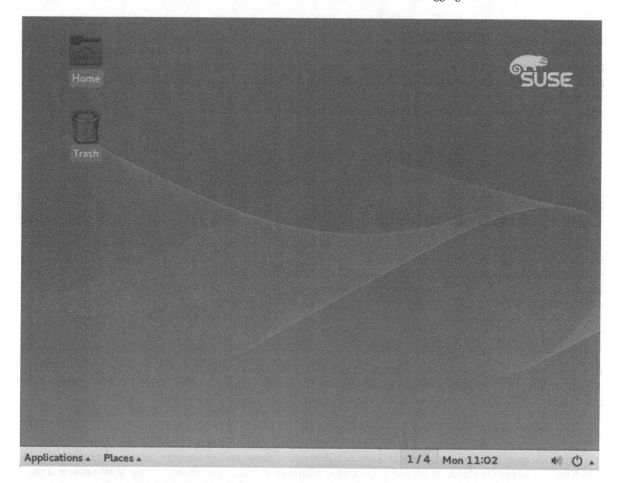

Figure 2-1. *The default GNOME 3 graphical interface*

You can see that the interface has a pretty clean configuration, to make it easy to find the items you need to work with. Basically, there are just a few things to be aware of to get you started with SUSE easily.

To begin with, the SUSE GNOME interface uses different workspaces. That means that the desktop is bigger than the part that you can see. By default, you're on workspace one out of four. If you click the 1/4 indicator (left from the time in the bar on the lower end of the screen), you can select a different workspace. Using workspaces makes it easy to work with multiple graphical applications.

A second part of the interface that is rather useful is the menu that pops up after clicking the right mouse button somewhere on the desktop. From this menu, you can easily access the most important part of the graphical interface: the terminal. Just click Open in Terminal to open as many terminals as you like (see Figure 2-2).

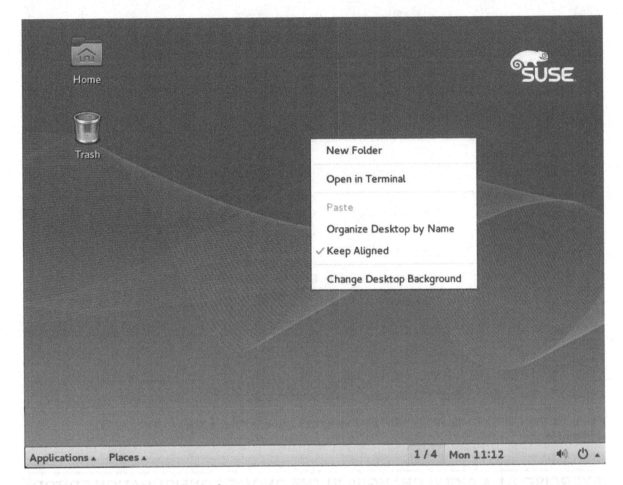

Figure 2-2. *Easy access to new terminals*

Third, there are a few menus in the lower-left part of the interface. The Applications menu provides access to some applications, and the Places menu allows you to easily gain access to folders on this server or from other locations. You should notice, however, that for a server administrator, the applications that are available from the menus are of limited use, and many more applications can be started directly from a terminal shell also. There are a few applications that can be useful anyway.

GNOME Configuration Editor

Not many people know it, but the GNOME interface comes with something that looks like a Windows Registry Editor. The GNOME Configuration Editor (see Figure 2-3) allows you to lock down or configure different parts of GNOME. Select, for example, the option desktop ➤ gnome ➤ applications ➤ terminal, and it gives access to the exec and exec_arg keys, which tell GNOME which binary to associate to the GNOME terminal and which startup arguments to use when running this binary. In Exercise 2-1, you'll learn how to apply a simple setting in the GNOME Configuration Editor.

35

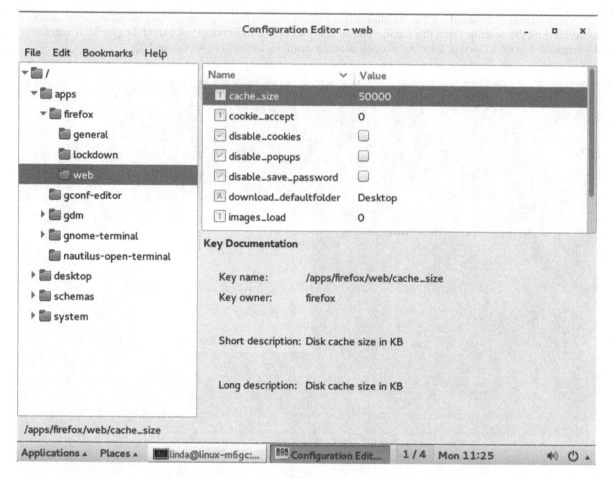

Figure 2-3. *The GNOME Configuration Editor provides access to many features to tune and limit graphical applications*

EXERCISE 2-1. MAKING CHANGES IN THE GNOME CONFIGURATION EDITOR

In this exercise, you'll work in the GNOME Configuration Editor to apply some simple changes to the GNOME configuration.

1. Log in as root and open System Tools ➤ GNOME Configuration Editor.

2. Browse to apps ➤ gdm ➤ simple-greeter.

3. You'll see that the disable_user_list currently is selected. This option makes sure that upon login in the graphical environment, you won't see a list of all users on your computer. De-select this option.

4. Another interesting candidate is in apps ➤ firefox ➤ lockdown. From there, click the options disable_extensions and disable_history. Using these options makes Firefox a little bit more secure.

5. Next, use apps ➤ firefox ➤ web and select the cache_size parameter. Click in the value to change it, and decrease it to 20000. This ensures that you have a bit less memory reserved for cache usages, which makes sense on a server.

6. Restart your server. You'll notice that the login screen is different. Next, start Firefox. Try to access the Firefox history. You'll note that it no longer works.

Network Tools

If you're a long-term Linux administrator, you'll probably know your tools, and you'll be able to fix network issues from the command line. If you don't know the different tools very well yet, you may like the Network Tools. This graphical program provides access to different useful functions that you can use to analyze the network. Figure 2-4 shows an overview of its default appearance. Note that you'll need to be root to get full access to the tools provided from this interface. Exercise 2-2 gives you an idea of what you can do with the Network Tools.

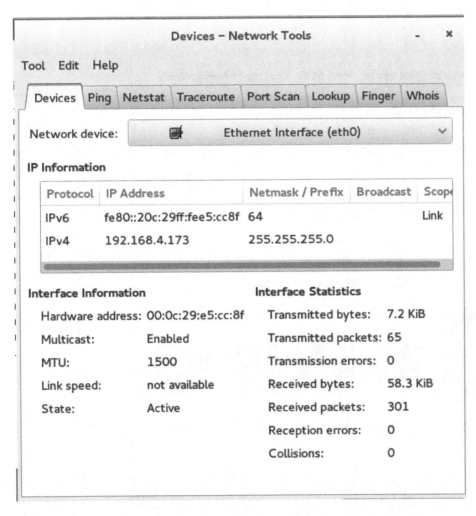

Figure 2-4. Network Tools provides an easy interface to test networking functionality

EXERCISE 2-2. USING THE GNOME NETWORK TOOLS

In this exercise, you'll explore some options that are provided from GNOME Network Tools.

1. Log in to your server as a normal user. From the Applications menu, select System Tools ➤ Network Tools. You'll open in the interface, from which you can select the network devices that are available. Use the drop-down list to have a look at the different network devices and find the IP address that is in use on your system.

2. Click the Ping tab and enter a network address that should be accessible. The default gateway, for example, will do well. Specify that you want to send only five requests and click Ping, to start pinging the other node. You'll get a nice overview of the round-trip time statistics while doing this (see Figure 2-5).

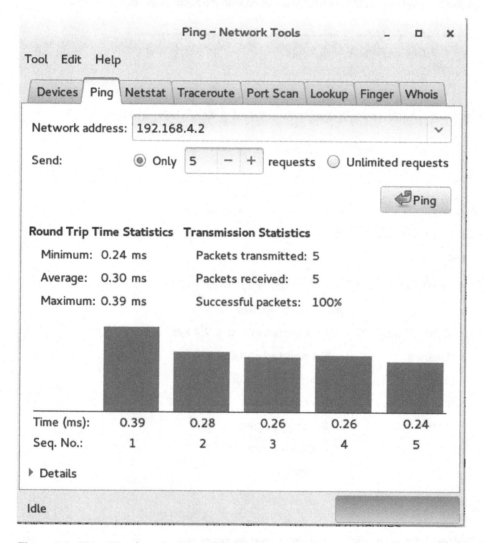

Figure 2-5. *Using Ping from the Network Tools*

3. On the Netstat tab, you can analyze networking configuration on your computer. Select Active Network Services, and next, click Netstat. This provides an overview of all the ports that are listening on your server. In subsequent chapters in this book, you'll learn more about configuring these services.

4. Last, click Port Scan. Enter an IP address and click Scan. This will tell you that nmap has to be installed to access this functionality. Open a terminal window and click su -. Next, enter the root password. You are now root, which allows you to install software. Type zypper in nmap to install the nmap port scanner. Go back to Network Tools and try to issue the port scan once again. You'll see that it now works, and if the target host you're scanning allows it, you'll get a list of all ports that are open on that host.

■ **Warning**   Port scanning is regarded by many network administrators as a malicious activity. You could be banned from the network—or worse—while performing a port scan. Use this on your own networks only, to analyze the availability and accessibility of services.

Settings

To make your GNOME desktop experience as good as it gets, you can access the GNOME Settings menu (see Figure 2-6). In this menu, you'll get access to different personalized GNOME settings. All of the settings that you configure here are written to your own user home directory. As an administrator who wants to provide default settings to users, you can change many of these settings and distribute them to other users. In Exercise 2-3, you'll learn how to change settings from this menu and distribute them to the home directories of other users.

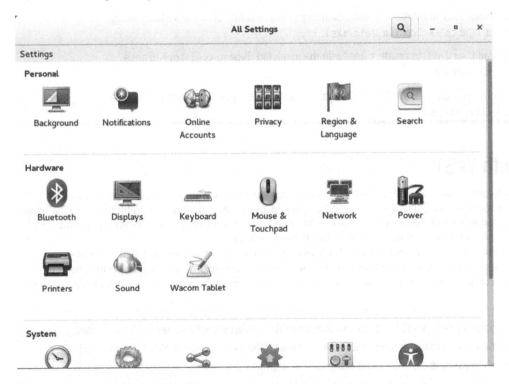

Figure 2-6. Changing GNOME settings

EXERCISE 2-3. CHANGING AND DISTRIBUTING GNOME USER SETTINGS

In this exercise, you'll lean how to change and distribute GNOME user settings. You'll work with some commands that are related to user management and which are discussed in more detail in Chapter 4.

1. Right-click the GNOME desktop to open a GNOME terminal. Type `su` - and enter the root password to become root.

2. Type `useradd -m user` to create a user with the name user. Use `passwd user` to set a password for this user. Set the password to "password." It will state that it's a bad password, but you can still set to this password.

3. Click the Off button in the lower-right part of the GNOME desktop. From the menu that appears now, click Log out.

4. Back on the login prompt, log in as the user you've just created.

5. As this user, access the GNOME Settings menu by selecting Applications ➤ System Tools ➤ Settings.

6. Click Displays; select your primary display; and make sure the display resolution is set to a minimum of 1024 × 768.

7. Select Background. From the window that opens, click Background, and from the next window, click Wallpapers. Select another wallpaper and close the Settings application.

8. Open a GNOME terminal, and type `su` - to become root. Enter the root password.

9. Use `cd /home/user` to access the home directory of the template user you've been using. From there, type `cp -R .config /etc/skel`.

10. Type `useradd -m lori`, to create a user with the name lori. Type `passwd lori` to set a password for user lori.

11. Log out and log in again as user lori. Note that the settings that you've changed for linda are applied for user lori also.

Working with YaST

Where other Linux distributions assume that their administrators want to work with command-line utilities and configuration files to configure their distribution, SUSE has created an extensive management platform with the name YaST (Yet another Sysadmin Tool). YaST offers easy access to many tasks in SUSE and makes it easy for administrators who are not expert at Linux administration to do what they have to do anyway.

In this section, you'll learn how to work with YaST. We won't go through every single utility that is available in YaST, but you'll get a generic overview that will help you in understanding how to use YaST in your environment. In subsequent chapters in this book, you'll get detailed information about many of the utilities that are available from YaST.

■ **Note** The official name of YaST is YaST (Yet another Sysadmin Tool). However, when referring to the binary, you'll also encounter `yast` and `yast2`. When referring to `yast`, you typically refer to the program file that starts YaST in a non-graphical mode, while `yast2` is the binary that starts YaST in a graphical mode.

YaST vs. Configuration Files

A common prejudice that is often heard from administrators who don't understand YaST is that working with YaST makes it impossible to apply changes directly to the configuration files. While glitches have existed in very old versions of SUSE Linux, this is no longer the case. For SUSE, it is top priority to make sure that YaST can be used as an easy interface to the configuration files. YaST is there to create a basic configuration, which gives the administrator a starting point to further fine-tune the configuration file.

In many cases, YaST will notice when an administrator has applied manual modifications. These modifications will, in most cases, be picked up by YaST automatically, so there will rarely be conflicts. If, however, the administrator has applied changes that are incompatible with the way YaST is working, a backup configuration file will be created, to make sure that the administrator does not lose his or her hard work, but can manually integrate the modifications made from YaST with his/her own modifications. In many configuration files, you'll also see clear instructions on how to act if you want to make manual modifications, to ensure that you don't have conflicts with what YaST has been doing. Listing 2-1 offers an example of the first few lines of the /etc/default/grub configuration file.

Listing 2-1. Integration Between YaST and Configuration Files

```
linux-m6gc:~ # head /etc/default/grub
# Modified by YaST2. Last modification on Mon Sep  1 07:31:52 EDT 2014
# THIS FILE WILL BE PARTIALLY OVERWRITTEN by perl-Bootloader
# For the new kernel it try to figure out old parameters. In case we are not able to recognize
it (e.g. change of flavor or strange install order ) it it use as fallback installation parameters
from /etc/sysconfig/bootloader

# If you change this file, run 'grub2-mkconfig -o /boot/grub2/grub.cfg' afterwards to update
# /boot/grub2/grub.cfg.
```

YaST in This Book

In this book, I want to promote the philosophy behind YaST as a tool that makes working with Linux a lot easier for the system administrator. Many topics will be configured from YaST first. Once YaST has created a basic configuration, you'll get to know the configuration file behind it and learn which parts in the configuration file are important and what they mean.

YaST Interfaces

To make working with YaST as easy as possible, there are three different appearances of YaST. First, there is the so-called ncurses interface, which is developed for use in a non-graphical environment. You can start this interface by typing yast or yast –ncurses. In Figure 2-7, you can see what this interface looks like. It is likely that you'll use this interface a lot, because it works perfectly over remote sessions such as PuTTY or other kinds of SSH connections.

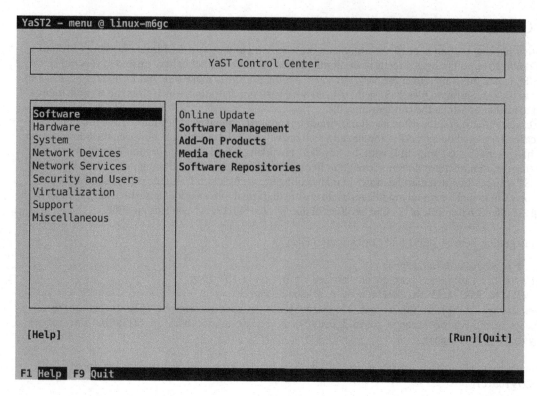

Figure 2-7. *The YaST ncurses interface*

To work with the ncurses interface, a few keys are important. First, there is the Tab key, which allows you to navigate between the main parts of the screen. Looking at the screen in Figure 2-7, you can see that there are a few main options. There's the pane on the left, from which you select the task category you want to work on. Within a task category, you'll see the different modules available in that task. Next, there are a couple of items available in the lower part of the screen. To navigate between these, use the Tab key, or use Shift+Tab to go backward.

If you're in one of the option panes, you need the arrow key, to move between options. Don't use the Tab key, because that will bring you to another pane of the YaST window. You'll also use the arrow keys to open drop-down lists. After selecting an option, you'll use the Enter key to open its further configuration. If within a certain window you find options to select or switch on/off, normally, you would use the Space bar to do that.

Also notice that on many occasions, there are shortcuts provided by function keys. F10, for example, is often used as the OK key, and F9 is used to Quit. Using these shortcuts makes it easier to make fast selections in YaST.

Apart from the ncurses interface, there are two graphical appearances of YaST, based on the QT and the GTK graphical user interfaces. The QT interface is the KDE interface, and as this interface is not supported on SLES, you won't use it. The GTK interface is what is needed in GNOME. An easy way to start YaST in GTK mode is by typing the command yast2. Alternatively, you can use yast --gtk to start it. (Depending on the software that is installed, this can generate an error message; it's safe to ignore that.) In Figure 2-8, you can see what the GTK interface looks like.

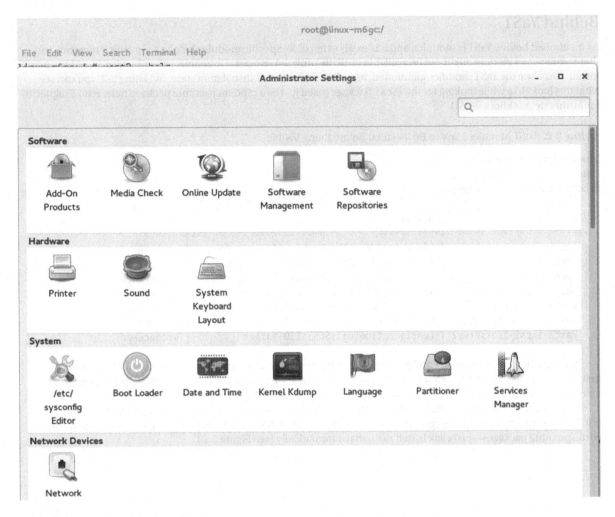

Figure 2-8. *The YaST GTK interface*

YaST Modules

YaST offers many different modules to accomplish a large diversity of tasks. That is convenient, because it allows you to browse, if you don't know exactly what you're doing. If, however, you're an experienced administrator who just wants to start a specific module, it's a waste of time to go through all the different menu options. There are a few solutions to that.

If you're using the GTK interface, there's a search bar in the upper-right corner. From this search bar, type a keyword, representing the kind of task that you want to perform. This will narrow the number of YaST modules that you see. If, for example, you type the text iscsi, it will only show the iSCSI management modules that are installed on your system, and nothing else.

Another approach is that you can directly call the module when starting YaST. If you type yast --list, a list of available modules is shown. From this list, you can look up the specific module that you need, and once you've found it, you can call it directly. If, for example, you want to start the Software Management utility directly, you can type yast sw_single. After closing the module, you won't see the main YaST window, but you'll get back to your starting terminal immediately.

Behind YaST

As mentioned before, YaST is modular, and it is easily extensible. Specific modules belong to specific programs, and that means that a module might not be available until the program using it is available. When looking for software to install, you'll see the YaST modules mentioned, as well as their current installation state. In Listing 2-2, you can see what this looks like while looking for the iscsi package (used just as a random example package here; read Chapter 16 for further details about iSCSI).

Listing 2-2. YaST Modules Have to Be Installed Before Being Visible

```
linux-m6gc:~ # zypper se iscsi
Loading repository data...
Reading installed packages...

S | Name                   | Summary                                   | Type
--+------------------------+-------------------------------------------+-----------
i | iscsiuio               | Linux Broadcom NetXtremem II iscsi server | package
i | open-iscsi             | Linux* Open-iSCSI Software Initiator       | package
  | open-iscsi             | Linux* Open-iSCSI Software Initiator       | srcpackage
i | yast2-iscsi-client     | YaST2 - iSCSI Client Configuration         | package
  | yast2-iscsi-client     | YaST2 - iSCSI Client Configuration         | srcpackage
  | yast2-iscsi-lio-server | Configuration of iSCSI LIO target         | package
  | yast2-iscsi-lio-server | Configuration of iSCSI LIO target         | srcpackage
```

So, imagine that you want to configure the iSCSI LIO target. You must install the corresponding YaST module first. To do that, use zypper in yast2-iscsi-lio-server. This will be explained in more detail in Chapter 5. To get an overview of all YaST modules that are available, type zypper search yast.

Some modules are so commonly used that they're installed by default. That is, the module is installed in YaST, but the software you need to configure the related service is not. If that is the case, you'll be prompted to install the corresponding packages—just click Install to do that automatically (see Figure 2-9).

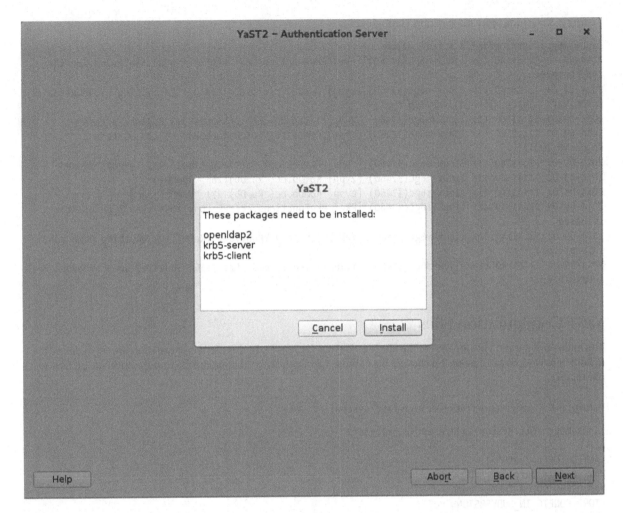

Figure 2-9. *Installing related software packages automatically*

An interesting part about YaST is that the modules it uses are written in perl. That means that if you're a perl programmer, you can easily create your own modules in YaST. YaST modules by default are installed in /usr/share/YaST2/modules. Have a look at them to get an impression on how they are organized.

YaST Logging

YaST activity is logged as well. You'll find the YaST2 logs in the directory /var/log/YaST2. Some modules have their own logging, which allows for detailed analysis of what they're doing. The generic yast log is /var/log/YaST2/y2log. In this log, you'll get detailed information about all the modules that were called by YaST and the status of that action (see Listing 2-3). If at any time YaST doesn't do what you expect it to, you can check here to find out what has happened.

Listing 2-3. Getting More Information Through y2log

```
linux-m6gc:/var/log/YaST2 # tail y2log
2014-09-01 12:41:40 <1> linux-m6gc(37460) [Pkg] PkgFunctions.cc(~PkgFunctions):158 Releasing the
zypp pointer...
2014-09-01 12:41:40 <1> linux-m6gc(37460) [zypp] RpmDb.cc(closeDatabase):734 Calling closeDatabase:
RpmDb[V4(X--)V3(---): '(/)/var/lib/rpm']
2014-09-01 12:41:40 <1> linux-m6gc(37460) [zypp] librpmDb.cc(blockAccess):328 Block access
2014-09-01 12:41:40 <1> linux-m6gc(37460) [zypp] RpmDb.cc(closeDatabase):765 closeDatabase:
RpmDb[NO_INIT]
2014-09-01 12:41:40 <1> linux-m6gc(37460) [zypp] TargetImpl.cc(~TargetImpl):953 Targets closed
2014-09-01 12:41:40 <1> linux-m6gc(37460) [zypp] RpmDb.cc(~RpmDb):268 ~RpmDb()
2014-09-01 12:41:40 <1> linux-m6gc(37460) [zypp] RpmDb.cc(~RpmDb):271 ~RpmDb() end
2014-09-01 12:41:40 <1> linux-m6gc(37460) [Pkg] PkgFunctions.cc(~PkgFunctions):160 Zypp pointer
released
2014-09-01 12:41:40 <1> linux-m6gc(37460) [Y2Ruby] binary/YRuby.cc(~YRuby):107 Shutting down ruby
interpreter.
2014-09-01 12:41:40 <1> linux-m6gc(37460) [Y2Perl] YPerl.cc(destroy):164 Shutting down embedded Perl
interpreter.
```

YaST Configuration Files

The main configuration file for YaST is the file /etc/sysconfig/yast2. In this file, some variables are set to define the default behavior of YaST. Listing 2-4 shows a list of those variables. You can open the file to see comments on how to use them.

Listing 2-4. Configuration Variables from /etc/sysconfig/yast2

```
linux-m6gc:/etc/sysconfig # grep -v ^\# yast2

WANTED_SHELL="auto"
WANTED_GUI="auto"
Y2NCURSES_COLOR_THEME="mono"
STORE_CONFIG_IN_SUBVERSION="no"
SUBVERSION_ADD_DIRS_RECURSIVE="no"
PKGMGR_ACTION_AT_EXIT="summary"
PKGMGR_AUTO_CHECK="yes"
PKGMGR_VERIFY_SYSTEM="no"
PKGMGR_REEVALUATE_RECOMMENDED="no"
USE_SNAPPER="no"
```

A setting that has been important in this book is Y2NCURSES_COLOR_THEME. By default, YaST is using light blue on a dark blue background, which may be very hard to read. By setting this variable to "mono", YaST displays in different shades of gray only, which in many situations, is much easier to read.

EXERCISE 2-4. WORKING WITH YAST

In this exercise, you'll explore some of the advanced YaST features. All tasks in this exercise have to be performed with root permissions.

1. Start YaST in GTK mode by typing `yast2` from a graphical environment. Use the search option in the upper-right part of the screen to look for iSCSI modules. You'll see one module only.

2. From a console, type `zypper se iscsi`. Install the iSCSI LIO server package, using `zypper in yast2-iscsi-lio-server`. Repeat step 1. You'll see that the package is now listed. (You must restart `yast` for this to work.)

3. Use `yast --list`, to find the module that allows you to manage users. Start it by specifying the module name as the argument.

4. Change YaST to use monochrome when started in ncurses mode. To do this, open the configuration file `/etc/sysconfig/yast2` and set `Y2NCURSES_COLOR_THEME="mono"`.

Summary

In this chapter, you've learned to work with some of the particulars of SUSE Linux Enterprise Server (SLES). First, you have explored the GNOME 3 graphical interface and worked with some of the most useful programs that it offers. Next, you've learned how to use YaST as the default tool for configuration of many aspects of SLES. In the next chapter, you'll learn how to manage file systems on SLES.

Administering SUSE Linux Enteprise Server

CHAPTER 3

■ ■ ■

Managing Disk Layout and File Systems

On a Linux server, the way in which the hard disk is organized—and in which the file systems are created on that hard disk—is essential. There are many choices to be made, and there is no single solution that fits all needs. In this chapter, you'll first assess if you have to work with partitions, or whether you're better off working with logical volumes. You'll also examine how partitions and volume behave differently on a master boot record (MBR) and on a globally unique identifier (GUID) partition table. Next, you'll discover how to create partitions and logical volumes. Once the storage volume has been created, you have to put a file system on it. In this chapter, you'll learn which file system best fits your needs and how to manage specific file-system features.

Creating a Storage Volume

When deciding on the design of hard disk layout, different options are available, depending on the hardware that is used. Options start with the type of disk that is used. On each disk, a boot loader is required. You'll have to decide between the classical master boot record and the newer globally unique identifier–based partition table. After making that choice, you'll have to decide whether to use partitions on logical volumes. This section explains your options.

The Partition Table: GUID vs. MBR

Since 1981, the MS-DOS-type boot sector has been used. With this type of boot sector, which is also known as a master boot record (MBR), a maximum disk size of 2TB is supported, and disk layout is based on partitions. As the amount of space in this type of boot sector is limited, a maximum amount of four partitions can be created. If more than four partitions are required, an extended partition is used, and within the extended partition, multiple logical partitions are created.

In current data centers, the maximum size of disks goes more and more frequently beyond 2TB. With the limited amount of address space that is available in MBR, this no longer can be addressed. That is why a new type of boot loader has been introduced. In this boot loader, the GUID Partition Table (GPT) is used. In this type of partition table, all partitions are primary partitions. Owing to the increased address space, the necessity to work with logical partitions has ceased.

A modern Linux distribution such as SUSE Linux Enterprise Server (SLES) can handle the difference between GPT and MBR. If partitions are created from YaST, the differences aren't even visible. If, however, you're using command-line utilities, you must be wary, because GPT partitions demand a different approach than MBR partitions. For the administrator, it's often not a choice whether to use GPT.

Partitions or Logical Volumes?

The other choice that you'll have to make as an administrator is between partitions and logical volumes. Partitions are the old way of organizing a disk, where every storage volume has a fixed size. Using partitions has a few disadvantages: you cannot easily resize them, and the maximum amount of partitions that can be created is limited.

Logical volumes, also referred to as LVM, have been introduced as an alternative. With LVM, it is relatively easy to resize the storage volume. Also, logical volumes aren't bound to the physical device they are created on. In LVM, all storage devices are grouped in the volume group, and logical volumes are created from the volume group. The result is that if a logical volume grows out of disk space, it is easy to add a disk to the volume group, which allows for growth of the logical volume.

While LVM is very flexible and offers important benefits, compared to traditional partitions, with the rise of the Btrfs file system, the need to create logical volumes has decreased. Many features that were previously supported only on LVM are now also supported in the Btrfs file system. So, if Btrfs is used, you can do without LVM. But, if on your server multiple file systems are used side by side, it can still be interesting to use LVM. To allow you to use the disk layout that works best for your environment, this chapter discusses both solutions.

Creating Partitions

If you're used to such tools as fdisk for managing partitions, you're welcome to do so on SLES. If you want to make it a bit easier, while having full access to all of the advanced options that exist when working with storage, you can use YaST as a partitioning tool. When creating partitions or logical volumes from YaST, everything is integrated, and after creating the partition, you can easily put a file system on it.

Creating Partitions from YaST

To start the partitioning utility from YaST, select System ➤ Partitioner. This will elicit a warning, from which you can select Yes to continue. You'll then see the Expert Partitioner screen, which is shown in Figure 3-1.

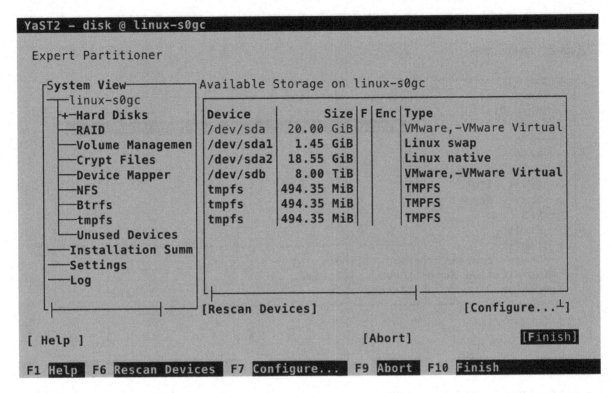

Figure 3-1. *The Expert Partitioner interface*

■ **Note** In this book, I prefer showing the ncurses interface of YaST, not because it is prettier, but because it is always available, no matter if you're working from a text-only session or a complete graphical environment.

To add a partition, from the Expert Partitioner window, you'll have to use the Tab key to navigate to the disk on which you want to create a partition. This gives access to the interface you see in Figure 3-2.

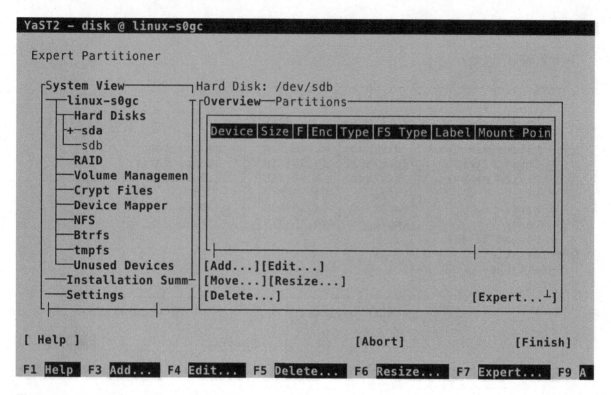

Figure 3-2. *Options for creating new partitions*

To add a new partition, select Add. This first opens a window, from which you can specify the size you want to use (see Figure 3-3). By default, all available disk space is selected, so if you don't want to use it all, specify the size you want to assign in MiB, GiB, or TiB. Note that the notation MiB (Mebibyte), and so forth, refers to a multiple of 1024 bytes. This is in contrast to MB, which is a multiple of 1000 bytes.

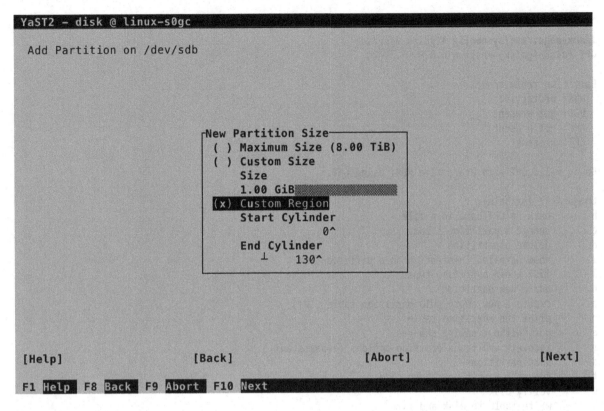

Figure 3-3. *Specifying partition size*

After specifying the partition size you want to use, you can select the role for the partition. Depending on the role you've selected, a preselection of file system and mount point will be made. You can also choose the option Raw Volume, which allows you to format the partition at a later stage. This can be useful if, for example, you want to reserve disk space for use as a storage back end for an iSCSI LUN or a virtual machine.

In the next screen, you can select the file system type and mount options. These topics are explained in detail later in this chapter. When you're back on the main screen of the Expert Partitioner, you'll see the new partition. It hasn't been committed to disk yet, however. To commit the changes to disk, select Next and Finish.

Creating Partitions from the Command Line

If you want to create partitions on an MBR disk, you have to use fdisk. To create partitions on a GUID disk, you'll have to use gdisk. The utilities are pretty similar, but the information that is written is different, so make sure to use the right tool. As GUID partitions are rapidly becoming more common, in this chapter, I'll explain gdisk and not fdisk.

To create a partition, type gdisk, followed by the name of the device you want to use. This gives you a message about the current disk partitioning and will next allow you to perform your manipulations on that disk. For an overview of available commands, type ? (see Listing 3-1).

Listing 3-1. Working from the gdisk Interface

```
linux-s0gc:/etc/sysconfig # gdisk /dev/sdb
GPT fdisk (gdisk) version 0.8.8

Partition table scan:
  MBR: protective
  BSD: not present
  APM: not present
  GPT: present

Found valid GPT with protective MBR; using GPT.

Command (? for help): ?
b       back up GPT data to a file
c       change a partition's name
d       delete a partition
i       show detailed information on a partition
l       list known partition types
n       add a new partition
o       create a new empty GUID partition table (GPT)
p       print the partition table
q       quit without saving changes
r       recovery and transformation options (experts only)
s       sort partitions
t       change a partition's type code
v       verify disk
w       write table to disk and exit
x       extra functionality (experts only)
?       print this menu

Command (? for help):
```

To create a new partition, type n. You can now select the partition number you want to create. The maximum amount of GUID partitions is 128, but you should number partitions in order, so normally, you can just press Enter to select the partition number that is proposed. Next, it asks for the first sector to use. A sector has a size of 512 bytes, and by default, the first sector that is used is 2048. You should not have your partition start anywhere else, unless you have a very good reason.

After selecting the starting point for the partition, you can specify the size. The easiest way to specify a size is by using a + sign, followed by an amount and the identifier K, M, G, T, or P, according to the amount of kilo-, mega-, giga-, tera-, or petabyte you want to assign. You next have to assign the partition type you want to use. For all normal Linux file systems, the default partition type 8300 works fine. Note that the partition type is *not* the same as the file system type. The partition type indicates the intended use of a partition, and in many cases, it's not necessary to set a specific partition type. After creating the partition, type p, for an overview. The result should resemble Listing 3-2.

Listing 3-2. Verifying Partition Creation

```
Command (? for help): p
Disk /dev/sdb: 17179869184 sectors, 8.0 TiB
Logical sector size: 512 bytes
Disk identifier (GUID): DF090B7D-9509-4B13-95E2-BC8D7E98B4C1
Partition table holds up to 128 entries
First usable sector is 34, last usable sector is 17179869150
Partitions will be aligned on 2048-sector boundaries
Total free space is 17177771965 sectors (8.0 TiB)

Number  Start (sector)    End (sector)   Size        Code  Name
1       2048              2099199        1024.0 MiB  8300  Linux filesystem

Command (? for help):
```

If you're happy with the results so far, press w to write the results to disk. If you're not happy after all, press q to get out without changing any of the new partitions.

■ **Warning**   It is extremely important that you not use gdisk on a partition that is configured to use MBR, if you are booting from that disk. Gdisk will overwrite the MBR, which makes your disk unbootable.

Creating Logical Volumes

As for partitions, you can also create logical volumes from YaST or from the command line. In this section, you'll learn how to do both.

Creating Logical Volumes from YaST

If you want to create logical volumes, YaST offers an easy-to-use interface. First, you should make sure that you have disk space available for creating logical volumes. That can be as a partition that you've created as partition type 0x8e. You're also fine if you have unallocated disk space available.

To create logical volumes, start from YaST ➤ System ➤ Partitioner. Click Yes when the warning is displayed, which opens Expert Partitioner. Before you're able to add new logical volumes, you need either a complete disk or a partition that has been set up with the partition type 0x8e. To create such a partition, from the YaST Expert Partitioner, select Hard Disks, and after selecting it, press the space bar. This will show you all available hard disks. Select the hard disk on which you want to work and press Enter. This opens the window that you can see in Figure 3-4.

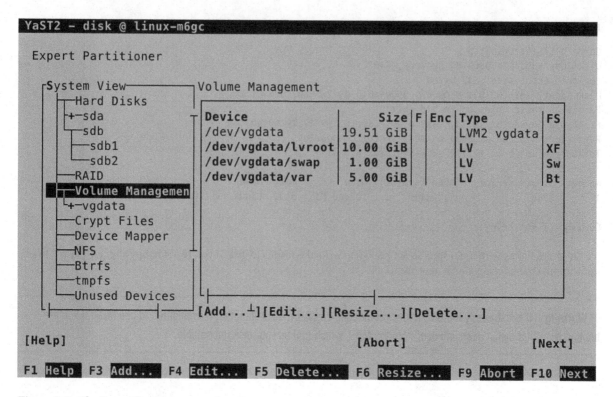

Figure 3-4. *The Expert Partitioner overview*

From this window, use the Tab key to select Add and create a new partition. By default, the Custom Size option is selected, which allows you to specify the intended partition size manually. Enter the partition size you'd like to use and select Next. You'll now see the screen on which you can select the partition role. From this screen, select Raw Volume (unformatted) and press Next. This will by default set the Linux LVM system ID. Click Finish to complete this part of the procedure.

After creating the LVM partition, you can move on to the Volume Management part in the Expert Partitioner. Select Volume Management and press Enter. This will open the Volume Management interface, which you can see in Figure 3-5.

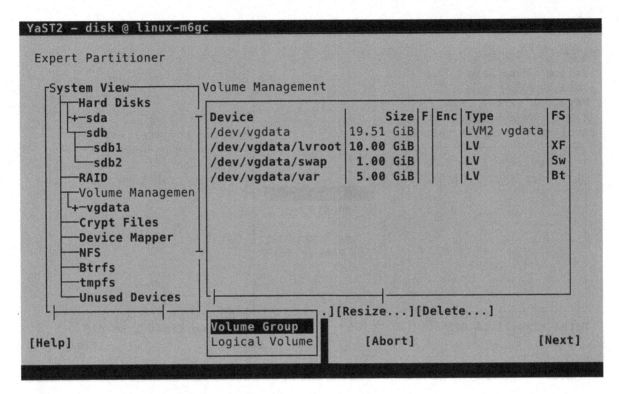

```
YaST2 - disk @ linux-m6gc

  Expert Partitioner

  ┌System View──────────┐ Volume Management
  │  ┬─Hard Disks       │ ┌──────────────────────────────────────────────┐
  │  ├+─sda            ┬│ │Device              Size│F│Enc│Type        │FS │
  │  ├─sdb             ││ │/dev/vgdata      19.51 GiB│ │   │LVM2 vgdata │   │
  │  ├─sdb1            ││ │/dev/vgdata/lvroot│10.00 GiB│ │  │LV          │XF │
  │  └─sdb2            ││ │/dev/vgdata/swap  │ 1.00 GiB│ │  │LV          │Sw │
  │  ─RAID             ││ │/dev/vgdata/var   │ 5.00 GiB│ │  │LV          │Bt │
  │  ─Volume Managemen  ││ │                                              │
  │  └+─vgdata          ││ │                                              │
  │  ─Crypt Files      ││ │                                              │
  │  ─Device Mapper    ││ │                                              │
  │  ─NFS              ┘│ │                                              │
  │  ─Btrfs            │ │                                              │
  │  ─tmpfs            │ │                                              │
  │  └─Unused Devices  │ └──────────────────────────────────────────────┘
  └─────────────────────┘         .][Resize...][Delete...]
                       ┌─────────────────┐
  [Help]               │Volume Group     │        [Abort]            [Next]
                       │Logical Volume   │
                       └─────────────────┘
```

Figure 3-5. *Creating LVM logical volumes from YaST*

From this interface, select Add. Depending on what has been created previously, you can now select between a volume group and a logical volume. In Figure 3-5, you can see an example of this window that was taken on a computer that was set up to use LVM. Before you can add a new logical volume, you must have a volume group. If no volume group exists yet, select Volume Group. If you already have an LVM set up on your computer, you can directly add a logical volume—if disk space is still available in the logical volume.

The volume group is the abstraction of all available disk space that can be assigned to LVM. You'll have to put disks in it (the so-called physical volumes), and once disk space has been assigned to the volume group, on the other end, you can create logical volumes out of it.

To create the volume group, you'll first have to specify a name. To make it easy to find the volume groups later, it's a good idea to start volume group names with the letters *vg*, but you're not required to do that. Next, you'll have to specify the physical extent size. These are the minimal building blocks that you're going to use in LVM. If you're planning on creating huge logical volumes, set the physical extent size to the maximum of 64MiB. Every logical volume you'll create will always have a size that is a multiple of 64MiB. For regular purposes, the default size of 4MiB does just fine.

After specifying the physical extent size, you must add physical volumes (disks or partitions) to the volume group. Make sure that you only select the intended disks or partitions, and after selecting them, click Add to add them to the set of selected physical volumes. At this point, you should see an interface that looks as in Figure 3-6.

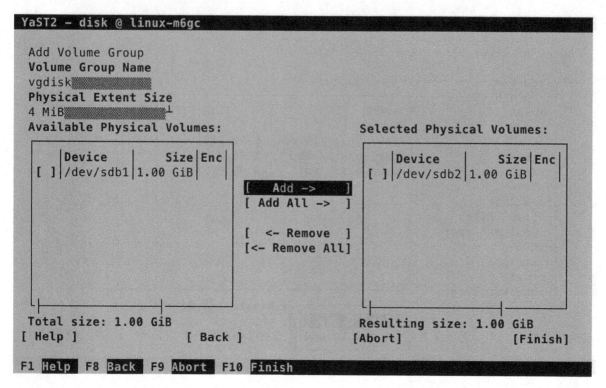

Figure 3-6. *Creating an LVM volume group*

After creating the volume group, you'll return to the Expert Partitioner main window. From this window, select the volume group that you've just created and use the Tab key on your keyboard to navigate to the Add option. From the drop-down list, select Logical Volume. This opens the screen that you see in Figure 3-7.

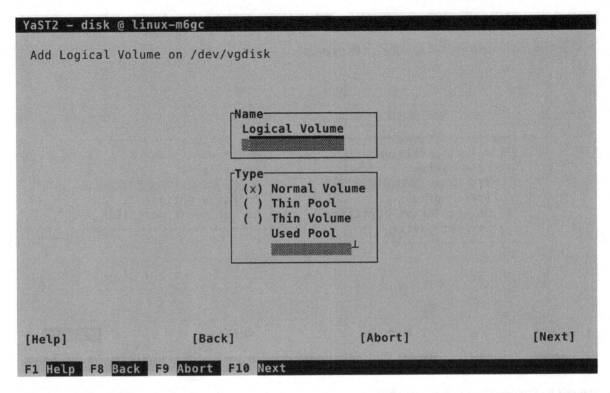

Figure 3-7. *Adding a logical volume*

To add a logical volume, you have to set the name of the logical volume and select the normal volume type. Then click Next and specify the size of the logical volume. By default, it wants to allocate the maximum size that is available in the volume group. That is not always a good idea, so you might be better off selecting a custom size. If there are multiple physical volumes in your volume group, you can also set the amount of stripes. By selecting an amount of stripes that is equal to the amount of physical volumes, you'll load-balance read and write requests to the logical volumes, which allows you to create a Redundant Array of Inexpensive Disks (RAID) set on top of LVM. If you have just one disk, set the stripe size to 1.

From the next screen, you'll have the opportunity to add a file system. As this will be discussed separately in a subsequent section, we'll skip it here. To step out without creating a file system now, select Raw Volume (unformatted) and in the next screen, make sure that Do not format partition and Do not mount partition are selected (see Figure 3-8).

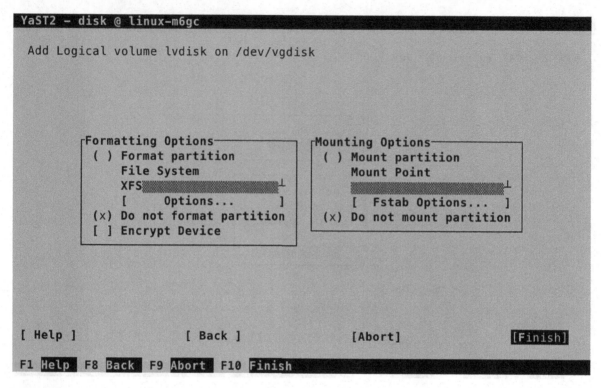

Figure 3-8. *Skipping File System creation for now*

Creating Logical Volumes from the Command Line

To create an LVM setup from the command line, you'll start by creating a partition. To do this, you can follow the directions that were given in the section "Creating Partitions from the Command Line." When gdisk asks which partition type to use, make sure to enter 8E00, which assigns the LVM partition type to the partition (see Listing 3-3).

Listing 3-3. Creating an LVM Partition Type

```
Command (? for help): n
Partition number (3-128, default 3): 3
First sector (34-17179869150, default = 4208640) or {+-}size{KMGTP}:
Last sector (4208640-17179869150, default = 17179869150) or {+-}size{KMGTP}: +1G
Current type is 'Linux filesystem'
Hex code or GUID (L to show codes, Enter = 8300): 8E00
Changed type of partition to 'Linux LVM'

Command (? for help):
```

Next, type w to write the partition to disk. If you're using fdisk to create the partition, you must first define the partition and next type t to change the partition type. Set the partition type to 8e and type w to write the changes to disk. Next, run partprobe to make sure that the kernel is updated with the new changes to the partition table.

After creating the partition, you have to make it a physical volume. To do that, you'll use the pvcreate command. The command is easy and straightforward to use: just type pvcreate, followed by the name of the partition you've just created, as in pvcreate /dev/sdb3. Next, type pvs to verify that you succeeded and the physical volume has been created (see Listing 3-4).

Listing 3-4. Verifying the Creation of Physical Volumes

```
linux-m6gc:~ # pvs
  PV         VG      Fmt  Attr PSize   PFree
  /dev/sda2  vgdata  lvm2 a--  19.51g   3.51g
  /dev/sdb2  vgdisk  lvm2 a--   1.00g 516.00m
  /dev/sdb3          lvm2 a--   1.00g   1.00g
```

In Listing 3-4, you can see that the physical volume has been added, but it's not a part of any volume group yet. To put it in a volume group, you can now use the vgcreate command. This command has two mandatory options: you'll have to specify the name of the volume group that you want to create, as well as the name of the device that you want to add to it, as in vgcreate vgsan /dev/sdb3. That would create the volume group for you, and you can verify that by using vgs or vgdisplay. Use vgs if you want to see a short summary of the volume groups on your system and their properties; use vgdisplay if you're looking for more extended information. In Listing 3-5, you can see the output of both commands.

Listing 3-5. Showing Volume Group Properties

```
linux-m6gc:~ # vgs
  VG      #PV #LV #SN Attr   VSize   VFree
  vgdata    1   3   0 wz--n- 19.51g   3.51g
  vgdisk    1   1   0 wz--n-  1.00g 516.00m
linux-m6gc:~ # vgdisplay vgdisk
  --- Volume group ---
  VG Name               vgdisk
  System ID
  Format                lvm2
  Metadata Areas        1
  Metadata Sequence No  2
  VG Access             read/write
  VG Status             resizable
  MAX LV                0
  Cur LV                1
  Open LV               0
  Max PV                0
  Cur PV                1
  Act PV                1
  VG Size               1.00 GiB
  PE Size               4.00 MiB
  Total PE              257
  Alloc PE / Size       128 / 512.00 MiB
  Free  PE / Size       129 / 516.00 MiB
  VG UUID               c2l6y9-ibIo-Zdp0-tWeE-WxZl-jmW9-YHaC1Y
```

In both commands, you can see how many physical volumes are added to the volume groups. You can also see the amount of logical volumes currently existing in the volume group and a summary of the total size and available free space in the volume groups.

Now that you have created the volume group, you can add a logical volume to it. To do that, you'll use the `lvcreate` command. This command requires at least two arguments: the size you want to use and the name of the volume group into which you want to put the logical volume. It is also a good idea to specify a name. If you don't do that, a random name will be generated. If, for example, you wanted to create a logical volume with a size of 500MB, the name lvdb, and put that in the volume group that uses the name vgdisk, the command to use is `lvcreate -L 500M -n lvdb vgdisk`. You can next use the command `lvs` to get an overview of the logical volume properties, or `lvdisplay`, if you want to see more details about it.

Creating and Mounting File Systems

At this point, you should have either a partition or a logical volume, and you're ready to create a file system on it. Before moving on and actually doing that, you'll have to know about differences between Linux file systems. In the next section, you can read about these. Next, you'll learn how to create a file system and how to make sure that the file system is automatically mounted on reboot.

Understanding File System Features

On Linux, many file systems are available, and recently some important changes have occurred, which leaves you with many choices for the file system that you want to use. Before moving on and teaching you how to actually create and manage a file system, we'll first discuss the different options, so that you can select the file system that fits your needs best.

Ext File Systems

Shortly after the release of Linux in 1992, the System Extended File version 2 (Ext2) was released. This file system perfectly met the data needs of the early days of Linux. Ext2 has been the default Linux file system for some years, until the need for journaling became more manifest.

A file system journal is used to keep track of all ongoing transactions on the file system. That means that if at any time something goes wrong on a server and the server crashes, the file system can be easily recovered from the journal. If a journal is present, recovering the file system is a matter of seconds. If no journal is present, for file system recovery, an extensive file system check has to be performed, and the consistency of every single file has to be verified. On a small file system, that can take a long time; on a modern file system, that can take days. That is why file system journaling is an essential need for any new file system.

The biggest improvement in Ext3, the successor of Ext2, is that it has a file system journal by default. Also, some improvements have been made to make the kernel module, as well as the indexing that is used in the file system, more efficient. Ext3 was the default file system in SUSE Linux Enterprise Server 11.

The major disadvantage of Ext3 is the way it organizes access to files. Ext3 keeps track of its files by using linear indexes. This makes the file system slower when more files are used in the file system. Unfortunately, stepping away from the way an Ext3 file system is organized would mean a radical redesign of the whole file system. That is why on the day the Ext3 successor Ext4 was released, it was already clear that this file system wasn't going to last, and something else would be needed to fit the needs of modern-day data centers.

Nevertheless, Ext4 has been, and still is, an important Linux file system. Compared to Ext3, the kernel module has been rewritten to make it faster and more efficient, and a new way of allocating blocks to the file system has been added: the use of extents.

An extent is a group of blocks that can be addressed and administered as one entity. The default size of an extent is 2MB. Compared to the often-used default file system block size of 4KB, using extents means an important reduction in the amount of blocks that has to be administered for a file. Imagine a file with a size of 2GB, for example. It would need 500,000 blocks for its administration, whereas only 1,000 extents are needed for its administration. Ext4 extents make the file system administration a lot more efficient, but it doesn't take away the inefficiency in addressing files. For that reason, on modern generation Linux distributions, new solutions have been introduced.

Even if new file systems have been introduced, Ext4 is still commonly used. To its credit is that it is a very stable file system, as well as a very well-known file system. That means that there is excellent tooling available to repair problems occurring on Ext4 and that many options are available for its optimum use.

ReiserFS

The first serious attempt to offer an alternative to the Ext file systems was made with ReiserFS. This file system was introduced in the late 1990s as the default file system used by SUSE. It was a revolutionary file system in its approach, as it was organized around a database, to keep track of file system administration, instead of the slow and inefficient linear tables that are used in Ext file systems.

Unfortunately, the integration of ReiserFS with the kernel was not optimal, and that is why with the release of SLES 11, SUSE has dropped ReiserFS as the default file system. Nevertheless, ReiserFS is still available on SLES 12, and if you need a file system that can deal with many small files in an efficient way, it still is a valid choice. You should realize, however, that it is not the most popular file system, which means that it may be difficult to get support, should you ever encounter serious trouble using it.

Btrfs

Since 2008, developer Chris Mason has been working on the next generation Linux file system: Btrfs. This file system is developed as a Copy on Write (CoW) file system, which means that old versions of files can be maintained while working on them. When writing block, the old block is copied to a new location, so that two different versions of the data block exist, which helps to prevent problems on the file system. In 2009, Btrfs was accepted in the Linux kernel, and since then, it is available in several Linux distributions. Since the beginning, SUSE has been one of the leading distributions to show support for Btrfs.

Apart from being a CoW file system, Btrfs has many other useful features. Among these features are the subvolumes. A subvolume can be seen as something that sits between a volume or logical partition and a directory. It is not a different device, but subvolumes can be mounted with their own specific mount options. This makes working with file systems completely different. Whereas on old Linux file systems you needed a dedicated device if you had to mount a file system with specific options, in Btrfs you can just keep it all on the same subvolume.

Another important feature of Btrfs are snapshots. A snapshot freezes the state of the file system at a specific moment, which can be useful if you must be able to revert to an old state of the file system, or if you have to make a backup of the file system.

Because Btrfs is a CoW file system, snapshots are very easy to create. While modifying files, a copy is made of the old file. That means that the state of the old file is still available, and only new data blocks have to be added to that. From the metadata perspective, it is very easy to deal with both of these, which is why it is easy to create snapshots and revert files to an earlier version.

Snapshots are useful if you want to revert to a previous version of a file, but they also come in handy for making backups. Files in a snapshot will never have a status of open. That means that files in a snapshot always have a stable state that can be used to create a backup. Because it is easy to create snapshots from Btrfs subvolumes, SLES takes care of this automatically. These snapshots are used from the snapper utility, a front-end utility that makes it easier to revert to earlier versions of a file. You can even select from the Grub boot menu, to revert to an earlier state of your system.

XFS

Where Btrfs definitely is the choice of the future, it's a relatively new file system, and not so long ago, it still had features that made many administrators question if it really was the best choice for their environment. That is why in SLES, the XFS file system is used as the default file system for operating system volumes.

XFS is a file system that was developed by SGI in the mid-1990s as a file system that organizes its metadata administration based on a database. It is a proven file system that has been around for a long time and is very flexible in the different options that can be used with it. XFS can be tuned for different environments. It is very usable for servers that have to deal with many small files but also for servers that have to be configured for streaming large files.

Creating and Mounting the File System

The easiest way to create a file system on SLES is from YaST. You can just follow the prompts that are provided when creating logical volumes or partitions. You can also add a new file system to a device that has been created previously, which you'll read about in this section.

Creating File Systems from YaST

To create a file system on a device, you first have to select the device. In the YaST Partitioner, you'll either open the Hard Disks view, or you'll open the Volume Management view, to select the device on which you want to create the file system. Select the device and, next, select Edit, to modify its properties in the interface, which you can see in Figure 3-9.

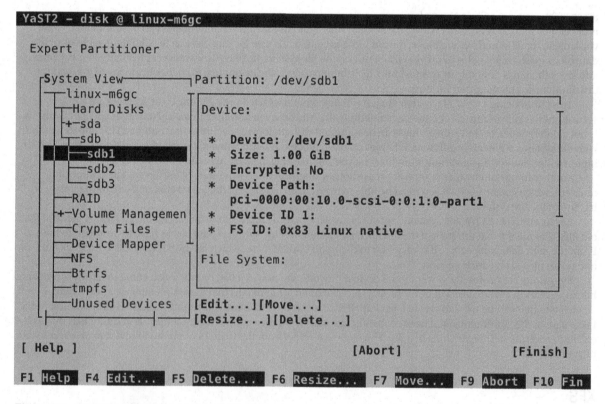

Figure 3-9. Creating a file system on an existing device

You'll now see the screen that you can see in Figure 3-10, on which you have to specify how you want to create the file system. In Formatting Options, select Format Partition. Next, use the down arrow key to select the file system you want to use, or accept the default selection of the Btrfs file system. You'll next have to specify a mount point also. This is the directory that users will go to to work with this file system.

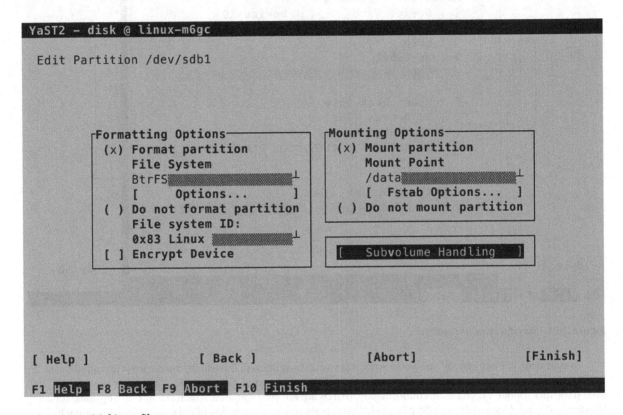

Figure 3-10. *Making a file system*

While creating a file system, you can specify specific fstab options. To make sure that the file system is automatically mounted on system boot, a reference to the file system is placed in the /etc/fstab file. YaST will take care of that automatically for you, but you can easily access different mount options, by selecting the fstab options, which you can see in Figure 3-11.

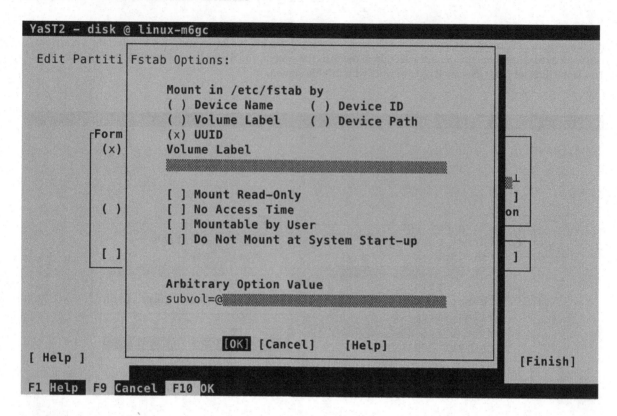

Figure 3-11. Specifying mount options

To start with, you can specify how you want the device to be mounted. By default, the device is mounted by its UUID. That is a universal unique ID that is written to the file system on the device and that will never change, not even if the disk topology is changed. Unfortunately, UUIDs are not very readable, which is why other options, such as the device ID and device path, are offered as well. You can also choose to use one of the more classical approaches, such as a mount that is based on device name (such as /dev/sdb1), or a mount that is based on a volume label that is written to the file system. From YaST, you can specify the volume label that you want to use (see Figure 3-11).

While mounting the file system, you can also select some mount options. The mount option No Access Time can be useful. This option makes it unnecessary for the file system metadata to be updated every time the file system is accessed, which is good for performance. There are many more mount options, however, that are not listed here, so if you have specific needs, you might want to edit the /etc/fstab file manually.

If you have elected to create a Btrfs file system, you can also create subvolumes from YaST. A subvolume is created as a subdirectory in the mount point that you're working on. To add a subvolume, specify its name in the YaST interface, shown in Figure 3-12, and select Add new. This will add the subvolume to the list (but won't do anything else with it). When done, select OK, to write the changes to disk. You have now added the file system to the /etc/fstab file, to ensure that it is mounted automatically on boot.

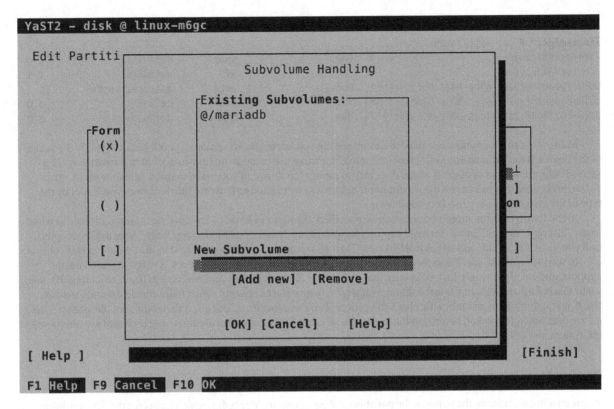

Figure 3-12. Adding subvolumes from YaST

Creating File Systems Manually

Instead of using YaST, you can also create file systems manually. This even adds some more flexibility, as from the command line, some tools are available that are not available from YaST. These allow you, for example, to create a ReiserFS file system, which you cannot do from YaST.

To add a file system from the command line, different utilities are available. To get an overview of these, type mkfs and hit the Tab key on your keyboard twice. This shows all commands that have a name beginning in *mkfs*. As each file system has different features and options, the options offered by these commands will be quite different from one another. If you want to create the file system the easy way, you can just type the name of the command, followed by the device name on which you want to create the file system, as in mkfs.ext4 /dev/sdb2. This will create a file system with default options for you, which, in most cases, will work just fine.

Making Manual Modifications to /etc/fstab

After creating the file system, you can put it in /etc/fstab for automatic mount after a reboot. In Listing 3-6, you can see an example of what the contents of /etc/fstab typically looks like.

Listing 3-6. Sample /etc/fstab Contents

```
linux-m6gc:~ # cat /etc/fstab
/dev/vgdata/swap                                    swap              swap        defaults            0 0
/dev/vgdata/lvroot                                  /                 xfs         defaults            1 1
UUID=781ab8eb-b1eb-49b4-b44a-8bf309e5b99c /boot                       ext4        acl,user_xattr      1 2
UUID=bab5beb7-02df-4697-809e-63d4a25d68bd /var                        btrfs       defaults            0 0
UUID=b0738048-2a89-4cd5-9d8e-dce32bc13f88 /data                       btrfs       defaults            0 0
```

In /etc/fstab, six columns are used to mount the file system. In the first column, you'll have to specify the name of the device. Read the next section, "Device Naming," for more information on how to do that in a smart way. The second column tells the system on which directory to mount the device. If you make manual adjustments to /etc/fstab, make sure that you create the mount point before you try mounting it! In the third column, you'll specify the type of file system you have used on this device.

In the fourth column, mount options can be specified. If you don't know of any specific mount options you want to use, just type "default," but if you need support for quota (see the section "Managing Quota," later in this chapter), or if you need support for access control lists (see Chapter 4), you can enter the required mount option in this column.

In the fifth column, you'll specify the backup option. This column needs to have a 1, if you want full backup support, and a 0, if you don't. Just make sure that on any real file system, this column has a 1. If you're using Btrfs, use a 0 in this column as well. In the last column, you'll specify how the file system needs to be checked during mount. Use 0, if you don't want an automatic check to occur or if you're using Btrfs. Use a 1, if this is the root file system. Using a 1 ensures that it is checked before anything else. On all other file systems that are not using Btrfs and are not the root file system, use a 2.

Device Naming

When creating a partition, the name of the partition will be similar to /dev/sdc1, which indicates the first partition on the third hard disk that will be found on the SCSI bus. Using device names such as /dev/sdc1 works perfectly in a scenario in which servers are connected to physical disks, and the storage topology never changes.

Nowadays, many servers are connected to a Storage Area Network (SAN) to access storage. This means that storage has become much more flexible and that storage topology can change, with the result that the device that was previously known as /dev/sdc1 will now be known as /dev/sdf1, or any other device name that you did not expect. That is why a more flexible approach to file system naming is needed. On modern Linux systems, three different alternatives for file system naming exist:

- UUID

- File System Labels

- /dev/disk naming

When a file system is created, the file system is automatically assigned a universal unique ID (UUID). This UUID is long and difficult to read, but it does have one benefit: it is bound to the file system, and it will never change spontaneously. If you're on a dynamic storage topology, it might be smart to use UUIDs. You can get a list of all UUIDs currently available on your system by typing the blkid command (see Listing 3-7).

Listing 3-7. Typing blkid for an Overview of UUIDs on Your System

```
linux-m6gc:~ # blkid
/dev/sda1: UUID="781ab8eb-b1eb-49b4-b44a-8bf309e5b99c" TYPE="ext4" PTTYPE="dos"
PARTLABEL="primary" PARTUUID="e1695ed9-f2db-495b-9fdd-b970eb7569a7"
/dev/sda2: UUID="Pteo9u-cBKv-3PG7-Vt1n-Mv2H-Tm53-EbK5Oi" TYPE="LVM2_member"
PARTLABEL="primary" PARTUUID="3ca331eb-c2fc-4d29-9dc7-ba3df66034f1"
```

```
/dev/sr0: UUID="2014-08-21-14-06-45-00" LABEL="SLE-12-Server-DVD-x86_6406991" TYPE="iso9660"
PTUUID="2663792f" PTTYPE="dos"
/dev/mapper/vgdata-swap: UUID="7e6db5e9-69cf-4292-b75a-24f4c4871a27" TYPE="swap"
/dev/mapper/vgdata-lvroot: UUID="f029648c-2218-403b-8d86-b2ef9b684c48" TYPE="xfs"
/dev/mapper/vgdata-var: UUID="bab5beb7-02df-4697-809e-63d4a25d68bd"
UUID_SUB="555f2b23-5d33-4ea6-8903-d66faf5b8a82" TYPE="btrfs"
/dev/sdb2: UUID="evADgP-Nb3w-X6cz-g9CD-fZrq-alPE-AjeERC" TYPE="LVM2_member" PARTLABEL="primary"
PARTUUID="4757de6c-7688-49c8-9a84-0c251381f361"
/dev/sdb3: UUID="qfCHtq-dK2Q-JSMG-GM8s-BdNM-K265-ZndJ3T" TYPE="LVM2_member" PARTLABEL="Linux LVM"
PARTUUID="dfe179c2-ed97-4cd2-829a-c619f8ee240c"
/dev/sdb1: UUID="b0738048-2a89-4cd5-9d8e-dce32bc13f88"
UUID_SUB="a5618c9e-ca89-4a6d-bc97-570e54b55276" TYPE="btrfs" PARTLABEL="Linux filesystem"
PARTUUID="927ec3f4-963f-41e1-a0e1-b34d69e1ff21"
```

Originally, UUIDs were assigned when creating the file system. If you're using GUIDs, there is an alternative to the file system UUID, and that is the partition UUID, which is displayed as PARTUUID in the output of the blkid command. To mount a file system based on its UUID, you can include UUID= in /etc/fstab; to mount it on its partition UUID, you can use PARTUUID= in /etc/fstab.

While UUIDs do serve their purpose and offer worldwide unique naming, they are not very user-friendly. If a problem occurs while mounting a file system, you won't be able to see at first sight that it is because of a wrong UUID. That is where file system labels may come in handy. Most mkfs utilities support the option -L to assign a human readable name to a file system. Using a label, you can specify a mount option such as LABEL=database in /etc/fstab. You can get an overview of labels currently defined by using the blkid command also.

Another option that ensures you have unique device naming is to use the names that are created in the /dev/disk directory. Depending on the specific configuration of the device, you'll find the device name represented in different ways. In Listing 3-8, you can see what the contents of the /dev/disk/by-path directory looks like. Using these names can be a relatively readable way to refer to devices.

Listing 3-8. Device Naming in /dev/disk/by-path

```
linux-m6gc:/dev/disk/by-path # \ls -l
total 0
lrwxrwxrwx 1 root root  9 Sep  9 12:52 pci-0000:00:10.0-scsi-0:0:0:0 -> ../../sda
lrwxrwxrwx 1 root root 10 Sep  8 16:57 pci-0000:00:10.0-scsi-0:0:0:0-part1 -> ../../sda1
lrwxrwxrwx 1 root root 10 Sep  8 16:57 pci-0000:00:10.0-scsi-0:0:0:0-part2 -> ../../sda2
lrwxrwxrwx 1 root root  9 Sep  9 13:39 pci-0000:00:10.0-scsi-0:0:1:0 -> ../../sdb
lrwxrwxrwx 1 root root 10 Sep  9 13:21 pci-0000:00:10.0-scsi-0:0:1:0-part1 -> ../../sdb1
lrwxrwxrwx 1 root root 10 Sep  9 12:18 pci-0000:00:10.0-scsi-0:0:1:0-part2 -> ../../sdb2
lrwxrwxrwx 1 root root 10 Sep  8 17:42 pci-0000:00:10.0-scsi-0:0:1:0-part3 -> ../../sdb3
lrwxrwxrwx 1 root root  9 Sep  8 16:57 pci-0000:02:05.0-ata-2.0 -> ../../sr0
```

EXERCISE 3-1. CREATING A FILE SYSTEM ON TOP OF LVM

Now that you've learned all about the file system creation basics, it's time to practice your skills in an exercise. To perform this exercise, you need to have available storage. If you're using a virtual machine, you can easily add a new disk to the machine. If you're working on physical hardware, you can use a USB key to work through this exercise. I will assume that the device you'll be working on is known to your computer as /dev/sdb. Make sure to change that, according to your specific hardware setup!

1. To find out the name of the storage device that you can use, type `cat /proc/partitions`. In this file, you'll get an overview of all disk devices that are attached to your computer.

2. Type `fdisk /dev/sdb` to open `fdisk` and add a new partition. Before changing anything, let's verify that there is nothing on the disk. Type p to show current partitioning. If any partitions do exist, and you are sure that you can use the entire disk in this exercise, type d to delete them.

3. Now type n to create a new partition. The utility next asks which type of partition you want to create. Type p to create a primary partition, and enter the partition number 1, which is suggested as the default partition. Now press Enter to accept the default starting point of the partition, and type +500M to create the partition as a 500MiB partition.

4. Verify that you have succeeded. Now type t to change the partition type, and set it to type 8e, which makes it usable for LVM. From the `fdisk` main menu, type w to write the changes to disk and quit `fdisk`.

5. To make sure that the kernel is updated with the modifications you've just applied, type the `partprobe` command. If you see anything that looks like an error, reboot your system to make sure that the kernel has been updated properly before continuing. Verify that your partition is known as `/dev/sdb1`.

6. Use `pvcreate /dev/sdb1` to mark the partition as an LVM physical volume.

7. Type `vgcreate vgdata /dev/sdb1` to put the partition in a volume group that has the name vgdata.

8. Type `lvcreate -n lvdata -l 50%FREE vgdata`. This command creates a volume with the name lvdata and allocates 50 percent of available disk space from vgdata to it.

9. Type the commands pvs, vgs, and lvs to verify the creation of the LVM devices.

10. If the LVM devices have been created properly, use `mkfs.btrfs -L fsdata /dev/vgdata/lvdata` to put a Btrfs file system on top of it, which uses the file system label fsdata.

11. Type `blkid` to verify that the file system has been created and the label can be read from the file system.

12. Use `mkdir /data` to create a mount point on which the file system can be mounted.

13. Enter the following line in `/etc/fstab`, to ensure that the file system can be mounted automatically:

    ```
    LABEL=fsdata    /data    btrfs    defaults        0 0
    ```

14. To test that all works well, type `mount -a`. This mounts all file systems that have an entry in `/etc/fstab` but haven't been mounted yet.

15. Type `mount` and `df -h` to verify that you can see the new mount.

Managing File Systems

As a Linux administrator, on occasion, you'll have to perform some file-system-management tasks as well. The exact tasks depend on the type of file system that you're using. In this section, we'll cover some of the more common of these tasks.

Checking and Repairing File Systems

An important responsibility of the administrator is to guarantee the integrity of the file systems in use. That means that on occasion, you'll have to check, and sometimes also repair, file systems on your systems. Fortunately, problems on file systems do not occur very frequently, but they do occur.

As the first line of defense, file systems are automatically checked while your system reboots—with the exception of the Btrfs file system, because the way it is organized makes a thorough check unnecessary. On occasion, the automated check may fail, and you'll have to perform a manual check using the fsck command. This is especially the case if you're using XFS or Ext4 file systems.

The Ext4 fsck utility has a few useful options. To start with, there is the option -p, which allows you to start an automatic repair where no questions are asked. If you add the option -y, you'll automatically answer "yes" to all questions asked. This is a good idea, because if serious problems have occurred, you may be prompted many times to confirm a repair action.

Other useful options are -c, which checks for bad blocks and marks them as such, and -f, which forces a file system check. Normally, when fsck is started, it won't do anything if the file system is considered clean, that is, free of problems. If there are problems, using the -f option is useful.

If serious problems have arisen on the file system, you can benefit from using an alternative superblock. On Ext4, the file system metadata is stored in the superblock, and the superblock is required to check and repair the file system. If the superblock is damaged, you cannot do anything to the file system anymore.

Fortunately, on any Ext file system, a backup superblock is stored. Typically, you'll find it on block 8193. To use this backup superblock, type fsck -b 8193 /dev/sda1. This allows your file system to be restored to the original state (see Listing 3-9).

Listing 3-9. Using fsck on the Backup Superblock

```
linux-m6gc:/dev/disk/by-path # fsck.ext4 -b 8193 /dev/sda1
e2fsck 1.42.11 (09-Jul-2014)
/dev/sda1 was not cleanly unmounted, check forced.
Pass 1: Checking inodes, blocks, and sizes
Pass 2: Checking directory structure
Pass 3: Checking directory connectivity
Pass 4: Checking reference counts
Pass 5: Checking group summary information
Block bitmap differences:  +(73729--73987) +(204801--205059) +(221185--221443) +(401409--401667)
Fix<y>?
```

Note that in Listing 3-9, you can see that some errors were encountered, and the fsck utility began prompting for confirmation, to verify that errors can be fixed automatically. If you don't want to press the y key many times, it's a good idea to interrupt the fsck utility, using Ctrl+C, and to start it again, using the -y option.

XFS Tools

When working with the XFS file system, there are a lot of XFS-specific tools that you can use to perform management tasks on the file system. You can get an overview of these by typing xfs[tab][tab] as root on the command line. Some of these tools are pretty common, and you'll use them on occasion. Some tools are not so common, and you will rarely use them.

To start with, there is the xfs_admin command. This command gives access to a few options, such as xfs_admin -l, which prints the file system label, or xfs_admin -L, which allows you to set a label on a file system. Note that when working with the XFS tools, some tools work on a device; other tools work on a mount point. So, on some occasions, you'll have to enter a device name, and with other tools, you'll have to use a directory name.

An interesting XFS tool is xfs_fsr, which will try to defragment an XFS file system. On some Linux distributions, you don't really have to do any defragmentation. On XFS, you do, and this tool works on a mounted file system.

The XFS file system also has its specific repair utility, xfs_repair. This utility can be used on unmounted devices only; it does not run at boot time. The fsck option in /etc/fstab will only replay the XFS journal if that is necessary. For performing a repair on an XFS file system, you'll have to make sure that the file system journal (which is referred to as the "log" in XFS) is clean. If you receive warnings about a dirty log, you can mount and unmount the file system, which, in general, will clean the log. If the journal is corrupt, just mounting and unmounting won't be sufficient. You'll have to use the command xfs_repair -L on your device to fix the problem.

In the section "Using LVM Snapshots," later in this chapter, you'll learn how to work with snapshots on LVM. If you don't use snapshots on LVM, it is good to know that the XFS file system allows you to temporarily freeze a file system, so that you can take a snapshot without changes being made to the file system at the same time.

To freeze an XFS file system, use xfs_freeze -f /mountpoint (use the mount point, not the device name). This will temporarily stall all writes, so that you can take a snapshot. Once completed, use xfs_freeze -u /mountpoint to unfreeze the file system and commit all writes to the file system.

Btrfs Tools and Features

As mentioned before, the Btrfs file system introduces many new features. Some of the Btrfs features make working with LVM unnecessary, and some new features have also been introduced. The key new features in Btrfs are that it is a copy on write file system. Because of this, it supports snapshots by itself, allowing users and administrators an easy rollback to a previous situation.

Also, Btrfs has support for multiple volumes. This means that when running out of disk space on a particular Btrfs volume, another volume can be added. Also, after adding or removing a volume from a Btrfs file system, online shrinking and growth of the file system is supported. The Btrfs file system also supports metadata balancing. This means that depending on the amount of volumes used, the file system metadata can be spread in the most efficient way. Apart from that, there are Btrfs subvolumes.

Understanding Subvolumes

A Btrfs subvolume is a namespace that can be mounted independently with specific mount options. Multiple subvolumes can reside on the same file system and allow administrators to create different mount points for specific needs. By default, all file systems have at least one subvolume, which is the file system device root, but additional subvolumes can also be created. Apart from the support of per-subvolume mount options, snapshots are created on subvolumes. After unmounting a subvolume, a rollback of the snapshot can be effected.

After a default installation of SLES 12, Btrfs is used on the root file system, and subvolumes are created automatically. In Listing 3-10, you can see how they are created from different mounts in the /etc/fstab file.

Listing 3-10. Btrfs Default Subvolumes

```
UUID=c7997ed8-2568-49c3-bb84-3d231978707c /btrfs defaults 0 0
UUID=c7997ed8-2568-49c3-bb84-3d231978707c /boot/grub2/i386-pc btrfs subvol=@/boot/grub2/i386-pc 0 0
UUID=c7997ed8-2568-49c3-bb84-3d231978707c /boot/grub2/x86_64-efi btrfs subvol=@/boot/grub2/x86_64-efi 0 0
UUID=c7997ed8-2568-49c3-bb84-3d231978707c /home btrfs subvol=@/home 0 0
UUID=c7997ed8-2568-49c3-bb84-3d231978707c /opt btrfs subvol=@/opt 0 0
UUID=c7997ed8-2568-49c3-bb84-3d231978707c /srv btrfs subvol=@/srv 0 0
UUID=c7997ed8-2568-49c3-bb84-3d231978707c /tmp btrfs subvol=@/tmp 0 0
UUID=c7997ed8-2568-49c3-bb84-3d231978707c /usr/local btrfs subvol=@/usr/local 0 0
UUID=c7997ed8-2568-49c3-bb84-3d231978707c /var/crash btrfs subvol=@/var/crash 0 0
UUID=c7997ed8-2568-49c3-bb84-3d231978707c /var/lib/mailman btrfs subvol=@/var/lib/mailman 0 0
UUID=c7997ed8-2568-49c3-bb84-3d231978707c /var/lib/named btrfs subvol=@/var/lib/named 0 0
UUID=c7997ed8-2568-49c3-bb84-3d231978707c /var/lib/pgsql btrfs subvol=@/var/lib/pgsql 0 0
UUID=c7997ed8-2568-49c3-bb84-3d231978707c /var/log btrfs subvol=@/var/log 0 0
UUID=c7997ed8-2568-49c3-bb84-3d231978707c /var/opt btrfs subvol=@/var/opt 0 0
UUID=c7997ed8-2568-49c3-bb84-3d231978707c /var/spool btrfs subvol=@/var/spool 0 0
UUID=c7997ed8-2568-49c3-bb84-3d231978707c /var/tmp btrfs subvol=@/var/tmp 0 0
UUID=c7997ed8-2568-49c3-bb84-3d231978707c /.snapshots btrfs subvol=@/.snapshots
```

Using these default subvolumes allows administrators to treat the most common directories that have been created with their own mount options and create snapshots for them as well, if required. The subvolumes are created on mount by including the Btrfs specific `subvol=@/some/name` option. Subvolumes can only be created if the parent volume is mounted first. You can see that in the first list of output in Listing 3-10, where the `/dev/sda2` device is mounted as a Btrfs device. For each subvolume after creation, specific mount options can be added to the mount options column in `/etc/fstab`.

From a shell prompt, you can request a list of subvolumes that are currently being used. Use the command `btrfs subvolume list /` to do so, which will give you a result like that in Listing 3-11.

Listing 3-11. Requesting a List of Current Subvolumes

```
linux-ia9r:~ # btrfs subvolume list /
ID 257 gen 48 top level 5 path @
ID 258 gen 39 top level 257 path boot/grub2/i386-pc
ID 259 gen 39 top level 257 path boot/grub2/x86_64-efi
ID 260 gen 42 top level 257 path home
ID 261 gen 28 top level 257 path opt
ID 262 gen 39 top level 257 path srv
ID 263 gen 45 top level 257 path tmp
ID 264 gen 39 top level 257 path usr/local
ID 265 gen 39 top level 257 path var/crash
ID 266 gen 39 top level 257 path var/lib/mailman
ID 267 gen 39 top level 257 path var/lib/named
ID 268 gen 39 top level 257 path var/lib/pgsql
ID 269 gen 48 top level 257 path var/log
ID 270 gen 39 top level 257 path var/opt
ID 271 gen 48 top level 257 path var/spool
ID 272 gen 41 top level 257 path var/tmp
ID 276 gen 39 top level 257 path .snapshots
```

Apart from the subvolumes that are created by default, an administrator can add new subvolumes manually. To do this, the command `btrfs subvolume create` is used, followed by the path of the desired subvolume. Use, for example, the command `btrfs subvolume create /root` to create a subvolume for the home directory of the user root.

After creating a subvolume, snapshots can be created. To do this, use the command `btrfs subvolume snapshot`, followed by the name of the subvolume and the name of the snapshot. Note that it is good practice, but not mandatory, to create snapshots within the same namespace as the subvolume. In Exercise 3-2, you'll apply these commands to work with snapshots yourself.

EXERCISE 3-2. WORKING WITH BTRFS SUBVOLUMES

In this exercise, you'll create a subvolume. You'll next put some files in the subvolume and create a snapshot in it. After that, you'll learn how to perform a rollback to the original state, using the snapshot you've just created.

1. On an existing Btrfs file system, type `btrfs subvolume create /test`.

2. Type `btrfs subvolume list /`. This will show all currently existing snapshots, including the snapshot you have just created.

3. Copy some files to `/test`, using the command `cp /etc/[abc]* /test`.

4. At this point, it's time to create a snapshot, using `btrfs subvolume snapshot /test / test/snap`.

5. Remove all files from `/test`.

6. To get back to the original state of the `/test` subvolume, use `mv /test/snap/* /test`.

Working with Multiple Devices in Btrfs

Another benefit of the Btrfs file system is that it allows you to work with multiple devices. By doing this, Btrfs offers a new approach to creating RAID volumes. To create a Btrfs volume that consists of multiple devices, type a command such as `mkfs.btrfs /dev/sda1 /dev/sda2 /dev/sda3`. To mount a composed device through /etc/fstab, you'll have to take a special approach. You'll have to refer to the first device in the composed device and specify the names of the other devices as a Btrfs mount option, as in the following sample line:

```
/dev/sda1       /somewhere      btrfs     device=/dev/sda1,device=/dev/sda2,device=/dev/sda3 0 0
```

Btrfs also allows you to add devices to a file system that is already created. Use `btrfs device add /dev/sda4 /somewhere` to do so. Notice that the `device add` command works on the name of the mount point and not the name of the volume. After adding a device to a Btrfs file system, you should rebalance the device metadata, using `btrfs filesystem balance /somewhere`. You can request the current status of a multi-device Btrfs volume by using the `btrfs device stats /somewhere` command.

A multivolume device, as just described, is just a device that consists of multiple volumes. If one of the devices in the volume gets damaged, there's no easy option to repair it. If you do want an easy option for repair, you should create a Btrfs RAID volume. The command `mkfs.btrfs -m raid1 /dev/sdb /dev/sdc /dev/sdd /dev/sde` will do that for you. If one of the devices in the RAID setup is missing, you'll first have to mount it in degraded state. That's for metadata consistency, and it allows you to remove the failing device. If, for example, /dev/sdb is showing errors, you would use the command `mount -o degraded /dev/sdb /mnt`. Notice that it must be mounted on a temporary mount and not on the mount point of the Btrfs RAID device. After mounting it, you can use `btrfs device delete missing /mnt` to remove it.

Managing Logical Volumes

You have previously learned how to create LVM logical volumes. Working with logical volumes adds some flexibility to your configuration, especially if no Btrfs file systems are used. Some important features that LVM was used for previously are now included in the Btrfs file system, however, which makes the need for LVM volumes less urgent. If you're not using Btrfs, configuring LVM can add useful features. In this section, you'll learn how to work with LVM snapshots and how to resize logical volumes.

Using LVM Snapshots

The purpose of LVM snapshots is to freeze the current state of a volume. That can be useful to make a backup. While creating a backup, open files cannot be backed up properly. It can also be useful, if you want to be able to easily revert to a previous configuration.

To create an LVM snapshot, you need available space in the volume group. The snapshot must be able to store the original blocks of all files that have changed during the lifetime of the snapshot. That means that if you're creating a snapshot just to make sure that your backup procedure will run smoothly, the size of the snapshot can be limited. If, however, you want to create a snapshot before setting up a complex test environment, so that in case all goes wrong you can easily get back to the original configuration, the size requirements for the snapshot will be considerably higher. If you're not sure, make certain that you have 10 percent of the size of the original volume. This will be sufficient in most cases.

While working with snapshots, you should be aware that a snapshot is not a replacement for a backup. Snapshots are linked to the original volume. If the original volume just dies, the snapshot will die with it. A snapshot is a tool to help you create a reliable backup.

To create a snapshot, you first have to make sure that you have a volume for which you want to create the snapshot and that you have available disk space in the volume group. Next, you have to make sure that no modifications are written to that volume at the moment that the snapshot is created. You can do this by stopping all services that are using the volume, or by using the XFS Freeze feature that was discussed earlier in this chapter. Next, use lvcreate -s -L 100M -n myvol-snap /dev/myvg/myvol. This creates a snapshot with a size of 100MiB for the volume myvol.

As discussed, LVM snapshots, in general, are created for two reasons: to create a backup or to revert to a previous situation. If you want to create a backup based on the snapshot volume you've just created, you should mount it somewhere. You can next take the backup of the mount point. Once the backup has been completed, the snapshot should be removed. This is important, because a snapshot that has not been removed will keep on claiming disk space until it is completely full and that will generate I/O errors on your system. To remove a snapshot, unmount it and, next, use lvremove /dev/yoursnapshot to remove it.

If you have created a snapshot to make it easier to revert to a previous state, you'll have to use the lvconvert utility. To revert to the original state, apply the following steps:

1. Unmount the volume that you want to revert.

2. Use lvconvert --merge /dev/yoursnapshot.

3. If the previous command complains that it cannot merge over an open origin volume, use lvchange -an /dev/yourvolume first.

4. At this point, the original volume will be reverted, and you can mount it again.

Resizing Logical Volumes

Another common task when working with LVM is the resizing of a volume. The size of an LVM volume can be increased as well as decreased, but you should know that not all file systems offer the same options. Btrfs, for example, can easily be resized in both directions, but an XFS file system can be grown, not reduced. So, before starting a resize operation, make sure that your file system fully supports it.

In some manuals, in fact, you'll read that you have to apply two different steps: the resizing of the file system and the resizing of the LVM volume. This is not the case. You can use the lvm commands to apply both steps in the same operation.

The most flexible utility for a resize operation is lvresize. Using this tool, you can grow as well as reduce a file system. Alternatively, you can use lvextend to grow an LVM volume or lvreduce to reduce its size. All of these commands honor the -r option, to resize the file system on the LVM volume at the same time, and the -L option, to specify the new size of the file system. The generic procedure for growing a file system is as follows:

1. Make sure that disk space is available in the volume group. If this is not the case, use vgextend to add disk space to the volume group. If, for example, you want to add the disk /dev/sdc to the volume group vgsan, you would use vgextend vgsan /dev/sdc.

2. At this point, you can grow the LVM volume. Use, for example, lvextend -L +1G -r /dev/vgsan/mylv, to add 1GiB of disk space to the volume mylv.

To reduce a file system, you'll use lvreduce; for example, use lvreduce -L -1G -r /dev/vgsan/mylv to reduce the size of a logical volume with 1GB. You should note that the success of this command differs according to the file system that you're using.

- To reduce the size of an Ext4 file system, the file system must be unmounted and checked before the actual reduce operation.

- XFS file systems cannot be reduced

- Btrfs file systems can be reduced while being online.

Instead of using the command line, you can also resize file systems easily from YaST. In YaST, select System ➤ Partitioner. Next, select the logical volume that you want to resize and navigate to the Resize option. This opens the window that you can see in Figure 3-13. From this window, specify the resulting size that you need. (Don't specify how much you want to add; specify how big you want the file system to be.) Next, select OK, to perform the resize operation.

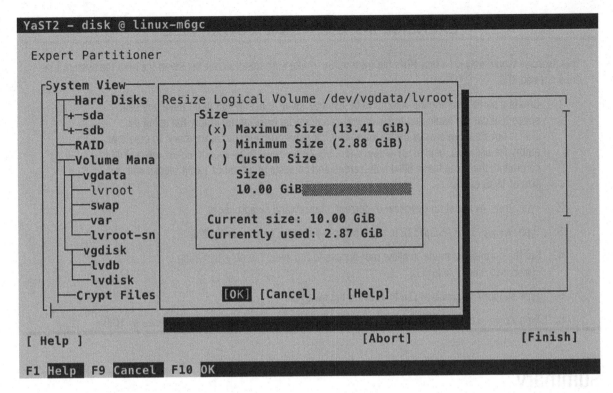

Figure 3-13. Resizing file systems from YaST

Creating Swap Space

On Linux, swap space is used in a very efficient way. If a shortage of memory arises, the Linux kernel moves memory pages that are not actively being used to swap, to make more memory available for processes that do really need it. On some occasions, you may find that all available swap space has been consumed. If that happens, you can add swap space to your computer. This can be done from YaST, as well as from the command line.

The procedure to add swap space from YaST is easy and intuitive. First, you have to create the storage device (partition or logical volume), and after doing that, you can format it as swap, by selecting the swap file system from the drop-down list. The procedure from the command line involves a couple of commands and is outlined in the following exercise.

EXERCISE 3-3. CREATING A SWAP FILE

This exercise works only on a non-Btrfs file system. So, make sure that you put the swap file on a file system that does not use XFS.

1. Create a partition or logical volume to be used as swap space. If you don't have any disk space that can be dedicated to swap, you can consider creating an empty file using dd. This is not ideal but always better than having a server running out of memory. To create an empty file using dd, use dd if=/dev/zero of=/root/swapfile bs=1M count=1024. In this command, the swap file is filled with zeroes and consists of a total of 1,024 blocks with a size of 1MiB each.

2. Type free -m to get an overview of current memory and swap usage.

3. Type mkswap/root/swapfile to put a swap file system on your swap file.

4. Set the permission mode to allow root access to the swap file only, by typing chmod 600/root/swapfile.

5. Type swapon/root/swapfile to activate the swap file.

6. Type free -m again. You'll see that the amount of available swap space has increased by 1GiB!

Summary

In this chapter, you have learned how to work with storage in the SUSE Linux Enterprise Server (SLES). You have read how to set up partitions as well as local volumes, and you have learned how to do that from YaST and from the command line. You've also read about common file-system-management tasks. In the next chapter, you'll learn how to work with users, groups, and permissions on SLES.

CHAPTER 4

■ ■ ■

User and Permission Management

On Linux, a difference is made between processes that run in kernel mode and processes that run without full permissions to the operating system. In the first case, the user needs to be running as root for most of these commands to work. In the latter case, user accounts are required. This chapter explains how to set up user and group accounts and how, after setting them up, they can be granted access to specific resources on the server, using permissions. The following topics are covered in this chapter:

- Creating and Managing User Accounts
- Creating and Managing Group Accounts
- Configuring Base Linux Permissions
- Configuring Special Permissions
- Working with Access Control Lists
- Working with Attributes

Creating and Managing User Accounts

In this chapter, you'll learn how to create and manage user accounts. Before diving into the details of user management, you'll read how users are used in a Linux environment.

Users on Linux

On Linux, there are two ways to look at system security. There are privileged users, and there are unprivileged users. The default privileged user is root. This user account has full access to everything on a Linux server and is allowed to work in system space without restrictions. The root user account is meant to perform system administration tasks and should only be used for that. For all other tasks, an unprivileged user account should be used.

On a typical Linux environment, two kinds of user accounts exist. There are user accounts for the people that need to work on a server and who need limited access to the resources on that server. These user accounts typically have a password that is used for authenticating the user to the system. There are also system accounts that are used by the services the server is offering. Both user accounts share common properties, which are kept in the files /etc/passwd and /etc/shadow. Listing 4-1 shows the contents of the /etc/passwd file. Note that the actual usernames depend upon users added and software installed.

Listing 4-1. Partial Contents of the /etc/passwd User Configuration File

```
linux:~ # tail -n 10 /etc/passwd
rtkit:x:492:491:RealtimeKit:/proc:/bin/false
rpc:x:491:65534:user for rpcbind:/var/lib/empty:/sbin/nologin
pulse:x:490:490:Pulse...:/var/lib/pulseaudio:/sbin/nologin
statd:x:489:65534:NFS statd daemon:/var/lib/nfs:/sbin/nologin
postfix:x:51:51:Postfix Daemon:/var/spool/postfix:/bin/false
scard:x:488:488:Smart Card...:/var/run/pcscd:/usr/sbin/nologin
gdm:x:487:487:Gnome Display ... daemon:/var/lib/gdm:/bin/false
hacluster:x:90:90:heartbeat processes:/var/lib/heartbeat/cores/hacluster:/bin/bash
lighttpd:x:486:486:user for ...:/var/lib/lighttpd:/bin/false
linda:x:1000:100::/home/linda:/bin/bash
```

As you can see, to define a user account, different fields are used in /etc/passwd. The fields are separated from one another by a colon. Below is a summary of these fields, followed by a short description of their purpose.

- *Username*: This is a unique name for the user. Usernames are important to match a user to his password, which is stored separately in /etc/shadow (see next).

- *Password*: In the old days, the second field of /etc/passwd was used to store the hashes password of the user. Because the /etc/passwd file is readable by all users, this poses a security threat, and for that reason, on current Linux systems, the hashes passwords are stored in /etc/shadow (discussed in the next section).

- *UID*: Each user has a unique User ID (UID). This is a numeric ID, and values from 0 to 65535 can be used. It is the UID that really determines what a user can do; when permissions are set for a user, the UID is stored in the file metadata (and not the username). UID 0 is reserved for root, the unrestricted user account. The lower UIDs (typically up to 499) are used for system accounts, and the higher UIDs (from 1000 on SUSE by default) are reserved for people who need a secure working environment on a server.

- *GID*: On Linux, each user is a member of at least one group. This group is referred to as the primary group, and this group plays a central role in permissions management, as will be discussed later in this chapter.

- *Comment field*: The comment field, as you can guess, is used to add comments for user accounts. This field is optional, but it can be used to describe what a user account is created for. Some utilities, such as the obsolete finger utility, can be used to get information from this field. The field is also referred to as the GECOS field, which stands for General Electric Comprehensive Operating System, and had a specific purpose for identifying jobs in the early 1970s when General Electric was still an important manufacturer of servers.

- *Directory*: This is the initial directory in which the user is placed after logging in, also referred to as the home directory. If the user account is used by a person, this is where the person would store his personal files and programs. For a system user account, this is the environment where the service can store files it needs while operating.

- *Shell*: This is the program that is started after the user has successfully connected to a server. For most users this will be /bin/bash, the default Linux shell. For system user accounts, it will typically be a shell such as /usr/bin/false or /sbin/nologin, to make sure that if by accident an intruder would be capable of starting a shell, he won't get access to the system environment.

A part of the user properties is kept in /etc/passwd, which was just discussed. Another part of the configuration of user properties is in /etc/shadow. Parameters in this file mostly refer to the user password. Typical for /etc/shadow is that no one except the superuser root has permission to access it, which makes sense, as it contains all the information that is required for connecting to a system. Listing 4-2 gives an overview of /etc/shadow fields.

Listing 4-2. Example Contents from /etc/shadow

```
linux:~ # tail -n 5 /etc/shadow
scard:!:16165:::::::
gdm:!:16165:::::::
hacluster:!:16168:::::::
lighttpd:!:16168:::::::
linda:$6$5mItSouz$Jkg5qdROahuN3nWJuIqUO/hXSdIwi9zjwpW2OL\
    X3cWOHN.XWCPO9jXNhDwSHdHRsNiWnV85Yju.:16171:0:99999:7:::
```

The following fields are used in /etc/shadow:

- *Login name*: Notice that /etc/shadow doesn't contain any UIDs, but usernames only. This opens a possibility for multiple users using the same UID but different passwords.

- *Encrypted password*: This field contains all that is needed to store the password in a secure way. The first part of it (6 in the example) indicates the encryption algorithm used. The second part contains the "salt" that is used to send an authentication token to a user wishing to authenticate. The last part has the encrypted password itself.

- *Days since Jan 1st 1970 that the password was last changed*: Many things on Linux refer to Jan 1st 1970, which on Linux is considered the beginning of days. It is also referred to as "epoch."

- *Days before password may be changed*: This allows system administrators to use a more strict password policy, whereby it is not possible to change back to the original password immediately after a password has been changed. Typically, this field is set to the value 0.

- *Days after which password must be changed*: This field contains the maximal validity period of passwords. Notice that by default, it is set to 99,999 (about 273 years).

- *Days before password is to expire that user is warned*: This field is used to warn a user when a forced password change is upcoming. Notice that the default is set to 7 (even if the password validity is set to 99,999 days!).

- *Days after password expires that account is disabled*: Use this field to enforce a password change. After password expiry, users can log in no longer.

- *Days since Jan 1st 1970 that account is disabled*: An administrator can set this field to disable an account. This is typically a better approach than removing an account, as all associated properties of the account will be kept, but it can be used no longer to authenticate on your server. An alternative would be to use userdel, which removes the user account but by default will keep the files the user has created.

- *A reserved field*: This will probably never be used.

Most of the password properties can be managed with the passwd or chage command, which are discussed later in this chapter.

Creating Users

There are many solutions for creating users on a Linux server. To start with, you can edit the contents of the /etc/passwd and /etc/shadow files directly (with the risk of making an error that could make logging in impossible to anyone). There's also useradd (called adduser on some distributions) and on some distributions, there are fancy graphical utilities available. What utility is used doesn't really matter, as the result will be the same anyway: a user account is added to the appropriate configuration files.

Modifying the Configuration Files

To add user accounts, it suffices that one line is added to /etc/passwd and another line is added to /etc/shadow, in which the user account and all of its properties are defined. It is not recommended, though. By making an error, you might mess up the consistency of the file and make logging in completely impossible to anyone. Also, you might encounter locking problems, if one administrator is trying to modify the file contents directly, while another administrator wants to write a modification with some tool.

If you insist on modifying the configuration files directly, you should use vipw. This command opens an editor interface on your configuration files, and more important, it sets the appropriate locks on the configuration files to prevent corruption. It does *not*, however, check syntax, so make sure you know what you're doing, because by making a typo, you might still severely mess up your server. If you want to use this tool to make modifications to the /etc/shadow file, use vipw -s.

Using useradd

The useradd utility is probably the most common tool on Linux for managing users. It allows you to add a user account from the command line by using many of its parameters. Use, for instance, the command useradd -m -u 1201 -G sales,ops linda to create a user, linda, who is a member of the groups sales and ops, with UID 1201, and add a home directory to the user account as well.

Using YaST2

On SUSE, users can also be created with the YaST2 management tool. Type yast2 users to access the user management tool directly. The interface offers easy access to all the options that can be used while creating users. Figure 4-1 shows the default interface that YaST2 uses to add user accounts.

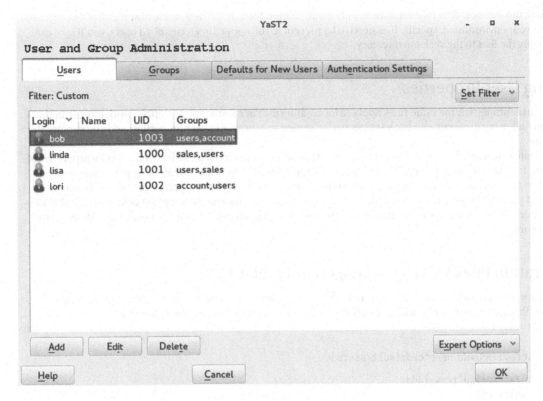

Figure 4-1. *Adding users with YaST*

YaST offers the options that are needed to add user accounts on four different tabs.

- *User Data*: Generic options to create the user account and set a password

- *Details*: More details, such as the default location of the user home directory and group membership

- *Password Settings*: Password-related settings that are stored in /etc/shadow

- *Plug-Ins*: Here, you can select additional user management plug-ins and configure additional properties. It offers, for instance, the Quota Manager plug-in, which allows you to set restrictions to the amount of files that users can create (needs support for quota on the file system; see Chapter 3 for more details on that).

Home Directories

Typically, users will have a home directory. For service accounts, the home directory is very specific. As an administrator, you'll normally not change home directory–related settings for system accounts, as they are created automatically from the RPM post installation scripts when installing the related software packages. If you have people that need a user account, you probably do want to manage home directory contents a bit.

If when creating user accounts you tell your server to add a home directory as well (for instance, by using useradd -m), the contents of the "skeleton" directory is copied to the user home directory. The skeleton directory is /etc/skel, and it contains files that are copied to the user home directory at the moment this directory is created. These files will also get the appropriate permissions to make sure the new user can use and access them.

By default, the skeleton directory contains mostly configuration files, which determine how the user environment is set up. If, in your environment, specific files need to be present in the home directories of all users, you'll take care of that by adding the files to the skeleton directory.

Managing User Properties

For changing user properties, the same rules apply as for creating user accounts. You can either work directly in the configuration files using vipw; you can use yast users for getting easy access to user properties; and you can use the command line.

The ultimate command line utility for modifying user properties is usermod. It can be used to set all properties of users as stored in /etc/passwd and /etc/shadow, plus some additional tasks, such as managing group membership. There's just one task it doesn't do well: setting passwords. Although usermod has an option, -p, which tells you to "use encrypted password for the new password," it expects you to do the password encryption before adding the user account. That doesn't make it particularly useful. If, as root, you want to change the user password, you'd better use the passwd command.

Configuration Files for User Management Defaults

When working with such tools as useradd, some default values are assumed. These default values are set in two configuration files: /etc/login.defs and /etc/default/useradd. Listing 4-3 shows the contents of /etc/default/useradd.

Listing 4-3. useradd Defaults in /etc/default/useradd

```
linux:~ # cat /etc/default/useradd
# useradd defaults file
GROUP=100
HOME=/home
INACTIVE=-1
EXPIRE=
SHELL=/bin/bash
SKEL=/etc/skel
CREATE_MAIL_SPOOL=yes
```

As can be seen from Listing 4-3, the /etc/default/useradd file contains some default values that are applied when using useradd.

In the file /etc/login.defs, different login-related variables are set. login.defs is used by different commands, and it relates to setting up the appropriate environment for new users. Following is a list of some of the most significant properties that can be set from /etc/login.defs:

MOTD_FILE: Defines the file that is used as "message of the day" file. In this file, you can include messages to be displayed after the user has successfully logged in to the server.

ENV_PATH: Defines the $PATH variable, a list of directories that should be searched for executable files after logging in

PASS_MAX_DAYS, PASS_MIN_DAYS, *and* PASS_WARN_AGE: Define the default password expiration properties when creating new users

UID_MIN: The first UID to use when creating new users

CREATE_HOME: Indicates whether or not to create a home directory for new users

USERGROUPS_ENAB: Set to "yes" to create a private group for all new users. That means that a new user has a group with the same name as the user as its default group. If set to "no," all users are made a member of the group "users."

Managing Password Properties

You have read about the password properties that can be set in /etc/shadow. There are two commands that you can use to change these properties for users: chage and passwd. The commands are rather straightforward; for instance, the command passwd -n 30 -w 3 -x 90 linda would set the password for user linda to a minimal usage period of 30 days and an expiry after 90 days, where a warning is generated 3 days before expiry.

Many of the tasks that can be accomplished with passwd can be done with chage also. For instance, use chage -E 2015-12-31 bob to have the account for user bob expire on December 31st of 2015. To see current password management settings, you can use chage -l (see Listing 4-4 for an example).

Listing 4-4. Showing Password Expiry Information with chage -l

```
linux:~ # chage -l linda
Last password change                               : Apr 11, 2014
Password expires                                   : Jul 10, 2014
Password inactive                                  : never
Account expires                                    : never
Minimum number of days between password change     : 30
Maximum number of days between password change     : 90
Number of days of warning before password expires  : 3
```

Creating a User Environment

When a user logs in, an environment is created. The environment consists of some variables that determine how the user environment is used. One such variable, for instance, is $PATH, which defines a list of directories that should be searched when a user types a command.

To construct the user environment, a few files play a role.

- /etc/profile: Used for default settings for all users when starting a login shell

- /etc/bash.bashrc: Used to define defaults for all users when starting a subshell

- ~/.profile: Specific settings for one user, applied when starting a login shell

- ~/.bashrc: Specific settings for one user, applied when starting a subshell

When logging in, the files are read in this order, and variables and other settings that are defined in these files are applied. If a variable or setting occurs in more than one file, the last one wins.

```
EXERCISE 4-1. CREATING USER ACCOUNTS
```

In this exercise, you will apply common solutions to create user accounts.

1. Type `vim /etc/login.defs` to open the configuration file `/etc/login.defs` and change a few parameters before you start creating logging. Look for the parameter `CREATE_HOME` and make sure it is set to "yes." Also, set the parameter `USERGROUPS_ENAB` to "no," which means that a new user is added to a group with the same name as the user and nothing else.

2. Use `cd /etc/skel` to go to the `/etc/skel` directory. Type `mkdir Pictures` and `mkdir Documents` to add two default directories to all user home directories. Also, change the contents of the file `.bashrc` to include the line `export EDITOR=/usr/bin/vim`, which sets the default editor for tools that have to modify text files.

3. Type `useradd linda` to create an account for user linda. Next, type `id linda` to verify that linda is a member of a group with the name linda and nothing else. Also, verify that the directories `Pictures` and `Documents` have been created in linda's home directory.

4. Use `passwd linda` to set a password for the user you've just created. Use the password *password*.

5. Type `passwd -n 30 -w 3 -x 90 linda` to change the password properties. This has the password expire after 90 days (`-x 90`). Three days before expiry, the user will get a warning (`-w 3`), and the password has to be used for at least 30 days before (`-n 30`) it can be changed.

6. Create a few more users—lisa, lori, and bob—using `for i in lisa lori bob; do useradd $i; done`.

Creating and Managing Group Accounts

Every Linux user has to be a member of at least one group. In this section, you'll learn how to manage settings for Linux group accounts.

Understanding Linux Groups

Linux users can be members of two different kinds of groups. First, there is the primary group. Every user must be a member of a primary group, and there is only one primary group. When creating files, the primary group becomes group owner of these files. (File ownership is discussed in detail in the section "Understanding File Ownership," later in this chapter.) Users can also access all files their primary group has access to.

Besides the mandatory primary group, users can be members of one or more secondary groups as well. Secondary groups are important for getting access to files. If the group a user is member of has access to specific files, the user will get access to these files also. Working with secondary groups is important, in particular in environments where Linux is used as a file server to allow people working for different departments to share files with one another.

Creating Groups

As is the case for creating users, there are also different options for creating groups. The group configuration files can be modified directly using vigr; the command line utility groupadd can be used; and graphical utilities are available, such as SUSE YaST. vi.

Creating Groups with vigr

With the vigr command, you open an editor interface directly on the /etc/group configuration file. In this file, groups are defined in four fields, per group (see Listing 4-5).

Listing 4-5. Example /etc/group Content

```
maildrop:x:59:postfix
scard:x:488:
ntadmin:x:71:
gdm:x:487:
haclient:x:90:
lighttpd:x:486:
sales:x:1000:linda,lisa
```

The following fields are used:

- *group name*: As is suggested by the name of the field, this contains the name of the group.

- *group password*: A feature that is hardly used anymore. A group password can be used by users who want to join the group on a temporary basis, so that access is allowed to files the group has access to.

- *group ID*: This is a unique numeric group identification number.

- *members*: In here, you find the names of users who are members of this group as a secondary group. Note that it does not show users who are members of this group as their primary group.

Using groupadd to Create Groups

Another method to create new groups is by using the groupadd command. This command is easy to use, just use groupadd, followed by the name of the group you want to add. There are some advanced options, but you'll hardly ever use them.

Creating Groups with YaST

SUSE YaST also provides an easy-to-use interface that is accessible from the yast2 users module, which you can see in Figure 4-2. It allows you to add a new group by entering its name and selecting its members directly, as well.

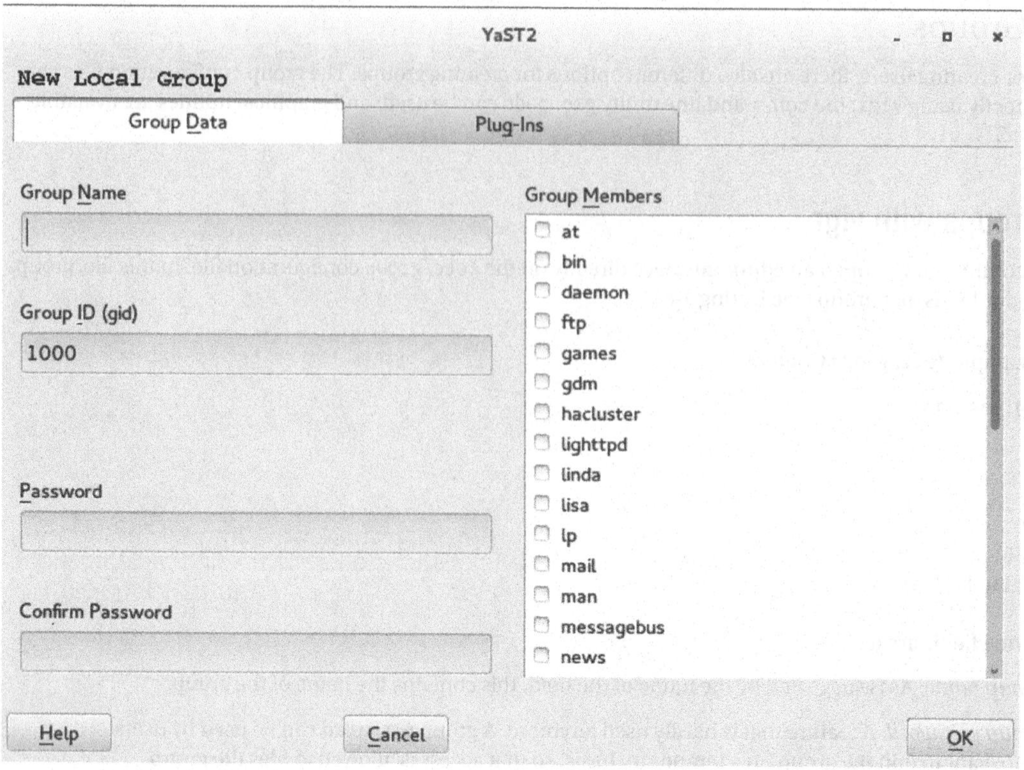

Figure 4-2. *Adding groups from YaST*

Managing Group Properties

To manage group properties, groupmod is available. You can use this command to change the name or Group ID of the group, but it doesn't allow you to add group members. To do this, you'll use usermod. As discussed before, usermod -aG will add users to new groups that will be used as their secondary group.

EXERCISE 4-2. WORKING WITH GROUPS

In this exercise, you'll create two groups and add some users as members to these groups.

1. Type groupadd sales, followed by groupadd account, to add groups with the names *sales* and *account*.

2. Use usermod to add users linda and lisa to the group sales, and lori and bob to the group account, as follows:

   ```
   usermod -aG sales linda
   usermod -aG sales lisa
   usermod -aG account lori
   usermod -aG account bob
   ```

3. Type id linda to verify that user linda has correctly been added to the group sales. In the results of this command, you'll see that linda is assigned to the group with gid=100(users). This is her primary group. With the groups parameter, all groups she is a member of as a secondary group are mentioned.

```
linux:~ # id linda
uid=1000(linda) gid=100(users) groups=1000(sales),100(users)
```

Configuring Base Linux Permissions

To determine which user can access which files, Linux uses permissions. Originally, a set of basic permissions was created, but over time, these didn't suffice. Therefore, a set of special permissions was added. These didn't seem to be enough either, and access control lists (ACLs) were added as well. Apart from these three solutions that relate to permissions, attributes can be used as well, to determine access to files and directories.

Understanding File Ownership

To understand file access security on Linux, you have to understand ownership. On Linux, each file has a user owner and a group owner. On each file, specific permissions are set for the user owner, the group owner, and "others," which refers to all other users. You can display current ownership with the ls -l utility. Listing 4-6 shows ownership on the user home directories in /home. You can see the specific users set as owners of their directories, and the name of the group users that is set as group owner.

Listing 4-6. Showing File Ownership with ls -l

```
linux:/home # ls -l
total 0
drwxr-xr-x 1 bob   users 258 Apr 11 23:49 bob
drwxr-xr-x 1 linda users 224 Apr 11 10:50 linda
drwxr-xr-x 1 lisa  users 258 Apr 11 23:49 lisa
drwxr-xr-x 1 lori  users 258 Apr 11 23:49 lori
```

To determine which access a user has to a specific file or directory, Linux adheres to the following rules:

1. If the user is owner of the file, apply related permissions and exit.

2. If the user is member of the group that is group owner of the file, apply its permissions and exit.

3. Apply the permissions assigned to "others."

Note that in specific cases, this may lead to surprises. Imagine the unusual permission where user linda is owner as file and as owner has no permissions, but she's also member of the group that is group owner, where the group owner has additional permissions to the file. In this case, she wouldn't have any permissions, because only the first match applies. Linda is user owner and, therefore, group ownership becomes irrelevant.

Changing File Ownership

To change file ownership, an administrator can use the chown and chgrp commands. You can use chown to set user as well as group owners. With chgrp, only group ownership can be modified.

Setting user ownership with chown is easy, just type chown username filename. To set group ownership with chown, make sure the name of the group is preceded by a dot or colon: chown :sales myfile would make the group sales group owner of "myfile." You can also use chown to set both user and group as group ownership to a file; chown linda:sales myfile would set user linda and group sales as the owners of myfile.

As an alternative to chown, you can use chgrp to change group ownership. The command chgrp sales myfile would do exactly the same as chown :sales myfile, which is setting the group sales as owner of myfile.

EXERCISE 4-3. CHANGING FILE OWNERSHIP

As a preparation for creating a directory structure that can be used in a shared group environment, this exercise shows you how to create the directories and set appropriate ownership.

1. Type mkdir -p /data/sales /data/account to create two shared group directories. Note the use of the option -p, which makes sure the /data directory is created if it didn't exist already.

2. Set group ownership for both directories by typing chgrp sales /data/sales and chgrp account /data/account.

Note that because the names of the groups match the names of the directories, you could also use a simple bash scripting structure to set the appropriate owners. This works only if /data is the active directory: for i in *; do chgrp $i $i; done. You can read this as "for each element in *" (which is sales and account), put the name of this element in a variable with the name i, and use that variable in the chgrp command. Don't worry if this looks too complicated at the moment, you'll learn lots more about Bash shell scripting in Chapter 15.

Understanding Base Linux Permissions

Now that ownership is set, it's time to take care of Linux permissions. There are three base Linux permissions, and they can be set on files as well as directories. Permissions can be changed by the user root and by the owner of the file. Table 4-1 gives an overview of these permissions.

Table 4-1. Base Permission Overview

Permission	Files	Directories
read	open the contents of the file	list the contents of the directory
write	modify the contents of an existing file	add files or remove files from a directory
execute	execute a file if it contains executable code	use cd to make the directory the active directory

Even if this overview looks rather straightforward, there are a few things that are often misunderstood. Try, for instance, to answer the following question:

1. The "others" entity has read and execute on the /data directory. Does that mean that any given user can read contents of files in that directory?

2. User root places a file in the home directory of user linda. User linda has read permissions only to that file. Can she remove it?

The answer to the first question is no. To determine if a user has read access to a file, the permissions on that file matter, and nothing else. Linux would first see if the user is owner and then if the user is a member of the group owner, and if neither is the case, Linux would apply the permissions assigned to "others." The fact that the user as part of "others" has read rights on the directory doesn't mean anything for what the user can do on the file.

The second question is answered wrongly by many. The important fact is that the file is in the home directory of user linda. Users normally have write permissions on their home directory, and this allows them to add and delete files in that directory. So, the fact that user linda cannot read the contents of the file doesn't matter. It's her home directory, so she will be allowed to remove it.

Applying Base Linux Permissions

Now that you understand a bit about permissions, let's see how they are applied. To set permissions on a directory, the chmod command is used. chmod can be used in absolute mode and in relative mode. In absolute mode, numbers are used to specify which permissions have to be set: read = 4, write = 2, and execute = 1. You'll specify for user, group, and others which permissions you want to assign. An example is chmod 764 myfile. In this command, user gets 7, group gets 6, and others get 4. To determine exactly what that means, you'll now have to do some calculations: 7 = 4 + 2 + 1, so user gets read, write, and execute; 6 = 4 + 2, so group gets read and write; and 4 is just 4, so others get read.

Another way to apply permissions is by using the relative mode. This mode explains itself best by using two examples. Let's start with chmod u=rwx,g-x,o+r myfile. In this command, you would set the user permissions to read, write, and execute; remove x from the current group permissions; and add read to the permissions for others. As you can see, this is not a particularly easy way to assign permissions. Relative mode is easy, though, if you just want to change file properties in general. Take, for instance, the command chmod +x myscript, which adds the execute permission to the myscript file to anyone. This is a fairly common way of assigning permissions in relative mode.

EXERCISE 4-4. ASSIGNING PERMISSIONS

In this exercise, we'll build further on the directories and groups that were added in the previous exercises. You'll make sure that the user and group owners have permissions to do anything in their relative group directories, while removing all permissions assigned to "others."

1. Use cd /data to make /data the current directory.

2. Use chmod 770 * to set grant all permissions to user and group and none to others.

3. Type ls -l to verify. The results should look as in Listing 4-7.

Listing 4-7. Directory Settings

```
linux:/data # ls -l
total 0
drwxr-xr-x 1 root account 0 Apr 12 00:03 account
drwxr-xr-x 1 root sales   0 Apr 12 00:03 sales
linux:/data # chmod 770 *
linux:/data # ls -l
total 0
drwxrwx--- 1 root account 0 Apr 12 00:03 account
drwxrwx--- 1 root sales   0 Apr 12 00:03 sales
```

Configuring Special Permissions

In some cases, the Linux base permissions cannot do all that is needed. That is why some special permissions have been added as well. They are called special permissions because they don't make up part of your default permissions tool. On occasion, you will use them, though, in particular, the Set Group ID (SGID) permission on directories and Sticky bit on directories. Table 4-2 gives an overview of the special permissions and their use.

Table 4-2. Special Permissions Overview

Permission	Files	Directories
SUID (4)	Execute with permissions of owner	-
SGID (2)	Execute with permissions of group owner	Inherit group owner to newly created items below
Sticky (1)	-	Allow deletion only for owner of the file or parent directory

So, let's discuss in some detail what these permissions are all about. The Set User ID (SUID) permission is a particularly dangerous but also very useful permission, in some cases. Normally, when a user executes a program, a subshell is started in which the program runs with the permissions of that user. If SUID is applied to a program file, the program runs with the permissions of the owner of the program file. This is useful in some cases, such as that of the passwd command that needs write access to /etc/shadow, which cannot even be read by ordinary users, but in most cases, it is a very dangerous permission. To be brief about it, even if you ever think about using it, just don't. There are other options, in most cases. SUID has no use on directories.

■ **Tip** As it opens good opportunities for potential evil-doers, the SUID permission is liked a lot by hackers. If a malicious program is installed that can access a shell environment with root permissions, the hacker would be able to take over your server completely. For that reason, it may be wise to periodically scan your server, to find out if any SUID permissions have been set that you don't know about yet. To do this, run find / -perm /4000. If you do this on a regular basis, you'll easily find files that have the SUID permission set but are not supposed to, by comparing with the output from when it was run previously.

Applied to files, the same explanation goes for SGID as for SUID. Applied to directories, however, it is a very useful permission. If SGID is set on a directory, all items created in that directory will get the same group owner as the directory. This is very useful for shared group directories, because it allows for easy access to the files created in that directory.

The Sticky bit permission has no use on files. On directories, it ensures that items in that directory can only be deleted by the user who is owner, or the user who is owner of the parent directory. Sticky bit is also a useful permission on shared group directories, as it prevents users from deleting files that they haven't created themselves.

To set the special permissions, you can use chmod. It works in either absolute or in relative mode. Absolute mode is a bit complicated, though; you'll be adding a fourth digit, and you'll have to make sure that permissions that were previously set are not overwritten by accident. Therefore, you're probably better off using relative mode. Use the following commands to set these permissions:

- chmod u+s myfile: Set SUID on "myfile."

- chmod g+s mydirectory: Set SGID on "mydirectory."

- chmod +t mydirectory: Set Sticky bit on "mydirectory."

If the special permissions are set to a file, you can see that using ls -l. In the original design of the output of ls -l, however, there is no place to show additional permissions. That is why the special permissions take the position where you can normally find the x for user, group, and others. If the special permission identifier is marked as an uppercase, it means that no execute permission is effective at that position. If it is marked as a lowercase, there is also an execute permission effective. The following examples show how it works:

- myfile has SUID but no execute: -rwSr--r-- myfile

- myfile has SUID and execute for user: -rwsr--r-- myfile

- myfile has SGID but not execute: -rw-r-Sr-- myfile

- myfile has SGID and execute for group: -rw-r-sr-- myfile

- myfile has Sticky bit but no execute: -rw-r--r-T myfile

- myfile has Sticky bit and execute for others: -rw-r--r-t myfile

EXERCISE 4-5. SETTING SPECIAL PERMISSONS

In this exercise, you'll learn how to further define your shared group environment, by setting special permissions on the environment that you've created in previous exercises in this chapter.

1. Use cd /data to go into the data directory.

2. Type chmod -R g+s * to set the SGID permission on the current directories and all files and subdirectories that might exist in them.

3. Type chmod -R +t * to apply Sticky bit as well.

4. Use su - linda to take the identity of user linda.

5. Use cd /data/sales, followed by touch linda, to create a file with the name "linda" in /data/sales.

6. Type ls -l. It will show that group sales is group owner of the file.

7. Type exit to go back to the root shell.

8. Type su - lisa to take the identity of user lisa.

9. From the /data/sales directory, type rm -f linda. You'll get an access denied message, because the Sticky bit permission is set on the directory.

10. Type touch lisa to create a file owned by lisa and type exit.

11. Assuming that linda is the manager of the sales department, it makes sense to make her owner of the sales directory. Use chown linda /data/sales.

12. Use su - linda to take the identity of user linda and type rm -f /data/sales/lisa. Because the owner of a directory may delete all files in that directory, there's nothing preventing linda from removing the file that was created by lisa.

Working with Access Control Lists

Another extension to the original Linux permission scheme is made by access control lists. This section describes how to use them.

Understanding ACLs

By adding the special permissions, Linux permissions were already made a bit better. Some functionality was still missing, though, and that is why access control lists (ACLs) were added as a new option. Adding ACLs makes it possible to give permissions to more than one user or group on a file or directory, which is useful, if you want to give full control to a directory for one group, read-only access to another group, and no permissions at all to others.

ACLs also allow you to set permission inheritance, also known as "default ACLs." That means that you can use them to create an environment in which permissions are set at the directory level, and these permissions will be applied automatically to all items that are created in that directory structure.

Imagine that you have a /data/sales directory, and you want all members of the group /data/account to be able to read all files that will ever be created in /data/sales. ACL permission inheritance will do that for you. When working with default ACLs, you should know that Linux will never, ever apply the execute permission to newly created files automatically. In ACLs, the mask takes care of that and filters out the execute permission on files. You'll see that in the next section, in which a default ACL makes read, write, and execute to be inherited on items created below, but the mask will show on files that read and write are used as effective permissions.

Applying ACLs

When applying ACLs, you'll normally apply them twice. The normal ACLs will take care of files that are already existing. To make sure permissions are set for newly created files also, you'll have to add a default ACL as well. To set an ACL, you'll use setfacl; to display current ACL settings, you'll use getfacl.

Before you start working with ACLs, you should know that they always are used as an addition to the normal permissions that are already set for a file or directory. So before taking care of ACLs, you should make sure to set the normal permissions. Next, when you apply the first default ACL to set inheritance, the normal permissions that are already set on that file will be inherited as well.

Let's have a look at how that works for the /data/sales directory that we've created previously. The current settings are that user linda is owner, and group sales is group owner and has all permissions to the directory. To add permissions by means of ACLs for the group account, you would use the following command:

```
setfacl  -R -m g:account:rx /data/sales
```

This, however, just means that members of the group account can list files in the directory and its contents, but if new files are created, account would have no access at all. To take care of that, now type setfacl -m d:g:account:rx /data/sales. This makes sure that members of account can read the contents of all new files that will be created.

Now let's see what this looks like from getfacl. The command getfacl /data/sales shows current settings (see Listing 4-8).

Listing 4-8. Showing Current ACL Assignments with getfacl

```
linux:/data # getfacl sales
# file: sales
# owner: root
# group: sales
user::rwx
group::rwx
group:account:r-x
mask::rwx
other::---
default:user::rwx
default:group::rwx
default:group:account:r-x
default:mask::rwx
default:other::---
```

As you can see, the output consists of two parts. The first part shows the permissions that apply to current users and groups (including groups that have gotten their permissions by means of ACLs). The second part shows the default permission settings.

Now let's create a new file in the /data/sales directory: touch myfile. Now look at the permissions that were set for this file: getfacl myfile. It should look as in Listing 4-9:

Listing 4-9. Showing ACL Assignments as Applied by Inheritance

```
linux:/data/sales # getfacl myfile
# file: myfile
# owner: root
# group: root
user::rw-
group::rwx                    #effective:rw-
group:account:r-x             #effective:r--
mask::rw-
other::---
```

As you can see, the permissions have been inherited to the new file. There's just one thing that isn't nice. User root has created this file, so the file has root:root as owners. That is why on a shared group environment, you would always want to set the SGID permission. It would make sure that new files are group-owned by the group that owns the /data/sales directory, with the effect that all members of the sales group have the appropriate permissions on the file.

In Listing 4-9 you can also see that the mask has become effective. For new files, the mask is set to rw-, which means that the execute permission will never be inherited for files created in a directory.

File System ACL Support

To work with ACLs, your file systems must offer support for them. A modern file system such as Btrfs does this by default, but for older file systems, this is not the case. The easiest way to add ACL support to your file system is by adding the acl mount option into the /etc/fstab file. If while working with ACLs you get an "Operation not supported" error, you'll have to do this. The following line shows an example of a file system that is mounted from /etc/fstab with ACL support.

/dev/sda3 /data ext4 acl 1 2

EXERCISE 4-6. APPLYING ACLS

In this exercise, you'll apply ACLs to allow members from the group "sales" to read files that were created by members of the group "account," and vice versa.

1. Type the command setfacl -m g:account:rx /data/sales and setfacl -m g:sales:rx /data/account. This sets the ACL assignments on the directories but not their contents.

2. Type setfacl -m d:g:account:rx /data/sales and setfacl -m d:g:account:rx /data/sales. This also sets the default ACL.

3. Use getfacl /data/sales to verify the ACL has been set correctly.

4. Use touch /data/sales/somefile to verify that the ACLs have been set correctly on the file as well.

Working with Attributes

A third system that can be used to manage what can be done with files are file system attributes. Attributes apply restrictions to files, no matter which user accesses the file. You can use chattr to set them and lsattr to list them.

Even if from the man page of chattr many attributes are listed, they don't all work. Also, some attributes are used internally by the operating system, and it doesn't make much sense switching them on or off manually. The e attribute, for instance, that is commonly applied on Ext4 file systems, stores files in extents instead of blocks, which makes for more efficient storage.

From a security perspective, there are a few restrictions that do matter and work well in general.

- *immutable* (i): makes it impossible to make any modification to the file

- *append only* (a): allows users to modify the file, but not to delete it

- *undeletable* (u): makes it impossible to delete files

So, if you would want to protect a configuration file in a user's home directory, chattr +i file.conf would do the trick. Even user root would no longer be able to modify the contents of the file. To remove attributes, use chattr -i on the file that has them set.

Summary

In this chapter, you have learned how to create users and groups. You have also learned how to work with permissions to create a secure working environment on your server. In the next chapter, you will learn how to perform common administration tasks, such as setting up printers, scheduling jobs, and configuring logging.

CHAPTER 5

■ ■ ■

Common Administration Tasks

In this chapter, you'll read how to perform some common administration tasks on SUSE Linux Enterprise Server. You'll read how to manage printers, software, and tasks and processes, and you'll also learn how to schedule tasks and set up an environment for logging.

Managing Printers

Even if printers, on many occasions, are connected to print servers, SUSE Linux Enterprise Server (SLES) contains everything that is needed to manage printers. Printers that are connected locally are supported, as is the case for printers that are connected to some other print server, no matter if that is a dedicated hardware print server or a software print server that is defined on another computer.

To communicate to printers, the Common UNIX Printing System (CUPS) is used. This is a process that monitors print queues for print jobs and forwards these jobs to the appropriate printer. In this section, you'll read how to manage printers from YaST as well as the command line.

Managing Printers from YaST

To manage printers from YaST, you have to select the Hardware ➤ Printer tool. Before doing anything, this tool will tell you that it is going to restart the CUPS daemon that is started by default upon installation. As you probably don't have any printers configured yet, that is no problem, so select Yes to proceed configuring printers.

At this point, you should see the interface that can be seen in Figure 5-1. From this interface, you can configure all properties of printers on your server.

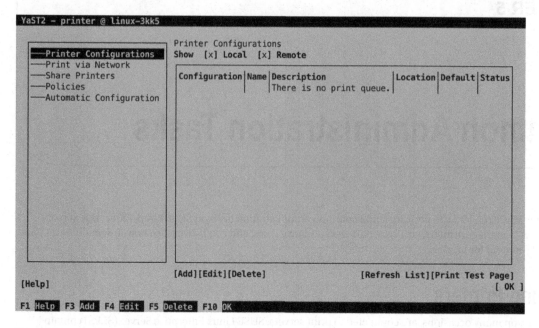

Figure 5-1. *Configuring printers from YaST*

To create new printers, you start from the Printer Configurations screen. From that screen, select Add to create a new printer. This starts a printer detection process. CUPS is rather good in detecting printers. If the printer is hardware connected to your server, the udev process (discussed in Chapter 8) will find it and initialize it. If it's on the network, the CUPS process will detect it.

For some types of printer connection, automatic detection doesn't work out well. If that is the case, you can manually start the Connection Wizard. From its first screen, you can first select the type of printer, after which you can specify the further printer properties. The options are divided into four different categories.

- *Directly Connected Device*: This is for any printer that is directly connected to your computer. In general, these types of printers will auto-install themselves, so normally, you won't have to configure any of these.

- *Network Printers*: These printers may need some help getting configured, as depending on the configuration of your network, the automatic detection may fail.

- *Print Server*: These are printers configured on another computer. They may require additional configuration also.

- *Special*: This is a rarely used option that allows administrators to configure special printer types, such as sending printer data directly to another program.

After configuring printers this way, the CUPS process on your server will give access to the printer, no matter if it is a local printer or a remote printer. You can next access it from the command line and from applications running on your computer.

Command-Line Printer Management Tools

Once printers have been installed—which, as you've read, can be done in quite an easy way—as an administrator, you might want to perform some management tasks on them. Managing the printer often relates to the print jobs that are in the queue. Some commands are available to manage print jobs, as follows:

- lpstat: Provides information about printers. This command offers many options that allow you to query the print queue. For example, use lpstat -l to show a list of printers, classes, or jobs, lpstat -W all for an overview of jobs and their current status, or lpstat -p to get a list of printers that are available on a specific host.

- lpr: The lpr command submits files for printing. It will send them to the default printer, unless the option -P is used to specify another destination to send print jobs to. While lpr is the old UNIX command, on Linux, the lp command normally is used to send print jobs to a printer.

- lpadmin: Allows administrators to create printers. Basically, everything that can be done from YaST can be done with lpadmin as well. The command has a large amount of options to specify exactly what needs to be done.

- lpq: Will show you which print jobs are in the print queue.

- lprm: Provides an easy-to-use interface to remove jobs from a print queue.

Managing Software

An important task for an SUSE Linux Enterprise Server (SLES) administrator is managing software. Two systems are available for software management: the old RPM and the new Zypper-based system. Before explaining the details of both systems, it's good to have some generic understanding of the use of repositories.

Understanding Repositories and Meta Package Handlers

When programmers write a program, they normally don't develop something that contains all that is required. Programmers tend to focus on specific functionality and will get the rest from libraries that have been written by someone else. This is called a dependency. In order to install a specific program, other items must already be available on the system where the program is installed.

These dependencies are reflected in software package management. An administrator may select to install a single package, but to install that package, all of its dependencies have to be installed as well. In the old days, when packages were installed directly, that often led to challenges. An administrator who wanted to install one package might get the response that some dependencies were missing, and these dependencies might even have had their own dependencies. This is what was referred to as dependency hell.

In current Linux distributions, meta package handlers are used. In a meta package handler, repositories are used for installing software. A repository is an installation source containing a collection of packages. The servers and workstations on which software has to be installed are normally configured to use multiple repositories and will regularly download an index of available packages. If when working with repositories administrators have to install software, all dependencies are looked up in the index files, and if the dependency is found, it is installed automatically.

In the way package management is organized on SUSE Linux, apart from repositories, there are also services involved. A service manages repositories or does some special task. Currently, the only type of service that is supported is the Repository Index Service (RIS). RIS contains a list of other repositories, which are indexed by using this list. This offers the benefit that in case many repositories are used, indexes don't have to be downloaded for every individual repository but can be downloaded for many repositories at the same time. This makes working with repositories faster.

On SUSE Linux Enterprise, packages can be installed individually as packages in the RPM format. They can also be installed from repositories, using Zypper or YaST. In the next subsection, you'll learn how to install packages using these tools.

Installing Software from YaST

YaST offers everything an administrator needs for installing and managing software. To configure the large amount of options available, you'll select the Software category from YaST. This shows the following different options:

- *Online Update*: This performs an update of your server against the repositories it has been configured to use.

- *Software Management*: Use this for common package management tasks, such as installing, deleting, updating, and more.

- *Add-On Products*: Add-On products such as the High Availability Extension are available for purchase on SLES. To install such an Add-On Product, this option from YaST is used.

- *Media Check*: This option can be used to verify that the installation medium does not contain any errors.

- *Software Repositories*: This option is used to define the repositories that will be used on this server

Apart from the options that are offered from this YaST interface, in large environments, SUSE Manager can be used for managing software. From SUSE Manager, multiple packages and patches can be selected, and these can be installed on multiple servers in an automated way. Using SUSE Manager is highly recommended in an environment in which many servers have to be managed. You can read more about SUSE Manager in Chapter 18.

Managing Repositories

Before an administrator can start managing software, software repositories must be available. After selecting the Software Repositories option from YaST, you'll see the screen shown in Figure 5-2. Normally in this list, you'll at least see the installation medium that was used while installing SLES. If your server is registered, you'll also see the SUSE update repositories, which are provided by SUSE to make sure that you'll always be using the latest version of available software.

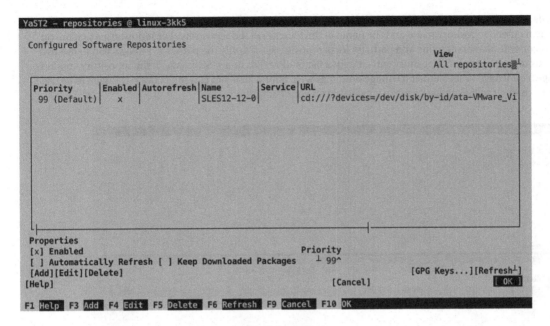

```
YaST2 - repositories @ linux-3kk5

Configured Software Repositories
                                                                    View
                                                                    All repositories▓↧

 ┌─────────┬───────┬───────────┬──────────┬──────────┬──────────────────────────────────┐
 │Priority │Enabled│Autorefresh│Name      │Service│URL                                   │
 │99 (Default)│  x  │           │SLES12-12-0│         │cd:///?devices=/dev/disk/by-id/ata-VMware_Vi│
 │         │       │           │          │          │                                  │
 │         │       │           │          │          │                                  │
 │         │       │           │          │          │                                  │
 │         │       │           │          │          │                                  │
 │         │       │           │          │          │                                  │
 │         │       │           │          │          │                                  │
 └┬────────────────────────────────────────────────────┬───────────────────────────────┘
  ⌐                                                      ⌐
Properties
[x] Enabled                                         Priority
[ ] Automatically Refresh [ ] Keep Downloaded Packages  ⊥ 99^
[Add][Edit][Delete]                                                    [GPG Keys...][Refresh↧]
[Help]                                             [Cancel]                        [ OK ]

F1 Help  F3 Add  F4 Edit  F5 Delete  F6 Refresh  F9 Cancel  F10 OK
```

Figure 5-2. *The Software Repositories management interface*

To add a new repository, you can select the Add option. This opens the screen that you can see in Figure 5-3. From this, you can specify the source of the repository. As you can see, every possible type of installation source is supported. To add a repository, you have to specify the URL for that specific repository. You can also specify whether you want to download repository description files. This is done by default, and it's a good idea to do it, because it makes the index of the selected repository available on your computer.

```
YaST2 - repositories @ linux-3kk5

Add On Product


          ( ) Scan Using SLP...
          ( ) Extensions and Modules from Registration Server...
          (x) Specify URL...
          ( ) FTP...
          ( ) HTTP...
          ( ) HTTPS...
          ( ) SMB/CIFS
          ( ) NFS...
          ( ) CD...
          ( ) DVD...
          ( ) Hard Disk...
          ( ) USB Mass Storage (USB Stick, Disk)...
          ( ) Local Directory...
          ( ) Local ISO Image...



          [x] Download repository description files



[Help]                  [Back]                  [Abort]                  [Next]

F1 Help  F8 Back  F9 Abort  F10 Next
```

Figure 5-3. *Selecting the source for the new repository*

After selecting which type of repository you want to add, the screen that you can see in Figure 5-4 opens. On this screen, you can enter a repository name and the name of the location of the repository. For repositories that are on a server, this consists of a server name and path; for local repositories, it's only the path. YaST allows you to use two different kinds of repositories. A repository can contain a list of RPM files or an ISO image. If the repository contains an ISO image, you'll have to select the ISO image option as well, after which you can select the ISO image to be used. This will loop-mount the ISO image, to make it available on your computer.

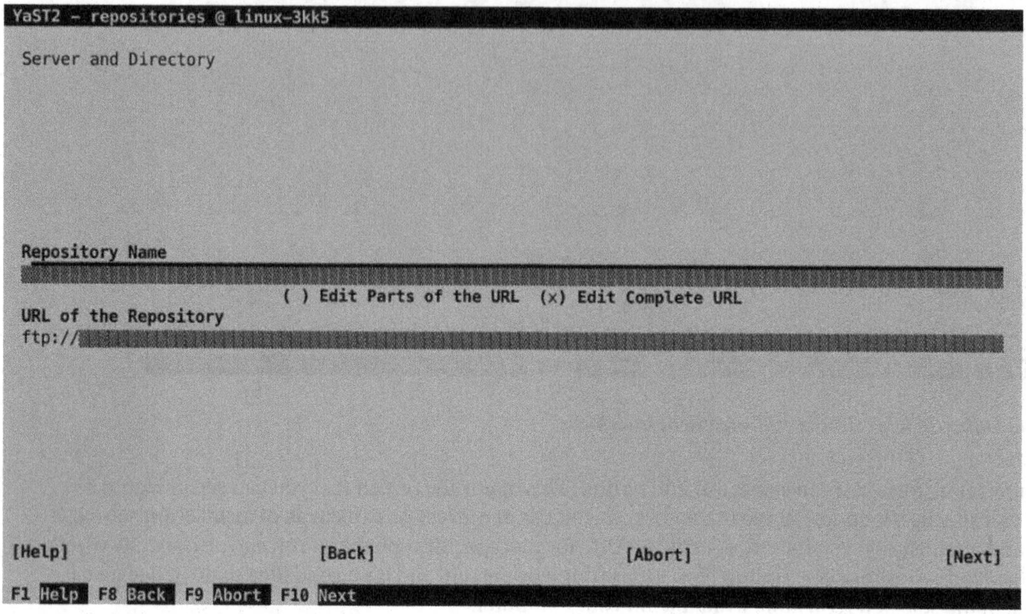

Figure 5-4. *Specifying repository properties*

From the list of available repositories, you can perform some management tasks as well. To start with, you can enable a repository. If you know that a repository will be unavailable for some time, it makes sense to tell it. If your server knows that a repository is temporarily unavailable, it won't try to install software from the repository. So, if you have to bring down a repository for maintenance, make sure to disable it as well.

The Autorefresh option makes sense on an online repository. This option tells your computer to fetch updated index files every day, so that your server is completely up to date about the most current state of packages. Another useful option is Priority. If you're working with multiple repositories, there is a risk that conflicts between package versions arise. In case of a conflict, the Priority option makes clear which package version takes precedence. The last option is Keep Downloaded Packages. If your Internet connection is slow, it may be beneficial to use this option in order to cache packages locally.

Managing Software Packages

After configuring the repositories, you can start managing software. For this purpose, YaST offers the interface that you can see in Figure 5-5. The most important item in this interface is the Filter option. By default, it is on Search, but by pressing the down arrow key, other options can be selected as well. Before you do anything, make sure to select the option you need from this list.

- *Patterns*: With the Patterns option, the software is presented in different categories. By selecting a pattern, you can easily select all the software you need for a specific purpose.

- *Languages*: Use this option if you need a specific language version of packages. The amount of packages available in a specific language often doesn't go much beyond the browser language.

- *RPM Groups*: RPM groups are another way of grouping RPM packages, as in the Patterns option. Use this option if you want to browse software according to the category of software packages.

- *Repositories*: Use this if you're looking for packages from a specific repository.

- *Search*: Use this option if you want to search for a package with a specific name.

- *Installation Summary*: This option summarizes the work to be done, before actually starting it.

- *Package Classification*: Every package, by default, has a classification. This classification gives a hint as to whether or not a package is needed on your server. Use this option to browse packages according to their current classification: Recommended, Suggested, Orphaned, or Unneeded.

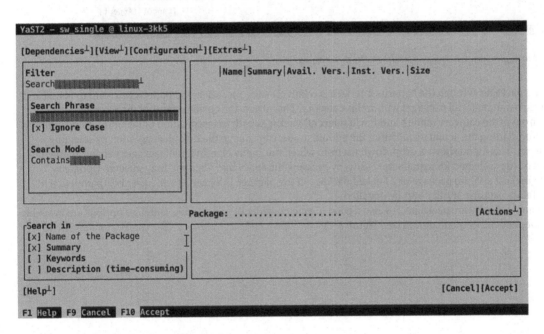

Figure 5-5. *Managing packages from YaST*

Installing Software Using the Patterns Option

The Patterns option provides a convenient way for installing software packages. This is the same interface as that used during the initial installation of SLES (see Figure 5-6).

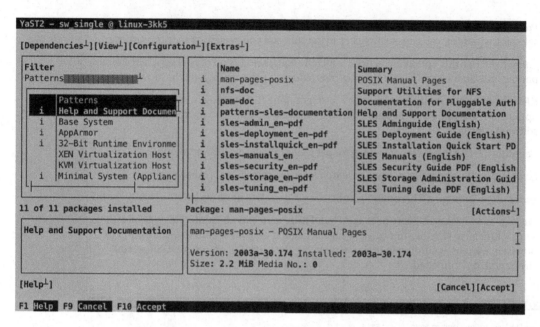

Figure 5-6. *Managing packages through the Patterns interface*

Managing packages through the Patterns interface is relatively easy. Just select the pattern you want to install and press the space bar to select all packages within this category. This makes the current status of the package category (a + is put in front of the category name), and it will select all packages with a classification of Recommended in this category. Before starting the actual installation, the administrator can change the default suggestion by selecting the Action menu. This menu shows a drop-down list from which the status of individual packages can be changed. Packages can be (de-)selected for installation easily, by pressing the space bar. Also, you may select to Update a package or to make it a Taboo package or a Locked package. If the package is locked, it will never be upgraded. If it's marked as a Taboo package, it will never be installed.

When managing software packages, it's also a good idea to consider dependencies. Different options are available through the Dependencies menu option (see Figure 5-7).

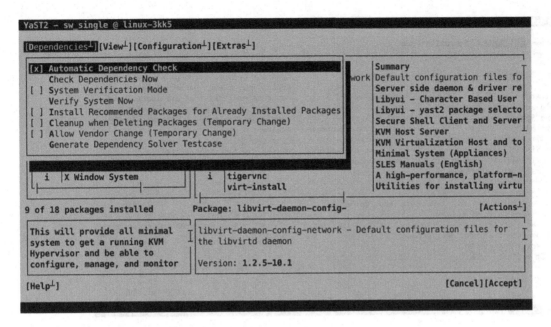

Figure 5-7. Managing package dependency options

The default setting is that dependencies are checked automatically. That means that before installing software packages, a check is performed to find out which requirements there are to install the selected package. Another useful option that is presented through the Dependencies menu is System Verification Mode. This mode allows you to verify that the state of the system is consistent with the actual packages that you have selected. You can set both of these options as default options, but it's also possible to run them on your system now, by selecting the appropriate option from the Dependencies menu.

While installing software through YaST, you can use the options in the View menu to get more information about selected packages (see Figure 5-8). This option goes into the RPM package itself to request specific installation. The most interesting of the view options are the File list and the Dependencies list. The File list shows the exact contents of the package, and by selecting Dependencies, you can manually examine what else is required on this system before the package can be installed. You'll see the results of the View option you have selected in the lower right part of the YaST package management screen.

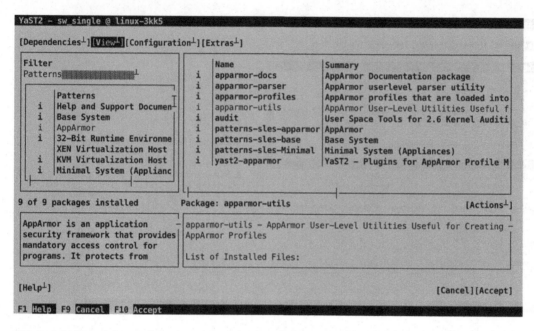

Figure 5-8. Examining package contents prior to installation

After selecting one or more packages for installation, an overview of Package Dependencies is provided. If there are problems preventing the package to be installed normally, you'll be prompted as to what to do. In general, the very first option listed is also the best option. In Figure 5-9, you can see an example of such a problem.

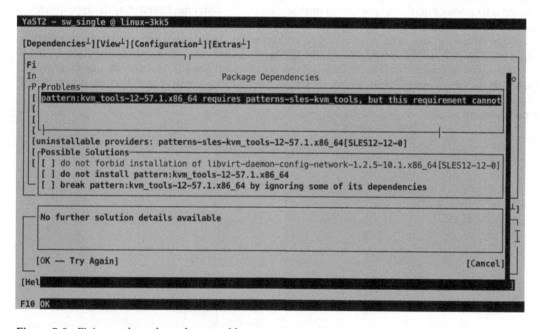

Figure 5-9. Fixing package dependency problems

If no problems became manifest, you'll see a window listing the automatic changes that will be applied. Read through the list of packages that is going to be installed, and if you're OK with it, press OK to start the installation.

Installing Software from the Command Line

While YaST offers an easy-to-use interface for packages installation, SUSE offers some good command-line utilities also. To work on individual packages, the rpm command is useful; to manage software, the zypper utility is what you need. You'll find yourself working with zypper more frequently than with rpm, because zypper offers all you need to install, update, and remove packages.

Managing Software Packages with zypper

zypper is the command-line tool that you want to use for installing, removing, and updating packages—and more. Typically, the first step to perform, if you have to install a package, is zypper se, which allows you to search packages. zypper search will also work, but why would you want to type a long command if there's a short alternative, right?

The zypper se command shows a list of results corresponding to what you were looking for, including the current state of the package. By default, zypper se performs a match on partial expressions. That means that if you type zypper se ap, you'll receive a list of all packages matching the string 'ap'. zypper also knows how to treat regular expressions: make sure the search string is between single quotes, if you're looking for a regex match.

Note that zypper se will search in the package name or description but not in the package contents. That means that you may be missing a specific package while looking for it with zypper se. If you want to look into the package, to look for a package containing a specific file, you can use zypper se --provides filename. Note that most binary files will also be found when using zypper se, but if you have to go down in a bit more detail, the --provides utility may be useful.

After finding the package you want to install with zypper se, you may want to get additional details about it. The command zypper info will do that for you. Type zypper info packagename, if you only want some generic information about the package (see Listing 5-1).

Listing 5-1. zypper info Provides Generic Information About a Specific Package

```
linux-3kk5:~ # zypper info nmap
Loading repository data...
Reading installed packages...

Information for package nmap:
----------------------------
Repository: SLES12-12-0
Name: nmap
Version: 6.46-1.62
Arch: x86_64
Vendor: SUSE LLC <https://www.suse.com/>
Installed: No
Status: not installed
Installed Size: 16.4 MiB
Summary: Portscanner
Description:
  Nmap is designed to allow system administrators and curious individuals
  to scan large networks to determine which hosts are up and what
  services they are offering. XNmap is a graphical front-end that shows
  nmap's output clearly.
  Find documentation in /usr/share/doc/packages/nmap
```

If you need more specific information about the package, you may appreciate some of the additional options that zypper info provides. You can, for example, receive information about a package from a specific repository, if zypper se has shown that the package is available from different repositories. Use zypper info -r, followed by the URL or name of the repository, to do that.

The zypper info command provides some other useful options also. Use zypper info --provides packagename, for example, to find out exactly what is in a package, or zypper info --requires packagename, to determine which software has to be installed for a package to be functional.

Of course you can use zypper to work with patterns also. Start by typing zypper pt, to show a list of all available patterns. This gives a result as in Listing 5-2.

Listing 5-2. The zypper pt Command Shows All Software Patterns

```
linux-3kk5:~ # zypper pt
Loading repository data...
Reading installed packages...
S | Name              | Version  | Repository     | Dependency
--+-------------------+----------+----------------+-----------
  | 32bit             | 12-57.1  | SLES12-12-0    |
i | 32bit             | 12-57.1  | @System        |
  | Basis-Devel       | 12-57.1  | SLES12-12-0    |
  | Minimal           | 12-57.1  | SLES12-12-0    |
i | Minimal           | 12-57.1  | @System        |
  | WBEM              | 12-57.1  | SLES12-12-0    |
  | apparmor          | 12-57.1  | SLES12-12-0    |
i | apparmor          | 12-57.1  | @System        |
  | base              | 12-57.1  | SLES12-12-0    |
i | base              | 12-57.1  | @System        |
  | dhcp_dns_server   | 12-57.1  | SLES12-12-0    |
  | directory_server  | 12-57.1  | SLES12-12-0    |
  | documentation     | 12-57.1  | SLES12-12-0    |
i | documentation     | 12-57.1  | @System        |
  | file_server       | 12-57.1  | SLES12-12-0    |
  | fips              | 12-57.1  | SLES12-12-0    |
  | gateway_server    | 12-57.1  | SLES12-12-0    |
  | gnome-basic       | 12-5.1   | SLES12-12-0    |
i | gnome-basic       | 12-5.1   | @System        |
  | kvm_server        | 12-57.1  | SLES12-12-0    |
i | kvm_server        | 12-57.1  | @System        |
  | kvm_tools         | 12-57.1  | SLES12-12-0    |
i | kvm_tools         | 12-57.1  | @System        |
  | lamp_server       | 12-57.1  | SLES12-12-0    |
  | mail_server       | 12-57.1  | SLES12-12-0    |
  | ofed              | 12-57.1  | SLES12-12-0    |
  | oracle_server     | 12-57.1  | SLES12-12-0    |
  | printing          | 12-57.1  | SLES12-12-0    |
  | sap_server        | 12-57.1  | SLES12-12-0    |
  | x11               | 12-57.1  | SLES12-12-0    |
i | x11               | 12-57.1  | @System        |
  | xen_server        | 12-57.1  | SLES12-12-0    |
  | xen_tools         | 12-57.1  | SLES12-12-0    |
```

Next, to find out what exactly is in the pattern, you can use zypper info -t pattern patternname, as in zypper info -t pattern fips, which shows a description and a list of all packages in the fips pattern.

After getting the required information about packages, you can move on and install them, using zypper in. You can, of course, just perform a basic installation, by using zypper in packagename, but you can also do a somewhat more sophisticated installation, such as zypper in vim -nano, which will install Vim and remove nano at the same time. Instead of installing individual packages, you can install patterns as well, as in zypper in -t pattern fips. In case your attempt to install packages results in an error message, you can insist a bit more by adding the -f option.

A specific case of installation is source packages. These are packages that don't contain ready-to-use binaries but the source code of these packages. On occasion, you may need these if you have to do some tweaking of the package source code. To install a source package, you'll use zypper si instead of zypper in.

A specific kind of package operation that you can do using zypper is patch management. That starts by typing zypper list-patches, to show a list of all patches that are available. To get more information about a specific patch, you can next type zypper info -t patch name. If you like all patches and want to install them, you can use zypper patch. This command, however, has some additional options also, such as zypper patch -b ###, in which ### is replaced with a bugzilla patch number. This command allows you to install patches as documented in a specific bugzilla patch number. Related to the patch commands is the up command, which just upgrades all packages that have an upgrade available.

When performing an update, normally all packages are updated. This is often OK, but on some occasions, it is not. A program might require a specific version of a package to be installed. To make sure a package will never be upgraded, you can create a lock. Use zypper addlock package to put a lock on a specific package name. This guarantees that it will never be updated. To get an overview of packages that are locked, use zypper ll.

EXERCISE 5-1. MANAGING SOFTWARE WITH ZYPPER

In this exercise, you'll learn how to work with some of the essential zypper commands.

1. Type zypper se nmap. This will search for packages containing nmap in their package name or description.

2. Type zypper info nmap to get more information about the nmap package. To see what will be installed with it, use zypper info --provides nmap, and to find out about its dependencies, type zypper info --requires nmap.

3. Now that you know more about the package, you can type zypper in nmap to install it.

4. Working with patterns is also convenient. Type zypper se -t pattern to show a list of all patterns that are available.

5. Request more information about the fips pattern, by typing zypper info -t pattern fips.

6. Assuming that you like what it is doing, install fips, using zypper in -t pattern fips.

7. To make sure that nmap will never be upgraded, type zypper addlock nmap. Verify that the lock has successfully been set, using zypper ll. To remove the lock again, use zypper rl nmap.

Querying Packages with rpm

The zypper command, in general, is used to manage software installations and upgrades. Once the software has been installed, the RPM database keeps track of it. On a modern Linux server such as SLES 12, you won't use the rpm command anymore to install, update, or remove software. It is still convenient, however, for querying software and its current state.

There are two types of RPM query that can be performed. The database can be queried, and package files can be queried. To query the database, you'll use rpm -q, followed by the specific query option. To query a package file, you'll use rpm -qp, followed by the specific query option. There are a few useful query options, as follows:

-l	Lists package contents
-i	Lists information about a package
-c	Lists configuration files included in the package
-d	Lists documentation provided by a package
-f	Lists the name of the RPM a specific file belongs to

In Exercise 5-2, you'll work with some of the most significant query options.

EXERCISE 5-2. USING RPM QUERIES

Have you ever been in a situation in which you needed to find the configuration file that is used by a specific binary? This exercise shows exactly what you can do in such cases. We'll use the vsftpd binary as an example.

1. To begin with, you need the exact name of the binary you want to query. Type which vsftpd to find out. It will show the name /usr/sbin/vsftpd.

2. Now we have to find out which RPM this file comes from. The command rpm -qf /usr/sbin/vsftpd will do that for us and show vsftpd as the RPM name. It shows a version number as well, but for querying the database, the version number is not important.

3. Now let's read the package description. Type rpm -qi vsftpd to get more information.

4. To get a list of all files in the package, type rpm -ql vsftpd.

5. To see which files are used for its configuration, use rpm -qc vsftpd.

6. And if you have to read some more documentation before you can begin, type rpm -qd vsftpd.

Managing Jobs and Processes

Most of the work that you'll be doing as a Linux administrator will be done from a terminal window. To start a task, you'll type a specific command. For example, you'll type ls to display a listing of files in the current directory. Every command you type, from the perspective of the shell, is started as a job. Most commands are started as a job in the foreground. That means the command is started; it shows its result on the terminal window; and then it exists. As many commands only take a short while to complete their work, you don't have to do any specific job management on them.

While some commands only take a few seconds to finish, other commands take much longer. Imagine, for example, the mandb command that is going to update the database that is used by the man -k command. This command can easily take a few minutes to complete. For commands such as these, it makes sense to start them as a background job, by putting an & sign (ampersand) at the end of the command, as in the following example:

mandb &

By putting an & at the end of a command, you start it as a background job. While starting a command this way, the shell gives its job number (between square brackets), as well as its unique process identification number, the PID. You can use these to manage your background jobs, as is explained in the following paragraphs.

The benefit of starting a job in the background is that the terminal is available to launch other commands, and that is good, if the job takes a long time to complete. At the moment the background job is finished, you'll see a message that it has completed, but this message is only displayed after you've entered another command to start.

To manage jobs that are started in the background, there are a few commands and key sequences that you can use (see Table 5-1).

Table 5-1. *Managing Shell Jobs*

Command/Key Sequence	Use
Ctrl+Z	Use this to pause a job. Once paused, you can put it in the foreground or in the background.
fg	Use this to start a paused job as a foreground job.
bg	Use this to start a paused job as a background job.
jobs	Use this to show a list of all current jobs.

Normally, you won't do too much job management, but in some cases, it does make sense to move a job you've already started to the background, so that you can make the terminal where it was started available for other tasks. Exercise 5-3 shows how to do this.

EXERCISE 5-3. MANAGING JOBS

In this exercise, you'll learn how to move a job that was started as a foreground job to the background. This can be especially useful for graphical programs that are started as a foreground job and occupy your terminal until they have finished.

1. From a graphical user interface, open a terminal, and from that terminal, start the gedit program. You will see that the terminal is now occupied by the graphical program you've just started, and at this moment, you cannot start any other programs.

2. Click in the terminal where you started gedit and use the Ctrl+Z key sequence. This temporarily stops the graphical program and gives back the prompt on your terminal.

3. Use the bg command to move the job you've started to the background.

4. From the terminal window, type the jobs command. This shows a list of all jobs that are started from this terminal. You should see just the gedit command. In the list that the jobs command shows you, every job has a unique job number. If you have only one job, it will always be job number 1.

5. To put a background job back in the foreground, use the fg command. By default, this command will put the last command you've started in the background back in the foreground. If you want to put another background job in the foreground, use fg, followed by the job number of the job you want to manage, for example, fg 1.

■ **Note** Job numbers are specific to the shell in which you've started the job. That means that if you have multiple terminals that are open, you can manage jobs in each of these terminals.

System and Process Monitoring and Management

In the preceding text, you've learned how to manage jobs that you have started from a shell. As mentioned, every command that you've started from the shell can be managed as a job. There are, however, many more tasks that are running on any given moment on your server. These tasks are referred to as processes.

Every command you enter or program you start from the shell becomes not only a job but also a process. Apart from that, when your server boots, many other processes are started to provide services on your server. These are the so called daemons—processes that are always started in the background and provide services on your server. If, for example, your server starts an Apache web server, this web server is started as a daemon.

For a system administrator, managing processes is an important task. You may have to send a specific signal to a process that doesn't respond properly anymore. Otherwise, on a very busy system, it is important to get an overview of your system and check exactly what it is doing. You will use a few commands to manage and monitor processes on your computer (see Table 5-2).

Table 5-2. *Common Process Management Commands*

Command	Use
ps	Used to show all current processes
kill	Used to send signals to processes, such as asking or forcing a process to stop
pstree	Used to give an overview of all processes, including the relation between parent and child processes
killall	Used to kill all processes, based on the name of the process
top	Used to get an overview of the current system activity

Managing Processes with ps

As an administrator, you might need to find out what a specific process is doing on your server. The ps command helps you with that. If started as root with the appropriate options, ps shows information about the current status of processes. Owing to historical reasons, the ps command can be used in two different modes: the BSD mode, in which options are not preceded by a - sign, and the System V mode, in which all options are preceded by a - sign. Between these two modes, there are options with an overlapping functionality.

Two of the most useful ways to use the ps commands are in the command ps fax, which gives a tree-like overview of all current processes, and ps aux, which gives an overview with lots of usage information for every process. Listing 5-3 shows a partial output of the ps aux command.

Listing 5-3. Partial Output of the ps aux Command

```
linux-3kk5:~ # ps aux | head -n 10
USER       PID %CPU %MEM    VSZ   RSS TTY     STAT START   TIME COMMAND
root         1  0.0  0.3  33660  3468 ?       Ss   Sep19   0:05
/usr/lib/systemd/systemd --switched-root --system --deserialize 19
root         2  0.0  0.0      0     0 ?       S    Sep19   0:00 [kthreadd]
root         3  0.0  0.0      0     0 ?       S    Sep19   0:00 [ksoftirqd/0]
root         5  0.0  0.0      0     0 ?       S<   Sep19   0:00 [kworker/0:0H]
root         7  0.0  0.0      0     0 ?       S    Sep19   0:00 [migration/0]
root         8  0.0  0.0      0     0 ?       S    Sep19   0:00 [rcu_bh]
root         9  0.0  0.0      0     0 ?       S    Sep19   0:01 [rcu_sched]
root        10  0.0  0.0      0     0 ?       S    Sep19   0:01 [watchdog/0]
root        11  0.0  0.0      0     0 ?       S    Sep19   0:00 [watchdog/1]
```

If using ps aux, process information is shown in different columns:

USER	The name of the user whose identity is used to run this process
PID	The process identification number (PID), a unique number that is needed to manage processes
%CPU	The percentage of CPU cycles used by this process
%MEM	The percentage of memory used by this process
VSZ	The Virtual Memory Size, the total amount of memory that is claimed by this process. It is normal that processes claim much more memory than the amount of memory they really need. That's no problem, because the memory in the VSZ column isn't used anyway
RSS	The Resident memory size, the total amount of memory that this process is really using
TTY	If the process is started from a terminal, the device name of the terminal is mentioned in this column
STAT	The current status of the process. The top three most common status indicators are S for sleeping, R for running, or Z for a process that has entered the zombie state
START	The time that the process was started
TIME	The real time in seconds that this process has used CPU cycles since it was started
COMMAND	The name of the command file that was used to start the process. If the name of this file is between brackets, it is a kernel process

Another common way to show process information is by using the command ps fax. The most useful addition in this command is the f option, which shows the relation between parent and child processes. For an administrator, this is important information to be aware of, because for process management purposes, this relation is important. Managing of processes goes via the parent process. That means that in order to kill a process, you must be able to contact the parent of that specific process. Also, if you kill a process that currently has active children, all of the children of the process are terminated as well. In Exercise 5-4, you can find out for yourself how this works.

Sending Signals to Processes with the kill Command

To manage processes as an administrator, you can send signals to the process in question. According to the POSIX standard—a standard that defines how UNIX-like operating systems should behave—different signals can be used. In practice, only a few of these signals are always available. It is up to the person who writes a program to determine which signals are available and which are not.

A well-known example of a command that offers more than the default signals is the dd command. When this command is active, you can send SIGUSR1 to the command, to show details about the current progress of the dd command.

Three signals are available at all times: SIGHUP (1), SIGKILL (9), and SIGTERM (15). Of these, SIGTERM is the best way to ask a process to stop its activity. If as an administrator you request closure of a program, using the SIGTERM signal, the process in question can still close all open files and stop using its resources.

A more brutal way of terminating a process is by sending it SIGKILL, which doesn't give any time at all to the process to cease its activity. The process is just cut off, and you risk damaging open files.

A completely different way of managing processes is by using the SIGHUP signal, which tells a process that it should reinitialize and read its configuration files again.

To send signals to processes, you will use the kill command. This command typically has two arguments: the number of the signal that you want to send to the process and the PID of the process to which you want to send a signal. An example is the command kill -9 1234, which will send the SIGKILL signal to the process with PID 1234.

When using the kill command, you can use the PIDs of multiple processes to send specific signals to multiple processes simultaneously. Another convenient way to send a signal to multiple processes simultaneously is by using the killall command, which takes the name of a process as its argument. For example, the command killall -SIGTERM vsftpd would send the SIGTERM signal to all active httpd processes.

EXERCISE 5-4. MANAGING PROCESSES WITH PS AND KILL

In this exercise, you will start a few processes to make the parent-child relation between these processes visible. Next, you will kill the parent process and see that all related child processes also disappear.

1. Open a terminal window (right-click the graphical desktop and select Open in Terminal).

2. Use the bash command to start bash as a subshell in the current terminal window.

3. Use ssh -X localhost to start ssh as a subshell in the bash shell you've just opened. When asked if you permanently want to add localhost to the list of known hosts, type "yes." Next, enter the password of the user root.

4. Type gedit & to start gedit as a background job.

5. Type ps efx to show a listing of all current processes, including the parent-child relationship between the commands you've just entered.

6. Find the PID of the SSH shell you've just started. If you can't find it, use ps aux | grep ssh. One of the output lines shows the ssh -X localhost command you've just entered. Note the PID that you see in that output line.

7. Use kill, followed by the PID number you've just found to close the SSH shell. As the SSH environment is the parent of the gedit command, killing ssh will kill the gedit window as well.

Using top to Show Current System Activity

The top program offers a convenient interface in which you can monitor current process activity and perform some basic management tasks. Figure 5-10 shows what a top window might look like.

```
top - 08:12:06 up 1 day,  1:18,  5 users,  load average: 0.00, 0.01, 0.05
Tasks: 220 total,   1 running, 219 sleeping,   0 stopped,   0 zombie
%Cpu(s):  0.0 us,  0.0 sy,  0.0 ni,100.0 id,  0.0 wa,  0.0 hi,  0.0 si,  0.0 st
KiB Mem:   1012440 total,   949100 used,    63340 free,      8 buffers
KiB Swap:  1517564 total,    30768 used,  1486796 free.   549624 cached Mem

  PID USER      PR  NI    VIRT    RES    SHR S  %CPU %MEM     TIME+ COMMAND
  793 root      20   0   84264   1408   1076 S 0.332 0.139   1:21.77 vmtoolsd
34157 root      20   0   13796   1544   1032 R 0.332 0.153   0:00.02 top
    1 root      20   0   33660   3468   1408 S 0.000 0.343   0:05.17 systemd
    2 root      20   0       0      0      0 S 0.000 0.000   0:00.01 kthreadd
    3 root      20   0       0      0      0 S 0.000 0.000   0:00.92 ksoftirqd/0
    5 root       0 -20       0      0      0 S 0.000 0.000   0:00.00 kworker/0:0H
    7 root      rt   0       0      0      0 S 0.000 0.000   0:00.04 migration/0
    8 root      20   0       0      0      0 S 0.000 0.000   0:00.00 rcu_bh
    9 root      20   0       0      0      0 S 0.000 0.000   0:01.22 rcu_sched
   10 root      rt   0       0      0      0 S 0.000 0.000   0:01.06 watchdog/0
   11 root      rt   0       0      0      0 S 0.000 0.000   0:00.75 watchdog/1
   12 root      rt   0       0      0      0 S 0.000 0.000   0:00.02 migration/1
   13 root      20   0       0      0      0 S 0.000 0.000   0:00.33 ksoftirqd/1
   15 root       0 -20       0      0      0 S 0.000 0.000   0:00.00 kworker/1:0H
   16 root       0 -20       0      0      0 S 0.000 0.000   0:00.00 khelper
   17 root      20   0       0      0      0 S 0.000 0.000   0:00.00 kdevtmpfs
   18 root       0 -20       0      0      0 S 0.000 0.000   0:00.00 netns
   19 root       0 -20       0      0      0 S 0.000 0.000   0:00.00 writeback
   20 root       0 -20       0      0      0 S 0.000 0.000   0:00.00 kintegrityd
   21 root       0 -20       0      0      0 S 0.000 0.000   0:00.00 bioset
```

Figure 5-10. *Monitoring system activity with* top

In the upper five lines of the top interface, you can see information about the current system activity. The lower part of the top window shows a list of the most active processes at the moment, which is refreshed every five seconds. If you notice that a process is very busy, you can press the k key from within the top interface to terminate that process. top will next first ask for the PID of the process to which you want to send a signal (PID to kill). After entering this, it will ask which signal you want to send to that PID, and next, it will operate on the requested PID immediately.

In the upper five lines of the top screen, you'll find a status indicator of current system performance. The most important information you'll find in the first line is the load average. This gives in three different figures the load average of the last minute, the last five minutes, and the last fifteen minutes.

To understand the load average parameter, you should understand that it reflects the average amount of processes in the run queue, which is the queue in which processes wait before they can be handled by the scheduler. The scheduler is the kernel component that ensures a process is handled by any of the CPU cores in your server. A rough starting point to estimate if your system can handle its workload is that roughly the amount of processes waiting in the run queue should never be higher than the total amount of CPU cores in your server. A quick way to find out how many CPU cores are in your server is by pressing the 1 key from the top interface. This will show you one line for every CPU core in your server.

In the second line of the top window, you'll see how many tasks your server is currently handling and what each of these tasks is currently doing. In this line, you may find four different status indications, as follows:

- *Running*: The number of processes that have been active in the last polling loop

- *Sleeping*: The number of processes that are currently loaded in memory but haven't issued any activity in the last polling loop

- *Stopped*: The number of processes that have been sent a stop signal but haven't freed all of the resources they were using

- *Zombie*: The number of processes that are in a zombie state. This is an unmanageable process state in which the parent of the zombie process has disappeared and the child still exists but cannot be managed anymore, because you need the parent of a process to manage that process.

A zombie process normally is the result of bad programming. If you're lucky, zombie processes will go away by themselves. Sometimes they don't, and that can be an annoyance. If that's the case, the only way to clean up your current zombie processes is by rebooting your server.

In the third line of top, you get an overview of the current processor activity. If you're experiencing a problem (which is typically expressed by a high load average), the %Cpu(s) line tells you exactly what the CPUs in your server are doing. When trying to understand current system activity, it is good to be aware that the %Cpu(s) line summarizes all CPUs in your system. For a per-CPU overview of the current activity, press the 1 key from the top.

In the %Cpu(s) line, you'll find the following information about CPU status:

us: The percentage of time your system is spending in user space, which is the amount of time your system is handling user-related tasks

sy: The percentage of time your system is working on kernel-related tasks in system space. This should on average be (much) lower than the amount of time spent in user space

ni: The amount of time your system has worked on handling tasks of which the nice value has been changed (see next section)

id: The amount of time the CPU has been idle

wa: The amount of time the CPU has been waiting for I/O requests. This is a very common indicator of performance problems. If you see an elevated value here, you can make your system faster by optimizing disk performance. See Chapter 15 for more details about performance optimization

hi: The amount of time the CPU has been handling hardware interrupts

si: The amount of time the CPU has been handling software interrupts

st: The amount of time that has been stolen from this CPU. You'll see this only if your server is a virtualization hypervisor host, and this value will increase at the moment that a virtual machine running on this host requests more CPU cycles

In the last two lines of the top status information, you'll find current information about memory usage. The first line contains information about memory usage; the second line has information about the usage of swap space. The formatting is not ideal, however. The last item on the second line gives information that really is about the usage of memory. The following parameters show how memory currently is used:

Mem: The total amount of memory that is available to the Linux kernel

used: The total amount of memory that currently is used

free: The total amount of memory that is available for starting new processes buffers: The amount of memory that is used for buffers. In buffers, essential system tables are stored in memory, as well as data that remains to be committed to disk

cached: The amount of memory that is currently used for cache

The Linux kernel tries to use system memory as efficiently as possible. To accomplish this goal, the kernel caches a lot. When a user requests a file from disk, it is first read from disk and copied to RAM. Fetching a file from disk is an extremely slow process, compared to fetching the file from RAM. For that reason, once the file is copied in RAM, the kernel tries to keep it there as long as possible. This process is referred to as *caching*.

From the top interface, you can see the amount of RAM that currently is used for caching of data. You'll notice that the longer your server is up, the more memory is allocated to cache, and this is good, because the alternative to use memory for caching would be to do nothing at all with it. The moment the kernel needs memory that currently is allocated to cache for something else, it can claim this memory back immediately.

Related to cache is the memory that is in buffers. In here, the kernel caches tables and indexes that it needs in order to allocate files, as well as data that still has to be committed to disk. Like cache, the buffer memory is also memory that can be claimed back by the kernel immediately, but you should make sure that a minimal amount of buffers, as well as cache, is available at all times. See Chapter 15 for further details.

As an administrator, you can tell the kernel to free all memory in buffers and cache immediately. Make sure that you do this on test servers only, however, because in some cases, it may lead to a crash of the server! To free the memory in buffers and cache immediately, as root, use the command echo 3 > /proc/sys/vm/drop_caches.

Managing Process Niceness

By default, every process is started with the same priority. On occasion, it may happen that some processes require some additional time, or can offer some of their processor time because they are not that important. In those cases, you can change the priority of the process by using the nice command.

When using the nice command, you can adjust the process niceness from -20, which is good for the most favorable scheduling, to 19 (least favorable). By default, all processes are started with a niceness of 0. The following example code line shows how to start the dd command with an adjusted niceness of -10, which makes it more favorable and, therefore, allows it to finish its work faster:

```
nice -n -10 dd if=/dev/sda of=/dev/null
```

Apart from specifying the niceness to use when starting a process, you can also use the renice command to adjust the niceness of a command that was already started. By default, renice works on the PID of the process whose priority you want to adjust, so you have to find this PID before using renice. The ps command, which was described earlier in this chapter, explains how to do this.

If, for example, you want to adjust the niceness of the find command that you've just started, you would begin by using ps aux | grep find, which gives you the PID of the command. Assuming that would give you the PID 1234, after finding it, you can use renice -10 1234 to adjust the niceness of the command.

Another method of adjusting process niceness is to do it from top. The convenience of using top for this purpose is that top shows only the busiest processes on your server, which typically are the processes whose niceness you want to adjust anyway. After identifying the PID of the process you want to adjust, from the top interface, press r. On the sixth line of the top window, you'll now see the message PID to renice:. Now, enter the PID of the process you want to adjust. Next, top prompts Renice PID 3284 to value:. Here, you enter the positive or negative nice value you want to use. Next, press Enter to apply the niceness to the selected process. In Exercise 5-5, you can apply these procedures.

```
EXERCISE 5-5. CHANGING PROCESS PRIORITY
```

In this exercise, you'll start four dd processes, which, by default, will go on forever. You'll see that all of them are started with the same priority and get about the same amount of CPU time and capacity. Next, you'll adjust the niceness of two of these processes from within top, which immediately shows the effect of using nice on these commands.

1. Open a terminal window and use su - to escalate to a root shell.

2. Type the command dd if=/dev/zero of=/dev/null & and repeat this four times.

3. Now start top. You'll see the four dd commands listed on top. In the PR column, you can see that the priority of all of these processes is set to 20. The NI column, which indicates the actual process niceness, shows a value of 0 for all of the dd processes, and in the TIME column, you can see that all of the processes use about the same amount of processor time.

4. Now, from within the top interface, press r. On the PID to renice prompt, type the PID of one of the four dd processes and press Enter. When asked to provide Renice PID <number> to value:, type 5 and press Enter.

5. With the preceding action, you have lowered the priority of one of the dd commands. You should immediately start to see the result in top, as one of the dd processes will receive a significantly lesser amount of CPU time.

6. Repeat the procedure to adjust the niceness of one of the other dd processes. Now use the niceness value of -15. You will notice that this process now tends to consume all of the available resources on your computer, which shows that you should avoid the extremes when working with nice.

7. Use the k command from the top interface to stop all processes for which you've just adjusted the niceness.

Scheduling Tasks

Up to now, you have learned how to start processes from a terminal window. For some tasks, it makes sense to have them started automatically. Think, for example, of a backup job that you want to execute automatically every night. To start jobs automatically, you can use cron.

cron consists of two parts. First, there is the cron daemon, a process that starts automatically when your server boots. This cron daemon checks its configuration every minute to see if there are any tasks that should be executed at that moment.

Some cron jobs are started from the directories /etc/cron.hourly, /etc/cron.daily, /etc/cron.weekly, and /etc/cron.monthly. Typically, as an administrator, you're not involved in managing these. Programs and services that require some tasks to be executed on a regular basis simply put a script in the directory where they need it, which ensures that the task is automatically executed. Some RPM packages will copy scripts that are to be executed by cron to the /etc/cron.d directory. The files in this directory contain everything that is needed to run a command through cron.

As an administrator, you can start cron jobs as a specific user, by first logging in as that user (or by using su - to take the identity of the user you want to start the cron job as). After doing that, you'll use the command crontab -e, which starts the crontab editor, which is a vi interface by default. That means that you work from crontab -e the way that you are used to working from vi.

As crontab files are created with crontab -e, you'll specify on separate lines which command has to be executed at which moment. Following, you can see an example of a line that can be used in crontab:

```
0 2 * * *       /root/bin/runscript.sh
```

It is very important that you start the definition of cron jobs at the right moment. To do this, five different positions can be used to specify date and time. Table 5-3, following, lists the time and date indicators that can be used.

Table 5-3. *cron Time Indicators*

Field	Allowed Value
minute	0–59
hour	0–23
day of month	1–31
month	1–12
day of week 0–7 (0 and 7 are Sunday)	

This means, for example, that in a crontab specification, the time indicator 0 2 3 4 * would translate to minute 0 of hour 2 (which is 2 a.m.) on the third day of the fourth month. Day of the week, in this example, is not specified, which means that the job would run on any day of the week.

In a cron job definition, you can use ranges as well. For example, the line */5 * * * 1-5 would mean that a job has to run every five minutes, but only from Monday until Friday.

After creating the cron configuration file, the cron daemon automatically picks up the changes and ensure that the job will run at the time indicated.

EXERCISE 5-6. CONFIGURING CRON JOBS

In this exercise, you'll learn how to schedule a cron job. You'll use your own user account to run a cron job that sends an e-mail message to user root on your system. In the final step, you'll verify that root has indeed received the message.

1. Open a terminal and make sure that you are logged in with your normal user account.

2. Type crontab -e to open the crontab editor.

3. Type the following line, which will write a message to syslog every five minutes:

    */5 * * * * logger hello,.

4. Use the vi command :wq! to close the crontab editor and safe your changes.

5. Wait five minutes. After five minutes, type tail -f /var/log/messages to verify that the message has been written to the logs.

6. Go back to the terminal where you are logged in with the normal user account and type crontab -r. This deletes the current crontab file from your user account.

Configuring Logging

On SLES 12, two different systems are used for logging. The rsyslog service takes care of writing log messages to different files, and the journald service works with systemd to fetch messages that are generated through systemd units and writes that information to the journal. Both can be interconnected also, to ensure that services that are handled by systemd do occur in the journal as well. In this section, you'll learn how to configure both of these services.

Understanding rsyslog

Since the old days of UNIX, the syslog service has been used for logging information. This service is compatible with many devices, which makes it a true log service that can take care of messages that are generated by multiple devices in the network. rsyslogd is the latest incarnation of syslog, providing full backward compatibility with syslog as well as new features.

The basis of the rsyslogd service configuration is in the file /etc/rsyslog.conf. In this file, logging is configured by the definition of facilities, priorities, and destinations. Also, modules are used to provide additional functionality.

Understanding Facilities

The rsyslog facilities define what needs to be logged. To maintain backward compatibility with syslog, the facilities are fixed, and it's not possible to add new ones. Table 5-4 gives an overview of facilities and their use.

Table 5-4. *Facilities and Their Use*

Facility	Use
auth	Messages related to authentication
authpriv	Same as auth
cron	Messages that are generated by the cron service
daemon	A generic facility that can log messages that are generated by daemons that don't have their own facilities
kern	Kernel-related messages
lpr	Printer-related messages
mail	Messages that are related to the mail system
mark	A special facility that can be used to write log information at a specified interval
news	Messages related to the NNTP news system
security	Same as auth
syslog	Relates to messages that are generated by the rsyslog service
user	User related messages
uucp	Messages related to the legacy uucp system
local0-local7	Facilities that can be assigned to services that don't have their own syslog facility

As you can see in Table 5-4, the facilities available are far from complete, and some commonly used services don't have their own facility. That is what the facilities local0 through local7 are created for. Many services that don't do syslog logging by default can be configured to log through one of these facilities. If, for example, an administrator wants Apache to write its log messages to syslog rather than directly to its configuration files, the line Errorlog syslog:local3 can be included in the Apache configuration file. Next in syslog, the local3 facility can be further defined, so that Apache-related log information is written to the right location.

Understanding Priorities

Where the facility defines what should be logged, the priority defines when information should be sent to a log file. Priorities can be debug, info, notice, warning, (or warn), err, (or error), crit, alert, emerg, or panic (which is equivalent to emerg).

While defining a syslog rule, you should always use a facility.priority pair, as in kern.debug, which specifies that the kernel facility should send everything with the priority debug (and higher) to the destination that is specified. When defining facilities and priorities, a scripting language can be used to select the exact conditions under which to write log messages.

Understanding Destinations

The destination defines where messages should be sent. Typically, this will be a file in the /var/log directory. Many alternatives can be used, too, such as the name of a specific console, a remote machine, a database, a specific user or all users who are logged in, and more. If used with output modules (see the next section), the possibilities are many.

Understanding Modules

Apart from facilities, priorities, and destinations, modules can be used. A module is an extension to the original syslog code and adds functionality. Many modules are available to allow syslog to receive messages from specific subsystems or to send messages to specific destinations.

In general, there are two types of modules. The Input Modules (which names that begin in *im*) are used to filter incoming messages, and the Output Modules (which have names starting with *om*) are used to send messages in a specific direction. Common modules are immark, which writes marker messages with a regular interval; imuxsock, which allows syslog to communicate to journald; and imudp, which allows for reception of messages from remote servers over UDP.

In Listing 5-4, following, you can see an example of the rsyslog.conf configuration file on SLES 12.

Listing 5-4. Sample rsyslog.conf Configuration File

```
$ModLoad immark.so
$MarkMessagePeriod      3600

$ModLoad imuxsock.so

$RepeatedMsgReduction   on

$ModLoad imklog.so
$klogConsoleLogLevel    1

$IncludeConfig /run/rsyslog/additional-log-sockets.conf
$IncludeConfig /etc/rsyslog.d/*.conf
```

```
if  ( \
        /* kernel up to warning except of firewall  */ \
        ($syslogfacility-text == 'kern')        and      \
        ($syslogseverity <= 4 /* warning */ ) and not  \
        ($msg contains 'IN=' and $msg contains 'OUT=') \
    ) or ( \
        /* up to errors except of facility authpriv */ \
        ($syslogseverity <= 3 /* errors  */ ) and not  \
        ($syslogfacility-text == 'authpriv')          \
    ) \
then {
    /dev/tty10
    |/dev/xconsole
}

*.emerg                         :omusrmsg:*

if ($syslogfacility-text == 'kern') and \
    ($msg contains 'IN=' and $msg contains 'OUT=') \
then {
    -/var/log/firewall
    stop
}

if ($programname == 'acpid' or $syslogtag == '[acpid]:') and \
    ($syslogseverity <= 5 /* notice */) \
then {
    -/var/log/acpid
    stop
}
if      ($programname == 'NetworkManager') or \
    ($programname startswith 'nm-') \
then {
    -/var/log/NetworkManager
    stop
}
mail.*                      -/var/log/mail
mail.info                  -/var/log/mail.info
mail.warning               -/var/log/mail.warn
mail.err                    /var/log/mail.err
news.crit                  -/var/log/news/news.crit
news.err                           -/var/log/news/news.err
news.notice                -/var/log/news/news.notice
*.=warning;*.=err          -/var/log/warn
*.crit                      /var/log/warn
*.*;mail.none;news.none    -/var/log/messages
local0.*;local1.*          -/var/log/localmessages
local2.*;local3.*          -/var/log/localmessages
local4.*;local5.*          -/var/log/localmessages
local6.*;local7.*          -/var/log/localmessages
```

As you can see from the sample file in the preceding listing, there is more than just the definition of facilities, priorities, and destinations. At the beginning of the file, some modules are defined. The immark module writes a marker message every hour, which helps verify that rsyslog is still operational. The imuxsock module allows syslog to receive messages from journald, and the RepeatedMsgReduction module ensures that repeated messages are not all written to the syslog files.

After the part where the modules are defined, two inclusions are defined. In particular the IncludeConfig/etc/rsyslog.d/*.conf line is important. This tells syslog to read additional configuration files as well. These configuration files may have been dropped in the /etc/rsyslog.d directory by software installation from RPM packages.

Next, there are a few lines that use scripting. In these scripting lines, especially the $msg contains lines are interesting. They allow syslog to read the contents of a message, which allows rsyslog to decide exactly what to do with the message.

The last part of the sample configuration file defines where messages should be written to. In most cases, the destination is a file name. The file name can be preceded by a -. This tells syslog that it's not necessary to write the message immediately, but that message can be buffered for better performance. Some other log destinations are defined as well. The destination :omusrmsg:*, for example, uses the output module user message, which sends the message to all users who are currently logged in.

Reading Log Files

The result of the work of rsyslog is in the log files. These log files are in the /var/log directory. According to the definitions in /var/log, different files are used, but the main log file is /var/log/messages. Listing 5-5 shows partial contents of this file.

Listing 5-5. Partial Contents of the /var/log/messages Files

```
2014-09-21T03:30:01.253425-04:00 linux-3kk5 cron[48465]: pam_unix(crond:session): session opened
for user root by (uid=0)
2014-09-21T03:30:01.255588-04:00 linux-3kk5 kernel: [160530.013392] type=1006
audit(1411284601.249:220): pid=48465 uid=0 old auid=4294967295 new auid=0 old ses=4294967295 new
ses=182 res=1
2014-09-21T03:30:01.293811-04:00 linux-3kk5 CRON[48465]: pam_unix(crond:session): session closed
for user root
2014-09-21T03:38:57.020771-04:00 linux-3kk5 wickedd-dhcp4[925]: eth0: Committed DHCPv4 lease with
address 192.168.4.210 (lease time 1800 sec, renew in 900 sec, rebind in 1575 sec)
2014-09-21T03:38:57.021297-04:00 linux-3kk5 wickedd[929]: eth0: address 192.168.4.210 covered by a
dhcp lease
2014-09-21T03:38:57.052381-04:00 linux-3kk5 wickedd[929]: eth0: Notified neighbours about IP address
192.168.4.210
2014-09-21T03:38:57.052774-04:00 linux-3kk5 wickedd[929]: route ipv4 0.0.0.0/0 via 192.168.4.2 dev
eth0 type unicast table main scope universe protocol dhcp covered by a ipv4:dhcp lease
2014-09-21T03:38:57.230038-04:00 linux-3kk5 wickedd[929]: Skipping hostname update, none available
2014-09-21T03:45:01.311979-04:00 linux-3kk5 kernel: [161429.729495] type=1006
audit(1411285501.307:221): pid=48669 uid=0 old auid=4294967295 new auid=0 old ses=4294967295 new
ses=183 res=1
2014-09-21T03:45:01.311470-04:00 linux-3kk5 cron[48669]: pam_unix(crond:session): session opened
for user root by (uid=0)
2014-09-21T03:45:01.338933-04:00 linux-3kk5 CRON[48669]: pam_unix(crond:session): session closed
for user root
2014-09-21T03:53:57.152972-04:00 linux-3kk5 wickedd-dhcp4[925]: eth0: Committed DHCPv4 lease with
address 192.168.4.210 (lease time 1800 sec, renew in 900 sec, rebind in 1575 sec)
2014-09-21T03:53:57.153516-04:00 linux-3kk5 wickedd[929]: eth0: address 192.168.4.210 covered by a
dhcp lease
```

```
2014-09-21T03:53:57.188390-04:00 linux-3kk5 wickedd[929]: eth0: Notified neighbours about IP address
192.168.4.210
2014-09-21T03:53:57.188638-04:00 linux-3kk5 wickedd[929]: route ipv4 0.0.0.0/0 via 192.168.4.2 dev
eth0 type unicast table main scope universe protocol dhcp covered by a ipv4:dhcp lease
2014-09-21T03:53:57.359250-04:00 linux-3kk5 wickedd[929]: Skipping hostname update, none available
2014-09-21T03:54:05.119585-04:00 linux-3kk5 dbus[790]: [system] Activating via systemd: service
name='org.freedesktop.PackageKit' unit='packagekit.service'
2014-09-21T03:54:05.124790-04:00 linux-3kk5 PackageKit: daemon start
2014-09-21T03:54:05.180829-04:00 linux-3kk5 dbus[790]: [system] Successfully activated service
'org.freedesktop.PackageKit'
2014-09-21T03:54:25.350410-04:00 linux-3kk5 PackageKit: daemon quit
2014-09-21T04:00:01.355931-04:00 linux-3kk5 kernel: [162329.431431] type=1006
audit(1411286401.349:222): pid=48878 uid=0 old auid=4294967295 new auid=0 old ses=4294967295 new
ses=184 res=1
2014-09-21T04:00:01.355448-04:00 linux-3kk5 cron[48878]: pam_unix(crond:session): session opened for
user root by (uid=0)
2014-09-21T04:00:01.397676-04:00 linux-3kk5 CRON[48878]: pam_unix(crond:session): session closed for
user root
```

Each message is structured in a similar way. It starts with the date and time the message has been logged. Next, the name of the host that has logged the message is printed (linux-3kk5, in this example). Then follows the name of the process and its PID, followed by the specific message that is logged.

You will note that services tend to have their own method of writing information to the syslog. You can see that some commands perform logging in a way that is rather difficult to read, while other log messages are easy to understand.

Configuring Remote Logging

In a large network environment, it makes sense to set up remote logging. This allows you to create one log server that is configured with a large amount of storage and will keep messages for a longer period. Other servers can be used as clients toward that server and maintain small logs for themselves.

To set up remote logging, you'll have to specify a remote log destination on the servers on which you want to do remote logging. The lines that do this follow:

```
*.*            @@remotehost.example.com
*.*            @remotehost.example.com
```

The first line tells rsyslog to send messages to the remote host specified, using TCP; the second line tells rsyslog to do the same, but using UDP. Sending messages via TCP is more secure. TCP is a connection-oriented protocol, so delivery of the log messages is guaranteed, and you can be sure that no messages will get lost. If you want to forward messages to a remote host that does not support TCP log reception, UDP can be used instead.

On the remote host, the file /etc/rsyslog.d/remote.conf must be used to enable log reception. The default remote.conf file on SLES contains many examples that show how to set up advanced remote log servers, on which it is even possible to use TLS for securing the message stream. The most important parameters that should be considered are the following:

```
@ModLoad imtcp.so
$TCPServerRun 514
@ModLoad imudp.so
$UDPServerRun 514
```

These lines enable the TCP as well as the UDP log reception modules and tell your server to listen for incoming messages on port 514.

Working with journal

On SLES 12, apart from rsyslog, journald is used for logging as well. The journald service keeps extensive information about services and other unit files that are managed through systemd (see Chapter 8 for further details). The information in journald must be considered as an addition to the information that is logged through rsyslog. By default, rsyslog is configured for receiving journald log messages. The line $ModLoad imuxsock.so takes care of this. There is not much need to configure the other way around, too, and have rsyslog write messages to journald. rsyslog should really be considered the central system for logging messages.

The journal is created at the moment that the journald service is started. That means that it won't survive a reboot, but the messages are forwarded to rsyslog anyway, so that shouldn't be a big deal. If you want to make the journal persistent, you can use the following procedure:

1. Create a journal directory using mkdir -p -m 2775 /var/log/journal.

2. Set the appropriate ownership: chown :systemd-journal /var/log/journal.

3. Restart the journal service using killall -USR1 systemd-journald.

The most important benefit of using a journal is that the journalctl command allows administrators to perform smart filtering on messages. To start with, an administrator can type the journalctl command, which will just show all messages, starting with the oldest. So, to see only the last five messages, the command journalctl -n 5 can be used. To see live messages scrolling by at the moment they are written, type journalctl -f. Also very useful is the option to filter according to the time the message was written, as, for example, journalctl --since-today, which shows all messages that were written since the start of the day.

To get even more specific information from the system, you can specify time ranges as well, as, for example, journalctl --since "2014-09-19 23:00:00" --until "2014-09-20 8:00:00". You can also filter for specific process information only, as in the case of journalctl _SYSTEMD_UNIT=sshd.service, or obtain detailed information, if you want, by adding -o verbose. And it is possible to make all this very specific, if, for example, you're looking for a detailed report on everything that has been logged by the sshd process in a specific date/time range. To do this, you can use a command such as journalctl --since "2014-09-19 23:00:00" --until "2014-09-20 8:00:00" _SYSTEMD_UNIT=sshd.service -o verbose.

When using journald logging, you should always remember that the journal is cleared at reboot. So, if you try to show messages that were logged too long ago, it may occur that they no longer exist, because you have rebooted in the meantime.

Configuring logrotate

On a very busy server, you may find that entries are added to your log files really fast. This poses a risk: your server may be quickly filled with log messages, which leaves no more place for normal files that have to be created. There are some solutions to this possible problem.

- To begin with, the directory /var/log should be on a dedicated partition or logical volume, so that in case too much information is written to the log files, this will never completely fill your server's file system.

- Always include the RepeatedMsgReduction module in rsyslog.conf. It will ensure that the volume of messages that are repeatedly written is reduced.

- Another solution that you can use to prevent your server from being filled up completely by log files that grow too big is logrotate. The logrotate command runs as a cron job by default once a day from /etc/cron.daily, and it helps you to define a policy whereby log files that grow beyond a certain age or size are rotated.

Rotating a log file basically means that the old log file is closed and a new log file is opened. In most cases, logrotate keeps a number of the old logged files, often stored as a compressed file on disk. In the logrotate configuration, you can define how exactly you want to handle the rotation of log files.

The configuration of logrotate is spread between two different locations. The main logrotate file is /etc/logrotate.conf. In this file, some generic parameters are stored, as well as specific parameters that define how specific files should be handled.

The logrotate configuration for specific files is stored in the directory /etc/logrotate.d. These scripts are typically put there when you install the service, but you can modify them as you like. The logrotate file for the apache2 services provides a good example that you can use, if you want to create your own logrotate file. You can see part of its contents in Listing 5-6.

Listing 5-6. Sample logrotate Configuration File

```
/var/log/apache2/error_log {
    compress
    dateext
    maxage 365
    rotate 99
    size=+1024k
    notifempty
    missingok
    create 644 root root
    postrotate
     /usr/bin/systemctl reload apache2.service
    endscript
}

/var/log/apache2/suexec.log {
    compress
    dateext
    maxage 365
    rotate 99
    size=+1024k
    notifempty
    missingok
    create 644 root root
    postrotate
     /usr/bin/systemctl reload apache2.service
    endscript
}
```

You can see that the contents of the configuration is pretty straightforward. It tells which files should be logged and how often they should be logged. This configuration shows that the maximum age of the file is set to 365, after which a rotation will follow. logrotate will keep a maximum of 99 rotated log files, which allows administrators to go a long way back in time.

EXERCISE 5-7. CONFIGURING LOGGING

In this exercise, you'll learn how to configure logging on your server. You'll first set up `rsyslogd` to send all messages that relate to authentication to the `/var/log/auth` file. Next, you'll set up `logrotate` to rotate this file on a daily basis and keep just one old version of the file.

1. Open a terminal and make sure that you have root permissions, by opening a root shell using `su -`.

2. Open the `/etc/rsyslog.conf` file in an editor and scroll down to the RULES section. Add the following line: `authpriv.*    /var/log/auth file` to the end of the file.

3. Close the log file and make sure to save the changes. Now, use the command `systemctl restart rsyslog` to ensure that `rsyslog` uses the new configuration.

4. Use the Ctrl+Alt+F4 key sequence to log in as a user. It doesn't really matter which user account you're using for this.

5. Switch back to the graphical user interface using Ctrl+Alt+F1 (or Ctrl+Alt+F7, depending on your configuration). From here, use `tail -f /var/log/auth`. This should show the contents of the freshly created file that contains authentication messages. Use Ctrl+C to close `tail -f`.

6. Create a file with the name `/etc/logrotate.d/auth` and make sure it has the following contents:

```
/var/log/auth {
      daily
      rotate 1
      compress }
```

7. Normally, you would have to wait a day until `logrotate` is started from `/etc/cron.daily`. As an alternative, you can run it from the command line, using the following command: `/usr/sbin/logrotate /etc/logrotate.conf`.

8. After one day, check the contents of the `/var/log` directory. You should see the rotated `/var/log/auth` file.

Summary

In this chapter, you've learned how to perform important daily system administration tasks. You've read how to work with printers and manage software. Next, you have learned how to manage processes and jobs and how to use `cron` to run processes at specific times. Following that, you have read how to configure logging on your server, to ensure that you can always find what has gone wrong and why.

CHAPTER 6

■ ■ ■

Hardening SUSE Linux

Before you start offering real services on your server, it's a good idea to think about how you can harden your SUSE Linux installation. In this chapter, you'll learn how to do that. We'll first have a look at the YaST Security Center and Hardening module, which provides some common options that are easy to apply. Next, you'll learn how to set up a sudo configuration that allows you to delegate tasks to specific users. Following that, you'll read about how to configure the Linux Audit Framework to get more detailed events about modifications that have been applied to your server. Then, you'll read how a pluggable authentication module (PAM) is used to make the authentication procedure modular. Last, you'll read about SELinux, an advanced way of profiling your system, so that only specific operations are allowed, while everything that is not specifically allowed will be denied.

In this chapter, the following topics are discussed:

- Using the YaST Security Center and Hardening
- Working with sudo
- The Linux Audit Framework
- Understanding PAM
- Configuring SELinux

SUSE offers different solutions for hardening a server. To give you a quick head start, the YaST Security Center and Hardening module is offered. After configuring basic settings using this module, you can use sudo to define which administrators are allowed access to which tasks.

Using the YaST Security Center and Hardening

The YaST Security Center and Hardening module was developed to provide an easy interface to set a secure server. It contains a list of security settings, which you can walk through to verify and set security parameters on your server.

After starting the module, you'll see the Security Overview section (see Figure 6-1). From here, you can easily see the current status and configure specific settings. The list contains a collection of security settings that can easily be accessed and modified from this list. For each of the settings, you can change the current status or get a description of what exactly the setting is doing on your server.

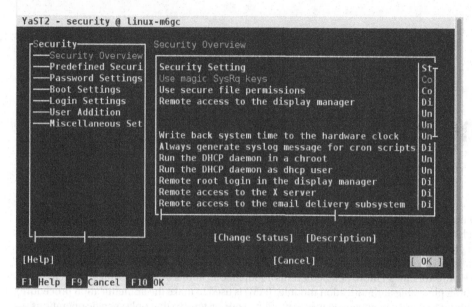

```
YaST2 - security @ linux-m6gc

┌Security─────────┐  Security Overview
│──Security Overview│ ┌────────────────────────────────────────────────┐
│──Predefined Securi│ │ Security Setting                          St┬│
│──Password Settings│ │ Use magic SysRq keys                      Co││
│──Boot Settings    │ │ Use secure file permissions               Co││
│──Login Settings   │ │ Remote access to the display manager       Di││
│──User Addition    │ │                                           Un││
│──Miscellaneous Set│ │                                           Un│┴
│                   │ │ Write back system time to the hardware clock  Un│
│                   │ │ Always generate syslog message for cron scripts│Di│
│                   │ │ Run the DHCP daemon in a chroot           Un│
│                   │ │ Run the DHCP daemon as dhcp user          Un│
│                   │ │ Remote root login in the display manager  Di│
│                   │ │ Remote access to the X server             Di│
│                   │ │ Remote access to the email delivery subsystem│Di│
│                   │ └────────────────────────────────────────────────┘
│                   │
└┴──────┴─────────┘      [Change Status]   [Description]

[Help]                         [Cancel]              [ OK ]

F1 Help  F9 Cancel  F10 OK
```

Figure 6-1. *The Security Overview gives easy access to a list of security settings*

On the Predefined Security Configurations section, you can choose between a few default security settings templates. The templates are Home Workstation, Networked Workstation, and Network Server, or Custom Settings. The settings relate to a few options related to booting, passwords, and file permissions. Home Workstation was created for computers that are not connected to any network (!); Networked Workstation is for end-user computers that are connected to a network; and Network Server offers the highest level of security setting. Don't use these options; they are too basic.

The Password Settings options provide access to a few of the options that can be set in the /etc/login.defs file and are related to passwords. You can set a minimal password length, specify the password encryption method, which by default is set to the robust SHA-512 algorithm, and you can set a minimal and maximal password age. The settings specified here are written to /etc/login.defs and will be applied for all new users that are created from that moment on.

On the Boot Settings option, you can find a few permissions that relate to booting. These options are old and obsolete. On the Login Settings section, you can specify the delay, after an incorrect login attempt, and specify whether or not you want to allow remote graphical login. User Addition specifies the minimum and maximum user IDs that are available for creation of users. On the Miscellaneous Settings section, you find a few settings that are of interest (see Figure 6-2).

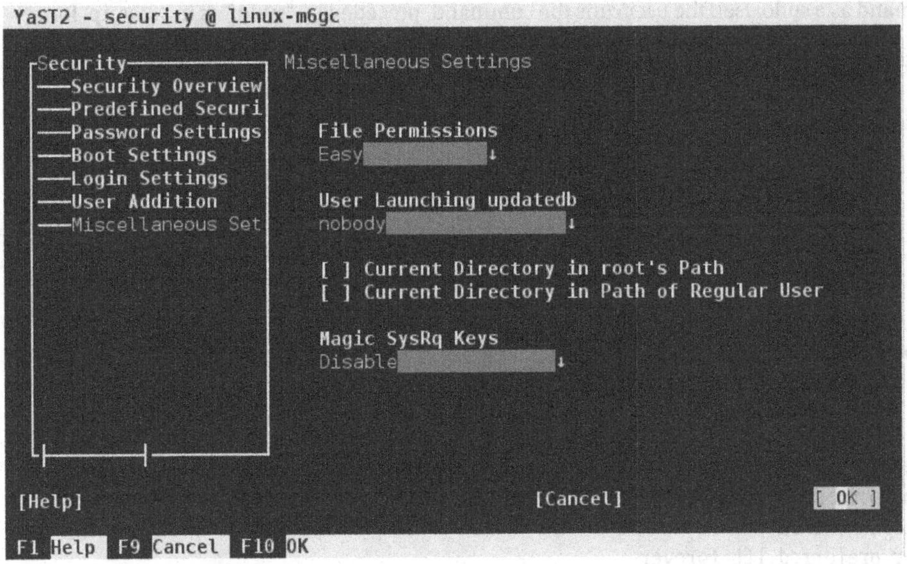

```
YaST2 - security @ linux-m6gc
 ┌─Security──────────┐ Miscellaneous Settings
 │ ───Security Overview│
 │ ───Predefined Securi│
 │ ───Password Settings│   File Permissions
 │ ───Boot Settings    │   Easy                    ↓
 │ ───Login Settings   │
 │ ───User Addition    │   User Launching updatedb
 │ ───Miscellaneous Set│   nobody                  ↓
 │                     │
 │                     │   [ ] Current Directory in root's Path
 │                     │   [ ] Current Directory in Path of Regular User
 │                     │
 │                     │   Magic SysRq Keys
 │                     │   Disable                ↓
 │                     │
 │ ┐                   │
 │ └─         ─┘        │
 └─────────────────────┘

 [Help]                          [Cancel]              [ OK ]
 F1 Help  F9 Cancel  F10 OK
```

Figure 6-2. *Miscellaneous security settings*

The file permissions option allows you to select one of the file permissions templates available in /etc/permissions.easy, permissions.local, permissions.secure and permissions.paranoid. In these files, standard permissions are set for a number of default configuration files, and by selecting them from YaST, you can easily set the permissions for many files on your computer. From the other options on this tab, the Magic SysRq Keys option is interesting. These options give access to some debugging and advanced administration options. These options can be used only by the root user by default, but having them enabled poses an increased risk. If enabled, the root user can use the command echo b > /proc/sysrq-trigger to write a "reset" trigger to sysrq, and other nasty options are available as well. In general, having these options enabled is useful but dangerous, which is why you might consider switching them off.

Working with sudo

By default, on Linux, there are two normal users who can log in directly. Apart from that, there are system users employed by the services that have been configured to run on your server. The user root is the privileged user; there are no limitations whatsoever for root. All other users have limited access to your system. To provide normal users access to performing tasks with administrator tasks, there is a middle way: using sudo. With sudo, you can define a list of tasks that can be performed by a specific list of users. That means that you can create a configuration in which user linda has permissions to shut down a server (which is normally a task that only root can do), but nothing else. In addition, using sudo, you can also specify that a user can run a task as any other user. For example, you can have user bob execute a tar job to create a backup of your Oracle databases as the Oracle user (an example of a user that can't normally log in directly), by using sudo.

Understanding sudo

Working with sudo offers a few important benefits from a security perspective. First, all commands that are executed with sudo can be logged, but that only works if Defaults log_output is enabled in the sudoers file. Therefore, it is possible to trace who has done what at which specific moment. Also, sudoreplay can be used to replay a sudo session, which allows administrators to see exactly what has happened during a sudo session.

When running a command as a sudo user, the user runs the command, preceded by "sudo," as in sudo ip, for example. The user will first see a warning and is next prompted for his/her password. After entering the correct password, the command will be executed (see Listing 6-1).

Listing 6-1. Using sudo to Run Commands

```
linda@ldap:~>sudo ip a

We trust you have received the usual lecture from the local System
Administrator. It usually boils down to these three things:

    #1) Respect the privacy of others.
    #2) Think before you type.
    #3) With great power comes great responsibility.

linda's password:
1: lo: <LOOPBACK,UP,LOWER_UP> mtu 65536 qdisc noqueue state UNKNOWN group default
    link/loopback 00:00:00:00:00:00 brd 00:00:00:00:00:00
    inet 127.0.0.1/8 scope host lo
       valid_lft forever preferred_lft forever
    inet6 ::1/128 scope host
       valid_lft forever preferred_lft forever
2: eth0: <BROADCAST,MULTICAST,UP,LOWER_UP> mtu 1500 qdisc pfifo_fast state UP group default qlen 1000
    link/ether 00:0c:29:82:a5:c9 brd ff:ff:ff:ff:ff:ff
    inet 192.168.4.180/24 brd 192.168.4.255 scope global eth0
       valid_lft forever preferred_lft forever
    inet6 fe80::20c:29ff:fe82:a5c9/64 scope link
       valid_lft forever preferred_lft forever
linda@ldap:~>
```

To create a sudo configuration, you can use YaST as well as visudo. For this command, I'll explain how to use visudo to create a configuration, because YaST doesn't add much to the ease of configuring sudo rules. In both cases, the configuration is written to the file /etc/sudoers, which should never be modified directly!

When creating a sudo configuration, the ultimate goal is to create rules such as the following:

```
linda ALL=/sbin/shutdown -h now
```

This command allows user linda to execute the command /sbin/shutdown -h now from all computers. When working with sudo, it is useful to work with Linux group names also. The following line gives an example on how you could do that:

```
%users ALL=/sbin/mount /mnt/cdrom, /sbin/umount /mnt/cdrom
```

This line ensures that all members of the group users (which typically are all users that are defined on this system) have permissions to mount and umount the /mnt/cdrom device. Note that with this command, an argument is specified, which means that users can only execute the command exactly as specified here; no other arguments are allowed.

Creating sudo Configuration Lines

The generic structure of any line in /etc/sudoers is

```
WHO FROM_WHERE=(AS_WHOM) WHICH_COMMANDS
```

The WHO part specifies the user or group that is allowed to run the commands. As an alternative, user aliases can be used as well. A User_Alias defines a group of users who are allowed to perform a specific task, but using user aliases is not very common, as Linux groups can be used instead. If you want to define a user alias, it should be defined as follows:

```
User_Alias ADMINS = linda, denise
```

After defining the alias, it can be referred to in a sudo rule as

```
ADMINS ALL=ALL
```

The FROM_WHERE part in /etc/sudoers specifies the hostname from which the user is allowed. In many cases, it is just set to ALL, which implements no host restrictions. If hostnames are used, these hostnames must be resolvable by using DNS or another hostname resolution mechanism. You can define a Host_Alias to make it easy to refer to a group of servers. The Host_Alias would look like the following:

```
Host_Alias WEBSERVERS = web1, web2
```

To use this alias, you would use a sudo rule such as

```
ADMINS WEBSERVERS=/usr/sbin/httpd
```

The AS_WHOM part is optional and specifies the use as whom the command is supposed to be executed. If nothing is specified here, the command will be executed as root. Optionally, you can specify another target user here. For this part also, an alias can be defined, which is the RunAs_Alias.

The final part specifies the commands that are allowed. This can be mentioned as a list of commands, and alternatively, a command alias can be used. Such an alias would look as follows:

```
Cmnd_Alias SOFTWARE = /bin/rpm, /usr/bin/zypper
```

And to use it in a rule, the rule would look like the following:

```
linda ALL=SOFTWARE
```

When configuring sudo on SUSE, there are two lines in particular that deserve attention. They are the following:

```
Defaults targetpw
ALL ALL = (ALL) ALL
```

The line Defaults targetpw asks for the password of user root in all cases. Next, the ALL ALL = (ALL) ALL line allows any user to run any command from any host as any target user. There's nothing wrong with this line, as long as the Defaults targetpw line is present. If it isn't any longer, this second line becomes very dangerous. For that reason, to prevent any errors from occurring, make sure to remove both lines before doing anything else in sudo.

Working in a sudo Shell

In many environments, root login is not permitted, and all root tasks have to be executed using sudo. That's not always seen as convenient, with the result that many administrators like using sudo -i. This opens a root shell, from which administrators can run any command they like, without passing through sudo every single time.

From an administrator perspective, using sudo -i is convenient, but from a security perspective, it's not very secure. If you want to disable the possibility of accessing shells using sudo -i, as well as the option to use sudo su to open a root shell, you can define two command aliases, two for which access can be denied using the exclamation point. The following three lines can be used to give access to all commands to all users who are members of the group wheel, with the exception of commands that are listed in the NSHELLS and NSU command aliases. When using these, make sure that the NSHELLS alias includes all shells that are installed on your server!

```
Cmnd_Alias    NSHELLS = /bin/sh, /bin/bash
Cmnd_Alias    NSU = /bin/su

%wheel ALL=ALL, !NSHELLS, !NSU
```

Replaying sudo Sessions

An important benefit of working with sudo is that sessions are logged, and it is easy to replay a sudo session, but note that this only works if the log_output entry is uncommented in the sudoers file. To do this, you can use the sudoreplay command. The command sudoreplay -l will give an overview of all sudo commands that have been issued and the time when they were used. In each of these commands, a session ID is specified, which can be identified by the TSID option. Using this session ID, a session can be replayed, which shows all output that has occurred in a sudo session. In Listing 6-2 you can see how sudoreplay can be used.

Listing 6-2. Using sudoreplay to Get Information About a sudo Session

```
ldap:~ # sudoreplay -l
Jul  6 06:54:59 2014 : linda : TTY=/dev/pts/0 ; CWD=/home/linda ; USER=root ; TSID=000001 ;
COMMAND=/sbin/ip a
ldap:~ # sudoreplay 000001
Replaying sudo session: /sbin/ip a
1: lo: <LOOPBACK,UP,LOWER_UP> mtu 65536 qdisc noqueue state UNKNOWN group default
    link/loopback 00:00:00:00:00:00 brd 00:00:00:00:00:00
    inet 127.0.0.1/8 scope host lo
       valid_lft forever preferred_lft forever
    inet6 ::1/128 scope host
       valid_lft forever preferred_lft forever
2: eth0: <BROADCAST,MULTICAST,UP,LOWER_UP> mtu 1500 qdisc pfifo_fast state UP group default qlen 1000
    link/ether 00:0c:29:82:a5:c9 brd ff:ff:ff:ff:ff:ff
    inet 192.168.4.180/24 brd 192.168.4.255 scope global eth0
       valid_lft forever preferred_lft forever
    inet6 fe80::20c:29ff:fe82:a5c9/64 scope link
       valid_lft forever preferred_lft forever
```

EXERCISE 6-1. CREATING A SUDO CONFIGURATION

1. Log in as root and enter the command visudo.

2. Locate the lines Defaults targetpw and ALL ALL = (ALL) ALL and put a comment sign (#) in front of both of them.

3. Add a command alias: Cmnd_Alias NETWORK = /usr/sbin/wicked, /sbin/ip.

4. Add the following line to allow all users who are members of the group users to run commands from the NETWORK alias: %users ALL = NETWORK.

5. Open a shell as any user on your system. Type sudo /sbin/ip addr show to run the ip addr show command with root permissions.

6. Open the sudo configuration again, using visudo.

7. Include the following lines to allow access to all commands, except shells and su, for all users who are members of the group wheel.

   ```
   Cmnd_Alias      NSHELLS = /bin/sh, /bin/bash
   Cmnd_Alias      NSU = /bin/su

   %wheel ALL=ALL, !NSHELLS, !NSU
   ```

8. Create a user, linda, and make her a member of the group wheel, using useradd linda; usermod -aG wheel linda.

9. Log in as linda and try to run the command sudo -i. You'll notice that it doesn't give you access to a root shell. It does not disallow the use of visudo, though, but at this point, you should be able to understand how that can be fixed.

The Linux Audit Framework

Logging is a part of hardening a server. By setting up logging, you make sure that you don't miss information about vital security incidents that have occurred. In Chapter 5, you have already learned how to configure logging on your server. In this section, we'll go one step further and talk about the Linux Audit Framework. The Linux Audit Framework allows administrators to set up the system for logging detailed messages, using the audit daemon (auditd).

Configuring Auditing from YaST

To configure auditing, you can start the Linux Audit Framework module from YaST ➤ Security and Users. After activating this module, you'll see a bit of a cryptic message, indicating the following:

The "apparmor" kernel module is loaded. The kernel uses a running audit daemon to log audit events to /var/log/audit/audit.log (default). Do you want to start the daemon now?

This message is talking about the AppArmor kernel module, because auditing takes care of messages generated by AppArmor but also messages generated by SELinux and other services that use the libaudit library, such as PAM login events.

If you just skip the part about the AppArmor kernel module (which isn't entirely relevant here), what matters is the part where it says that the audit module has to be started. Just select Yes to make sure that the audit module is started, and it will start logging messages to /var/log/audit.

You'll now see a screen from which you can configure the different aspects of the working of Linux auditing. The screen that you see in Figure 6-3 allows you to specify log file properties. In the General Settings section, you'll specify what will be logged and how it will be logged there. The default audit log file is /var/log/audit/audit.log, and there is no reason to change that. Next, you must specify the format. The RAW format is the only format that makes sense here. It makes sure that messages are logged exactly the way they were generated by the kernel.

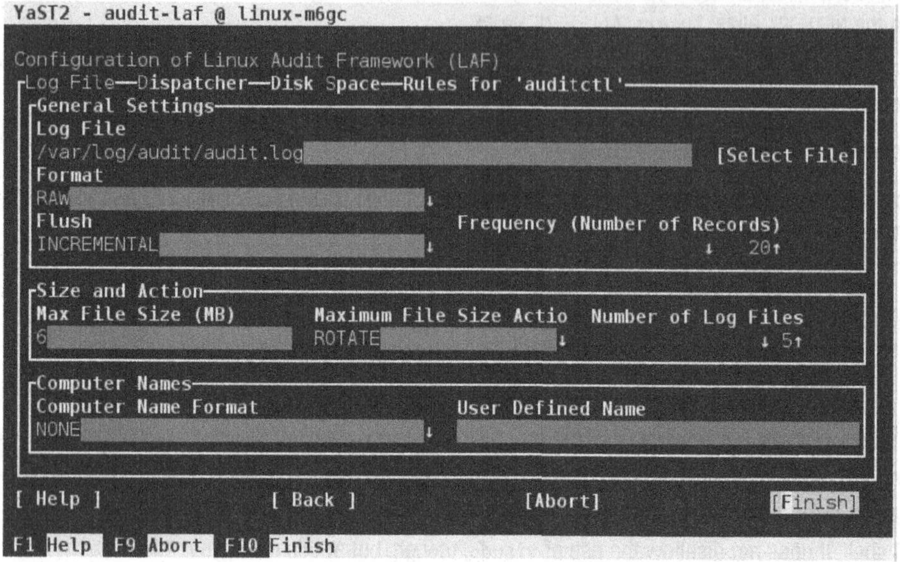

Figure 6-3. *Specifying log file properties*

The Flush parameter determines how data is written to disk. The default setting of INCREMENTAL specifies an amount of records that is flushed all at once. Use the frequency parameter to specify how many these are. Select NONE, if you don't want the audit daemon to make an effort to flush data; DATA, if you want complete synchronization where the risk of losing log events is minimized; and SYNC, if you want to keep metadata and data fully synchronized, which provides minimal risk of losing data.

In the Size and Action section, you can specify the maximum size of the log file. By default, it is set to 6MB. When that size is reached, the Maximum File Size Action determines what will happen. If set to ROTATE, the log file will be rotated, and the maximum number of log files that is kept is specified in the Number of Log Files option. Other options after reaching the maximum log file size are the following:

- Ignore: Nothing will happen if the maximal size is reached.

- Syslog: A message is sent to syslog, indicating that the maximum size has been reached.

- Susped: The audit daemon stops writing messages to disk.

- Keep_logs: Logs are rotated, but without a limit on the maximum amount of files that is kept.

In the Computer Names section, you can specify if and, if so, how computer names are used in log messages. As auditing is typically set up locally, the default setting is NONE, but you can select to log a hostname, the FQDN, or a user-specified name to the log file.

On the Dispatcher tab (see Figure 6-4), you can specify how the dispatcher is used to handle log messages. The dispatcher is a program that is started with the audit daemon. It takes audit events and sends them to child programs that can analyze the events in real time. These child programs are specified in /etc/audisp/plugins.d and make sure that action is taken if something happens to the audit daemon. One of the dispatcher modules, for example, is syslog, which makes sure that events related to the audit daemon are treated by syslogd as well.

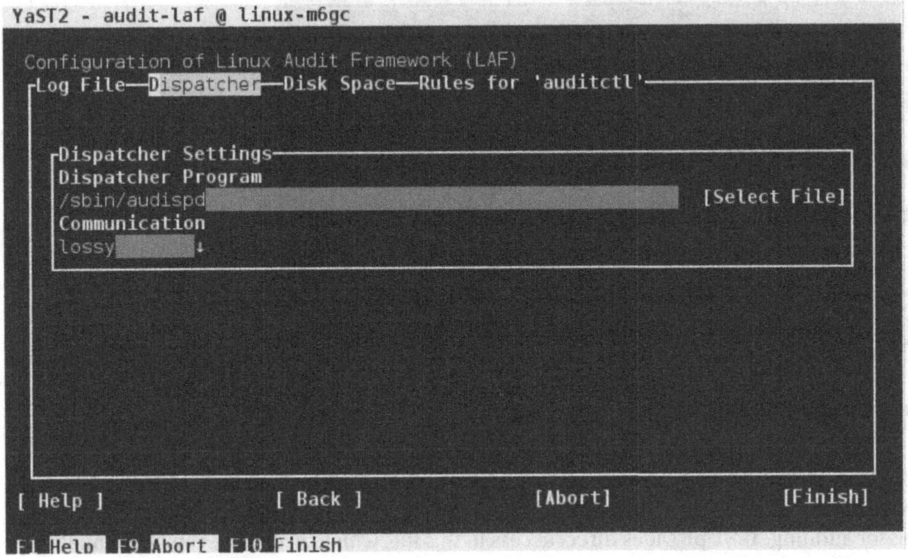

Figure 6-4. *Configuring the dispatcher*

On the Dispatcher tab, you can specify which program is used as the default dispatcher program and how that program should communicate to its child programs. Normally, there is no reason to change this program. The communication method, by default, is set to lossy, which means that a 128KB queue is filled, and once this queue is full, events will be discarded. Use lossless for fewer chances of losing events handled by the dispatcher.

Auditd can also monitor the availability of disk space on the log partition. To do this, use the settings on the Disk Space tab, which you can see in Figure 6-5. On this tab, you can set a warning threshold and a minimal threshold. On reaching the warning threshold, a message is written to syslog, and on reaching the minimal threshold, the audit system shuts down.

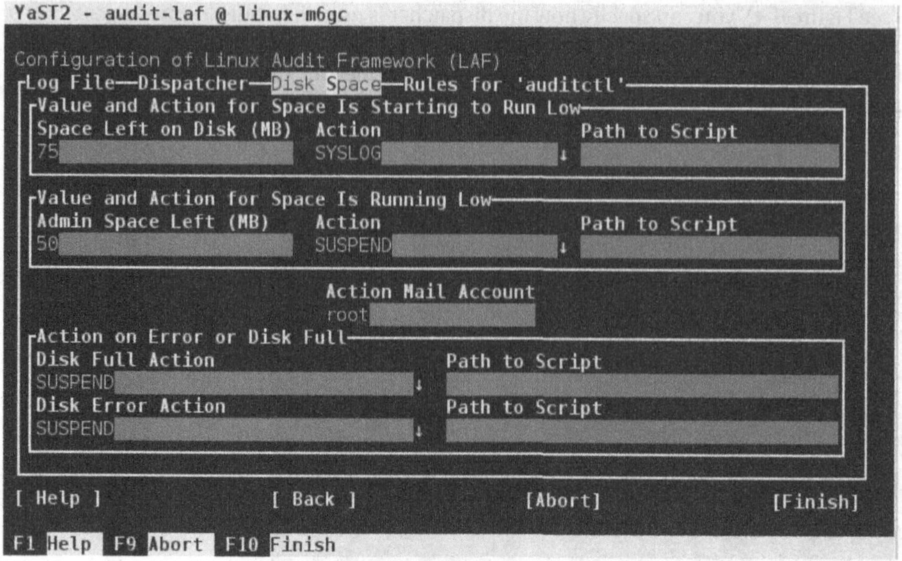

Figure 6-5. *Specifying what to do when the disk is full*

On the Rules for auditctl tab, you can specify how additional rules are processed by the Linux Auditing Framework. To start with, you have to set Auditing to enabled, and next you can edit the contents of the audit.rules file to define additional rules for auditing. YaST provides direct access to this file, which, of course, can be manually edited as well. The rules specified here contain parameters that are directly passed to the auditctl process. Read the man page for this process for more information on how to use these options.

After configuring the auditing system, you can see audit messages in the /var/log/audit/audit.log file. You'll notice that these messages are hard to read in some cases, because they are messages that have been generated by the kernel. For working with some subsystems, in particular with SELinux, they provide an important source of information on what is happening on your server.

Understanding PAM

On Linux, many programs require access to information that relates to authentication. To make accessing this information easy, Linux uses pluggable authentication modules (PAMs). The authentication-related programs are configured to use the libpam.so and libpam_misc.so libraries. These libraries tell the program to look in the /etc/pam.d directory for a corresponding configuration file. From this directory, different authentication plug-ins from the directory /lib64/security can be included to implement specific login behavior (see Figure 6-6).

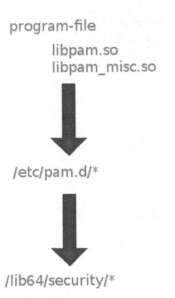

program-file

libpam.so
libpam_misc.so

/etc/pam.d/*

/lib64/security/*

Figure 6-6. PAM schematic overview

In Exercise 6-2, you'll explore what the PAM configuration for the su program looks like.

EXERCISE 6-2. EXPLORING PAM CONFIGURATION

1. Open a root shell and type ldd $(which su). This command lists the libraries that are used by the su command. You'll see that they include libpam and libpam_misc.

2. Type cat /etc/pam.d/su. This shows the following configuration (the contents is explained after this exercise):

```
ldap:/etc/pam.d # cat su
#%PAM-1.0
auth      sufficient    pam_rootok.so
auth      include       common-auth
account   sufficient    pam_rootok.so
account   include       common-account
password  include       common-password
session   include       common-session
session   optional      pam_xauth.so
```

3. From the previous step of the exercise, you have seen that some common files are included. Type cat /etc/pam.d/common-auth, to show the contents of one of these common files. It will show you something as in the following code:

```
ldap:/etc/pam.d # cat common-auth
#%PAM-1.0
#
# This file is autogenerated by pam-config. All changes
# will be overwritten.
#
# Authentication-related modules common to all services
#
# This file is included from other service-specific PAM config files,
# and should contain a list of the authentication modules that define
# the central authentication scheme for use on the system
# (e.g., /etc/shadow, LDAP, Kerberos, etc.). The default is to use the
# traditional Unix authentication mechanisms.
#
auth    required      pam_env.so
auth    optional      pam_gnome_keyring.so
auth    sufficient    pam_unix.so        try_first_pass
auth    required      pam_sss.so         use_first_pass
```

4. Use cd /lib64/security and type ls to display all the PAM modules that are listed in this directory. You'll see that all modules that the configuration files refer to are listed here.

5. Type less /usr/share/doc/packages/pam/Linux-PAM_SAG.txt. This gives access to the PAM System Administrator Guide, in which all the PAM modules are explained, including the parameters that can be used when using these modules.

PAM Configuration Files

In the preceding exercise, you have looked at the contents of a PAM configuration file. In each configuration file, the authentication process is defined in four different phases. In each phase, different PAM files can be included, and there are different ways to include the PAMs.

The following phases are defined in authentication:

- auth: This is where the authentication is initialized.

- account: This refers to the phase in authentication where account settings are checked.

- password: This is for checking password-related settings.

- session: This defines what happens after authentication, when the user wants to access specific resources.

When calling a PAM file, it can be called in different ways.

- required: The conditions that are implemented by this PAM library file must be met. If this is not the case, the rest of the procedure is followed, but access will be denied.

- requisite: With this, the conditions implemented by the PAM library file must also be met. If this is not the case, the authentication procedure stops immediately.

- sufficient: Conditions imposed by this PAM file don't have to be met, but if they are met, that is sufficient, and further PAM files in this phase of the authentication don't have to be processed anymore. This is useful if you want users to authenticate on an LDAP server first, but if that is not successful, to continue local authentication. This would look as follows:

```
...
auth    sufficient    pam_ldap.so
auth    required      pam_unix2.so
...
```

- optional: Used to include functionality that typically doesn't deal with the real authentication process. Use this, for example, to display the contents of a text file, or anything else that is nonessential.

- include: This is used to include the contents of another PAM configuration file.

In Exercise 6-3, you'll change the PAM configuration to include the pam_securetty file. This file can be used to define the names of terminals (TTYs) that are considered to be secure and where the user root can log in. In the exercise, you'll first use su on tty4 (virtual terminal 4, which can be accessed by using the Ctrl+Alt+F4 key sequence) when the pam_securetty.so file is not included. Next, you will include the pam_securetty.so file in the login sequence and modify the contents of /etc/securetty to disable root access on tty4.

EXERCISE 6-3. USING PAM TO LIMIT SU

1. Use the key sequence Ctrl+Alt+F4. On the login prompt, log in as user linda and type su - to become root. Enter the root password. You will authenticate. Type *exit* twice to log out both from the su session and from the session in which you are user linda.

2. Open a root shell and type vim /etc/pam.d/su.

3. As the second entry (make sure it is before the line where common-auth is included), add the line auth   required   pam_securetty.so.

4. Open the file /etc/securetty in an editor and make sure the line tty4 is removed.

5. Repeat step 1 of this exercise. It will no longer work.

Understanding nsswitch

PAM is related to authentication and specifies where the authentication process should look for user-related information and more. PAM doesn't help you to get information from nonlocal sources when they are not directly related to authentication. For that purpose, there is nsswitch, which uses the /etc/nsswitch.conf configuration file. In Listing 6-3, you can see what its contents looks like.

Listing 6-3. Sample /etc/nsswitch.conf Contents

```
passwd:          files sss
group:           files sss

hosts:           files dns
networks:        files dns

services:        files
protocols:       files
rpc:             files
ethers:          files
netmasks:        files
netgroup:        files
publickey:       files

bootparams:      files
automount:       files
aliases:         files
passwd_compat:   files
group_compat:    files
```

By default, all information about users, but also about network hosts and much more, is looked up in local configuration files. If you want utilities that require access to such information to look beyond, you will tell them, in the /etc/nsswitch.conf file, where to look. You can see, for instance, that password-related information is looked for in files, but also in sss. This refers to sssd, which is used to get user information from network authentication sources. (sssd configuration is discussed in more detail in the section about LDAP in Chapter 11.) In addition, you can see that for host- and network-related information, first the local configuration files are checked, after which DNS is consulted.

The information in /etc/nsswitch is used by all utilities that require access to dispersed information but that don't deal with authentication. Two examples of such utilities are id and host. The id utility can show user-related information and get information about that user from any source that is specified in /etc/nsswitch.conf. The host utility will retrieve host information from local configuration files and also from DNS (if /etc/nsswitch.conf indicates that DNS should be used). In the example in Listing 6-4, you can see how the id command shows information about a user, linda, that is defined in LDAP and how host gets information from DNS.

Listing 6-4. Using nsswitch.conf-Related Information

```
ldap:~ # id linda
uid=1001(linda) gid=100(users) groups=100(users)
ldap:~ # host www.sandervanvugt.nl
www.sandervanvugt.nl has address 213.124.112.46
```

Securing SLES 12 with SELinux

The Linux kernel offers a security framework in which additional security restrictions can be imposed. This framework can be used to filter activity on the lowest level, by allowing or denying system calls, as they are issued by the Linux kernel.

In SUSE Linux Enterprise Server 12, there are two different solutions that implement this kind of security. First, there is AppArmor, which has been the default solution in SUSE Linux Enterprise Server since Novell purchased the company that developed AppArmor back in 2006. A recent alternative is SELinux. As the AppArmor code hasn't really changed since it was included in 2006, we'll just have a look at the way that SELinux can be configured.

■ **Note** The current state of kernel-level security framework support in SLES is rather unclear. When I wrote this, I was working on RC1 of SLES 12, which normally contains all features that will be included in the final release. In this version of the software, serious functionality was missing from the AppArmor implementation, and at the same time, the SELinux code wasn't complete either. Because SUSE is planning to offer AppArmor support for current customers and seems to be gradually shifting toward SELinux, I've chosen to discuss only SELinux configuration in this section, even if it is far from complete in the current release of the software. For that reason, you should realize that everything discussed from here on, isn't about stable software but the future directions, which might very well have been implemented by the time you're reading this.

SELinux Backgrounds

Security in Linux was inherited from UNIX security. UNIX security is basically oriented toward file permissions: users are allowed to read, write, or execute files, and that's all in the original UNIX permission scheme. An example explains why in some cases that isn't enough.

> One morning, I found out that my server was hacked. The server was running SLES 10 at the time and was fully patched up to the latest level. A firewall was configured on it and no unnecessary services were offered by this server. After further analyzing the hack, it became clear that the hacker had come in through a flaky PHP script that was a part of one of the Apache virtual hosts that was running on this server. Through this script, the intruder had managed to get access to a shell, using the wwwrun account that was used by the webserver. Using the legal permissions of this account, the intruder had created several scripts in the /var/tmp and /tmp directories, that were a part of a botnet that was launching Distributed Denial of Services attacks against multiple servers.

The interesting lesson that can be drawn from this hack is that nothing really was wrong on this server. The main issue that the hacker had taken advantage of was the fact that every user is allowed to create and run scripts in the /tmp and /var/tmp directories. At the time that the UNIX security model was originally developed, this was good enough. Now that servers are connected to the Internet, it's no longer good enough. That's why the kernel security framework has been developed.

There are two solutions built on the Linux kernel security framework: AppArmor and SELinux. SUSE has been offering AppArmor since SUSE Linux Enterprise Server 9 and has recently introduced support for SELinux as well. This is because SELinux has become the market standard, and in many environments, SELinux security is a requirement for Linux servers.

The basic principle of SELinux is that all system calls are blocked by default on a system on which SELinux is enabled. That means that if nothing else is done, the kernel will generate a kernel panic at a very early stage, and everything halts. Everything that is allowed on a server is defined in the SELinux policy, in which many security rules are set to strictly define what is allowed and what isn't.

To define the rules in the policy, SELinux uses labels on different objects on the system. Labels can be set to files, processes, ports, and users. These labels define what kind of object it is, and if an object with a specific kind of label needs access to another object, this is only allowed if in the policy a rule exists allowing such access. This means that, by default, an intruder that breaks in via the web server would be in an environment that is labeled as the web server environment and would, therefore, never get access to either the /tmp or the /var/tmp directory.

Understanding SELinux Components

Before starting the configuration of SELinux, you should know a bit about how SELinux is organized. Three components play a role:

- The security framework in the Linux kernel

- The SELinux libraries and binaries

- The SELinux policy

Since SUSE Linux Enterprise 11 SP 2, SLES comes with the standard support for SELinux in the Linux kernel and the tools that are needed to manage the SELinux solution. You will shortly learn how to install these tools on your server. The most important part of the work of the administrator with regard to SELinux is managing the policy.

In the SELinux policy, security labels are applied to different objects on a Linux server. These objects typically are users, ports, processes, and files. Using these security labels, rules are created that define what is and what isn't allowed on a server. Remember: By default, SELinux denies all syscalls, and by creating the appropriate rules, you can again allow the syscalls that you trust. Rules, therefore, should exist for all programs that you want to use on a system. Alternatively, you might want to configure parts of a system to run in unconfined mode, which means that specific ports, programs, users, files, and directories are not protected at all by SELinux. This mode is useful, if you only want to use SELinux to protect some essential services but don't specifically care about other services. To get a completely confined system, you should try to avoid this.

To ensure the appropriate protection for your system, you need an SELinux policy. This must be a tailor-made policy in which all files are provided with a label, and all services and users have a security label as well, to express which files and directories can be accessed by which user and process on the server. Developing such a policy requires technical expertise and a significant amount of work.

At the time this was written, the SELinux framework was supported, and there was no policy on SUSE Linux Enterprise. That means that you will have to create your own policy or use one of the standard policies that are available for free. Do be aware, however, that a freely available SELinux policy might work on your server, but it will never offer complete protection for all aspects of security on your server! Also, SUSE does not support these policies. You may, however, contact SUSE to discuss your options.

The Policy

As mentioned, the policy is the key component in SELinux. It defines rules that specify which objects can access which files, directories, ports, and processes on a system. To do this, a security context is defined for all of these. On an SELinux system on which the policy has been applied to label the file system, you can use the ls -Z command on any directory to find the security context for the files in that directory. Listing 6-5 shows the security context settings for the directories in the / directory of an SLES system with an SELinux labeled file system.

Listing 6-5. Showing Security Context Settings Using ls -Z

```
mmi:/ # ls -Z
system_u:object_r:default_t .autorelabel
system_u:object_r:file_t .viminfo
system_u:object_r:bin_t bin
system_u:object_r:boot_t boot
system_u:object_r:device_t dev
system_u:object_r:etc_t etc
system_u:object_r:home_root_t home
system_u:object_r:lib_t lib
system_u:object_r:lib_t lib64
system_u:object_r:lost_found_t lost+found
```

```
system_u:object_r:mnt_t media
system_u:object_r:mnt_t mnt
system_u:object_r:usr_t opt
system_u:object_r:proc_t proc
system_u:object_r:default_t root
system_u:object_r:bin_t sbin
system_u:object_r:security_t selinux
system_u:object_r:var_t srv
system_u:object_r:sysfs_t sys
system_u:object_r:tmp_t tmp
system_u:object_r:usr_t usr
system_u:object_r:var_t var
system_u:object_r:httpd_sys_content_t www
```

The most important line in the security context is the context type. This is the part of the security context that ends in _t. It tells SELinux which kind of access is allowed to the object. In the policy, rules are specified to define which type of user or which type of role has access to which type of context. For example, this can be defined by using a rule such as the following:

allow user_t bin_t:file {read execute gettattr};

This sample rule states that the user who has the context type user_t (this user is referred to as the source object) is allowed to access the file with the context type bin_t (the target), using the permissions read, execute, and getattr. Later in this section, you will learn how to use a standard policy to apply this kind of security context settings to the file system on your server.

The standard policy that you are going to use contains a huge amount of rules. To make it more manageable, policies are often applied as modular policies. This allows the administrator to work with independent modules that allow him or her to switch protection on or off for different parts of the system. When compiling the policy for your system, you will have a choice to work either with a modular policy or with a monolithic policy, in which one huge policy is used to protect everything on your system. It is strongly recommended that you use a modular policy and not a monolithic policy. Modular policies are much easier to manage.

Installing SELinux on SUSE Linux Enterprise 12 FCS

SELinux still doesn't come as the default option for security. If you want to use it, you'll have to install it yourself. This section discusses how to do that. Configuring SELinux on SLES 12 consists of three phases:

- Install all SELinux packages
- Enable GRUB Boot options
- Install a policy

Installing SELinux Packages and Modifying GRUB

The easiest way to make sure that all SELinux components are installed is by using YaST2. The following procedure outlines what to do on an installed SLES 11 SP2 server.

1. Log in to your server as root and start YaST2.

2. Select Software ➤ Software Management.

3. Select Filter ➤ Patterns and select the entire C/C++ Compiler and Tools software category for installation.

4. Select Filter ➤ Search and make sure that Search in Name, Keywords and Summary is selected. Now enter the keyword "selinux" and click Search. You now see a list of packages.

5. Make sure that all packages you've found are selected, then click Accept to install them.

After installing the SELinux packages, you have to modify the GRUB2 boot loader. To do this, from YaST, select System ➤ Boot Loader. On the Kernel Parameters tab, select the line that contains the Optional Kernel Command Line Parameters and add the following to the end of that line: `security=selinux selinux=1 enforcing=0`.
The preceding options are used for the following purposes:

- `security=selinux`: This option tells the kernel to use SELinux and not AppArmor.

- `selinux=1`: This option switches on SELinux.

- `enforcing=0`: This option puts SELinux in permissive mode. In this mode, SELinux is fully functional but doesn't enforce any of the security settings in the policy. Use this mode for configuring your system, and once it is fully operational, change it to `enforcing=1`, to switch on SELinux protection on your server.

After installing the SELinux packages and enabling the SELinux GRUB boot options, reboot your server to activate the configuration. You may notice that while rebooting, an error is displayed, mentioning that the policy file could not be loaded. At this point in the configuration, the error is normal, and you can safely ignore it. It will disappear once you have compiled the policy.

Compiling the Policy

As mentioned, the policy is an essential component of SELinux, but no default policy is available for SUSE Linux Enterprise. That means that you'll have to obtain a policy from somewhere else. The best choice is to get a policy from the OpenSUSE download site at `software.opensuse.org`. In the Package Search bar presented at this site, type "selinux-policy" to get access to a list of all open source policy packages presented at openSUSE.org. Download the policy for OpenSUSE 13.1 to your server and install it. Do not use the One-click install. Instead, use the `rpm` command from the command line to install both packages. Note that you need two packages: the `selinux-policy` package and the `selinux-policy-targeted` package.

After rebooting the system, you now have to perform a few additional tasks to finalize your work. First, open /etc/passwd with an editor and change the shell of the user, nobody, to /sbin/nologin. Next, you should use the command `pam-config -a --selinux` to make the PAM aware of SELinux.

At this point, all prerequisites have been met, and you are ready to start file system labeling. To do this, use the command `restorecon -Rv /`. This command starts the /sbin/setfiles command to label all files on your system. To do this, the input file /etc/selinux/refpolicy/contexts/files/file_contexts is used. Because there currently is no SELinux policy for SUSE Linux Enterprise, this is a delicate part of the configuration. The file_contexts file has to match your actual file system as much as possible, so if it goes wrong, it is likely to go wrong at this point. This can lead to a completely unbootable system. If that happens, tune the contents of the file_contexts file to match the structure of the file system your server is using. Before doing this, make sure to read the rest of this article, so that you fully understand how context type is applied to files and directories (and don't forget to make a backup of the file_contexts file before starting). At the end of this section, you'll find tips to help you troubleshoot SELinux and create a system that fully works with your SELinux policy.

■ **Note** If while using `semanage` you receive a message that complains about the user nobody's home directory, you can change the login shell of user nobody to /sbin/nologin. This ensures that the user nobody's settings match the current policy settings.

After another reboot, SELinux should be operational. To verify this, use the command `sestatus -v`. It should give you an output that looks like that in Listing 6-6.

Listing 6-6. Verifying That SELinux Is Functional, by Using `sestatus -v`, After Labeling the File System

```
mmi:/ # sestatus -v
SELinux status:                 enabled
SELinuxfs mount:                /selinux
Current mode:                   permissive
Mode from config file:          permissive
Policy version:                 26
Policy from config file:        refpolicy

Process contexts:
Current context:                root:staff_r:staff_t
Init context:                   system_u:system_r:init_t
/sbin/mingetty                  system_u:system_r:sysadm_t
/usr/sbin/sshd                  system_u:system_r:sshd_t

File contexts:
Controlling term:               root:object_r:user_devpts_t
/etc/passwd                     system_u:object_r:etc_t
/etc/shadow                     system_u:object_r:shadow_t
/bin/bash                       system_u:object_r:shell_exec_t
/bin/login                      system_u:object_r:login_exec_t
/bin/sh                         system_u:object_r:bin_t -> system_u:object_r:shell_exec_t
/sbin/agetty                    system_u:object_r:getty_exec_t
/sbin/init                      system_u:object_r:init_exec_t
/sbin/mingetty                  system_u:object_r:getty_exec_t
/usr/sbin/sshd                  system_u:object_r:sshd_exec_t
/lib/libc.so.6                  system_u:object_r:lib_t -> system_u:object_r:lib_t
/lib/ld-linux.so.2              system_u:object_r:lib_t -> system_u:object_r:ld_so_t
```

Configuring SELinux

At this point, you have a completely functional SELinux system, and it is time to further configure the system. In the current status, SELinux is operational but not in enforcing mode. That means that it doesn't limit you to do anything. It just logs everything that it should be doing if it were in enforcing mode. This is good, because, based on the log files, you can find what it is that it would prevent you from doing. As a first test, it is a good idea to put SELinux in enforcing mode and find out if you can still use your server after doing that. Before doing so, modify GRUB so that it has two boot options: one where no SELinux configuration is used at all, and one that contains all SELinux configuration. This makes it easier to revert to a working situation, in case your SELinux configuration doesn't work. (See Chapter 8 for detailed instructions on how to modify GRUB parameters).

To do this, open the Kernel Parameters option from the YaST module for GRUB configuration and make sure that the `enforcing=1` option is set as one of the Optional Kernel Command Line Parameters. Reboot your server and see if it still comes up the way you expect it to. If it does, leave it like that and start modifying the server in such a way that everything works as expected. Chances are, though, that you won't even be able to boot the server properly. If that is the case, switch back to the mode in which SELinux is not enforcing and start tuning your server.

Verifying the Installation

Before you start tuning your server, it is a good idea to verify the SELinux installation. You have already used the command sestatus -v to view the current mode and process and file contexts. Next, use semanage boolean -l, which shows a list of all Boolean switches that are available and, at the same time, verifies that you can access the policy. Listing 6-7 shows a part of the output of this command.

Listing 6-7. Use semanage boolean -l to Get a List of Booleans and Verify Policy Access

```
mmi:~ # semanage boolean -l
SELinux boolean                         Description

ftp_home_dir                      -> off    ftp_home_dir
mozilla_read_content              -> off    mozilla_read_content
spamassassin_can_network          -> off    spamassassin_can_network
httpd_can_network_relay           -> off    httpd_can_network_relay
openvpn_enable_homedirs           -> off    openvpn_enable_homedirs
gpg_agent_env_file                -> off    gpg_agent_env_file
allow_httpd_awstats_script_anon_write -> off    allow_httpd_awstats_script_anon_write
httpd_can_network_connect_db      -> off    httpd_can_network_connect_db
allow_user_mysql_connect          -> off    allow_user_mysql_connect
allow_ftpd_full_access            -> off    allow_ftpd_full_access
samba_domain_controller           -> off    samba_domain_controller
httpd_enable_cgi                  -> off    httpd_enable_cgi
virt_use_nfs                      -> off    virt_use_nfs
```

Another command that should produce output at this stage is semanage fcontext -l. This command shows the default file context settings, as provided by the policy (see Listing 6-8 for a partial output of this command).

Listing 6-8. Use semanage fcontext -l to Get File Context Information

```
/var/run/usb(/.*)?              all files      system_u:object_r:hotplug_var_run_t
/var/run/utmp                   regular file   system_u:object_r:initrc_var_run_t
/var/run/vbe.*                  regular file   system_u:object_r:hald_var_run_t
/var/run/vmnat.*                socket         system_u:object_r:vmware_var_run_t
/var/run/vmware.*               all files      system_u:object_r:vmware_var_run_t
/var/run/vpnc(/.*)?             all files      system_u:object_r:vpnc_var_run_t
/var/run/watchdog\.pid          regular file   system_u:object_r:watchdog_var_run_t
/var/run/winbindd(/.*)?         all files      system_u:object_r:winbind_var_run_t
/var/run/wnn-unix(/.*)          all files      system_u:object_r:canna_var_run_t
/var/run/wpa_supplicant(/.*)?   all files      system_u:object_r:NetworkManager_var_run_t
/var/run/wpa_supplicant-global  socket         system_u:object_r:NetworkManager_var_run_t
/var/run/xdmctl(/.*)?           all files      system_u:object_r:xdm_var_run_t
/var/run/yiff-[0-9]+\.pid       regular file   system_u:object_r:soundd_var_run_t
```

Managing SELinux

Now that the base SELinux configuration is operational, it's time to start configuring it in a way that secures your server. First, let's resume what SELinux is all about. In SELinux, an additional set of rules is used to define exactly which process or user can access which files, directories, or ports. To accomplish this, SELinux applies a context to every file, directory, process, and port. This context is a security label that defines how this file, directory, process, or port should be treated. These context labels are used by the SELinux policy, which defines exactly what should be done with the context labels. By default, the policy blocks all non-default access, which means that, as an administrator, you have to enable all features that are non-default on your server.

Displaying the Security Context

As mentioned, files, folders, and ports can be labeled. Within each label, different contexts are used. To be able to perform your daily administration work, the type context is what you're most interested in. As an administrator, you'll mostly work with the type context. Many commands allow you to use the -Z option to show a list of current context settings. In Listing 6-9, you can see what the context settings are for the directories in the root directory.

Listing 6-9. The Default Context for Directories in the Root Directory

```
[root@hnl /]# ls -Z
dr-xr-xr-x. root root system_u:object_r:bin_t:s0        bin
dr-xr-xr-x. root root system_u:object_r:boot_t:s0       boot
drwxr-xr-x. root root system_u:object_r:cgroup_t:s0     cgroup
drwxr-xr-x+ root root unconfined_u:object_r:default_t:s0 data
drwxr-xr-x. root root system_u:object_r:device_t:s0     dev
drwxr-xr-x. root root system_u:object_r:etc_t:s0        etc
drwxr-xr-x. root root system_u:object_r:home_root_t:s0 home
dr-xr-xr-x. root root system_u:object_r:lib_t:s0        lib
dr-xr-xr-x. root root system_u:object_r:lib_t:s0        lib64
drwx------. root root system_u:object_r:lost_found_t:s0 lost+found
drwxr-xr-x. root root system_u:object_r:mnt_t:s0        media
drwxr-xr-x. root root system_u:object_r:autofs_t:s0     misc
drwxr-xr-x. root root system_u:object_r:mnt_t:s0        mnt
drwxr-xr-x. root root unconfined_u:object_r:default_t:s0 mnt2
drwxr-xr-x. root root unconfined_u:object_r:default_t:s0 mounts
drwxr-xr-x. root root system_u:object_r:autofs_t:s0     net
drwxr-xr-x. root root system_u:object_r:usr_t:s0        opt
dr-xr-xr-x. root root system_u:object_r:proc_t:s0       proc
drwxr-xr-x. root root unconfined_u:object_r:default_t:s0 repo
dr-xr-x---. root root system_u:object_r:admin_home_t:s0 root
dr-xr-xr-x. root root system_u:object_r:bin_t:s0        sbin
drwxr-xr-x. root root system_u:object_r:security_t:s0   selinux
drwxr-xr-x. root root system_u:object_r:var_t:s0        srv
-rw-r--r--. root root unconfined_u:object_r:swapfile_t:s0 swapfile
drwxr-xr-x. root root system_u:object_r:sysfs_t:s0      sys
drwxrwxrwt. root root system_u:object_r:tmp_t:s0        tmp
-rw-r--r--. root root unconfined_u:object_r:etc_runtime_t:s0 tmp2.tar
-rw-r--r--. root root unconfined_u:object_r:etc_runtime_t:s0 tmp.tar
drwxr-xr-x. root root system_u:object_r:usr_t:s0        usr
drwxr-xr-x. root root system_u:object_r:var_t:s0        var
```

In the preceding listing, you can see the complete context for all directories. It consists of a user, a role, and a type. The s0 settings indicate the security level in multilevel security (MLS) environments. These environments are not discussed in this section, so just make sure that it is set to s0, and you'll be fine. The Context Type defines what kind of activity is permitted in the directory. Compare, for example, the /root directory, which has the admin_home_t context type, and the /home directory, which has the home_root_t context type. In the SELinux policy, different kinds of access are defined for these context types.

Multilevel security is the application of a computer system to process information with incompatible classifications (i.e., at different security levels), permit access by users with different security clearances and needs-to-know, and prevent users from obtaining access to information for which they lack authorization. There are two contexts for the use of MLS. One is to refer to a system that is adequate to protect itself from subversion and has robust mechanisms to separate information domains, that is, trustworthy. Another context is to refer to an application of a computer that will require the computer to be strong enough to protect itself from subversion and possess adequate mechanisms to separate information domains, that is, a system we must trust. This distinction is important, because systems that have to be trusted are not necessarily trustworthy (Wikipedia, "Multilevel security," http://en.wikipedia.org/wiki/Multilevel_security).

Security labels are not only associated with files, but also with other items, such as ports and processes. In Listing 6-10, for example, you can see the context settings for processes on your server.

Listing 6-10. Showing SELinux Settings for Processes

```
mmi:/ # ps Zaux
LABEL                             USER      PID %CPU %MEM    VSZ  RSS TTY  STAT START  TIME COMMAND
system_u:system_r:init_t          root        1  0.0  0.0  10640  808 ?    Ss   05:31  0:00 init [5]
system_u:system_r:kernel_t        root        2  0.0  0.0      0    0 ?    S    05:31  0:00 [kthreadd]
system_u:system_r:kernel_t        root        3  0.0  0.0      0    0 ?    S    05:31  0:00 [ksoftirqd/0]
system_u:system_r:kernel_t        root        6  0.0  0.0      0    0 ?    S    05:31  0:00 [migration/0]
system_u:system_r:kernel_t        root        7  0.0  0.0      0    0 ?    S    05:31  0:00 [watchdog/0]
system_u:system_r:sysadm_t        root     2344  0.0  0.0  27640  852 ?    Ss   05:32  0:00 /usr/sbin/mcelog
                                                                           --daemon --config-file /etc/mcelog/mcelog.conf
system_u:system_r:sshd_t          root     3245  0.0  0.0  69300 1492 ?    Ss   05:32  0:00 /usr/sbin/sshd -o
                                                                           PidFile=/var/run/sshd.init.pid
system_u:system_r:cupsd_t         root     3265  0.0  0.0  68176 2852 ?    Ss   05:32  0:00 /usr/sbin/cupsd
system_u:system_r:nscd_t          root     3267  0.0  0.0 772876 1380 ?    Ssl  05:32  0:00 /usr/sbin/nscd
system_u:system_r:postfix_master_t root    3334  0.0  0.0  38320 2424 ?    Ss   05:32  0:00 /usr/lib/postfix/
                                                                                                master
system_u:system_r:postfix_qmgr_t postfix  3358  0.0  0.0  40216 2252 ?    S    05:32  0:00 qmgr -l -t fifo -u
system_u:system_r:crond_t         root     3415  0.0  0.0  14900  800 ?    Ss   05:32  0:00 /usr/sbin/cron
system_u:system_r:fsdaemon_t      root     3437  0.0  0.0  16468 1040 ?    S    05:32  0:00 /usr/sbin/smartd
system_u:system_r:sysadm_t        root     3441  0.0  0.0  66916 2152 ?    Ss   05:32  0:00 login -- root
system_u:system_r:sysadm_t        root     3442  0.0  0.0   4596  800 tty2 Ss+  05:32  0:00 /sbin/mingetty tty2
```

Selecting the SELinux Mode

In SELinux, three different modes can be used:

- *Enforcing*: This is the default mode. SELinux protects your server according to the rules in the policy, and SELinux logs all of its activity to the audit log.

- *Permissive*: This mode is useful for troubleshooting. If set to Permissive, SELinux does not protect your server, but it still logs everything that happens to the log files. Also, in permissive mode, the Linux kernel still maintains the SELinux labels in the file system. This is good, because it prevents your system from relabeling everything after turning SELinux on again.

- *Disabled*: This mode is to be inactivated. In disabled mode, SELinux is switched off completely, and no logging occurs. The file system labels, however, are not removed from the file system.

You have already read how you can set the current SELinux mode from GRUB while booting, using the enforcing boot parameter.

Modifying SELinux Context Types

An important part of the work of an administrator is setting context types on files, to ensure appropriate working of SELinux.

If a file is created within a specific directory, it inherits the context type of the parent directory by default. If, however, a file is moved from one location to another, it retains the context type that it had in the former location.

To set the context type for files, you can use the semanage fcontext command. With this command, you write the new context type to the policy, but it doesn't change the actual context type immediately! To apply the context types that are in the policy, you have to run the restorecon command afterward.

The challenge when working with semanage fcontext is to find out which context you actually need. You can use semanage fcontext -l to show a list of all contexts in the policy, but because it is rather long, it might be a bit difficult to find the actual context you need from that list (see Listing 6-11).

Listing 6-11. Displaying Default File Contexts with semanage fcontext -l

```
[root@hnl ~]# semanage fcontext -l | less
SELinux fcontext                          type            Context

/                                         directory       system_u:object_r:root_t:s0
/.*                                       all files       system_u:object_r:default_t:s0
/[^/]+                                     regular file    system_u:object_r:etc_runtime_t:s0
/\.autofsck                               regular file    system_u:object_r:etc_runtime_t:s0
/\.autorelabel                            regular file    system_u:object_r:etc_runtime_t:s0
/\.journal                                all files       <<None>>
/\.suspended                              regular file    system_u:object_r:etc_runtime_t:s0
/a?quota\.(user|group)                    regular file    system_u:object_r:quota_db_t:s0
/afs                                      directory       system_u:object_r:mnt_t:s0
/bin                                      directory       system_u:object_r:bin_t:s0
/bin/.*                                   all files       system_u:object_r:bin_t:s0
```

There are three ways to find out which context settings are available for your services.

1. Install the service and look at the default context settings that are used. This is the easiest and recommended option.

2. Consult the man page for the specific service. Some services have a man page that ends in _selinux, which contains all the information you need to find the correct context settings.

After finding the specific context setting you need, you just have to apply it using semanage fcontext. This command takes the -t context type as its first argument, followed by the name of the directory or file to which you want to apply the context settings. To apply the context to everything that already exists in the directory in which you want to apply the context, you add the regular expression (/.*)? to the name of the directory, which. This means: optionally, match a slash followed by any character. The examples section of the semanage man page has some useful applicable examples for semanage.

3. Use seinfo -t to display a list of all type contexts that are available on your system, combined with grep to find the type context you need for a specific purpose. The amount of information provided with seinfo -t is a bit overwhelming; about 3,000 type contexts are available by default!

Applying File Contexts

To help you apply the SELinux context properly, the following procedure shows how to set a context, using semanage fcontext and restorecon. You will notice that at first attempt, the web server with a non-default document root doesn't work. After changing the SELinux context it will.

1. Use zypper in apache2.

2. Use mkdir /web and then go to that directory using cd /web.

3. Use a text editor to create the file /web/index.html, which contains the text "welcome to my website."

4. Open the file /etc/apache2/default-server.conf with an editor and change the DocumentRoot line to DocumentRoot /web. Also change the <Directory> statement in this file, to validate for the directory /web.

5. Start the Apache Web server, using systemctl start apache2.

6. Use w3m localhost to open a session to your local web server. You will receive a connection refused message. Press Enter and then *q*, to quit w3m.

7. Use ls -Z /srv/www to find the current type context for the default Apache DocumentRoot, which is /srv/www/htdocs. It should be set to httpd_sys_content_t.

8. Use semanage fcontext -a -t httpd_sys_content_t '/web(/.*) ?' to set the new context in the policy and press Enter.

9. Now use restorecon /web to apply the new type context.

10. Use ls -Z /web to show the context of the files in the directory /web. You'll see that the new context type has been set properly to the /web directory, but not to its contents.

11. Use restorecon -R /web to apply the new context recursively to the /web directory. The type context has now been set correctly.

12. Restart the web server, using rcapache2 restart. You should now be able to access the content of the /web directory.

Configuring SELinux Policies

The easiest way to change the behavior of the policy is by working with Booleans. These are on-off switches that you can use to change the settings in the policy.

To find out which Booleans are available, you can use the semanage boolean -l command. It will show you a long list of Booleans, with a short description of what each of these will do for you. Once you have found the Boolean you want to set, you can use setsebool -P, followed by the name of the Boolean that you want to change. It is important to use the -P option at all times when using setsebool. This option writes the setting to the policy file on disk, and this is the only way to make sure that the Boolean is applied automatically after a reboot.

The following procedure provides an example of changing Boolean settings.

1. From a root shell, type semanage boolean -l | grep ftp. This shows a list of Booleans that are related to FTP servers.

2. Use setsebool allow_ftpd_anon_write off to make sure this Boolean is off. Note that it doesn't take much time to write the change. Use semanage boolean -l grep ftpd_anon to verify that the Boolean is indeed turned on. (If you don't succeed with this step, use semodule -e ftp first.)

3. Reboot your server.

4. Check again to see if the `allow_ftpd_anon_write` Boolean is still turned on. As it hasn't yet been written to the policy, you'll see that it is off at the moment.

5. Use `setsebool -P allow_ftpd_anon_write` on to switch on the Boolean and write the setting to the policy.

Working with SELinux Modules

You have compiled SELinux as modular. That means that the policy that implements SELinux features is not just one huge policy, but it consists of many smaller modules. Each module covers a specific part of the SELinux configuration. The concept of the SELinux module was introduced to make it easier for third-party vendors to make their services compatible with SELinux. To get an overview of the SELinux modules, you can use the `semodule -l` command. This command shows a list of all current modules in use by SELinux and their version numbers.

As an administrator, you can switch modules on or off. This can be useful if you want to disable only a part of SELinux and not everything, to run a specific service without SELinux protection. Especially when building your own policy, it makes sense to switch off all modules that you don't need, so that you can focus on the services that really do require SELinux protection. To switch off an SELinux module, use `semodule -d modulename`. If you want to switch it on again, you can use `semodule -e modulename`. Using this command will change the current state of the module in the `/etc/selinux/refpolicy/policy/modules.conf` file. Alternatively, you could also edit this file by hand.

To handle policy modules properly, it helps to understand what you're dealing with. In the end, a policy module is a compiled policy file that you can load using the `semodule -e` command. You can recognize these files by the extension they use: `*.pp` (which stands for "Policy Package"). In some cases, it can be useful to modify modules to have them do exactly what you need them to. If all the sources of the SELinux policy are installed, three different kinds of files are used as input files for policy modules, and you can find them in subdirectories of the `/etc/selinux/refpolicy/policy/modules` directory, as follows:

- `te` files contain transition rules. These rules tell the policy how to deal with specific subprocesses that are started. You won't often change these as administrator.

- `if` files define what exactly the policy should be doing. As an administrator, you don't typically change the contents of this file.

- `fc` files contain the labeling instructions that apply to this policy. As an administrator, you might want to change the contents of the `.fc` files to modify the default behavior of policies.

In Listing 6-12, you can see the first 20 lines of the `apache.fc` file. This is the file that contains the default file contexts that are used for the Apache server.

Listing 6-12. The First 20 Lines from the `apache.fc` File

```
mmi:/etc/selinux/refpolicy/policy/modules/services # head -n 20 apache.fc
HOME_DIR/((www)|(web)|(public_html))(/.+)? gen_context(system_u:object_r:httpd_user_content_t,s0)

/etc/apache(2)?(/.*)?             gen_context(system_u:object_r:httpd_config_t,s0)
/etc/apache-ssl(2)?(/.*)?         gen_context(system_u:object_r:httpd_config_t,s0)
/etc/htdig(/.*)?                  gen_context(system_u:object_r:httpd_sys_content_t,s0)
/etc/httpd                 -d     gen_context(system_u:object_r:httpd_config_t,s0)
/etc/httpd/conf.*                 gen_context(system_u:object_r:httpd_config_t,s0)
/etc/httpd/logs                   gen_context(system_u:object_r:httpd_log_t,s0)
/etc/httpd/modules                gen_context(system_u:object_r:httpd_modules_t,s0)
/etc/vhosts                --     gen_context(system_u:object_r:httpd_config_t,s0)
```

```
/srv/([^/]*/)?www(/.*)?                    gen_context(system_u:object_r:httpd_sys_content_t,s0)
/srv/gallery2(/.*)?                        gen_context(system_u:object_r:httpd_sys_content_t,s0)

/usr/bin/htsslpass              --         gen_context(system_u:object_r:httpd_helper_exec_t,s0)

/usr/lib/apache-ssl/.+          --         gen_context(system_u:object_r:httpd_exec_t,s0)
/usr/lib/cgi-bin(/.*)?                      gen_context(system_u:object_r:httpd_sys_script_exec_t,s0)
/usr/lib(64)?/apache(/.*)?                 gen_context(system_u:object_r:httpd_modules_t,s0)
/usr/lib(64)?/apache2/modules(/.*)?        gen_context(system_u:object_r:httpd_modules_t,s0)
```

In the `fc` file, you'll be able to recognize different elements. First is the name of the directory or file to which the file context will apply. As you can see, variables can be used (as is the case of the first line, which starts with `HOME_DIR`), and typically, regular expressions will be used as well. Next, the `gen_context` command tells the policy to which context the files related to the policy module should be set. This is the same context setting as that you can see when using `ls -Z` on the file or directory.

As an administrator, you don't typically change the contents of the policy files that come from the SELinux Policy RPM. You would rather use `semanage fcontext` to change file contexts. If you are using `audit2allow` to generate policies for your server, you might want to change the policy files after all. If you want to change the contents of any of the policy module files, you'll need to compile the changes into a new policy module file. To do this, copy or link the SELinux Makefile from `/etc/selinux/refpolicy` to the directory that contains the policy module input files and run the following command to compile the module:

`make && make install && make load`

Once the `make` command has completed, you can manually load the modules into the system, using `semodule -e`.

Troubleshooting SELinux

By default, if SELinux is the reason why something isn't working, a log message to that effect is sent to the `/var/log/audit/audit.log` file. That is, if the auditd service is running. If you see an empty `/var/log/audit`, start the auditd service using `service auditd start`, and put it in the runlevels of your system, using `chkconfig auditd on`. In listing 6-13, you can see a partial example of the contents of `/var/log/audit/audit.log`.

Listing 6-13. Example Lines from `/var/log/audit/audit.log`

```
type=DAEMON_START msg=audit(1348173810.874:6248): auditd start, ver=1.7.7 format=raw kernel=3.0.13-
0.27-default auid=0 pid=4235 subj=system_u:system_r:auditd_t res=success
type=AVC msg=audit(1348173901.081:292): avc:  denied  { write } for  pid=3426 comm="smartd"
                    name="smartmontools" dev=sda6 ino=581743 scontext=system_u:system_r:fsdaemon_t
                                                  tcontext=system_u:object_r:var_lib_t tclass=dir
type=AVC msg=audit(1348173901.081:293): avc:  denied  { remove_name } for  pid=3426 comm="smartd"
name="smartd.WDC_WD2500BEKT_75PVMT0-WD_WXC1A21E0454.ata.state~" dev=sda6 ino=582390 scontext=system_
                          u:system_r:fsdaemon_t tcontext=system_u:object_r:var_lib_t tclass=dir
type=AVC msg=audit(1348173901.081:294): avc:  denied  { unlink } for  pid=3426 comm="smartd"
name="smartd.WDC_WD2500BEKT_75PVMT0-WD_WXC1A21E0454.ata.state~" dev=sda6 ino=582390 scontext=system_
                          u:system_r:fsdaemon_t tcontext=system_u:object_r:var_lib_t tclass=file
type=AVC msg=audit(1348173901.081:295): avc:  denied  { rename } for  pid=3426 comm="smartd"
name="smartd.WDC_WD2500BEKT_75PVMT0-WD_WXC1A21E0454.ata.state" dev=sda6 ino=582373 scontext=system_
                          u:system_r:fsdaemon_t tcontext=system_u:object_r:var_lib_t tclass=file
type=AVC msg=audit(1348173901.081:296): avc:  denied  { add_name } for  pid=3426 comm="smartd"
name="smartd.WDC_WD2500BEKT_75PVMT0-WD_WXC1A21E0454.ata.state~" scontext=system_u:system_r:fsdaemon_
                          t tcontext=system_u:object_r:var_lib_t tclass=dir
```

```
type=AVC msg=audit(1348173901.081:297): avc:  denied  { create } for pid=3426 comm="smartd"
name="smartd.WDC_WD2500BEKT_75PVMT0-WD_WXC1A21E0454.ata.state" scontext=system_u:system_r:fsdaemon_t
                                         tcontext=system_u:object_r:var_lib_t tclass=file
type=AVC msg=audit(1348173901.081:298): avc:  denied  { write open } for  pid=3426 comm="smartd"
name="smartd.WDC_WD2500BEKT_75PVMT0-WD_WXC1A21E0454.ata.state" dev=sda6 ino=582390 scontext=system_
                           u:system_r:fsdaemon_t tcontext=system_u:object_r:var_lib_t tclass=file
type=AVC msg=audit(1348173901.081:299): avc:  denied  { getattr } for pid=3426 comm="smartd"
     path="/var/lib/smartmontools/smartd.WDC_WD2500BEKT_75PVMT0-WD_WXC1A21E0454.ata.state" dev=sda6
  ino=582390 scontext=system_u:system_r:fsdaemon_t tcontext=system_u:object_r:var_lib_t tclass=file
type=AVC msg=audit(1348173901.309:300): avc:  denied  { append } for  pid=1316
            comm="syslog-ng" name="acpid" dev=sda6 ino=582296 scontext=system_u:system_r:syslogd_t
            tcontext=system_u:object_r:apmd_log_t tclass=file
```

At first look, the lines in audit.log are a bit difficult to read. However, on closer examination, they are not that hard to understand. Every line can be broken down in some default sections. Let's have a look at the different sections in the last line.

- type=AVC: Every SELinux-related audit log line starts with the type identification type=AVC (Access Vector Cache).

- msg=audit(1348173901.309:300): This is the timestamp, which, unfortunately, is written in epoch time, the number of seconds that have passed since January 1, 1970. You can use date -d on the part up to the dot in the epoch time notation, to find out when the event has occurred, as follows:

  ```
  mmi:~ # date -d @1348173901
  Thu Sep 20 16:45:01 EDT 2012
  ```

- avc: denied { append }: The specific action that was denied. In this case, the system has denied to append data to a file. While browsing through the audit log file, you can see other system actions, such as write open, getattr, and more.

- for pid=1316: The process ID of the command or process that initiated the action

- comm="syslog-ng": The specific command that was associated with that PID

- name="acpid": The name of the subject of the action

- dev=sda6 ino=582296: The block device and inode number of the file that was involved

- scontext=system_u:system_r:syslogd_t: The source context, which is the context of the initiator of the action

- tcontext=system_u:object_r:apmd_log_t: The target context, which is the context set on the file on which the action was initiated

- tclass=file: A class identification of the subject

Instead of interpreting the events in audit.log yourself, there is another approach. You can use the audit2allow command, which helps analyze the cryptic log messages in /var/log/audit/audit.log. An audit2allow troubleshooting session always consists of three different commands. First, you would use audit2allow -w -a, to present the audit information in a more readable way. The audit2allow -w -a, by default, works on the audit.log file. If you want to analyze a specific message in the audit.log file, copy it to a temporary file and analyze that, using audit2allow -w -i filename (see Listing 6-14).

Listing 6-14. Analyzing Audit Messages Using `audit2allow`

```
mmi:/var/log/audit # audit2allow -w -i testfile
type=AVC msg=audit(1348173901.309:300): avc:  denied  { append } for  pid=1316 comm="syslog-ng"
name="acpid" dev=sda6 ino=582296 scontext=system_u:system_r:syslogd_t
tcontext=system_u:object_r:apmd_log_t tclass=file

        Was caused by:
                Missing type enforcement (TE) allow rule.

                You can use audit2allow to generate a loadable module to allow this access.
```

To find out which specific rule has denied access, you can use `audit2allow -a`, to show the enforcing rules from all events that were logged to the `audit.log` file, or `audit2allow -i filename`, to show it for messages that you have stored in a specific file (see Listing 6-15).

Listing 6-15. Using `audit2allow` to See Which Lines Have Denied Access

```
mmi:/var/log/audit # audit2allow -i testfile

#============= syslogd_t ==============
allow syslogd_t apmd_log_t:file append;
```

As the last part, use `audit2allow -a -M mymodule` to create an SELinux module with the name mymodule that you can load in order to allow the access that was previously denied. If you want to do this for all events that have been logged to the `audit.log`, use the `-a -M` command arguments. To do it only for specific messages that are in a specific file, use `-i -M`, as in the example in Listing 6-16.

Listing 6-16. Use `audit2allow` to Create a Policy Module That Will Allow the Action Previously Denied

```
mmi:/var/log/audit # audit2allow -i testfile -M auditresult
******************** IMPORTANT ************************
To make this policy package active, execute:

semodule -i auditresult.pp
```

As indicated by the `audit2allow` command, you can now run this module by using the `semodule -i` command, followed by the name of the module that `audit2allow` has just created for you.

Switching to Enforcing Mode

With everything you've done so far, you still cannot switch SELinux to enforcing mode. This is because of a misconfiguration in the context types for some files. When you switch to enforcing mode now, you can see that many AVC denied messages have been written that are related to the `tmpfs`, and following these messages, your system hangs.

The messages that you'll see just before the system stops, look as follows:

> [5.595812] type=1400 audit(1361363803.588:3): avc: denied { read write } for pid=431
> comm="sh" name="console" dev=tmpfs ino=2513 scontext=system_u:system_r:sysadm_t tc
> ontext=system_u:object_r:tmpfs_t tclass=chr_file

> [5.607734] type=1400 audit(1361363803.604:4): avc: denied { read write } for pid=431
> comm="sh" path="/dev/console" dev=tmpfs ino=2513 scontext=system_u:system_r:sysad
> m_t tcontext=system_u:object_r:tmpfs_t tclass=chr_file

As you can see, this message is repeated several times.

To fix this problem, reboot your computer in permissive mode. Copy the /var/log/audit/audit.log file to a temporary file (such as /var/log/audit/audit.2allow) and remove all lines, with the exception of the lines that contain the audit.log messages for the errors listed above (use grep denied audit.log > audit2allow to find them). Assuming that the name of the log file that you've created is audit.2allow, you should now run the following command:

```
audit2allow -i audit.2allow -M bootme
```

This creates a policy module file with the name bootme.pp. Make sure that this module is included in your SELinux configuration by using semodule -i bootme.pp. Now reboot your computer in enforcing mode. You will be able to boot and log in as root in your SELinux-protected system. If this is not the case, you'll have to repeat this procedure until you have no more messages in your audit.log that refer to path="/dev/console" dev=tmpfs. This may involve several reboots.

From here, the fine-tuning begins. You will notice that many items on your system don't work yet. You'll have to fix them one by one. The approach to fix all of these errors is by using audit2allow, as described in the preceding example, and by setting the appropriate context on files and directories on your system. Until a supported version of the SELinux policy is provided with SUSE Linux Enterprise, you'll have to follow this approach to get it to work. At least using this procedure does allow you to configure a computer with the very detailed security settings that are offered with SELinux and will make your system more secure than when using other solutions.

Summary

In this chapter, you have read how to harden an SLES 12 server. You've read about different approaches to hardening, starting with the relatively simple YaST security module, then working through such essentials as configuration of auditing and sudo, up to the application of advanced security settings with SELinux. Using all of the information in this chapter, you should be able to create a relatively safe basic server installation!

■ ■ ■

## CHAPTER 7

Managing Virtualization on SLES

Even if SUSE Linux Enterprise Server (SLES) is not developed as a specific virtualization platform, it's a Linux distribution, and the Linux kernel includes embedded virtualization options. This chapter provides an overview of the available options and goes into further detail about setting up a Kernel-based Virtual Machine (KVM) host platform.

Understanding Linux Virtualization Solutions

In Linux, no less than three approaches are available to create virtual machines. Before going into detail about the most significant virtualization approach, let's have a look at available techniques.

The first virtualization hype on Linux started with the introduction of Xen in the early 2000s. The Xen virtualization platform used a modified Linux kernel that offered virtualization extensions. Because Xen allowed virtual machines to address hardware directly, by using an approach that was known as paravirtualization, it took a long time before the Xen virtualization extension really got integrated into the Linux kernel, which has stimulated the rise of an alternative virtualization solution: KVM.

KVM is the Linux Kernel-based Virtual Machine, a kernel module that offers support for creating virtual machines. Because KVM is so simple in its design and approach, it has been a huge success since the moment it was launched. At present, KVM is the de facto virtualization solution on Linux.

Apart from Xen and KVM, which both are tightly integrated into the Linux kernel, there is also container virtualization. In container virtualization, one kernel is used, and on top of that kernel, different isolated environments are created. Each of these environments behaves as an independent machine, but it isn't. They all depend on the same kernel, and that also means that it's not possible to run different operating systems in such an environment. In Linux, LXC (Linux Containers) is the default solution for offering container-based virtualization.

Understanding the KVM Environment

To set up a KVM environment, a few elements are needed. To start with, you'll need hardware support for virtualization. That means that the CPU that is needed on the hypervisor platform requires virtualization extensions. In general, this is the case for mid- to high-end CPUs. It can be verified by checking the contents of the `/proc/cpuinfo` file; in the CPU, flags `vmx` (intel) or `svm` (AMD) should be listed. If they are not, your CPU does not offer support for virtualization, and KVM cannot be used. Listing 7-1 shows sample contents of the `/proc/cpuinfo` file for a CPU that does offer virtualization support.

Listing 7-1. The Availability of Virtualization Support in the CPU Is Shown in /proc/cpuinfo

```
processor       : 1
vendor_id       : GenuineIntel
cpu family      : 6
model           : 58
model name      : Intel(R) Core(TM) i7-3740QM CPU @ 2.70GHz
stepping        : 9
microcode       : 0x15
cpu MHz         : 2693.694
cache size      : 6144 KB
fpu             : yes
fpu_exception   : yes
cpuid level     : 13
wp              : yes
flags           : fpu vme de pse tsc msr pae mce cx8 apic sep mtrr pge mca cmov pat pse36 clflush
dts mmx fxsr sse sse2 ss syscall nx rdtscp lm constant_tsc arch_perfmon pebs bts nopl xtopology
tsc_reliable nonstop_tsc aperfmperf eagerfpu pni pclmulqdq vmx ssse3 cx16 pcid sse4_1 sse4_2 x2apic
popcnt aes xsave avx f16c rdrand hypervisor lahf_lm ida arat epb xsaveopt pln pts dtherm tpr_shadow
vnmi ept vpid fsgsbase smep
bogomips        : 5387.38
clflush size    : 64
cache_alignment : 64
address sizes   : 40 bits physical, 48 bits virtual
power management :
```

If the CPU extensions for virtualization are available, the required kernel modules can be loaded. These are kvm and kvm_intel or kvm_amd, depending on the hardware platform that is used.

To manage a virtual machine, libvirt is used. libvirtd is a daemon that is started on the hypervisor platform and offers management support for different virtualization platforms. Using libvirtd, KVM can be managed, but other virtualization platforms can be used as well, such as Xen or LXC. libvirtd is also the interface that is used by different management utilities. Common management utilities that can work on top of libvirt are the graphical utility virt-manager and the command-line utility virsh.

Creating KVM Virtual Machines

Using SLES 12 as a KVM host is not difficult. It is started by selecting the software pattern from the Software option in YaST. There's a pattern for Xen as well as for KVM, as SUSE believes it is important to continue supporting customers who have a current infrastructure on top of Xen and, at the same time, wants to offer full KVM support.

After installing the KVM software pattern, YaST will show a Virtualization option (see Figure 7-1). From this virtualization menu, the following three options are available:

- *Create Virtual Machines for Xen and KVM*: This option helps you to configure virtual machines from YaST.

- *Install Hypervisor and Tools*: This is the option you'll have to use first, as it ensures that all of the required components are available.

- *Relocation Server Configuration*: Use this option if you have multiple KVM host platforms and you want to be able to use live migration, whereby a running virtual machine can be migrated from one platform to the other hardware platform.

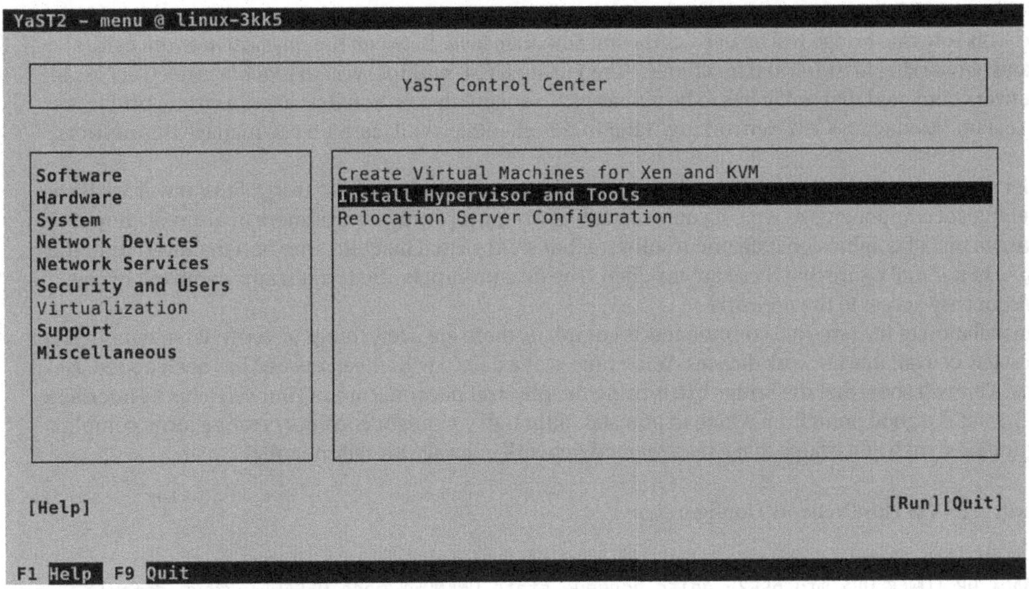

```
YaST2 - menu @ linux-3kk5

                        YaST Control Center

   Software            Create Virtual Machines for Xen and KVM
   Hardware            Install Hypervisor and Tools
   System              Relocation Server Configuration
   Network Devices
   Network Services
   Security and Users
   Virtualization
   Support
   Miscellaneous



   [Help]                                              [Run][Quit]

 F1 Help  F9 Quit
```

Figure 7-1. *YaST virtualization options*

Configuring the KVM Host

When selecting the Install Hypervisor and Tools option, you can select between the three different virtualization platforms (see Figure 7-2). For using KVM, select the KVM server, as well as the KVM tools to be installed, and select Accept, to proceed.

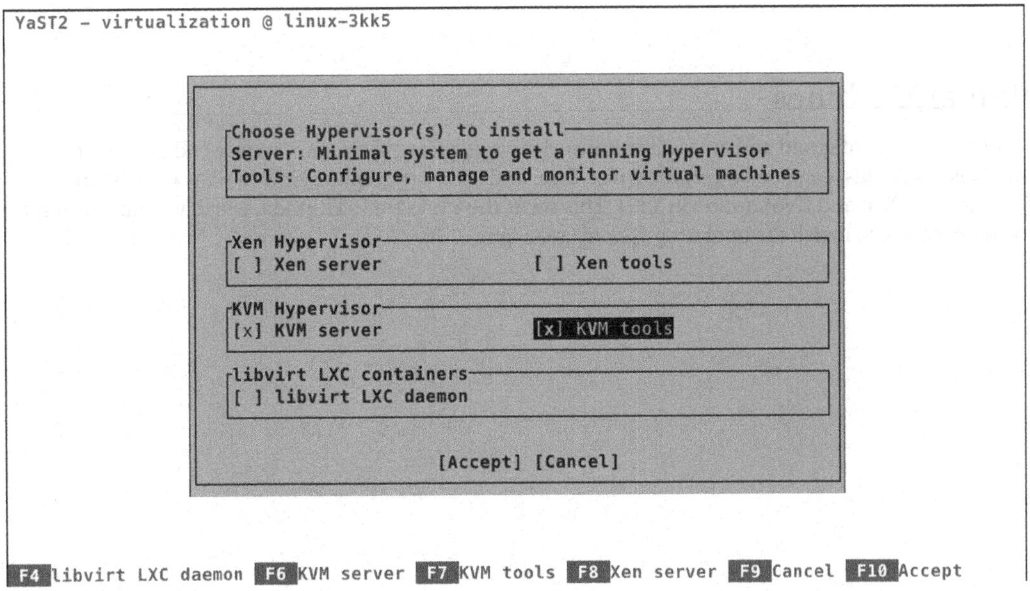

```
YaST2 - virtualization @ linux-3kk5


            ┌Choose Hypervisor(s) to install─────────
            Server: Minimal system to get a running Hypervisor
            Tools: Configure, manage and monitor virtual machines


            ┌Xen Hypervisor──────────────
            [ ] Xen server              [ ] Xen tools

            ┌KVM Hypervisor──────────────
            [x] KVM server              [x] KVM tools

            ┌libvirt LXC containers──────
            [ ] libvirt LXC daemon


                        [Accept] [Cancel]



 F4 libvirt LXC daemon  F6 KVM server  F7 KVM tools  F8 Xen server  F9 Cancel  F10 Accept
```

Figure 7-2. *Selecting your hypervisor of choice*

While installing the KVM environment, multiple things will occur. An important element is the creation of a software bridge. This software bridge will be used as the intermediate layer between the physical network card(s) in your server and networking in the virtual machines. When using KVM, multiple virtual machines need access to one physical network card, and that traffic has to be managed. To ensure that no conflicts arise, a virtual bridge is created. In the section "Managing KVM Networking," later in this chapter, you'll learn how to manage this network environment.

The installer may prompt a few times, depending on the exact configuration you're using. First, it will ask if you want to install graphical components as well. If you're installing from a text-only environment, it normally doesn't make much sense to install graphical management software, but KVM virtual machines are best managed from the graphical tools, so better make sure that these are installed. The next prompt is about setting up a network bridge. You must do this for easy access to the network.

Once the installation of the required components is complete, there are a few things to verify. First, type `ip link show`, for an overview of available network devices. You'll note that a device with the name br0 has been added. Next, type `brctl show`. This will show that the bridge br0 is using the physical network card in your server as its interface. (See Listing 7-2). That is a good point from which to proceed (although you might consider creating more complex network configurations, such as a bridge that uses a teamed network interface for redundancy).

Listing 7-2. Verifying KVM Host Network Configuration

```
linux-3kk5:~ # ip link show
1: lo: <LOOPBACK,UP,LOWER_UP> mtu 65536 qdisc noqueue state UNKNOWN mode DEFAULT group default
    link/loopback 00:00:00:00:00:00 brd 00:00:00:00:00:00
2: eth0: <BROADCAST,MULTICAST,UP,LOWER_UP> mtu 1500 qdisc pfifo_fast master br0 state UP mode
DEFAULT group default qlen 1000
    link/ether 00:0c:29:aa:91:f2 brd ff:ff:ff:ff:ff:ff
3: br0: <BROADCAST,MULTICAST,UP,LOWER_UP> mtu 1500 qdisc noqueue state UP mode DEFAULT group default
    link/ether 00:0c:29:aa:91:f2 brd ff:ff:ff:ff:ff:ff
linux-3kk5:~ # brctl show
bridge name       bridge id               STP enabled        interfaces
br0               8000.000c29aa91f2       no                 eth0
```

Creating Virtual Machines

Once the KVM host has been configured and at least the network bridging is in place, you can proceed and create some virtual machines. To do this, you need a graphical interface, and from the graphical interface, you can start the Create Virtual Machines for Xen and KVM option in YaST. This starts the `virt-install` utility, which will now prompt you about how you would like to install the operating system (see Figure 7-3).

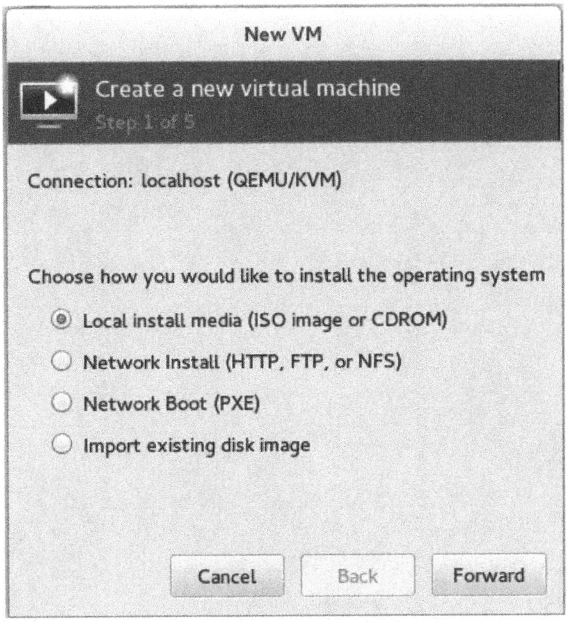

Figure 7-3. *Starting virtual machine installation*

To make installation of virtual machines easy, it's a good idea to use network installation. You might want to set up an installation server through HTTP, FTP, or NFS, that offers the repositories required for installation of the virtual machine and configure PXE as well, to ensure that the machines can boot from the network and get an installation image delivered automatically. Read Chapter 17 for more details on setting up such an environment.

If no installation server is available, select Local install media. This allows you to install the virtual machine from a physical DVD or an ISO image that is available on the KVM host.

After selecting the installation source you want to use, you can provide more details on where exactly the installation files can be found. If you have selected to install from a DVD or ISO, you'll select the disk you want to use (see Figure 7-4), or if you have selected to install from an installation server, you have to provide a URL to make sure that the files installation packages can be located (see Figure 7-5).

Figure 7-4. *Providing the path to access an installation disk or ISO*

Figure 7-5. *Providing details about the installation server*

After specifying details about the installation source you want to use, you'll have to provide information about the amount of RAM and CPUs you want to assign to the virtual machine (see Figure 7-6). You'll understand that it's not possible to go beyond the physical limits of available RAM and CPUs on your computer, but the total of all RAM that is used by your virtual machines doesn't have to be less than the total amount of RAM in the host.

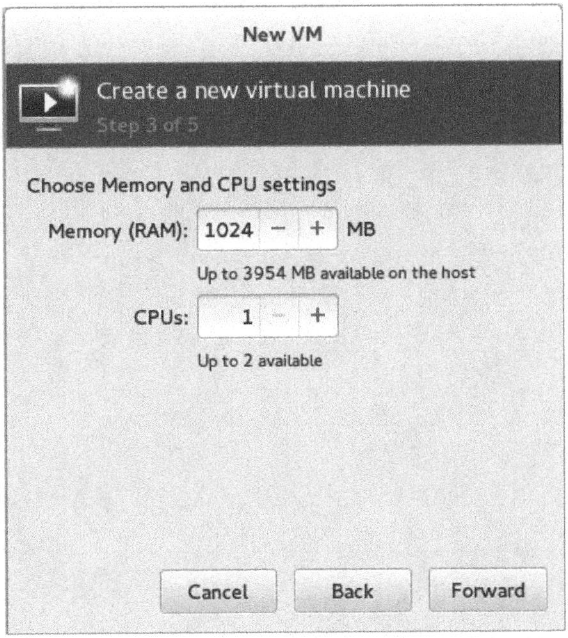

Figure 7-6. *Allocating virtual machine RAM and CPUs*

In KVM, a smart feature that is known as Kernel Shared Memory (KSM) is used. Using KSM makes it possible to load memory pages that are addressed multiple times once only, as shared memory. That means that if you have four virtual machines that are all using the same Linux kernel, you don't physically have to load that kernel four times as well, which means that the total amount of RAM that is configured on your virtual machines can go beyond the total amount of RAM in the host.

After allocating RAM and CPUs to the virtual machine, you'll have to configure storage (see Figure 7-7). The easy solution is to create a disk image on the computer's hard drive. That option will create a disk file for each virtual machine. This is an easy option, if you don't want to take additional measures at the storage level. If you want a more advanced setup for storage, it makes sense to create an LVM logical volume for each virtual machine and configure that as storage, using Select managed or other existing storage options.

Figure 7-7. *Selecting storage*

After selecting which storage to use, you'll see a summary screen. From this screen, you can start the installation of your virtual machine.

Managing KVM Virtual Machines

Once the virtual machine has been installed, you can start using it. On operational virtual machines, there are a few parameters that can be managed as well. Many of these can be managed from the graphical interfaces that are offered through the virt-managerb utility. These include networking and virtual machine properties. Alternatively, the virsh command-line utility can be used for performing basic management tasks.

Managing KVM Networking

Networking is an important part of virtual machine management. The network properties can be accessed through Virtual Machine Manager, by selecting the local hypervisor, which is indicated as localhost (qemu). After selecting this, you'll see the window shown in Figure 7-8, from which the network interfaces and the virtual networks can be managed.

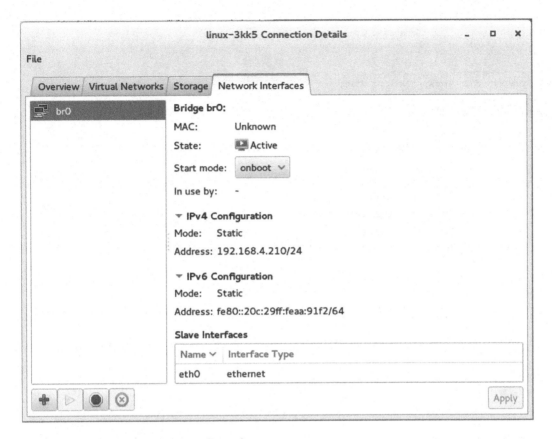

Figure 7-8. *Managing virtual network interfaces*

By default, the virtual bridge that is active on the KVM host offers networking through NAT. On the virtual network, a private IP address is ranged, and users in the same network can access other hosts in that network. External users, however, cannot access hosts in the NATted network directly. The default IP address for the internal NATted network is 192.168.4.0/24.

In many cases, the default NATted network works well, but in some cases, it does not, and you might require something else. To create an alternative network configuration, select the Virtual Networks tab (see Figure 7-9). On this tab, you can create different virtual network configurations that can be connected to the network interfaces seen on the Network Interfaces tab.

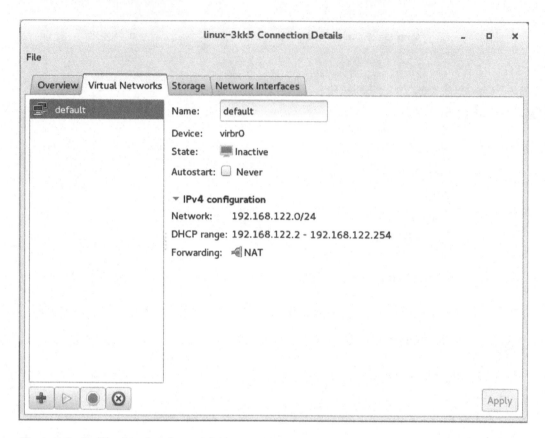

Figure 7-9. *Configuring virtual networks*

When adding new virtual networks, you'll walk through a small wizard. The last screen in the window asks how you want to be connected to the physical network. On this screen, you can select between an Isolated virtual network and Forwarding to physical network. The Isolated virtual network is what it says it is: a network that is connected to nothing else. If you want to connect the network to the outside world, you'll have to select the Forwarding to physical network option. This option first lets you select the physical network to connect to and, next, has you select a mode. You can choose between NAT and routed modes. In NAT mode, the network configuration of virtual machines is set up automatically, which ensures an easy connection to external computers. If selecting Routed networking, you'll have to manually configure routing between the internal virtual network and external networks (see Figure 7-10).

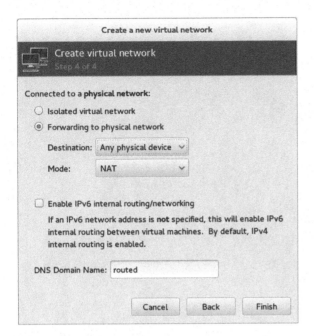

Figure 7-10. *Setting up virtual networking*

Managing Virtual Machine Properties

On a virtual machine, much virtual hardware is available. This hardware can be managed and changed by opening the virtual machine in virt-manager and clicking the lightbulb. This gives the interface that can be seen in Figure 7-11.

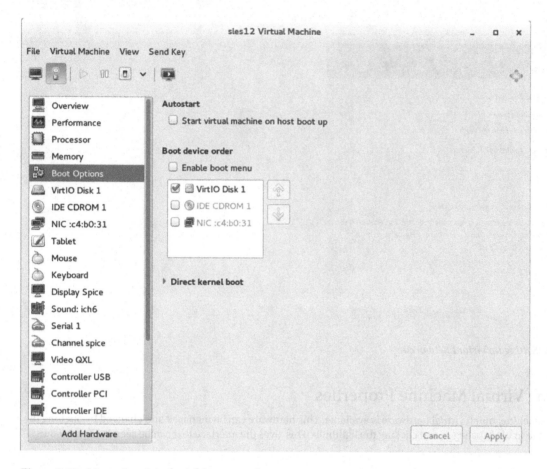

Figure 7-11. *Managing virtual machine properties*

As you can see in Figure 7-11, an interface is available for all elements of the hardware that is configured in the virtual machine, and many properties of the devices can be managed. This includes advanced settings, such as properties of hardware devices, but also more basic settings, such as the amount of RAM or hard disks allocated to a virtual machine. Note that for many changes in the virtual hardware configuration, the virtual machine must be rebooted. There are also hardware settings that can only be changed while the virtual machine is powered off.

Managing Virtual Machines from the Command Line

In addition to the options that are offered from the graphical interface, virtual machines can be managed from the command line as well, using the `virsh` utility. `virsh` offers a shell interface with a huge amount of options that allow advanced administrators to perform any possible manipulation on virtual machines. To start with, there is `virsh list`, which shows a list of all virtual machines that are currently running. It doesn't show virtual machines that are not operational, however. Use `virsh list --all` to see them too.

From the command line, the state of a virtual machine can be managed also. Type `virsh shutdown vmname` to shut down a virtual machine gracefully. If that doesn't work, you can use `virsh destroy vmname`, which halts it immediately, as if you have pulled the power plug.

The virtual machine itself is stored in a configuration file, which is in /etc/libvirt/qemu. All settings of the virtual machine are stored in that configuration file. You can see an example of it in Listing 7-3.

Listing 7-3. Sample Virtual Machine Configuration File

```
linux-3kk5:/etc/libvirt/qemu # cat sles12.xml
<!--
WARNING: THIS IS AN AUTO-GENERATED FILE. CHANGES TO IT ARE LIKELY TO BE
OVERWRITTEN AND LOST. Changes to this xml configuration should be made using:
  virsh edit sles12
or other application using the libvirt API.
-->

<domain type='kvm'>
  <name>sles12</name>
  <uuid>c0352e07-795d-404c-86a6-bf045f7aa729</uuid>
  <memory unit='KiB'>1048576</memory>
  <currentMemory unit='KiB'>1048576</currentMemory>
  <vcpu placement='static'>1</vcpu>
  <os>
    <type arch='x86_64' machine='pc-i440fx-2.0'>hvm</type>
    <boot dev='hd'/>
  </os>
  <features>
    <acpi/>
    <apic/>
    <pae/>
  </features>
  <cpu mode='custom' match='exact'>
    <model fallback='allow'>Westmere</model>
  </cpu>
  <clock offset='utc'>
    <timer name='rtc' tickpolicy='catchup'/>
    <timer name='pit' tickpolicy='delay'/>
    <timer name='hpet' present='no'/>
  </clock>
  <on_poweroff>destroy</on_poweroff>
  <on_reboot>restart</on_reboot>
  <on_crash>restart</on_crash>
  <pm>
    <suspend-to-mem enabled='no'/>
    <suspend-to-disk enabled='no'/>
  </pm>
  <devices>
    <emulator>/usr/bin/qemu-system-x86_64</emulator>
    <disk type='file' device='disk'>
      <driver name='qemu' type='qcow2'/>
      <source file='/var/lib/libvirt/images/sles12.qcow2'/>
      <target dev='vda' bus='virtio'/>
      <address type='pci' domain='0x0000' bus='0x00' slot='0x07' function='0x0'/>
    </disk>
```

```
<disk type='block' device='cdrom'>
  <driver name='qemu' type='raw'/>
  <target dev='hda' bus='ide'/>
  <readonly/>
  <address type='drive' controller='0' bus='0' target='0' unit='0'/>
</disk>
<controller type='usb' index='0' model='ich9-ehci1'>
  <address type='pci' domain='0x0000' bus='0x00' slot='0x05' function='0x7'/>
</controller>
<controller type='usb' index='0' model='ich9-uhci1'>
  <master startport='0'/>
  <address type='pci' domain='0x0000' bus='0x00' slot='0x05' function='0x0' multifunction='on'/>
</controller>
<controller type='usb' index='0' model='ich9-uhci2'>
  <master startport='2'/>
  <address type='pci' domain='0x0000' bus='0x00' slot='0x05' function='0x1'/>
</controller>
<controller type='usb' index='0' model='ich9-uhci3'>
  <master startport='4'/>
  <address type='pci' domain='0x0000' bus='0x00' slot='0x05' function='0x2'/>
</controller>
<controller type='pci' index='0' model='pci-root'/>
<controller type='ide' index='0'>
  <address type='pci' domain='0x0000' bus='0x00' slot='0x01' function='0x1'/>
</controller>
<controller type='virtio-serial' index='0'>
  <address type='pci' domain='0x0000' bus='0x00' slot='0x06' function='0x0'/>
</controller>
<interface type='bridge'>
  <mac address='52:54:00:c4:b0:31'/>
  <source bridge='br0'/>
  <model type='virtio'/>
  <address type='pci' domain='0x0000' bus='0x00' slot='0x03' function='0x0'/>
</interface>
<serial type='pty'>
  <target port='0'/>
</serial>
<console type='pty'>
  <target type='serial' port='0'/>
</console>
<channel type='spicevmc'>
  <target type='virtio' name='com.redhat.spice.0'/>
  <address type='virtio-serial' controller='0' bus='0' port='1'/>
</channel>
<input type='tablet' bus='usb'/>
<input type='mouse' bus='ps2'/>
<input type='keyboard' bus='ps2'/>
<graphics type='spice' autoport='yes'/>
<sound model='ich6'>
  <address type='pci' domain='0x0000' bus='0x00' slot='0x04' function='0x0'/>
</sound>
```

```
    <video>
      <model type='qxl' ram='65536' vram='65536' heads='1'/>
      <address type='pci' domain='0x0000' bus='0x00' slot='0x02' function='0x0'/>
    </video>
    <redirdev bus='usb' type='spicevmc'>
    </redirdev>
    <redirdev bus='usb' type='spicevmc'>
    </redirdev>
    <redirdev bus='usb' type='spicevmc'>
    </redirdev>
    <redirdev bus='usb' type='spicevmc'>
    </redirdev>
    <memballoon model='virtio'>
      <address type='pci' domain='0x0000' bus='0x00' slot='0x08' function='0x0'/>
    </memballoon>
    <rng model='virtio'>
      <backend model='random'>/dev/random</backend>
      <address type='pci' domain='0x0000' bus='0x00' slot='0x09' function='0x0'/>
    </rng>
  </devices>
</domain>
```

As is mentioned in the configuration file, its contents should not be edited directly, but by using the `virsh edit vmname` command, which ensures that all modifications are applied correctly. From the XML file, new virtual machines can be created easily as well: use `virsh create vmname.xml` to generate a new virtual machine from the XML code.

Summary

In this chapter, you've read how SUSE uses virtualization to make it easy to run multiple virtual hosts on one hardware box. You've read about the different virtualization technologies that exist and how KVM can be used to configure SUSE as a versatile hypervisor environment.

CHAPTER 8

Managing Hardware, the Kernel, and the Boot Procedure

As a Linux administrator, you have to know a bit about Linux server internals. That includes kernel management, hardware management, and the boot procedure on SUSE Linux Enterprise Server (SLES). In this chapter, you will read about how they all work.

Managing the Linux Kernel

The Linux kernel is the heart of the Linux operating system. It's the layer that sits between the processes that are running on a Linux server and the commands users are issuing, at one end, and the hardware in the computer, at the other end. It is the kernel that allows your computer to do smart things.

Glibc and System Calls

To be able to communicate to the operating system, commands, applications, and processes generate system calls. These system calls are provided through libraries, of which the glibc (also known as the C library) provides the most important functions. Because all commands, applications, and processes on Linux are compiled to use the C library, they can send uniform system calls to the operating system kernel. The kernel then uses these instructions to perform specific tasks (see Figure 8-1).

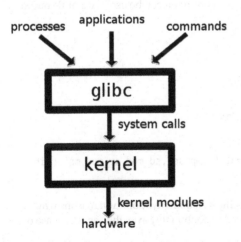

Figure 8-1. *Schematic Linux OS overview*

The Modular Kernel

In the old days of Linux, the kernel was monolithic. That meant that in order to access specific functionality, the functionality had to be compiled into the kernel. The modern Linux kernel is modular, and it is no longer necessary to compile the Linux kernel on a modern Linux distribution such as the SUSE Linux Enterprise Server (SLES). On the contrary, recompiling the kernel will most likely break the supportability of your installation. For that reason, you won't find the kernel sources and compiler tools easily.

For an SLES administrator, there are two common approaches to changing the way the kernel works. There is the /proc file system, and there are the kernel modules. Kernel modules can be seen as drivers that are loaded when needed. The /proc file system is a generic interface that contains tunables that an administrator can change to modify kernel behavior (see Figure 8-2). In Chapter 15, you can read in detail how to perform kernel optimization through /proc.

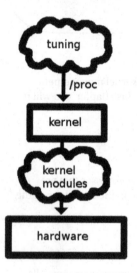

Figure 8-2. *Kernel modules and /proc overview*

lsmod and Kernel Module Dependencies

To get an overview of the kernel modules that are currently loaded, the lsmod command can be used. A sample output of this command can be seen in Listing 8-1.

Listing 8-1. Partial lsmod Output

```
vmwgfx              143303  2
ttm                  92240  1 vmwgfx
drm                 322623  3 ttm,vmwgfx
libata              235807  4 ahci,libahci,ata_generic,ata_piix
floppy               73522  0
sg                   40629  0
scsi_mod            244354  8 sg,scsi_transport_spi,libata,mptctl,mptspi,sd_mod,sr_mod,mptscsih
autofs4              42930  2
```

Speaking in a generic way, kernel modules are loaded to provide specific functionality. Common reasons why kernel modules are needed include addressing hardware and making specific functionality available, as is the case of file system drivers.

When loading kernel modules, dependencies are considered. A dependency exists when some other kernel modules are required to load a specific kernel module. The lsmod command shows an overview of these kernel module dependencies. You can see, for example, that the ttm module is needed by the vmwgfx module, and the ttm module, in turn, needs the drm module to be present. Normally, as a Linux administrator, you don't have to consider kernel module dependencies, as they are taken care of automatically. If, however, you wanted to unload a kernel module that is still needed by another kernel module, it would fail, because of that dependency. This is also why some kernel modules can never be unloaded and that to apply changes to the kernel, a reboot may be required.

Getting More Kernel Module Information

As an administrator, on occasion, you have to get more information about specific kernel modules. That is, in particular, because many kernel modules have parameters. These are tunable options that can be set while loading the kernel module. Parameters are used for fine-tuning kernel module behavior. By switching certain parameters on or off, the administrator can have the kernel module work in a more efficient way.

An example of how kernel module parameters can be useful is configuring a driver for a wireless network card. Often, these drivers offer support for multiple options, including options that you don't need on your server. By switching these options off, you might get better performance on your network card. To get a complete list of parameters that are supported by your hardware, use the modinfo command, as in modinfo e1000, which would give information about parameters supported by the e1000 kernel module. Listing 8-2 shows a partial output of that command.

Listing 8-2. Partial Output of modinfo e1000

```
linux-ia9r:~ # modinfo e1000
filename:       /lib/modules/3.12.26-3-default/kernel/drivers/net/ethernet/intel/e1000/e1000.ko
version:        7.3.21-k8-NAPI
license:        GPL
description:    Intel(R) PRO/1000 Network Driver
author:         Intel Corporation, <linux.nics@intel.com>
srcversion:     2C5D1F29B48A7A94A8F5D29
alias:          pci:v00008086d00002E6Esv*sd*bc*sc*i*
...
depends:
supported:      yes
intree:         Y
vermagic:       3.12.26-3-default SMP mod_unload modversions
signer:         SUSE Linux Enterprise Secure Boot Signkey
sig_key:        3F:B0:77:B6:CE:BC:6F:F2:52:2E:1C:14:8C:57:C7:77:C7:88:E3:E7
sig_hashalgo:   sha256
parm:           TxDescriptors:Number of transmit descriptors (array of int)
parm:           RxDescriptors:Number of receive descriptors (array of int)
parm:           Speed:Speed setting (array of int)
parm:           Duplex:Duplex setting (array of int)
parm:           AutoNeg:Advertised auto-negotiation setting (array of int)
parm:           FlowControl:Flow Control setting (array of int)
parm:           XsumRX:Disable or enable Receive Checksum offload (array of int)
parm:           TxIntDelay:Transmit Interrupt Delay (array of int)
parm:           TxAbsIntDelay:Transmit Absolute Interrupt Delay (array of int)
parm:           RxIntDelay:Receive Interrupt Delay (array of int)
parm:           RxAbsIntDelay:Receive Absolute Interrupt Delay (array of int)
parm:           InterruptThrottleRate:Interrupt Throttling Rate (array of int)
parm:           SmartPowerDownEnable:Enable PHY smart power down (array of int)
parm:           copybreak:Maximum size of packet that is copied to a new buffer on receive (uint)
parm:           debug:Debug level (0=none,...,16=all) (int)
```

In the output of the `modprobe` command, it is the `parm` lines that are of particular interest. These describe the available parameters and the values that can be given to them. In the next section, you'll read how you can use these parameters while loading kernel modules.

Loading and Unloading Kernel Modules

As an administrator, you normally don't have to manually load kernel modules to get the hardware support you need. Upon boot, hardware is detected automatically, and the appropriate kernel module will be loaded. When a system has already booted and new hardware devices are plugged in, the udev kernel helper process detects the hardware and will initiate it automatically, which includes the loading of kernel modules. So, under normal circumstances, as an administrator, you'll rarely have to load any kernel modules by hand. It may be useful for testing purposes, though.

To manually mount a kernel module, you'll use the `modprobe` command. So, if you want to check out the `ecryptfs` kernel module, for example, you would use `modprobe ecryptfs`. Using `modprobe` automatically considers all dependencies, so if any dependencies exist, `modprobe` will take care of them and automatically load them as well. To remove a kernel module that has been loaded, you'd use `modprobe -r`, followed by the name of the kernel module. So, in the case of the `ecryptfs` module, `modprobe -r ecryptfs` would do the trick. If a module is currently in use, however, you cannot manually unload it. The only way to get rid of used kernel modules is by rebooting your server (or by analyzing all of its dependencies, using `lsmod`, and seeing if you can manually unload all of them).

While loading a module using `modprobe`, you can also pass kernel module options. To do this, you first have to look up the option, using `modinfo`. Next, as an argument, you can specify the option with its desired value, while loading the kernel module. In the case of `ecryptfs`, for example, you could use `modprobe ecryptfs ecryptfs_verbosity=1`. If you want a module to be loaded with a specific option at all times, you can use `modprobe.conf`, as explained in the next section.

Using modprobe.d

To automate the loading of kernel module options, you can use the `modprobe.d` directory. In this directory, different configuration files can be created, containing relevant options, while loading kernel modules. The files in this directory are numbered and processed in order. That makes that, by default, the `00-system.conf` file is processed first, and the `99-local.conf` file is processed last, which ensures that options that are used in the `99-local.conf` file will overrule the options that were specified before it.

Specifying module options through `modprobe.d` is easy. You'll create a configuration file in `/etc/modprobe.d`, or modify the contents of the `99-local.conf` file, and specify an options line, followed by the name of the kernel module, the arguments you want to use, and the values you want to set for the parameters you've specified. So, in the case of the `ecryptfs_verbosity` module that was used before, you could put the following line in `/etc/modprobe.d/99-local.conf`:

```
options ecryptfs ecryptfs_verbosity=1
```

EXERCISE 8-1. WORKING WITH KERNEL MODULES

In this exercise, you'll manually load a kernel module, find out which options it supports, and, after that, automate the loading of the kernel module, together with the selected options.

1. Type modinfo ecryptfs to show available options for the ecryptfs kernel module.

2. Type modprobe ecryptfs ecryptfs_verbosity=1 to load the kernel module with increased verbosity.

3. Open the file /etc/modprobe.d/99-local and enter the following line:

    options ecryptfs ecryptfs_verbosity=1

4. Type modprobe -r ecryptfs, followed by modprobe ecryptfs. The module should now be loaded with increased verbosity.

5. Type dmesg to see kernel messages about the kernel module that was just loaded. This should confirm the increased verbosity setting.

Managing Hardware

As an administrator, you normally don't have to do much hardware management. If hardware isn't initializing properly, it is nice to be familiar with some of the tools that allow you to analyze the hardware setup that is used. To start with, there are the ls- utilities. I'm not talking about ls, which shows the contents of directories, but utilities such as lspci, pscpu, and lsusb. Apart from that, there is information you can get from udev and the /sys file system.

Using lspic, lsusb, and lscpu

Using the lspci command, you can get details about hardware that is installed on the PCI bus. The result of this command does not show you if the hardware can be used on Linux; it just shows which hardware has been probed. You can request further details about that hardware by using lspci -v, for verbose mode, or lspci -k, to show only kernel modules that have been loaded for specific devices. So, if, for example, you want to find out which kernel module is used for the network card that is installed on your server, use lscpi -k (see Listing 8-3).

Listing 8-3. Showing Kernel Module Information with lspci -k

```
02:01.0 Ethernet controller: Intel Corporation 82545EM Gigabit Ethernet Controller (Copper) (rev 01)
        Subsystem: VMware PRO/1000 MT Single Port Adapter
        Kernel driver in use: e1000
        Kernel modules: e1000
02:02.0 Multimedia audio controller: Ensoniq ES1371 / Creative Labs CT2518 [AudioPCI-97] (rev 02)
        Subsystem: Ensoniq AudioPCI 64V/128 / Creative Sound Blaster CT4810
        Kernel driver in use: snd_ens1371
        Kernel modules: snd_ens1371
02:03.0 USB controller: VMware USB2 EHCI Controller
        Subsystem: VMware USB2 EHCI Controller
        Kernel driver in use: ehci-pci
        Kernel modules: ehci_pci
```

```
02:05.0 SATA controller: VMware SATA AHCI controller
        Subsystem: VMware SATA AHCI controller
        Kernel driver in use: ahci
        Kernel modules: ahci
```

For finding information about USB devices, there is the lsusb command. When used without arguments, this command will only list the devices found on your computer. You can also use it in tree mode, to find out information about relations between devices using lsusb -t. Using lsusb, you won't see which kernel module is loaded, however. If you must know that, you'll have to use the usb-devices command. Partial output of this command is shown in Listing 8-4.

Listing 8-4. Getting Details About USB Devices with usb-devices

```
T:  Bus=02 Lev=01 Prnt=01 Port=00 Cnt=01 Dev#=  2 Spd=12   MxCh= 0
D:  Ver= 1.10 Cls=00(>ifc ) Sub=00 Prot=00 MxPS= 8 #Cfgs=  1
P:  Vendor=0e0f ProdID=0003 Rev=01.03
S:  Manufacturer=VMware
S:  Product=VMware Virtual USB Mouse
C:  #Ifs= 1 Cfg#= 1 Atr=c0 MxPwr=0mA
I:  If#= 0 Alt= 0 #EPs= 1 Cls=03(HID  ) Sub=01 Prot=02 Driver=usbhid

T:  Bus=02 Lev=01 Prnt=01 Port=01 Cnt=02 Dev#=  3 Spd=12   MxCh= 7
D:  Ver= 1.10 Cls=09(hub  ) Sub=00 Prot=00 MxPS= 8 #Cfgs=  1
P:  Vendor=0e0f ProdID=0002 Rev=01.00
S:  Product=VMware Virtual USB Hub
C:  #Ifs= 1 Cfg#= 1 Atr=e0 MxPwr=0mA
I:  If#= 0 Alt= 0 #EPs= 1 Cls=09(hub  ) Sub=00 Prot=00 Driver=hub

T:  Bus=02 Lev=02 Prnt=03 Port=00 Cnt=01 Dev#=  4 Spd=12   MxCh= 0
D:  Ver= 2.00 Cls=e0(wlcon) Sub=01 Prot=01 MxPS=64 #Cfgs=  1
P:  Vendor=0e0f ProdID=0008 Rev=01.00
S:  Manufacturer=VMware
S:  Product=Virtual Bluetooth Adapter
S:  SerialNumber=000650268328
C:  #Ifs= 2 Cfg#= 1 Atr=c0 MxPwr=0mA
I:  If#= 0 Alt= 0 #EPs= 3 Cls=e0(wlcon) Sub=01 Prot=01 Driver=btusb
I:  If#= 1 Alt= 0 #EPs= 2 Cls=e0(wlcon) Sub=01 Prot=01 Driver=btusb
```

Another useful hardware-related command is lscpu. This command shows you properties of the CPUs in use on your computer. Use this command to find out if specific features are supported. In Listing 8-5, you can see partial output of this command.

Listing 8-5. Listing CPU Information with lscpu

```
linux-3kk5:~ # lscpu
Architecture:          x86_64
CPU op-mode(s):        32-bit, 64-bit
Byte Order:            Little Endian
CPU(s):                2
On-line CPU(s) list:   0,1
Thread(s) per core:    1
Core(s) per socket:    1
```

```
Socket(s):              2
NUMA node(s):           1
Vendor ID:              GenuineIntel
CPU family:             6
Model:                  58
Model name:             Intel(R) Core(TM) i7-3740QM CPU @ 2.70GHz
Stepping:               9
CPU MHz:                2693.694
BogoMIPS:               5387.38
Hypervisor vendor:      VMware
Virtualization type:    full
L1d cache:              32K
L1i cache:              32K
L2 cache:               256K
L3 cache:               6144K
NUMA node0 CPU(s):      0,1
```

The lscpu command summarizes information about the CPU. If you need further details, you'll have to go to the /proc/cpuinfo file. This file gets detailed information about your CPU directly from the kernel, and it gives much more information about specific features in use on your CPU.

Understanding udev

To initialize hardware, the kernel is helped by the udev process. This process is started early during the boot procedure, and it will help the kernel loading hardware devices. What it comes down to is that the kernel detects a hardware event—such as connecting a USB device—and it will pass information to udev, which can act upon the hardware event.

To determine how hardware should be initialized, udev uses rules. The default rules are in /usr/lib/udev/rules.d, and the system administrator can create custom rules in /etc/udev/rules.d. The contents of the udev rules consists of scripts in which a specific syntax is used for initializing devices. Listing 8-6 gives an example of such a file, the contents of the 70-printers.rules file. From the rules in this file, you can see that the trigger is an action on a specific USB interface, containing the ID 0701. Based on that number, a printer can be recognized. The result of detecting a printer is that systemd should be activated, to run the con-printer service. This passes the initialization over to systemd, which takes care about further hardware initialization. (See the section "Working with systemd," later in this chapter, for more details about systemd).

Listing 8-6. Sample Contents of a udev Rules File

```
linux-3kk5:/usr/lib/udev/rules.d # cat 70-printers.rules
# Low-level USB device add trigger
ACTION=="add", SUBSYSTEM=="usb", ENV{DEVTYPE}=="usb_device", ENV{ID_USB_INTERFACES}=="*:0701??:*",
TAG+="systemd", ENV{SYSTEMD_WANTS}="con-printer@usb-$env{BUSNUM}-$env{DEVNUM}.service"
# Low-level USB device remove trigger
ACTION=="remove", SUBSYSTEM=="usb", ENV{ID_USB_INTERFACES}=="*:0701*:*",
RUN+="udev-configure-printer remove %p"
```

A useful command to use to determine what's happening in udev is udevadm. In particular, udevadm monitor, which gives information about the hardware events that udev has dealt with. In Listing 8-7, you can see a partial output of this command, which allows you to trace the initialization of a hardware device, from the moment it is plugged to the computer until the moment that the related block devices have been initialized.

Listing 8-7. Tracing udev Activity with udevadm monitor

```
linux-3kk5:~ # udevadm monitor
monitor will print the received events for:
UDEV - the event which udev sends out after rule processing
KERNEL - the kernel uevent

KERNEL[1906.571563] add        /devices/pci0000:00/0000:00:11.0/0000:02:03.0/usb1/1-1 (usb)
KERNEL[1906.715316] add        /devices/pci0000:00/0000:00:11.0/0000:02:03.0/usb1/1-1/1-1:1.0 (usb)
KERNEL[1906.715356] add        /devices/pci0000:00/0000:00:11.0/0000:02:03.0/usb1/1-1/1-1:1.1 (usb)
UDEV  [1906.821560] add        /devices/pci0000:00/0000:00:11.0/0000:02:03.0/usb1/1-1 (usb)
KERNEL[1906.932148] add        /module/usb_storage (module)
KERNEL[1906.933266] add        /devices/pci0000:00/0000:00:11.0/0000:02:03.0/usb1/1-1/1-1:1.0/host33
(scsi)
...
        /devices/pci0000:00/0000:00:11.0/0000:02:03.0/usb1/1-1/1-1:1.1/host34/target34:0:0/34:0:0:0/
bsg/34:0:0:0 (bsg)
KERNEL[1907.941389] add        /devices/virtual/bdi/8:16 (bdi)
KERNEL[1907.941698] add        /devices/virtual/bdi/11:1 (bdi)
UDEV  [1907.941709] add        /devices/virtual/bdi/11:1 (bdi)
UDEV  [1907.941715] add        /devices/virtual/bdi/8:16 (bdi)
KERNEL[1907.941854] add        /devices/pci0000:00/0000:00:11.0/0000:02:03.0/usb1/1-1/1-1:1.1/host34/
                               target34:0:0/34:0:0:0/block/sdb (block)
KERNEL[1907.941867] add        /devices/pci0000:00/0000:00:11.0/0000:02:03.0/usb1/1-1/1-1:1.0/host33/
                               target33:0:0/33:0:0:0/block/sr1 (block)
KERNEL[1907.941874] add        /devices/pci0000:00/0000:00:11.0/0000:02:03.0/usb1/1-1/1-1:1.0/host33/
                               target33:0:0/33:0:0:0/scsi_device/33:0:0:0 (scsi_device)
...
KERNEL[1907.946186] change     /devices/pci0000:00/0000:00:11.0/0000:02:03.0/usb1/1-1/1-1:1.1/host34/
                               target34:0:0/34:0:0:0/block/sdb (block)
UDEV  [1907.983312] add        /devices/pci0000:00/0000:00:11.0/0000:02:03.0/usb1/1-1/1-1:1.1/host34/
                               target34:0:0/34:0:0:0/block/sdb (block)
UDEV  [1908.019997] add        /devices/pci0000:00/0000:00:11.0/0000:02:03.0/usb1/1-1/1-1:1.0/host33/
                               target33:0:0/33:0:0:0/block/sr1 (block)
UDEV  [1908.023783] change     /devices/pci0000:00/0000:00:11.0/0000:02:03.0/usb1/1-1/1-1:1.1/host34/
                               target34:0:0/34:0:0:0/block/sdb (block)
UDEV  [1908.148729] change     /devices/pci0000:00/0000:00:11.0/0000:02:03.0/usb1/1-1/1-1:1.0/host33/
                               target33:0:0/33:0:0:0/block/sr1 (block)
KERNEL[1918.432972] change     /devices/pci0000:00/0000:00:11.0/0000:02:03.0/usb1/1-1/1-1:1.0/host33/
                               target33:0:0/33:0:0:0/block/sr1 (block)
UDEV  [1918.536263] change     /devices/pci0000:00/0000:00:11.0/0000:02:03.0/usb1/1-1/1-1:1.0/host33/
                               target33:0:0/33:0:0:0/block/sr1 (block)
```

The /dev Directory

Ultimately, the activity of udev results in the creation of device files (also referred to as device nodes) in the /dev directory. These device nodes allow users to communicate with devices that are managed by the kernel. From the kernel perspective, a device is managed through a major:minor number. To make it easier for users to work with devices, device files are provided. Listing 8-8 gives a partial overview of some content of the /dev directory.

Listing 8-8. Devices, As Seen from the /dev Directory

```
linux-3kk5:/dev # ls -ld s*
brw-rw----  1 root disk   8,   0 Sep 19  2014 sda
brw-rw----  1 root disk   8,   1 Sep 19  2014 sda1
brw-rw----  1 root disk   8,   2 Sep 19  2014 sda2
brw-rw----  1 root disk   8,  16 Sep 19 04:33 sdb
crw-rw----+ 1 root cdrom 21,   0 Sep 19  2014 sg0
crw-rw----  1 root disk  21,   1 Sep 19  2014 sg1
crw-rw----  1 root disk  21,   2 Sep 19 04:33 sg2
crw-rw----+ 1 root cdrom 21,   3 Sep 19 04:33 sg3
drwxrwxrwt  2 root root       160 Sep 19 04:02 shm
crw-------  1 root root  10, 231 Sep 19  2014 snapshot
drwxr-xr-x  3 root root       200 Sep 19  2014 snd
brw-rw----+ 1 root cdrom 11,   0 Sep 19  2014 sr0
brw-rw----+ 1 root cdrom 11,   1 Sep 19 04:33 sr1
lrwxrwxrwx  1 root root        15 Sep 19  2014 stderr -> /proc/self/fd/2
lrwxrwxrwx  1 root root        15 Sep 19  2014 stdin -> /proc/self/fd/0
lrwxrwxrwx  1 root root        15 Sep 19  2014 stdout -> /proc/self/fd/1
```

If you look at Listing 8-8, you can see the device major and monitor just before the column that shows the date the device file was created. Note, for example, that there are devices for sda and sdb (the first two hard drives connected to this computer). Each of these files uses the major number 8, and you can see that device sda is on 8,0, whereas device sdb is on 8,16. The numbers between 0 and 16 (that is, from 1 up to 15) can be used to refer to partitions. That also means that the maximum amount of partitions that can be used in this way is limited to 15.

In the /dev directory, you'll find four different kinds of files, which can be recognized by the first character in the ls -l output (b,c,l,d). If this shows a b, you're looking at a block device. This device type is a storage device, what can be addressed in blocks. If you see a c, it's a character device, which normally deals with streams of characters that are sent to and from the device. Then there are also links and directories that refer to devices in other locations.

Understanding the /sys File System

To keep track of all the device-related information, the Linux kernel uses the /sys file system. This file system contains a few directories that allow administrators to look at devices from different perspectives. There is, for example, the /sys/module directory, which allows you to look up information from the device kernel module, or /dev/bus, which allows you to go through the hardware bus that the device is connected to.

For each device, different configuration files are created on the fly, containing device parameters. For an administrator who wants to trace device information, these files can be useful. When looking for specific information, you should consider the top-level directories as entry points that allow you to look up information in a specific way. Because different entry points are used to refer to the same information, you'll see that many symbolic links are used in this structure as well.

In the files in /sys, you will find that the information that is shown is not standardized. That means that on some occasions, you will find the information you're looking for in this file system, and sometimes you won't. Take, for example, the information about kernel modules on your system. In /sys/module/e1000/parameters, you can find all kernel modules that don't use their default values, but in the ecryptfs kernel module directory, there is no parameters subdirectory showing you this information. This makes the /sys file system of limited use for looking up specific information.

Managing the Boot Procedure

In the boot procedure, the Linux kernel is started, and from that, all services that are required for full functionality have to be initialized. In this section, you'll read all there is to know about the SUSE Linux Enterprise Server 12 startup procedure.

Understanding the Boot Procedure

Basically, three things are happening in the boot procedure of your SLES 12 system. It starts with the boot loader GRUB2 that is started from the boot sector of your hard drive—no matter whether UEFI or BIOS is used. The boot loader, in turn, will load the kernel and the initramfs, and from there, systemd is started. systemd is responsible for starting everything else, including all services that are used on your server.

Configuring GRUB2

GRUB2 is the boot loader. Its task is to start the operating system, which means that it loads the kernel with all of the options that have been specified while loading it. You can configure GRUB2 from YaST as well as from the command line, both of which will be covered in this section.

Configuring GRUB2 from YaST

To configure GRUB2 from YaST, select System ➤ Bootloader. This opens the screen shown in Figure 8-3. On this screen, you can set generic parameters on the Boot Code Options screen, specific kernel boot parameters on the Kernel Parameters part of the screen, and generic options to determine how the boot loader menu is displayed on the Bootloader Options screen.

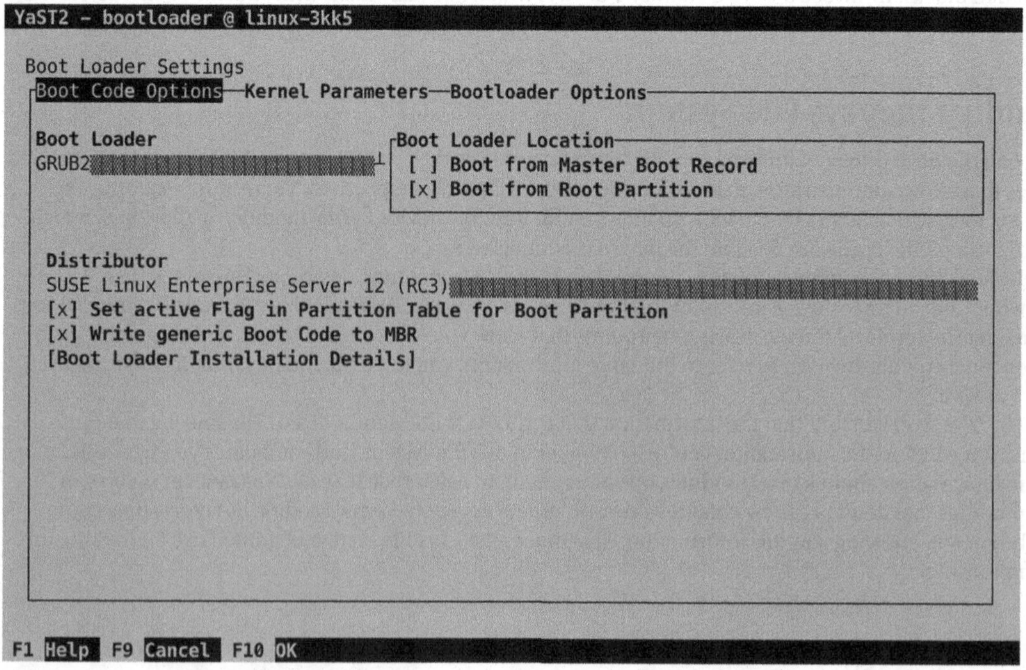

Figure 8-3. *Configuring GRUB2 from YaST*

On the Boot Code Options screen, you can first select which boot loader you want to use. GRUB2 is the default, and as an alternative, GRUB2-EFI can be selected. The latter is needed on a server that boots from a server that uses not BIOS but the Extended Firmware Interface (EFI) for booting. This is not normally something that you would change on a running system, however, as the appropriate boot loader will be selected while installing your server.

Next, you can select the Boot Loader Location from the Boot Code Options screen. You can choose between either booting from the master boot record or from the root partition. Note that "Boot from Master Boot Record" is also found on hard disks that use GPT (which don't have a Master Boot Record anymore). So, if you're on GPT, this option is still relevant.

By default, SLES 12 boots from the root partition. This protects your boot loader against accidental overwriting of the master boot record and makes it easier to configure a dual-boot system. To be able to boot from the boot loader that is installed in the root partition, that partition must be set as the active partition in the partition table. If you want to configure booting in a more straightforward way, you might as well select Boot from Master Boot Record option.

Also from the Boot Code Options screen, you can select the distribution you want to use. This makes sense if multiple versions of the kernel are installed and you want to switch to something that is not the default kernel. The Boot Loader Installation Details option is normally not used. It defines the order in which your hard disks are detected by GRUB2. Don't change this; it is fine if GRUB2 uses the first hard disk first and the second hard disk only after that.

From Kernel Parameters, shown in Figure 8-4, you can specify different options to pass to the kernel while booting. This is not the place to apply one-time-only changes to the kernel parameters. Use this for kernel parameters that you want loaded at all times. The Vga Mode options are useful if your display cannot handle the default resolution that is used. In general, Unspecified works fine. Use the down arrow key to select from among a list of available Vga Modes.

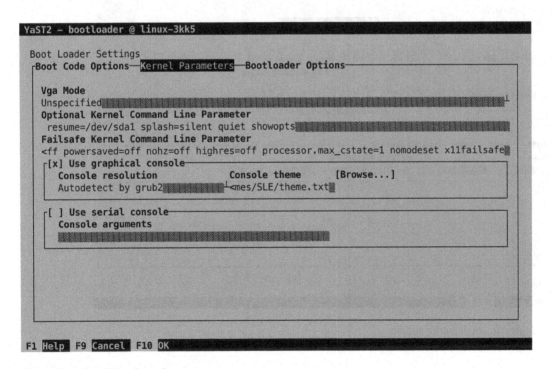

Figure 8-4. *Specifying kernel parameters*

Next, there are two Kernel Command Line Parameter lines: one for the default kernel that is started and the other for the failsafe kernel that you can use in case your server cannot boot normally anymore. If you have specific options to load, you'll do it here. You may like taking out the `splash=silent quiet showopts` part, which all do their part in hiding what is happening during boot.

The last part of the Kernel Parameters specifies which console to use. By default, a graphical console is used. Notice that "graphical console" in this case means a console that is directly attached; it doesn't necessarily mean that your server has to start with a graphical interface. If you don't want to see anything graphical on boot, make sure to set the Vga Mode to Text only.

The alternative to a graphical console is the serial console. This is useful if you want to connect your server to a remote console over a modem connection or if you want to use uncommon hardware, such as a braille terminal, which has to interface a serial console as well.

On the Bootloader Options screen (see Figure 8-5), you can specify generic options for GRUB2. These options relate to the boot menu that is shown and to how it is shown. To begin, you set a timeout. This is the time you have to do something if you don't want the server to be started with default options. You may elect to probe for a foreign OS, but that is most useful on a dual-boot system, where, for example, Windows is used besides Linux. As this is not typically used on a Linux server, you won't need this option. For use on an end-user desktop, you may like the Hide Menu on Boot option, so that end users won't get confused by the boot menu that is for experts only. On a server, it normally is fine to show this menu.

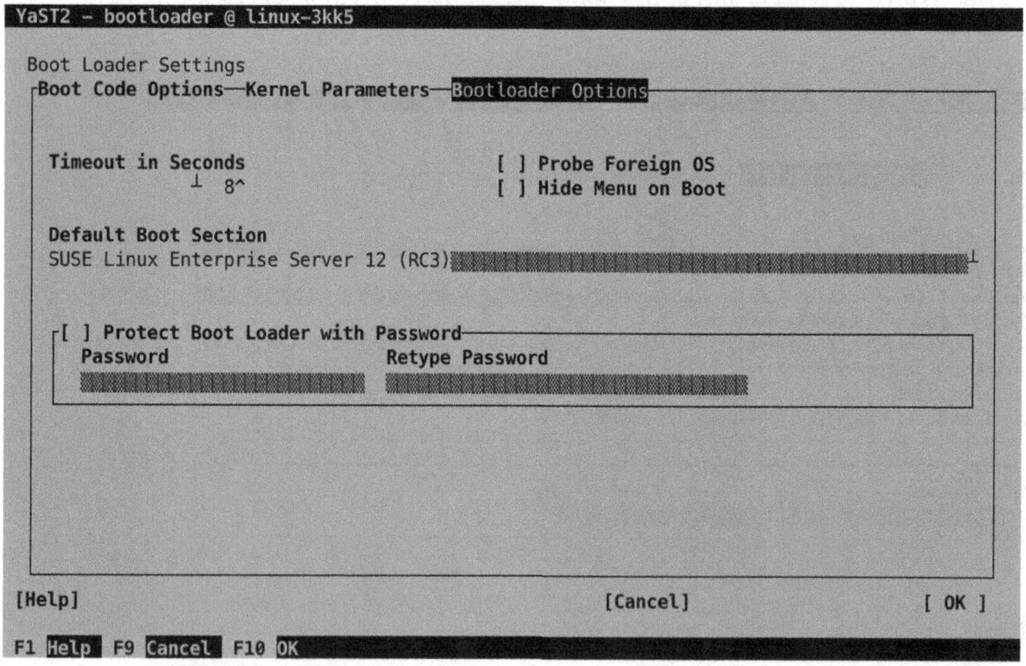

```
 YaST2 — bootloader @ linux-3kk5

  Boot Loader Settings
  ┌Boot Code Options—Kernel Parameters—Bootloader Options┐
  │                                                       │
  │                                                       │
  │   Timeout in Seconds             [ ] Probe Foreign OS │
  │            ⊥ 8^                  [ ] Hide Menu on Boot │
  │                                                       │
  │   Default Boot Section                                │
  │   SUSE Linux Enterprise Server 12 (RC3)▓▓▓▓▓▓▓▓▓▓▓⊥  │
  │                                                       │
  │   ┌[ ] Protect Boot Loader with Password─────────────┐│
  │   │ Password              Retype Password            ││
  │   │ ▓▓▓▓▓▓▓▓▓▓▓▓▓▓▓▓▓▓     ▓▓▓▓▓▓▓▓▓▓▓▓▓▓▓▓▓▓        ││
  │   └──────────────────────────────────────────────────┘│
  │                                                       │
  │                                                       │
  │                                                       │
  │                                                       │
  │                                                       │
  │                                                       │
  │                                                       │
 [Help]                     [Cancel]              [ OK ] │
  F1 Help  F9 Cancel  F10 OK
```

Figure 8-5. *Configuring boot loader options*

Next, you can select which operating system is started by default. Use the down arrow key to select from the drop-down list. Also, you can protect the boot loader with a password. This is a wise option to use, because it will prompt for a password before any options can be modified on the boot prompt.

Configuring GRUB2 Manually

The good thing about configuring GRUB2 from YaST is that you'll not see much difference between SLES 12 and previous versions. If you access the GRUB2 configuration from the command line, you'll notice that it's a completely different approach.

To understand working with GRUB2, you should know that the starting point of anything you want to change is the /etc/default/grub configuration file. This is the easy interface to modify common options you want to modify. After making modifications to this file, you'll use the grub2-mkconfig > /boot/grub2/grub.cfg command to write the results to the GRUB configuration file that is used while booting. Don't ever write modifications directly to /boot/grub2/grub.cfg, because you will break your configuration! While writing the GRUB2 configuration, the files in the /etc/grub.d directory are involved as well. In this file, GRUB2 specifics, such as menu options, are written.

Starting systemd

In the boot process, after loading the kernel, the systemd process is loaded, and it will take care of initializing everything else, including services on your computer. As systemd is about much more than just loading services, you'll find more details about it in the next section.

Applying Essential Troubleshooting Skills

Normally, your server will just boot. On some occasions, it might not, because something is wrong. If that is the case, you can perform some troubleshooting operations from the GRUB2 boot menu. What you'll basically have to do from the GRUB2 boot menu is tell GRUB2 to start something else. You'll do this from the GRUB boot menu, shown in Figure 8-6.

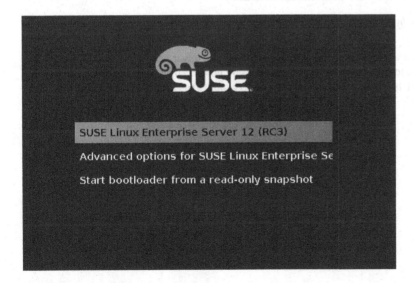

Figure 8-6. *The GRUB2 boot menu*

In the GRUB2 boot menu, you'll normally see three (at least) options. The first, default option allows you to start your server with default settings. The advanced options boot menu entry lets you boot your server with limited hardware support, which increases chances of booting successfully. The last option allows you to boot from a Btrfs snapshot.

In the Btrfs file system, snapshots are created to keep the state of your server. Each time you make modifications from YaST, the old state of the server is written to a snapshot, and all these snapshots are available from the GRUB2 boot menu. This makes it easy to revert to a previous configuration. In the snapshot boot loader menu, you can see the different snapshot states existing on your server, and you only have to select it (see Figure 8-7). You should realize that by selecting to boot from a snapshot, all modifications that have been applied after the snapshot will get lost.

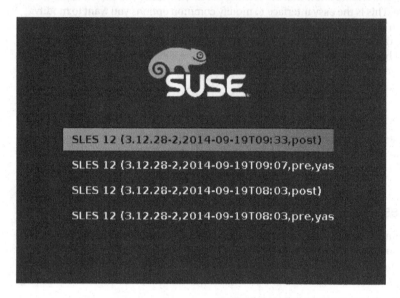

Figure 8-7. *Reverting to a previous state by selecting a snapshot*

If you want to specify kernel options while booting, you can type them in the lower part of the screen. If a GRUB password has been enabled, you'll have to press *e* to open the GRUB2 menu editor. This opens the interface that you can see in Figure 8-8 (which, in fact, is just the contents of the /boot/grub2/grub.cfg file that has been loaded in memory).

```
                        GNU GRUB   version 2.02~beta2

 setparams 'SUSE Linux Enterprise Server 12 (RC3)'

        load_video
        set gfxpayload=keep
        insmod gzio
        insmod part_msdos
        insmod btrfs
        set root='hd0,msdos2'
        if [ x$feature_platform_search_hint = xy ]; then
            search --no-floppy --fs-uuid --set=root --hint-bios=hd0,msdos2\
 --hint-efi=hd0,msdos2 --hint-baremetal=ahci0,msdos2 --hint='hd0,msdos2'\
 7541b53d-2f53-44f5-8f28-155804b69de1
        else
            search --no-floppy --fs-uuid --set=root 7541b53d-2f53-44f5-8f2\
 8-155804b69de1                                                          ↓


     Minimum Emacs-like screen editing is supported. TAB lists
     completions. Press Ctrl-x or F10 to boot, Ctrl-c or F2 for a
     command-line or ESC to discard edits and return to the GRUB
     menu.
```

Figure 8-8. *Modifying GRUB options at boot time*

To add specific boot options, you'll have to find the line that starts with linux /boot/vmlinuz. This is the line that loads the kernel. At the end of this line, you can specify the options you need to get your server back in a working state. If, for example, your server is in a nonoperational state, you may add the boot argument systemd.unit=emergency.target, which starts the server in emergency mode. After entering specific boot options, use the Ctrl+X key sequence to boot. If you have just entered emergency mode by adding the emergency.target option, you'll be prompted for the root password. After entering the root password successfully, you'll get access to the server and can start repairing it (see Figure 8-9).

```
[    4.974067] sd 30:0:0:0: [sda] Assuming drive cache: write through
[    4.976179] sd 30:0:0:0: [sda] Assuming drive cache: write through
[    4.977604] sd 30:0:0:0: [sda] Assuming drive cache: write through
Welcome to emergency mode! After logging in, type "journalctl -xb" to view
system logs, "systemctl reboot" to reboot, "systemctl default" to try again
to boot into default mode.
Give root password for maintenance
(or press Control-D to continue):
```

Figure 8-9. *Entering emergency mode*

While entering the emergency.target mode, you have to specify the password for the user root. If you don't have the root password for the server you want to connect to, you'll have to apply a different procedure. This procedure is summarized in Exercise 8-2.

EXERCISE 8-2. CHANGING THE ROOT PASSWORD

1. At the GRUB2 boot prompt, add the kernel argument rd.break. This will stop the boot process at the last stages of initializing the inird process and drop a root shell in which you don't have to enter any password.

2. At this very early stage of the boot process, the root file system has not been mounted on the / directory yet. It is on the temporary /sysroot directory, where it is mounted read-only. To get read/write access to it, type mount -o remount,rw /sysroot.

3. Now you need to make your root file system accessible on the / directory. To do this, type chroot /sysroot. This will make the contents of the /sysroot directory the a ctual system root.

4. At this point, you can type passwd, to change the root password.

Working with systemd

In previous versions of SUSE Linux Enterprise Server (SLES), many scripts were involved to start all services on a Linux computer. In SLES 12, this has changed. systemd is used, and systemd is basically responsible for starting everything. This section explains how systemd is organized and how as an administrator you can work with systemd.

Understanding systemd

After loading the Linux kernel, systemd is the first process that is started. It is responsible for starting everything else. systemd is responsible for starting much more than just services; it initializes sockets, mounts, and many other items. To take care of all this, systemd works with unit files. A unit in a systemd context can be best described as a thing. That isn't very specific, but it gets exactly to the point because so many different things can be managed from systemd. To get an overview of the different things that F can manage, use the systemctl -t help command (see Listing 8-9).

Listing 8-9. Overview of systemd Unit Files

```
linux-3kk5:~ # systemctl -t help
Available unit types:
service
socket
busname
target
snapshot
device
mount
automount
swap
timer
path
slice
scope
```

The unit files in systemd are stored in two locations. The directory /usr/lib/systemd/system contains the default unit files that are copied to your server on installation. The /etc/systemd/system directory contains configuration that is specific for your server or configuration that you have modified yourself. In SLES 12, it is important to distinguish between this default configuration and custom configuration settings.

Understanding Unit File Contents

As systemd provides a common interface for loading unit files, the unit file itself can be fairly simple. In Listing 8-10, you can see sample contents for one of the unit files.

Listing 8-10. Contents of the apache2.service File

```
[Unit]
Description=The Apache Webserver
Wants=network.target nss-lookup.target
After=network.target nss-lookup.target
Before=getty@tty1.service

[Service]
Type=notify
PrivateTmp=true
EnvironmentFile=/etc/sysconfig/apache2
ExecStart=/usr/sbin/start_apache2 -D SYSTEMD -DFOREGROUND -k start
ExecReload=/usr/sbin/start_apache2 -D SYSTEMD -DFOREGROUND -k graceful
ExecStop=/usr/sbin/start_apache2 -D SYSTEMD -DFOREGROUND -k graceful-stop

[Install]
WantedBy=multi-user.target
Alias=httpd.service
```

In the unit files, there are three generic sections. The first section describes the unit file itself. It defines ordering dependencies, and it defines the so-called wants. Wants define other units that are required by this specific unit file. In the sample configuration file, you can see that there are wants for different targets. For now, we'll consider a target as a group of unit files. More details are provided later in this chapter.

After the unit parameters, there are the parameters that define how the service should be started. In this part, the environment is defined, as well as the command that is used to start, reload, or stop the unit files. The six lines in the Service section of the unit file in Listing 8-10 basically replace hundreds of lines of code that were used in old-style init scripts. systemd can do this, because it defines the common interface for working with unit files.

In the last part of the unit file, the Install section defines what should happen when the unit file is enabled (see the next section). When it is enabled, it is WantedBy the collection of unit files known as the multi-user.target.

Understanding Targets

To define dependencies and make sure that unit files are started at the right moment, systemd uses targets. A target is a group of unit files. Between targets, dependency relations can be defined by means of wants. That allows administrators to chain targets together to get a server in a desired state.

Two important targets in systemd are the multi-user.target and the graphical.target. Starting these targets brings the server into a fully operational state in which the multi-user.target doesn't use a graphical interface, whereas in the graphical.target, a full graphical interface is started. The definition of the target file itself is relatively simple, as you can see from Listing 8-11.

Listing 8-11. Contents of the `multi-user.target` File

```
[Unit]
Description=Multi-User System
Documentation=man:systemd.special(7)
Requires=basic.target
Conflicts=rescue.service rescue.target
After=basic.target rescue.service rescue.target
AllowIsolate=yes
```

Understanding Wants

As you can see, the target does not know by itself about the unit files that are included. It just defines dependency relations. In the case of the `multi-user.target`, that means that it knows that it should be started after the `basic.target`, and that's all. To find out what is included in a target, there are wants. Wants exists as a directory in the file system. For the `multi-user.target`, for example, the default wants is in `/usr/lib/systemd/system/multi-user.target.wants`. This, however, does not contain everything that should be started with this target. The directory in `/usr/lib/systemd/system` only shows the items that are always wanted in the `multi-user.target`, no matter which services are started.

Apart from the wants files in `/usr/lib/systemd/system`, there are wants files in `/etc/systemd/system/multi-user.target.wants`. These are the files that are specific to this system, and in here, you'll find the typical services that will be started. If the administrator is enabling services, a corresponding wants file will be created in this directory.

Because the unit files define in which target a service is typically wanted, and the wants define that a service should indeed be started in a specific target, a complex hierarchy of dependencies is created. To get an overview of these dependencies, you can use the command `systemctl list-dependencies multi-user.target`, for example. This will show which targets will be started by starting the `multi-user target` and which unit files are included in these targets.

Understanding Other Unit Files

For an administrator, the service unit files are the most important types of files to work with. This is what changes between different servers. There are many other unit files also, but these won't be manipulated as often by administrators. Think of mount, path, swap, but also of slightly more exotic unit files, such as sockets, timers, and slices. Just don't bother about them too much. They are there, and upon installation of your server, they are related to the relevant wants and targets, and there's not much else an administrator needs to do with them.

Managing systemd Services

Even if `systemd` uses a sophisticated construction to make those system parts available that have to be available, for an administrator, managing services in `systemd` is not that difficult. The `systemctl` command is used to do this. This command has many options, but for managing `systemd` services, the `start`, `stop`, `status`, and `restart` options are the most significant.

To start the `apache2.service`, for example, you would use `systemctl start apache2`. To request its current status, you would use `systemctl status apache2`, and to stop it, the command `systemctl stop apache2` would be used. In Listing 8-12, you can see what the result of the `systemctl status apache2` command looks like.

Listing 8-12. Monitoring Service Status with `systemctl`

```
linux-3kk5:~ # systemctl status -l apache2
apache2.service - The Apache Webserver
   Loaded: loaded (/usr/lib/systemd/system/apache2.service; disabled)
   Active: active (running) since Fri 2014-09-19 07:27:16 EDT; 4s ago
 Main PID: 3047 (httpd2-prefork)
   Status: "Processing requests..."
   CGroup: /system.slice/apache2.service
           ├─3047 /usr/sbin/httpd2-prefork -f /etc/apache2/httpd.conf -D SYSTEMD -DFOREGROUND -k start
           ├─3068 /usr/sbin/httpd2-prefork -f /etc/apache2/httpd.conf -D SYSTEMD -DFOREGROUND -k start
           ├─3069 /usr/sbin/httpd2-prefork -f /etc/apache2/httpd.conf -D SYSTEMD -DFOREGROUND -k start
           ├─3070 /usr/sbin/httpd2-prefork -f /etc/apache2/httpd.conf -D SYSTEMD -DFOREGROUND -k start
           ├─3071 /usr/sbin/httpd2-prefork -f /etc/apache2/httpd.conf -D SYSTEMD -DFOREGROUND -k start
           ├─3073 /usr/sbin/httpd2-prefork -f /etc/apache2/httpd.conf -D SYSTEMD -DFOREGROUND -k start

Sep 19 07:27:11 linux-3kk5 start_apache2[3047]: AH00557: httpd2-prefork: apr_sockaddr_info_get()
failed for linux-3kk5
Sep 19 07:27:11 linux-3kk5 start_apache2[3047]: AH00558: httpd2-prefork: Could not reliably
determine the server's fully qualified domain name, using 127.0.0.1. Set the 'ServerName' directive
globally to suppress this message
```

As you can see, the `systemctl status` command not only shows if the service is running, it also gives detailed information about the process itself and errors that may have occurred while trying to start the service. `systemd` can do that because of `journald`, a `systemd` component that takes care of logging system information and writing it to the journal (a kind of log) from the very first stage of booting on.

Apart from starting and stopping services, `systemctl` is also used to enable or disable services. This means that with `systemctl`, you'll create a wants that starts the service in its default target. To create such a wants, use `systemctl enable apache2`, and to remove it again, use `systemctl disable apache2`. In Exercise 8-3, you can use these commands to find out for yourself what is happening.

EXERCISE 8-3. MANAGING SYSTEMD SERVICES

In this exercise, you'll install the `vsftpd` service, start it, and enable it.

1. Type `zypper in vsftpd`. This installs the `vsftpd` services (or tells you that it has already been installed).

2. Type `cd /etc/systemd/system/multi-user.target.wants` to change to the wants directory for the `multi-user.target`.

3. Type `ls` to see which wants are currently in there. There are no wants for the `vsftpd.service` file.

4. Type `systemctl start vsftpd`, followed by `systemctl status vsftpd`. This shows the current status overview for the `vsftd` service.

5. To make sure the service is restarted automatically on reboot, type `systemctl enable vsftpd`. Use the `ls` command again in the `multi-user.target.wants` directory. You'll see that a symbolic link is created to make sure the service is started automatically on reboot.

Working with systemd Targets

As an administrator, there's a limited amount of tasks related to management of targets as well. First, you can start your server in a different target, by entering the target name as a boot argument on the GRUB2 command line. You have seen how the boot argument `systemd.unit=rescue.target` will start your server in the rescue target mode.

You might want to change the default target also. The relevant targets that can be used as a default target and for troubleshooting are as follows:

- `emergency.target`: The most minimal target that starts a very basic system for troubleshooting

- `rescue.target`: A somewhat less minimal target, for rescue purposes only

- `multi-user.target`: What you want to get full functionality but no graphical interface on a server

- `graphical.target`: Gives a fully functional server with a GNOME graphical interface

To manage targets, you'll use the `systemctl get-default` target, which shows the current default target. Use `systemctl set-default graphical.target` to set the default target to the `graphical.target` (or any target you'd like to use).

Summary

In this chapter, you have learned how to manage hardware on your Linux server. You've also learned how to work with the kernel and how to manage the boot procedure. In addition, you have seen how to work in a GRUB2 environment and how to work with the new `systemd` solution.

■ ■ ■

## PART III

Networking SUSE Linux Enterprise Server

CHAPTER 9

■ ■ ■

Configuring Network Access

In this chapter, you'll learn all there is to know about networking in SLES. We'll cover the required information about manual network configuration, which makes clear which commands to use and which not to. Then you'll read how to perform configuration automated from YaST. You'll also learn which configuration files are related. Next, you'll read how the completely new wicked tool is used to configure network settings, as an alternative to the approach that can be taken using YaST. At the end of the chapter, you'll discover how to set up and work with Secure Shell (SSH), for secure remote network connections.

This chapter covers the following:

- Manual NIC Configuration
- Using YaST to Configure Networking
- Understanding Wicked
- Troubleshooting Networking
- Configuring SSH

It doesn't make sense to install a server if you don't have networking up and running. This chapter teaches all you need to know about networking.

Manual NIC Configuration

In all cases, your server should be configured to start the network interfaces automatically. In many cases, however, it's also useful if you can manually create a configuration for a network card. This is especially useful if you're experiencing problems and want to test if a given configuration works, before writing it down to a configuration file.

The classic tool for manual network configuration and monitoring is ifconfig. This command conveniently provides an overview of the current configuration of all network cards, including some usage statistics that show how much traffic has been handled by the network card since it was activated. But it has been deprecated, since the release of Linux 2.0 kernels (back in the mid-1990s), so you shouldn't use it anymore. Listing 9-1 shows what the ifconfig output typically looks like.

Listing 9-1. ifconfig Output

```
linux-kscc:~ # ifconfig
ens33     Link encap:Ethernet  HWaddr 00:0C:29:3E:D8:59
          inet addr:192.168.4.12  Bcast:192.168.4.255  Mask:255.255.255.0
          inet6 addr: fe80::20c:29ff:fe3e:d859/64 Scope:Link
          UP BROADCAST RUNNING MULTICAST  MTU:1500  Metric:1
          RX packets:80 errors:0 dropped:0 overruns:0 frame:0
```

```
          TX packets:52 errors:0 dropped:0 overruns:0 carrier:0
          collisions:0 txqueuelen:1000
          RX bytes:12186 (11.9 Kb)  TX bytes:7473 (7.2 Kb)

lo        Link encap:Local Loopback
          inet addr:127.0.0.1  Mask:255.0.0.0
          inet6 addr: ::1/128 Scope:Host
          UP LOOPBACK RUNNING  MTU:65536  Metric:1
          RX packets:20 errors:0 dropped:0 overruns:0 frame:0
          TX packets:20 errors:0 dropped:0 overruns:0 carrier:0
          collisions:0 txqueuelen:0
          RX bytes:1376 (1.3 Kb)  TX bytes:1376 (1.3 Kb)
```

Even if the ifconfig output is easy to read, you shouldn't use it anymore on modern Linux distributions. The ip tool is the default tool for manual network configuration and monitoring. While setting and reading information that is related to the network card, it addresses libraries and regions in memory that aren't used with ifconfig. All modern utilities are using the same approach as ip; therefore, you risk not seeing modifications to networking if you're only looking with the ifconfig utility.

Exercise 9-1 shows you how to use this tool and also demonstrates why you shouldn't use ifconfig anymore.

EXERCISE 9-1. CONFIGURING A NETWORK INTERFACE WITH IP

In this exercise, you'll add a secondary Internet Protocol (IP) address to a network card, using the ip tool. Using secondary IP addresses can be useful if you have multiple services running on your server and you want to make a unique IP address available for each of these services. (Think of Apache virtual servers, for example.) You will next check your network configuration with ifconfig and note that the secondary IP address is not visible. Next, you'll use the ip tool to display the current network configuration, and you'll see that using this tool does show you the secondary IP address you've just added.

1. Open a terminal and make sure that you have root permissions.

2. Use the command ip addr show to display the current IP address configuration. What matters at this point is that you find the name of the network card. In Listing 9-2, this name is ens33.

Listing 9-2. Showing the Current Network Configuration with ip addr show

```
linux-kscc:~ # ip addr show
1: lo: <LOOPBACK,UP,LOWER_UP> mtu 65536 qdisc noqueue state UNKNOWN group default
    link/loopback 00:00:00:00:00:00 brd 00:00:00:00:00:00
    inet 127.0.0.1/8 scope host lo
       valid_lft forever preferred_lft forever
    inet6 ::1/128 scope host
       valid_lft forever preferred_lft forever
2: ens33: <BROADCAST,MULTICAST,UP,LOWER_UP> mtu 1500 qdisc pfifo_fast state UP group
            default qlen 1000
    link/ether 00:0c:29:3e:d8:59 brd ff:ff:ff:ff:ff:ff
    inet 192.168.4.12/24 brd 192.168.4.255 scope global ens33
       valid_lft forever preferred_lft forever
    inet6 fe80::20c:29ff:fe3e:d859/64 scope link
       valid_lft forever preferred_lft forever3.
```

In the preceding listing, you can see that the Ethernet network card is known as ens33 on this system. Knowing this, you can now add an IP address to this network card, using the command `ip addr add dev ens33 192.168.4.71/24` (make sure that you're using a valid unique IP address!).

3. Now use the command `ping 192.168.4.71` to check the availability of the IP address you've just added. You should see echo reply packets coming in.

4. Use `ifconfig` to check the current network configuration. You won't see the secondary IP address you've just added.

5. Use `ip addr show` to display the current network configuration. This will show you the secondary IP address.

One reason why many administrators who have been using Linux for years don't like the `ip` command is because it's not very intuitive. That's because the `ip` command works with subcommands, referred to as *objects* in the help of the command. Using these objects makes the `ip` command very versatile but difficult, at the same time.

If you type "ip help," you'll see a help message, showing all objects that are available with `ip` (see Listing 9-3).

Listing 9-3. Using `ip help` to Get an Overview of All Available Objects

```
linux-kscc:~ # ip help
Usage: ip [ OPTIONS ] OBJECT { COMMAND | help }
       ip [ -force ] -batch filename
where  OBJECT := { link | addr | addrlabel | route | rule | neigh | ntable |
                   tunnel | tuntap | maddr | mroute | mrule | monitor | xfrm |
                   netns | l2tp | tcp_metrics | token }
       OPTIONS := { -V[ersion] | -s[tatistics] | -d[etails] | -r[esolve] |
                    -f[amily] { inet | inet6 | ipx | dnet | bridge | link } |
                    -4 | -6 | -I | -D | -B | -0 |
                    -l[oops] { maximum-addr-flush-attempts } |
                    -o[neline] | -t[imestamp] | -b[atch] [filename] |
                    -rc[vbuf] [size]}
```

As you can see, many objects are available, but there are only three that really are interesting: `ip link` is used to show link statistics; `ip addr` is used to show and manipulate the IP addresses on network interfaces; and `ip route` can be used to show and manage routes on your server.

Managing Device Settings

Let's begin by having a look at `ip link`. By using this command, you can set device properties and monitor the current state of a device. If you use the command `ip link help`, you'll receive a nice overview of all of the available options (see Listing 9-4).

Listing 9-4. Using `ip link help` to Show All Available `ip link` Options

```
linux-kscc:~ # ip link help
Usage: ip link add [link DEV] [ name ] NAME
                   [ txqueuelen PACKETS ]
                   [ address LLADDR ]
                   [ broadcast LLADDR ]
                   [ mtu MTU ]
```

```
                    [ numtxqueues QUEUE_COUNT ]
                    [ numrxqueues QUEUE_COUNT ]
                    type TYPE [ ARGS ]
        ip link delete DEV type TYPE [ ARGS ]

        ip link set { dev DEVICE | group DEVGROUP } [ { up | down } ]
                        [ arp { on | off } ]
                        [ dynamic { on | off } ]
                        [ multicast { on | off } ]
                        [ allmulticast { on | off } ]
                        [ promisc { on | off } ]
                        [ trailers { on | off } ]
                        [ txqueuelen PACKETS ]
                        [ name NEWNAME ]
                        [ address LLADDR ]
                        [ broadcast LLADDR ]
                        [ mtu MTU ]
                        [ netns PID ]
                        [ netns NAME ]
                        [ alias NAME ]
                        [ vf NUM [ mac LLADDR ]
                                 [ vlan VLANID [ qos VLAN-QOS ] ]
                                 [ rate TXRATE ] ]
                                 [ spoofchk { on | off} ] ]
                                 [ state { auto | enable | disable} ] ]
                        [ master DEVICE ]
                        [ nomaster ]
        ip link show [ DEVICE | group GROUP ] [up]

TYPE := { vlan | veth | vcan | dummy | ifb | macvlan | macvtap |
          can | bridge | bond | ipoib | ip6tnl | ipip | sit |
          vxlan | gre | gretap | ip6gre | ip6gretap | vti }
TYPE := { vlan | veth | vcan | dummy | ifb | macvlan | can }
```

To start with, ip link show gives all current parameters on the device specified, or on all devices, if no specific device has been specified. If you don't like some of the options you see, you can use ip link set on the device to change properties of the device. A rather common option, for example, is ip link set ens33 mtu 9000, which sets the maximal size of packets sent on the device to 9000 bytes, something that is particularly useful if the device connects to an iSCSI SAN.

Be sure, however, to check that your device supports the setting you intend to change. If it doesn't, you'll see an Invalid Argument error, and the setting won't be changed.

Managing Address Configuration

To manage the current address allocation to a device, you use ip addr. If used without argument, this command shows the current address configuration, as is the case if you use the command ip addr show (see also the preceding Listing 9-2, in Exercise 9-1).

To set an IP address, you need `ip addr add`, followed by the name of the device and the address you want to set. Make sure that the address is always specified with the subnet mask you want to use, if it isn't, a 32-bit subnet mask is used, and that makes it impossible to communicate with any other node on the same network. As you've seen before, to add an IP address 192.168.0.72 to the network device with the name ens33, you would use `ip addr add dev ens33 192.168.0.72/24`.

Another common task you might want to perform is deleting an IP address. This is very similar to adding an IP address. To delete the IP address 192.168.0.72, for example, you would use `ip addr del dev ens33 192.168.0.72/24`.

Managing Routes

To communicate on a network, your server has to know which node to use as the default gateway, also known as the default router. To see the current settings, you can use `ip route show` (see Listing 9-5).

Listing 9-5. Using `ip route show` to Show Current Routing Information

```
linux-kscc:~ # ip route show
default via 192.168.4.1 dev ens33
192.168.4.0/24 dev ens33   proto kernel   scope link   src 192.168.4.12
```

On a typical server, you won't see much routing information. There's only a direct route for the networks your server is connected to directly. In Listing 9-5, this is evident in the first line, where the network 192.168.4.0 is identified with the scope link (which means it is directly attached) and accessible through the network card ens33.

Apart from the directly attached routers, there should be a default route on every server. In Listing 9-5, you can see that the default route is the node with IP address 192.168.4.1. This means all traffic to networks not directly connected to this server is sent to IP address 192.168.4.1.

As a server administrator, you occasionally have to set a route from the command line. You can do this using the `ip route add` command, which must be followed by the required routing information. Typically, in this routing information, you must specify which host is identified as a router and which network card is used on this server to reach this host.

So, if there is a network 10.0.0.0, which can be reached through IP address 192.168.4.253, which is accessible by using the network card ens34, you can add the route using `ip route add 10.0.0.0 via 192.168.4.253 dev ens33`.

Nothing you'll do with the `ip` command is automatically saved. That means that you only have to restart a network card to lose all information you've manually set using `ip`. In the next sections, you'll learn how to make the configuration persistent.

Name Resolving

From the command line, you can set the IP address and the address of the default router for temporary use. You cannot do this with the DNS resolver; this must be configured in a configuration file. On SLES 12, the starting point for such configuration is the file `/etc/sysconfig/network/config`. This file contains settings for several services, including DNS resolving. In Listing 9-6, you can see a list of the different DNS-related configuration options in this file.

Listing 9-6. DNS Name Lookup Options in `/etc/sysconfig/network/config`

```
linux-kscc:~ # grep DNS /etc/sysconfig/network/config
# Defines the DNS merge policy as documented in netconfig(8) manual page.
# Set to "" to disable DNS configuration.
NETCONFIG_DNS_POLICY="auto"
# Defines the name of the DNS forwarder that has to be configured.
NETCONFIG_DNS_FORWARDER="resolver"
NETCONFIG_DNS_FORWARDER_FALLBACK="yes"
```

```
# List of DNS domain names used for host-name lookup.
NETCONFIG_DNS_STATIC_SEARCHLIST=""
# List of DNS nameserver IP addresses to use for host-name lookup.
# When the NETCONFIG_DNS_FORWARDER variable is set to "resolver",
NETCONFIG_DNS_STATIC_SERVERS=""
# Allows to specify a custom DNS service ranking list, that is which
NETCONFIG_DNS_RANKING="auto"
NETCONFIG_DNS_RESOLVER_OPTIONS=""
NETCONFIG_DNS_RESOLVER_SORTLIST=""
```

From the configuration file, the changes are pushed to the appropriate configuration files. In the case of DNS name resolution, there are two methods to push the configuration: you can restart the Wicked service, which is responsible for managing network configuration, using systemctl restart wicked. Alternatively, you can use the command netconfig update -f.

Note that you should not edit the contents of the /etc/resolv.conf file manually. This will break the functionality that is provided from /etc/sysconfig/network/config, and modifications that are applied from such services as Wicked and YaST risk not functioning anymore as well.

Understanding Wicked

One of the major component changes in SLES 12 is with regards to network management. Wicked now is the central service that takes care of managing all scripts that store network configuration. These are mainly the following scripts:

- The ifcfg scripts in the directory /etc/sysconfig/network. These scripts contain the configuration for all of the individual network interfaces. Listing 9-7 shows the contents of a typical script.

- The /etc/sysconfig/network/config script. This script contains generic settings that are not specific to particular network cards.

- The /etc/sysconfig/network/routes script. All routes are stored in this script.

Listing 9-7. Network Configuration in an ifcfg Script

```
BOOTPROTO='static'
BROADCAST=''
ETHTOOL_OPTIONS=''
IPADDR='192.168.4.12/24'
MTU=''
NAME='82545EM Gigabit Ethernet Controller (Copper)'
NETWORK=''
REMOTE_IPADDR=''
STARTMODE='auto'
```

When modifications to the configuration files are made, the Wicked service must be restarted or reloaded. Apart from that, the wicked command can be used to request current status information about network interfaces. In Exercise 9-2, you'll learn how to perform basic operations using the wicked tool.

EXERCISE 9-2. MANAGING NETWORK INTERFACES WITH WICKED

1. Type `wicked show all` to get an overview of the current interface configuration. This provides information such as that in Listing 9-8.

    Listing 9-8. Showing Interface Information with `wicked show`

    ```
    linux-kscc:/etc/sysconfig/network # wicked show all
    lo              up
            link:   #1, state up
            type:   loopback
            cstate: network-up
            config: compat:/etc/sysconfig/network/ifcfg-lo
            leases: ipv4 static granted
            addr:   ipv4 127.0.0.1/8
            addr:   ipv6 ::1/128

    ens33           up
            link:   #2, state up, mtu 1500
            type:   ethernet, hwaddr 00:0c:29:3e:d8:59
            cstate: network-up
            config: compat:/etc/sysconfig/network/ifcfg-ens33
            leases: ipv4 static granted
            addr:   ipv4 192.168.4.12/24
    ```

2. With an editor, open the file `/etc/sysconfig/network/ifcfg-YOURINTERFACE` and add the line `IPADDR2='192.168.4.13/24'` (or anything that meets your current network configuration).

3. Type `wicked ifreload ens33`, to activate the network card configuration.

4. Type `wicked check resolve www.sandervanvugt.com`. It should show you the IP address associated with this host.

5. Type `wicked check route 8.8.8.8`. It will show you whether the server with IP address 8.8.8.8 is reachable.

As you have seen in the exercise, the Wicked service provides a generic interface that helps you to manage most aspects of the network configuration. As such, it can be used as an alternative to many old utilities that were used to change network configuration in the past and to modify network parameters as well. Some of these tools should not be used anymore. In particular, these are the `ifdown` and `ifup` tools, which were written to interact with the old style of network configuration files.

Another tool that should not be used anymore is `NetworkManager`. `NetworkManager`, in previous versions of SLES and on other Linux distributions, was used to manage network configuration and network cards. It consisted of a service (the NetworkManager service) and a front-end utility `NetworkManager`. Wicked has completely replaced this utility.

Using YaST for NIC Configuration

In general, Linux administrators prefer to modify configuration files manually. In some cases, that makes sense; in other cases, it just doesn't. Especially not, because YaST provides many options to create network configurations, even some relatively complicated configurations. Therefore, even the most hard-core Linux administrator should know thoroughly the YaST options that relate to network configuration. In this section, you'll get an overview.

■ **Note**   Graphical or not? Most Linux servers are used without a graphical interface. On these text-only installations, the Text User Interface (TUI) of YaST can be used. As using this interface is the reality for most administrators, I'm discussing its use in this chapter. All steps described here will work in the graphical interface as well.

Accessing Basic Network Configuration from YaST

To access the basic network configuration settings from YaST, start YaST and select Network Devices ➤ Network Settings. This brings you to the main network configuration interface (see Figure 9-1).

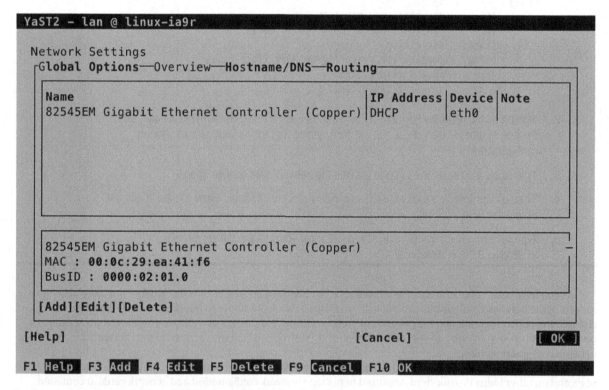

Figure 9-1. Accessing network configuration from YaST

In the first configuration window, you see an overview of network cards that are currently available. It shows configured network interfaces, as well as interfaces that haven't been configured yet. To select a network card and enter its detailed configuration, you should first use the Tab key, to highlight the network card, and then select Edit, to access its configuration. You can use either the Tab key or the Alt+I key sequence to select the Edit option. This brings you to the Network Card Setup window that you can see in Figure 9-2.

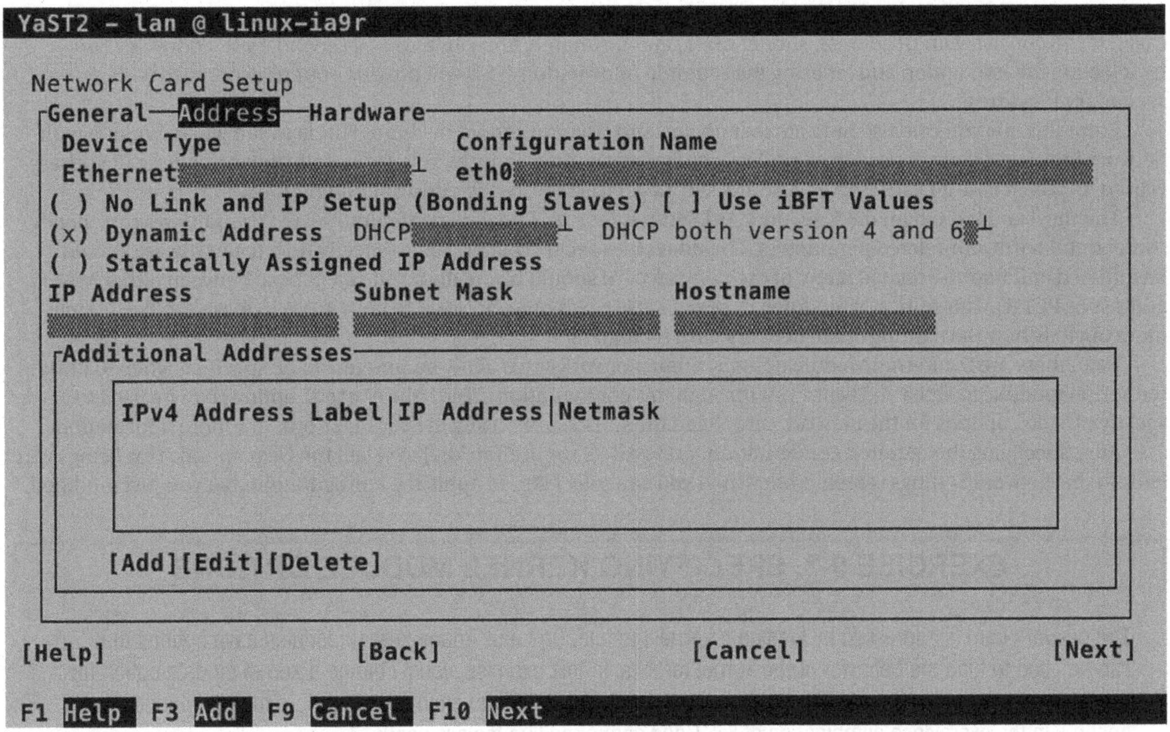

```
YaST2 - lan @ linux-ia9r
Network Card Setup
┌General──Address──Hardware─────────────────────────────────────────────────┐
  Device Type                    Configuration Name
  Ethernet▓▓▓▓▓▓▓▓▓▓▓▓▓▓▓▓▓⊥ eth0▓▓▓▓▓▓▓▓▓▓▓▓▓▓▓▓▓▓▓▓▓▓▓▓▓▓▓▓▓▓▓▓▓▓▓▓
  ( ) No Link and IP Setup (Bonding Slaves) [ ] Use iBFT Values
  (x) Dynamic Address   DHCP▓▓▓▓▓▓▓▓▓⊥  DHCP both version 4 and 6▓⊥
  ( ) Statically Assigned IP Address
  IP Address              Subnet Mask              Hostname
  ▓▓▓▓▓▓▓▓▓▓▓▓▓▓▓▓▓▓    ▓▓▓▓▓▓▓▓▓▓▓▓▓▓▓▓      ▓▓▓▓▓▓▓▓▓▓▓▓▓▓▓▓
  ┌Additional Addresses─────────────────────────────────────────────────┐
  │                                                                      │
  │  IPv4 Address Label│IP Address│Netmask                               │
  │                                                                      │
  │                                                                      │
  │                                                                      │
  │                                                                      │
  │                                                                      │
  │  [Add][Edit][Delete]                                                 │
  └──────────────────────────────────────────────────────────────────────┘
└───────────────────────────────────────────────────────────────────────────┘

[Help]              [Back]                   [Cancel]              [Next]

F1 Help  F3 Add  F9 Cancel  F10 Next
```

Figure 9-2. *The YaST Network Card Setup interface*

You should notice that from the Network Card Setup window, you can access all configuration settings that apply to the selected network card. In fact, these are the options that will be written to the related /etc/sysconfig/network/ifcfg-xxx file. From this interface, you cannot access the routing or DNS configuration.

The Network Card Setup screen consists of three different tabs, which you can select using the Tab key. On the Address tab, which is selected by default, you can enter network addresses and related configuration. The Hardware tab allows you to specify parameters that define how the network interface is used, and the General tab allows you to specify generic settings.

On the General tab, the following three different options can be arranged:

- *Device Activation*: This defines when the network card will be activated. Typically, you might want this to happen at boot time, but alternatively, you can indicate that it is activated on a specific event only, for example, when a cable is connected. Also, you can specify that a network card should never be activated, which can be useful if you have to make sure a specific interface is excluded at all times.

- *Firewall Zone*: In SUSE Firewall, you can add network interfaces to specific zones, which makes it easy to apply some default security settings to the interface. You can choose among either the Internal Zone, which leaves it in unprotected mode, the Demilitarized Zone, and the External Zone.

- *Set MTU*: This option allows you to specify Maximum Transfer Unit (MTU), which is the maximal size of Ethernet packets. If you don't do anything, a default size of 1500 bytes is used. You can increase the size to a maximum of 9000 bytes, which makes sense if this network card is used to access an iSCSI SAN.

On the Address tab, you can specify information that is related to the configuration of the IP address. In many cases, it will consist of an IP address, subnet mask, and hostname. You can also add secondary IP addresses here, by selecting the Add option and entering the required information. This will provide your network card with a secondary IP address.

From this tab, you can also indicate that no link and IP setup should be done. This is useful when working with network interfaces that are used in a bonding configuration. Alternatively, you can specify that a dynamic IP address is used, in which case a DHCP server is addressed, to get the required IP address configuration.

The third and last tab on the Network Card Setup screen is Hardware configuration. On this tab, you can specify some useful hardware-related parameters. The udev rules section allows you to specify how the hardware should be initiated and how the related name of the network card should be created. You can choose between either MAC address or PCI ID. This option is modified in specific use cases only, because in both ways, it doesn't make it much more obvious how the naming of the network card is created.

Next, there are the Kernel Module options. Some network cards allow parameters to be specified when loading the kernel module. Exercise 9-3 walks you through this configuration. Third, the ethtool options can be used to specify ethtool options for the network card. Read the subsection "Using ethtool Options," for more information.

After specifying the required configuration, press Alt+N (or the Tab key) to select the Next option. This brings you back to the Network Settings screen, from which you can select OK, to apply the configuration that you just modified.

EXERCISE 9-3. SPECIFYING KERNEL MODULE OPTIONS

The network card is addressed by loading a kernel module. On Linux, many kernel modules have options that can be used to tune the behavior of the kernel module. In this exercise, you'll change a kernel module option for the driver of your network card. This exercise also teaches you how to change parameters for kernel modules in general. In the exercise, a combination of YaST and command line tools is used.

1. On the command line, type lspci -k. This gives an overview of everything that was found on the PCI bus, including the kernel modules that are used to address the PCI device. Look for the Ethernet controller, which is your network card.

   02:01.0 Ethernet controller: Intel Corporation 82545EM Gigabit Ethernet Controller (Copper) (rev 01)

   Subsystem: VMware PRO/1000 MT Single Port Adapter

   Kernel driver in use: e1000

   Kernel modules: e1000

2. The last two lines show which kernel modules are in use. In this case, the e1000 module.

3. Type modinfo e1000 (make sure the name matches the name of your kernel module). Look at the end of the output, where you probably will see a few lines starting with "parm." These are the parameters that you can use for this specific kernel module.

```
parm:           TxDescriptors:Number of transmit descriptors (array of int)
parm:           RxDescriptors:Number of receive descriptors (array of int)
parm:           Speed:Speed setting (array of int)
parm:           Duplex:Duplex setting (array of int)
parm:           AutoNeg:Advertised auto-negotiation setting (array of int)
parm:           FlowControl:Flow Control setting (array of int)
parm:           XsumRX:Disable or enable Receive Checksum offload (array of int)
```

```
parm:          TxIntDelay:Transmit Interrupt Delay (array of int)
parm:          TxAbsIntDelay:Transmit Absolute Interrupt Delay (array of int)
parm:          RxIntDelay:Receive Interrupt Delay (array of int)
parm:          RxAbsIntDelay:Receive Absolute Interrupt Delay (array of int)
parm:          InterruptThrottleRate:Interrupt Throttling Rate (array of int)
parm:          SmartPowerDownEnable:Enable PHY smart power down (array of int)
parm:          copybreak:Maximum size of packet that is copied to a new buffer on
               receive (uint)
parm:          debug:Debug level (0=none,...,16=all) (int)
```

4. Start YaST and select Network Devices ➤ Network Settings. Access the properties for your network card and select the Hardware tab. On this tab, select NameOptions and set the debugging level to 16, by typing debug=16 (see Figure 9-3). Note that this specific parameter may not be available on the type of network card that you are using—kernel module parameters are specific to the device you're using.

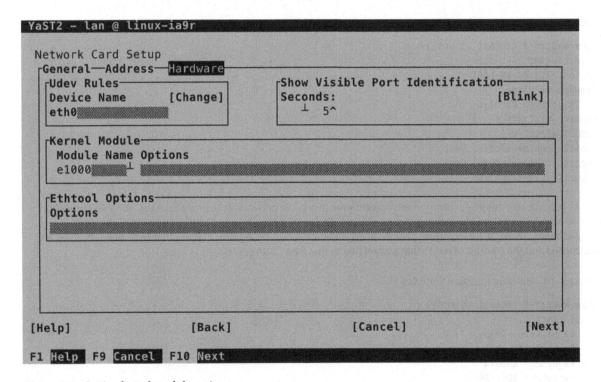

Figure 9-3. *Setting kernel module options*

5. Select Next, OK, and Quit to write the settings to your server. Back on the console of your server, use cat /etc/modprobe.d/50-yast.conf. You'll see that this file contains the line options e1000 debug=16, which ensures that the kernel module option is applied every time the kernel module is loaded.

In the previous exercise, you have applied an option to a kernel module. Unfortunately, there is no good way of verifying that the parameter has indeed been applied. On some occasions, you can type dmesg to see the output that was generated when loading the kernel module. On other occasions, you can check the contents of the /sys/module/yourmodule directory, which sometimes contains a file with the name parameters, containing all parameters that were used when loading this kernel module.

Using ethtool Options

The ethtool utility can be used to set and monitor device properties for Ethernet cards. Notice that it works on the Ethernet devices only, and not on devices such as bonds or bridges. Also, the operations that are supported will be different between different devices. Some devices allow many operations; other devices only allow for a few manipulations. So, before applying the ethtool options you want to use in YaST, make sure to find out which options are supported by your device.

To start with, let's request some device information using ethtool -i eth0 (see Listing 9-9). (Make sure to replace the generic network device name eth0 with the name of the device as it is used in your environment.)

Listing 9-9. Showing Interface Options

```
linux-kscc:~ # ethtool -i ens33
driver: e1000
version: 7.3.21-k8-NAPI
firmware-version:
bus-info: 0000:02:01.0
supports-statistics: yes
supports-test: yes
supports-eeprom-access: yes
supports-register-dump: yes
supports-priv-flags: no
```

As you can see, this gives some generic information about the network device you're using. You can request more specific information about the device as well, which is useful for advanced troubleshooting of the device. Using ethtool -S eth0, for example, gives detailed statistics about the amount of bytes that have been received and transmitted and the amount of errors that was related to that (see Listing 9-10).

Listing 9-10. Showing Interface Statistics

```
linux-kscc:~ # ethtool -S ens33
NIC statistics:
     rx_packets: 5030
     tx_packets: 3332
     rx_bytes: 489074
     tx_bytes: 1082759
     rx_broadcast: 0
     tx_broadcast: 0
     rx_multicast: 0
     tx_multicast: 0
     rx_errors: 0
     tx_errors: 0
     tx_dropped: 0
     multicast: 0
     collisions: 0
```

```
rx_length_errors: 0
rx_over_errors: 0
rx_crc_errors: 0
rx_frame_errors: 0
rx_no_buffer_count: 0
rx_missed_errors: 0
tx_aborted_errors: 0
tx_carrier_errors: 0
tx_fifo_errors: 0
tx_heartbeat_errors: 0
tx_window_errors: 0
tx_abort_late_coll: 0
tx_deferred_ok: 0
tx_single_coll_ok: 0
tx_multi_coll_ok: 0
tx_timeout_count: 0
tx_restart_queue: 0
rx_long_length_errors: 0
rx_short_length_errors: 0
rx_align_errors: 0
tx_tcp_seg_good: 47
tx_tcp_seg_failed: 0
rx_flow_control_xon: 0
rx_flow_control_xoff: 0
tx_flow_control_xon: 0
tx_flow_control_xoff: 0
rx_long_byte_count: 489074
rx_csum_offload_good: 4999
rx_csum_offload_errors: 0
alloc_rx_buff_failed: 0
tx_smbus: 0
rx_smbus: 0
dropped_smbus: 0
```

With ethtool, you can perform some tests as well. First, it may be useful to identify your network card. This makes sense on a server with multiple network cards. Use ethtool -p eth0 5, which lets the leds on your eth0 device blink for five seconds. At least you'll be sure which cable to pull and which one to leave alone!

In some cases, you may have to change device parameters, to get the best out of your network card. To do this, you first have to get an overview of all options that are supported by your specific network card. To get this overview, just type ethtool eth0. The output will look like Listing 9-11.

Listing 9-11. Showing Supported Device Settings

```
linux-kscc:~ # ethtool ens33
Settings for ens33:
        Supported ports: [ TP ]
        Supported link modes:   10baseT/Half 10baseT/Full
                                100baseT/Half 100baseT/Full
                                1000baseT/Full
        Supported pause frame use: No
        Supports auto-negotiation: Yes
```

```
Advertised link modes:   10baseT/Half 10baseT/Full
                         100baseT/Half 100baseT/Full
                         1000baseT/Full
Advertised pause frame use: No
Advertised auto-negotiation: Yes
Speed: 1000Mb/s
Duplex: Full
Port: Twisted Pair
PHYAD: 0
Transceiver: internal
Auto-negotiation: on
MDI-X: off (auto)
Supports Wake-on: d
Wake-on: d
Current message level: 0x00000007 (7)
                         drv probe link
Link detected: yes
```

If you don't like one of these parameters, you can change it. To do this from the command line, you can run a command such as ethtool -s eth0 speed 1000. This will set a fixed speed of 1000Mbps on your network card. Although this will work, the setting will have disappeared after a reboot. This is where YaST comes in.

To make ethtool settings permanent, you can put them in YaST. Select the Hardware tab on the Network Card Setup and from there, enter the ethtool options you want to use, such as speed 1000. Next, apply the changes and quit YaST. You can find these options written to the ifcfg file for your interface, as you can see in Listing 9-12.

Listing 9-12. ethtool Options Made Permanent

```
linux-kscc:~ # cat /etc/sysconfig/network/ifcfg-ens33
BOOTPROTO='static'
BROADCAST=''
ETHTOOL_OPTIONS='speed 1000'
IPADDR2='192.168.4.13/24'
IPADDR='192.168.4.12/24'
MTU=''
NAME='82545EM Gigabit Ethernet Controller (Copper)'
NETWORK=''
REMOTE_IPADDR=''
STARTMODE='auto'
```

Changing Routing and Name Resolution from YaST

When setting properties for network devices, you can set the address and related properties on the Overview tab of the Network Settings module. Information that relates to Hostname/DNS and Routing is on different tabs. In Figure 9-4, you can see the Hostname/DNS tab.

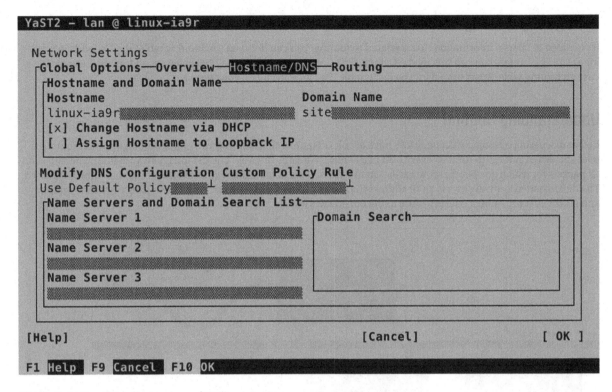

Figure 9-4. *Specifying hostname and DNS properties*

Modifying Hostname- and DNS-Related Information

On the Hostname/DNS tab, you first have to change the hostname, if you haven't done that yet. Make sure to set both the hostname and domain name, to ensure that identification of your host on the Internet works smoothly. If your host gets its IP configuration from a DHCP server, you can leave Change Hostname via DHCP on, but if you don't have a DHCP server in your network that has been set up for that purpose, that's fine as well. Optionally, you can also specify whether to assign the hostname to the loopback IP address.

Next, you can specify the DNS Configuration. At least you want to specify one or more DNS name servers. To make hostname lookup in common domains easier, you can specify the names of these domains in the Domain Search box. This is useful if you want to be able to address hosts based on their partial name, instead of their fully qualified DNS hostname.

Related to DNS Configuration, you can also specify a policy. The policy determines how DNS servers should be treated in an environment in which fixed DNS servers are set, but there's also a DHCP server handing out DNS server configuration. You can choose from among the following three options:

- *Only Manually*: The DNS server settings that are handed out by a DHCP server will be ignored.

- *Use Default Policy*: This adds DNS Server information to manually configured DNS servers.

- *Use Custom Policy*: This allows you to choose between STATIC and STATIC_FALLBACK. The STATIC policy setting uses manually configured DNS servers only; the STATIC_FALLBACK options use manually configured DNS servers, if DHCP fails to hand out DNS configuration options.

The options that you will set on the DNS and routing tabs will be written to the /etc/sysconfig/network/config file, and from there, they are pushed to the appropriate configuration files on your server.

Configuring Routing Parameters

If you need to change information that is related to routing, you can do so on the Routing tab of the Network Settings interface. On this tab, you can specify the Default IPv4 Gateway, as well as the IPv6 gateway, and you can also create a custom routing table. Apart from that, you can enable IPv4 forwarding on your server.

Understanding Routing

Before discussing routing parameters, let's have a look at Figure 9-5, which shows a configuration in which routing is relevant. When setting up routing, every host has to have a default gateway. The default gateway defines where to send all packets for which no specific route exists. On most hosts, the default gateway is the only route that must be defined. The default gateway in all cases is an IP address that exists on the same network as the host using the default gateway, and it's the first router on a packet's route to the outside world.

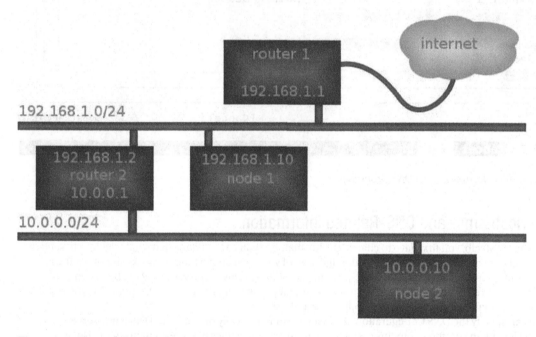

Figure 9-5. Network Routing Overview

Let's have a look at node2 first. The default gateway for this node is 10.0.0.1. From there, node2 doesn't care anymore, as router2 takes over. Router2, in turn, also needs to know where to send packets that have a destination on the Internet. As you can guess, the default gateway on the 192.168.1.0/24 network would be 192.168.1.1, from which packets can be sent to the Internet.

For all hosts on the 10.0.0.0/24 network, it's enough to specify the address 10.0.0.1 as the default gateway. For nodes on the network 192.168.1.0/24, additional information is required. With just the address of the default gateway 192.168.1.1, these hosts wouldn't be able to send packets to hosts on the 10.0.0.10 network. To fix this, these nodes need a specific route to the 10.0.0.0 network, which goes via router2 at IP address 192.168.1.2.

In this simple network diagram, the configuration for router2 isn't very difficult. It just has to have its routing enabled. As router 2 is directly attached to both the 192.168.0.0/24 and the 10.0.0.0/24 networks, enabling routing on that node is sufficient.

Modifying Routing Parameters

From the Network Settings ➤ Routing tab in YaST, it's easy to add a custom routing table (see Figure 9-6). Select Add and specify a value for each of the requested parameters, as follows:

- *Destination*: The network to which you want to define a route

- *Gateway*: The gateway that is needed to access that network. Note that this should always be an IP address that is on a network the machine is directly connected to.

- *Genmask*: The netmask in CIDR notation (24, not 255.255.255.0)

- *Options*: Advanced options, such as the metric that can be used to define the costs of a specific route

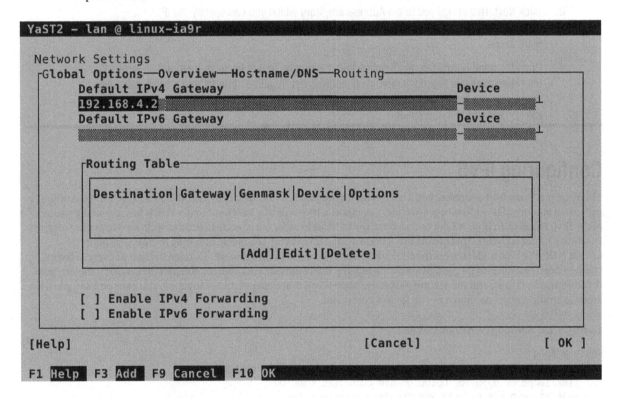

Figure 9-6. *Defining routing options*

If you want to use the machine as a router, you should select one or both of the Enable IPv4/IPv6 Forwarding options.

Managing Interfaces from YaST

From the Network Settings ➤ Overview tab, you can see all network interfaces that are currently available on your server. Normally, all hardware interfaces are detected and added automatically. Not all interfaces, however, are hardware interfaces. Software interfaces are commonly used as well, such as a bridge in a virtual environment, or a bonded interface that allows you to bundle multiple physical network cards to create a redundant logical network interface that is backed by two physical interfaces. From YaST, it is relatively easy to add such a logical interface. In Exercise 9-4, you can walk through the steps that are required for creating such an interface.

EXERCISE 9-4. CREATING A BOND INTERFACE FROM YAST

In this exercise, you'll learn how to create a bond interface. Normally, behind a logical bond interface, there are at least two physical network interfaces. To allow you to perform the steps in this exercise even if you have only one physical interface, you'll create a bond interface that is backed by one physical device only.

1. From the Network Settings ➤ Overview tab, select Add, to open the screen that allows you to add a new network interface.

2. From the Device Type drop-down list, select the Bond Device Type (press the down arrow to open the drop-down list). Leave the configuration name at 0, which will create the device as bond0.

3. Click Next. This brings you to the Address tab, from which you can specify the IP configuration that you want to use on the bonded interface. Specify the address that you want to use.

4. Open the Bond Slaves tab. You'll notice that it is empty. That is because there are no network interfaces available that don't have an IP address set. To add an interface to a bond, you have to clear its current IP configuration. To do this, select the interface you want to add and select the No Link and IP Setup option.

Configuring IPv6

There are not many IPv4 addresses left. That is why, for the past few decades, IPv6 has been available. In IPv6, a virtually unlimited amount of IP addresses is available. Configuring IPv6 typically isn't hard to do. This is because of the nature of the IPv6 protocol. In IPv6, it's not necessary to set an IP address for every node in the network. IPv6 uses the Neighbor Discovery Protocol (NDP). That means that a node in an IPv6 network is capable of setting its own IPv6 address.

In NDP, the IPv6 node detects the IPv6 address that is in use on its network. That means that in every network, you just need one node to be configured with a reliable IPv6 address. This address consists of two parts: the first part is the network address, and the second part is the node ID on that network. In Listing 9-13, you can see a sample IPv6 address configuration, as shown by the `ip a s` command.

Listing 9-13. Showing IPv6 Configuration

```
web:~ # ip a
1: lo: <LOOPBACK,UP,LOWER_UP> mtu 16436 qdisc noqueue state UNKNOWN
    link/loopback 00:00:00:00:00:00 brd 00:00:00:00:00:00
    inet 127.0.0.1/8 brd 127.255.255.255 scope host lo
    inet 127.0.0.2/8 brd 127.255.255.255 scope host secondary lo
    inet6 ::1/128 scope host
       valid_lft forever preferred_lft forever
2: eth0: <BROADCAST,MULTICAST,UP,LOWER_UP> mtu 1500 qdisc pfifo_fast state UNKNOWN qlen 1000
    link/ether 00:16:3e:37:ea:cd brd ff:ff:ff:ff:ff:ff
    inet 87.253.155.186/25 brd 87.253.155.255 scope global eth0
    inet6 2a01:7c8:c127:1216::3/64 scope global
       valid_lft forever preferred_lft forever
    inet6 fe80::216:3eff:fe37:eacd/64 scope link
       valid_lft forever preferred_lft forever
```

As you can see in the preceding sample listing, on interface eth0, two IPv6 addresses are set. First, there is the address that starts with 2a01; next, there is the address starting with fe80. The first address is a registered worldwide unique address that was handed out by an Internet provider. The address starting with fe80 is an IPv6 address that is for internal use only. You will see one of these addresses on every node that has IPv6 enabled.

In IPv6 addresses, a total of 128 bits is used to create an address that consists of 8 groups of 2 bytes, written in a hexadecimal way. Because IPv6 has an enormous available address space, there is no need to use subnet masks. It is possible, however, to use subnet masks to define several networks within the address space of one registered IP network address. Normally, the first half of the address is used for the network, and the second half of the address is used for the node part. That means that in the imaginary address fe80:1234:bad:cafe:216:3eff:fe37:eacd, the part up to cafe is the network address, and the part that starts with 216 is the node ID on the network.

If you look carefully at the node ID of the IPv6 address, you will see that it includes the MAC address of the network card on which the IPv6 address is set. You can see it in the preceding listing, in which the MAC address 00:16:3e:37:ea:cd is easily recognized in the node part of the fe80 address, which is 216:3eff:fe:37:eacd. As the MAC address by default is just 6 bytes, the node ID is padded with the bytes ff:fe to make it an 8-byte address in the 16-byte IPv6 address.

Now that you know how IPv6 uses the MAC address in the node ID of the address, it's easy to imagine how NDP works. The NDP protocol detects the network address on use on this network and just adds the node ID to this network. So, if you want to use IPv6 in your network, just make sure that there is a router announcing IPv6 addresses that can be picked up by your server.

Troubleshooting Networking

When using a network, you may experience many different configuration problems. In this section, you'll learn how to work with some common tools that help you to fix these problems.

Checking the Network Card

Before using any tool to fix a problem, you should know what exactly is wrong. A common approach is to work from the network interface to a remote host on the Internet. That means you first check the configuration of the network card, by looking if the network card is up at all, and if it has an IP address currently assigned to it. The ip addr command shows all this. In Listing 9-14, you can see an overview of current network settings as shown with ip addr.

Listing 9-14. Checking the Current State of a Network Interface

```
linux-kscc:~ # ip addr
1: lo: <LOOPBACK,UP,LOWER_UP> mtu 65536 qdisc noqueue state UNKNOWN group default
    link/loopback 00:00:00:00:00:00 brd 00:00:00:00:00:00
    inet 127.0.0.1/8 scope host lo
      valid_lft forever preferred_lft forever
    inet6 ::1/128 scope host
      valid_lft forever preferred_lft forever
2: ens33: <BROADCAST,MULTICAST,DOWN,LOWER_UP> mtu 1500 qdisc pfifo_fast state UP group default qlen 1000
    link/ether 00:0c:29:3e:d8:59 brd ff:ff:ff:ff:ff:ff
    inet 192.168.4.13/24 brd 192.168.4.255 scope global ens33
      valid_lft forever preferred_lft forever
    inet 192.168.4.12/24 brd 192.168.4.255 scope global secondary ens33
      valid_lft forever preferred_lft forever
    inet6 fe80::20c:29ff:fe3e:d859/64 scope link
      valid_lft forever preferred_lft forever
```

If you have confirmed that the problem is related to the local network card, it's a good idea to see if you can fix it without changing the actual configuration files. Basically, the following tips will help you with that.

- Use `wicked ifup` on your network card to try to change its status to up. If it fails, check the physical connection. (Is the network cable plugged in?)

- Use `ip addr add` to manually add an IP address to the network card. If this fixes the problem, you probably have a DHCP server that's not working properly or a misconfiguration in the network card's configuration file.

After allegedly fixing the problem, you should perform a simple test to see whether you can really communicate to an outside host. To do this, pinging the default gateway is typically a good idea. Just use the `ping` command, followed by the IP address of the node you want to ping, for instance, `ping 192.168.0.254`.

Once you've got the network card up again, you should check its configuration files. You may have a misconfiguration in the configuration file, or else the DHCP server might be down.

Checking Routing

If the local network card is not the problem, you should check external hosts. The first step is to ping the default gateway. If that works, you can ping a host on the Internet, if possible, by using its IP address. Use 8.8.8.8, the Google DNS server, for example. It has never failed any of my ping tests.

In case your favorite ping host on the Internet doesn't reply, it's time to check routing. The following three common steps should normally give a result.

1. Use `ip route show` to show your current routing configuration. You should see a line that indicates which node is used as the default gateway. If you don't, you should manually add it.

2. If you do have a default router set, verify that you don't have a local firewall blocking access. To do this, use `iptables -L` as root. If it shows something similar to Listing 9-15, you're good. If it gives you lots of output, you do have a firewall that's blocking access. In that case, use `systemctl stop iptables` to stop it, and repeat your test. If it now works, you have a firewall issue. In that case, read Chapter 10 to make sure the firewall is configured correctly. If possible, turn the firewall on again (after all, it does protect you!), by using `service iptables start`.

Listing 9-15. Verifying Firewall Configuration

```
linux-kscc:~ # iptables -L
Chain INPUT (policy ACCEPT)
target     prot opt source              destination

Chain FORWARD (policy ACCEPT)
target     prot opt source              destination

Chain OUTPUT (policy ACCEPT)
target     prot opt source              destination
```

3. If you don't have a firewall issue, there might be something wrong between your default gateway and the host on the Internet you're trying to reach. Use `traceroute`, followed by the IP address of the target host (for example, `traceroute 8.8.8.8`). This command shows how far you get and possibly indicates where the fault occurs. But if the error is at your Internet provider, there's nothing you can do anyway.

Checking DNS

The third usual suspect in network communications errors is DNS. A useful command to check DNS configuration, is dig. Using dig, you can find out if a DNS server is capable of finding an authoritative answer to your query about DNS hosts.

The problem that many users have with the dig utility is that it provides lots of information in the answer. Consider the example in Listing 9-16, following, which is the answer dig gave to the command dig www.suse.com. The most important part in this example is the Got answer section. This means that the DNS server was able to provide an answer. In the line directly under the Got answer line, you can see the status of the answer is NOERROR. That's good; we didn't only get an answer, but also, there was no error in the answer. What follows is lots of details about the answer.

Listing 9-16. What dig Tells You If All Is Well

```
linux-kscc:~ # dig www.suse.com

; <<>>DiG 9.9.4-rpz2.13269.14-P2 <<>>www.suse.com
;; global options: +cmd
;; Got answer:
;; ->>HEADER<<- opcode: QUERY, status: NOERROR, id: 3590
;; flags: qr rd ra; QUERY: 1, ANSWER: 1, AUTHORITY: 0, ADDITIONAL: 1

;; OPT PSEUDOSECTION:
; EDNS: version: 0, flags:; udp: 512
;; QUESTION SECTION:
;www.suse.com.                  IN      A

;; ANSWER SECTION:
www.suse.com.           17161   IN      A       130.57.66.10

;; Query time: 29 msec
;; SERVER: 8.8.8.8#53(8.8.8.8)
;; WHEN: Fri May 30 23:24:44 CEST 2014
;; MSG SIZE  rcvd: 57
```

In the QUESTION SECTION, you can see the original request was for www.redhat.com. In the ANSWER SECTION, you can see exactly what the answer consisted of. This section provides details that you probably aren't interested in, but it enables the eager administrator to analyze exactly which DNS server provided the answer and how it got there.

In the sample in Listing 9-17, following, a request was made for the address of the nonexisting server hweg.skdhv.df. The important part, again, is in the Got answer section. This means that a DNS server did give an answer, it just wasn't very useful. This can be seen from the line that begins with HEADER. Especially important in this line is the status, which is indicated as NXDOMAIN. This means "No Such Domain." From the answer that dig provides here, you can see that a DNS server could be contacted. In the AUTHORITY SECTION, you can even see that a DNS server of the DNS root domain was queried. From this query, however, no useful answer followed.

Listing 9-17. What dig Shows You for a Nonexisting Host

```
linux-kscc:~ # dig hweg.skdhv.df

; <<>>DiG 9.9.4-rpz2.13269.14-P2 <<>>hweg.skdhv.df
;; global options: +cmd
;; Got answer:
;; ->>HEADER<<- opcode: QUERY, status: NXDOMAIN, id: 3278
;; flags: qr rd ra ad; QUERY: 1, ANSWER: 0, AUTHORITY: 1, ADDITIONAL: 1
```

```
;; OPT PSEUDOSECTION:
; EDNS: version: 0, flags:; udp: 512
;; QUESTION SECTION:
;hweg.skdhv.df.                    IN      A

;; AUTHORITY SECTION:
.                           1799    IN      SOA     a.root-servers.net. nstld.verisign-grs.com.
2014053001 1800 900 604800 86400

;; Query time: 40 msec
;; SERVER: 8.8.8.8#53(8.8.8.8)
;; WHEN: Fri May 30 23:26:07 CEST 2014
;; MSG SIZE  rcvd: 117
```

In the two dig examples that were just discussed, a DNS server has been reached. You might also encounter situations in which no DNS server can be reached. If that occurs, the answer dig provides is much shorter, as you can see in Listing 9-18. If there's a failure in contacting the DNS server, you'll also notice it takes a long time before it gives an answer.

Listing 9-18. dig Answer When DNS Is Not Available

linux-kscc:~ # dig www.suse.com

```
; <<>>DiG 9.9.4-rpz2.13269.14-P2 <<>>www.suse.com
;; global options: +cmd
;; connection timed out; no servers could be reached
```

The answer is loud and clear here: no DNS servers could be reached, which means that the error is probably in the local DNS configuration. That means that you have to check the /etc/resolv.conf file, which typically contains a list of DNS servers to be contacted. In Listing 9-19, you can see an example of what this file should look like. If it doesn't look good, check the contents of the /etc/sysconfig/network/config file and correct where necessary.

Listing 9-19. Sample /etc/resolv.conf File

linux-kscc:~ # cat /etc/resolv.conf
```
### /etc/resolv.conf file autogenerated by netconfig!
#
# Before you change this file manually, consider to define the
# static DNS configuration using the following variables in the
# /etc/sysconfig/network/config file:
#     NETCONFIG_DNS_STATIC_SEARCHLIST
#     NETCONFIG_DNS_STATIC_SERVERS
#     NETCONFIG_DNS_FORWARDER
# or disable DNS configuration updates via netconfig by setting:
#     NETCONFIG_DNS_POLICY=''
#
# See also the netconfig(8) manual page and other documentation.
#
# Note: Manual change of this file disables netconfig too, but
# may get lost when this file contains comments or empty lines
# only, the netconfig settings are same with settings in this
# file and in case of a "netconfig update -f" call.
#
```

```
### Please remove (at least) this line when you modify the file!
search example.com sandervanvugt.nl
nameserver 8.8.8.8
nameserver 4.4.4.4
```

In the sample file, you can see that two name servers are used. That means that if the first name server cannot be contacted, your server tries to contact the second DNS server. In the error in Listing 9-15, you can see that no servers could be reached. That indicates a problem in the local network configuration; it is very unlikely that two DNS name servers experience an error at the same time.

Configuring SSH

Most servers are in data centers, environments that are hostile to humans, because they are noisy and cold. That means that as an administrator of a SUSE Linux Enterprise Server, you probably want to access the server from a distance. The Secure Shell (SSH) protocol is the default service to get remote access to a server.

To use SSH, you need an SSH server and an SSH client. The SSH server is a process that runs on your server. On most Linux distributions, the name of this process is sshd. To connect to it from a client computer, you can use the ssh client utility, if the client is Linux, or PuTTY, if you're using a Windows client.

Enabling the SSH Server

When a SUSE Linux Server is installed, you can indicate whether you want to start sshd by default. If it is started, and the firewall isn't blocking access, you can access it immediately. (In Chapter 10, you will learn how to configure the firewall to accept SSH traffic, if it is blocking it.) To check if it is available, use the command systemctl status sshd.service, as in Listing 9-20.

Listing 9-20. Checking sshd Status

```
linux-kscc:~ # systemctl status sshd.service
sshd.service - OpenSSH Daemon
   Loaded: loaded (/usr/lib/systemd/system/sshd.service; enabled)
   Active: active (running) since Fri 2014-05-30 12:21:05 CEST; 11h ago
 Main PID: 950 (sshd)
   CGroup: /system.slice/sshd.service
           └─950 /usr/sbin/sshd -D

May 30 12:21:05 linux-kscc sshd-gen-keys-start[936]: Checking for missing server keys in /etc/ssh
May 30 12:21:05 linux-kscc systemd[1]: Started OpenSSH Daemon.
May 30 12:21:05 linux-kscc sshd[950]: Server listening on 0.0.0.0 port 22.
May 30 12:21:05 linux-kscc sshd[950]: Server listening on :: port 22.
May 30 12:50:29 linux-kscc sshd[33306]: Accepted keyboard-interactive/pam for root from 192.168.4.1
    port 50134 ssh2
May 30 12:50:29 linux-kscc sshd[33306]: pam_unix(sshd:session): session opened for user root by (uid=0)
May 30 15:54:02 linux-kscc sshd[37712]: Accepted keyboard-interactive/pam for root from 192.168.4.1
    port 50270 ssh2
May 30 15:54:02 linux-kscc sshd[37712]: pam_unix(sshd:session): session opened for user root by (uid=0)
```

If the sshd service isn't running, you can use systemctl start sshd.service, followed by systemctl enable sshd.service. These two commands make sure that sshd is started and will be started when rebooting as well. In Exercise 9-5, you can read how to test, start, and enable the SSH service.

```
┌──────────────────────────────────────────────────────────────────────┐
│        EXERCISE 9-5. ENABLING AND TESTING THE SSH SERVER               │
└──────────────────────────────────────────────────────────────────────┘
```

In this exercise, you'll enable the SSH server and test connectivity to it from your own local server.

1. From root shell, use the command `systemctl status sshd.service`. Verify that the result looks as in the preceding Listing 9-20. If it does, you don't have to do anything.

2. If the `sshd` service is not running, you need to start it. Use `systemctl start sshd.service` to do this.

3. Use `systemctl enable sshd.service` to enable the SSH. This ensures that the SSH server also comes up after rebooting the server.

4. Now it's time to test the SSH server: open a new terminal window and, from there, use `ssh root@localhost` to open an SSH session in which you're logging in as root. Enter the password when prompted.

5. You're now in an SSH session. In this example, you've tested the connection from your own local machine. You can also test the connection from a remote machine (more about this is in the following sections).

6. Type "exit" to close the SSH sessions.

You have noticed that it's not hard to enable SSH on your server. An SSH server that has been enabled with all the default settings isn't a secure SSH server, however. To make the SSH server secure, there are at least two modifications you should make to the `/etc/ssh/sshd_config` file.

■ **Note** There are two configuration files: `/etc/ssh/ssh_config` is the configuration file in which you put default settings for the `ssh` client utility; in `/etc/ssh/sshd_config`, you specify default settings for the Secure Shell server.

Make sure that you consider at least the following SSH security settings:

- Port: By default, SSH listens on port 22. Every script kiddy on the Internet knows that as well. That means that if you offer SSH services on port 22 of your server, and it is connected directly to the Internet, you are likely to get visitors in not too much time. So, if you're directly on the Internet, change the SSH port to something less obvious. I like putting it on port 443, if the same server doesn't require HTTPS (the average script kiddy expects HTTPS to be offered on that port and, therefore, will launch an HTTPS attack, which will never work). The disadvantage of using port 443, however, is that you can't use HTTPS anymore. A safe choice is a port like 2022. Which exact port you're using doesn't really matter, as long as its number is above 1024. Using a port above 1024 has the advantage of the service not needing to be root to bind to that port.

- ListenAddress: By default, the SSH server offers its services on all IP addresses. In some cases, you might want to restrict this to just the IP addresses that are visible from the internal network, and not from the Internet. If this is the case, change 0.0.0.0 to the specific IP address on which your SSH server should offer its services.

- PermitRootLogin: This parameter, by default, allows the user root to log in to your SSH server. This is not a good idea. If root is permitted to log in, the potential hacker only has to guess the root password to get access. Better to switch off RootLogin, by giving this parameter the value no. That means you'll have to connect as an ordinary user, and once connected, you'll have to use su - to escalate your privileges to the root level.

- ChallengeResponseAuthentication: This parameter, by default, allows users to log in using passwords. If you have created public/private key pairs, you might consider switching off password authentication completely. Be careful, however. Switching off password authentication also makes it difficult for you to log in from an unknown machine on which your private key is not available.

- AllowUsers: This is a very nice parameter that is not in sshd_config by default. Everyone should use it and add a list of only those users they want to allow to log in to their SSH server. This really makes it hard for a hacker, because he'll have to guess the name of that user before he can start his evil work! Notice that by using this parameter, you'll allow only users that are listed here to connect. That means that root also won't have access, if he's not on the list of users specified here.

Apart from these important parameters that relate to security, there are a few that you might want to consider, to ensure that the client session will stay open, even if there's not much activity on it. These are the following settings:

- ClientAliveInterval: The amount of time in minutes that SSH should check, if a connection is still alive. By default, it is set to 0, which means that client sessions will get disconnected after being inactive for too long. It's a good idea to set this to 10.

- ClientAliveCountMax: The amount of packets the SSH service should send to the client before disconnecting a session that is no longer alive. If this is set to the default of 3, and ClientAliveInterval is set to 10, client sessions will stay alive for at least 30 minutes.

You can change the default sshd behavior with many other parameters as well. The preceding parameters are generally considered the most important, however. In Exercise 9-6, you'll learn how to change some of these important parameters.

EXERCISE 9-6. SECURING THE SSH SERVER

In this exercise, you'll change some parameters that help you to secure the SSH server. You'll also create two user accounts to test the AllowUsers parameter. Note that we're using the password "password" in the exercise. It's a very bad idea to use an insecure password such as that for real, but for working through the exercises, the strength of the password doesn't really matter. Using the same (simple) password throughout the book ensures that you'll never run into a situation in which you no longer remember which password was used.

1. Open a root shell on your server and use the commands useradd linda and useradd lisa, to add two users to your server. Next, set the password for these users to "password," by using passwd linda and, next, passwd lisa.

2. Use vim /etc/ssh/sshd_config to open the sshd configuration file.

3. Change the Port parameter and give it the value 443. Next, set the PermitRootLogin parameter to the value no, and add the parameter AllowUsers and give it the value linda.

4. Close the vim editor, using the :wq! command and restart the sshd process, using systemctl restart sshd.service.

5. Connect as root on SSH port 443, using ssh -p 443 root@localhost. Access should be denied. Try to connect as lisa, using ssh -p 443 lisa@localhost. Access should also be denied. Now try to connect as linda, using ssh -p 443 linda@localhost. You should be granted access.

Using the SSH Client

On every Linux computer, an SSH client is available. Also, on Mac OS, you'll have an SSH client by default, which works exactly the same way as the Linux SSH client. Using it is easy: just enter the name of the server you want to connect to as the argument, and a connection will be established. For example, use ssh 192.168.0.1 to establish an SSH session with SSH host 192.168.0.1.

By default, SSH connects with the same user ID as the user ID you are currently logged in with. You can specifically tell the SSH client to connect as a different user, using username@servername as the argument, while using the SSH command. For example, to connect as user linda to server 192.168.0.1, you can use ssh linda@192.168.0.1.

Using PuTTY on Windows Machines

Every Linux computer has an SSH client by default. If you're on Windows, you can also establish SSH sessions, by using the free SSH client PuTTY. You can download a free copy of PuTTY from www.putty.org or from its official web site at www.chiark.greenend.org.uk/~sgtatham/putty and install it on your Windows computer. After starting PuTTY, you'll see its main interface. From there, you can enter the IP address or name of the server you want to connect to and click Open to establish the connection.

Alternatively, you can enter different properties of the SSH session you want to establish using PuTTY, including font sizes and other parameters, and specify a name under Saved Sessions. Next, click Save, to save the parameters, which creates an entry on the list of saved sessions. By using these, you can easily reestablish a session to a host you frequently use.

Configuring Key-Based SSH Authentication

In SSH, the default authentication method is password-based. That means that when connecting to a server, you have to enter the password of the user you are connecting with. There are two reasons why this might not be ideal:

- There is a risk that someone guesses your password.

- If you must connect to the same server frequently, it's a waste of time to enter the same password over and over.

There is an alternative: you can use key-based authentication. When SSH key-based authentication is used, you have to make sure that for all users who need to use this technology, a public key is available on the servers on which they want to log in. When logging in, the user creates an authentication request that is signed with the user's private key. This authentication request is matched to the public key of the same user on the server on which that user wants to authenticate. If it matches, the user is allowed to come in; if it doesn't, the user is denied access.

Public/private-key-based authentication is enabled by default on SUSE Linux Enterprise Server; therefore, only when no keys are present does the server prompt the user for a password. The following summarizes what happens when a user is trying to establish an SSH session with a server:

1. If public key authentication is enabled, which by default is the case, SSH checks the .ssh directory in the user's home directory, to see if a private key is present.

2. If a private key is found, SSH creates a packet with some data in it (the salt), encrypts that packet with the private key, and next sends it to the server. With this packet, the public key is sent as well.

3. The server now checks if a file with the name authorized_keys exists in the home directory of the user. If it doesn't, the user cannot authenticate with his keys. If this file does exist, and the public key is an allowed key and identical to the key that was previously stored on the server, the server uses this key to check the signature.

4. If the signature can be verified, the user is granted access. If it can't, the server will prompt the user, who then tries to connect with his or her password (assuming that password authentication is permitted).

In Exercise 9-7, you'll learn how to set up key-based authentication.

EXERCISE 9-7. SETTING UP KEY-BASED AUTHENTICATION

To use key-based authentication, you'll first have to create a key pair. Next, you will have to copy the key you want to use to the host to which you want to create a connection. You would normally do this between two hosts. That means that in order to perform this exercise, you need a second host that has SUSE Linux Enterprise Server installed. In this exercise, the remote host is referred to as the server. If you don't have a second host to work on, replace the hostname server with localhost, and it will also work.

1. Open a root shell and from there, use ssh server. You will be prompted for a password.

2. Type exit to close the SSH session.

3. Now generate the public/private key pair, using ssh-keygen (see Listing 9-21). You will be prompted as to which file you want to save the private key in. Press Enter to accept the default, which saves the key in /root/.ssh/id_rsa. Next, press Enter twice, to save the key without a passphrase. This completes the procedure and creates two files: id_rsa and id_rsa.pub. In id_rsa, the private key is stored, and in id_rsa.pub, the public key is stored.

Listing 9-21. Creating a Public/Private Key Pair

```
linux-kscc:~ # ssh-keygen
Generating public/private rsa key pair.
Enter file in which to save the key (/root/.ssh/id_rsa):
Enter passphrase (empty for no passphrase):
Enter same passphrase again:
Your identification has been saved in /root/.ssh/id_rsa.
Your public key has been saved in /root/.ssh/id_rsa.pub.
The key fingerprint is:
f1:a2:14:36:5b:b0:2b:df:87:38:08:0a:83:f7:1f:62 [MD5] root@suse
The key's randomart image is:
+--[ RSA 2048]----+
|        .        |
|       o         |
|      = o        |
|.    . * o       |
|+ o . + S .      |
|.+o = + o        |
|.   E * o .      |
|   . o o .       |
|      .          |
+--[MD5]----------+
```

4. Now you need to copy the public key over to the server on which you want to use it. To do this, use ssh-copy-id server. This copies the public key to the server and generates some messages.

5. Use ssh server to connect to the server again. You'll notice that you won't be prompted for a password, because the SSH keys are used to establish the connection.

In the preceding exercise, you established a key-based session in which no further protection was used for the keys. When prompted to enter a passphrase for the key, you just pressed Enter. This is convenient for use in a trusted environment, but it is not very secure.

If you create a public/private key pair to make connection to a server easier, you should consider using a passphrase. Without a passphrase, anyone who copies your private key can forge your identity. With a passphrase, no one can use your private key without knowing the passphrase as well. To use a passphrase, just enter it when prompted for it by ssh-keygen.

There is an inconvenience about using a passphrase, however. You will have to enter it every time you connect to the server. To make it a bit easier, you can use ssh-agent to cache the passphrase for the duration of the session. To do this, you run ssh-agent, with the name of the shell for which you want to cache the passphrase. Run, for instance, ssh-agent /bin/bash. You will be prompted for a passphrase next. Enter it, and it will be cached as long as you keep on working in the same shell. When you type "exit," the passphrase will be forgotten, and you'll have to repeat the same procedure, if you want to start caching your passphrase again. In Exercise 9-8, you'll create a private key that is secured with a passphrase and next use ssh-agent to cache this passphrase.

EXERCISE 9-8. SETTING UP KEY-BASED SSH AUTHENTICATION PROTECTED WITH A PASSPHRASE

In this exercise, you'll generate an SSH public/private key pair. You'll protect the private key by adding a passphrase. Next, you will start ssh-agent, to cache the passphrase.

1. Open a root shell and type "ssh-keygen." When asked where to save the file, press Enter. You will be prompted that the file /root/.ssh/id_rsa already exists. Type "y," to confirm that you want to overwrite this file.

2. Now enter a passphrase and press Enter to confirm. Type the same passphrase again and, once more, press Enter. The key will now be saved.

3. Copy the new public key to your server, using ssh-copy-id server. You must enter your password once, to perform this copy.

4. Establish an SSH session to your server, using ssh server. Enter the passphrase when prompted for. Next, type "exit," to close this session.

5. Type "ssh-agent /bin/bash." Next, type "ssh-add," to add your current passphrase. Type the passphrase, and you will see a confirmation: "Identity added."

6. Type "ssh server." You'll notice that at this point, you can enter a session without entering a passphrase.

7. Type "exit," to close the current ssh session.

8. Type "exit," to close the ssh-agent session. By doing this, the passphrase will be forgotten.

9. Type "ssh server," to establish a new session. You'll notice that you'll be prompted to enter the passphrase again.

Using Graphical Applications with SSH

By default, you cannot use graphical programs over an SSH session. To use them anyway, you have to enable X-Forwarding on the SSH client. To do this, use ssh -X instead of just ssh, when establishing a connection.

As an alternative to using ssh -X, you can also set X Forwarding for all users. To do this, you have to modify the /etc/ssh/ssh_config file. This file contains the parameter ForwardX11. Make sure to enable this parameter and give it the value yes. The next time you start a graphical program from an SSH session, it will work automatically.

Using SSH Port Forwarding

SSH can also be used for port forwarding. That means that you connect a local port on your server to a remote port on some other machine.

In the sample network shown in Figure 9-7, there are three nodes. Node AMS is the node from which the administrator is working. ATL is the node in the middle. AMS has a direct connection to ATL, but not to SLC, which is behind a firewall. ATL, however, does have a direct connection—not obstructed by any firewall—to SLC.

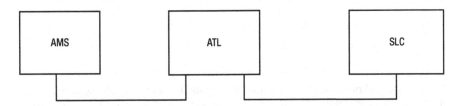

Figure 9-7. *Sample network*

An easy example of port forwarding is one in which the following command is given:

```
linda@AMS:~>ssh -L 4444:ATL:110 linda@ATL
```

In this example, user linda forwards connections to port 4444 on her local host to port 110 on the host ATL, as user linda on that host. This is what you would use, for example, to establish a secure session to the insecure POP service on that host. The local host first establishes a connection to the SSH server running on ATL. This SSH server connects to port 110 at ATL, whereas ssh binds to port 4444 on the local host. Now, an encrypted session is established between local port 4444 and server port 110: everything sent to port 4444 on the local host would really go to port 110 at the server. If, for example, you configured your POP mail client to get its mail from local port 4444, it would really get it from port 110 at ATL. Notice, in this example, that a non-privileged port is used. Only user root can connect to a privileged port with a port number lower than 1024. No matter what port you are connecting to, you should always check in the services configuration file /etc/services, in which port numbers are matched to the names of services that the port is normally used for (if any) and use netstat -patune | grep <your-intended-port> to ensure that the port is not already in use.

A little variation on the local port forwarding seen previously is remote port forwarding. If you use that, you will be forwarding all connections to a given port on the remote port to a local port on your machine. To do so, use the -R option, as in the following example:

```
linda@AMS:-> ssh -R 4444:AMS:110 linda@ATL.
```

In this example, user linda connects to host ATL (see the last part of the command). On this host, port 4444 is addressed by using the construction -R 4444. This remote port is redirected to port 110 on the local host. As a result, anything going to port 4444 on ATL is redirected to port 110 on AMS. This example would be useful if ATL were the client and AMS the server running a POP mail server that linda wanted to connect to.

227

Another very useful example is when the host you want to forward to cannot be reached directly, for example, because it is behind a firewall. In that case, you can establish a tunnel to another host that is reachable with SSH. Imagine that in our example in Figure 9-7 the host SLC is running a POP mail server that user linda wants to connect to. This user would use the following command:

```
linda@AMS:~>ssh -L 4444:SLC:110 linda@ATL
```

In this example, linda forwards connections to port 4444 on her local host to server ATL, which is running ssh. This server would, in turn, forward the connection to port 110 on server SLC. Note that in this scenario, the only requirement is that ATL have the SSH service activated; no sshd is required on SLC for this to work. Also note that there is no need for host AMS to get in direct contact with SLC, because this would happen from host ATL on.

In the preceding examples, you have learned how to use the ssh command to perform port forwarding. This isn't your only option. If a port forwarding connection has to be established all the time, you can put it in the ssh configuration file at the client computer. Put it in .ssh/config in your home directory, if you want it to work for your user account only, or in /etc/ssh/ssh_config, if you want it to apply for all users on your machine. The parameter that should be used as an alternative to ssh -L 4444:ATL:110 would be the following:

```
LocalForward 4444 ATL:110
```

Summary

In this chapter, you have learned all you have to know about networking. The chapter began by explaining how to set up network connections manually. Next you read how to use the wicked command line tool or YaST, to configure network connections permanently. Following that, you read how you can troubleshoot network connections that aren't working properly. At the end of the chapter, you learned how you can configure SSH for remote access to your server. In Chapter 10, you'll learn how to set up security for your Internet services.

■ ■ ■

Securing Internet Services: Certificates and SUSE Firewall

Every server that is connected to the Internet needs security. Security is required at the point of entry; hence, you need a firewall. You'll also have to secure services that are offered by your server, which is why you need certificates. In this chapter, you'll learn how to set up a firewall, using SUSE Firewall, and how to use certificates, with the YaST integrated certificate authority.

Setting Up a Firewall

As with any other Linux distribution, SUSE uses Linux kernel security features, where netfilter is offering firewall services. The default interface to manage the SUSE firewall is by using the YaST firewall module, which you can find in Security and Users ➤ Firewall. This interface offers a clear and straight method for setting up firewall configurations, while still being compatible with the iptables command that administrators can use to configure firewalls from the command line.

SUSE Firewall or iptables?

You have to make a choice when setting up firewalls. While iptables provides an excellent interface to manage firewalls that works the same on all Linux distributions, you don't want to manage with iptables a firewall that was created from YaST. That is because in iptables, the firewall rules, which are easily set from the YaST module, are represented in a complicated way, in which many custom firewall chains are called. In Figure 10-1, you can see what the firewall configuration looks like from SUSE Firewall. In Listing 10-1, you can see the same, but from the iptables interface.

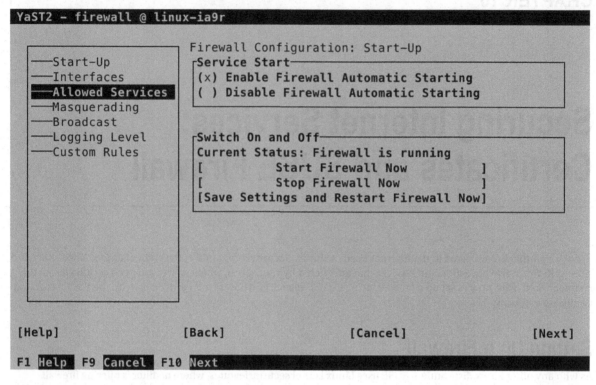

Figure 10-1. *Firewall rules, as seen from SUSE Firewall*

Listing 10-1. The Same Rules, As Seen with `iptables`

```
ldap:~ # iptables -L
Chain INPUT (policy DROP)
target     prot opt source            destination
ACCEPT     all  -- anywhere           anywhere
ACCEPT     all  -- anywhere           anywhere            ctstate ESTABLISHED
ACCEPT     icmp -- anywhere           anywhere            ctstate RELATED
input_ext  all  -- anywhere           anywhere
LOG        all  -- anywhere           anywhere            limit: avg 3/min burst 5 LOG level
warning tcp-options ip-options prefix "SFW2-IN-ILL-TARGET "
DROP       all  -- anywhere           anywhere

Chain FORWARD (policy DROP)
target     prot opt source            destination
LOG        all  -- anywhere           anywhere            limit: avg 3/min burst 5 LOG level
warning tcp-options ip-options prefix "SFW2-FWD-ILL-ROUTING "

Chain OUTPUT (policy ACCEPT)
target     prot opt source            destination
ACCEPT     all  -- anywhere           anywhere
```

```
Chain forward_ext (0 references)
target     prot opt source              destination

Chain input_ext (1 references)
target     prot opt source              destination
DROP       all  -- anywhere             anywhere             PKTTYPE = broadcast
ACCEPT     icmp -- anywhere             anywhere             icmp source-quench
ACCEPT     icmp -- anywhere             anywhere             icmp echo-request
LOG        tcp  -- anywhere             anywhere             limit: avg 3/min burst 5 tcp
dpt:kerberos-adm flags:FIN,SYN,RST,ACK/SYN LOG level warning tcp-options ip-options prefix "SFW2-
INext-ACC-TCP "
ACCEPT     tcp  -- anywhere             anywhere             tcp dpt:kerberos-adm
LOG        tcp  -- anywhere             anywhere             limit: avg 3/min burst 5 tcp dpt:ldap
flags:FIN,SYN,RST,ACK/SYN LOG level warning tcp-options ip-options prefix "SFW2-INext-ACC-TCP "
ACCEPT     tcp  -- anywhere             anywhere             tcp dpt:ldap
LOG        tcp  -- anywhere             anywhere             limit: avg 3/min burst 5 tcp dpt:ldaps
flags:FIN,SYN,RST,ACK/SYN LOG level warning tcp-options ip-options prefix "SFW2-INext-ACC-TCP "
ACCEPT     tcp  -- anywhere             anywhere             tcp dpt:ldaps
LOG        tcp  -- anywhere             anywhere             limit: avg 3/min burst 5 tcp dpt:ssh
flags:FIN,SYN,RST,ACK/SYN LOG level warning tcp-options ip-options prefix "SFW2-INext-ACC-TCP "
ACCEPT     tcp  -- anywhere             anywhere             tcp dpt:ssh
ACCEPT     udp  -- anywhere             anywhere             udp dpt:kpasswd
ACCEPT     udp  -- anywhere             anywhere             udp dpt:kerberos
ACCEPT     udp  -- anywhere             anywhere             udp dpt:loadav
ACCEPT     udp  -- anywhere             anywhere             udp dpt:ldap
DROP       all  -- anywhere             anywhere             PKTTYPE = multicast
DROP       all  -- anywhere             anywhere             PKTTYPE = broadcast
LOG        tcp  -- anywhere             anywhere             limit: avg 3/min burst 5 tcp
flags:FIN,SYN,RST,ACK/SYN LOG level warning tcp-options ip-options prefix "SFW2-INext-DROP-DEFLT "
LOG        icmp -- anywhere             anywhere             limit: avg 3/min burst 5 LOG level
warning tcp-options ip-options prefix "SFW2-INext-DROP-DEFLT "
LOG        udp  -- anywhere             anywhere             limit: avg 3/min burst 5 ctstate NEW
LOG level warning tcp-options ip-options prefix "SFW2-INext-DROP-DEFLT "
DROP       all  -- anywhere             anywhere

Chain reject_func (0 references)
target     prot opt source              destination
REJECT     tcp  -- anywhere             anywhere             reject-with tcp-reset
REJECT     udp  -- anywhere             anywhere             reject-with icmp-port-unreachable
REJECT     all  -- anywhere             anywhere             reject-with icmp-proto-unreachable
```

Setting Up a Firewall with SUSE Firewall

To keep things simple, in this book, you'll learn how to configure a firewall, using SUSE Firewall.

Understanding SUSE Firewall Core Components

SUSE Firewall is based on a few core principles. If you want to set up a firewall successfully, you have to know how to handle each of the following:

- *Interfaces*: These are the network cards the firewall is using.

- *Zones*: Each interface is configured in a zone. The zone configuration allows users to make an easy distinction between secure environments, partially secured environments, and insecure environments.

- *Services*: Services are the basic entities that you want to add to firewall zones.

Before starting firewall configuration in the SUSE Firewall YaST module, let's have a look at what is behind it. First, there is the file /etc/sysconfig/SuSEfirewall2. This file contains all settings that you'll be making with YaST. The file behaves as a typical /etc/sysiconfig script: it is processed at the time the firewall starts, and all variables that are defined in the script are activated. Even if you can modify this script manually, you shouldn't, because the YaST module provides an excellent method to do exactly the same.

Next, there are the service definition files in /etc/sysconfig/SuSEfirewall2.d/services. In these files, properties of specific services are defined. By default, a limited amount of services is defined, but it is relatively easy to add your own services. In Listing 10-2, you can see the contents of the sander service file I created:

Listing 10-2. Example of a Service File

```
ldap:/etc/sysconfig/SuSEfirewall2.d/services # cat sander
## Name: sander
## Description: Opens ports for the sander Server (sander).

# space separated list of allowed TCP ports
TCP="sander"

# space separated list of allowed UDP ports
UDP="sander"

# space separated list of allowed RPC services
RPC=""

# space separated list of allowed IP protocols
IP=""

# space separated list of allowed UDP broadcast ports
BROADCAST=""
```

As you can see, the service file is relatively simple. As a starting point, it contains only the TCP and UDP ports that have to be opened. In the example, file names are used. These names match the definitions in /etc/services, in which I have added TCP and UDP ports 778 as ports for the sander service. The service files also allow for additional configuration, such as a specification of RPC services (used in NFS environments) or very rarely used IP services that are allowed to the service. The services files created in /etc/sysconfig/SuSEfirewall2.d/services are all available in the YaST firewall module, which allows you to configure the firewall in an easy but consistent manner.

Using YaST to Set Up a Firewall

From YaST, you'll select Security and Users ➤ Firewall to create a firewall configuration. This opens the interface that you see in Figure 10-2.

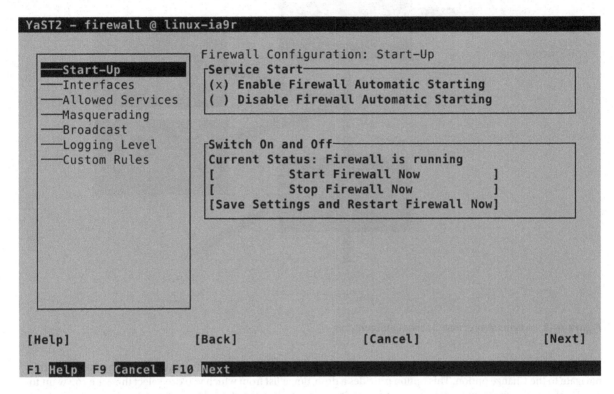

Figure 10-2. *Configuring a firewall from YaST*

On the Start-Up tab, you'll enable the firewall. If you haven't disabled it during installation, it will be enabled by default. On the Interfaces tab, you can see the network interfaces that were found on your computer and the zone they are currently configured in. As services are allowed or denied in zones, you should make sure to configure a zone for each interface. Three zones are available:

- *Internal*: This is the trusted network, where no restrictions are required.

- *External*: This is the Internet zone, where security needs to be at the highest level.

- *Demilitarized*: This is the zone behind the internal and the external zone, where typically, web services and other services that have to be publicly available reside.

Figure 10-3 gives a schematic overview of the different zones.

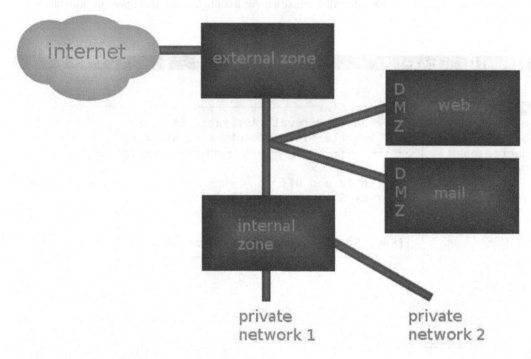

Figure 10-3. *Schematic overview of zone configuration*

Your first task as a firewall administrator is to assign each interface to a zone. To do this, select the Interface and navigate to the Change option. This option provides a drop-down list from which you can select the zone you want to use. Working with zones makes it easy to assign services to multiple network cards.

Allowed Services

The Allowed Services tab (see Figure 10-4) allows you to select services and add them to a zone. From this interface, you can also add your own services, as an alternative to modifying the configuration file directly, as described earlier in this chapter.

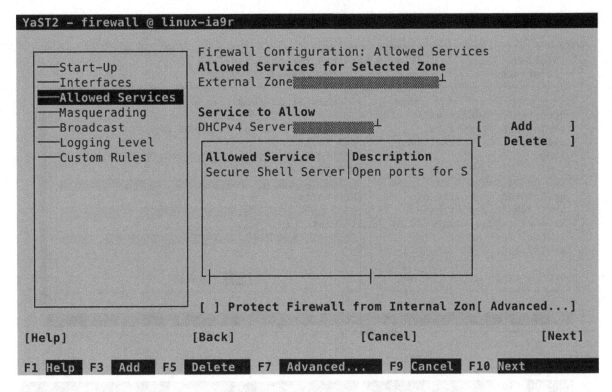

Figure 10-4. Managing services

To manage a service, you first select the zone you want to add the service to. Make sure it corresponds to the network interface you want the services to be allowed on. You will notice that in the Internal Zone, all services are allowed, and no restriction is applied by default. In the External Zone and the Demilitarized Zone, you will have to specify which services you want to allow yourself.

After selecting the zone you want to configure, you can select the service you want to allow. To do this, use the Service to Allow drop-down list and select Add, to add it. You will now see it in the list of allowed services.

The Advanced option on the Allowed Services tab makes it possible to define your own services (see Figure 10-5). This can be useful if you have to set up more complicated services that aren't available by default. You can specify multiple ports and even IP protocols. (This is useful if you're interested in such protocols as esp, smp, or chaos. If you have no clue what these are—as is the case for the majority of Linux admins on this planet—you don't need them.)

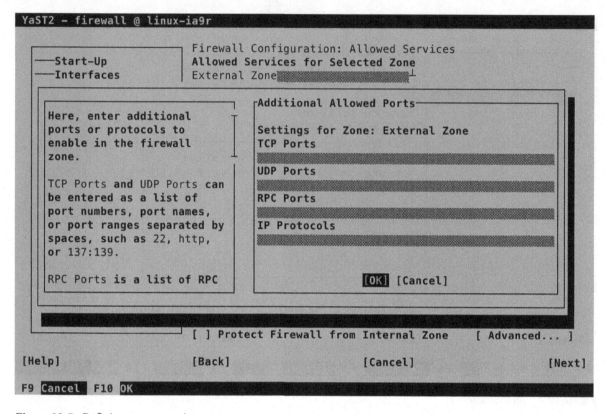

Figure 10-5. *Defining custom services*

Understanding Masquerading

Before setting up Masquerading, you have to know what you're dealing with. Figure 10-6 gives a schematic overview. In IP Masquerading, also known as Network Address Translation (NAT), you'll always have an external and an internal network. On the external network, public IP addresses, which can be reached directly, are used. On the private network, IP addresses from the private IP address ranges can be reached. These addresses are not directly accessible from the Internet. The following IP address ranges can be used as private IP addresses. These addresses will never be routed on the Internet.

- 10.0.0.0/8

- 172.168.16.0/20

- 192.168.0.0/16

In Masquerading, two solutions are used.

- Internal clients can use the public IP address of the Masquerading router to go out on the Internet. This solution is referred to as dynamic NAT.

- Port forwarding can be used to define publicly accessible ports on the router, which are forwarded to private IP addresses on the internal network. This solution is referred to as port forwarding.

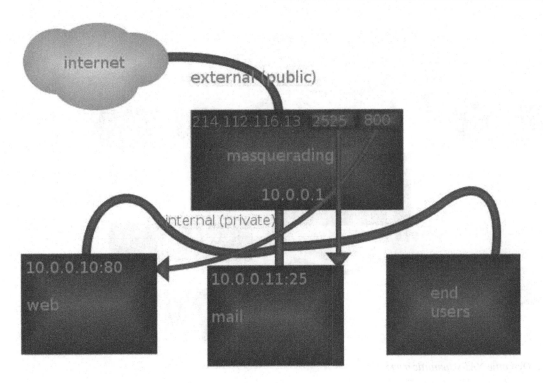

Figure 10-6. *NAT schematic overview*

In both solutions, the Linux kernel routes packets between networks and is configured to keep track of connections in the NAT table. In the schematic overview in Figure 10-6, you can see that on the NAT router, a public IP address, 214.112.116.13, is used. In this IP address, two ports are available: 2525 and 800. Behind these ports there must be a port-forwarding configuration that tells the NAT router that all traffic coming in on port 2525 is forwarded to 10.0.0.11:25 and all traffic addressed to port 800 is forwarded to 10.0.0.10:80.

In dynamic NAT, it is the end user who initiates the traffic. Have a look at Figure 10-7, for a schematic overview. In this overview, a user at IP address 10.0.0.60 issues a request to go to http://www.sander.fr. As this name resolves to IP address, in step 2, a packet is created with the destination address 217.70.184.38:80. The source address in this packet is 10.0.0.60:2345, in which the dynamic port 2345 is used as an identifier when the answering packet comes back from the target web server.

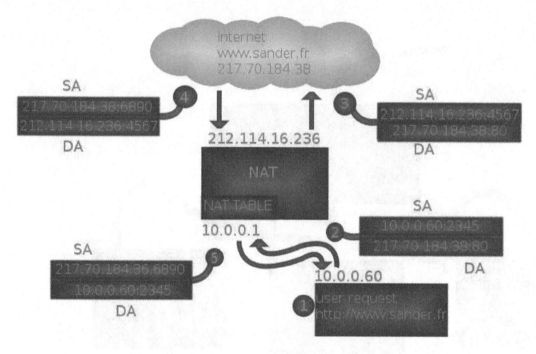

Figure 10-7. *Dynamic NAT schematic overview*

Before it can be further processed, the packet arrives at the NAT router. This router takes out the source address and stores it in an internal table, in which all outstanding NAT requests are stored. Next, the NAT router can re-create the packet, where, in step 3, the destination address is still the same, but the packet source address is now replaced with the IP address of the NAT router.

When the packet arrives at its destination, the destination server knows no better than that the packet comes from 212.114.16.236:4567, so the answer is sent back to that IP address in step 4. When the packet arrives on the NAT router, it uses port 4567 to identify the NAT request in the NAT table, which allows it to find the original request from the NAT client. This allows the NAT router in step 5 to send back a packet to the original client, who isn't aware at all of everything that has happened to the packet.

Setting Up Masquerading

Setting up Masquerading from YaST is easy. In the Firewall module, select the Masquerading tab and select Masquerade Networks. This is all you have to do to set up dynamic NAT.

To configure port forwarding, you select Add, from the YaST Masquerading module. This opens the interface that you see in Figure 10-8. With this interface, the following options are available:

- *Source Network*: This option allows you to specify the allowed source network addresses. The address 0/0 opens the port-forwarding rule to any client.

- *Protocol*: Select TCP, UDP, or any other upper layer client protocol.

- *Requested IP*: This optional option allows you to make this rule available on one specific public IP address only.

- *Requested Port*: This is the port that must be available on the public IP address of your IP Masquerading router.

- *Redirection*: The private IP address that the request has to be forwarded to

- *Redirect to Port*: The port on the target IP address the request has to be forwarded to.

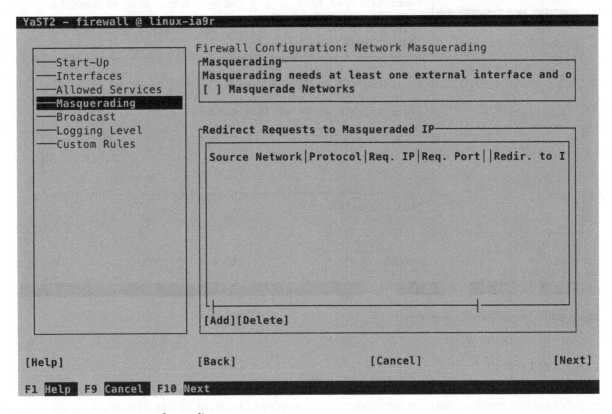

Figure 10-8. *Setting up port forwarding*

Notice that the option Redirect to Port is optional. Without this option, requests will be directed to the same port. This allows you, for example, to open port 80 on the Masquerading router and forward that to the same port on the IP address in the internal network.

Broadcast

A specific case that must be handled by a firewall is broadcast packets. Some services, such as CUPS printing, need broadcast to announce and discover the availability of services. If you have opened the firewall for a service that needs broadcast packets, it will automatically be added to the Broadcast overview screen that you see in Figure 10-9. Be careful setting up broadcast services yourself, because this is not typically what you want on an Internet connection.

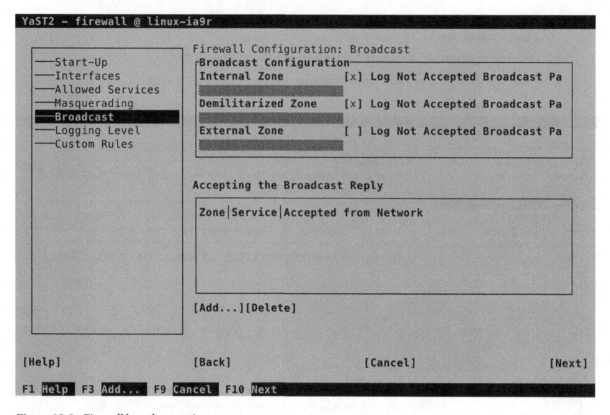

Figure 10-9. *Firewall broadcast settings*

Logging Level

In a firewall, it is possible to log all packets. Believe me, you don't want that, because the log system will get overwhelmed with messages. You do, however, want to see entries occurring in the log files, if something critical happens. That is exactly what is configured in the Logging Level tab. If you need more information, you can use the drop-down lists to select another log level for logging of accepted packets, as well as logging of not accepted packets (see Figure 10-10).

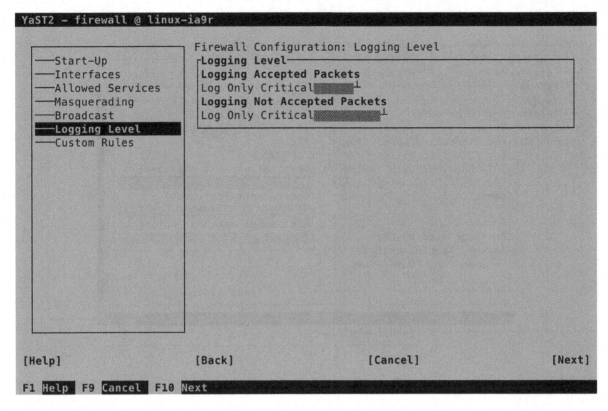

Figure 10-10. *Specifying the log level*

Custom Rules

SUSE Firewall allows you to specify custom rules as well. In a custom rule, you can specify exactly what you want the firewall to allow or disallow. To start with, it permits you to open a source network, allowing or denying packets from that specific network only. Next, you can specify source and destination ports, as well as some of the advanced additional options that can be used with `iptables`.

Custom rules can be used, if you have specific needs. Imagine that you want to open the web service, but only for hosts coming from the network 10.0.0.0/24. You would define the source network 10.0.0.0/24, specify TCP as the protocol, and add the destination port 80 (see Figure 10-11).

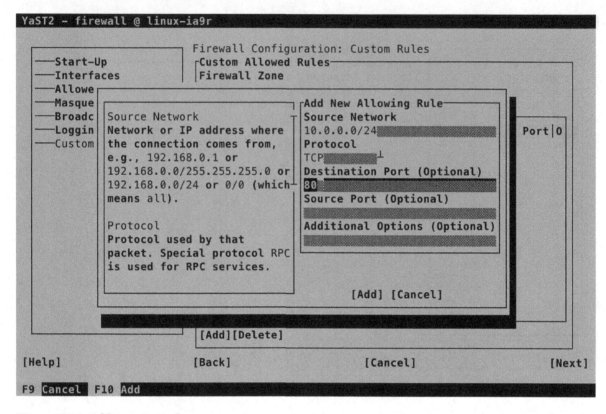

Figure 10-11. *Adding custom rules*

Before writing the firewall configuration, you'll see a summary of selected settings. This brings all you have configured so far together in one interface. If the summary doesn't provide you with enough detail, make sure to select the Show Details option as well. This option provides valuable additional information, as you can see in Figure 10-12. After confirming that all is configured the way you want it to be, select Finish, to write the configuration to your system.

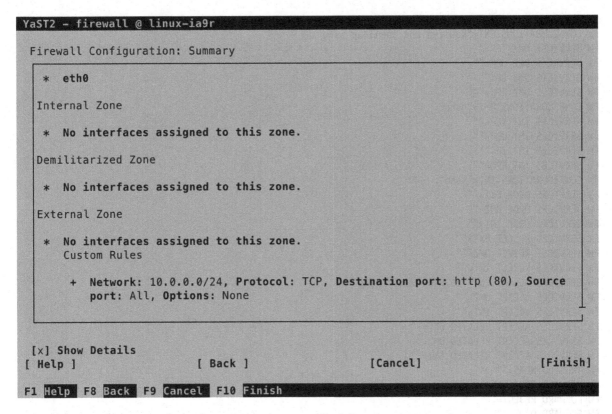

Figure 10-12. *Before writing the configuration, make sure to check the summary*

Checking SUSE Firewall Configuration

As an administrator, it is always good to know where you can find the configuration you have created. In the case of SUSE Firewall, most of the settings are stored in the file /etc/sysconfig/SuSEfirewall2. You can see that Listing 10-3 contains, in particular, many of the Masquerading options, which are easily recognized by the letters *FW*.

Listing 10-3. Checking Firewall Configuration

```
ldap:/etc/sysconfig # cat SuSEfirewall2 | grep -v ^# | grep -v '^$'
FW_DEV_EXT="eth0"
FW_DEV_INT="eth1"
FW_DEV_DMZ=""
FW_ROUTE="yes"
FW_MASQUERADE="yes"
FW_MASQ_DEV=""
FW_MASQ_NETS=""
FW_NOMASQ_NETS=""
FW_PROTECT_FROM_INT="no"
FW_SERVICES_EXT_TCP=""
FW_SERVICES_EXT_UDP=""
FW_SERVICES_EXT_IP=""
```

```
FW_SERVICES_EXT_RPC=""
FW_CONFIGURATIONS_EXT="kadmind kdc openldap sshd"
FW_SERVICES_DMZ_TCP=""
FW_SERVICES_DMZ_UDP=""
FW_SERVICES_DMZ_IP=""
FW_SERVICES_DMZ_RPC=""
FW_CONFIGURATIONS_DMZ="sshd"
FW_SERVICES_INT_TCP=""
FW_SERVICES_INT_UDP=""
FW_SERVICES_INT_IP=""
FW_SERVICES_INT_RPC=""
FW_CONFIGURATIONS_INT="sshd"
FW_SERVICES_DROP_EXT=""
FW_SERVICES_DROP_DMZ=""
FW_SERVICES_DROP_INT=""
FW_SERVICES_REJECT_EXT=""
FW_SERVICES_REJECT_DMZ=""
FW_SERVICES_REJECT_INT=""
FW_SERVICES_ACCEPT_EXT="10.0.0.0/24,tcp,80"
FW_SERVICES_ACCEPT_DMZ=""
FW_SERVICES_ACCEPT_INT=""
FW_SERVICES_ACCEPT_RELATED_EXT=""
FW_SERVICES_ACCEPT_RELATED_DMZ=""
FW_SERVICES_ACCEPT_RELATED_INT=""
FW_TRUSTED_NETS=""
FW_FORWARD=""
FW_FORWARD_REJECT=""
FW_FORWARD_DROP=""
FW_FORWARD_MASQ="0/0,10.0.0.20,tcp,2525,25"
FW_REDIRECT=""
FW_LOG_DROP_CRIT="yes"
FW_LOG_DROP_ALL="no"
FW_LOG_ACCEPT_CRIT="yes"
FW_LOG_ACCEPT_ALL="no"
FW_LOG_LIMIT=""
FW_LOG=""
FW_KERNEL_SECURITY=""
FW_STOP_KEEP_ROUTING_STATE=""
FW_ALLOW_PING_FW=""
FW_ALLOW_PING_DMZ=""
FW_ALLOW_PING_EXT=""
FW_ALLOW_FW_SOURCEQUENCH=""
FW_ALLOW_FW_BROADCAST_EXT="no"
FW_ALLOW_FW_BROADCAST_INT="no"
FW_ALLOW_FW_BROADCAST_DMZ="no"
FW_IGNORE_FW_BROADCAST_EXT="yes"
FW_IGNORE_FW_BROADCAST_INT="no"
FW_IGNORE_FW_BROADCAST_DMZ="no"
FW_ALLOW_CLASS_ROUTING=""
FW_CUSTOMRULES=""
FW_REJECT=""
```

```
FW_REJECT_INT=""
FW_HTB_TUNE_DEV=""
FW_IPv6=""
FW_IPv6_REJECT_OUTGOING=""
FW_IPSEC_TRUST="no"
FW_ZONES=""
FW_ZONE_DEFAULT=''
FW_USE_IPTABLES_BATCH=""
FW_LOAD_MODULES="nf_conntrack_netbios_ns"
FW_FORWARD_ALWAYS_INOUT_DEV=""
FW_FORWARD_ALLOW_BRIDGING=""
FW_WRITE_STATUS=""
FW_RUNTIME_OVERRIDE=""
FW_LO_NOTRACK=""
FW_BOOT_FULL_INIT=""
```

EXERCISE 10-1. CONFIGURING A FIREWALL

This exercise allows you to apply some firewall settings. It assumes nothing has been configured yet.

1. From a root shell, type "yast firewall," to start the YaST firewall module directly.

2. On the Start-Up tab, select Enable Firewall Automatic Starting.

3. Configure your network card in the external zone, using the options on the Interfaces tab.

4. On the Allowed Services list, add at least the Secure Shell Server. There is no need to do anything else, because while configuring the individual modules, you'll use the options on the Start-Up tab to open the firewall for the specific service.

Working with SSL Certificates

For many services that are offered by a modern server, additional security is a requirement. By using this security, you can make sure that traffic to the server is encrypted and that the identity of the server is guaranteed. To realize this security, SSL is the standard. Before talking about setting up SSL certificates, you'll now first read how the public/private key is used in common cryptography.

Understanding SSL

When thinking about SSL, many people think about web servers only. SSL certificates, however, are used by other servers as well. Without SSL, anyone can capture passwords that are sent between a POP or IMAP mail client and the mail server, and also, LDAP is commonly protected with SSL, to make sure that the passwords that are sent over cannot be captured when authenticating against an LDAP server. This makes creation and distribution of certificates an essential task for administrators.

If a user wants to establish a connection to a site, this connection must be protected. To ensure a protected connection, public and private keys are used. These keys can be used for the following three different reasons:

- To encrypt traffic from and to a server

- To prove the identity of another party

- To verify that a message has not been tampered with

Let's take an example in which public/private keys are used to encrypt traffic that is sent to a server, something that is common during Internet use.

1. When the connection to the server is first initialized, the server sends its public key infrastructure (PKI) certificate. This contains the public key of the server and is signed with the private key of the certificate authority (CA) that the owner of the server has used.

2. To verify that the PKI certificate can be trusted, the signature of the CA that is in the certificate is checked. If the signature can be traced back to a public key that already is known to the client, the connection is considered to be trusted.

3. Now that the connection is trusted, the client can send encrypted packets to the server. To encrypt the data traffic, the public key of the server is used.

4. As public/private-key encryption is one-way encryption, only the server is capable of decrypting the traffic, by using its private key.

The essential part in working securely with SSL is the certificate. The certificate contains the public key of the server that users are going to employ to establish a secured connection, and it contains a "proof of identity," which is normally provided by a CA. This CA can be a commonly trusted external server, or it can be an internal service that is used to create self-signed certificates.

The use of public/private keys is a great improvement in security on the Internet. But there is a challenge. How can the receiver be sure that the public key that is received really comes from the server that it is supposed to come from and not from a hacker who has hijacked the connection? This is where the CA comes in.

To guarantee the authenticity of a public key, a CA is used. The role of the CA is to sign certificates. A certificate can be generated by just any server, and it is the role of the CA to sign these certificates with its private key. This, however, only is useful if the public key of the CA is known to the client that receives the certificate. If this is not the case, the user will see a message indicating that he's using an untrusted connection and will probably close the connection. So, for common use on the Internet, you better make sure that the CA is known to everyone. For private internal use, an in-house CA can be used as well.

If you want to create your own CA, you better make sure that the users that are going to use it will also trust it. You can accomplish this by having its certificates signed by a commonly known CA. Because the public keys of these commonly known CAs are available in most client applications, the CA that uses it will transparently be accepted. The only drawback is that, in general, you need to pay the CA that is going to sign your certificates. If you don't want or don't need to do that, you can use a self-signed certificate.

In case you are creating a certificate that is to be trusted, you need to have it signed. To do this, you'll send a certificate signing request. You'll learn in this chapter how you can do this.

In this section, you will learn how to run your own CA. If you do that, you can have its certificates signed by a trusted root. Alternatively, you can use self-signed certificates. This is the kind of certificate in which you mention "You can trust me, because I say so." Not really the kind of security that you want to show your customers on the Internet, but for internal use it works well.

If you're using self-signed certificates anywhere in the chain, the first time a user uses it, he or she will get a message indicating that there is a problem with the trustworthiness of the certificate. If your users are mainly internal users, you can deal with that, by importing the certificates on the users' workstations. If they are external users, you have to convince them in some way that the certificate is to be trusted. If you're offering an SSL-protected web server for your local hockey club, that's not too hard to do, but you don't really want to do this for the customers of your web shop on the Internet.

Configuring the YaST Certificate Authority

On the YaST Security and Users tab, the option CA Management is offered (see Figure 10-13). You may find an already existing certificate authority (CA), or you can create one for yourself. To allow for the management of certificates in your own environment, it's a good idea to create your own CA. To do this, select Create Root CA.

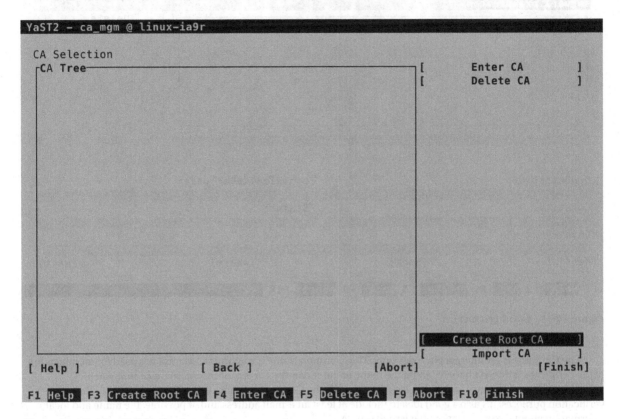

Figure 10-13. *The CA Selection interface*

On the Create New Root CA screen (see Figure 10-14), you have to enter the properties of the CA. The amount of completeness depends on what you're going to use the CA for. If you're using it for internal purposes only, it suffices to specify CA Name and Common Name. If you want to use it for signing external certificates as well, it's a good idea to be as complete as possible, to make it easy for users to identify your CA.

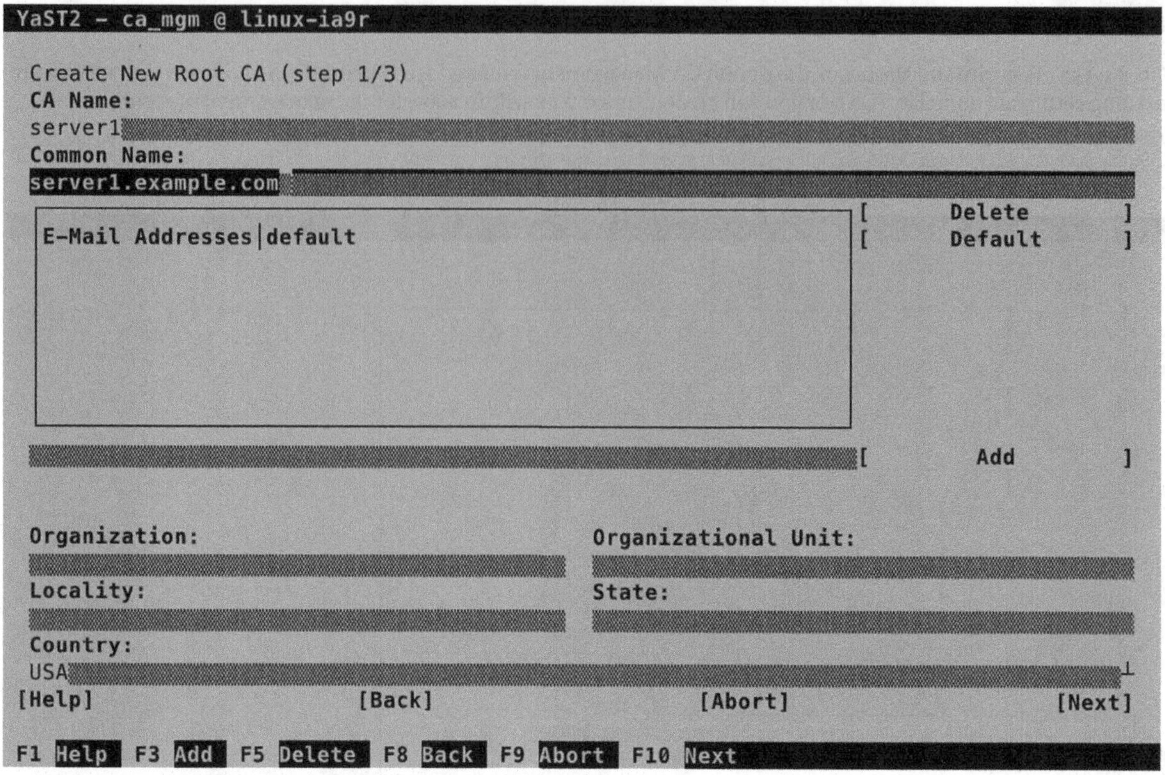

```
YaST2 - ca_mgm @ linux-ia9r

  Create New Root CA (step 1/3)
  CA Name:
  server1
  Common Name:
  server1.example.com
                                                          [    Delete    ]
    E-Mail Addresses|default                              [    Default   ]




                                                          [     Add      ]


  Organization:                      Organizational Unit:


  Locality:                          State:


  Country:
  USA
                                                                        ⊥
  [Help]              [Back]                   [Abort]          [Next]

 F1 Help  F3 Add  F5 Delete  F8 Back  F9 Abort  F10 Next
```

Figure 10-14. *Creating a root CA*

The CA Name is for internal purposes only. The Common Name is important, because it is used for identification of the certificate. It doesn't have to match the name of the server the CA is running on, so make sure you pick something that makes sense and makes it easy to identify the CA from a certificate that it has signed. For these verification purposes, it's also a good idea to include at least an e-mail address and, if possible, the name and local information about the organization that issued the CA.

On the second screen of the Create New Root CA procedure, you'll enter a password that protects the CA, a key length, and a validity period. The password is mandatory, so choose wisely. The key length, by default, is set to 2048 bits, and the standard validity is 3650 days. In general, there is no reason to change these parameters.

If you have advanced requirements for setting up the properties of the CA, you can do so by selecting Advanced Options. This opens the screen shown in Figure 10-15, on which you can set a wide variety of usage options. In general, you don't need them for setting up your own CA for internal usage.

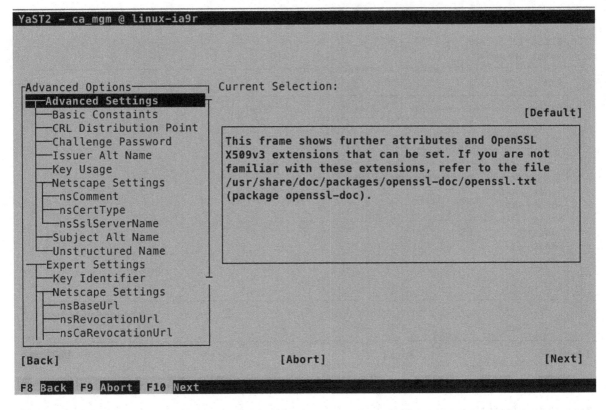

Figure 10-15. *Specifying advanced CA options*

Before selecting Create on the last screen of the procedure, you can verify the summary of all options that have been selected. Once the CA is created, you go back to the CA Selection screen, from which you can enter the CA, to issue certificates. Remember that a CA by itself doesn't serve any purpose other than to sign the certificates that your services are going to use.

Creating Certificates

Now that you have your own certificate authority (CA), you can go on and create certificates. To understand what you are doing, it's good to remember the big picture and make sure you understand what the certificates are used for.

- Every service that requires security services needs access to a private key as well as a public key.

- When a client connects to that service, he or she needs access to the public key certificate of the CA that signed the service certificate.

- If the certificate is signed by a commonly known CA, often no additional work is required. If the certificate is self-signed, the client application needs access to the CA certificate as well.

To create certificates, from the YaST CA Management main screen, you first have to enter the CA. After supplying the CA password, you gain access to all CA Management options (see Figure 10-16).

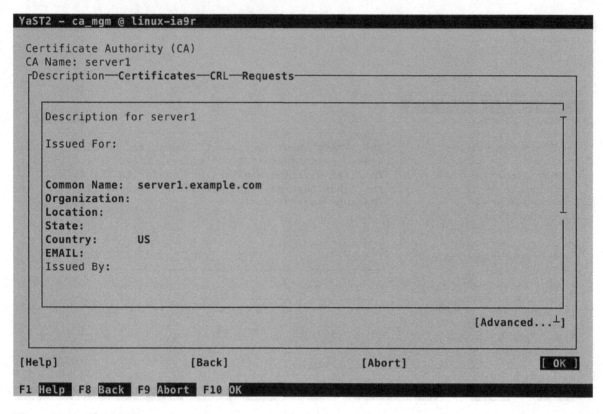

Figure 10-16. *The CA Management screen*

To create a certificate, activate the Certificates tab and select Add. This shows a small drop-down list from which you can specify whether to create a Server Certificate or a Client Certificate. From this drop-down list, select Add Server Certificate. This opens the screen shown in Figure 10-17.

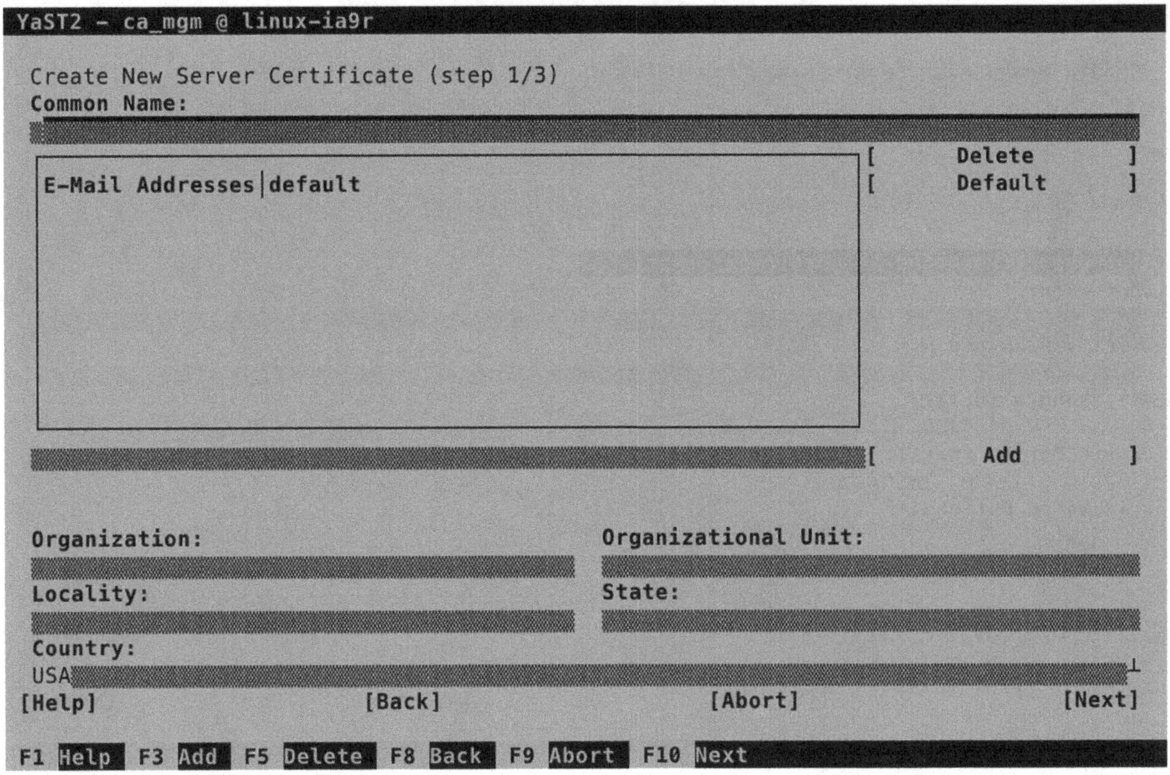

```
 YaST2 - ca_mgm @ linux-ia9r

  Create New Server Certificate (step 1/3)
  Common Name:

  ┌────────────────────────────────────────────────────┐  [     Delete          ]
  │ E-Mail Addresses│default                            │  [     Default         ]
  │                                                      │
  │                                                      │
  │                                                      │
  │                                                      │
  │                                                      │
  │                                                      │
  └────────────────────────────────────────────────────┘ [       Add            ]


  Organization:                        Organizational Unit:

  Locality:                            State:

  Country:
  USA
 [Help]                 [Back]                    [Abort]                   [Next]

 F1 Help  F3 Add  F5 Delete  F8 Back  F9 Abort  F10 Next
```

Figure 10-17. Specifying certificate properties

The single most important option when creating a new certificate is the Common Name. This must match the name of the server that is going to use the certificate. If it doesn't match, it will most likely be rejected by the client who is going to receive the certificate. In general, you have two options here.

- Use the name as returned by the uname -ncommand, to use the certificate as a common server certificate. If you're not sure which option is best, select this option.

- Use the name that is similar to the service that is being configured to use it. So, if your server name is server.example.com, but you're going to use the certificate on ldap.example.com, the common name should be ldap.example.com.

On the second screen (see Figure 10-18), you'll have to set a password to protect the private key that you are going to generate. Consider this a mandatory activity: the password is going to protect the key from physical theft. To make it easy, you can also use the CA password as the certificate password. After specifying the password, you can select a Key Length and a Valid Period. A longer key length means better protection, but it's more complex and, therefore, can make the services that are using it a bit slower. The default key length of 2048 bits works well for most uses.

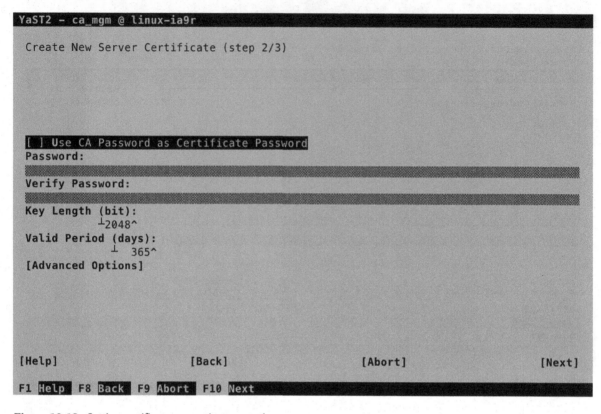

Figure 10-18. *Setting certificate encryption properties*

An option to consider favorably is the Valid Period. By default, it is set to 365 days, which means that you'll have to create and generate new certificates every 365 days. For security reasons, it is good to have a validity period of only 365 days, but that means you'll have to be prepared to replace all keys after a year. So, you better put a notification in your agenda, if you don't want to find out one year from now that your keys have expired, which makes authentication of all users on your LDAP server impossible.

As is the case for the CA, when creating a server certificate, you can specify many advanced options as well. For most uses, you don't need them, and that's why I'm not explaining them here either. After specifying all required properties, press Next, verify all settings in the overview screen, and click Create, to create the certificate.

Understanding Certificate Exports

Merely creating a certificate isn't enough. You'll have to do something with it, and that means that you have to export it. This is where certificate management often goes wrong. The reason is that there are many different kinds of exports that can be performed, and they are often mixed up. Let's first line up the different scenarios.

- You want to use the certificate you've just created on the server where you've created it.

- You want to use the certificate you've just created on another server.

- You have to make sure that client applications can use the certificate you've just created.

The first scenario is the easiest. If you want to use the certificate you've just created on the same server, you can just export it as the default server certificate. This will at least allow your applications to access the certificate in an easy way. As the certificates we've just created are self-signed certificates, you will have a problem with client applications, however. Fix this by exporting the CA certificate as well, and make it available to client applications that have to use it.

If you're using one CA in your network to create certificates for use on other servers, you'll have to export the certificate to files and make these files available on the other server. In this case, you still have to make sure that the CA certificate is available for use by the clients.

In any case, as the certificates you've created here are self-signed certificates, you'll have to make the CA certificate available to clients as well. This step is often skipped, which inevitably poses problems when using services that are set up to use your certificates.

Note that in all the preceding cases described, you'll have to export the CA certificate for use on the client computers. That is because the certificates that have been created here are self-signed certificates, and the validity of the certificates cannot be traced back to the signing CA by the clients. That's why you have to do it manually.

If you have your certificates signed by an external certificate authority, the signing CA can be traced back to a known CA by the client application. On the client, the applications that require certificates have access to the certificates of commonly known CAs. These certificates are installed locally on the client, and that means that the certificates you've issued can be verified without any further intervention. Later in this chapter, you can read how to set up your CA to use certificates that are externally signed.

Setting Up a Default Server Certificate

The easiest scenario is to set the certificates you've just created as the default server certificates. To do this, after entering the CA, select the Certificates tab and click Export. Then select Export as Common Server Certificate (see Figure 10-19) and enter the password that you've used when creating the certificate pair.

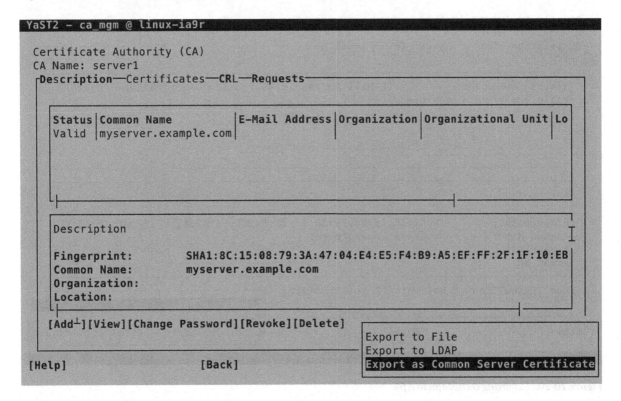

Figure 10-19. Setting common server certificates

As a result of this export action, two certificates have been created in the directory /etc/ssl/servercerts. The servercert.pem file contains the public key certificate. This is what services are going to offer to clients wanting to establish an SSL session. The serverkey.pem file contains the private key of the server. It needs the highest level of protection, and therefore, it is accessible by the root user only. Consider the location /etc/ssl/servercerts a temporary location, but you will further configure the certificate locations when setting up services to use the certificates.

Exporting Certificates for Use on Another Server

In a corporate environment, it makes sense to run one CA only. Preferably, this CA is not even network-connected and is used to generate public/private key pairs for all of the servers needing access to PKI certificates. If that is the case, from the CA server, you have to export the certificates. Here again, two options are available.

- Export the public key certificate as well as the private key of the certificate to files.

- Export both public key certificates as private key to an LDAP server, from which it can easily be accessed.

To export the certificates to a file, from the Certificate Authority management screen, select Certificates, then Export, and then Export to File (see Figure 10-20).

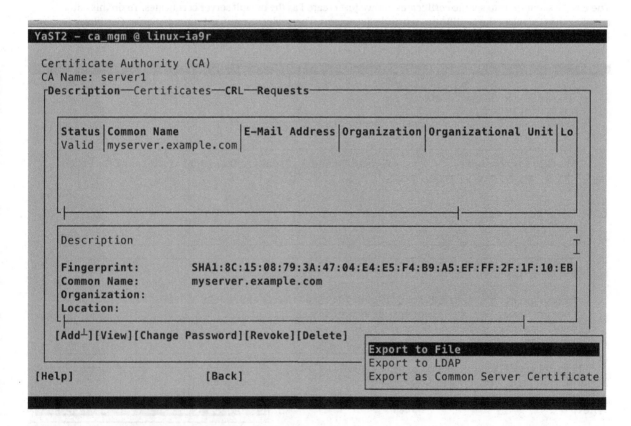

Figure 10-20. Exporting certificates to a file

You'll now see the Export Certificate to File screen (see Figure 10-21), from which you can choose from multiple options. From among these options, you will have to make a few choices, which are described as follows:

- *File format*: Depending on the application that is going to use the certificates, you can choose between PEM, DER, and PKCS12 formats. As long as your application supports it, it doesn't really matter what you select here. PEM is by far the most common format.

- *Encryption level*: If you want to add additional protection to the certificates while they are in transit, make sure to export them as encrypted certificates.

- If you want client users to have access to all certificates, select an option that includes the CA Chain. This copies over the certificate of the signing CA as well.

- Select if you want to export the key, the certificate, or both of them.

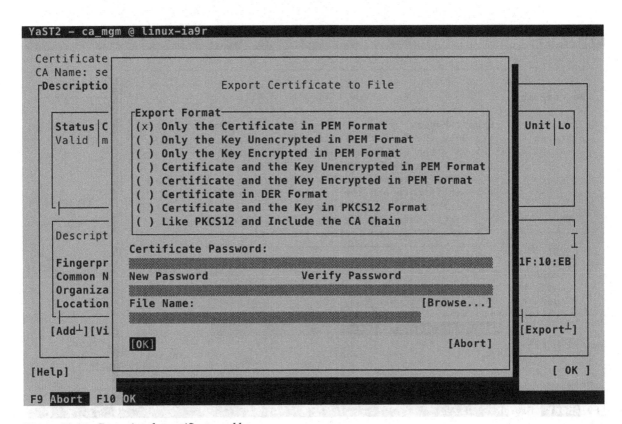

Figure 10-21. *Exporting the certificate and key*

Next, you can specify the password that was used when creating the private key (assuming that you have selected to export the private key as well). Make sure you also export the name of the destination file. For use of the certificates on another server, it's a good idea to put them in a location where the other server can easily access them, like an FTP server. Be careful, though, when transferring private keys!

■ **Tip**   Even if it is convenient to export the key as well as the certificate in one run, it means you'll have to extract them as well, which isn't always obvious. To make it easy to use the certificates on the other server, I recommend that you first export the certificate to a file and then export the key to another file.

Making Certificates Available for Use on Clients

Now that you've made the certificates available to use on other servers, you have to make the certificate authority (CA) certificate available to client applications using these certificates as well. To do this, from the YaST CA Selection screen, choose Enter CA. Once in the Certificate Authority screen, select Advanced ➤ Export CA to File (see Figure 10-22).

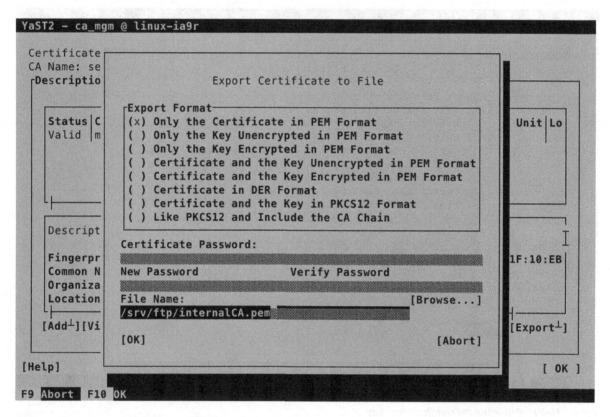

Figure 10-22.   *Exporting the CA certificate*

Next, in the Export Format box, select Only the Certificate in PEM Format and export it to a commonly accessible location.

Working with Externally Signed Certificates

Up to now, you have read how to create certificates for use within your own network environment. The certificates are self-signed, but that doesn't matter, as you have control over the clients as well, and you can make the CA certificates easily available to the clients. In an Internet environment in which the client often is anonymous, you better work with certificates that are externally signed. To do this, from the YaST Certificate Authority screen, select Requests and add a new request. Export the request to files and send these over to the signing certificate authority. Next, you have to wait until you get them back.

Alternatively, you can often enter a management interface on the certificate authority and generate the certificate from there. Make sure to export both the key and the certificate into one file. To use them on your server, you have to make the certificate files physically available on the server. Next, from YaST, select Security and Users ➤ Common Server Certificate. This allows access to the screen shown in Figure 10-23. From this screen, select Import/Replace.

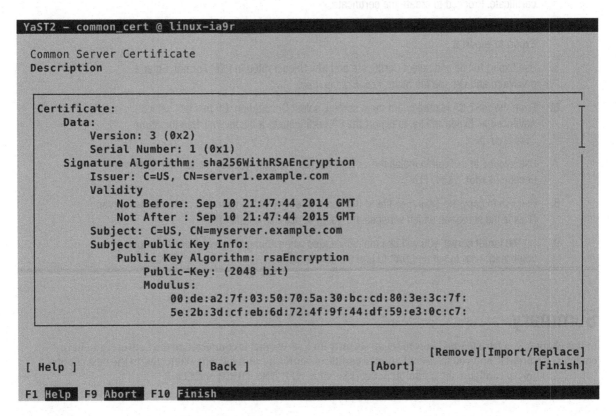

Figure 10-23. *Importing externally signed certificates*

From here, you can select the file you have received from the external CA. Enter the password and select Next, which allows you to specify the location where you want to put the certificate file and its associated private key.

EXERCISE 10-2. CONFIGURING A CERTIFICATE ENVIRONMENT

In this exercise, you'll set up a certificate environment. You will first enter the default CA and create a certificate as well as a key. Next, you will export these to a file, to import them on another server. You will also make the certificate of the signing CA available, by putting it in an FTP server document root.

1. On the server that you want to use as a CA, start the YaST CA Management utility and enter the CA.

2. Select the Certificates tab and use Add to add a new certificate. Select Add Server Certificate.

3. As the common name, use the fully qualified DNS name of the server that is going to use the certificate. Proceed to create the certificate.

4. Still from the CA Management module, select the certificate you've just created and select Export to export it.

5. Use Export to File and select Certificate and Key Unencrypted in PEM Format. Enter a password and use the file name /root/ldap.pem.

6. From the YaST CA Management main screen, select Description. On this tab, select Advanced ➤ Export to File, to export the CA certificate to a file as well. Use the name /root/ca.pem.

7. Use zypper in vsftpd to install the vsftpd server. Copy the ca.pem file to the FTP server document root /srv/ftp.

8. Use ssh to copy the ldap.pem file to the home directory of the user root on the target server. (This is the server on which services are going to use this certificate.)

9. On the target server, you will use the certificates when configuring services. In Chapter 11, you'll learn how to set up LDAP to use the certificates.

Summary

In this chapter, you have learned how to set up security for a server that is connected to the network. You have configured a firewall, and you have configured a certificate authority with related certificates. In the next chapter, you'll learn how to configure the common network services NTP, DNS, DHCP, and LDAP.

■ ■ ■

Basic Network Services: xinetd, NTP, DNS, DHCP, and LDAP

SUSE Linux Enterprise Server (SLES) can be used very effectively to provide different services on the network. In this chapter, you'll learn how to work with such elementary services as NTP, DNS, DHCP, and LDAP. You'll also learn how to set up different network services. We'll begin with the xinetd service, also known as the Internet super service. This service can be used to listen on different ports and to start the related service as a request comes in on its port. Next, you'll learn how to set up your server to synchronize time on the Internet. Following that, you'll learn how to set up a DNS server, as well as a DHCP server, for automatic provision of IP-related settings to nodes. In the last section of this chapter, you'll learn how to use LDAP as a centralized authentication service.

xinetd

In the days when servers had limited amounts of RAM, it was important not to waste the available resources. One way of doing this was by using the Internet super service inetd, which later was replaced with a more advanced version, known as xinetd.

The Internet super service is configured to listen on different ports, for a number of different protocols. At the moment that a request comes in on one of its ports, the associated service is started, and if the service hasn't been used for an amount of time, the Internet super service can also shut it down.

To use xinetd, a few parts are involved. First there is the xinetd service; next, there is the generic configuration file /etc/xinetd.conf; and there are include files in the directory /etc/xinetd.d that are used to load specific services.

The xinetd Service

By default, no services are enabled for use with xinetd, which is why the xinetd service is also not started by default. To start and enable it, use systemctl start xinetd and systemctl enable xinetd. Once started, the systemctl status -l xinetd command gives detailed information about what it is doing. In its output (shown in Listing 11-1), you can see which service files have been processed and which services have been loaded.

Listing 11-1. Using systemctl status –l xinetd to Get Status Information

```
dbx:/etc/xinetd.d # systemctl status -l xinetd
xinetd.service - Xinetd A Powerful Replacement For Inetd
   Loaded: loaded (/usr/lib/systemd/system/xinetd.service; disabled)
   Active: active (running) since Sat 2014-07-05 07:06:43 EDT; 6s ago
```

```
 Main PID: 7345 (xinetd)
   CGroup: /system.slice/xinetd.service
           └─7345 /usr/sbin/xinetd -stayalive -dontfork
Jul 05 07:06:43 dbx systemd[1]: Starting Xinetd A Powerful Replacement For Inetd...
Jul 05 07:06:43 dbx systemd[1]: Started Xinetd A Powerful Replacement For Inetd.
Jul 05 07:06:44 dbx xinetd[7345]: Reading included configuration file: /etc/xinetd.d/chargen
[file=/etc/xinetd.conf] [line=60]
Jul 05 07:06:44 dbx xinetd[7345]: Reading included configuration file: /etc/xinetd.d/chargen-udp
[file=/etc/xinetd.d/chargen-udp] [line=14]
Jul 05 07:06:44 dbx xinetd[7345]: Reading included configuration file: /etc/xinetd.d/cups-lpd
[file=/etc/xinetd.d/cups-lpd] [line=15]
Jul 05 07:06:44 dbx xinetd[7345]: Reading included configuration file: /etc/xinetd.d/daytime
[file=/etc/xinetd.d/daytime] [line=11]
Jul 05 07:06:44 dbx xinetd[7345]: Reading included configuration file: /etc/xinetd.d/daytime-udp
[file=/etc/xinetd.d/daytime-udp] [line=14]
Jul 05 07:06:44 dbx xinetd[7345]: Reading included configuration file: /etc/xinetd.d/discard
[file=/etc/xinetd.d/discard] [line=15]
Jul 05 07:06:44 dbx xinetd[7345]: Reading included configuration file: /etc/xinetd.d/discard-udp
[file=/etc/xinetd.d/discard-udp] [line=14]
Jul 05 07:06:44 dbx xinetd[7345]: Reading included configuration file: /etc/xinetd.d/echo
[file=/etc/xinetd.d/echo] [line=15]
Jul 05 07:06:44 dbx xinetd[7345]: Reading included configuration file: /etc/xinetd.d/echo-udp
[file=/etc/xinetd.d/echo-udp] [line=14]
Jul 05 07:06:44 dbx xinetd[7345]: Reading included configuration file: /etc/xinetd.d/netstat
[file=/etc/xinetd.d/netstat] [line=15]
Jul 05 07:06:44 dbx xinetd[7345]: Reading included configuration file: /etc/xinetd.d/rsync
[file=/etc/xinetd.d/rsync] [line=16]
Jul 05 07:06:44 dbx xinetd[7345]: Reading included configuration file: /etc/xinetd.d/servers
[file=/etc/xinetd.d/servers] [line=12]
Jul 05 07:06:44 dbx xinetd[7345]: Reading included configuration file: /etc/xinetd.d/services
[file=/etc/xinetd.d/services] [line=14]
Jul 05 07:06:44 dbx xinetd[7345]: Reading included configuration file: /etc/xinetd.d/systat
[file=/etc/xinetd.d/systat] [line=14]
Jul 05 07:06:44 dbx xinetd[7345]: Reading included configuration file: /etc/xinetd.d/time
[file=/etc/xinetd.d/time] [line=17]
Jul 05 07:06:44 dbx xinetd[7345]: Reading included configuration file: /etc/xinetd.d/time-udp
[file=/etc/xinetd.d/time-udp] [line=15]
Jul 05 07:06:44 dbx xinetd[7345]: Reading included configuration file: /etc/xinetd.d/vnc
[file=/etc/xinetd.d/vnc] [line=15]
Jul 05 07:06:44 dbx xinetd[7345]: Service discard will use IPv6 or fallback to IPv4
Jul 05 07:06:44 dbx xinetd[7345]: xinetd Version 2.3.15 started with libwrap loadavg options
compiled in.
Jul 05 07:06:44 dbx xinetd[7345]: Started working: 1 available service
```

The xinetd.conf File

To set main xinetd parameters, you can modify the xinetd.conf file. This file contains generic settings that allow you to quickly enable or disable services, to specify logging, and to configure the default address that the xinetd service should be listening on. In Listing 11-2, you can see its default contents on SLES 12.

Listing 11-2. xinetd.conf Contents

```
defaults
{
# The next two items are intended to be a quick access place to
# temporarily enable or disable services.
#
#       enabled        =
#       disabled       =

# Previous default in SUSE - please don't forget to use the logrotate. The
# sample configuration is in /usr/share/packages/doc/xinetd/logrotate
#       log_type       = FILE /var/log/xinetd.log

# Define general logging characteristics.
        log_type       = SYSLOG daemon info
        log_on_failure = HOST ATTEMPT
        log_on_success = HOST EXIT DURATION

# Define access restriction defaults
#
#       no_access      =
#       only_from      = localhost
#       max_load       = 0
        cps            = 50 10
        instances      = 30
        per_source     = 10


#
# The specification of an interface is interesting, if we are on a firewall.
# For example, if you only want to provide services from an internal
# network interface, you may specify your internal interfaces IP-Address.
#
#       bind           = 127.0.0.1

# Address and networking defaults
#
#       bind           =
#       mdns           = yes
        v6only         = no

# setup environmental attributes
#
#       passenv        =
        groups         = yes
        umask          = 002

# Generally, banners are not used. This sets up their global defaults
#
#       banner         =
#       banner_fail    =
#       banner_success =
}

includedir /etc/xinetd.d
```

The xinetd Include Files

To determine which services are enabled with xinetd, you will use the include files in /etc/xinetd.d. Some default include files have been copied there upon installation, and as administrator, you can add your own include files also. In Listing 11-3, you can see a sample include file for the systat service.

In each include file, you'll find a couple of interesting parameters. First, there is disable, which specifies whether the service should be offered or not. Next, the user employed to run this service can be set, after which the server parameter tells xinetd which service process it should start. If the server uses arguments, these can be specified using the server_args parameter.

Listing 11-3. Sample xinetd Configuration File

```
service systat
{
        disable         = yes
        socket_type     = stream
        protocol        = tcp
        wait            = no
        user            = nobody
        server          = /bin/ps
        server_args     = -auwwx
}
```

EXERCISE 11-1. WORKING WITH XINETD

1. Open the /etc/xinetd.d/netstat configuration file to enable the systat service in xinetd.

2. Use systemctl start xinetd to start xinetd.

3. Use systemctl status -l xinetd to give current usage information about the xinetd service.

NTP

On modern servers, many services can be used. Many of these services are very time-sensitive, which is why you must take care of time synchronization. A difference of just a few seconds may be enough for your database not to replicate or synchronize its data to other servers, which is why proper time synchronization is primordial. On SUSE Linux Enterprise Server (SLES), the Network Time Protocol is used to synchronize time between the local server and some time sources on the Internet.

Understanding Linux Time

In addition to the NTP server, the difference between the computer's hardware clock and system clock also plays an important role. When a server boots, the hardware clock is read. Typically, this is the BIOS clock that is on the motherboard of the computer. Based on the current hardware clock setting, the system clock is set. Next, the ntpd process loads and seeks synchronization with an Internet time source. If there is a deviance, the system clock will synchronize with the Internet time. Changes that are made to the local clock are not synchronized back to the hardware clock. Such a synchronization can be forced, using the hwclock --systohc command (see Figure 11-1).

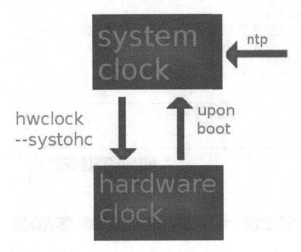

Figure 11-1. *Linux time overview*

To prevent changes from getting lost, this normally is a slow process. If, for instance, a ten-minute difference is found, the local system clock will increase or decrease its speed, to reach full synchronization after some time. This process can be sped up by using the iburst option in the NTP configuration file.

It is also important to know that the difference between a local clock and the time that is provided by an NTP server cannot be too great. If the difference is more than 15 minutes, the time source is considered to be insane and won't be a candidate to synchronize with. For that reason, it is important to set local time to more or less the correct time, before starting synchronization.

Setting Time on SLES

To set time on SLES, YaST can be used. The YaST module for NTP configuration is available in Network Services ➤ NTP Configuration. This shows the screen in Figure 11-2.

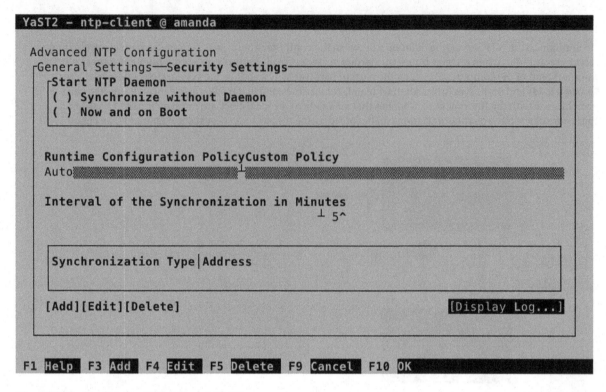

Figure 11-2. *Configuring NTP settings in YaST*

To start with, you should set the NTP daemon startup option. By default, it won't be started. To have it started automatically, select Now and on Boot. Next, select Add, to add time servers to synchronize with. This offers the following five different synchronization types:

- *Server* is used to add an NTP server to synchronize with. Your server will just copy the time of the server to its local system clock.

- *Peer* is used to set another NTP node as peer. In a negotiation between peers, time is compared, and if there is a difference, both nodes will synchronize toward each other.

- *Radio Clock* is used to synchronize time with a local clock that is directly connected to your computer.

- *Outgoing Broadcast* is used to have your server broadcast time on the network.

- *Incoming Broadcast* is used to configure your server to accept time that is broadcast by other nodes on the network.

Between these options, the most common option is to configure an NTP server. Common NTP servers are available through pool.ntp.org. When selecting an NTP server in the screen that is shown in Figure 11-3, you can test that the server can be reached, before configuring access to it. Also, you can specify options that should be used in synchronization. The iburst option is common. It tells your server not to synchronize slowly but to synchronize local time as fast as possible with the time provided by the NTP server.

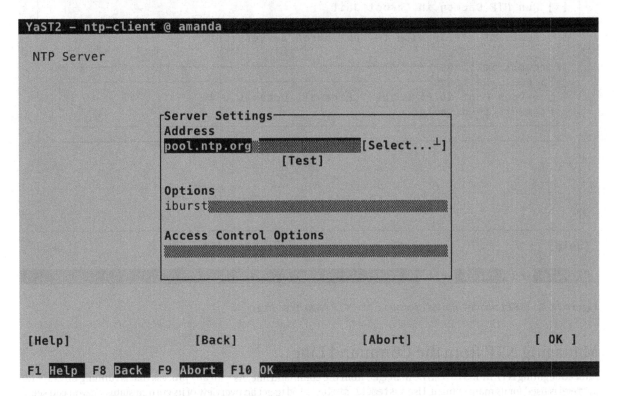

Figure 11-3. *Specifying the server to synchronize with*

When setting up NTP configuration, YaST also gives access to a limited amount of security settings (see Figure 11-4). By default, the option Run NTP Daemon in Chroot Jail is set. This means that the process is running in the w fake root directory. That means that if an intruder got shell access through a misconfiguration in the process, that intruder would only see configuration files related to the NTP server itself. Other security settings are best applied through the /etc/ntp.conf configuration file.

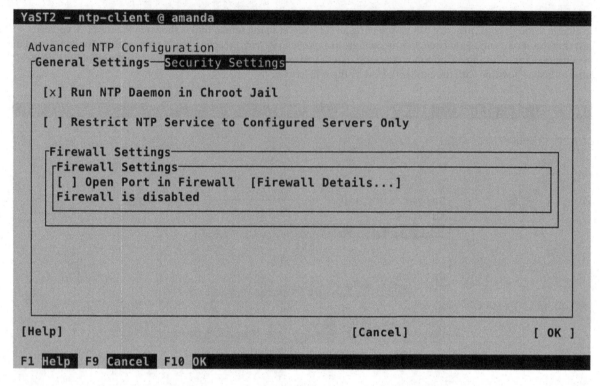

Figure 11-4. YaST provides limited access to a few NTP security settings

Managing NTP from the Command Line

After configuring NTP in YaST, it can be managed from the command line. As with any process that is running on SLES 12, systemd is used for its management. Use systemctl status ntpd to get an overview of its current status. As you can see in Listing 11-4, this command tells you if the process is active and, if it is, on which interfaces it is listening.

Listing 11-4. Checking ntpd Availability with systemctl status nptd

```
dbx:/etc # systemctl status -l ntpd
ntpd.service - NTP Server Daemon
   Loaded: loaded (/usr/lib/systemd/system/ntpd.service; enabled)
   Active: active (running) since Sat 2014-07-05 07:49:27 EDT; 1min 33s ago
     Docs: man:ntpd(1)
  Process: 8388 ExecStart=/usr/sbin/start-ntpd start (code=exited, status=0/SUCCESS)
 Main PID: 8401 (ntpd)
   CGroup: /system.slice/ntpd.service
           └─8401 /usr/sbin/ntpd -p /var/run/ntp/ntpd.pid -g -u ntp:ntp -i /var/lib/ntp -c
             /etc/ntp.conf

Jul 05 07:49:27 dbx systemd[1]: Started NTP Server Daemon.
Jul 05 07:49:27 dbx ntpd[8401]: ntp_io: estimated max descriptors: 1024, initial socket boundary: 16
Jul 05 07:49:27 dbx ntpd[8401]: Listen and drop on 0 v4wildcard 0.0.0.0 UDP 123
Jul 05 07:49:27 dbx ntpd[8401]: Listen and drop on 1 v6wildcard :: UDP 123
```

```
Jul 05 07:49:27 dbx ntpd[8401]: Listen normally on 2 lo 127.0.0.1 UDP 123
Jul 05 07:49:27 dbx ntpd[8401]: Listen normally on 3 eth0 192.168.4.175 UDP 123
Jul 05 07:49:27 dbx ntpd[8401]: Listen normally on 4 lo ::1 UDP 123
Jul 05 07:49:27 dbx ntpd[8401]: Listen normally on 5 eth0 fe80::20c:29ff:feff:f1fd UDP 123
Jul 05 07:49:27 dbx ntpd[8401]: peers refreshed
Jul 05 07:49:27 dbx ntpd[8401]: Listening on routing socket on fd #22 for interface updates
```

To start and enable the NTP service, you can use systemctl start ntpd, followed by systemctl enable ntpd.

While configuring the NTP server, configuration is written to /etc/npt.conf. Listing 11-5 shows what its contents looks like after applying the settings from YaST that were just discussed.

Listing 11-5. The ntp.conf Configuration File

```
# Clients from this (example!) subnet have unlimited access, but only if
# cryptographically authenticated.
# restrict 192.168.123.0 mask 255.255.255.0 notrust


##
## Miscellaneous stuff
##

driftfile /var/lib/ntp/drift/ntp.drift
# path for drift file

logfile /var/log/ntp
# alternate log file
# logconfig =syncstatus + sysevents
# logconfig =all

# statsdir /tmp/                 # directory for statistics files
# filegen peerstats  file peerstats  type day enable
# filegen loopstats  file loopstats  type day enable
# filegen clockstats file clockstats type day enable


#
# Authentication stuff
#
keys /etc/ntp.keys
# path for keys file
trustedkey 1
# define trusted keys
requestkey 1
server pool.ntp.org iburst
# key (7) for accessing server variables
# controlkey 15              # key (6) for accessing server variables
```

From the `ntp.conf` file, you can apply additional security settings, using the `restrict` parameter. Using this parameter, you can specify different synchronization parameters. Using this parameter, you can also specify specific options for an IP network address, including mask, which is followed by different flags. The following flags can be applied:

- `ignore`: All packets are denied.

- `kod`: If an access violation occurs, a "Kiss of Death" packet is sent back to the originator. A maximum of one kod packet is sent per second.

- `nomodify`: Access attempting to modify the current state of this server is denied.

- `noquery`: No `ntpq` and `ntpdc` queries are allowed.

- `nopeer`: This server cannot be configured as a peer.

- `noserve`: All packets are denied, with the exception of `ntpq` and `ntpdc` queries.

- `notrust`: Deny all packets, unless cryptographically authenticated.

- `version`: Only allow packets that were sent using the same NTP version as on this server.

Using ntpq and ntpdc for NTP Server Management

To manage NTP Server information, you can use `ntpq` and `ntpdc`. The `ntpq` command is useful for displaying NTP usage information on the current host. It offers many options to display information, of which the option -p is the most common. It shows status information about the server and peers the server is using for setting up time synchronization. In Listing 11-6, you can see what its output looks like.

Listing 11-6. Using `ntp -p` to Show Current Synchronization Information

```
dbx:/etc # ntpq -p
     remote           refid      st t when poll reach   delay   offset  jitter
==============================================================================
 server01.coloce 87.195.109.207   3 u    1   64    1  30.099 -137.74   0.409
 D57C702B.static .INIT.          16 u    -   64    0   0.000   0.000   0.000
```

In the preceding listing, you can see that this server is set up to synchronize with two different servers. For each server, an identification is given in the remote column. Once synchronization has been established, this is often the DNS name of the server that synchronization has been established with. This is followed by the `refid`, which contains either the IP address of that server or the current synchronization state. To establish synchronization, a server typically goes through a number of states: the state `if INIT` means that this server has just initialized; the state STEP means that it is looking to contact the other server, but first contact has not been established yet. If first contact with the other server has been established, you'll see an IP address in the `refid` column.

In the third column of `ntpq -p` output, the stratum of the other NTP server is indicated. Stratum is a fundamental concept in NTP. It indicates the reliability of the NTP server. Servers with a low stratum number are more reliable than servers with a high stratum number. If multiple servers are available for synchronization, the local NTP process will always prefer the server with the lowest possible number. If a stratum of 16 is indicated, it means that the server has not been available for synchronization. The meanings of the other columns in `ntpq -p` output are provided in the following list:

- `poll`: The number of seconds between polls on the server

- `when`: The number of seconds since the last answer was received from the server

- `reach`: An octal bitmap indicating how successful communication with the server had been the last 8 polls. The value 377 means that the previous 8 attempts were successful; the number 0 means that none of them had been successful.

- delay: The amount of milliseconds it takes a round trip to the NTP server. Shorter delays are always better.

- offset: The difference in milliseconds between your clock and the clock of the server

- jitter: The dispersion of successive time values from the remote server. A lower value indicates a higher stability of the remote clock.

Whereas the ntpq -p command gives generic information, more detailed information can be obtained by using the ntpdc command. This command can be used as an interactive interface or as a command-line utility. You should note, however, that it only works on servers that haven't been configured to deny ntpdc commands, using the noquery restriction. Unfortunately, many NTP servers won't reveal much on ntpdc. You can also use ntpdc to get more information about the local time configuration. You can use, for example, the ntpdc -c loopinfo command, to display in seconds how far off the system time is, or ntpdc -c kerninfo, to display the current correction that still has to be applied to the local clock (see Listing 11-7).

Listing 11-7. Using ntpdc to Get Detailed Information About NTP Configuration

```
dbx:/etc # ntpdc -c loopinfo
offset:             0.000000 s
frequency:          -186.674 ppm
poll adjust:        0
watchdog timer:     35 s
dbx:/etc # ntpdc -c kerninfo
pll offset:         0 s
pll frequency:      -186.674 ppm
maximum error:      16 s
estimated error:    16 s
status:             0041   pll unsync
pll time constant:  7
precision:          1e-06 s
frequency tolerance: 500 ppm
```

EXERCISE 11-2. CONFIGURING NTP

1. Type date to show the current time on your machine.

2. Type hwclock to see the difference between system time and hardware time.

3. Open the /etc/ntp.conf file with an editor and add the following line:

   server   pool.ntp.org   iburst

4. Use systemctl restart ntpd.

5. Show current information about the service, using systemctl status -l ntpd.

6. Show current synchronization information, using ntpq -p.

7. Use ntpdc -c loopinfo and ntpdc -c kerninfo to get more information about the current state of your clock.

8. Once the local clock has been synchronized sufficiently, use hwclock --systohc to write the system time to the hardware clock.

DNS

Even if hosted DNS servers are becoming more and more common, SUSE offers great options to configure your own internal DNS server. All types of DNS are supported: DNS master servers, DNS slave servers, and Cache-only servers. As, in setting up DNS, many configuration files relate to one another, it makes sense to set up a base DNS configuration with YaST, after which you can manually modify the related configuration files.

Setting Up DNS with YaST

To set up DNS with YaST, select Network Services ➤ DNS Server. This will start the bind packages for you, after which the configuration of DNS can be started. Next, you'll go through a wizard to complete all steps of the DNS configuration. In the first screen of this wizard (see Figure 11-5), you can configure a forwarder.

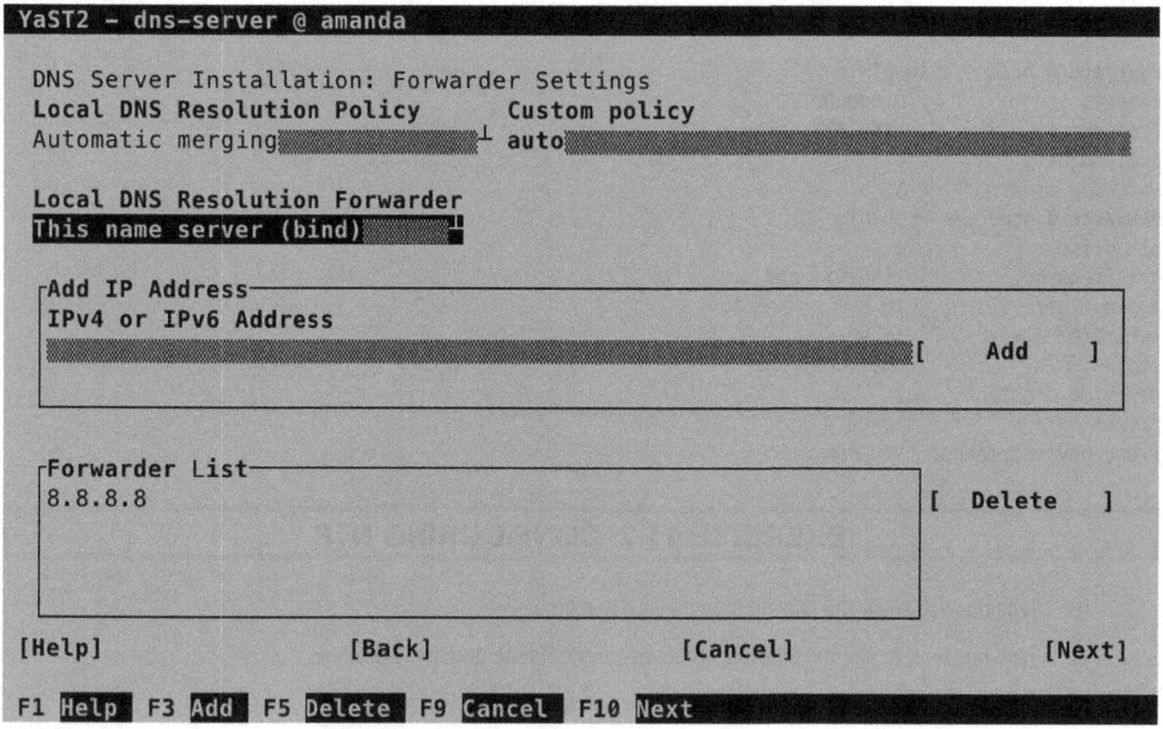

```
 YaST2 - dns-server @ amanda

  DNS Server Installation: Forwarder Settings
  Local DNS Resolution Policy      Custom policy
  Automatic merging▓▓▓▓▓▓▓▓▓▓▓▓▓⊥ auto▓▓▓▓▓▓▓▓▓▓▓▓▓▓▓▓▓▓▓▓▓▓▓▓▓▓▓▓

  Local DNS Resolution Forwarder
  This name server (bind)▓▓▓▓▓▓▓▓⊥

  ┌Add IP Address──────────────────────────────────────────────
  │IPv4 or IPv6 Address
  │▓▓▓▓▓▓▓▓▓▓▓▓▓▓▓▓▓▓▓▓▓▓▓▓▓▓▓▓▓▓▓▓▓▓▓▓▓▓▓▓▓▓[    Add     ]
  │


  ┌Forwarder List──────────────────────────────────
  │8.8.8.8                                            [  Delete   ]
  │



  [Help]              [Back]              [Cancel]              [Next]

  F1 Help  F3 Add  F5 Delete  F9 Cancel  F10 Next
```

Figure 11-5. *DNS forwarder configuration*

Using a DNS forwarder is optional. By default, the named process that is running on your server will access a name server of the DNS root domain on the Internet, if it receives a request regarding a resource record that is not known. If you have access to a fast DNS server nearby, it makes sense to specify a forwarder. All unknown resource records will then be sent to the forwarder, which takes care of the further name-resolving process. Using a forwarder makes sense if you're not on a fast Internet connection, or if you want to forward all requests to the main DNS server in your environment.

In the next screen of the DNS setup wizard (see Figure 11-6), you can add a new zone. That will be a zone that this DNS server is responsible for. Typically, that would be your local domain or other domains within your environment. Just add the name of the zone, specify the type, and select Add to add the zone. When starting to set up your own

DNS zone, you'll create a master zone. If it's a master zone, your server is responsible for the resource records in the zone. For redundancy purposes, slave zones can be used also. A slave zone is typically a replicated database that can be used by DNS clients but cannot handle modifications by itself. You can also configure a forward zone, which directs a specific zone to a specific forwarder.

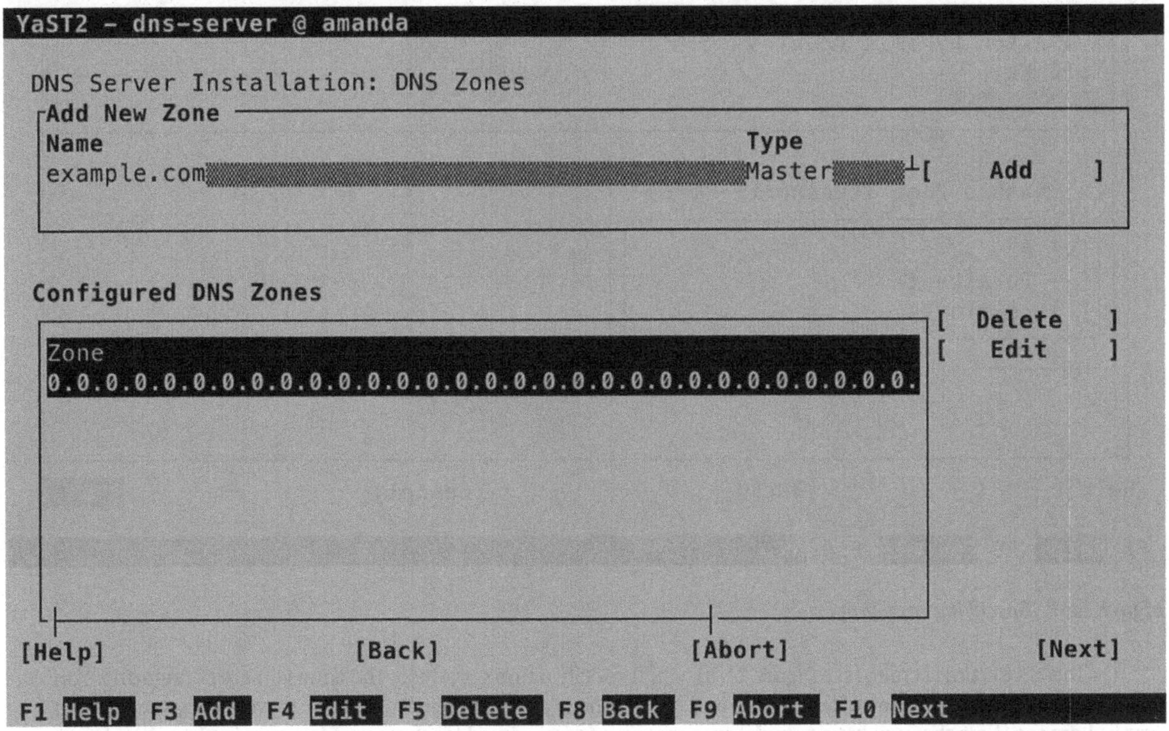

```
 YaST2 - dns-server @ amanda

   DNS Server Installation: DNS Zones
   ┌Add New Zone ─────────────────────────────────────────────────────────────
   │ Name                                            Type
   │ example.com▓▓▓▓▓▓▓▓▓▓▓▓▓▓▓▓▓▓▓▓▓▓▓▓▓▓▓▓▓▓▓▓▓▓▓▓▓Master▓▓▓▓▓┴[    Add    ]


   Configured DNS Zones
   ┌──────────────────────────────────────────────────────────┐ [  Delete   ]
   │Zone                                                        │ [   Edit    ]
   │0.0.0.0.0.0.0.0.0.0.0.0.0.0.0.0.0.0.0.0.0.0.0.0.0.0.0.0.0.0.│
   │                                                            │
   │                                                            │
   │                                                            │
   │                                                            │
   │                                                            │
   └─                                                          ─┘

   [Help]              [Back]                [Abort]               [Next]

 F1 Help  F3 Add  F4 Edit  F5 Delete  F8 Back  F9 Abort  F10 Next
```

Figure 11-6. Creating your own zones

After adding your zones, you can add resource records to it. To do this, select the zone in the Configured DNS Zones pane and next select Edit. This brings you to the Zone Editor, which you can see in Figure 11-7. On this screen, there are different options available. The first screen you'll get into contains the Basics settings. These include the following:

- *Allow Dynamic Updates*: Use this option if you want to use Dynamic DNS. This is the configuration in which updates are sent from a DHCP server to the DNS server. This means that after receiving new configuration from the DHCP server, a node can update its information in DNS.

- *TSIG Key*: To use Dynamic DNS, a security key must be used. This is the TSIG key. Make sure to select a TSIG key, if you want to use Dynamic DNS. You'll learn how to create a TSIG key later in this chapter.

- *Enable Zone Transport*: In zone transport, the entire DNS database is downloaded to another host. As this has some implications for security, zone transport is not enabled by default. Check this option if you want to enable zone transport, and make sure to select an ACL next.

- *ACLs*: If zone transports are allowed, you have to specify which hosts are allowed to perform a zone transport. Select between any, localhost, or localnets.

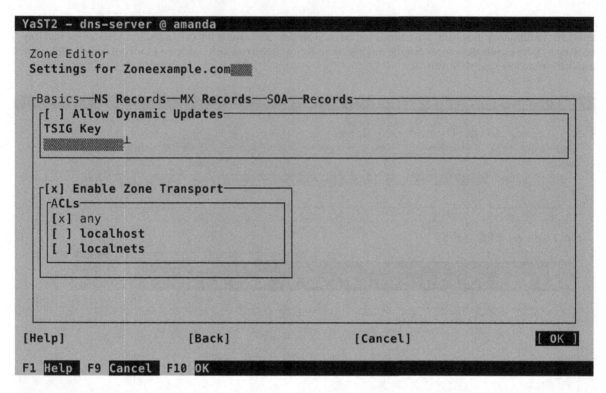

Figure 11-7. *Specifying zone properties*

On the NS Records screen (see Figure 11-8), you'll specify name servers for the zone you are configuring. You must at least include the name of this server, and if this zone is going to have Slave name servers also, specify their names here too. Note that you have to make sure that an address record for the name you're using here is going to be created as well; otherwise, the name server cannot be reached. Also, you must be sure to use the correct naming, which has a dot at the end of the name. (So use dbx.example.com. and not dbx.example.com.) The dot at the end of the name ensures that this name is matched against the root of the DNS structure.

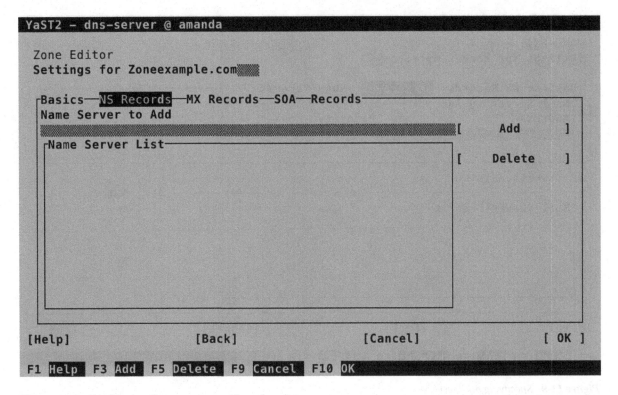

Figure 11-8. *Configuring the name servers for a domain*

On the MX Records screen (see Figure 11-9), you'll include the Mail Exchange record. This is the address of the mail servers that are used by this DNS domain. Specifying these is important, if your domain has e-mail users employing that domain as well. When a remote mail server is looking up the mail server for a specific domain, this record is used to find out which server should be contacted.

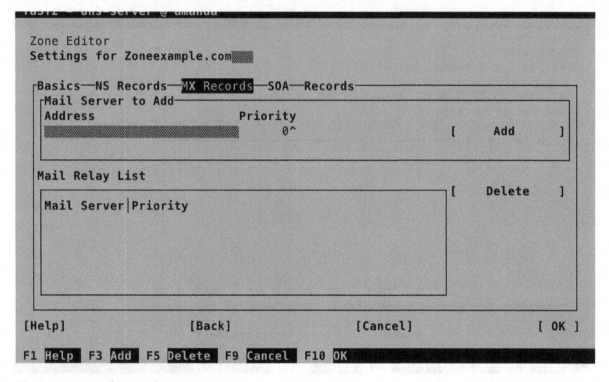

Figure 11-9. *Specifying mail servers*

When specifying the mail server, you must use a valid DNS name. Also, each mail server can be configured with a priority. The mail server with the lowest priority is contacted first, other mail servers may be configured for redundancy purposes.

On the SOA screen, which you can see in Figure 11-10, you'll specify default time-out settings. You don't have to specify anything, as the default settings will work well, but if you want to, you can specify the following settings:

- *Serial*: A number that you can change on the master server to indicate to slave servers that the contents of the DNS database has been modified.

- *TTL*: The Time To Live (the validity time) of all records in the zone that don't have specific TTL settings.

- *Refresh*: Specifies how often the zone should be synchronized from the master to the slave name servers.

- *Expiration*: Indicates how long it takes for a zone to expire on the slave server, if no successful synchronization has occurred. If a slave zone is expired, the slave server will stop servicing its records.

- *Minimum*: Specifies how long negative answers should be cached on a DNS server. Make sure not to set this too high!

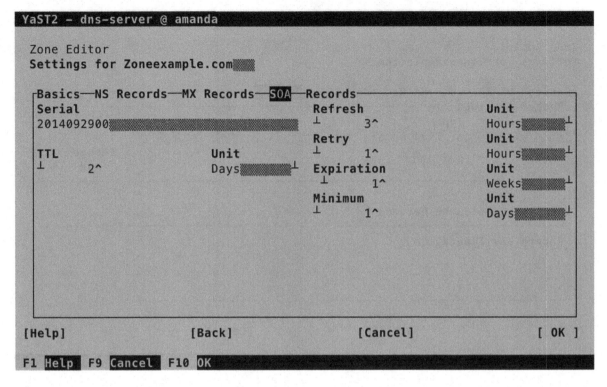

Figure 11-10. *Setting synchronization properties on the SOA tab*

It is from the Records tab that you'll do the real work and create the resource records. Numerous resource records can be set, of which the most common types (following) are available from YaST.

- *A*: This is the address field, used to get the IP address that belongs with a name in IPv4. Every DNS server must be configured with at least A records for its name servers.

- *AAAA*: The A record for IPv6 addresses.

- *CNAME*: A canonical name. This is an alias that can be specified for a hostname.

- *NS*: Name Server. These are the name servers that are configured in this zone.

- *MX*: The mail server responsible for this domain.

- *SRV*: An optional resource record that can be used to register services.

- *TXT*: An optional resource record that can be used to keep notes in DNS.

- *SPF*: The sender policy framework resource record contains a list of authorized mail servers for this zone. This resource record is used in spam protection. Mail from a mail server that is not listed in the SPF record for a domain will be refused.

Adding a resource record is not difficult. You first have to specify the resource record type you want to add. Next, specify the record key and the value. For an A record, for instance, the record key would be the hostname relative to this zone, and the value would be the IP address of the hostname (see Figure 11-11).

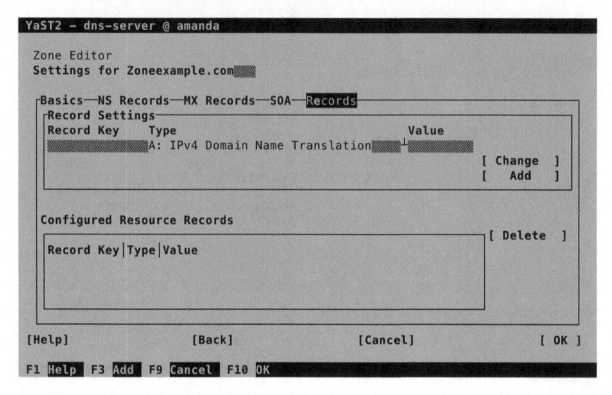

Figure 11-11. Adding resource records to DNS

After creating the base DNS configuration, YaST brings you to the last step of the wizard. On this screen, you can specify startup behavior and open firewall ports. Also, you can enable LDAP support, which makes DNS resource records to be replicated by an LDAP server. Also on this screen, which is shown in Figure 11-12, you get access to the DNS Server Expert Configuration.

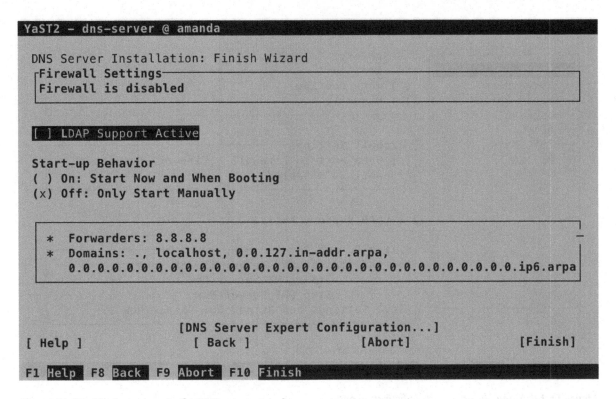

Figure 11-12. *The last screen in the DNS setup wizard*

From the Expert Configuration screen, shown in Figure 11-13, you'll have access to all the options you've just created. In addition, on a DNS server that has already been configured, this is the default management interface for all settings. It adds additional options, such as logging and ACL configuration, and the TSIG Keys tab.

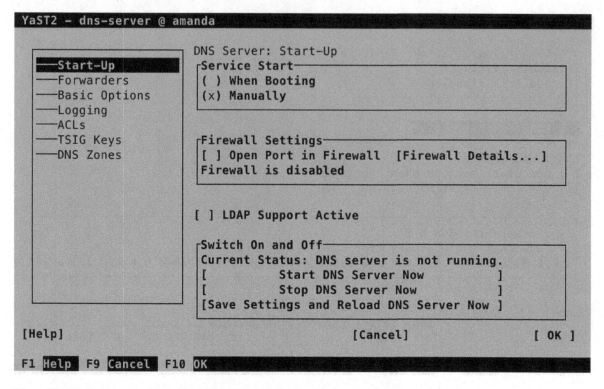

Figure 11-13. *Managing advanced configuration options*

TSIG keys are used to set up trusted connections between DNS servers and between DNS servers and DHCP servers that are configured for Dynamic DNS. From the TSIG Keys tab, you can easily create these keys. On the tab, in the Create a New TSIG Key box, you must enter a key ID, which is used as an identifier for the key. Next, specify the name of the file the key should be written to and select Generate the key. This creates the TSIG key and automatically adds it to the list of current TSIG keys.

Manual DNS Server Management

Manual management of the DNS server on SUSE starts with the named process. DNS is implemented by the named process. Use systemctl start named to start it and systemctl enable named to make sure it is started automatically when your server reboots. Next, you can use systemctl status -l named to get information about its current status. This doesn't just show you that it is running but also gives information about inconsistencies that appear in the zone configurations (see Listing 11-8).

Listing 11-8. Showing DNS Status Information

```
dbx:~ # systemctl status -l named
named.service - LSB: Domain Name System (DNS) server, named
   Loaded: loaded (/etc/init.d/named)
   Active: active (running) since Sat 2014-07-05 09:54:55 EDT; 2min 17s ago
  Process: 13670 ExecStart=/etc/init.d/named start (code=exited, status=0/SUCCESS)
   CGroup: /system.slice/named.service
           └─13736 /usr/sbin/named -t /var/lib/named -u named
```

```
Jul 05 09:54:55 dbx named[13736]: managed-keys-zone: loaded serial 0
Jul 05 09:54:55 dbx named[13736]: zone 0.0.127.in-addr.arpa/IN: loaded serial 42
Jul 05 09:54:55 dbx named[13736]: zone localhost/IN: loaded serial 42
Jul 05 09:54:55 dbx named[13736]: zone 0.0.0.0.0.0.0.0.0.0.0.0.0.0.0.0.0.0.0.0.0.0.0.0.0.0.0.0.0.0.0.0
.ip6.arpa/IN: loaded serial 42
Jul 05 09:54:55 dbx named[13736]: zone example.com/IN: example.com/MX 'mail.example.com' has no
address records (A or AAAA)
Jul 05 09:54:55 dbx named[13736]: zone example.com/IN: loaded serial 2014070500
Jul 05 09:54:55 dbx named[13736]: all zones loaded
Jul 05 09:54:55 dbx systemd[1]: Started LSB: Domain Name System (DNS) server, named.
Jul 05 09:54:55 dbx named[13670]: ..done
Jul 05 09:54:55 dbx named[13736]: running
```

The main configuration file of DNS is in /etc/named.conf. In Listing 11-9, following, you can see its configuration after a base DNS server has been configured from YaST.

Listing 11-9. /etc/named.conf Contents

```
dbx:~ # cat /etc/named.conf | grep -v '#'
options {
    directory "/var/lib/named";
    managed-keys-directory "/var/lib/named/dyn/";
    dump-file "/var/log/named_dump.db";
    statistics-file "/var/log/named.stats";
    listen-on-v6 { any; };
    notify no;
    disable-empty-zone "1.0.0.0.0.0.0.0.0.0.0.0.0.0.0.0.0.0.0.0.0.0.0.0.0.0.0.0.0.0.0.0.IP6.ARPA";
    include "/etc/named.d/forwarders.conf";
};

zone "." in {
    type hint;
    file "root.hint";
};

zone "localhost" in {
    type master;
    file "localhost.zone";
};

zone "0.0.127.in-addr.arpa" in {
    type master;
    file "127.0.0.zone";
};

zone "0.0.0.0.0.0.0.0.0.0.0.0.0.0.0.0.0.0.0.0.0.0.0.0.0.0.0.0.0.0.0.0.ip6.arpa" in {
    type master;
    file "127.0.0.zone";
};
```

```
include "/etc/named.conf.include";
zone "example.com" in {
    allow-transfer { any; };
     file "master/example.com";
     type master;
};
```

The configuration file consists of two main parts. First, there is the options section, which defines where all important DNS configuration can be found. For example, it specifies the directory setting, which indicates the default DNS root. All files that the configuration file refers to further on are related to this directory.

The second important part of the configuration is the definition of the zone files. All zone files that exist on this server are referred to from the /etc/named.conf file. Also note the use of the /etc/named.conf.include file, a configuration file that may contain additional configuration settings.

The second important part of the DNS configuration is in the directory /var/lib/named. In here, you'll find all that the DNS server needs. This makes it easy to run the DNS server in a chroot jail. Typically, this directory contains a file with the name root.hint, which has a list of all root DNS servers that should be used. Also, it has the subdirectories master and slave, which are used for storage of configuration of master zones and slave zones that are hosted by this server.

In Listing 11-10, you can see what the contents of a zone configuration file may look like.

Listing 11-10. Sample Contents of a Zone Configuration File

```
dbx:/var/lib/named/master # cat example.com
$TTL 2d
@                   IN SOA          dbx.example.com.          root.dbx.example.com. (
                                    2014070501                ; serial
                                    3h                        ; refresh
                                    1h                        ; retry
                                    1w                        ; expiry
                                    1d )                      ; minimum

example.com.        IN NS           dbx.example.com.
example.com.        IN MX           10 mail.example.com.
dbx                 IN A            192.168.4.175
lisa                IN A            192.168.4.176
mail                IN A            192.168.4.175
```

EXERCISE 11-3. CONFIGURING DNS

In this exercise, you'll learn how to set up a DNS server and configure it with resource records for the zone example.org.

1. Use `systemctl status -l named` to get the current status of the DNS name server. If it is currently running, stop it, using `systemctl stop named`.

2. Make sure the named package is installed, using `zypper in bind`.

3. Open the file `/etc/named.conf` and include the following lines:

```
zone "example.org" in {
        allow-transfer { any; } ;
        file "master/example.org";
        type master;
};
```

4. Create a file with the name `/var/lib/named/master/example.org` and give it a contents like the following (make sure to modify settings to match the configuration you're using, and make sure it contains at least an entry for "server.example.org"):

```
dbx:/var/lib/named/master # cat example.org
$TTL 2d
@               IN SOA          server.example.org.            root.server.example.org. (
                                2014070501                     ; serial
                                3h                             ; refresh
                                1h                             ; retry
                                1w                             ; expiry
                                1d )                           ; minimum

example.org.    IN NS           server.example.org.
example.org.    IN MX           10 mail.example.org.
server          IN A            192.168.4.175
lisa            IN A            192.168.4.176
mail            IN A            192.168.4.175
```

5. Use `systemctl start named` followed by `systemctl enable named` to start the DNS server, and make sure it is started automatically when your server reboots.

6. Open the file `/etc/sysconfig/network/config` with an editor and modify the following lines to use your server as the DNS server.

```
NETCONFIG_DNS_FORWARDER="resolver"
NETCONFIG_DNS_STATIC_SERVERS="192.168.4.175"
```

7. Use the command `netconfig update -v` to update your network configuration.

8. Type `ping server.example.org` to verify the working of your DNS server. It does not matter if you don't get an answer, but you should see the name resolving in process and the `ping` command pinging the IP address of the server (see Listing 11-11).

Listing 11-11. Testing DNS Functionality with ping

```
dbx:~ # ping server.example.org
PING server.example.org (192.168.4.175) 56(84) bytes of data.
64 bytes from 192.168.4.175: icmp_seq=1 ttl=64 time=0.022 ms
64 bytes from 192.168.4.175: icmp_seq=2 ttl=64 time=0.044 ms
64 bytes from 192.168.4.175: icmp_seq=3 ttl=64 time=0.049 ms
^C
--- server.example.org ping statistics ---
3 packets transmitted, 3 received, 0% packet loss, time 2001ms
rtt min/avg/max/mdev = 0.022/0.038/0.049/0.012 ms
```

DHCP

Even if the Dynamic Host Configuration Protocol (DHCP) is provided by many network devices too, it can easily be configured on SUSE Linux Enterprise Server (SLES). In this section, you'll learn how to set it up using YaST and how to manually tune the configuration from the command line.

Understanding DHCP

Some people think that DHCP is used only for handing out IP addresses and some related configuration. DHCP can do so much more! Using different DHCP types, more than 100 parameters can be handed out to DHCP clients! Before starting the configuration of these parameters, however, you should make sure that they are supported by the receiving IP stack. It is good that you can easily set a time server using DHCP, but you will find there's a lack of support for many of the DHCP features by its clients.

DHCP is a broadcast-based protocol. A DHCP client will send a DHCP broadcast on its local network. That will be captured by any DHCP server that is listening. This means that there can be one DHCP server per network only. If (by accident) another DHCP server is also present, it will be unclear which server hands out the IP address configuration to clients. So, make sure that you don't have two DHCP servers on the same network (this is especially true when setting up test environments).

If a network consists of multiple subnets that are connected by a router or a layer 3 switch, DHCP broadcasts that were issued on one network won't be received on the other network. If you want to forward DHCP requests between networks, you have to run a DHCP agent on each network. Typically, this is something you would configure on the router. The DHCP agent captures DHCP requests and sends them through to the DHCP server that is configured for your network.

Configuring DHCP with YaST

The YaST module for DHCP server configuration is available in Network Services ➤ DHCP. After you have launched the module, it will start a short wizard for setting up the DHCP server. If it is not installed, then it prompts to install dhcp-server and installs the package. In the first screen of the wizard (see Figure 11-14), you have to select the network interface or interfaces that the DHCP server will be listening on.

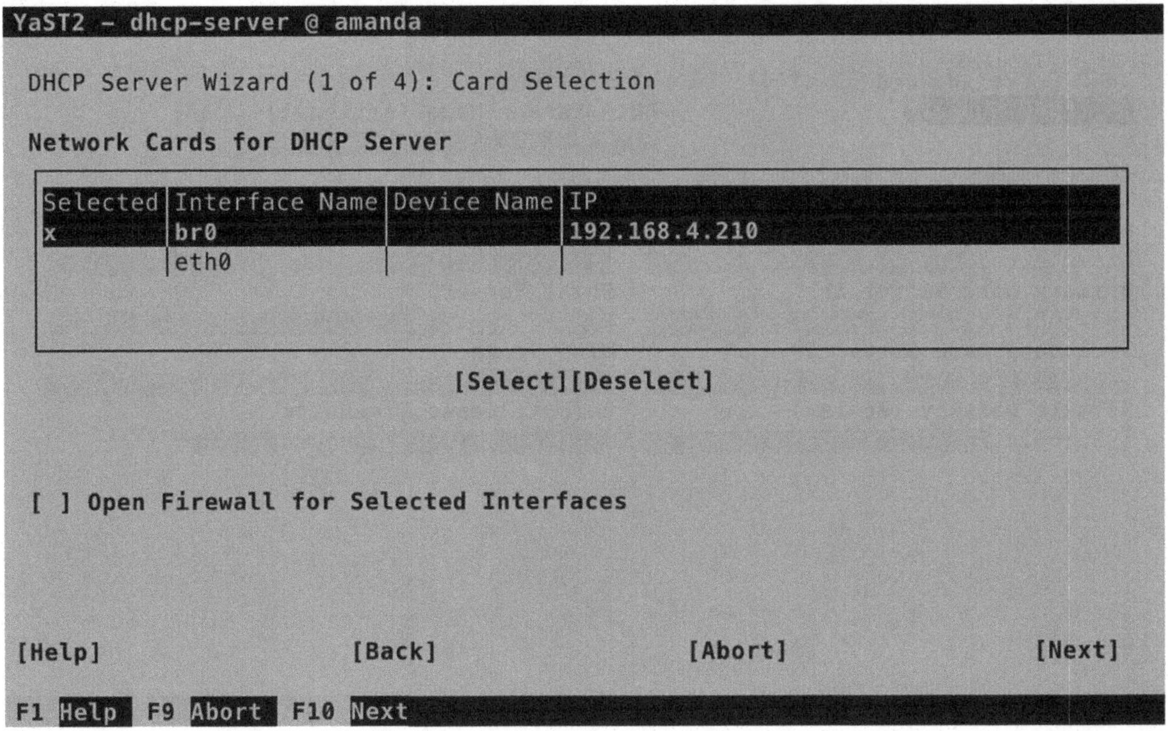

```
YaST2 - dhcp-server @ amanda

DHCP Server Wizard (1 of 4): Card Selection

Network Cards for DHCP Server

┌──────────────────────────────────────────────────────────────────────┐
│Selected│Interface Name│Device Name│IP                                  │
│x       │br0           │           │192.168.4.210                       │
│        │eth0          │           │                                    │
│                                                                        │
│                                                                        │
└──────────────────────────────────────────────────────────────────────┘

                        [Select][Deselect]



[ ] Open Firewall for Selected Interfaces




[Help]              [Back]                  [Abort]              [Next]

F1 Help  F9 Abort  F10 Next
```

Figure 11-14. *Selecting the interface on which the DHCP server will be listening*

In the second screen (see Figure 11-15), you'll set up the base configuration that will be handed out by the DHCP server. You will normally configure it at least with a (DNS) Domain Name, a Primary Name Server IP address, and a Default Gateway. Other options are the NTP Time Server, Print Server, and WINS Server. These settings are supported by most Linux clients, but you may have a hard time using them on other platforms. Also, you can specify the Default Lease Time. Notice that the default value of four hours is relatively short. If a node doesn't succeed in renewing its lease within that period, it will lose its IP configuration.

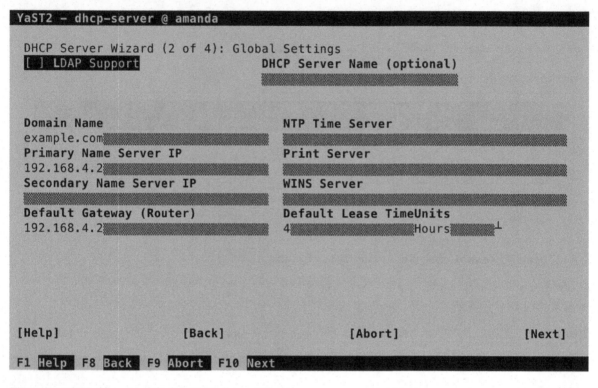

Figure 11-15. *Configuring default DHCP server settings*

In the next screen, shown in Figure 11-16, you'll configure the IP addresses that are to be handed out. To start with, you need a subnet configuration. This is configured by default, because you have selected the interface on which you want to offer DHCP services. You cannot modify the subnet information, as it contains only the network properties of the subnet you are working on.

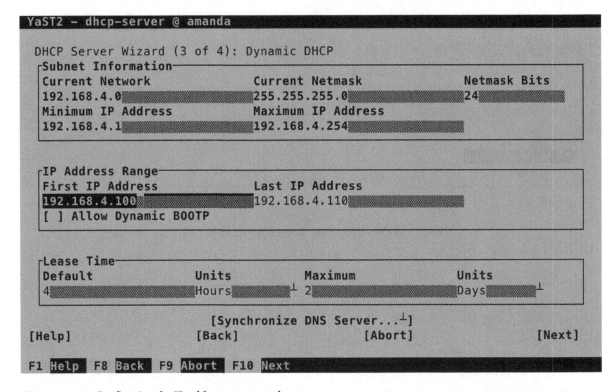

Figure 11-16. *Configuring the IP address ranges and more*

The most important part of the DHCP server configuration is the IP Address Range. You'll enter the First IP Address that can be handed out, up to the Last IP Address. It is a good idea not to use all the available IP addresses within the subnet but only to specify a select range of IP addresses and leave some other IP addresses within the range available for fixed IP address assignments. You can also select if you want to allow Dynamic BOOTP. BOOTP is often required if you want to allow clients who perform a PXE boot, in which the client boots from the network card and listens to a DHCP server handing out the required configuration. If you want to enable your server for automatic installations, it's a good idea to enable BOOTP.

Next, you'll specify the Lease Time for this zone. Note that this will overwrite the server-wide DHCP lease time. The lease time consists of a default lease, which is four hours, and a maximum lease, which is set to two days. If within the period that is specified as the maximum lease a client isn't able to renew his or her lease, it will expire, and the client will fall back to an address from the APIPA (Automatic Private IP Addresses Assignment) range, which starts with 169.254. (This normally means that the client cannot communicate on the network anymore).

Also on this screen is an option to synchronize the configuration with the DNS server. This is if you have set up your DNS server for Dynamic DNS, and it uploads all current IP address assignment information to the DNS server.

On the final screen of the wizard, you can specify how to start the server. Note that you do NOT want to start it automatically if there's another DHCP server already active on this network! From this screen, you can also get access to the DHCP Server Expert Configuration, which you can see in Figure 11-17.

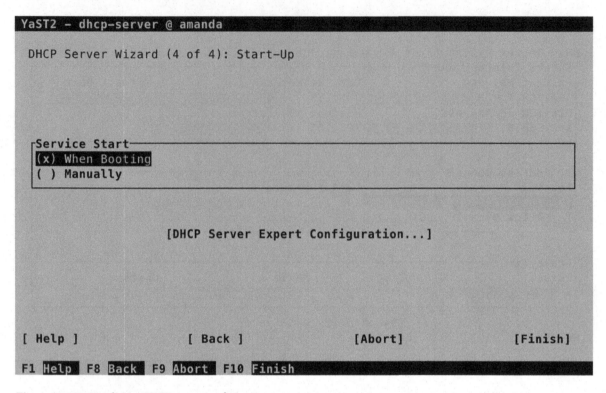

Figure 11-17. Finalizing DHCP server configuration

On the advanced DHCP Server Configuration screen, select DHCP Server Expert Configuration (see Figure 11-18), which gives access to some additional options. First, there is Run DHCP Server in Chroot Jail, which is enabled by default, and that is good. This means that if an intruder manages to break through the DHCP server and gets shell access, he or she will have gained entry to a very limited environment only.

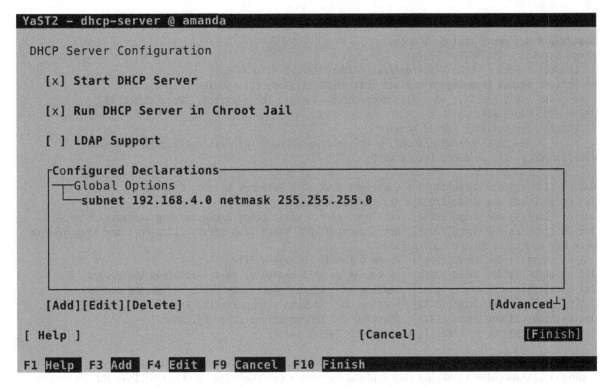

Figure 11-18. *DHCP expert options*

Also from this screen, you can enable LDAP support. This only works if the DHCP server has been able to find the current hostname it is running on. If that's not the case, you cannot configure LDAP support. The advantage of having LDAP support is that the DHCP configuration is stored in an LDAP directory. That is not just the settings but also the information about current leases, and that allows for more redundancy. The LDAP server can replicate information between servers, which makes the configuration more available.

From the Advanced Configuration screen, you can select each subnet the DHCP server is currently servicing and add new subnets, if that is needed. After selecting a subnet, you get access to the subnet options. From here, you can add many more configuration parameters to be handed out to DHCP clients, including some parameters that are not supported by many clients. So, find out if your client supports it before adding it!

Also from the subnet options, you'll get access to the Dynamic DNS Setup. This is because setup of dynamic DNS is per subnet. To connect your DHCP server to a DNS server, you have to select a TSIG key. If this key has been created while setting up the DNS server, you can select it from here; otherwise, you can create a new key (which must be configured for use on the DNS server also).

Manual DHCP Configuration

To manage the DHCP server, you must start and enable the dhcpd process, using systemctl start dhcpd, followed by systemctl enable dhcpd. After a successful start, you can verify the operations of the DHCP server, using systemctl status -l dhcpd (see Listing 11-12).

Listing 11-12. Verifying DHCP Server Operation

```
dbx:/etc # systemctl status -l dhcpd
dhcpd.service - ISC DHCPv4 Server
   Loaded: loaded (/usr/lib/systemd/system/dhcpd.service; enabled)
   Active: active (running) since Sat 2014-07-05 11:05:33 EDT; 5s ago
  Process: 21925 ExecStart=/usr/lib/dhcp/dhcpd -4 start (code=exited, status=0/SUCCESS)
 Main PID: 22053 (dhcpd)
   CGroup: /system.slice/dhcpd.service
           └─22053 /usr/sbin/dhcpd -4 -cf /etc/dhcpd.conf -pf /var/run/dhcpd.pid -chroot
/var/lib/dhcp -lf /db/dhcpd.leases eth0

Jul 05 11:05:33 dbx dhcpd[22052]: Copyright 2004-2014 Internet Systems Consortium.
Jul 05 11:05:33 dbx dhcpd[22052]: All rights reserved.
Jul 05 11:05:33 dbx dhcpd[22052]: For info, please visit https://www.isc.org/software/dhcp/
Jul 05 11:05:33 dbx dhcpd[22052]: Not searching LDAP since ldap-server, ldap-port and ldap-base-dn
were not specified in the config file
Jul 05 11:05:33 dbx dhcpd[22052]: Wrote 0 leases to leases file.
Jul 05 11:05:33 dbx dhcpd[22052]: Listening on LPF/eth0/00:0c:29:ff:f1:fd/192.168.4.0/24
Jul 05 11:05:33 dbx dhcpd[22052]: Sending on   LPF/eth0/00:0c:29:ff:f1:fd/192.168.4.0/24
Jul 05 11:05:33 dbx dhcpd[22052]: Sending on   Socket/fallback/fallback-net
Jul 05 11:05:33 dbx dhcpd[21925]: Starting ISC DHCPv4 Server [chroot]..done
Jul 05 11:05:33 dbx systemd[1]: Started ISC DHCPv4 Server.
```

The configuration of the DHCP server is written to the file /etc/dhcpd.conf, which is relatively easy to read. Listing 11-13 shows what it looks like after applying the settings previously discussed in YaST. From this file, you can change all settings that have to be adjusted.

Listing 11-13. Contents of the dhcpd.conf Configuration File

```
option domain-name "example.com";
option domain-name-servers 192.168.4.175;
option routers 192.168.4.2;
default-lease-time 14400;
ldap-dhcp-server-cn "dhcpserver";
ddns-update-style none;
subnet 192.168.4.0 netmask 255.255.255.0 {
  option pop-server 192.168.4.2;
  range dynamic-bootp 192.168.4.50 192.168.4.75;
  default-lease-time 14400;
  max-lease-time 172800;
}
```

Monitoring and Testing DHCP Functionality

Testing DHCP functionality is not difficult. Messages about DHCP requests are sent to rsyslog, so you can easily access information about the working of the DHCP server by opening a trace to /var/log/messages, using tail -f /var/log/messages. In Listing 11-14, you can see what occurs in the /var/log/messages file on the DHCP server when a machine boots.

Listing 11-14. Analyzing DHCP Log Information

```
2014-07-05T11:14:36.797964-04:00 dbx dhcpd: DHCPREQUEST for 192.168.4.175 (192.168.4.254) from
00:0c:29:ff:f1:fd via eth0: unknown lease 192.168.4.175.
2014-07-05T11:14:51.782009-04:00 dbx dhcpd: DHCPDISCOVER from 00:0c:29:b9:8b:55 via eth0
2014-07-05T11:14:52.781707-04:00 dbx dhcpd: DHCPREQUEST for 192.168.4.191 (192.168.4.254) from
00:0c:29:b9:8b:55 via eth0: unknown lease 192.168.4.191.
2014-07-05T11:14:52.782687-04:00 dbx dhcpd: DHCPOFFER on 192.168.4.50 to 00:0c:29:b9:8b:55 via eth0
2014-07-05T11:14:57.792148-04:00 dbx dhcpd: DHCPREQUEST for 192.168.4.142 from 00:0c:29:b9:8b:55 via
eth0: unknown lease 192.168.4.142.
```

A normal DHCP request will always start with a DHCPREQUEST. This is the broadcast that is issued by the DHCP client when it starts up. If the client has used an IP address before, it will ask to use that specific IP address again. In the preceding listing you can see two clients requesting information for specific IP addresses.

The DHCPREQUEST is normally followed by a DHCPOFFER. This is your DHCP server offering a specific IP address. Next, it is up to the client to confirm that he or she wants to use that address. If that occurs, a DHCPACK follows as the confirmation that the client does want to use the address that was offered.

What is interesting in the preceding configuration sample is that the DHCPACK did never follow. The logical explanation is that the listening DHCP server was not able to offer the requested IP address. If this would have been the only address that is offered to the client, it would have accepted it anyway. As the client in this case didn't get back with an acknowledgment that he or she wanted to use the IP address offered, that can only mean that there is another DHCP server on this network that did offer the requested IP address!

Configuring the DHCP Relay Service

As mentioned previously, you can have only one DHCP server per network, and a DHCP server is required on each network. On networks that don't have their own DHCP server, you can configure the DHCP Relay Agent. Setting it up is easy.

1. Use zypper in dhcp-relay to install the dhcp-relay package.

2. Edit the contents of the /etc/sysconfig/dhcrelay configuration file and make sure it contains a DHCRELAY_INTERFACES parameter listing the network interfaces the DHCP Relay Agent should listen on. Also, it should have a DHCRELAY_SERVERS parameter, configured with the IP address of the DHCP server.

3. Use systemctl start dhcrelay, followed by zypper enable dhcrelay, to start and enable the DHCP Relay Agent.

```
EXERCISE 11-4. SETTING UP A DHCP SERVER
```

It is highly recommended that this exercise be performed only in an isolated network! If not, you may mess up the working of a currently functional DHCP server!

1. Use `zypper in dhcp-server dhcp` to install the packages that are required for setting up a DHCP server.

2. Open the configuration file `/etc/dhcpd.conf` with an editor, and give it the following contents, making sure that the address you're employing is used on a local connected interface;if not, the DHCP server will refuse to start:

```
INTERFACES=ëtho"
option domain-name "example.org";
option domain-name-servers 192.168.4.175;
option routers 192.168.4.2;
default-lease-time 14400;
ldap-dhcp-server-cn "dhcpserver";
ddns-update-style none;
subnet 192.168.4.0 netmask 255.255.255.0 {
  option pop-server 192.168.4.2;
  range dynamic-bootp 192.168.4.50 192.168.4.75;
  default-lease-time 14400;
  max-lease-time 172800;
}
```

3. Use `systemctl start dhcpd` to start the DHCP server. Don't enable it to make sure that it is not started automatically. (This is to avoid having conflicts with other DHCP servers on your network).

4. Start a client that is configured to use DHCP. Verify that the logs are appearing in `/var/log/messages`.

LDAP

If you've got only one server to administer, it's easy to keep track of the user accounts in your environment. Just create your users as local users, and all will be fine. If you have dozens of servers, that approach doesn't work well. In such cases, you can benefit from a centralized directory server, such as an LDAP directory server. In this section, you will learn how to set up LDAP for this purpose.

Understanding LDAP

The Lightweight Directory Access Protocol (LDAP) was initially developed as an access protocol, allowing users to request information from a directory server that was based on the X.500 protocol. Over the years, LDAP has evolved into a protocol to structure such directory servers as well. In SUSE Linux, OpenLDAP is well integrated and allows you to set up a centralized service that can be used for authentication and much more.

An LDAP setup is hierarchical, in the way that DNS is hierarchical. That means that in LDAP, different domains are used, too, which makes it easy to differentiate between objects in different locations or that serve different purposes. As in DNS, in LDAP databases also can be created for each domain that is in use. The relation between domains is established by using referrals, which are pointers to the next child or parent domain. This approach allows a huge directory service to be set up, which can include the entire planet, if necessary.

For redundancy purposes, the databases in LDAP can be set up as replicated databases, in which a master-slave model is used. The databases are writable on the master copy, and changes are replicated to the slave database, which makes it easy to make the setup available at different sites, while offering redundancy at the same time.

When setting up an LDAP server, there are a few things to be aware of. First, in LDAP, you have to specify a base domain. This is the entry point from which clients should start searching for information in the LDAP directory. This domain name is written with a type indication. As a result, a domain that in DNS would be known as example.com is known in LDAP as dc=example,dc=com.

When setting up LDAP clients, it is also necessary to specify the LDAP server that the client should connect to. This is typically only one server. If redundancy is required, it can be offered by using techniques such as high-availability (HA) clusters, as described in Chapter 14.

When establishing contact with the LDAP servers, TLS certificates are also mandatory. So, before setting up an LDAP server with certificates, administrators should make sure they have configured certificates for use on the LDAP server.

Setting Up an LDAP Server with YaST

To set up an LDAP server from YaST, select Network Services ➤ Authentication Server. This will install openldap2 as well as the Kerberos packages krb5-server and krb5-client. (Kerberos is not really required, but as LDAP can use Kerberos as an authentication service, there is a dependency anyway).

After installation of the packages, a setup wizard will guide you through some of the most important settings. To start with, set Start LDAP Server to Yes, to make sure it automatically starts up while booting. You can also indicate that it should register at an SLP daemon, which makes it easier to relocate the LDAP server on the network. SLP clients can query the SLP server on which the LDAP service is registered, and thus have an easy method of locating an available LDAP server.

When setting up an LDAP server, you can choose different roles. In this chapter, you'll read how to set up LDAP as a stand-alone server. Alternatively, you can set it up as a master server or as a slave server in a network environment (see Figure 11-19). Setting up a master/slave configuration provides redundancy but is more complicated, and for that reason, this is not covered in this chapter.

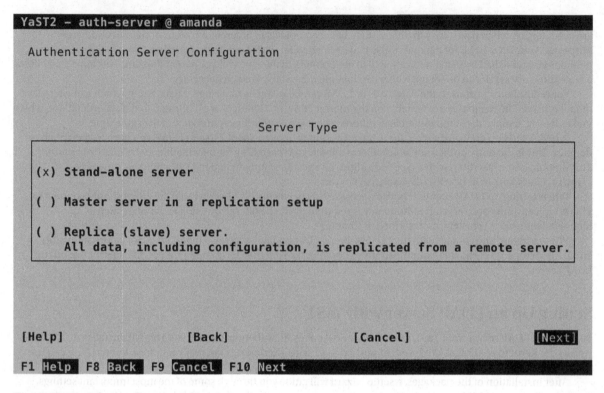

Figure 11-19. Selecting the server role

Specifying Security Settings

When working with LDAP, security is important. In Figure 11-20 you can see the screen from which you take care of setting security options. By default, only the option Enable LDAP over SSL (ldaps) interface is selected. This allows LDAP clients to connect to port 636 to establish a secure connection. With the option Enable TLS, the client also can connect to port 389 and open a TLS-secured session from there. This is the recommended option, so make sure to select Enable TLS.

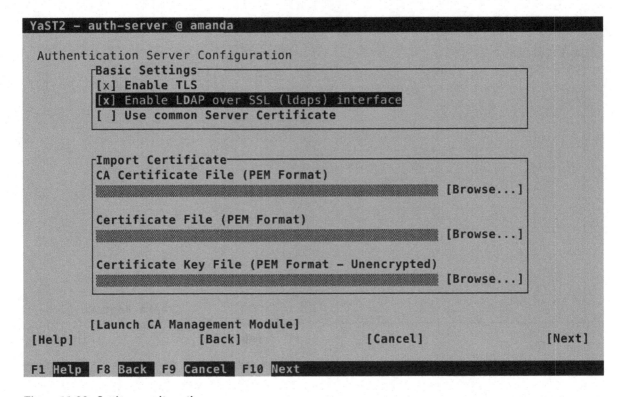

Figure 11-20. *Setting security options*

When working with TLS, you need TLS certificates as well. These are taken care of from the CA Management Module. So, before you specify anything, select Launch CA Management Module to create certificates. In Chapter 10, you can read in detail about using certificates. In this section, I'll only explain what you need to do to set up TLS certificates for use with LDAP on a server that doesn't have any certificates configured yet. If your server already has TLS certificates, you can select them there.

From the CA Selection screen, you can enter the Root CA, or Create a Root CA, if it doesn't exist yet. On the screen shown in Figure 11-21, no root certificate currently exists, so select Create Root CA to create one. (In Chapter 10, you can find more detailed instructions on setting up a Certificate Authority [CA] and working with certificates.)

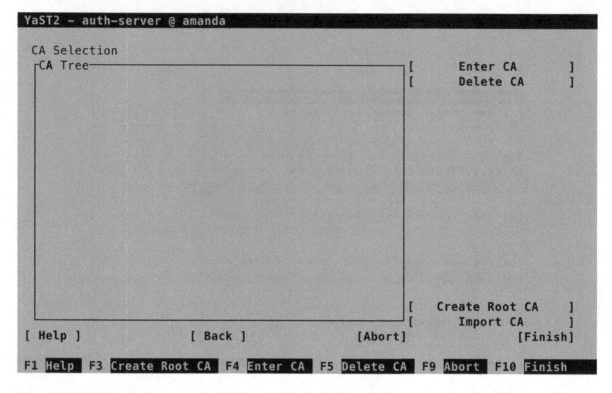

Figure 11-21. *CA properties*

From the Create New Root CA screen, you have to enter at least a CA name and a common name. The CA Name is the name that will be used in the certificate files, so make sure to choose a name that is easy to recognize later. The Common Name is the name of this server. All other options are discretionary, so you can skip them (see Figure 11-22).

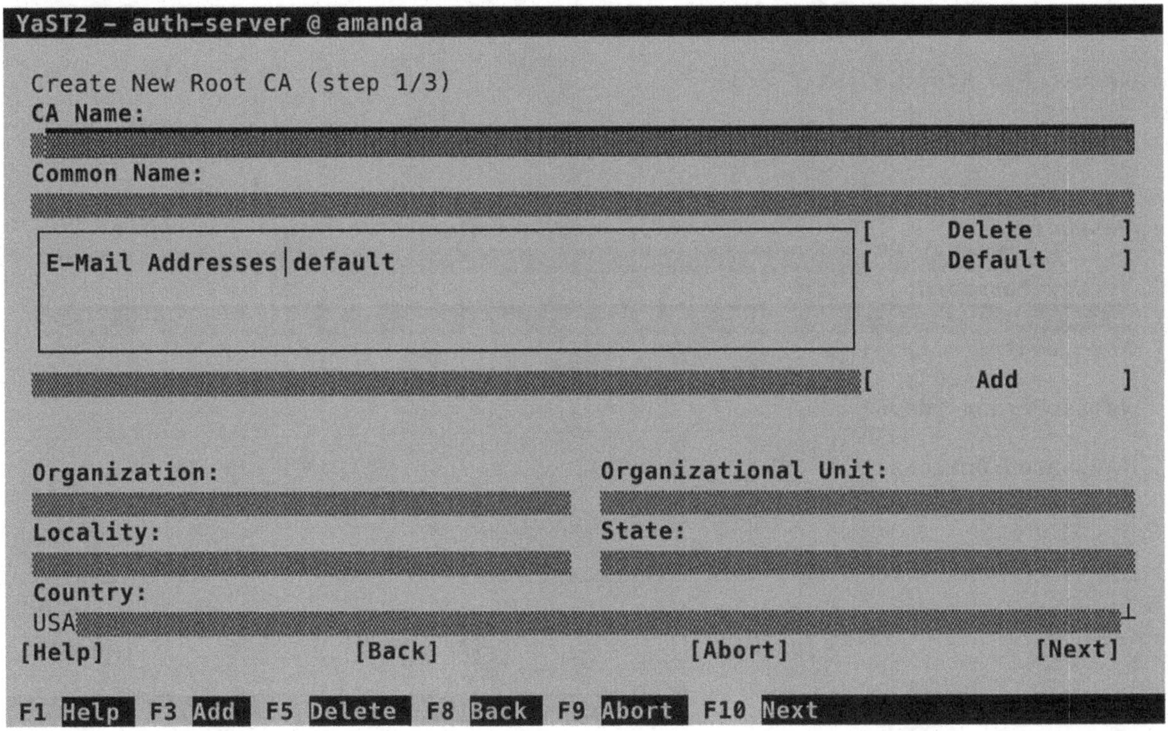

```
 YaST2 - auth-server @ amanda

  Create New Root CA (step 1/3)
  CA Name:
  ░░░░░░░░░░░░░░░░░░░░░░░░░░░░░░░░░░░░░░░░░░░░░░░░░░░░░░░░░░░░░░░░░░░░░░░░░░░░░░
  Common Name:
  ░░░░░░░░░░░░░░░░░░░░░░░░░░░░░░░░░░░░░░░░░░░░░░░░░░░░░░░░░░░░░░░░░░░░░░░░░░░░░░
  ┌──────────────────────────────────────────────────────────┐ [   Delete    ]
  │ E-Mail Addresses│default                                  │ [   Default   ]
  │                                                            │
  │                                                            │
  │                                                            │
  └──────────────────────────────────────────────────────────┘
  ░░░░░░░░░░░░░░░░░░░░░░░░░░░░░░░░░░░░░░░░░░░░░░░░░░░░░░░░░░░░░░ [    Add       ]


  Organization:                      Organizational Unit:
  ░░░░░░░░░░░░░░░░░░░░░░░░░░░░░░░░░░░  ░░░░░░░░░░░░░░░░░░░░░░░░░░░░░░░░░░░░░░
  Locality:                          State:
  ░░░░░░░░░░░░░░░░░░░░░░░░░░░░░░░░░░░  ░░░░░░░░░░░░░░░░░░░░░░░░░░░░░░░░░░░░░░
  Country:
  USA░░░░░░░░░░░░░░░░░░░░░░░░░░░░░░░░░░░░░░░░░░░░░░░░░░░░░░░░░░░░░░░░░░░░░░░░⊥
  [Help]            [Back]                    [Abort]                [Next]

 F1 Help  F3 Add  F5 Delete  F8 Back  F9 Abort  F10 Next
```

Figure 11-22. *Creating the root CA*

In the next screen (Figure 11-23), you set the properties for the root CA. These are a password that has to be entered when starting the root CA, a key length, and a validity period. For the purpose of creating certificates for an LDAP server, you must enter a password, and for the rest, you can select all default options and Next, to proceed to the following screen. You'll now see an overview of the selected settings. Review them and click Create to proceed.

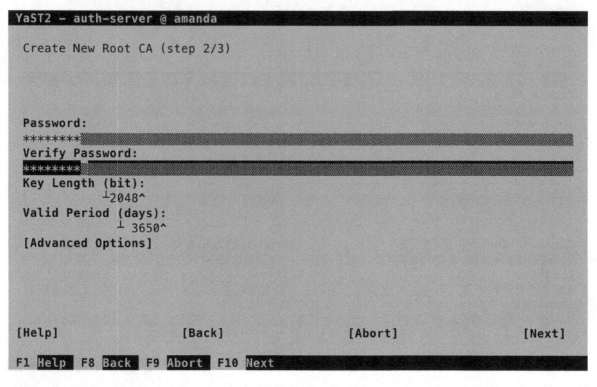

Figure 11-23. *Setting the root CA password and certificate validity*

Back on the CA Selection screen, you can now select Enter CA to enter the CA and create the certificates that the LDAP server is going to use.

You are now on the Certificate Authority (CA) screen (see Figure 11-24). From here, select Certificates ➤ Add to add a new certificate. From the drop-down list, select Add Server Certificate.

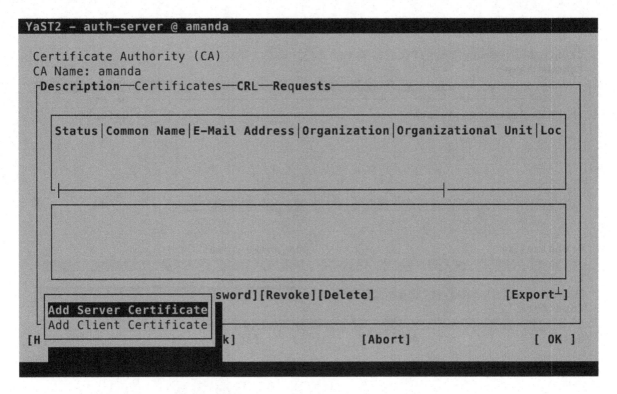

Figure 11-24. *Adding a server certificate to the CA*

The most important parameter when adding a new certificate is the Common Name. You can set this on the screen shown in Figure 11-25. This name is used to identify the host that the client is connecting to, and for that reason, it should be similar to the hostname. All other parameters are optional.

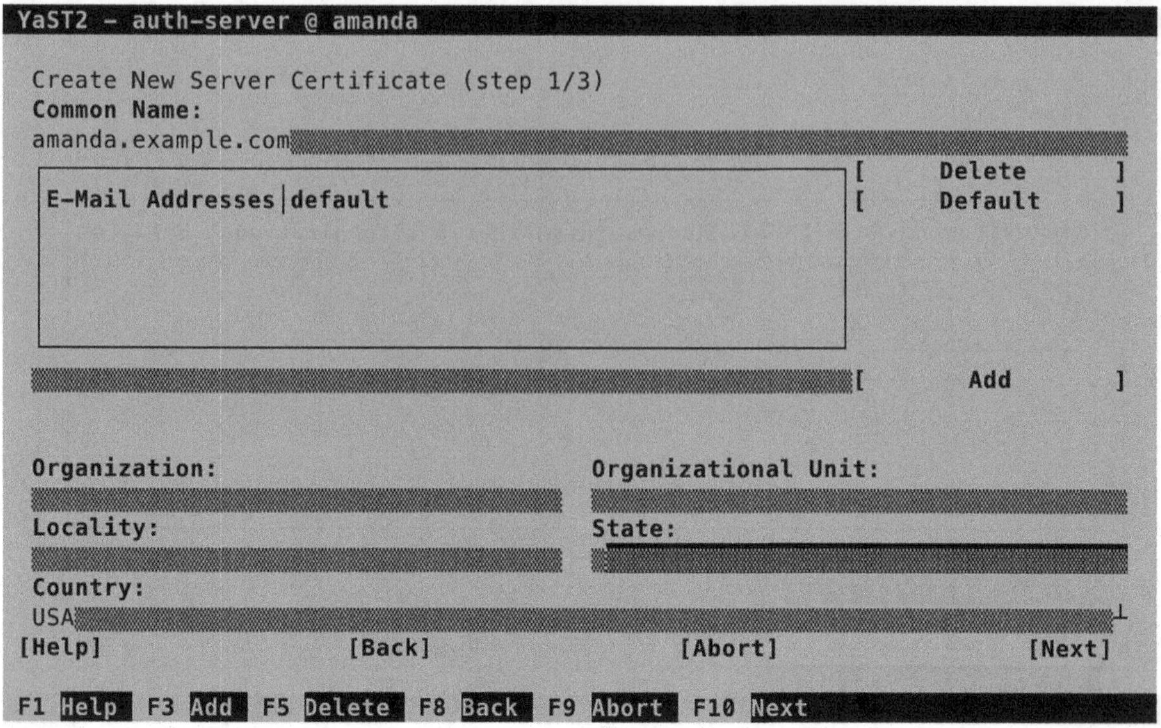

```
YaST2 - auth-server @ amanda

  Create New Server Certificate (step 1/3)
  Common Name:
  amanda.example.com▓▓▓▓▓▓▓▓▓▓▓▓▓▓▓▓▓▓▓▓▓▓▓▓▓▓▓▓▓▓▓▓▓▓▓▓▓▓▓
  ┌─────────────────────────────────────────────┐ [    Delete     ]
  │ E-Mail Addresses│default                     │ [    Default    ]
  │                                              │
  │                                              │
  │                                              │
  │                                              │
  └─────────────────────────────────────────────┘
  ▓▓▓▓▓▓▓▓▓▓▓▓▓▓▓▓▓▓▓▓▓▓▓▓▓▓▓▓▓▓▓▓▓▓▓▓▓▓▓▓▓▓▓▓ [      Add       ]


  Organization:                  Organizational Unit:
  ▓▓▓▓▓▓▓▓▓▓▓▓▓▓▓▓▓▓▓▓▓▓▓▓▓       ▓▓▓▓▓▓▓▓▓▓▓▓▓▓▓▓▓▓▓▓▓▓▓▓▓▓▓▓▓▓
  Locality:                      State:
  ▓▓▓▓▓▓▓▓▓▓▓▓▓▓▓▓▓▓▓▓▓▓▓▓▓       ▓▓▓▓▓▓▓▓▓▓▓▓▓▓▓▓▓▓▓▓▓▓▓▓▓▓▓▓▓▓
  Country:
  USA▓▓▓▓▓▓▓▓▓▓▓▓▓▓▓▓▓▓▓▓▓▓▓▓▓▓▓▓▓▓▓▓▓▓▓▓▓▓▓▓▓▓▓▓▓▓▓▓▓▓▓▓▓▓▓▓▓
  [Help]             [Back]              [Abort]           [Next]

  F1 Help  F3 Add  F5 Delete  F8 Back  F9 Abort  F10 Next
```

Figure 11-25. *Specifying the certificate common name*

In the next step, you have to set a password and enter the certificate validity period. By default, certificates are valid for 365 days only. This is secure, but inconvenient, as you will have to create new certificates every year. You, therefore, might want to increase the validity period (see Figure 11-26).

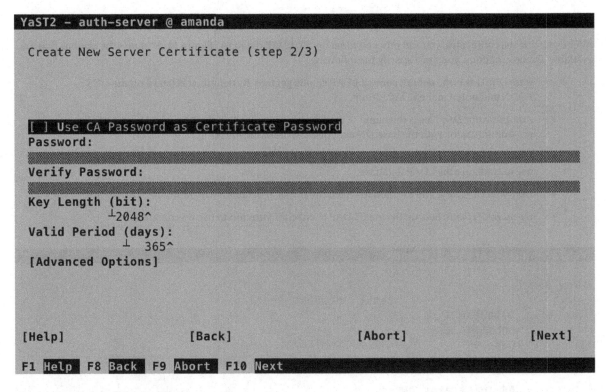

Figure 11-26. *Specifying certificate properties*

Once created, you'll get back to the Certificate Authority screen. From here, you have to export it. There are three different kinds of exports that must be performed.

- The LDAP server needs access to the private key of the server certificate you've just created.

- The LDAP server needs access to hand out to clients the public key of the server certificate you've just created.

- LDAP clients need access to the public key of the Certificate Authority.

From the Export option, you can select to export to File, to LDAP, or to export as a common server certificate. A common server certificate can be used by different services and provides an easy way of securing multiple services. Therefore, export as a common server certificate and close down the CA Management utility.

■ **Note**   If the common server certificate didn't exist when you first started YaST to configure the LDAP server, you won't be able to select it directly after creation. Stop YaST and start it again, and you will see the common server certificate selected.

Setting Up the LDAP Database

After exporting the certificates, you can proceed to set up the LDAP database. Figure 11-27 shows the options that are available. Of these options, you must specify the following:

- *Base DN*: This is the default context LDAP clients get into. By default, it is based on the DNS FQDN and noted in the LDAP format.

- *Administrator DN*: This is the name of the administrator. By default, the administrator will be cn=Administrator, with the base DN appended to make the full name.

- *LDAP Administrator Password*: In here, you'll set the password the administrator is going to use to configure the LDAP database.

- *Database Directory*: The location in which the physical database will be stored.

- *OpenLDAP clients*: Sets up the local LDAP client configuration to use this database.

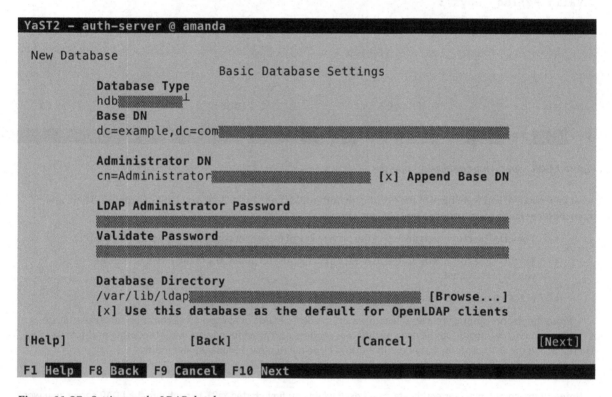

Figure 11-27. Setting up the LDAP database

On the next screen, you'll specify whether you want to use Kerberos Authentication. For increased security where Kerberos tickets are used instead of LDAP Password, select Yes. For setting up a basic LDAP server, leave this setting to No and select Next to proceed. You'll now see the LDAP server overview window. Click Finish to create the LDAP database and start it.

At this point, it's a good idea to verify the working of the LDAP server. The ldapsearch utility provides a solution to do that. Use ldapsearch -D "cn=Administrator,dc=example,dc=com" -W -x -b "dc=example,dc=com". It should, at this point, give you a result, as you can see in Listing 11-15.

Listing 11-15. Using ldapsearch to Verify LDAP Accessibility

```
suse:~ # ldapsearch -D "cn=Administrator,dc=example,dc=com" -b "dc=example,dc=com" -W -x
Enter LDAP Password:
# extended LDIF
#
# LDAPv3
# base <dc=example,dc=com> with scope subtree
# filter: (objectclass=*)
# requesting: ALL
#

# search result
search: 2
result: 32 No such object

# numResponses: 1
```

Populating the LDAP Database

The classic way of adding users to an LDAP server is by using LDIF files. These are files in which user accounts have to be specified, with all of the properties that the users require to do whatever they need to do on the server. Before doing that, however, you have to create a base structure. This is also accomplished by using an LDIF file, such as the one shown in Listing 11-16.

Listing 11-16. LDIF to Create the Base LDAP Structure

```
dn: ou=users,dc=example,dc=com
objectClass: organizationalUnit
objectClass: top
ou: users

dn: ou=groups,dc=example,dc=com
objectClass: organizationalUnit
objectClass: top
ou: groups
```

To add the contents of this file to the LDAP directory, you can use the ldapadd command, as in ldapadd -x -D "cn=Administrator,dc=example,dc=com" -W -f ~/base.ldif.

Once the base structure has been added to the LDAP database, LDIF files containing users can be added to the service. The contents of such an LDIF file may resemble Listing 11-17.

Listing 11-17. Sample LDIF Configuration File

```
dn: uid=lisa,ou=users,dc=example,dc=com
objectClass: top
objectClass: account
objectClass: posixAccount
objectClass: shadowAccount
cn: lisa
uid: lisa
uidNumber: 5001
```

```
gidNumber: 5001
homeDirectory: /home/lisa
loginShell: /bin/bash
gecos: lisa
userPassword: {crypt}x
shadowLastChange: 0
shadowMax: 0
shadowWarning: 0
```

After creating the LDIF file, it must be imported to the LDAP directory, using a command such as `ldapadd -x -D "cn=Administrator,dc=example,dc=com" -W -f ~/users.ldif`. To verify that the import has been successful, you can use the `ldapsearch` command, as in `ldapsearch -x -D "cn=Administrator,dc=example,dc=com" -W -b "dc=example,dc=com" "(objectclass=*)"`.

Because setting up users in this way can hardly be called intuitive, YaST provides an alternative approach. The steps below describe how to set up a newly installed LDAP Directory Server for adding user accounts.

1. Start YaST and select Security and Users ➤ User and Group Management.

2. First, select Expert Options ➤ LDAP User and Group Configuration. From the screen that you see now (see Figure 11-28), make sure that Home Directories on This Machine is selected and, next, select Configure User Management Settings. The last option doesn't show you anything, but it does create the required information in the LDAP directory. Next, press OK to return to the User and Group Management main screen.

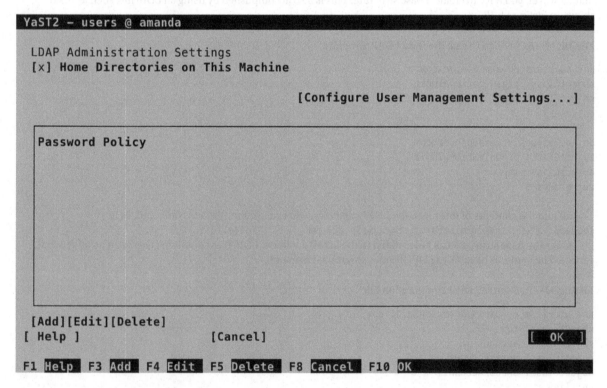

Figure 11-28. *Enabling YaST for managing LDAP users*

3. From the User and Group Administration interface, select Set Filter. From the drop-down list, select LDAP Users and enter the BindDN and password, to connect to the LDAP Server (see Figure 11-28).

4. At this point, continue and create the users as normal. This will add the users to the database with all the required properties. To verify, you can use ldapsearch -x -D "cn=A dministrator,dc=example,dc=com" -W -b "dc=example,dc=com" "(objectclass=*)". This does not guarantee that you can log in as the LDAP user (you have to set up the LDAP client to do that), but at least it shows that the user has been added to the directory, including some additional configuration.

LDAP Client Configuration

To use an LDAP server, you have to notify your server or the LDAP client that you want to configure. An Authentication Client is available in YaST. Select Network Services ➤ Authentication Client to configure it. The first thing you have to configure is an authentication domain. Consider the domain a collection of settings that tells the authentication process where to go to do its work. From the screen that you see in Figure 11-29, select Add to configure the authentication domain.

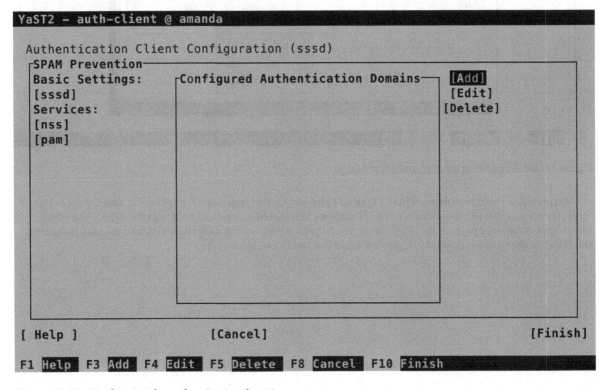

Figure 11-29. Configuring the authentication domain

From the screen that opens now (see Figure 11-30), enter a name for the domain. It doesn't really matter which name you use, so enter something like "ldap," for example. Next, make sure that the identification provider as well as the authentication provider are set to ldap and press OK.

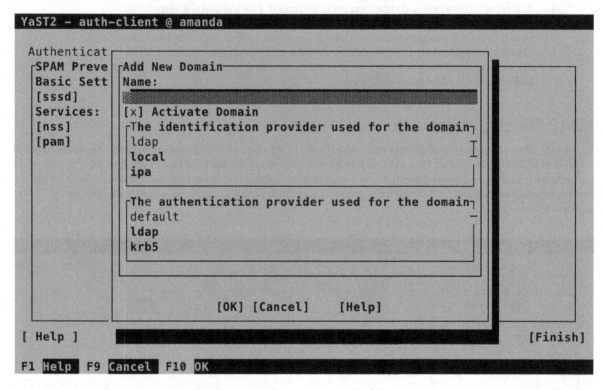

Figure 11-30. Configuring the authentication domain

At this point, you'll have to provide an LDAP URI and an LDAP Search Base. The URI is the name of the LDAP server (make sure that you use a name, not an IP address, and that this name can be resolved in DNS). The LDAP search base is the entry point in the LDAP hierarchy. If the LDAP server is at ldap.example.com, use that as the URI, and if the search_base is dc=example,dc=com, enter that here (see Figure 11-31).

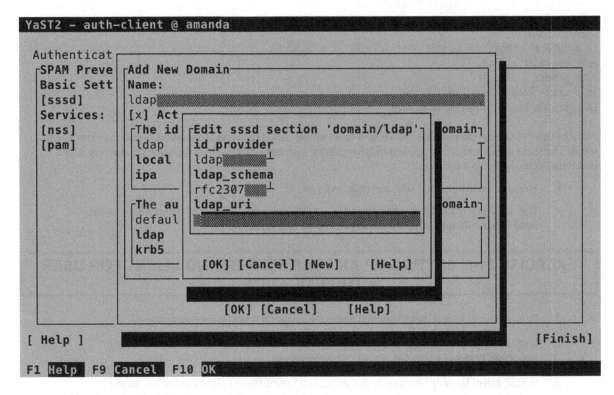

Figure 11-31. Entering the LDAP URI and search base

Back in the main screen of the Authentication Client Configuration, select Finish to finish and write the configuration. At this point, you're ready to test the configuration, for example, by using the command su - linda (assuming that linda is your LDAP user). You will be authenticated as that user now.

While setting up the LDAP Client with YaST, the sssd service has been configured. Use systemctl status -l sssd to check that it is running. This service reads a configuration file, which is in /etc/sssd/sssd.conf. In Listing 11-18, you can see what its contents should look like, based on the settings that were entered from YaST.

Listing 11-18. Checking the Contents of the /etc/sssd/sssd.conf File

```
ldap:/etc/sssd # cat sssd.conf
[sssd]
config_file_version = 2
services = nss, pam
domains = ldap
# SSSD will not start if you do not configure any domains.
# Add new domain configurations as [domain/<NAME>] sections, and
# then add the list of domains (in the order you want them to be
# queried) to the "domains" attribute below and uncomment it.
; domains = LDAP

[nss]
filter_users = root
filter_groups = root
```

```
[pam]
[domain/ldap]
id_provider = ldap
auth_provider = ldap
ldap_schema = rfc2307
ldap_uri = ldap://ldap.example.com
ldap_search_base = dc=example,dc=com
```

The preceding configuration has shown how to set up the LDAP client on the server that also runs the LDAP server. The same procedure can be applied to other clients. Just make sure to enter the same parameters, and if problems occur, verify the following:

- You are able to ping the LDAP server by its name.

- The certificate of the CA that has signed the LDAP server certificate is available on the client. Read Chapter 10 for more information on how to organize this.

EXERCISE 11-5. SETTING UP AN LDAP SERVER AND CLIENT FOR USER AUTHENTICATION

1. Open /etc/hosts and make sure that hostname resolving is set up for your server.

2. Create a Certificate Authority and create default server certificates from it. Make sure the server certificates are installed in their default locations.

3. In YaST, select Network Services ➤ Authentication Server. Press Enter to install the required packages.

4. On the General Settings screen, press Enter to accept the default settings. Next, select Stand-alone server as the default Server Type.

5. On the TLS Settings screen, accept all basic settings. Make sure that the three certificate files are present at the locations where they are mentioned. By default, the YaST-CA.pem file is not present at the location that is mentioned. Export it from the root CA to a PEM file that contains only the certificate and copy the file you have exported to the directory /etc/ssl/certs/YaST-CA.pem.

6. On the Basic Database Settings screen, enter a password for the LDAP administrator user.

7. On the Kerberos Authentication screen, accept the default settings.

8. Press Finish to close the Authentication Server module.

9. Still from YaST, select Security and Users ➤ User and Group Management.

10. Select Expert Options ➤ LDAP User and Group Configuration. From the screen that appears now, select Configure User Management Settings and then press OK.

11. Back on the main User and Group Administration screen, select Set Filter; select LDAP Users; and log in to the LDAP server. Now add a user account to the LDAP database.

12. Use `ldapsearch` to check that the user account and related information have been created successfully.

13. Select Network Services ➤ Authentication Client and then Add to add a new authentication domain.

14. Set the `id_provider, and auth_provider` to ldap; set the LDAP URI to the name of your LDAP server (make sure the URI starts with `ldap://`); and specify the LDAP Search Base.

15. Close the Authentication Client Configuration window and log in as your LDAP user. If this does not work, open the `/etc/sssd/sssd.conf` file and split the URI into `ldap_uri` and `ldap_search_base` entries.

Summary

In this chapter, you have learned how to configure core network services. You have learned how to configure xinetd, NTP, DNS, and DHCP. In the last part of the chapter, you have learned how to set up an LDAP server for centralized user authentication. In the next chapter, you'll learn how to configure core Internet services on your server.

CHAPTER 12

■ ■ ■

Setting Up a LAMP Server

LAMP, which stands forLinux, Apache, MySQL, and PHP, is what has made Linux the most-used operating system in the data center. Even if the database and scripting solution may be different in your environment, LAMP still plays a significant role in Enterprise Linux. In this chapter, you'll learn how to configure it.

Configuring Apache from YaST

From YaST, you can easily configure an Apache web server. YaST offers options to configure a web server with basic settings, as well as advanced configurations, such as virtual hosts or Secure Sockets Layer (SSL)–enabled web servers. In the next sections, you'll read about the different configuration options.

Setting Up a Web Server with Basic Settings

As is the case for many services in the SUSE Linux Enterprise Server (SLES), YaST offers the most convenient way to get a server in an operational state. To start the Apache configuration from YaST, select Network Services ➤ HTTP Server. If the Apache software hasn't been installed yet, you are now prompted to start the installation. Once installed, you will see the screen shown in Figure 12-1.

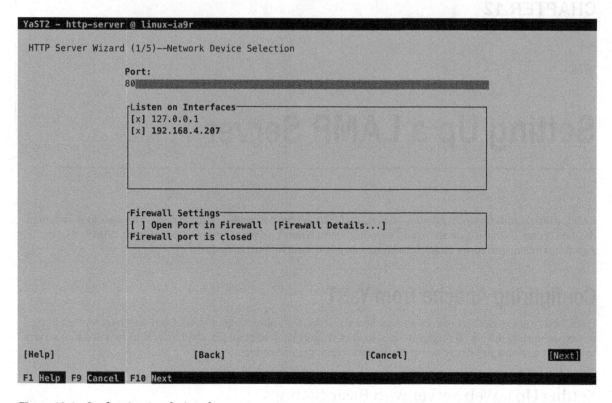

```
 YaST2 - http-server @ linux-ia9r

 HTTP Server Wizard (1/5)--Network Device Selection

                    Port:
                    80

                    ┌Listen on Interfaces─────────────────────────────────┐
                    │[x] 127.0.0.1                                         │
                    │[x] 192.168.4.207                                     │
                    │                                                      │
                    │                                                      │
                    │                                                      │
                    └──────────────────────────────────────────────────────┘

                    ┌Firewall Settings────────────────────────────────────┐
                    │[ ] Open Port in Firewall  [Firewall Details...]      │
                    │Firewall port is closed                               │
                    └──────────────────────────────────────────────────────┘




  [Help]                       [Back]                    [Cancel]                    [Next]

  F1 Help  F9 Cancel  F10 Next
```

Figure 12-1. *Configuring Apache interfaces*

To start with, you have to specify how Apache should offer its services. By default, it will be configured to listen on port 80 and all available network interfaces, which you can change here, if so desired. You'll also have to open Apache ports in the firewall. This does not happen by default.

In the next screen, you can specify whether Apache should have scripting enabled. You can choose between PHP5, Perl, and Python scripting. It is recommended that you select only the scripting type that you really intend to be using, as allowing unnecessary scripting types increases the security risks on your server. Most of the Apache security breaches that occur are in some way related to scripting, so you better disable scripting types that are not really needed (see Figure 12-2).

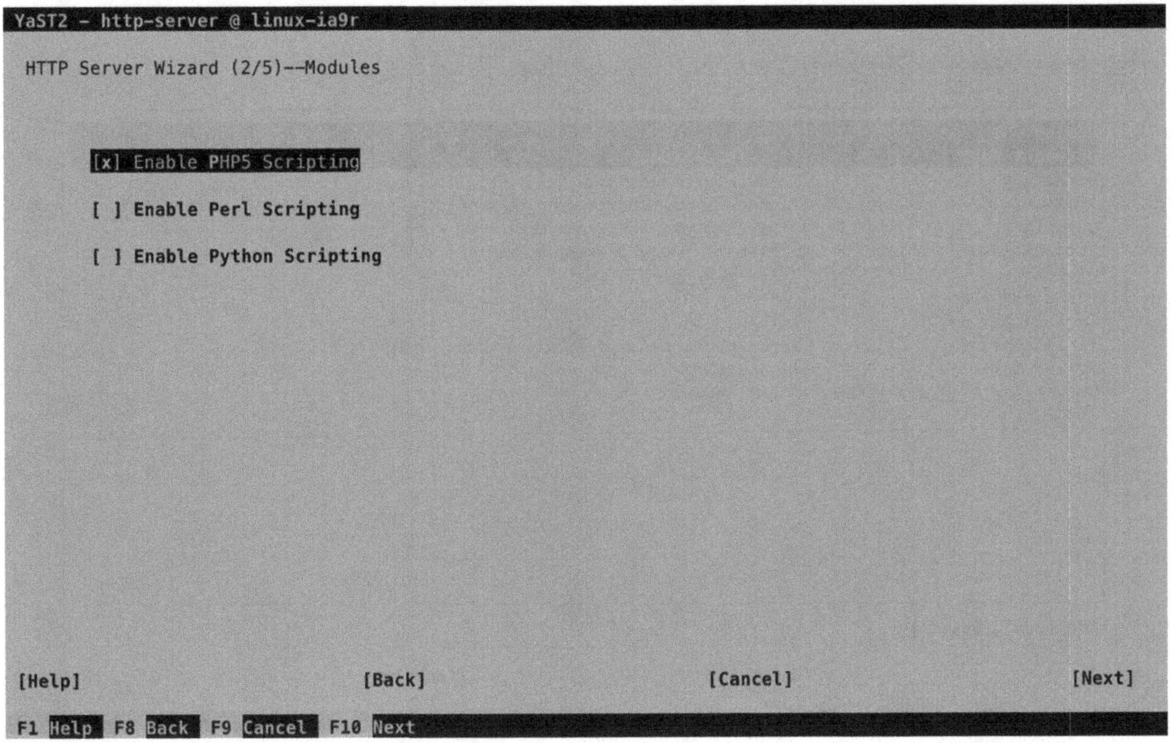

```
YaST2 - http-server @ linux-ia9r

HTTP Server Wizard (2/5)--Modules


        [x] Enable PHP5 Scripting

        [ ] Enable Perl Scripting

        [ ] Enable Python Scripting














[Help]                    [Back]                        [Cancel]                        [Next]
F1 Help  F8 Back  F9 Cancel  F10 Next
```

Figure 12-2. *Make sure to allow only the scripting types you really need*

In the next screen (see Figure 12-3), you'll configure default host settings. The settings that are specified and explained in Table 12-1 relate directly to settings that you can find in the main Apache configuration file /etc/apache2/default-server.conf and related files (see the next section, "Manual Apache Configuration," for more details about the configuration files that are used).

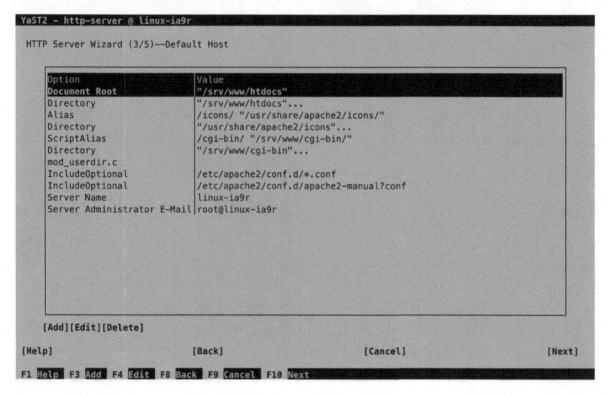

Figure 12-3. Specifying default configuration options

Table 12-1. Common Apache Configuration Options

Option	Use
DocumentRoot	The default location where the Apache server is looking for web content files such as index.html.
Directory	Directory settings are used to specify security settings that are specific to a particular directory.
Alias	An alias defines a subdirectory that a user or Apache module can use when looking for specific items. The default alias /icons, for example, can be accessed as http://yourhost/icons.
ScriptAlias	This default alias specifies the default location for scripts that the Apache server can start.
IncludeOptional	This directive refers to additional configuration files that can be included. By default, included files are in /etc/apache2/conf.d.
ServerName	The name of this server
Server Administrator E-mail	The e-mail address of the administrator of this server

Apart from the configuration options that are listed by default and discussed in Table 12-1, an administrator can add additional configuration settings. To do this, select Add. This opens a window in which you can select options from a drop-down list. Press the arrow key to see the contents of this list (see Figure 12-4).

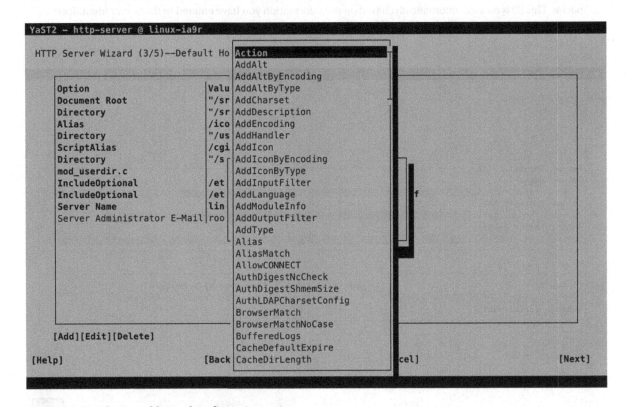

Figure 12-4. *Selecting additional configuration options*

In the next window, the configuration utility prompts for the virtual hosts you want to create. Creating virtual hosts is discussed in the next subsection in this chapter. Next, you'll see the overview of settings selected so far. From this overview, you can select Stat Apache2 Server When Booting to make sure it starts automatically on boot. Next, select Finish, to write the configuration. Depending on the selections that you've made, you can now be prompted to install some additional packages.

At this point, you have configured a basic Apache web server. It doesn't have any content yet, though. To create content for your web server, you can produce a file with the name index.html and put it in the directory /srv/www/htdocs. The contents of this file (which may be plain ASCII text) will be displayed by users who are connecting to the web server.

Configuring Virtual Hosts

On a server, several Apache web sites can be hosted, each using a different domain name. You have to configure DNS so that requests to a particular web site will be received on your server, and the Apache process will next decide where to forward the request to. This decision is based on the configuration of virtual hosts on Apache. Virtual hosts are easily configured from YaST. The following procedure explains how to do it.

From YaST, select the module to configure Apache. From the main screen, select Hosts and select Add. This opens the window that you can see in Figure 12-5, from which you can put the identification of the virtual host you want to create. The server identification field defines the name and document root for the web server, as well as the administrator e-mail address. In the Server Resolution box, you'll specify the name of the VirtualHost as it will be used by Apache. This ID is created automatically, based on the information you have entered in the Server Identification, but if required, you can select Change VirtualHost ID to change it here.

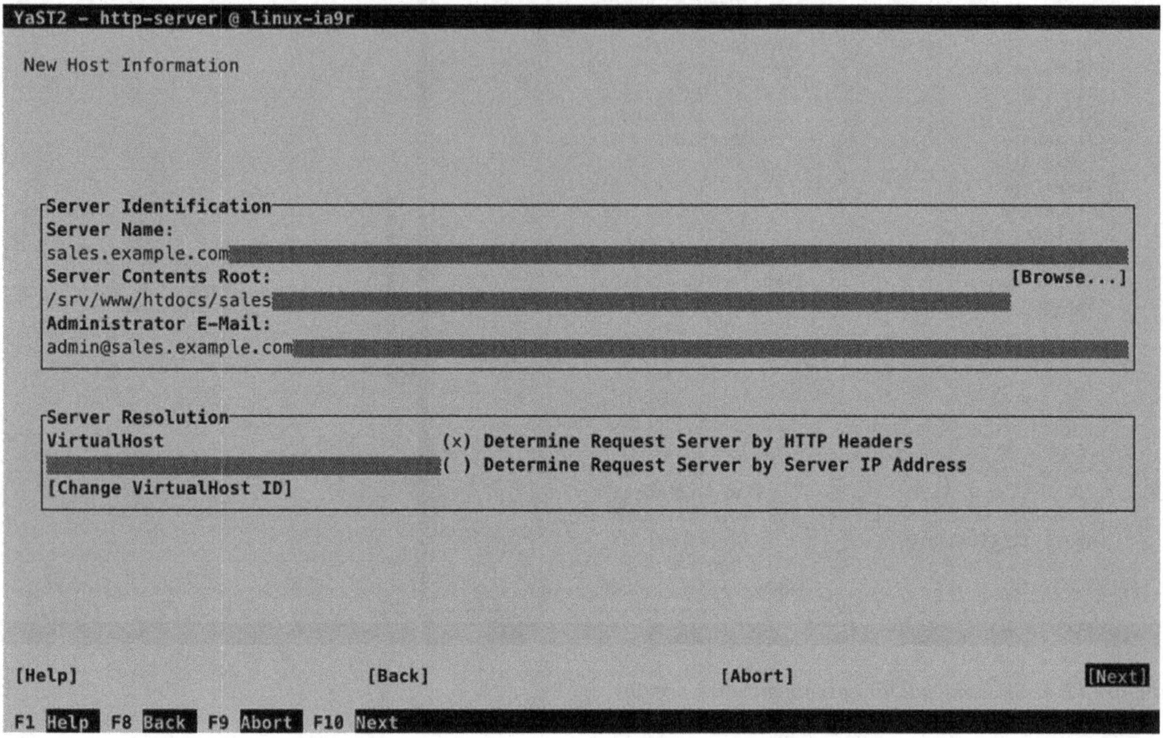

```
 YaST2 - http-server @ linux-ia9r

  New Host Information




    ┌Server Identification──────────────────────────────────────────────────────────┐
    │Server Name:                                                                     │
    │sales.example.com▓▓▓▓▓▓▓▓▓▓▓▓▓▓▓▓▓▓▓▓▓▓▓▓▓▓▓▓▓▓▓▓▓▓▓▓▓▓▓▓▓▓▓▓▓▓▓▓▓▓▓▓▓▓▓▓▓▓▓▓▓│
    │Server Contents Root:                                                 [Browse...]│
    │/srv/www/htdocs/sales▓▓▓▓▓▓▓▓▓▓▓▓▓▓▓▓▓▓▓▓▓▓▓▓▓▓▓▓▓▓▓▓▓▓▓▓▓▓▓▓▓▓▓▓▓               │
    │Administrator E-Mail:                                                            │
    │admin@sales.example.com▓▓▓▓▓▓▓▓▓▓▓▓▓▓▓▓▓▓▓▓▓▓▓▓▓▓▓▓▓▓▓▓▓▓▓▓▓▓▓▓▓▓▓▓▓▓▓▓▓▓▓▓▓▓▓▓│
    └────────────────────────────────────────────────────────────────────────────────┘

    ┌Server Resolution──────────────────────────────────────────────────────────────┐
    │VirtualHost                        (x) Determine Request Server by HTTP Headers  │
    │▓▓▓▓▓▓▓▓▓▓▓▓▓▓▓▓▓▓▓▓▓▓▓▓▓▓▓▓▓▓▓▓▓▓▓( ) Determine Request Server by Server IP Address │
    │[Change VirtualHost ID]                                                          │
    └────────────────────────────────────────────────────────────────────────────────┘




  [Help]                    [Back]                      [Abort]                [Next]
  F1 Help  F8 Back  F9 Abort  F10 Next
```

Figure 12-5. *Specifying new host information*

While creating virtual hosts, you can choose between two different approaches. Select Determine Request Server by HTTP Headers to configure a name-based virtual host or select Determine Request Server by Server IP Address to configure an IP-based virtual host. A name-based virtual host allows you to configure several hosts who are listening on the same IP address. To configure IP-based virtual hosts, you need a dedicated IP address for each virtual host. That is why name-based virtual hosts, in general, are more commonly used.

After specifying virtual host settings, you can configure advanced options on the screen shown in Figure 12-6. To start with, you can specify whether you want to enable CGI for this virtual host. By selecting this option, the virtual host will be available to start scripts. If you need this functionality, you'll also have to specify the CGI Directory Path, which is the name of the directory on which the script files will be stored.

```
 YaST2 - http-server @ linux-ia9r

  Virtual Host Details


    ┌CGI Options──────────────────────────────────────────────────────────────┐
    │[ ] Enable CGI for This Virtual Host                                       │
    │CGI Directory Path                                              [Browse...] │
    │                                                                           │
    └───────────────────────────────────────────────────────────────────────────┘

    ┌SSL Support──────────────────────────────────────────────────────────────┐
    │[ ] Enable SSL Support for This Virtual Host                               │
    │Certificate File Path                                          [Browse...] │
    │                                                                           │
    │Certificate Key File Path                                      [Browse...] │
    │                                                                           │
    └───────────────────────────────────────────────────────────────────────────┘

    ┌Directory Options────────────────────────────────────────────────────────┐
    │Directory Index                                                            │
    │                                                                           │
    └───────────────────────────────────────────────────────────────────────────┘

    ┌Public HTML──────────────────────────────────────────────────────────────┐
    │[ ] Enable Public HTML                                                     │
    └───────────────────────────────────────────────────────────────────────────┘

  [Help]                       [Back]                    [Abort]          [Next]
 F1 Help  F8 Back  F9 Abort  F10 Next
```

Figure 12-6. *Specifying advanced virtual host options*

If you need SSL Support on the virtual host as well, select Enable SSL Support for This Virtual Host. To offer SSL support, you have to specify access to the Certificate File and the Certificate Key File (read Chapter 10 for more information about SSL Certificates).

The Directory Index option that is under Directory Options is used to specify which files in the document root the Apache server should be looking for as HTML documents. By default, it will be looking for an index.html. If you need anything else, you can specify it here. Last, the Public HTML option is used to allow access to HTML documents in the home directories of users. If enabled, the user has to put the HTML documents in his or her home directory in a subdirectory with the name .public_html.

When working with virtual hosts, you should consider specifying a default virtual host. This default setting is important for packets that do reach your server but do not match a specific virtual host. That can happen if you have configured a virtual host for a site such as www.example.com. If you have configured your server in a way that packets addressed to example.com (without www) arrive at your server as well, but there is no matching virtual host configuration, then the packet will be delivered at the default virtual host.

Normally, the first host that is listed in alphabetical order is used as the default virtual host. If, instead, you want packets to be sent to a specific virtual host, you can use the Set as Default option to designate a specific host as default virtual host.

Apache Modules

Apache is a modular web server. That means that to offer specific functionality, modules have to be enabled. An example of such a module is mod_sssl. Without this module, no SSL support is available on your Apache web server. As with this module, many others are also available.

In some cases (like mod_ssl), configuration of a module is a transparent process. If you select SSL configuration from YaST, mod_ssl will automatically be loaded. For other modules, you have to specifically enable them. You can do this from the HTTP Server Configuration ➤ Server Modules screen (see Figure 12-7). From this screen, you can toggle the use of a module on or off, but no further configuration is possible from this screen. If you want to fine-tune an Apache module, you have to access the module-specific configuration file, which cannot be done from YaST.

```
YaST2 - http-server @ linux-ia9r

HTTP Server Configuration
┌Listen Ports and Addresses──Server Modules──Main Host──Hosts─────────────────────

  ┌────────────────────────────────────────────────────────────────────────────┐
  │Name            Status     Description                                        │
  │dav_fs          Disabled   File system provider for mod_dav                   │
  │deflate         Disabled   Compress content before it is delivered to the client│
  │disk_cache      Disabled   Content cache storage manager keyed to URIs        │
  │echo            Disabled   A simple echo server to illustrate protocol modules│
  │ext_filter      Disabled   Pass the response body through an external program before delivery to t│
  │file_cache      Disabled   Caches a static list of files in memory           │
  │headers         Disabled   Customization of HTTP request and response headers │
  │imagemap        Enabled    Server-side image map processing                  │
  │info            Enabled    Provides a comprehensive overview of the server configuration│
  │ldap            Disabled   LDAP connection pooling and result caching services for use by other LD│
  │authnz_ldap     Disabled   Allows an LDAP directory to be used to store the database for HTTP Basi│
  │logio           Disabled   Logging of input and output bytes per request     │
  │mem_cache       Disabled   Content cache keyed to URIs                        │
  │mime_magic      Disabled   Determines the MIME type of a file by looking at a few bytes of its con│
  │proxy           Disabled   HTTP/1.1 proxy/gateway server                     │
  │proxy_ajp       Disabled   AJP support module for mod_proxy                  │
  │proxy_connect   Disabled   mod_proxy extension for CONNECT request handling   │
  └────────────────────────────────────────────────────────────────────────────┘

  [Toggle Status]                                                    [Add Module]


[ Help ]                [ Back ]                    [Abort]                  [Finish]

F1 Help  F9 Abort  F10 Finish
```

Figure 12-7. *Enabling Apache modules from YaST*

Although it seems tempting to enable many modules, there is a security risk. With every unnecessary module that is enabled, you increase chances that security issues will occur. For that reason, you should not enable modules that you don't specifically need.

Manual Apache Configuration

Some Linux distributions put all of the Apache configuration in one file. This is not the case for SUSE Linux Enterprise (SLES). On SLES, you'll have to work through multiple configuration files to configure Apache the way you want.

default-server.conf

The starting point of all the configuration files is /etc/apache2/default-server.conf, which you can see in the contents of Listing 12-1 (for legibility, all comment lines included in this file are removed).

Listing 12-1. Apache Configuration in /etc/apache2/default-server.conf

linux-ia9r:/etc/apache2 # cat default-server.conf | grep -v '#'

```
DocumentRoot "/srv/www/htdocs"

<Directory "/srv/www/htdocs">
Options None
AllowOverride None
Order allow,deny
 Allow from all
</Directory>

Alias /icons/ "/usr/share/apache2/icons/"

<Directory "/usr/share/apache2/icons">
 Options Indexes MultiViews
 AllowOverride None
 Order allow,deny
 Allow from all
</Directory>

ScriptAlias /cgi-bin/ "/srv/www/cgi-bin/"

<Directory "/srv/www/cgi-bin">
 AllowOverride None
 Options +ExecCGI -Includes
 Order allow,deny
 Allow from all
</Directory>

<IfModule mod_userdir.c>
UserDir public_html
Include /etc/apache2/mod_userdir.conf
</IfModule>


IncludeOptional /etc/apache2/conf.d/*.conf

IncludeOptional /etc/apache2/conf.d/apache2-manual?conf
ServerName linux-ia9r

ServerAdmin root@linux-ia9r
NameVirtualHost *
```

Table 12-2 provides an overview of the important configuration lines that you can find in this configuration file.

Table 12-2. Configuration Parameters Overview

Parameter	Explanation
DocumentRoot	The location where the Apache server looks for its web content
Directory	Specific settings for a directory
Options	Options to consider for a specific directory
AllowOverride	Set to None, if you don't want security settings that are specified for this directory to be overwritten at a lower level
Order allow,deny	Specifies that Allow directives should be read before Deny directives
Alias	Defines an alias relative to the document root. The alias can be accessed as a subdirectory on the web server.
ScriptAlias	An alias that is specific for web scripts
IfModule	Configuration options that are for a specific module only
IncludeOptional	Refers to names of directories of files that contain additional configuration. Contents of these will always be included while running the web server.
ServerAdmin	The e-mail address of the web server administrator
NameVirtualHost	Specifies that name-based virtual hosts should be used
ServerName	The name of this web server

httpd.conf

The default-server.conf file contains configuration for the default web server. It is not the starting point for all configuration, however. The first configuration file to be considered is /etc/apache2/httpd.conf. This file mainly contains includes to other files that should be read. The contents of this file is displayed in Listing 12-2.

Listing 12-2. httpd.conf Contents

```
linux-ia9r:/etc/apache2 # cat httpd.conf | grep -v '#'
Include /etc/apache2/uid.conf
Include /etc/apache2/server-tuning.conf
ErrorLog /var/log/apache2/error_log
Include /etc/apache2/sysconfig.d/loadmodule.conf
Include /etc/apache2/listen.conf
Include /etc/apache2/mod_log_config.conf
Include /etc/apache2/sysconfig.d/global.conf
Include /etc/apache2/mod_status.conf
Include /etc/apache2/mod_info.conf
Include /etc/apache2/mod_reqtimeout.conf
Include /etc/apache2/mod_usertrack.conf
Include /etc/apache2/mod_autoindex-defaults.conf
TypesConfig /etc/apache2/mime.types
Include /etc/apache2/mod_mime-defaults.conf
Include /etc/apache2/errors.conf
Include /etc/apache2/ssl-global.conf
```

```
<Directory />
    Options None
    AllowOverride None
    Order deny,allow
    Deny from all
</Directory>

AccessFileName .htaccess
<Files ~ "^\.ht">
    Order allow,deny
    Deny from all
</Files>

DirectoryIndex index.html index.html.var

Include /etc/apache2/default-server.conf
Include /etc/apache2/sysconfig.d/include.conf
IncludeOptional /etc/apache2/vhosts.d/*.conf
```

As you can see, the `httpd.conf` mainly contains includes to read other files and contents of other directories. The most important configuration file that is included is `default-server.conf`, which was discussed in the previous section. Apart from this, there are configuration files that are specific to different modules (all of them start with `mod`). Another important include is on the last line, where all virtual host configuration files are included.

Virtual Host Configuration Files

On SUSE Linux Enterprise Server, virtual host configuration files are stored in separate configuration files, one for each virtual host that is defined. In Listing 12-3, you can see the contents of a sample virtual host configuration file.

Listing 12-3. Virtual Host Example

```
<VirtualHost *>
 DocumentRoot /srv/www/htdocs/account
 ServerName account.example.com
 ServerAdmin account@example.com
 <Directory /srv/www/htdocs/account>
  AllowOverride None
  Order allow,deny
  Allow from all
 </Directory>
</VirtualHost>
```

To allow administrators to configure virtual hosts easily, two template files are also provided. These are `vhost-ssl.template` and `vhost.template`. If an administrator wants to create a virtual host manually, it suffices to copy the contents of these template files and work from there.

SSL Configuration Files

To make configuration of SSL easy, a template file is provided to create an SSL-based virtual host. The contents of this file is in Listing 12-4.

Listing 12-4. Sample Template File for SSL Configuration

linux-ia9r:/etc/apache2/vhosts.d # cat vhost-ssl.template | grep -v '#'

```
<IfDefine SSL>
<IfDefine !NOSSL>

<VirtualHost _default_:443>
      DocumentRoot "/srv/www/htdocs"
      ErrorLog /var/log/apache2/error_log
      TransferLog /var/log/apache2/access_log
      SSLEngine on
      SSLProtocol all -SSLv2 -SSLv3
      SSLCertificateFile /etc/apache2/ssl.crt/server.crt
      SSLCertificateKeyFile /etc/apache2/ssl.key/server.key
<FilesMatch "\.(cgi|shtml|phtml|php)$">
        SSLOptions +StdEnvVars
</FilesMatch>
<Directory "/srv/www/cgi-bin">
        SSLOptions +StdEnvVars
</Directory>
      BrowserMatch "MSIE [2-5]" \
       nokeepalive ssl-unclean-shutdown \
       downgrade-1.0 force-response-1.0
      CustomLog /var/log/apache2/ssl_request_log    ssl_combined
</VirtualHost>
```

Although there are more options in an SSL configuration file than in a regular Apache configuration file, it is not that hard to read. The most important lines in this file are the lines in which the location of the certificate file and the certificate key file are specified: SSLCertificateFile and SSLCertificateKeyFile. These by default point to /etc/apache2/ssl.crt for the certificate and /etc/apache2/ssl.key for the key file. Typically, after creating SSL certificates that match the name of your server, you should manually copy the files to this location.

Setting Up Authentication

On some occasions, it may be useful to set up authenticated web servers or to protect access to specific directories through authentication. To do this, you must set up a user authentication file, as well as a section that prompts for credentials when accessing a secured area.

To start with, you'll need user accounts. The easiest way to set up these user accounts is by creating them with the htpasswd command. If you would want to add a user linda, the corresponding command would be htpasswd2 -c / etc/apache2/htpasswd linda. This will add user linda to the file /etc/apache2/htpasswd. Note that you're free to select the file name from which the user accounts will be created. There's no default or standard; the only thing that counts is that you refer to the same file name while setting up the protected environment. Instead of setting up a user file on each server, you could also use an LDAP server containing the usernames and passwords you'd like to use.

After creating the user account, you have to set up a protected environment. The sample code from Listing 12-5 shows how you can do this. Add this code to the appropriate vhost file:

Listing 12-5. Adding Security to a Directory

```
<Directory /srv/www/htdocs/secret>
     AuthType Basic
     AuthName "secret files"
     AuthUserFile /etc/apache2/htpasswd
     Require user linda
</Directory>
```

In this section, just four lines are used to make it a protected directory. To start with, the parameter AuthType Basic enables basic authentication. Next, AuthName defines a name that will be displayed to users accessing the protected environment. The most important line is AuthUserFile, which refers to the file that you've created for setting up authentication. The name of this file must match the name of the file you've created with the htpasswd command. In the last line, Require user linda specifies the name of the user account that has access. Instead of mentioning names of specific users, you can also use valid-user, which will only open the share to any user who exists in the password file.

If you want to set up your web server to authenticate against an LDAP server, that's also possible. You'll just need some more information in the Apache configuration. Listing 12-6 shows what the code to enable LDAP authentication would look like.

Listing 12-6. Setting Up LDAP Authentication

```
<Directory /srv/www/htdocs/private>
     AuthName Private Directory
     AuthType Basic
     AuthBasicProvider ldap
     AuthLDAPUrl "ldap://yourserver.example.com/dc=example,dc=com TLS"
     Require valid-user
</Directory>
```

As you can see, compared to Listing 12-5, only two parameters have changed. First, the AuthBasicProvider is now set to ldap, which tells Apache to expect an answer from an LDAP server. Next, the AuthLDAPUrl specifies the URL that can be used to get the credentials. This URL consists of two parts. The first part specifies the name for the LDAP server to use, which is followed by the LDAP context to use. The suffix TLS tells Apache that TLS security is required to get the credentials from LDAP.

Apache Logs

When things don't work out the way they should, you can use the log files that are created by the Apache server. By default, Apache does not use syslog but writes directly to its own log files. On SLES, you can find these log files in /var/log/apache2. If you're running only one web server, you'll find a file with the name access_log containing information about users accessing your server and an error_log that shows details about errors that have occurred on your server. If virtual hosts are used, you have the option to configure each virtual host with its own log file (which is highly recommended).

If you want to centralize log handling on Apache, you can set up Apache to go through syslog. To do this, change the lines in /etc/apache2/httpd.log in which log handling is defined to look as follows:

```
ErrorLog       syslog:local1
AccessLog      syslog:local1
```

These lines ensure that log information is sent to syslog, using the local1 facility. Read Chapter 5 of this book for more information on how to configure this in syslog.

EXERCISE 12-1. SETTING UP AN AUTHENTICATED APACHE ENVIRONMENT

This exercise is a lab exercise that allows you to apply the skills that you've acquired so far.

Configure your server to host two virtual web servers: sales.example.com and account.example.com. Make these servers accessible through port 443 only. Use the YaST certificate module to obtain the certificates that are required for accessing the servers over TLS. Next, set up authentication for sales.example.com on the DocumentRoot of that server. Create at least one user with the name lisa and the password password. Allow access for all users who have been set up in the Apache password file.

Configuring the Database Part of the LAMP Server

Apache servers are commonly configured to work with databases. In previous releases of SLES, MySQL was the default database solution. MySQL, however, has been acquired by Oracle, and for licensing reasons, an open source fork of MySQL has been created with the name MariaDB. You'll note from many things (including the name of the script file used to start the service) that MariaDB essentially is the same as MySQL, but in the future, both might develop in different directions.

MariaDB Base Configuration

To start with, you must install MariaDB and apply basic settings. In this section, you'll learn how to do that, by installing the software, securing it, and making small changes to the database configuration file /etc/my.cnf. You will see that many of the components of MariaDB have names that refer to MySQL. That is normal, because MariaDB is a derivative of the MySQL database software.

To install MariaDB, apply the following steps:

1. Use zypper in mariadb on the server on which you want to install the software.

2. Type systemctl start mysql, followed by systemctl enable mysql, to start and enable the database service.

3. Verify that MariaDB is running by using systemctl status mysql.

After installing MariaDB, it's a good idea to secure it as well. To do this, run the mysql_secure_installation command. This will apply a few security settings. First, it removes root accounts that are accessible from outside, just keeping root access open from localhost. It will also set a password for the root user account, and it removes anonymous user accounts as well as the test database. The command will do this in an interactive command sequence, in which all of these steps are applied one by one.

MariaDB can be used locally only, or it can be accessed over the network. There are advantages to both. If MariaDB is accessible over the network, it is easy to set up a service stack on which the database is running on one server and related services are running somewhere else. This offers the maximum possible performance for the database, but it also increases the risk that things go wrong, because the database is accessible over the network. If you care to elevate the security to a maximum, you may want to consider switching off network access completely. That implies that all services that are using the database are available on the same server.

To determine if MariaDB is going to use networking, you'll modify a few parameters in the /etc/my.cnf configuration file (which is the MariaDB main configuration file). In the [mysqld] section, you'll find the following settings:

- bind-address: The address on which the database service will be listening. Set to :, if you want to enable access through all IP addresses (IPv4 as well as IPv6), or leave blank to enable access over IPv4 only. Alternatively, you can specify the IP addresses of specific interfaces to which the database should bind.

- skip-networking: Set to 1 to disable all networking. Communications with other local processes in that case will go through sockets, which by default are in /var/lib/mysql/mysql.sock. When using this approach, the client software also needs to access the database through sockets and cannot use localhost and IP for local database access.

- port: Specifies the port to listen on for TCP/IP connections

---

EXERCISE 12-2. INSTALLING MARIADB

In this exercise, you will perform a base installation of MariaDB. You'll also disable network access and apply security settings. Next, you'll verify that some default system databases are available.

1. Type zypper in mariadb to install the database software.

2. Use systemctl start mysql; systemctl enable mysql to start and enable the MariaDB software.

3. Verify that MariaDB is listening, using netstat -tulpen | grep mysql. You should see a mysqld process listening on port 3306.

4. Disable networking by adding the line skip_networking=1 to /etc/my.cnf and restart MariaDB using systemctl restart mysql.

5. Start securing MariaDB, by using mysql_secure_installation. Set the password for the database root user to "password", disable remote root access, and remove the test database and any anonymous users.

6. Type mysql -u root -p to log in to the database as root and have the database prompt for a password.

7. From the MariaDB interactive shell prompt, type show databases; to display databases that are currently available.

8. Type exit; to quit the MariaDB interactive shell interface.

Performing Simple Database Administration Tasks

Even if you're a Linux administrator, it is useful to have basic knowledge of database administration commands. That doesn't make you a database administrator, but it does help you perform basic configuration tasks.

To start working with databases, you must connect to the database first. To do this, you'll use the mysql command, as in mysql -u root -h localhost -p. This command will log you in as user root to server "localhost" and will next prompt for a password. After logging in, you'll enter the MySQL interactive shell, from which you will work with databases. You've already seen the command show databases;, which displays a list of available databases. Note that in the MySQL shell, commands are not case sensitive (but names of databases and tables are case sensitive!). In addition, note that all commands are terminated with a semicolon (;).

Working with databases looks a little like working with directories. The database administrator will create a database, start using the database, and then enter the contents of the database. The USE command is used like the cd command from a bash shell. Whereas cd allows you to switch between directories easily, the USE command allows you to switch between databases. Try, for example, the following commands (after logging in to the MySQL shell environment as root):

1. Type CREATE DATABASE addressbook; to create a database with the name addressbook.

2. Type USE addressbook; to start using the addressbook database.

3. Type SHOW TABLES; to show its current tables. You should see none.

4. Now type USE mysql; to switch to the mysql database.

5. Type SHOW TABLES;, which will show many tables, including a table with the name user.

6. Type DESCRIBE user; to get column names from the user table. This gives a detailed description, as you can see in Listing 12-7. It tells you which fields are available in a table, what type of data is expected in a field, and provides some more attributes on the table contents.

Listing 12-7. Showing Table Contents

```
MariaDB [mysql]> describe user;
+-----------------+-------------------+------+-----+---------+-------+
| Field           | Type              | Null | Key | Default | Extra |
+-----------------+-------------------+------+-----+---------+-------+
| Host            | char(60)          | NO   | PRI |         |       |
| User            | char(16)          | NO   | PRI |         |       |
| Password        | char(41)          | NO   |     |         |       |
...          |
| max_connections | int(11) unsigned  | NO   |     | 0       |       |
| max_user_connect| int(11)           | NO   |     | 0       |       |
| plugin          | char(64)          | NO   |     |         |       |
| authent_string  | text              | NO   |     | NULL    |       |
+-----------------+-------------------+------+-----+---------+-------+
42 rows in set (0.00 sec)
```

In MariaDB, as well as in MySQL, you'll be using Structured Query Language (SQL) to manipulate data in the database. The basic commands allow you to create, read, update, and delete. These commands are also referred to as the CRUD operations: create, select, update, and delete. Before inserting data in a database, you'll have to find out which are the attributes of a table. Use DESCRIBE to do this, as in the DESCRIBE user; command that you've previously used.

Once you've found out which attributes are needed to create data in a table, you can use the INSERT command to add them: INSERT INTO user (Host,User,Password) VALUES ('localhost',linda,password);. In this command you'll first refer to the name of the table in which data has to be added, list the specific attributes you want to fill, and, next, list the values that you want to enter in those specific attributes.

To delete data, you'll use the DELETE command, as in DELETE FROM user WHERE User = rick;. Note that in this command, it is very important not to forget the WHERE part; if you omit it, all records in the table will be erased.

To change data, you'll use the UPDATE command: UPDATA user SET password=secret WHERE User = linda;. Note that in this command, you have to use the WHERE statement to tell MariaDB which record to use and the SET command to specify the attribute you want to change, with its new value.

To read records, you'll use the SELECT command: SELECT Host,User FROM user;. Alternatively, you can select to show all attributes, using *: SELECT * FROM user;, and using where, you can create simple queries, filtering by specific results: SELECT * FROM user WHERE name = johnson;.

When using where clauses, different operators can be used, as follows:

=	Equal
<>	Not equal
>	Greater than
>=	Greater than or equal
<	Less than
>=	Less than or equal
BETWEEN	Between a range
LIKE	Search for a pattern
IN	Specify multiple possible values in a column

Managing Users

In MariaDB, you can create users and groups to restrict access to databases and tables. Alternatively, MariaDB can use PAM for authentication. By default, users are stored in the user table in the mysql database. To create new users, you'll use CREATE USER. As the user who creates the new user, you'll need the CREATE USER or INSERT privilege in the mysql database. While creating a user, you'll typically include @hostname in the username. That allows you to distinguish between users who can log in from localhost only and those who can log in from other hosts.

If, for example, you want to create a user lisa, use CREATE USER lisa@localhost IDENTIFIED BY 'password';. This creates a user with the name lisa and the password 'password'. Passwords are stored encrypted in the MariaDB database. In the hostname specification, you have multiple options. You can use a hostname or IP address and the % sign as a wildcard. For example, lisa@% would refer to user lisa, who can log in from any host. When the user is no longer needed, use DROP USER user@host; to remove the user. Note that users who are currently active on the system won't be deleted immediately.

When creating a user, the user, by default, is created with no privileges. That means that the user can connect but won't be able to use any command. The privileges can be granted on specific tables but also on the entire database. As root, for example, use GRANT SELECT, UPDATE, DELETE, INSERT on addressbook.names to lisa@localhost; to grant user lisa the basic permissions to the names table in the addressbook database. Let's look at some more examples where privileges are granted.

GRANT SELECT ON database.table TO user@host;: Gives SELECT privilege to a specific table in a specific database

GRANT SELECT ON database.* TO user@host;: Gives SELECT privilege to all tables in "database".

GRANT SELECT ON *.* TO user@host;: Gives privileges to all tables in all databases

GRANT CREATE, ALTER, DROP ON database.* to user@host;: Gives privilege to create, alter, and drop databases

GRANT ALL PRIVILEGES ON *.* to user@host;: Creates a superuser

When working with privileges, it is important to reload all privileges after changing them. To do that, use the FLUSH PRIVILEGES; command. To show privileges that are assigned to a specific user, you can use SHOW GRANTS FOR user@host;.

In Exercise 12-3, you'll create a simple database and work with user privileges on it.

EXERCISE 12-3. CREATING A DATABASE

1. Type `mysql -u root -p` to log in as root.

2. Type `create database videos;` to create a database with the name videos.

3. Type `USE videos;` to switch to the videos database.

4. Now let's enter some columns: `CREATE TABLE videos(title VARCHAR(40), actor VARCHAR(40), year INT, registration INT);`.

5. Let's enter some data: `INSERT INTO videos (registration,title,actor,year) VALUES(1,'Basic Instinct','Sharon Stone', 1992);`.

6. Repeat this to enter the following videos as well:

   Pretty Woman, Julia Roberts, 1990

   The Terminator, Arnold Schwarzenegger, 1984

   Patriot Games, Harrison Ford, 1992

7. Type `SELECT * from videos;` to show an overview of all database. You should see a result as in Listing 12-8.

   Listing 12-8. `SELECT *` Result

```
MariaDB [videos]> INSERT INTO videos (registration, title, actor,year) VALUES
(1,'Basic Instincts', 'Sharon Stone', 1992);
Query OK, 1 row affected (0.01 sec)

MariaDB [videos]> INSERT INTO videos (registration, title, actor,year) VALUES
(2, 'Pretty Woman', 'Julia Roberts', 1990);
Query OK, 1 row affected (0.00 sec)

MariaDB [videos]> INSERT INTO videos (registration, title, actor,year) VALUES
(3, 'The Terminator', 'Arnold Schwarzenegger', 1984);
Query OK, 1 row affected (0.01 sec)

MariaDB [videos]> INSERT INTO videos (registration, title, actor,year) VALUES
(4, 'Patriot Games', 'Harrison Ford', 1992);
Query OK, 1 row affected (0.00 sec)

MariaDB [videos]> select * from videos;
+----------------+-----------------------+------+--------------+
| title          | actor                 | year | registration |
+----------------+-----------------------+------+--------------+
| Basic Instincts| Sharon Stone          | 1992 |            1 |
| Pretty Woman   | Julia Roberts         | 1990 |            2 |
| The Terminator | Arnold Schwarzenegger | 1984 |            3 |
| Patriot Games  | Harrison Ford         | 1992 |            4 |
+----------------+-----------------------+------+--------------+
4 rows in set (0.00 sec)
```

8. Create a user using `CREATE USER julia@'%' IDENTIFIED BY 'secret';`.

9. Grant permissions to user julia using `GRANT SELECT,INSERT,UPDATE,DELETE ON videos.* TO julia@'%';`.

10. Type `FLUSH PRIVILEGES;` to update the privileges.

11. Type `DESCRIBE videos;` to show an overview of records in the videos database.

12. Insert another new video: `INSERT INTO videos(registration,title,actor,year) VALUES (5,'The Last Stand', 'Arnold Schwarzenegger', 2013);`.

13. Show a list of all records where the value of the `'actor'` field is set to Arnold Schwarzenegger: `SELECT * FROM videos WHERE actor = 'Arnold Schwarzenegger';`.

14. Type `quit` to close the MySQL shell interface.

MariaDB Backup and Restore

When making backups of MariaDB, there are two approaches to follow. You can create a physical backup, in which you'll have a raw copy of the database directories and folders. This backup is fast and portable, but only to machines that are using similar hardware and software. To make a physical backup, the database service should be offline, or the tables in the database should be locked, to prevent data from changing during the backup.

As an alternative, you can make a logical backup. In a logical backup, the database structure is retrieved by querying the database. Such a backup is relatively slow, because the database must be accessed and converted into a logical format. It does have two huge benefits, however: (1) you can create a logical backup on an operational database; and (2) logical databases are portable to other database providers as well. In a logical backup, however, log and configuration files are not included.

To make a logical database backup, you can use the `mysqldump` (shell) command. If, for example, you want to create a backup of the videos database and write that to the file `/root/videos-db.dump`, you would use the following command: `mysqldump -u root -p videos > /root/videos-db.dump`. The `mysqldump` command can also be used to create a backup of all databases, using `mysqldump -u root -p --all-databases > /root/all-db.dump`.

To create physical backups, it's a good idea to use LVM volumes. In LVM, you can create a snapshot, which contains the actual state of the LVM volume at the moment the snapshot was created. The physical backup itself will next be made from the snapshot and not from the actual open LVM volume. In Exercise 12-4, you can read how to create a physical database backup.

EXERCISE 12-4. CREATING A PHYSICAL MYSQL DATABASE BACKUP

1. To start with, you have to make sure where the actual database is stored. To do this, use `mysqladmin -u root -p variables | grep datadir`. This command will show the directory in the file system where data is stored. Typically, the result would be the directory `/var/lib/mysql`.

2. Use the `df /var/lib/mysql` command to find out which LVM volume is used to host this location. (This will, of course, only work if during installation an LVM volume was created to host the physical database.)

3. Verify that within the volume group hosting the database volume unallocated disk space is still available, using `vgs vgname`.

4. At this point, you must temporarily freeze the database, so that no modifications can be applied while the snapshot is created. To do this, connect to the database as root, using `mysql -u root -p`, and type `FLUSH TABLES WITH READ LOCK;`. Do *NOT* close this session, because it will remove the lock!

5. In *another* terminal session, create the LVM snapshot. The following command assumes that the name of the volume group is `vgdata` and the name of the LVM volume hosting the database is `lvmariadb`: `lvcreate -L 2G -s -n lvmariadb-snapshot /dev/vgdata/lvmariadb`. Make sure that the snapshot size is large enough to hold the backup.

6. Get back to the MariaDB session, and type `UNLOCK TABLES;` to remove the locks.

7. Get back to the other session and mount the snapshot `mkdir /mnt/snapshot; mount /dev/vgdata/lvmariadb-snapshot /mnt/snapshot`.

8. Use `tar -cvf /root/mariadb.tar /mnt/snapshot` to create the backup.

9. Once the backup has been successfully created, you have to unmount and remove the snapshot: `umount /mnt/snapshot; lvremove /dev/vgdata/lvmariadb-snapshot`.

To restore a backup, it depends which kind of backup you have. To restore a logical backup, you would use a command such as `mysql -u root -p videos < /root/videos-db.dump`. To restore a physical backup, you must first stop the MariaDB service, after which you can use `tar` to restore the backup, as follows:

1. `systemctl stop mysql`

2. `rm -rf /var/lib/mysql/*`

3. `tar xvf /root/mariadb.tar -C /`

Make sure that you verify the contents of the archive file before restoring the backup!

EXERCISE 12-5. WORKING WITH MARIADB DATABASES

Install MariaDB. Set the password of user root to `'secret'`. Create a database with the name `'addressbook'`. In this database, make sure you include the following fields:

first name

last name

street

number

city

zip

telephone

Enter the following records:

first name	last name	street	number	city	zip	telephone
Linda	Thomsen	State Street	14578	Provo	48261	651 555 432
Lori	Smith	Main Street	11	Sunnyvale	78025	453 555 667
Marlet	Joanes	Ocean Boulevard	124	Honolulu	99301	108 999 555
Marsha	Smith	Long Street	7812	Honolulu	99303	108555 431

Make a logical backup of the database and write it to `/tmp/address-db.dump`.

Summary

In this chapter, you've learned how to set up a LAMP server. You've read about the configuration of Apache and MariaDB for database services. You haven't read much about setting up scripting, apart from how to enable the required modules in Apache for using PHP, Perl, or Python. Scripting itself is an art that requires a book dedicated exclusively to the subject; therefore, it has not been covered in this chapter.

■ ■ ■

## CHAPTER 13

File Sharing: NFS, FTP, and Samba

On SUSE Linux Enterprise Server, different solutions for file sharing are available. In this chapter you'll learn how to configure the most significant of these services. You'll learn how to share files with other Linux users using NFS, with anonymous Internet users using FTP and how to create a file server that can be used by Windows clients using Samba.

This chapter covers the following:

- Setting up NFS
- Using FTP for File Sharing
- Sharing Files with Samba
- Configuring Automount

Introducing the File Sharing Protocols

On Linux, there are different protocols available for file sharing. This can make it difficult for an administrator to select the most appropriate solution. Of the three solutions discussed in this chapter, Network File Services (NFS) is the classic UNIX way to share files. In recent Linux distributions, it is much enhanced and remains a very common solution for file sharing. It is especially useful for sharing files between servers or for mounting home directories.

The File Transfer Protocol (FTP)is a very common solution for use on the Internet. It allows not only authenticated users but also gives good options for making files available to anonymous users. It can even be used as a dropbox for anonymous users.

Samba file services, also known as Common Internet File Sharing (CIFS) services, are common in an environment in which interoperability with Windows is required. It offers many configuration options, which doesn't always make it easy to configure, but for sharing files with endusers, Samba has become the defacto standard.

Also in this chapter, you'll read about Automount, a service that can be used to mount network file systems automatically, when access is needed, which facilitates the work of the system administrator, as it is no longer necessary to set up every share in the /etc/fstab file.

NFS

For most tasks that a SUSE Linux administrator has to accomplish, YaST offers a good management utility for setting NFS servers as well as NFS clients. In this section, you'll read how to start setting up an NFS server with YaST, after which we'll have a look at the configuration files that are created during setup as well.

Setting Up an NFS Server with YaST

From YaST, select Network Services ➤ NFS Server. This shows the interface with which you can set up basic NFS server settings (see Figure 13-1).

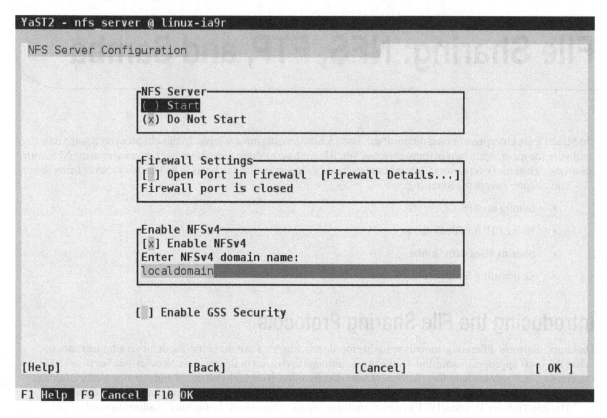

Figure 13-1. *Setting up an NFS server from YaST*

On the first screen of the YaST NFS server setup module, there are a couple of choices to make. First is whether you want to enable NFSv4. NFSv4 still has the reputation of being a new solution, as opposed to the older NFSv3 solution, but NFSv4 has been around since the mid-1990s. Still, however, some clients can make only much simpler NFSv3 mounts. If you want to set up an NFS server for such clients, you might consider not enabling NFSv4, but normally, you would want to use NFSv4.

Also on the NFS server configuration screen is the option to enable GSS Security. In old versions of NFS, security was dealt with in a very basic way, which is why a more advanced Kerberos-based security has been added. Using authentication tickets instead of sending over passwords in clear text makes an NFS server much more secure. However, many Linux administrators don't need the complexity that is added with this option, which is why a vast majority of servers still come without GSS Security.

The last option you need to consider on the NFS server setup screen is the domain name. This domain name is used by the idmap daemon, an NFS helper process that tries to match usernames. Set it to the fully qualified domain name of this host, to make ID mapping work.

ID mapping is an important part of the NFS configuration, because it tries to match user IDs on an NFS client with user IDs on an NFS server. The default setting is that a user on the NFS client will connect with the same UID on the server. So, if on the client, user linda has UID 600, but on the NFS server, user bob has UID 600, the client user linda will be granted access to files on the server that are owned by bob. To prevent these kinds of mess-ups, an NFS server should either use a common authentication service, such as LDAP, or the idmap daemon. When setting up an NFS server from YaST, the idmap daemon is started automatically as well.

The second screen of the NFS server setup module in YaST allows you to specify which directories you want to export and which hosts are granted access to those directories (see Figure 13-2).

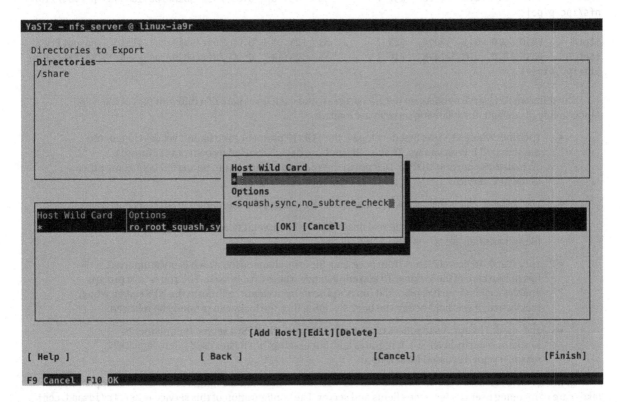

Figure 13-2. *Setting up NFS shared directories*

Managing the NFS Service

Setting up a basic NFS server isn't very difficult. You basically need just two things: a file that defines what needs to be shared and the NFS services. To start the NFS server, you have to run the command systemctl start nfs, and to enable it, you add systemctl enable nfs afterward. In Chapter 17 of this book, you will learn that systemctl has become the default for NFS service management. The NFS service, however, is still managed by an in it script with the name /etc/init.d/nfs. From this in it script, different services can be started to make up the NFS service.

You can easily recognize the NFS-related services; all of their names begin with rpc. Use ps aux | greprpc to get an overview of all the services that are currently loaded, which should show a result as in Listing 13-1.

Listing 13-1. Showing NFS Services

```
suse:~ # ps aux | grep rpc | grep -v grep
rpc       4712  0.0  0.0  47092   660 ?      Ss  23:06  0:00 /sbin/rpcbind -w -f
root      4760  0.0  0.0      0     0 ?      S<  23:06  0:00 [rpciod]
root      8903  0.0  0.0  14928   152 ?      Ss  23:08  0:00 /usr/sbin/rpc.idmapd -p /var/lib/
nfs/rpc_pipefs
root      8907  0.0  0.1  40476   780 ?      Ss  23:08  0:00 /usr/sbin/rpc.mountd
statd     8910  0.0  0.1  36004   988 ?      Ss  23:08  0:00 /usr/sbin/rpc.statd --no-notify
root      9615  0.0  0.0  31416   416 ?      Ss  23:13  0:00 /usr/sbin/rpc.gssd -D -p /var/lib/
nfs/rpc_pipefs
```

The different RPC services make up the NFS process, and each takes care of a different part of the NFS functionality. By default, the following services are loaded:

- rpcbind: When NFS was first developed, the TCP/IP protocol suite hadn't yet developed into the standard it is nowadays. That is why in those days, NFS used its own port addresses. To map these ports to UDP or TCP ports, the rpcbind service has to be started before any other of the RPC services.

- rpc.idmapd: This is the part of NFS that takes care of mapping usernames to UIDs and vice versa.

- rpc.mountd: This makes up the real heart of the NFS server. It takes care of exporting the local file systems that are accessible to NFS clients.

- rpc.statd: To prevent users from accessing files simultaneously, which is not supported, NFS has to take care of file locking. To accomplish this, rpc.statd is used. The rpc.statd process enables a client who has rebooted (on purpose or by accident) to inform the NFS server, which locks where it was held before the boot. By doing this, the locks can properly be released.

- rpc.gssd: The rpc.gssd process is a standard part of the NFSv4 server. It implements Kerberos security in NFSv4. It requires additional setup, but it isn't used often, for which reason it's not discussed further here.

Of the services discussed previously, there is one that has an additional configuration: the ID Mapper, which takes care of mapping user IDs between clients and server. The configuration of this service is in /etc/idmapd.conf. In this file, you can match usernames, as used by the NFS client, to local usernames on your server. This isparticularly useful in case the client uses other local usernames as the ones in use on the NFS server. In Listing 13-2, you can see the default contents of this configuration file.

Listing 13-2. The /etc/idmapd.conf File Can Be Used to Match Client Usernames to NFS Server Usernames

```
[General]

Verbosity = 0
Pipefs-Directory = /var/lib/nfs/rpc_pipefs
Domain = suse.example.com

[Mapping]

Nobody-User = nobody
Nobody-Group = nobody
```

Creating Shares in /etc/exports

To define the file systems that have to be exported, the /etc/exports file is used. In this file, lines are defined that contain the following three elements:

- The directory to export

- The nodes to which this export is available

- The options with which the share is exported

In Listing 13-3, you can see what the contents of this file may look like.

Listing 13-3. Defining Exported File Systems

```
/home  *(ro,root_squash,sync,no_subtree_check)
```

When setting up an NFS share, you will have to define the options that are used for the export. Many options can be used, of which the man (5) exports give an overview. Some of the more common options are listed below.

- rw: Allow read/write access on the shared file system.

- ro: Allow read-only access on the shared file system (this is the default setting).

- sync: This makes the NFS server secure with regard to file modifications.A reply to a request will only be sent once the changes have been committed to storage.

- async: Opposite of the sync option described above. Using this option is faster but not as secure.

- no_subtree_check: This is a performance-related option, which defines that exact location of files in an exported NFS subtree does not have to be verified. Use this option on all exports that normally have many modifications. On a file system that is mostly read-only, it should be exported with the subtree_check option.

- root_squash: This option "squashes" root user access. This means that the user root on the NFS client will be mapped to user "nobody" on the NFS server. Use of this option on all shares is highly recommended.

Mounting NFS Shares

Getting access to an NFS share is easy: you can mount it from any client that supports the NFS protocol. If on server a directory /data is exported, a client can mount it on the /mnt directory with the following command:

```
mount server:/data /mnt
```

While mounting an NFS share, different mount options can be used to define how the share should be accessed. The following list shows the most important mount options in use:

- nfsvers=n: Specifies which version of the NFS protocol should be used when accessing an NFS mount. If this option is not specified, the client will negotiate the protocol, trying version 4 first and working down to versions 3 and 2, if that is unsuccessful.

- soft/hard: hard is the default NFS mount option. This option means that the NFS client will re-try indefinitely if a mount gets lost. This may mean that an application hangs forever, waiting for a response from the NFS server. To prevent this, use the soft mount option, which will generate a failure after trying three times.

- rsize/wsize: This can be used to specify the default block size employed in NFS communication.

When mounting an NFS share from a client, you can find out which shares are offered. To do this, use the `showmount -e` command, followed by the name of the NFS server.

EXERCISE 13-1. SETTING UP AN NFS SERVER

In this exercise, you'll set up an NFS server. To allow you to perform this exercise using only one computer, you'll use your host as the client also.

1. Use the command `mkdir /data` to create a directory with the name /data.

2. Copy some files to the /data directory, using `cp /etc/a* /data`.

3. Open the file /etc/exports with an editor and add the following line:
    `/data *(rw,root_squash)`.

4. Type `systemctl start nfs.service`, followed by `systemctl enable nfs.service`.

5. Type `showmount -e localhost` to get an overview of the exported mounts on your local computer.

6. Use the command mount `localhost:/data /mnt` to mount the NFS export on the local directory /mnt.

FTP

You can use FTP to offer an easy way to share files over the Internet. Both authenticated local users are supported, as are anonymous users who use your server over the Internet. In this section, you'll read how to set up an FTP server from YaST and how to further fine-tune it, using the configuration files.

Setting Up an FTP Server from YaST

To set up an FTP server, select Network Services ➤ FTP Server, from YaST. This asks if you want to use `vsftpd` or `pure-ftpd` as the FTP server. In this procedure, I'll describe the use of `vsftpd`, so select `vsftpd`. This opens the generic FTP server setup screen that you can see in Figure 13-3. On this screen, five different configuration screens are accessible, all from the pane on the left side of the screen. By default, the Start-up page is active.

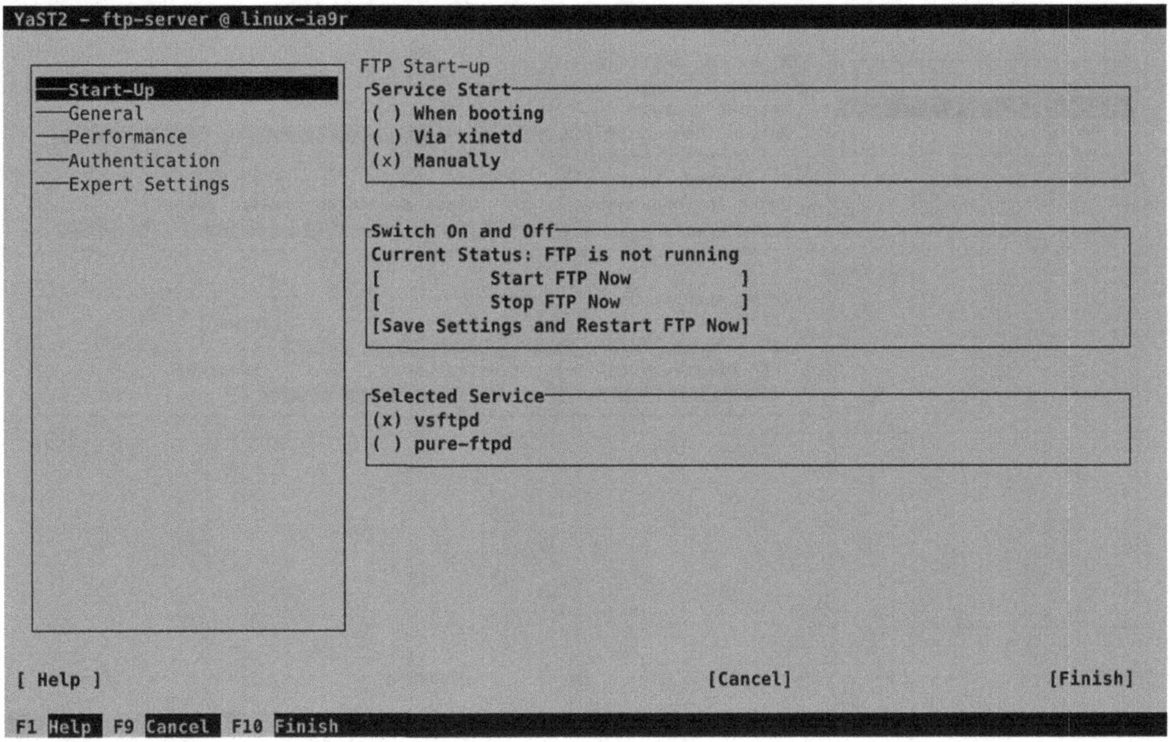

```
YaST2 - ftp-server @ linux-ia9r

                              FTP Start-up
 ┌────────────────────┐      ┌Service Start────────────────────────────────────────────────┐
 │────Start-Up         │      │( ) When booting                                              │
 │────General          │      │( ) Via xinetd                                                │
 │────Performance      │      │(x) Manually                                                  │
 │────Authentication   │      └──────────────────────────────────────────────────────────────┘
 │────Expert Settings  │
 │                     │      ┌Switch On and Off──────────────────────────────────────────────┐
 │                     │      │Current Status: FTP is not running                              │
 │                     │      │[              Start FTP Now            ]                       │
 │                     │      │[              Stop FTP Now             ]                       │
 │                     │      │[Save Settings and Restart FTP Now]                            │
 │                     │      └──────────────────────────────────────────────────────────────┘
 │                     │
 │                     │      ┌Selected Service───────────────────────────────────────────────┐
 │                     │      │(x) vsftpd                                                      │
 │                     │      │( ) pure-ftpd                                                   │
 │                     │      └──────────────────────────────────────────────────────────────┘
 │                     │
 │                     │
 │                     │
 │                     │
 │                     │
 └────────────────────┘

 [ Help ]                                           [Cancel]                    [Finish]

 F1 Help  F9 Cancel  F10 Finish
```

Figure 13-3. *The YaST FTP Server setup window*

On the Start-up screen, you'll first have to select how to start the FTP server. By default, it is not started automatically. If the FTP server is only going to be used occasionally, select Via xinetd, to have it managed by the xinetd service (read Chapter 11 for further details). To have it available on a permanent basis, select When booting. Also on this screen, you can select which FTP service you want to use. By default, the vsftpd service is used.

Next, there is the General Settings screen, on which you can specify some general settings for the server (see Figure 13-4). On this screen, you'll set some important security-related settings. To start with, there is the Welcome message, which is often used to display a legal message, informing accidental users that unauthorized use is prohibited. The Chroot Everyone option ensures that all users come in a chrooted directory. This ensures that authenticated users cannot browse to the directories of other users and makes your FTP server more secure.

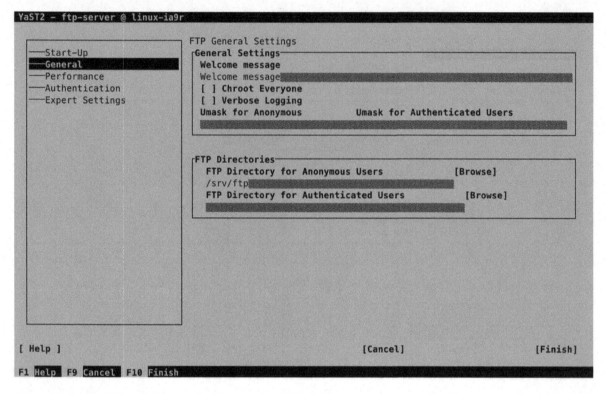

Figure 13-4. *The FTP server General Settings screen*

If you want detailed information on what is happening on the server, you can consider selecting Verbose Logging. In general, it's not the best idea to set up verbose logging, because logs will be created for every individual file that is uploaded or downloaded. The last general settings determine the umask for Anonymous, as well as for authenticated users. By specifying this, you'll tell the FTP server which default permissions should be used.

In the FTP Directories box, you specify where FTP users will go to work with their files. On SLES, anonymous users will access the directory /srv/ftp, which is also the home directory of the FTP user. Authenticated users, by default, will go to their home directory.

On the Performance Settings screen (see Figure 13-5), you can set performance-related settings. These settings ensure that not too many unused connections are staying open. By default, a maximum of 10 clients can exist. Make sure to change this parameter on a heavy-use FTP server, because it's not enough if you're running a popular server. The maximal idle time of 15 minutes, in general, is reasonable, because a user who hasn't been downloading or uploading files for more than 15 minutes can be disconnected as well.

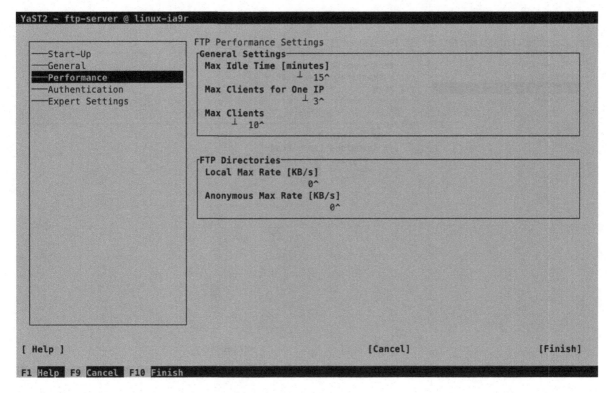

Figure 13-5. FTP server Performance Settings screen

Also interesting are the options to limit bandwidth use. You can set these in the amount of kilobytes per second, where a difference can be applied between local (authenticated) users and anonymous users.

On the Authentication tab (see Figure 13-6), you can specify which kinds of users are allowed. The default setting, which you can change if needed, allows anonymous users as well as authenticated users. By default, uploading files is not allowed. If you have to do this, make sure to switch on the Enable Upload option, to allow uploading for authenticated users. If you want to allow uploads for anonymous users as well, you have to select the Anonymous Can Upload option too.

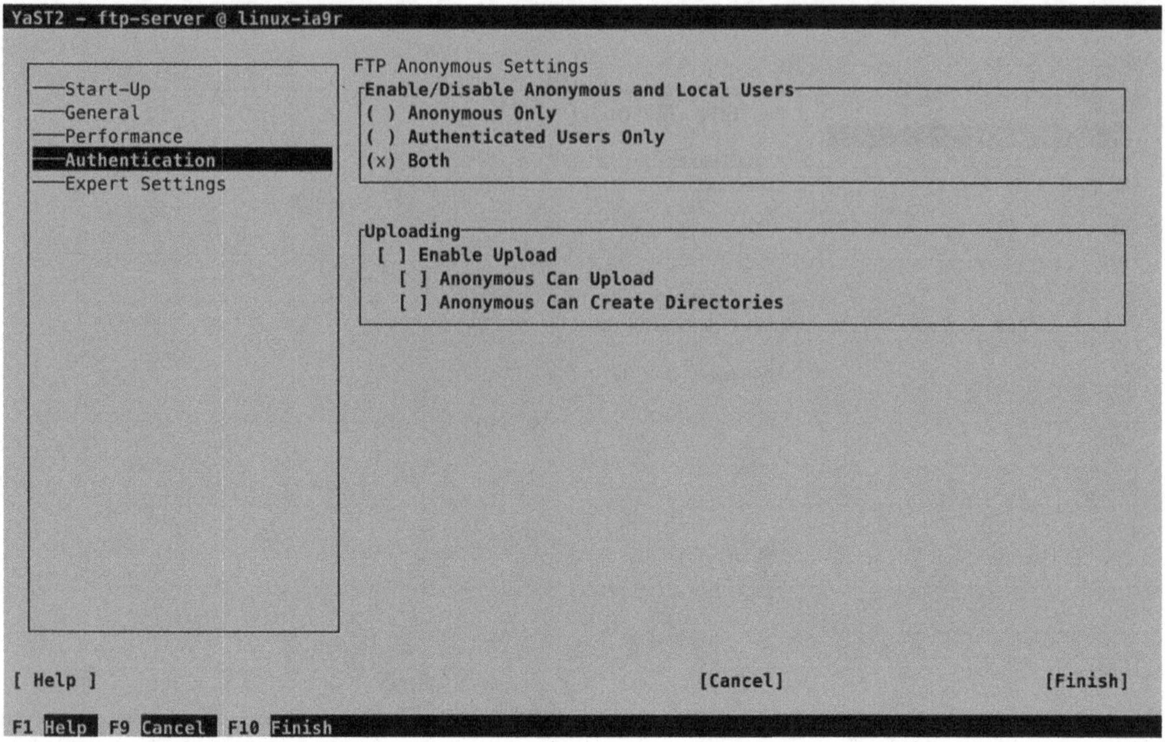

```
YaST2 - ftp-server @ linux-ia9r

                          FTP Anonymous Settings
   ──Start-Up             ┌Enable/Disable Anonymous and Local Users──────────────┐
   ──General              │( ) Anonymous Only                                    │
   ──Performance          │( ) Authenticated Users Only                          │
   ──Authentication       │(x) Both                                              │
   ──Expert Settings      │                                                      │
                          └──────────────────────────────────────────────────────┘

                          ┌Uploading─────────────────────────────────────────────┐
                          │ [ ] Enable Upload                                     │
                          │   [ ] Anonymous Can Upload                            │
                          │   [ ] Anonymous Can Create Directories                │
                          └──────────────────────────────────────────────────────┘




 [ Help ]                                        [Cancel]              [Finish]

 F1 Help  F9 Cancel  F10 Finish
```

Figure 13-6. *FTP server Authentication options*

When allowing anonymous uploads, you may wish to use some additional security settings, or else you may find that your server is very soon being abused as a platform to exchange illegal content between users. If you want to create an anonymous user dropbox server on which anonymous users can upload files but cannot see the files that are uploaded, you have to change the umask on uploaded files. Set this on the General tab, and make sure the upload umask is set to 600, which takes away from anonymous users all permissions on uploaded files.

On the Expert Settings (see Figure 13-7) tab, you'll find some options that are rarely modified. It can be interesting to enable SSL and/or TLS for your FTP server. If you do this, make sure to select a DSA certificate for establishing encrypted connections. After specifying all settings for your FTP server, get back to the General tab and press the Finish button. This saves the configuration and starts the FTP server with the new settings.

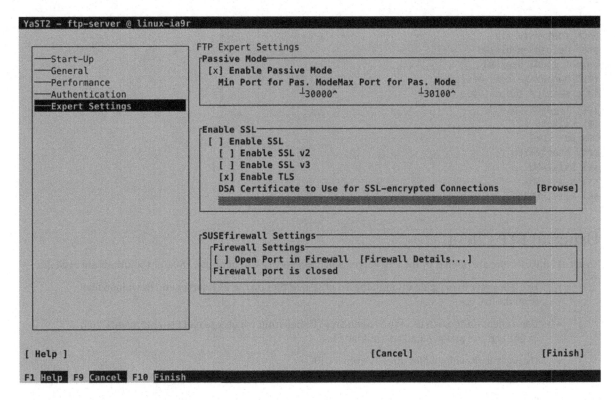

Figure 13-7. *FTP server Expert Settings*

Manually Configuring the vsftpd Server

To manage the vsftpd server, two parts are involved. First, there is the systemctl script /usr/lib/systemd/system/ vsftpd.service, which runs the /usr/sbin/vsftpd process. This process gets its configuration from the /etc/vsftpd.conf file. By using the YaST interface, you'll write modifications directly to this file, but you can also change it manually. In Listing 13-4, you can see the default contents of this file.

Listing 13-4. Default FTP Settings As Defined in /etc/vsftpd.conf

```
suse:~ # cat /etc/vsftpd.conf | grep -v ^#
write_enable=NO
dirmessage_enable=YES
nopriv_user=ftpsecure
local_enable=YES
anonymous_enable=YES
anon_world_readable_only=YES
syslog_enable=NO
connect_from_port_20=YES
ascii_upload_enable=YES
pam_service_name=vsftpd
listen=YES
ssl_enable=NO
pasv_min_port=29997
pasv_max_port=30100
```

```
anon_mkdir_write_enable=NO
anon_root=/srv/ftp
anon_upload_enable=NO
chroot_local_user=NO
ftpd_banner=Welcome message
idle_session_timeout=900
log_ftp_protocol=NO
max_clients=10
max_per_ip=3
pasv_enable=YES
ssl_sslv2=NO
ssl_sslv3=NO
ssl_tlsv1=YES
```

Using an FTP Client

To access the files that are offered by the FTP server, you need an FTP Client utility. Different solutions are available.

- Use a browser to navigate through the list of shared files on the FTP server and download files from the list.

- Use a client utility such as lftp to open an FTP shell from which you can use commands such as get and put to download and upload files.

- Use wget to download files directly from a URL.

About sftp

Apart from using the vsftpd server, alternatives are available. Among these is the sftp server, which offers FTP services through the SSH daemon. This service has been relatively popular in the past, but its need has been decreased with the rise of vsftpd, which offers security features as well. You should, however, be aware that a default FTP session is not secure, and neither data nor authentication tokens are protected with encryption.

EXERCISE 13-2. CONFIGURING A VSFTPD SERVER

In this exercise, you'll configure the vsftpd service. After configuring the service, you'll use the lftp client to connect to the FTP server and test the functionality.

1. Use zypper in vsftpd to install the vsftpd server.

2. Open the configuration file /etc/vsftpd.conf and use the following parameters to enable access to anonymous as well as authenticated users, but write access to authenticated users only:

```
write_enable=YES
local_enable=YES
chroot_local_user=YES
anonymous_enable=YES
```

---

3. Start and enable the FTP server, using systemctl start vsftpd.service and systemctl enable vsftpd.service.

4. Install the lftp client utility, using zypper in lftp.

5. Connect as the user user, using lftpuser@localhost.

6. Type help to get an overview of commands that are available.

7. Type bye to close the session to your FTP server.

Samba

Not so long ago, the file server was an important server in the corporate network. Windows file servers were the standard, and Linux offered an alternative by introducing Samba, also referred to as CIFS (Common Internet File Services). This service implements Windows file services.

The purpose of Samba and CIFS is to provide file sharing for Windows clients. Samba, however, has evolved to support more than only Windows clients. CIFS has become a standard for offering access to shared files, and other types of clients, such as Apple and Linux, are supported as well.

Whereas, at some point in time, lots of effort was put into developing Samba, the momentum has passed. This is due to the fact that file servers, as such, are not that important anymore. A large part of corporate data has moved away from the file server to the cloud or a dedicated application that manages data. Also, NAS appliances have become increasingly popular. In these, embedded Samba services are used to offer access to shared files. Even with these developments, Samba services can still be offered on Linux, and in this section, you'll learn how to do it.

Configuring Samba with YaST

A quick and easy way to get started with Samba is by using YaST. In YaST, select Network Services ➤ Samba, to access the Samba configuration options. If no Samba configuration exists currently, you'll have to provide a workgroup or domain name first. This is the simple method of providing access to shared files. Every Samba client is configured with a workgroup or domain name and will look for services that are offered in the same workgroup or domain.

Initial Setup

From a Samba perspective, there is no real difference between the workgroup and domain name, so when setting up a Samba server, you'll just set up a workgroup. The security option (which is discussed later in this chapter) determines whether your Samba server functions in a workgroup mode (which basically is a peer-to-peer networking model) or in a domain mode, where a domain controller or an Active Directory controller is used. You should set the workgroup name to something different from *Workgroup* (see Figure 13-8). *Workgroup* is the default workgroup name on most Samba implementations, and by using it, you might unconsciously be sharing files with too many others.

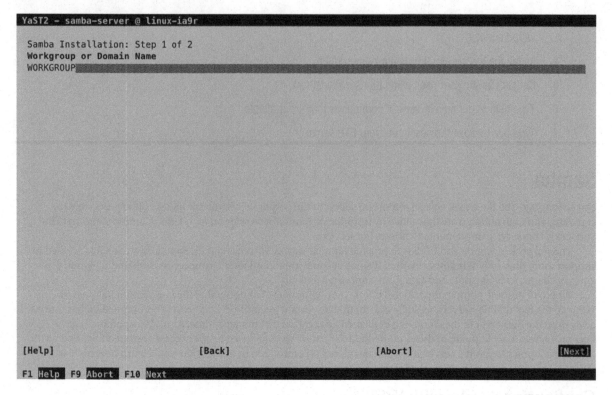

Figure 13-8. *To start with, change the workgroup name*

In the next step of the Samba setup, you'll specify which type of domain controller you'll be using (see Figure 13-9). In a Windows environment, a domain controller is a central server that handles authentication requests. Samba domain controllers are based on the Windows NT4 Domain Controller model, which was released in the early 1990s. If many Samba servers are used, it makes sense to configure a domain controller, which makes it possible to manage user accounts on one central location. The Primary Domain Controller is the server on which user accounts are managed, and they are replicated to Backup Domain Controllers. Users can authenticate against Primary and Backup Domain Controllers.

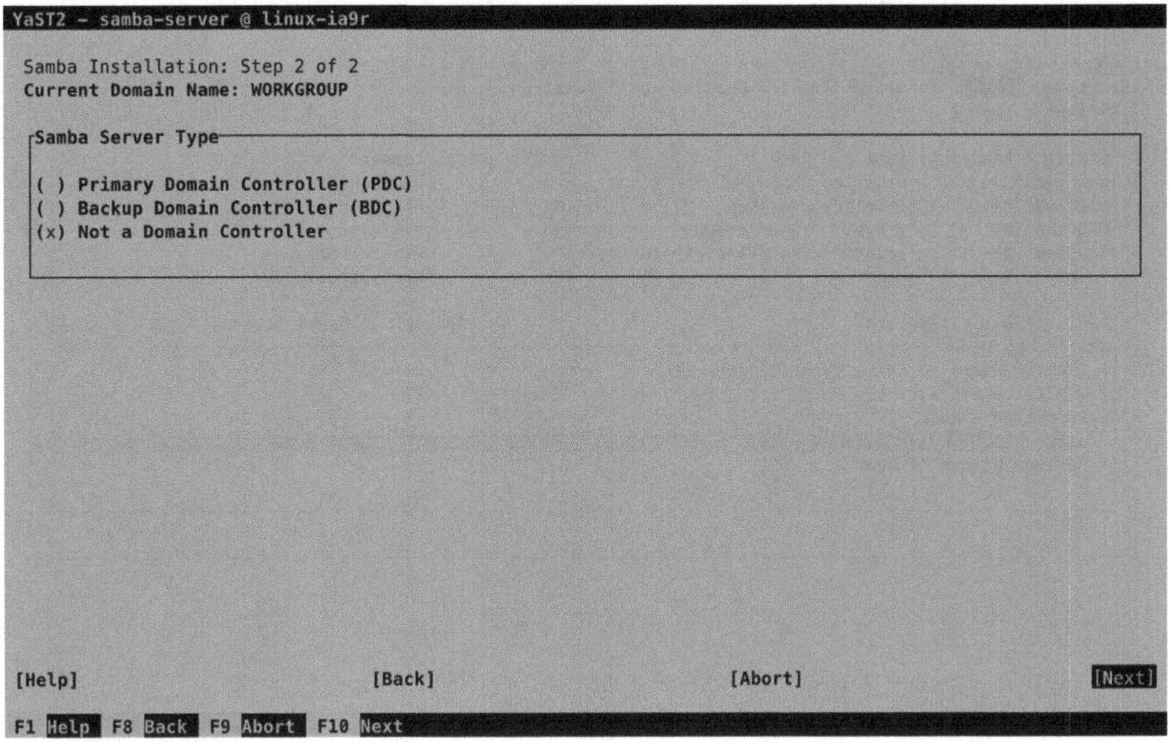

```
YaST2 - samba-server @ linux-ia9r

 Samba Installation: Step 2 of 2
 Current Domain Name: WORKGROUP

 ┌Samba Server Type─────────────────────────────────────────────────────────────┐
 │                                                                                │
 │ ( ) Primary Domain Controller (PDC)                                            │
 │ ( ) Backup Domain Controller (BDC)                                             │
 │ (x) Not a Domain Controller                                                    │
 │                                                                                │
 └────────────────────────────────────────────────────────────────────────────────┘




















 [Help]                         [Back]                         [Abort]                    [Next]
 F1 Help  F8 Back  F9 Abort  F10 Next
```

Figure 13-9. *Selecting the Domain Controller Type*

If you just want to set up a single server environment in which shared files are offered to Samba clients, you don't have to use a domain controller. Working with domain controllers is discussed in greater detail later in this chapter. In the remainder of this procedure, it is assumed that you have selected the option Not a Domain Controller.

■ **Note**   Setting up a domain controller is a Windows-oriented way of working. As a more flexible alternative, you can also use an LDAP server for centralized user management. In this setup, you'll construct an LDAP server (see Chapter 12 for further details) and connect the Samba servers to the LDAP server.

After specifying the basic settings, you'll gain access to the Samba Configuration screen, on which many other Samba configuration options can be specified. From the Start Up screen, you select how to start the Samba service. Don't forget to change to During Boot, if you want your Samba server to start automatically when your server starts up.

Creating Shares

The most important part of setting up a Samba server is the configuration of shares. A share provides a method with which to access resources such as printers and directories. Figure 13-10 gives an overview of the default shares that are offered.

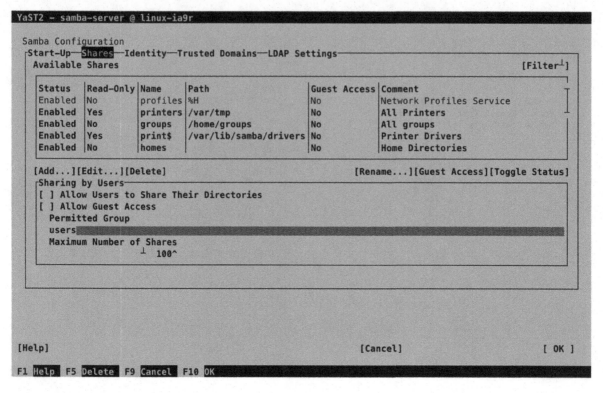

Figure 13-10. *Default sharesconfiguration*

In every share, a few properties are set, as follows:

- *Status*: Use this to toggle share access on or off.

- *Read-Only*: Use this to set share level access to read-only or not.

- *Name*: This is the name of the share.

- *Path*: The path to the share. Some administrative shares, such as the netlogon share, which is needed for a domain controller setup, don't require a path. Some other shares use variables, such as %H for home directories.

- *Guest Access*: This indicates whether or not to allow guest access to shares. A guest is a user who can access the share without authentication.

- *Comment*: An optional comment that makes it easier to identify a share.

To add access for a new share, you can select Add. This opens the screen that you can see in Figure 13-11.

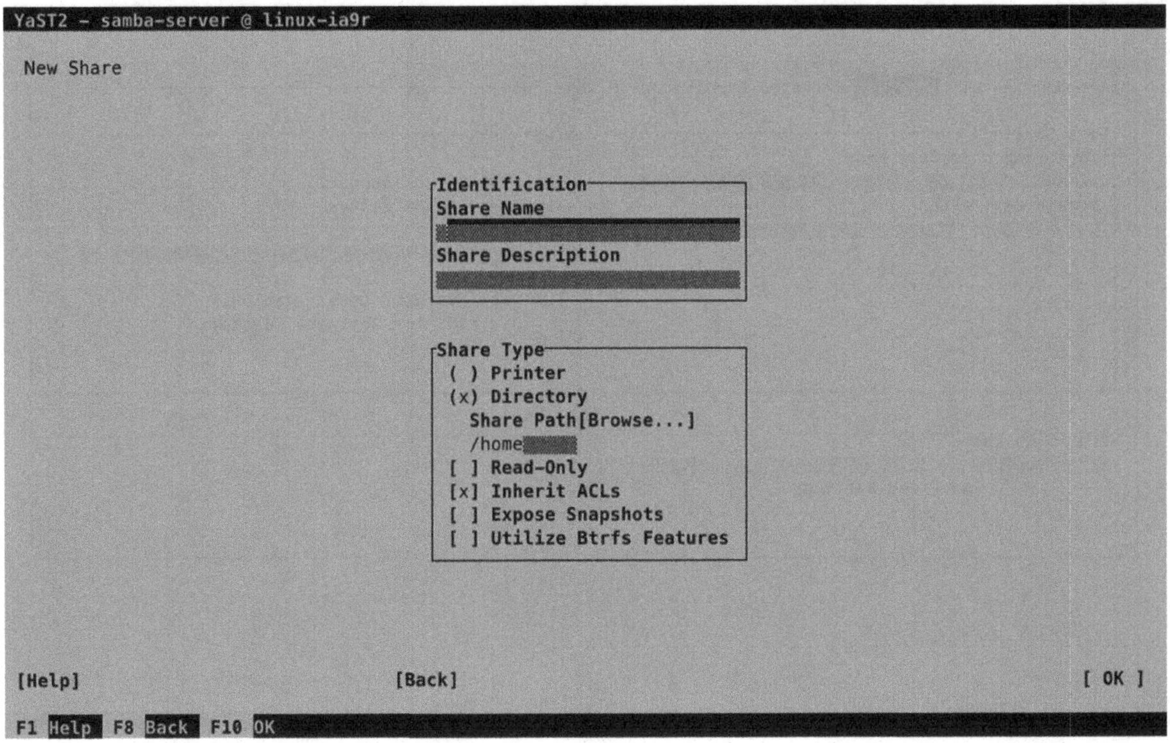

```
┌─────────────────────────────────────────────────────────────────────────────┐
│ YaST2 - samba-server @ linux-ia9r                                             │
│                                                                               │
│   New Share                                                                   │
│                                                                               │
│                                                                               │
│                         ┌Identification──────────────┐                        │
│                         │Share Name                  │                        │
│                         │▓▓▓▓▓▓▓▓▓▓▓▓▓▓▓▓▓▓▓▓▓▓▓▓▓▓▓▓▓│                        │
│                         │Share Description           │                        │
│                         │▓▓▓▓▓▓▓▓▓▓▓▓▓▓▓▓▓▓▓▓▓▓▓▓▓▓▓▓▓│                        │
│                         └────────────────────────────┘                        │
│                                                                               │
│                         ┌Share Type──────────────────┐                        │
│                         │ ( ) Printer                │                        │
│                         │ (x) Directory              │                        │
│                         │     Share Path[Browse...]  │                        │
│                         │     /home▓▓▓▓▓▓▓            │                        │
│                         │ [ ] Read-Only              │                        │
│                         │ [x] Inherit ACLs           │                        │
│                         │ [ ] Expose Snapshots       │                        │
│                         │ [ ] Utilize Btrfs Features │                        │
│                         └────────────────────────────┘                        │
│                                                                               │
│                                                                               │
│                                                                               │
│  [Help]                            [Back]                             [ OK ]  │
│  F1 Help  F8 Back  F10 OK                                                      │
└─────────────────────────────────────────────────────────────────────────────┘
```

Figure 13-11. *Creating a share*

To start with, every share needs a name. From the Identification box, you can also enter an optional Share Description. In Share Type, you can enter the other share properties. The most important property is the Share Path, which specifies the name of the directory you want to share. Here, you can enter the name of the directory you want to share, or use the browser that is integrated in YaST. If you enter a directory name that doesn't yet exist, YaST will show a prompt suggesting that you create the path now. Another important setting that you can select here is Inherit ACLs. This allows the share to inherit Linux file system ACLs, which allows you to set up security using Linux ACLs. After specifying all required options, select OK, to write the configuration.

On Samba shares, many different share options are available. The Create Share interface doesn't show all of them. To gain access to additional share options, create the share, select it, and then click Edit. This opens the Selected Option box, from which you can use the down arrow key to select from among a long list of options the one you want to use. Select an option from this list, and then press Enter to add it to the list. Next, you can specify the value that you want to assign to this option.

On each share, many options can be selected. For more information, you can consult man 5 smb.conf. One option that is of use when setting up shares is the valid users option. This allows you to specify the names of users or groups that you want to give access to the share. As argument, you'll specify the name of allowed users or groups. When specifying a group name, you have to start the group name with a @ sign, to make sure it is recognized as a group name.

Samba Server Options

On the Identity, Trusted Domains, and LDAP Settings tabs, you can specify further Samba configuration options. The Identity tab (see Figure 13-12) allows you to set the workgroup or domain name and change the current role as Domain Controller. The WINS and NetBIOS options are old and shouldn't be used anymore. Pre-Windows 2000 clients needed NetBIOS and WINS to find Samba servers, but on current configurations, DNS is used for looking up hostnames.

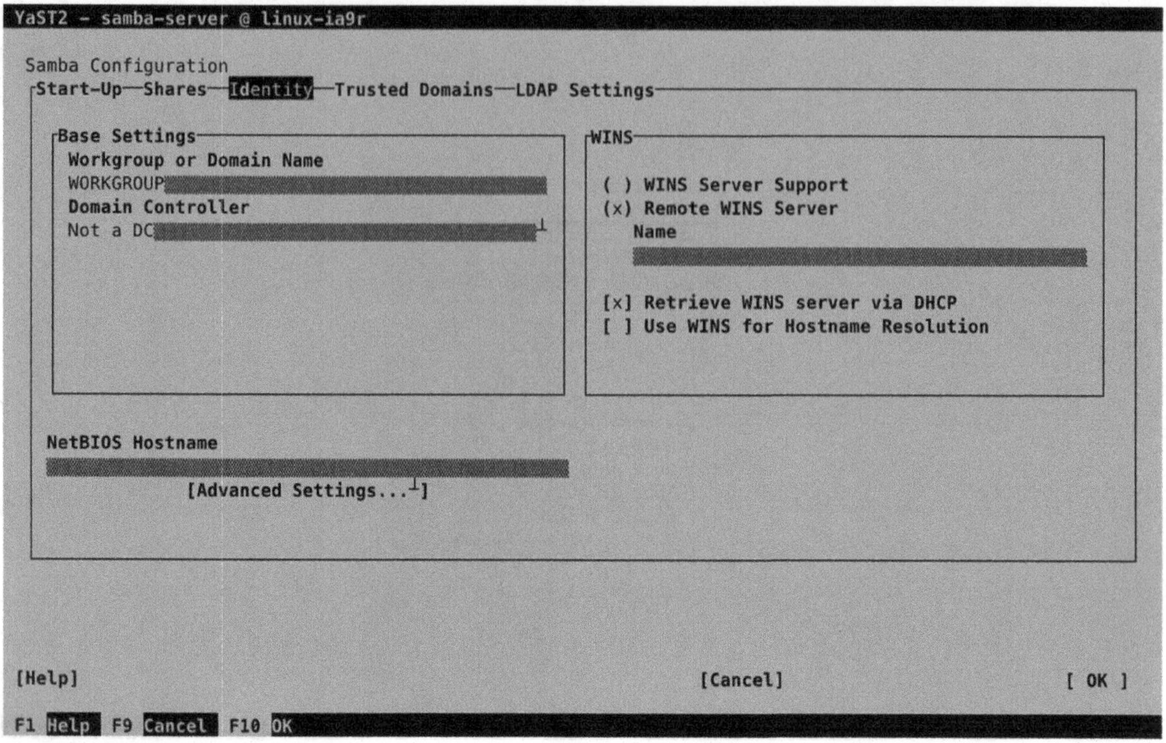

```
YaST2 - samba-server @ linux-ia9r

 Samba Configuration
 ┌Start-Up──Shares──Identity──Trusted Domains──LDAP Settings────────────────────┐
 │┌Base Settings──────────────────────┐ ┌WINS─────────────────────────────────┐│
 ││ Workgroup or Domain Name          │ │                                     ││
 ││ WORKGROUP▓                         │ │ ( ) WINS Server Support             ││
 ││ Domain Controller                 │ │ (x) Remote WINS Server              ││
 ││ Not a DC▓▓▓▓▓▓▓▓▓▓▓▓▓▓▓▓▓▓▓▓▓▓▓▓┘  │ │     Name                            ││
 ││                                    │ │     ▓▓▓▓▓▓▓▓▓▓▓▓▓▓▓▓▓▓▓▓▓▓▓▓▓▓▓▓▓▓   ││
 ││                                    │ │                                     ││
 ││                                    │ │ [x] Retrieve WINS server via DHCP   ││
 ││                                    │ │ [ ] Use WINS for Hostname Resolution││
 ││                                    │ │                                     ││
 │└────────────────────────────────────┘ └─────────────────────────────────────┘│
 │ NetBIOS Hostname                                                              │
 │ ▓▓▓▓▓▓▓▓▓▓▓▓▓▓▓▓▓▓▓▓▓▓▓▓▓▓▓▓▓▓▓▓▓▓▓▓▓▓                                        │
 │            [Advanced Settings...┘]                                           │
 │                                                                              │
 │                                                                              │
 │                                                                              │
 └──────────────────────────────────────────────────────────────────────────────┘


 [Help]                                    [Cancel]                      [ OK ]
 F1 Help  F9 Cancel  F10 OK
```

Figure 13-12. *Specifying Identity options*

The Trusted Domains interface allows you to set up trust relations between Windows domains. Make sure the Windows domain has been set up for trust relationships and, next, select Add to define a new trusted domain relationship. Enter the name of the Trusted Domain and the password to establish the trust.

Connecting Samba to LDAP

If an LDAP server is available in your environment, and if the LDAP client has been set up correctly, you can connect the Samba server to the LDAP server, using the LDAP Settings option (see Figure 13-13).

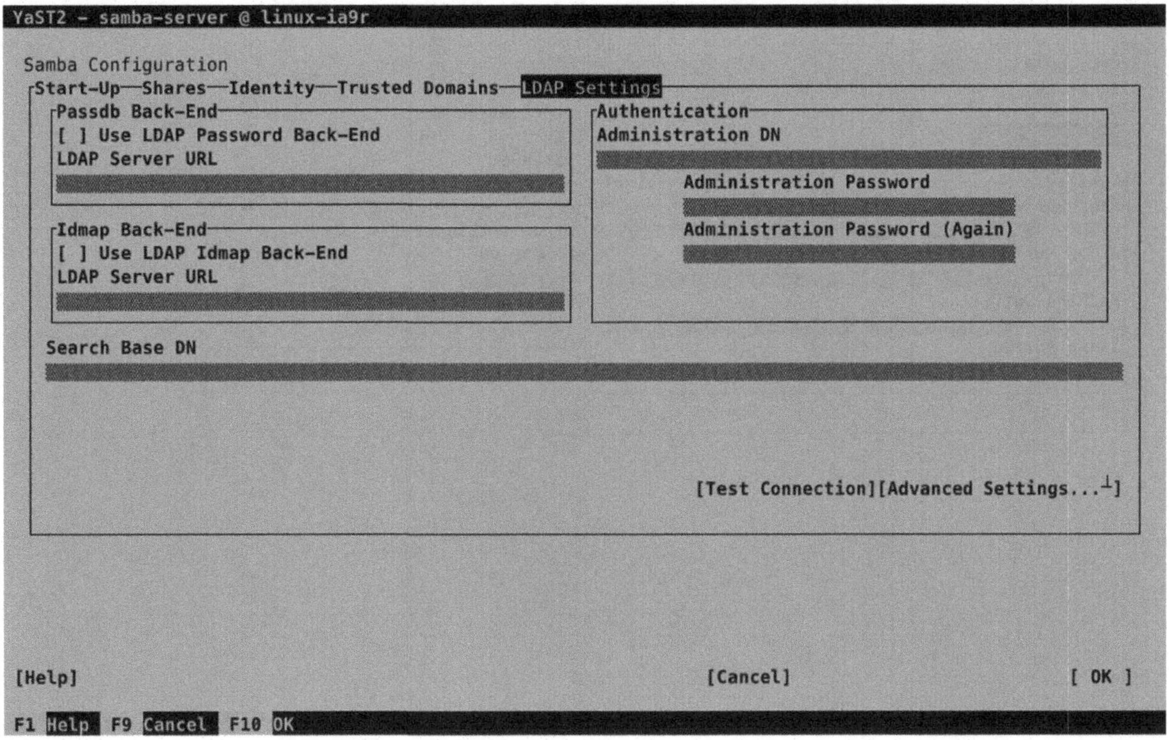

```
 YaST2 - samba-server @ linux-ia9r

 Samba Configuration
 ┌Start-Up──Shares──Identity──Trusted Domains──LDAP Settings┐
 │┌Passdb Back-End──────────────────────────┐ ┌Authentication──────────────────────┐
 ││[ ] Use LDAP Password Back-End           │ │Administration DN                    │
 ││LDAP Server URL                          │ │▓▓▓▓▓▓▓▓▓▓▓▓▓▓▓▓▓▓▓▓▓▓▓▓▓▓▓▓▓▓▓▓▓▓▓▓▓ │
 ││▓▓▓▓▓▓▓▓▓▓▓▓▓▓▓▓▓▓▓▓▓▓▓▓▓▓▓▓▓▓▓▓▓▓▓▓▓▓▓▓▓ │ │    Administration Password           │
 ││                                         │ │    ▓▓▓▓▓▓▓▓▓▓▓▓▓▓▓▓▓▓▓▓▓▓▓▓▓▓▓▓▓▓▓▓▓▓ │
 │┌Idmap Back-End───────────────────────────┐ │    Administration Password (Again)  │
 ││[ ] Use LDAP Idmap Back-End              │ │    ▓▓▓▓▓▓▓▓▓▓▓▓▓▓▓▓▓▓▓▓▓▓           │
 ││LDAP Server URL                          │ │                                     │
 ││▓▓▓▓▓▓▓▓▓▓▓▓▓▓▓▓▓▓▓▓▓▓▓▓▓▓▓▓▓▓▓▓▓▓▓▓▓▓▓▓▓ │ └─────────────────────────────────────┘

   Search Base DN
   ▓▓▓▓▓▓▓▓▓▓▓▓▓▓▓▓▓▓▓▓▓▓▓▓▓▓▓▓▓▓▓▓▓▓▓▓▓▓▓▓▓▓▓▓▓▓▓▓▓▓▓▓▓▓▓▓▓▓▓▓▓▓▓▓▓▓▓▓▓▓▓▓▓



                                        [Test Connection][Advanced Settings...⊥]



 [Help]                                          [Cancel]              [ OK ]
 F1 Help  F9 Cancel  F10 OK
```

Figure 13-13. *LDAP Settings*

To start with, you have to enter all properties that are required to make the connection to the LDAP server. The Passdb backend allows you to store user passwords in LDAP. Enter the URL to the LDAP server, to configure the password back end. The Idmap back end is used for getting user IDs from LDAP as well. Next, you must specify the basic entry point in the LDAP server, by configuring the Search Base DN. Following that, you have to enter the Administrator account on LDAP, which allows the Samba module to log in to LDAP, to get and store Samba-related information in LDAP. Before going on, use Test Connection to make sure that the selected settings are operational and allow you to make connection.

Next, select the Expert LDAP options to define communications between Samba and the LDAP server. This gives you, within the LDAP Base DN, options to define the security setting (SSL or TLS) and suffixes that are used for storing users, groups, machines, and additional information (see Figure 13-14). Normally, the default settings will do fine here.

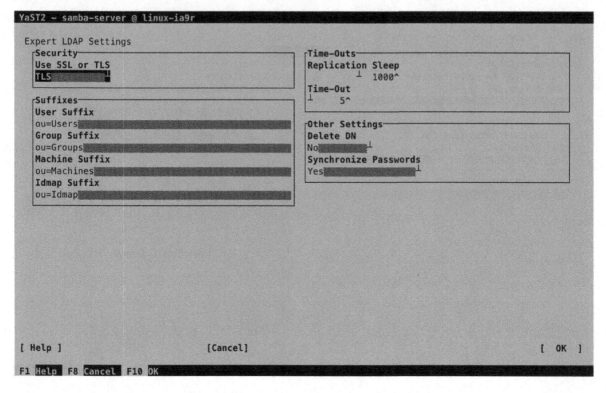

Figure 13-14. *Advanced options for connecting to LDAP*

Adding Samba Users to LDAP

By setting up the connection to the LDAP server, the Samba server will get authentication credentials from this server (see Figure 13-15). This assumes that users and groups have been added to the LDAP server also, using the YaST User and Group Administration module. In Exercise 13-3, you'll learn how to create Samba users in LDAP from YaST.

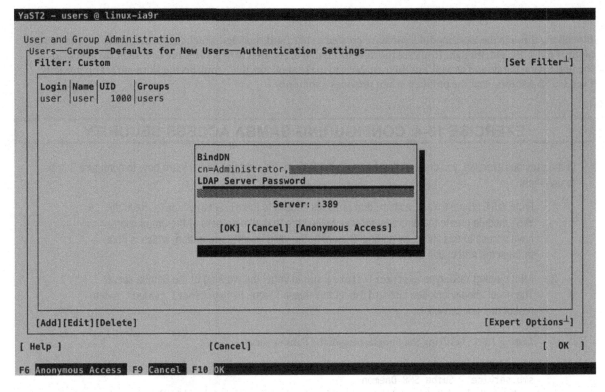

Figure 13-15. *Connecting to the LDAP server*

EXERCISE 13-3. CREATING SAMBA LDAP USERS FROM YAST

In this exercise, you'll create LDAP users that can be used in Samba. This advanced approach for dealing with authentication allows you to set up a Samba server that is ready for use in large corporate environments.

1. Start YaST and select Security and Users ➤ User and Group Management.

2. By default, you'll see local user administration. Select Set Filter ➤ LDAP Users. You'll now be prompted to log in to the LDAP server. The name of the administrative user should already be filled in (if not, read the section about LDAP in Chapter 11), so you only have to enter the LDAP Server Password to connect.

3. Click Add to add a new user. Make sure to enter at least a username and a password the user can use to connect with.

4. Do not select OK yet, but activate the Plug-Ins tab. On this tab, you see the Manage Samba account parameters option. Select this option and launch it.

5. From the next screen, you can enter the different Samba-related parameters and store them in LDAP. Don't change anything; just select Next to continue.

6. Select OK, OK, and Quit to write the Samba user account to LDAP. You have now successfully connected Samba to LDAP.

Understanding Samba Security Settings

By walking through the YaST module, you have created a share and specified which users can access the share. This alone is not sufficient, though. To access the directories that are shared with Samba, the user requires access to the underlying file system as well. For this, you have to make sure, too, that Linux permissions are set up properly. Exercise 13-4 shows what the problem is and provides a solution.

EXERCISE 13-4. CONFIGURING SAMBA ACCESS SECURITY

In the previous exercise, you created Samba users in LDAP. In this exercise, you'll learn how to configure Samba to use them.

1. From YaST, create a Samba share that provides access to the directory /data. Have the YaST module create the directory for you. Make sure that all members of the group users have access to this share, by adding @users to the valid users share option, which is done through the Add option in the edit share page.

2. After quitting YaST, type systemctl status smb to verify the working of the Samba server. The result should look like Listing 13-5. (If this doesn't work, use systemctl restart smb to restart the smb service.

   Listing 13-5. Verifying the Functioning of the Samba Server

   ```
   suse:/ # systemctl status smb
   smb.service - Samba SMB Daemon
      Loaded: loaded (/usr/lib/systemd/system/smb.service; disabled)
      Active: active (running) since Sun 2014-06-08 16:09:35 CEST; 7s ago
     Process: 31256 ExecStart=/usr/sbin/smbd $SMBDOPTIONS (code=exited, status=0/SUCCESS)
     Process: 31246 ExecStartPre=/usr/share/samba/update-apparmor-samba-profile
             (code=exited, status=0/SUCCESS)
    Main PID: 31259 (smbd)
      CGroup: /system.slice/smb.service
    ├─31259 /usr/sbin/smbd -D
    └─31261 /usr/sbin/smbd -D

   Jun 08 16:09:35 suse systemd[1]: Starting Samba SMB Daemon...
   Jun 08 16:09:35 suse systemd[1]: PID file /run/samba/smbd.pid not readable (yet?) aft...rt.
   Jun 08 16:09:35 suse systemd[1]: Started Samba SMB Daemon.
   ```

3. Type smbclient -L //localhost to verify the availability of shares. It should look just as in Listing 13-6 and include the data share in the list.

Listing 13-6. Verifying the Availability of Shares **suse:/ #** smbclient -L //localhost

```
Enter root's password:
Domain=[SUSE] OS=[Unix] Server=[Samba 4.1.7-5.1-3238-SUSE-SLE_12-x86_64]

        Sharename       Type        Comment
        ---------       ----        -------
        profiles        Disk        Network Profiles Service
        users           Disk        All users
        groups          Disk        All groups
        print$          Disk        Printer Drivers
        data            Disk        group data
        IPC$            IPC         IPC Service (Samba 4.1.7-5.1-3238-SUSE-SLE_12-x86_64)
Domain=[SUSE] OS=[Unix] Server=[Samba 4.1.7-5.1-3238-SUSE-SLE_12-x86_64]

        Server                  Comment
        ------                  -------


        Workgroup               Master
        ---------               ------
```

4. Up to now, you haven't set up the user accounts on your system for authentication on Samba. To do this, you have to use smbpasswd -a user for each user that has to be able to log in to the Samba server. You can only do this for valid Linux users, and this command creates a corresponding Samba user account with an associated password.

5. Now, access the share you have created by mounting it in the local file system. The command mount -o username=user //localhost/data /mnt should do that for you. Make sure to replace the name of the user with a user account name that is valid on your system. Even if you still see a root prompt, at this point, you have connected the /mnt directory to the Samba share, and you'll access the share as the user you've just configured.

```
suse:/ # mount -o username=user //localhost/data /mnt
Password for user@//localhost/data:  ********
suse:/ # cd /mnt
```

6. Try to write a file to the /mnt directory, by using the command touch hello. You'll get a Permission denied error.

```
suse:/mnt # touch hello
touch: cannot touch 'hello': Permission denied
```

7. Type ls -ld /data. You'll notice the directory is owned by user and group root, and the others entity has just read an execute permissions on this directory.

```
suse:/ # ls -ld /data
drwxr-xr-x 1 root root 0 Jun  8 12:22 /data
```

8. Type chmod 777 /data to set permissions on the Linux file system wide open. (This isn't very elegant, but it proves the point, and that's all we need now.)

9. Get back in the /mnt directory and type touch myfile. You'll notice that at this point, you can create the file without any problem.

In the preceding exercise, you have seen that additional setup is needed to allow users access to Samba shares. Let's resume what you have to do to set up permissions correctly.

- Make sure you have a Samba user account for each Linux user that needs access to Samba shares. Use smbpasswd -a to set up these accounts and give them a password.

- For a Samba user to access a Linux share, a Linux user account that has permissions on the Linux file system is needed.

- Use Linux users, groups, and permissions to set the appropriate permissions to the Linux file system.

- Use Samba configuration to allow write access to Samba shares.

Manually Setting Up Samba

Until now, you have used YaST for setting up the Samba server. Like any other service on Linux, you can also configure the service manually. There are two main parts involved: the smb service provides access to Samba shares, and the /etc/samba/smb.conf file defines how access should be provided. To manage the service, you can use the systemctl command: use systemctl status smb to check the current status of the Samba service. You'll notice that this command also gives detailed information about any existing error conditions. You can see this in Listing 13-7, in which the command is used with the -l option, to provide detailed information about the status of the Samba services.

Listing 13-7. Providing Information About the Samba Processes Using systemctl status -l

```
suse:/etc/samba # systemctl status smb -l
smb.service - Samba SMB Daemon
   Loaded: loaded (/usr/lib/systemd/system/smb.service; disabled)
   Active: active (running) since Sun 2014-06-08 16:09:35 CEST; 34min ago
  Process: 31256 ExecStart=/usr/sbin/smbd $SMBDOPTIONS (code=exited, status=0/SUCCESS)
  Process: 31246 ExecStartPre=/usr/share/samba/update-apparmor-samba-profile (code=exited,
           status=0/SUCCESS)
 Main PID: 31259 (smbd)
   CGroup: /system.slice/smb.service
           ├─31259 /usr/sbin/smbd -D
           ├─31261 /usr/sbin/smbd -D
           └─31349 /usr/sbin/smbd -D

Jun 08 16:10:35 suse smbd[31261]: [2014/06/08 16:10:35.720507,  0] ../source3/printing/print_
                                  cups.c:528(cups_async_callback)
Jun 08 16:10:35 suse smbd[31261]: failed to retrieve printer list: NT_STATUS_UNSUCCESSFUL
Jun 08 16:23:36 suse smbd[31375]: [2014/06/08 16:23:36.381112,  0] ../source3/printing/print_
                                  cups.c:151(cups_connect)
Jun 08 16:23:36 suse smbd[31375]: Unable to connect to CUPS server localhost:631 - Bad file
                                  descriptor
```

```
Jun 08 16:23:36 suse smbd[31261]: [2014/06/08 16:23:36.383102,  0] ../source3/printing/
                                  print_cups.c:528(cups_async_callback)
Jun 08 16:23:36 suse smbd[31261]: failed to retrieve printer list: NT_STATUS_UNSUCCESSFUL
Jun 08 16:36:37 suse smbd[31435]: [2014/06/08 16:36:37.004921,  0] ../source3/printing/
                                  print_cups.c:151(cups_connect)
Jun 08 16:36:37 suse smbd[31435]: Unable to connect to CUPS server localhost:631 - Bad file descriptor
Jun 08 16:36:37 suse smbd[31261]: [2014/06/08 16:36:37.006867,  0] ../source3/printing/
                                  print_cups.c:528(cups_async_callback)
Jun 08 16:36:37 suse smbd[31261]: failed to retrieve printer list: NT_STATUS_UNSUCCESSFUL
suse:/etc/samba #
```

Use systemctl start smb to start it, followed by systemctl enable smb, which ensures that it is restarted when your computer restarts.

As an administrator, it is important to understand the contents of the /etc/samba/smb.conf file. Listing 13-8 shows the contents of this file as it has been created, based on the previous manipulations from YaST.

Listing 13-8. Sample smb.conf File

```
[global]
        workgroup = SUSE
        passdb backend = tdbsam
        printing = cups
        printcap name = cups
        printcap cache time = 750
        cups options = raw
        map to guest = Bad User
        include = /etc/samba/dhcp.conf
        logon path = \\%L\profiles\.msprofile
        logon home = \\%L\%U\.9xprofile
        logon drive = P:
        usershare allow guests = No
        add machine script = /usr/sbin/useradd  -c Machine -d /var/lib/nobody -s /bin/false %m$
        domain logons = No
        domain master = No
        security = user
        wins support = No
        ldap admin dn = cn=Administrator,dc=example,dc=com
ldap group suffix = ou=Groups
        ldap idmap suffix = ou=Idmap
        ldap machine suffix = ou=Machines
        ldap passwd sync = Yes
        ldap suffix = dc=example,dc=com
        ldap user suffix = ou=Users
wins server =
[homes]
        comment = Home Directories
        valid users = %S, %D%w%S
        browseable = No
        read only = No
        inherit acls = Yes
[profiles]
```

```
        comment = Network Profiles Service
        path = %H
        read only = No
        store dos attributes = Yes
        create mask = 0600
        directory mask = 0700
[users]
        comment = All users
        path = /home
        read only = No
        inherit acls = Yes
        veto files = /aquota.user/groups/shares/
[groups]
        comment = All groups
        path = /home/groups
        read only = No
        inherit acls = Yes
[printers]
        comment = All Printers
        path = /var/tmp
        printable = Yes
        create mask = 0600
        browseable = No
[print$]
        comment = Printer Drivers
        path = /var/lib/samba/drivers
        write list = @ntadmin root
        force group = ntadmin
        create mask = 0664
        directory mask = 0775

[data]
        comment = group data
        inherit acls = Yes
        path = /data
        read only = No
        valid users = @users


## Share disabled by YaST
# [netlogon]
```

Let's quickly review the configuration of the sample smb.conf file. The file starts with a [global] section. This defines the behavior of the Samba server in general. It deals with settings such as the name of the workgroup, Samba Printing, and connection to external authentication mechanisms such as LDAP, which is used in this example.

Following the [global] section are the individual shares. Many shares are existing by default, such as the [home] share, which gives users access to their home directories; the [profiles] share, which is used for logging in on domain controllers; some more generic shares; and shares that enable users to use printers on Samba. In these shares, you can use configuration settings that apply only to that share. Table 13-1 gives an overview of the most useful settings that haven't been covered before.

Table 13-1. *Samba share parameters*

Setting	Use
valid users	Specifies which user accounts get access
browseable	Prevents users from navigating to directories outside of their own environment
read-only	Set to No to give write access to shares. By default, users have read-only access only
inherit acls	This setting has Samba respect ACLs that are configured on the Linux file system
store dos attributes	Offers support for Windows attributes through Samba. Useful for offering the full file sharing experience to Windows users
create mask	A umask that sets default permissions to new files
directory mask	A umask that sets default permissions to new directories
veto files	Names of files that will never be shown in the share
printable	Used on printer shares to enable printing from the share
path	The name of the directory or resource that is shared
write list	If read-only is set to yes, this can be used to allow write access to specific users and/or groups
force group	Makes sure new items are owned by the group that is specified here

Samba Printing

Apart from giving access to directories, Samba can be used to give access to printers as well. Setting this up is easy to do: by default, Samba gives access to all printers that are available through CUPS. That means that Windows users will see the shared printers through Samba. This is useful in an environment in which users exist who don't have access to CUPS printers by default. If your server is used in an environment where users can access printers directly or through CUPS, it doesn't provide any additional value to set up CUPS as well.

Summary

In this chapter, you have learned how to configure your server for file sharing using NFS, FTP, or Samba. This was the last chapter in the section "Networking SUSE Linux Enterprise Server." The following section is about "Advanced SUSE Linux Enterprise Server Administration," and the first chapter in this section explains how to use shell scripting on Linux.

## PART IV

Advanced SUSE Linux Enterprise Server Administration

CHAPTER 14

■ ■ ■

Introduction to Bash Shell Scripting

Once you are really at ease working on the command line, you'll want more. You've already learned how to combine commands using pipes, but if you truly want to get the best out of your commands, there is much more you can do. In this chapter, you'll get an introduction to the possibilities of Bash shell scripting, which helps you accomplish difficult tasks in an easy way. Once you understand shell scripting with Bash, you'll be able to automate many tasks and, thus, do your work much faster and more efficiently.

The following topics are discussed:

- Shell Scripting Fundamentals
- Working with Variables and Input
- Performing Calculations
- Using Control Structures

Getting Started: Shell Scripting Fundamentals

A shell script is a text file that contains a sequence of commands. So, basically, anything that can run a bunch of commands can be considered a shell script. Nevertheless, there are some basic recommendations that ensure that you'll create decent shell scripts. These are scripts that will not only perform the task you've written them for but also be readable by others and organized in an efficient manner.

At some point in time, you'll be glad of the habit of writing readable shell scripts. Especially if your scripts get longer and longer, you will notice that when a script does not meet the basic requirements of readability, even you risk not being able to understand what it is doing.

Elements of a Good Shell Script

When writing a script, make sure that you heed the following recommendations:

- Give the script a unique name.
- Include the shebang (#!), to tell the shell which sub shell should execute the script.
- Include comments, lots of comments.
- Use the exit command to tell the shell that executes the script that the script has executed successfully.
- Make your scripts executable.

In Exercise 14-1, you'll create a shell script that meets all of the basic requirements.

EXERCISE 14-1. CREATING A BASIC SHELL SCRIPT

1. Use `mkdir ~/bin` to create in your home directory a subdirectory in which you can store scripts.

2. Type the following code and save it with the name *hello* in the `~/bin` directory:

```
#!/bin/bash
# this is the hello script
# run it by typing ./hello in the directory where you've found it

clear
echo hello world
exit 0
```

You have just created your first script. In this script, you've used some elements that you'll use in many future shell scripts that you'll write.

Let's talk about the name of the script first. You'll be amazed at how many commands exist on your computer. So, you have to make sure that the name of your script is unique. For example, many people like to give the name test to their first script. Unfortunately, there's an existing command with the name *test* (see later in this chapter). If your script has the same name as an existing command, the existing command will be executed, and not your script (unless you prefix the name of the script with `./`). So, make sure that the name of your script is not already in use. You can find out if the name already exists by using the `which` command. For example, if you want to use the name *hello* and want to be sure that it's not already in use, type `which hello`. Listing 14-1 shows the result of this command.

Listing 14-1. Use `which` to Find Out If the Name of Your Script Is Not Already in Use

```
nuuk:~ # which hello
which: no hello in
(/sbin:/usr/sbin:/usr/local/sbin:/opt/gnome/sbin:/root/bin:/usr/local/bin:/usr/bin:/usr/X11R6/bin:
/bin
:/usr/games:/opt/gnome/bin:/opt/kde3/bin:/usr/lib/mit/bin:/usr/lib/mit/sbin)
```

Let's have a look at the content of the script you've created in Exercise 14-1. In the first line of the script, you can find the shebang. This scripting element tells the parent shell which subshell should be used to run this script. This may sound rather cryptic, but it is not too hard to understand.

If you run a command from a shell, the command becomes the child process of the shell. You can verify that by using a command such as `ps fax` or `pstree`. Likewise, if you run a script from the shell, the script becomes a child process of the shell. This makes scripts portable and ensures that even if you're using korn shell as your current shell, a Bash script can still be executed.

To tell your current shell which subshell should be executed when running the script, include the shebang. The shebang always starts with `#!` and is followed by the name of the subshell that should execute the script. In Exercise 14-1, you used `/bin/bash` as the subshell. By doing this, you can run this script from any shell, even if it contains items that are specific only to Bash. In the example from Listing 14-1, you could have done without the shebang, because there is not really any Bash-specific code in it, but it's a good habit to include a shebang in any script you like.

You will notice that not all scripts include a shebang, and in many cases, even if your script doesn't include a shebang, it will still run. The shell just executes the script using the same shell for the subshell process. However, if a user who uses a shell other than /bin/bash tries to run a script without a shebang, it will probably fail. You can avoid this by always including a shebang. So, just make sure it's in there!

The second part in the sample script in Exercise 14-1 includes two lines of comment. As you can guess, these comment lines explain to the user what the purpose of the script is and how to use it. There's only one rule regarding the comment lines: they should be clear and explain what's happening. A comment line always starts with a #, followed by anything.

■ **Note**   You may ask why the shebang, which also starts with a #, is not interpreted as a comment. That is because of its position and the fact that it is immediately followed by an exclamation point. This combination at the very start of a script tells the shell that it's not a comment but a shebang.

Following the comment lines in the script you have created in Exercise 14-1, there is the body of the script itself, which contains the code that the script should execute. In the example, the code consists of two simple commands: first, the screen is cleared, and next, the text "hello world" is echoed to the screen.

As the last part of the script, the command exit 0 is used. It is good habit to use the exit command in all your scripts. This command exits the script and next tells the parent shell how the script has executed. If the parent shell reads exit 0, it knows the script executed successfully. If it encounters anything other than exit 0, it knows there is a problem. In more complex scripts, you could even start working with different exit codes. Use exit 1 as a generic error message, and exit 2 etcetera to specify that a specific condition was not met. When applying conditional loops later, you'll see that it may be very useful to work with exit codes. From the parent shell, you can check the exit status of the last command by using the command echo $?.

Executing the Script

Now that your first shell script is written, it's time to execute it. There are different ways of doing this:

- Make it executable and run it as a program.
- Run it as an argument of the bash command.
- Source it.

Making the Script Executable

The most common way to run the shell script is by making it executable. To do this with the hello script from the sample in Exercise 14-1, you would use the following command:

```
chmod +x hello
```

After making the script executable, you can run it, just like any other normal command. The only limitation is the exact location in the directory structure where your script is. If it is in the search path, you can run it by typing any command. If it is not in the search path, you have to run it from the exact directory where it is. That means that if linda created a script with the name hello that is in /home/linda, she has to run it using the command /home/linda/hello. Alternatively, if she is already in /home/linda, she could use ./hello to run the script. In the latter example, the dot and the slash tell the shell to run the command from the current directory.

> ■ **Tip** Not sure if a directory is in the path or not? Use echo $PATH to find out. If it's not, you can add a directory to the path by redefining it. When defining it again, you'll mention the new directory, followed by a call to the old path variable. For example, to add the directory /something to the PATH, you would use PATH=$PATH:/something.

Running the Script As an Argument of the bash Command

The second way to run a script is by specifying its name as an argument of the bash command. For instance, our example script hello would run by using the command bash hello. The advantage of running the script in this way is that there is no need to make it executable first.

When running the script this way, make sure that you are using a complete path to where the script is. It has to be in the current directory, or you will have to use a complete path to the directory where it is. That means that if the script is /home/linda/hello, and your current directory is /tmp, you should run it using the command bash /home/linda/hello.

Sourcing the Script

The third way of running the script is completely different. You can source the script. By sourcing a script, you don't run it as a subshell, but you are including it in the current shell. This may be useful if the script contains variables that you want to be active in the current shell (this happens often in the scripts that are executed when you boot your computer).

If you source a script, you cannot use the exit command. Whereas in normal scripts the exit command is used to close the subshell, if used from a script that is sourced, it would close the parent shell, and normally, that is not what you want.

There are two ways to source a script: you can use the .command (yes, that is just a dot!), or you can use the source command. In Exercise 14-2, you will create two scripts that use sourcing. In the script, you are defining a variable that is used later. In the next section of this chapter you'll read more about using variables in scripts.

EXERCISE 14-2. USING SOURCING

1. In ~/bin, create a script with the name *color* and the following contents:

   ```
   COLOR=blue
   ```

2. Also in ~/bin, create a script with the name *sourceme* and the following contents:

   ```
   #!/bin/bash
   # example script that demonstrates sourcing

   .  ~/bin/color
   echo the color is $COLOR
   ```

3. Run the script sourceme. To do this, first make it executable with the command chmod +x sourceme, and next, run it typing ./sourceme. You will see the script using the variable that you have defined in the script color.

4. Change the value of the variable COLOR in ~/bin/color and run the script again.

Working with Variables and Input

Variables are essential to efficient shell scripting. The purpose of using variables is to have scripts work with changing data. The value of a variable depends on how it is used. You can have your script get the variable itself, for example, by executing a command, by making a calculation, by specifying it as a command-line argument for the script, or by modifying some text string. You can also set it yourself, as you've seen in the sample script from Exercise 14-2. In this section, you'll learn all the basics about variables.

Understanding Variables

A variable is a value that you define somewhere specific and use in a flexible way later. You can do that in a script, but you don't have to. You can define a variable in the shell as well. To define a variable, you use VARNAME=value. To get the value of a variable later on, you can call its value by using the echo command. Listing 14-2 gives an example of how a variable is set on the command line and how its value is used in the next command.

Listing 14-2. Setting and Using a Variable

```
nuuk:~ # HAPPY=yes
nuuk:~ # echo $HAPPY
yes
```

■ **Note** The method described here works for the bash command. Not every shell supports this. For instance, on TCSH, you have to use the set command to define a variable. For example, use set happy=yes to give the value yes to the variable happy.

Variables play a very important role on Linux. When booting, lots of variables are defined and used later when you work with your computer. For example, the name of your computer is in a variable; the name of the user account you logged in with is in a variable, as is the search path.

When starting a computer, the environment, which contains all of these variables, is set for users. You can use the env command to get a complete list of all the variables that are set for your computer.

When defining variables, it is a good idea to use uppercase. If your script gets longer, using variables in uppercase makes the script more readable. This is, however, in no way a requirement. An environment variable can very well be in lowercase.

The advantage of using variables in shell scripts is that you can use them in different ways to treat dynamic data. Here are some examples:

- A single point of administration for a certain value

- A value that a user provides in some way

- A value that is calculated dynamically

In many scripts, all the variables are defined in the beginning of the script. This makes administration easier, because all the flexible content is easily accessible and referred to later in the script. Variables can also be stored in files, as you have seen in Exercise 14-2. Let's have a look at the example in Listing 14-3.

Listing 14-3. Understanding the Use of Variables

```
#!/bin/bash
#
# dirscript
#
# Script that creates a directory with a certain name
# next sets $USER and $GROUP as the owners of the directory
# and finally changes the permission mode to 770

DIRECTORY=/blah
USER=linda
GROUP=sales

mkdir $DIRECTORY
chown $USER $DIRECTORY
chgrp $GROUP $DIRECTORY
chmod 770 $DIRECTORY

exit 0
```

As you can see, after the comment lines, this script starts by defining all the variables that are used. I've specified them in all uppercase letters, because they're more readable. In the second part of the script, the variables are referred to by preceding their name with a $ sign.

You will notice that many scripts work in this way. Apart from defining variables in this static way, you can also define variables dynamically, by using command substitution. You'll read more about this later in this chapter.

Variables, Subshells, and Sourcing

When defining variables, you should be aware that a variable is defined for the current shell only. That means that if from the current shell you start a subshell, the variable won't be there anymore. And if in a subshell you define a variable, it won't be there anymore once you've quit the subshell and returned to the parent shell. Listing 14-4 shows how this works.

Listing 14-4. Variables Are Local to the Shell Where They Are Defined

```
nuuk:~/bin # HAPPY=yes
nuuk:~/bin # echo $HAPPY
yes
nuuk:~/bin # bash
nuuk:~/bin # echo $HAPPY

nuuk:~/bin # exit
exit
nuuk:~/bin # echo $HAPPY
yes
nuuk:~/bin #
```

In the preceding listing, I've defined a variable with the name HAPPY. Next, you can see that its value is correctly echoed. In the third command, a subshell is started, and as you can see, when asking for the value of the variable HAPPY in this subshell, it isn't there, because it simply doesn't exist. But when the subshell is closed by using the exit command, we're back in the parent shell, where the variable still exists.

In some cases, you may want to set a variable that is present in all subshells as well. If this is the case, you can define it by using the export command. For instance, the command export HAPPY=yes would define the variable HAPPY and make sure that it is available in all subshells from the current shell on, until you next reboot the computer. There is, however, no way to define a variable and make that available in the parent shells in this way.

In Listing 14-5, you can see the same commands as used in Listing 14-4, but now with the value of the variable being exported.

Listing 14-5. By Exporting a Variable You Can Make It Available in Subshells As Well

```
nuuk:~/bin # export HAPPY=yes
nuuk:~/bin # echo $HAPPY
yes
nuuk:~/bin # bash
nuuk:~/bin # echo $HAPPY
yes
nuuk:~/bin # exit
exit
nuuk:~/bin # echo $HAPPY
yes
nuuk:~/bin #
```

Working with Script Arguments

In the preceding section, you have learned how you can define variables. Up to now, you've seen how to create a variable in a static way. In this subsection, you'll learn how to provide values for your variables in a dynamic way, by specifying them as an argument for the script when running the script on the command line.

Using Script Arguments

When running a script, you can specify arguments to the script on the command line. Consider the script dirscript that you've seen in sample Listing 14-3. You could run it with an argument on the command line as well, as in the following example:

dirscript /blah

Now wouldn't it be nice if in the script, you could do something with its argument /blah? The good news is that you can. You can refer to the first argument that was used when launching the script by using $1 in the script. The second argument is $2, and so on, up to $9. You can also use $0 to refer to the name of the script itself. In Exercise 14-3, you'll create a script that works with arguments and see how it works for yourself.

EXERCISE 14-3. CREATING A SCRIPT THAT WORKS WITH ARGUMENTS

In this exercise, you'll create a script that works with arguments. Type the following code and execute it, to find out what it does. Save the script, using the name ~/bin/argscript. First, run it without any arguments. Next, see what happens if you put one or more arguments after the name of the script.

```
#!/bin/bash
#
# argscript
#
# Script that shows how arguments are used

ARG1=$1
ARG2=$2
ARG3=$3
SCRIPTNAME=$0

echo The name of this script is $SCRIPTNAME
echo The first argument used is $ARG1
echo The second argument used is $ARG2
echo The third argument used is $ARG3
exit 0
```

In Exercise 14-4, you'll make a rewrite of the script dirscript that you've used before. You'll rewrite it to use arguments. This changes dirscript from a rather static script that can create only one directory to a dynamic script that can create any directory and assign any user and any group as an owner of that directory.

EXERCISE 14-4. REFERRING TO COMMAND-LINE ARGUMENTS IN A SCRIPT

The following script shows a rewrite of the dirscript that you've used before. In this new version, the script works with arguments instead of fixed variables, which makes it a lot more flexible!

```
#!/bin/bash
#
# dirscript
#
# Script that creates a directory with a certain name
# next sets $USER and $GROUP as the owners of the directory
# and finally changes the permission mode to 770
# Provide the directory name first, followed by the username and
# finally the groupname.

DIRECTORY=$1
USER=$2
GROUP=$3
```

```
mkdir $DIRECTORY
chown $USER $DIRECTORY
chgrp $GROUP $DIRECTORY
chmod 770 $DIRECTORY

exit 0
```

To execute the script from Exercise 14-4, you would use a command, as in the next sample code line:

dirscript somedir denise sales

This line shows you how the dirscript has been made more flexible now, but at the same time, it also shows you the most important disadvantage: it has become less obvious as well. You can imagine that for a user it is very easy to mix up the right order of the arguments and type dirscript kylie sales /somedir instead. So it becomes important to provide good help information on how to run this script. Do this by including comments at the beginning of the script. That explains to the user what exactly you are expecting.

Counting the Number of Script Arguments

On some occasions, you'll want to check the number of arguments that is provided with a script. This is useful if you expect a certain number of arguments and want to make sure that the required amount of arguments is present before running the script. To count the number of arguments provided with a script, you can use $#. Used all by itself, $# doesn't really make sense. Combined with an if statement (about which you'll read more later in this chapter), it does make sense. You could, for example, use it to show a help message, if the user hasn't provided the correct amount of arguments. In Exercise 14-5, you see the contents of the script countargs, in which $# is used. Directly following the code of the script, you also see a sample running of it.

EXERCISE 14-5. COUNTING ARGUMENTS

One useful technique to check whether the user has provided the expected number of arguments is to count these arguments. In this exercise, you'll write a script that does just that.

```
#!/bin/bash
#
# countargs
# sample script that shows how many arguments were used

echo the number of arguments is $#

exit 0
```

If you run the script from Exercise 14-5 with a number of arguments, it will show you how many arguments it has seen. The following code listing shows what to expect:

```
nuuk:~/bin # ./countargs a b c d e
the number of arguments is 5
nuuk:~/bin #.
```

Referring to All Script Arguments

So far, you've seen that a script can work with a fixed number of arguments. The script that you've created in Exercise 14-4 is hard-coded to evaluate arguments as $1, $2, and so on. But what if the number of arguments is not known beforehand? In that case, you can use $@ in your script. Let's show how this is used by creating a small for loop.

A **for** loop can be used to test all elements in a string of characters. Listing 14-6 shows how a for loop and $@ are used to evaluate all arguments that were used when starting a script.

Listing 14-6. Evaluating Arguments

```
#!/bin/bash
# showargs
# this script shows all arguments used when starting the script

echo the arguments are $@

for i in $@
do
        echo $i
done

exit 0
```

When running this script, you can see that an echo command is executed for every single argument. The for loop takes care of that. You can read the part for i in as "for every element in. . .". So, it processes all variables and starts an operation for each of them. When looping through the list of arguments, the argument is stored in the variable i, which is used in the command echo $i, which is executed for every argument that was encountered.

Prompting for Input

Another way to get user data is just to ask for it. To do this, you can use read in the script. When using read, the script waits for user input and puts that in a variable. In Exercise 14-6, you are going to create a simple script that first asks the input and then shows the input that was provided by echoing the value of the variable. Directly following the sample code, you can see also what happens when you run the script.

EXERCISE 14-6. PROMPTING FOR INPUT WITH READ

Create the script ~/bin/askinput containing the following contents:

```
#!/bin/bash
#
# askinput
# ask user to enter some text and then display it

echo Enter some text
read SOMETEXT
echo -e "You have entered the following text:\t $SOMETEXT"

exit 0
```

Now let's see what happens if you run the script code from the previous exercise.

```
nuuk:~/bin # ./askinput
Enter some text
hi there
You have entered the following text: hi there
nuuk:~/bin #
```

As you can see, the script starts with an echo line that explains to the user what it expects the user to do. Next, in the line read SOMETEXT, it will stop to allow the user to enter some text. This text is stored in the variable SOMETEXT. In the following line, the echo command is used to show the current value of SOMETEXT. As you see in this sample script, I've used echo with the option -e. This option allows you to use some special formatting characters, in this case, the formatting character \t, which enters a tab in the text. Using formatting such as this, you can ensure that the result is displayed in a nice manner.

As you can see, in the line that has the command echo -e, the text that the script needs to be echoed is between double quotes. That is to prevent the shell from interpreting the special character \t before echo does. Again, if you want to make sure that the shell does not interpret special characters such as this, put the string between double quotes.

In the previous script, two new items have been introduced: formatting characters and escaping. By escaping characters, you can make sure they are not interpreted by the shell. This is the difference between echo \t and echo "\t". In the former, the \ is treated as a special character, with the result that only the letter *t* is displayed. In the latter, double quotes are used to tell the shell not to interpret anything that is between the double quotes; hence, it shows \t. But in the script, we've used echo -e, which tells the script to understand \t as a formatting character.

When running shell scripts, you can use formatting. We've done that by using the formatting character \t with the command echo -e. This is one of the special characters that you can use in the shell, and this one tells the shell to display a tab. But to make sure that it is not interpreted by the shell when it first parses the script (which would result in the shell just displaying a *t*), you have to put any of these special formatting characters between double quotes. Let's have a look at how this works, in Listing 14-7.

Listing 14-7. Escaping and Special Characters

```
SYD:~ # echo \t
t
SYD:~ # echo "\t"
\t
SYD:~ # echo -e \t
t
SYD:~ # echo -e "\t"

SYD:~ #
```

When using echo −e, you can use the following special characters:

```
\0NNN  the character whose ASCII code is NNN (octal).
\\ , backslash. Use this if you want to show just a backslash.
\a, alert (BEL). If supported by your system, this will let you hear a beep.
\b, backspace
\c, suppress trailing newline
\f, form feed
```

```
\n, new line
\r, carriage return
\t, horizontal tab
\v, vertical tab
```

Using Command Substitution

In command substitution, you'll use the result of a command in the script. It makes an excellent way of working with variable content. For example, by using this technique, you can tell the script that it should only execute if a certain condition is met (you would have to use a conditional loop with if to accomplish this). To use command substitution, put the command that you want to use between back quotes (also known as back ticks), or within $(...). The following sample code line shows how it works:

```
nuuk:~/bin # echo "today is `date +%d-%m-%y`"
today is 24-05-14
nuuk:~/bin # echo "today is $(date +%d-%m-%y)"
today is 24-05-14
```

Both the back quotes will work as the $(...) construction, but you may want to consider that using $(...) makes the script more readable: it is easy to mix up back quotes with single quotes, which are also common in shell scripts.

In the previous example, the date command is used with some of its special formatting characters. The command date +%d-%m-%y tells date to present its result in the day, month, year format. In this example, the command is just executed. You can, however, also put the result of the command substitution in a variable, which makes it easier to perform operations on the result later in the script. The following sample code shows how to do that:

```
nuuk:~/bin # TODAY=`date +%d-%m-%y`
nuuk:~/bin # echo today=$TODAY
today=08-09-14
```

Substitution Operators

Within a script, it may be important to check if a variable really has a value assigned to it, before the script continues. To do this, Bash offers substitution operators. By using substitution operators, you can assign a default value, if a variable doesn't have a value currently assigned, and much more. Table 14-1 provides an overview of the most common substitution operators with a short explanation of their use.

Table 14-1. *Substitution Operators*

Operator	Use
${parameter:-value}	Shows a value, if the parameter is not defined.
${parameter=value}	Assigns a value to the parameter, if the parameter does not exist at all. This operator does nothing if the parameter exists but doesn't have a value.
${parameter:=value}	Assigns a value, if the parameter currently has no value or doesn't exist at all.
${parameter:?value}	Shows a message that is defined as a value, if the parameter doesn't exist or is empty. Using this construction will force the shell script to be aborted immediately.
${parameter:+value}	If the parameter does have a value, the value is displayed. If it doesn't have a value, nothing happens.

Substitution operators can be hard to understand. To make it easier to see how they work, Listing 14-8 provides some examples. In all of these examples, something happens to the $BLAH variable. You'll see that the result of the given command is different, depending on the substitution operator that's used. To make it easier to discuss what happens, I've added line numbers to the listing. Notice that, when trying this yourself, you should omit the line numbers.

Listing 14-8. Using Substitution Operators

```
1.  sander@linux %> echo $BLAH
2.
3.  sander@linux %> echo ${BLAH:-variable is empty}
4.  variable is empty
5.  sander@linux %> echo $BLAH
6.
7.  sander@linux %> echo ${BLAH=value}
8.  value
9.  sander@linux %> echo $BLAH
10. value
11. sander@linux %> BLAH=
12. sander@linux %> echo ${BLAH=value}
13.
14. sander@linux %> echo ${BLAH:=value}
15. value
16. sander@linux %> echo $BLAH
17. value
14. sander@linux %> echo ${BLAH:+sometext}
19. sometext
```

The example in Listing 14-8 starts with the following command:

```
echo $BLAH
```

This command reads the variable BLAH and shows its current value. Because BLAH doesn't have a value yet, nothing is shown in line 2. Next, a message is defined in line 3 that should be displayed if BLAH is empty. This happens with the following command:

```
sander@linux %> echo ${BLAH:-variable is empty}
```

As you can see, the message is displayed in line 4. However, this doesn't assign a value to BLAH, and you can see in lines 5 and 6, in which the current value of BLAH is requested again.

```
3. sander@linux %> echo ${BLAH:-variable is empty}
4 variable is empty
5. sander@linux %> echo $BLAH
6.
```

In line 7, BLAH finally gets a value, which is displayed in line 8.

```
7. sander@linux %> echo ${BLAH=value}
8. value
```

The shell remembers the new value of BLAH, which you can see in lines 9 and 10, in which the value of BLAH is referred to and displayed.

```
 9. sander@linux %> echo $BLAH
10. value
```

In line 11, BLAH is redefined, but it gets a null value.

```
11. sander@linux %> BLAH=
```

The variable still exists; it just has no value here. This is demonstrated when echo ${BLAH=value} is used in line 12. BecauseBLAH has a null value at that moment, no new value is assigned.

```
12. sander@linux %> echo ${BLAH=value}
13.
```

Next, the construction echo ${BLAH:=value} is used to assign a new value to BLAH. The fact that BLAH really gets a value from this is shown in lines 16 and 17.

```
14. sander@linux %> echo ${BLAH:=value}
15. value
16. sander@linux %> echo $BLAH
17. value
```

Finally, the construction in line 18 is used to display sometext, if BLAH currently does have a value.

```
18. sander@linux %> echo ${BLAH:+sometext}
19. sometext
```

Note that this doesn't change anything in the value that is assigned to BLAH at that moment; sometext just indicates that it has a value, and that's all.

Changing Variable Content with Pattern Matching

You've just seen how substitution operators can be used to do something if a variable does not have a value. You can consider them a rather primitive way of handling errors in your script. A pattern-matching operator can be used to search for a pattern in a variable and, if that pattern is found, modify the variable. This can be very useful, because it allows you to define a variable exactly the way you want. For example, think of the situation in which a user enters a complete path name of a file, but only the name of the file itself (without the path) is needed in your script.

The pattern-matching operator is the way to change this.

Pattern-matching operators allow you to remove part of a variable automatically. In Exercise 14-7, you'll write a small script that uses pattern matching.

EXERCISE 14-7. WORKING WITH PATTERN-MATCHING OPERATORS

In this exercise, you'll write a script that uses pattern matching.

```
#!/bin/bash
# stripit
# script that extracts the file name from a filename that includes the complete path
# usage: stripit <complete file name>

filename=${1##*/}
echo "The name of the file is $filename"

exit 0
```

When executing the code you've just written, the script will show the following result:

```
sander@linux %> ./stripit /bin/bash
the name of the file is bash
```

Pattern-matching operators always try to locate a given string. In this case, the string is */. In other words, the pattern-matching operator searches for a /, preceded by another character (*). In this pattern-matching operator, ## is used to search for the longest match of the provided string, starting from the beginning of the string. So, the pattern-matching operator searches for the last / that occurs in the string and removes it and everything that precedes the / as well. You may ask how the script comes to remove everything in front of the /. It's because the pattern-matching operator refers to */ and not to /. You can confirm this by running the script with a name such as /bin/bash as an argument. In this case, the pattern that's searched for is in the last position of the string, and the pattern-matching operator removes everything.

This example explains the use of the pattern-matching operator that looks for the longest match. By using a single #, you can let the pattern-matching operator look for the shortest match, again, starting from the beginning of the string. If, for example, the script you've created in Exercise 14-7 used filename=${1#*/}, the pattern-matching operator would look for the first / in the complete file name and remove that and everything before it. I would recommend applying this modification to the shell script in Exercise 14-7 and seeing what the result is like.

You should realize that in these examples, the * is important. The pattern-matching operator ${1#*/} removes the first / found and anything in front of it. The pattern-matching operator ${1#/} removes the first / in $1 only if the value of $1 starts with a /. However, if there's anything before the /, the operator will not know what to do. So, make sure that all of your pattern-matching operators are using *.

In these examples, you've seen how a pattern-matching operator is used to start searching from the beginning of a string. You can start searching from the end of a string as well, which is useful if you want to remove a pattern from the end of a string. Remember: The purpose of pattern-matching operators is to remove parts of a string. To remove patterns from the end of a string, a % is used instead of a #. This % refers to the shortest match of the pattern, and %% refers to the longest match. The script in Listing 14-9 shows how this works.

Listing 14-9. *Using Pattern-Matching Operators to Start Searching at the End of a String*

```
#!/bin/bash
# stripdir
# script that isolates the directory name from a complete file name
# usage: stripdir <complete file name>

dirname=${1%%/*}
echo "The directory name is $dirname"

exit 0
```

While executing, you'll see that this script has a problem:

```
sander@linux %> ./stripdir /bin/bash
The directory name is
```

As you can see, the script does its work somewhat too enthusiastically and removes everything. Fortunately, this problem can be solved by first using a pattern-matching operator that removes the / from the start of the complete file name (but only if that / is provided) and then removing everything following the first / in the complete file name. The example in Listing 14-10 shows how this is done.

Listing 14-10. *Fixing the Example from Listing 14-9*

```
#!/bin/bash
# stripdir
# script that isolates the directory name from a complete file name
# usage: stripdir <complete file name>

dirname=${1#/}
dirname=${dirname%%/*}
echo "The directory name is $dirname"

exit 0
```

As you can see, the problem is solved by using ${1#/}. This construction starts searching from the beginning of the file name to a /. Because no * is used here, it looks for a / only at the very first position of the file name and does nothing if the string starts with anything else. If it finds a /, it removes it. So, if a user enters usr/bin/passwd instead of /usr/bin/passwd, the ${1#/} construction does nothing at all.

In the line after that, the variable dirname is defined again to do its work on the result of its first definition in the preceding line. This line does the real work and looks for the pattern /*, starting at the end of the file name. This makes sure that everything after the first / in the file name is removed and that only the name of the top-level directory is echoed. Of course, you can easily edit this script to display the complete path of the file: just use dirname=${dirname%/*} instead.

To make sure that you are comfortable with pattern-matching operators, the script in Listing 14-11 gives another example. This time, however, the example does not work with a file name but with a random text string. I don't want you to think that you can use pattern-matching operators only on file names; they work on any string.

Listing 14-11. Another Example with Pattern Matching

```
#!/bin/bash
#
# generic script that shows some more pattern matching
# usage: pmex
BLAH=babarabaraba
echo BLAH is $BLAH
echo 'The result of ##ba is '${BLAH##*ba}
echo 'The result of #ba is '${BLAH#*ba}
echo 'The result of %%ba is '${BLAH%ba*}
echo 'The result of %ba is '${BLAH%%ba*}

exit 0
```

When running it, the script gives the result shown in Listing 14-12.

Listing 14-12. The Result of the Script in Listing 14-11

```
root@RNA:~/scripts# ./pmex
BLAH is babarabaraba
The result of ##ba is
The result of #ba is barabaraba
The result of %%ba is babarabara
The result of %ba is
root@RNA:~/scripts#
```

EXERCISE 14-8. APPLYING PATTERN MATCHING ON A DATE STRING

In this exercise, you'll apply pattern matching on a date string. You'll see how to use pattern matching to filter out text in the middle of a string. The purpose of this exercise is to write a script that works on the result of the command date +%d-%m-%y. Next, it should show three separate lines, echoing today's day is..., the month is..., and the year is.... The code below shows what this script should look like.

```
#!/bin/bash
#
DATE=$(date +%d-%m-%y)
TODAY=${DATE%%-*}
THISMONTH=${DATE%-*}
THISMONTH=${THISMONTH#*-}
THISYEAR=${DATE##*-}
echo today is $TODAY
echo this month is $THISMONTH
echo this year is $THISYEAR
```

Performing Calculations

Bash offers some options that allow you to perform simple calculations from scripts. Of course, you're not likely to use them as a replacement for your spreadsheet program, but performing simple calculations from Bash can be useful. For example, you can use calculation options to execute a command a number of times or to ensure that a counter is incremented when a command executes successfully. The script in Listing 14-13 provides an example of how counters can be used.

Listing 14-13. Using a Counter in a Script

```
#!/bin/bash
# counter
# script that counts until infinity
counter=1
    counter=$((counter + 1))
    echo counter is set to $counter
exit 0
```

This script consists of three lines. The first line initializes the variable counter with a value of one. Next, the value of this variable is incremented by one. In the third line, the new value of the variable is shown.

Of course, it doesn't make much sense to run the script this way. It would make more sense if you included it in a conditional loop, to count the number of actions that are performed until a condition is true. In the section "Using while," later in this chapter, I provide an example that shows how to combine counters with while.

So far, we've dealt with only one method to perform script calculations, but you have other options as well. First, you can use the external expr command to perform any kind of calculation. For example, the following line produces the result of 1 + 2:

sum=`expr 1 + 2`; echo $sum

In this example, a variable with the name sum is defined, and this variable gets the result of the command expr 1 + 2 by using command substitution. A semicolon is then used to indicate that what follows is a new command. (Remember the generic use of semicolons? They're used to separate one command from the next command.) After the semicolon, the command echo $sum shows the result of the calculation.

The expr command can work with addition, and other types of calculations are supported as well. Table 14-2 summarizes the options.

Table 14-2. expr Operators

Operator	Meaning
+	Addition (1 + 1 = 2)
-	Subtraction (10 - 2 = 8)
/	Division (10 / 2 = 5)
*	Multiplication (3 * 3 = 9)
%	Modulus; this calculates the remainder after division. This works because expr can handle integers only (11 % 3 = 2).

When working with these options, you'll see that they all work fine, with the exception of the multiplication operator *. Using this operator results in the following syntax error:

```
linux: ~>expr 2 * 2
expr: syntax error
```

This seems curious but can be easily explained. The * has a special meaning for the shell, as in ls -l *. When the shell parses the command line, it interprets the *, and you don't want it to do that here. To indicate that the shell shouldn't touch it, you have to escape it. Therefore, change the command as follows:

expr 2 * 2

Another way to perform some calculations is to use the internal command let. Just the fact that let is internal makes it a better solution than the external command expr: it can be loaded from memory directly and doesn't have to come all the way from your computer's hard drive. Using let, you can make your calculation and apply the result directly to a variable, as in the following example:

let x="1 + 2"

The result of the calculation in this example is stored in the variable x. The disadvantage of working this way is that let has no option to display the result directly, as can be done when using expr. For use in a script, however, it offers excellent capabilities. Listing 14-14 shows a script that uses let to perform calculations.

Listing 14-14. Performing Calculations with let

```
#!/bin/bash
# calcscript
# usage: calc $1 $2 $3
# $1 is the first number
# $2 is the operator
# $3 is the second number

let x="$1 $2 $3"
echo $x

exit 0
```

Following, you can see what happens if you run this script:

```
SYD:~/bin # ./calcscript 1 + 2
3
SYD:~/bin #
```

Using Control Structures

Up until now, you haven't read much about the way in which the execution of commands can be made conditional. The technique for enabling this in shell scripts is known as flow control. Bash offers many options to use flow control in scripts.

- if: Use if to execute commands only if certain conditions are met. To customize the working of if some more, you can use else to indicate what should happen if the condition isn't met.

- case: Use case to handle options. This allows the user to further specify the working of the command when he or she runs it.

- for: This construction is used to run a command for a given number of items. For example, you can use for to do something for every file in a specified directory.

- while: Use while as long as the specified condition is met. For example, this construction can be very useful to check if a certain host is reachable or to monitor the activity of a process.

- until: This is the opposite of while. Use until to run a command until a certain condition has been met.

The following subsections cover flow control in more detail. Before going into these details, however, you can first read about the test command, which plays an important role in flow control. This command is used to perform many checks to see, for example, if a file exists or if a variable has a value. Table 14-3 shows some of the more common test options.

Table 14-3. *Common Options for the test Command*

Option	Use
test -e $1	Checks if $1 is a file, without looking at what particular kind of file it is
test -f $1	Checks if $1 is a regular file and not (for example) a device file, a directory, or an executable file
test -f $1	Checks if $1 is a directory
test -x $1	Checks if $1 is an executable file. Note that you can test for other permissions as well. For example, -g would check to see if the SGID permission is set
test $1 -nt $2	Controls if $1 is newer than $2
test $1 -ot $2	Controls if $1 is older than $2
test $1 -ef $2	Checks if $1 and $2 both refer to the same inode. This is the case if one is a hard link to the other.
test $1 -eq $2	Sees if the integer values of $1 and $2 are equal
test $1 -ne $2	Checks if the integers $1 and $2 are not equal
test $1 -gt $2	Is true if integer $1 is greater than integer $2
test $1 -lt $2	Is true if integer $1 is less than integer $2.
test -z $1	Checks if $1 is empty. This is a very useful construction to find out whether a variable has been defined.
test $1	Gives the exit status 0 if $1 is true
test $1=$2	Checks if the strings $1 and $2 are the same. This is most useful in comparing the value of two variables.
test $1 != $2	Checks if the strings $1 and $2 are not equal to each other. You can use ! with all other tests as well, to check for the negation of the statement.

You can use the test command in two ways. First, you can write the complete command, as in test -f $1. You can also rewrite this command as [-f $1]. Frequently, you'll see the latter option only, because people who write shell scripts like to work as efficiently as possible.

Using if...then...else

Possibly, the classic example of flow control consists of constructions that use if...then...else. Especially if used in conjunction with the test command, this construction offers various interesting possibilities. You can use it to find out if a file exists, if a variable currently has a value, and much more. Listing 14-15 provides an example of a construction with if...then...else.

Listing 14-15. Using if to Perform a Basic Check

```
#!/bin/bash
# testarg
# test to see if argument is present

if [ -z $1 ]
then
    echo You have to provide an argument with this command
    exit 1
fi

echo the argument is $1

exit 0
```

The simple check from the Listing 14-15 example is used to see if the user who started your script provided an argument. Here's what you see if you run the script:

```
SYD:~/bin # ./testarg
You have to provide an argument with this command
SYD:~/bin #
```

If the user didn't provide an argument, the code in the if loop becomes active, in which case, it displays the message that the user has to provide an argument and then terminates the script. If an argument has been provided, the commands within the loop aren't executed, and the script will run the line echo the argument is $1, and in this case, echo the argument to the user's screen.

Also, note how the syntax of the if construction is organized. First, you have to open it with if. Then, separated on a new line (or with a semicolon), then is used. Finally, the if loop is closed with a fi statement. Make sure all those ingredients are used all the time, or your loop won't work.

The example in Listing 14-15 is rather simple. It's also possible to make if loops more complex and have them test for more than one condition. To do this, use else or elif. By using else within the control structure, you can make sure that something happens if the condition is met, but it allows you to check another condition if the condition is not met. You can even use else in conjunction with if (elif) to open a new control structure, if the first condition isn't met. If you do that, you have to use then after elif. Listing 14-16 is an example of the latter construction.

Listing 14-16. Nesting if Control Structures

```
#!/bin/bash
# testfile

if [ -f $1 ]
then
     echo "$1 is a file"
elif [ -d $1 ]
then
     echo "$1 is a directory"
else
     echo "I don't know what \$1 is"
fi

exit 0
```

Following, you can see what happens when you run this script:

```
SYD:~/bin # ./testfile /bin/blah
I don't know what $1 is
SYD:~/bin #
```

In this example, the argument that was entered when running the script is checked. If it is a file (if [-f $1]), the script tells the user that. If it isn't a file, the part under elif is executed, which basically opens a second control structure. In this second control structure, the first test performed is to see if $1 is perhaps a directory. Notice that this second part of the control structure becomes active only if $1 is not a file. If $1 isn't a directory either, the part after else is executed, and the script reports that it has no idea what $1 is. Note that, for this entire construction, only one fi is needed to close the control structure, but after every if (that includes all elif as well), you have to use then.

Looping constructions based on if are used in two different ways. You can write out the complete construction as in the previous examples, or you can use && and ||. These so-called logical operators are used to separate two commands and establish a conditional relationship between them. If && is used (the logical AND), the second command is executed only if the first command is executed successfully (in other words, if the first command has returned an exit status 0). If || is used, the second command is executed only if the first command has returned an exit status that is not 0. So, with one line of code, you can find out if $1 is a file and echo a message if it is.

[-f $1] && echo $1 is a file

Note that this can be rewritten differently as well.

[! -f $1] || echo $1 is a file

■ Note   The preceding example only works as a part of a complete shell script because of the $1, which refers to the first argument that was used when starting the script. Listing 14-17 shows how the example from Listing 14-16 is rewritten, if you want to use this syntax.

Listing 14-17. The Example from Listing 14-16 Rewritten with && and ||

```
([ -z $1 ] && echo please provide an argument; exit 1) || (([ -f $1 ] && echo $1 is a file) ||
([ -d $1 ] && echo $1 is a directory || echo I have no idea what $1 is))
```

The code in the second example (where || is used) performs a test to see if $1 is not a file. (The ! is used to test if something is not the case.) Only if the test fails (which is the case if $1 is a file), it executes the part after the || and echoes that $1 is a file.

This sample listing does the same as the script code from Listing 14-16; however, you should be aware of a few things. First, I've added a [-z $1] test to give an error if $1 is not defined. Next, the example in Listing 14-17 is all on one line. This makes the script more compact, but it also makes it harder to understand what is going on. I've used parentheses to increase the readability a little bit and also to keep the different parts of the script together. The parts between parentheses are the main tests, and within these main tests, some smaller tests are used as well.

Let's have a look at some other examples with if...then...else. Consider the following line, for example:

rsync -vaze ssh --delete /var/ftp 10.0.0.20:/var/ftp || echo "rsync failed" | mail admin@mydomain.com

In this single script line, the rsync command tries to synchronize the content of the directory /var/ftp with the content of the same directory on some other machine. If this succeeds, no further evaluation of this line is attempted. If something happens, however, the part after the || becomes active and makes sure that user admin@mydomain.com gets a message.

Another, more complex example could be the following script, which checks whether available disk space has dropped below a certain threshold. The complex part lies in the sequence of pipes used in the command substitution.

```
if [ `df -m /var | tail -n1 | awk '{print $4} '` -lt 120 ]
then
    logger running out of disk space
fi
```

The important part of this piece of code is in the first line, in which the result of a command is used in the if loop, by using command substitution, and that result is compared with the value 120. Note that the back tick notation for command substitution doesn't really make the script readable. You could consider using $(...) instead.

If the result is less than 120, the following section becomes active. If the result is greater than 120, nothing happens. As for the command itself, it uses the df command to check available disk space on the volume where /var is mounted, filters out the last line of that result, and from that last line, filters out the fourth column only, which in turn is compared to the value 120. And, if the condition is true, the logger command writes a message to the system log file. This example isn't really well organized. The following rewrite does exactly the same, but using a different syntax:

[$(df -m /var | tail -n1 | awk '{print $4}') -lt $1] && logger running out of disk space

This rewrite shows why it's fun to write shell scripts: you can almost always make them better.

Case

Let's start with an example this time. In Exercise 14-9 you'll create a script, run it, and then try to explain what it's done.

EXERCISE 14-9. SAMPLE SCRIPT WITH CASE

Type the scripting code below, execute it a few times, and try to explain what it does.

```
#!/bin/bash
# soccer
# Your personal soccer expert
# predicts world championship football

cat << EOF
Enter the name of the country you think will be world soccer champion in
EOF

read COUNTRY
# translate $COUNTRY into all uppercase
COUNTRY=`echo $COUNTRY | tr a-z A-Z`

# perform the test
case $COUNTRY in
     NEDERLAND | HOLLAND | NETHERLANDS)
     echo "Yes, you are a soccer expert "
     ;;
     DEUTSCHLAND | GERMANY | MANNSCHAFT)
     echo "No, they are the worst team on earth"
     ;;
     ENGLAND | AUSTRALIA | FRANCE | BRAZIL)
     echo "hahahahahahaha, you must be joking"
     ;;
     *)
     echo "Huh? Do they play soccer?"
     ;;
esac

exit 0
```

In case you didn't guess, this script can be used to analyze the next World Cup championship (of course, you can modify it for any major sports event you like). It will first ask the person who runs the script to enter the name of the country that he or she thinks will be the next champion. This country is put in the $COUNTRY variable. Note the use of uppercase for this variable; it's a nice way to identify variables easily, if your script becomes rather long.

Because the case statement that's used in this script is case sensitive, the user input in the first part is translated into all uppercase using the tr command. Using command substitution with this command, the current value of $COUNTRY is read, translated to all uppercase, and assigned again to the $COUNTRY variable using command substitution. In addition, note that I've made it easier to distinguish the different parts of this script, by adding some additional comments.

The body of this script consists of the `case` command, which is used to evaluate the input the user has entered. The generic construction used to evaluate the input is as follows:

```
alternative1 | alternative2)
command
;;
```

So, the first line evaluates everything that the user can enter. Note that more than one alternative is used on most lines, which makes it easier to handle typos and other situations in which the user hasn't typed exactly what you were expecting him/her to type. Then on separate lines come all the commands that you want the script to execute. In the example, only one command is executed, but you can enter a hundred lines to execute commands, if you like. Finally, the test is closed by using `;;`. Don't forget to use double semicolons to close all items; otherwise, the script won't understand you. The `;;`(double semicolons) can be on a line by themselves, but you can also put them directly after the last command line in the script (which might make it a bit less readable).

When using `case`, you should make it a habit to handle "all other options." Hopefully, the user who runs the script will enter something that you expect. But what if he or she doesn't? In that case, you probably do want the user to see something. This is handled by the `*)` at the end of the script. So, in this case, for everything the user enters that isn't specifically mentioned as an option in the script, the script will echo `"Huh? Do they play soccer?"` to the user.

Using while

You can use `while` to run a command, as long as a condition is met. Listing 14-18 shows how `while` can be used to monitor the activity of an important process.

Listing 14-18. Monitoring Process Activity with `while`

```
#!/bin/bash
# procesmon
# usage: monitor <processname>

while ps aux | grep $1
do
     sleep 1
done

logger $1 is no longer present

exit 0
```

The body of this script consists of the command `ps aux | grep $1`. This command monitors for the availability of the process whose name was entered as an argument when starting the script. As long as the process is detected, the condition is met, and the commands in the loop are executed. In this case, the script waits one second and then repeats its action. When the process is no longer detected, the `logger` command writes a message to syslog.

As you can see from this example, `while` offers an excellent method to check if something (such as a process or an IP address) still exists. If you combine it with the `sleep` command, you can start your script with `while` as a kind of daemon and perform a check repeatedly. In Exercise 14-10, you'll write a message to syslog if, due to an error, the IP address suddenly gets lost.

```
┌─────────────────────────────────────────────────────────────────────────────┐
│        EXERCISE 14-10. CHECKING IF THE IP ADDRESS IS STILL THERE              │
└─────────────────────────────────────────────────────────────────────────────┘
```

The script code below offers an option to monitor the availability of an IP address. Write the code to a script and run it a few times to understand how it works.

```bash
#!/bin/bash
# ipmon
# script that monitors an IP address
# usage: ipmon <ip-address>

while ip a s | grep $1/ > /dev/null
do
      sleep 5
done

logger HELP, the IP address $1 is gone.

exit 0
```

Using until

Where while does its work as long as a certain condition is met, until is used for the opposite: it runs until the condition is met. This can be seen in Listing 14-19, in which the script monitors if the user, whose name is entered as the argument, is logged in.

Listing 14-19. Monitoring User Login

```bash
#!/bin/bash
# usermon
# script that alerts when a user logs in
# usage: ishere <username>

until who | grep $1 >> /dev/null
do
     echo $1 is not logged in yet
     sleep 5
done

echo $1 has just logged in

exit 0
```

In this example, the who | grep $1 command is executed repeatedly. In this command, the result of the who command that lists users currently logged in to the system is searched for the occurrence of $1. As long as that command is not true (which is the case if the user is not logged in), the commands in the loop will be executed. As soon as the user logs in, the loop is broken, and a message is displayed to say that the user has just logged in. Note the use of redirection to the null device in the test, ensuring that the result of the who command is not echoed on the screen.

Using for

Sometimes it's necessary to execute a series of commands, whether for a limited or an unlimited number of times. In such cases, for loops offer an excellent solution. Listing 14-20 shows how you can use for to create a counter.

Listing 14-20. Using for to Create a Counter

```
#!/bin/bash
# counter
# counter that counts from 1 to 9

for (( counter=1; counter<10; counter++ )); do
     echo "The counter is now set to $counter"
done

exit 0
```

The code used in this script isn't difficult to understand: the conditional loop determines that, as long as the counter has a value between one and ten, the variable counter must be automatically incremented by one. To do this, the construction counter++ is used. As long as this incrementing of the variable counter continues, the commands between do and done are executed. When the specified number is reached, the loop is left, and the script will terminate and with exit 0 indicate to the system that it has done its work successfully.

Loops with for can be pretty versatile. For example, you can use them to do something on every line in a text file. The example in Listing 14-21 illustrates how this works (as you will see, it has some problems, though).

Listing 14-21. Displaying Lines from a Text File

```
#!/bin/bash
# listusers
# faulty script that tries to show all users in /etc/passwd

for i in `cat /etc/passwd`
do
     echo $i
done

exit 0
```

In this example, for is used to display all lines in /etc/passwd one by one. Of course, just echoing the lines is a rather trivial example, but it's enough to show how a for statement works. If you're using for in this way, you should notice that it cannot handle spaces in the lines. A space would be interpreted as a field separator, so a new field would begin after the space.

Following is one more example with for, here, used to ping a range of IP addresses. This is a script that one of my clients likes to run to see if a range of machines is up and running. Because the IP addresses are always in the same range, starting with 192.168.1, there's no harm in including these first three bits in the IP address itself.

```
#!/bin/bash
for i in $@
do
     ping -c 1 192.168.1.$i
done
```

Summary

In this chapter, you've learned how to write shell scripts. You've worked with some of the basic shell scripting technologies, which should allow you to get around shell scripting and start experimenting with this technique and create your own more advanced scripts. Also, based on the information in this chapter, you should now be able to understand what most of the start up scripts on your server are doing.

CHAPTER 15

■ ■ ■

Performance Monitoring and Optimizing

An installed Linux server comes with default performance settings. That means that it will perform well for an average workload. Unfortunately, many servers are going beyond average, which means that optimization can be applied. In this chapter, you'll read how to monitor and optimize performance. The first part of this chapter is about performance monitoring. In the second part, you'll learn how to optimize performance.

The following topics are covered in this chapter:

- Performance Monitoring
- Optimizing Performance
- Optimizing Linux Performance Using Cgroups

Performance Monitoring

Before you can actually optimize anything, you have to know what's going on. In this first section of the chapter, you'll learn how to analyze performance. We'll start with one of the most common but also one of the most informative tools: top.

Interpreting What's Going On: top

Before starting to look at details, you should have a general overview of the current state of your server. The top utility is an excellent tool to help you with that. Let's start by having a look at a server that is used as a virtualization server, hosting multiple virtual machines (see Listing 15-1).

Listing 15-1. Using top on a Busy Server

```
top - 10:47: 49 up 1 day, 16:56, 3 users, load average: 0.08, 0.06, 0.10
Tasks:  409 total, 1 running, 408 sleeping, 0 stopped, 0 zombie
%Cpu(s): 1.6 us, 0.4 sy, 0.0 ni, 98.0 id, 0.0 wa, 0.0 hi, 0.0 si, 0.0 st
KiB Mem: 16196548 total, 13197772 used, 2998776 free, 4692 buffers
KiB Swap: 4194300 total, 0 used, 4194300 free. 4679428 cached Mem
```

PID	USER	PR	NI	VIRT	RES	SHR	S	%CPU	%MEM	TIME+	COMMAND
1489	root	20	0	1074368	23568	11836	S	3.3	0.1	51:18.32	libvirtd
12730	root	20	0	6018668	2.058g	56760	S	2.7	13.3	52:07.62	virt-manager
19586	qemu	20	0	1320328	532616	8028	S	2.0	3.3	23:08.54	qemu-kvm
13719	qemu	20	0	1211512	508476	8028	S	1.7	3.1	23:42.33	qemu-kvm
18450	qemu	20	0	1336528	526252	8016	S	1.7	3.2	23:39.71	qemu-kvm
18513	qemu	20	0	1274928	463408	8036	S	1.7	2.9	23:28.97	qemu-kvm
18540	qemu	20	0	1274932	467276	8020	S	1.7	2.9	23:32.23	qemu-kvm
19542	qemu	20	0	1320840	514224	8032	S	1.7	3.2	23:03.55	qemu-kvm
19631	qemu	20	0	1315620	501828	8012	S	1.7	3.1	23:10.92	qemu-kvm
24773	qemu	20	0	1342848	547784	8016	S	1.7	3.4	23:38.80	qemu-kvm
3572	root	20	0	950484	148812	42644	S	1.3	0.9	39:24.33	firefox
16388	qemu	20	0	1275076	465400	7996	S	1.3	2.9	22:51.46	qemu-kvm
18919	qemu	20	0	1318728	510000	8020	S	1.3	3.1	23:46.81	qemu-kvm
28791	**root**	**20**	**0**	**123792**	**1876**	**1152**	**R**	**0.3**	**0.0**	**0:00.03**	**top**
1	root	20	0	53500	7644	3788	S	0.0	0.0	0:07.07	systemd
2	root	20	0	0	0	0	S	0.0	0.0	0:00.13	kthreadd
3	root	20	0	0	0	0	S	0.0	0.0	0:03.27	ksoftirqd/0
5	root	0	-20	0	0	0	S	0.0	0.0	0:00.00	kworker/0:0H
7	root	rt	0	0	0	0	S	0.0	0.0	0:00.19	migration/0
8	root	20	0	0	0	0	S	0.0	0.0	0:00.00	rcu_bh
9	root	20	0	0	0	0	S	0.0	0.0	0:00.00	rcuob/0
10	root	20	0	0	0	0	S	0.0	0.0	0:00.00	rcuob/1
11	root	20	0	0	0	0	S	0.0	0.0	0:00.00	rcuob/2

CPU Monitoring with top

When analyzing performance, you start at the first line of the top output. The load average parameters at the end of the line are of special interest. There are three of them, indicating the load average for the last minute, the last five minutes, and the last fifteen minutes. The load average gives the average amount of processes that were in the run queue. Stated otherwise, the load average gives that which is actually being handled, or waiting to be handled. As ultimately a CPU core can handle one process at any moment only, a load average of 1.00 on a 1-CPU would be the ideal load, indicating that the CPU is completely busy.

Looking at load average in this way is a little bit too simple, though. Some processes don't demand that much from the CPU; other processes do. So, in some cases, performance can be good on a 1-CPU system that gives a load average of 8.00, while on other occasions, performance might be suffering, if load average is only at 1.00. Load average is a good start, but it's not good enough just by itself.

Consider, for example, a task that is running completely on the CPU. You can force such a task by entering the following code line:

```
while true; do true; done
```

This task will completely claim one CPU core, thus causing a workload of 1.00. Because, however, this is a task that doesn't do any input/output (I/O), the task does not have waiting times, and therefore, for a task like this, 1.00 is considered a heavy workload, because if another task is started, processes will have to be queued owing to of a lack of available resources.

Let's now consider a task that is I/O intensive, such as a task in which your complete hard drive is copied to the null device (dd if=/dev/sda of=/dev/null). This task will also easily cause a workload that is 1.00 or higher, but because there is a lot of waiting for I/O involved in a task like that, it's not as bad as the while true task. That is because while waiting for I/O, the CPU can do something else. So don't be too quick in drawing conclusions from the load line.

When seeing that your server's CPUs are very busy, you should further analyze. First, you should relate the load average to the amount of CPUs in your server. By default, top provides a summary for all CPUs in your server. Press the 1 on the keyboard, to show a line for each CPU core in your server. Because most modern servers are multi-core, you should apply this option, as it gives you information about the multiprocessing environment as well. In Listing 15-2, you can see an example in which usage statistics are provided on a four-core server:

Listing 15-2. Monitoring Performance on a Four-Core Server

```
top - 11:06:29 up 1 day, 17:15, 3 users, load average: 6.80, 4.20, 1.95
Tasks : 424 total, 3 running, 421 sleeping, 0 stopped, 0 zombie
%Cpu0 : 84.9 us, 11.7 sy, 0.0 ni, 2.0 id, 0.7 wa, 0.0 hi, 0.7 si, 0.0 st
%Cpu1 : 86.6 us,  9.4 sy, 0.0 ni, 3.0 id, 0.3 wa, 0.0 hi, 0.7 si, 0.0 st
%Cpu2 : 86.6 us,  9.7 sy, 0.0 ni, 2.7 id, 0.7 wa, 0.0 hi, 0.3 si, 0.0 st
%Cpu3 : 88.0 us,  9.0 sy, 0.0 ni, 2.7 id, 0.3 wa, 0.0 hi, 0.0 si, 0.0 st
KiB Mem: 16196548 total, 16021536 used, 175012 free, 3956 buffers
KiB Swap: 4194300 total, 10072 used, 4184228 free. 3700732 cached Mem


PID   USER     PR  NI  VIRT     RES      SHR   S  %CPU  %MEM  TIME+      COMMAND
29694 qemu     20   0  1424580  658276   8068  S  72.6  4.1   3:30.70    qemu-kvm
29934 qemu     20   0  1221208  614936   8064  S  69.7  3.8   1:08.35    qemu-kvm
29863 qemu     20   0  1386616  637948   8052  S  56.7  3.9   1:54.51    qemu-kvm
29627 qemu     20   0  1417552  643716   8064  S  56.1  4.0   4:37.15    qemu-kvm
29785 qemu     20   0  1425656  657500   8064  S  54.7  4.1   2:39.03    qemu-kvm
12730 root     20   0  7276512  2.566g   70496 R  26.5  16.6  54:20.94   virt-manager
 3225 root     20   0  1950632  215728   35300 S  25.2  1.3   14:52.82   gnome-shell
 1489 root     20   0  1074368  23600    11836 S  6.6   0.1   52:09.98   libvirtd
 1144 root     20   0  226540   51348    35704 S  6.3   0.3   4:19.12    Xorg
18540 qemu     20   0  1274932  467276   8020  R  6.0   2.9   23:47.89   qemu-kvm
18450 qemu     20   0  1336528  526252   8016  S  2.3   3.2   23:55.18   qemu-kvm
18919 qemu     20   0  1318728  510000   8020  S  1.0   3.1   24:02.42   qemu-kvm
19631 qemu     20   0  1315620  501828   8012  S  1.0   3.1   23:26.65   qemu-kvm
24773 qemu     20   0  1334652  538816   8016  S  1.0   3.3   23:54.71   qemu-kvm
 3572 root     20   0  950484   172500   42636 S  0.7   1.1   39:36.99   firefox
28791 root     20   0  123792   1876     1152  R  0.7   0.0   0:03.25    top
  339 root      0 -20  0        0        0     S  0.3   0.0   0:04.00    kworker/1:1H
  428 root     20   0  0        0        0     S  0.3   0.0   0:39.65    xfsaild/dm-1
  921 root     20   0  19112    1164     948   S  0.3   0.0   0:09.19    irqbalance
26424 root     20   0  0        0        0     S  0.3   0.0   0:00.13    kworker/u8:2
```

When considering exactly what your server is doing, the CPU lines are an important indicator. In there, you can monitor CPU performance, divided in different performance categories. In the following list, you can see these options summarized:

us: This refers to a workload in user space. Typically, this relates to processes that are started by end users and don't run with root priorities. If you see a high load in here, that means that your server is heavily used by applications.

sy: This refers to the work that is done in system space. These are important tasks in which the kernel of your operating system is involved as well. Load average in here should, in general, not be too high. You can see it elevated when particular jobs are executed, for example, a large compiling job. If the load here is high, it can indicate elevated hardware activity.

ni: This indicator relates to the amount of jobs started with an adjusted nice value.

id: Here you can see how busy the idle loop is. This special loop indicates the amount of time that your CPU is doing nothing. Therefore, a high percentage in the idle loop means a CPU that is not too busy.

wa: This is an important indicator. The wa parameter refers to the amount of time that your CPU is waiting for I/O. If the value that you see here is often above 30 percent, that could indicate a problem on the I/O-channel, which involves storage and network. See the sections "Monitoring Storage Performance" and "Understanding Network Performance" later in this chapter to find out what may be happening.

hi: The hi parameter relates to the time the CPU spends handling hardware interrupts. You will see some utilization here when a device is particularly busy (optical drives do stress this parameter from time to time), but normally you won't ever see it above a few percent.

si: This parameter relates to software interrupts. Typically, these are lower priority interrupts that are created by the kernel. You will probably never see a high utilization in this field.

st: The st parameter relates to an environment in which virtualization is used. In some virtual environments, a virtual machine can take ("steal," hence "st") CPU time from the host operating system. If this occurs, you will see some utilization in the st field. If the utilization here starts getting really high, you should consider off-loading virtual machines from your server.

Memory Monitoring with top

The second set of information to get from top concerns the lines about memory and swap usage. The memory lines contain five parameters (of which the last is in the swap line). These are

total: This is the total amount of physical memory installed in your server.

used: The amount of memory that is currently in use by something. This includes memory in buffers and cache.

free: The amount of memory that is not currently in use. On a typical server that is operational for more than a couple of hours, you will always see that this value is rather low (see, for example, Listing 15-2, in which it has dropped down to next to nothing).

buffers: This parameter relates to the write cache that your server uses. It also contains file system tables and other unstructured data that the server has to have in memory. All data that a server has to write to disk is written to the write cache first. From there, the disk controller takes care of this data when it has time to write it. The advantage of using write cache is that from the perspective of the end user, the data is written, so the application the user is using does not have to wait anymore. This buffer cache, however, is memory that is used for nonessential purposes, and when an application requires more memory and can't allocate that from the pool of free memory, the write cache can be written to disk (flushed), so that memory that was used by the write cache is available for other purposes. Essentially, write cache is a good thing that makes your server performing faster.

cached: When a user requests a file from the server, the file normally has to be read from the hard disk. Because a hard disk is typically about 1,000 times slower than RAM, this process causes major delays. For that reason, every time, after fetching a file from the server hard drive, the file is stored in cache. This is a read cache and has one purpose only: to speed up reads. When memory that is currently allocated to the read cache is needed for other purposes, the read cache can be freed immediately, so that more memory can be added to the pool of available ("free") memory. Your server will typically see a high amount of cached memory. Especially if your server is used for reads mostly, this is considered good, as it will speed up your server. In case your server is used for reads mostly, and this parameter falls below 30 percent of total available memory, you will most likely get a slowed-down performance. Add more RAM if this happens. Be aware that there are exceptions, though. Servers running large databases typically don't have a very high read cache, as the data are stored in memory that is claimed by the database, and they are not managed by the Linux kernel.

Understanding swap

When considering memory usage, you should also consider the amount of swap that is being allocated. Swap is RAM that is emulated on disk. That may sound like a bad idea that really slows down server performance, but it doesn't have to be.

To understand swap usage, you should understand the different kinds of memory that are in use on a Linux server. Linux distinguishes between active and inactive memory, and between file and anon memory. You can get these parameters from the /proc/meminfo file (see Listing 15-3).

Listing 15-3. Getting Detailed Memory Information from /proc/meminfo

```
[root@lab ~]# cat /proc/meminfo
MemTotal:       16196548 kB
MemFree:         1730808 kB
MemAvailable:    5248720 kB
Buffers:            3956 kB
Cached:          4045672 kB
SwapCached:            0 kB
Active:         10900288 kB
Inactive:        3019436 kB
Active(anon):    9725132 kB
Inactive(anon):   627268 kB
Active(file):    1175156 kB
Inactive(file):  2392168 kB
Unevictable:       25100 kB
Mlocked:           25100 kB
SwapTotal:       4194300 kB
SwapFree:        4194300 kB
```

Anon (anonymous) *memory* refers to memory that is allocated by programs. *File memory* refers to memory that is used as cache or buffers. On any Linux system, these two kinds of memory can be flagged as active or inactive. Inactive file memory typically exists on a server that doesn't need the RAM for anything else. If memory pressure arises, the kernel can clear this memory immediately to make more RAM available. Inactive anon memory is memory that has to be allocated. However, as it hasn't been used actively, it can be moved to a slower kind of memory. That exactly is what swap is used for.

If in swap there's only inactive anon memory, swap helps optimizing the memory performance of a system. By moving out these inactive memory pages, more memory becomes available for caching, which is good for the overall performance of a server. Hence, if a Linux server shows some activity in swap, that is not a bad sign at all.

EXERCISE 15-1. MONITORING BUFFER AND CACHE MEMORY

In this exercise, you'll monitor how buffer and cache memory are used. To start with a clean image, you'll first restart your server, so that no old data is in buffers or cache. Next, you'll run some commands that will cause the buffer and cache memory to be filled. At the end, you'll clear the total amount of buffer and cache memory by using /proc/sys/vm/drop_caches.

1. Reboot your server.

2. After rebooting, open two root console windows. In one window, start top, so that you'll have a real-time overview of what's happening. Note the current memory allocation. Buffers and cache should be low, and your server should have a relatively large amount of free memory available.

3. Run the following script to read data, which will fill your server cache.

```
cd /etc
for I in *
do
    cat $I
done
```

4. You should now see an increase in cache (probably not much, as the contents of the /etc directory typically isn't that high).

5. Run the following command to fill the buffer cache: ls -Rl / > /dev/null &.

6. You'll notice that the buffer cache has filled a bit as well.

7. Optionally, you can run some more commands that will fill buffers as well as cache, such as dd if=/dev/sda of=/dev/null & (which has a much greater impact than the previous commands).

8. Once finished, type free -m, to observe the current usage of buffers and cache.

9. Tell the kernel to drop all buffers and cache that it doesn't really need at this moment, by using echo 2 > /proc/sys/vm/drop_caches.

Process Monitoring with top

The lower part of top is reserved for information about the most active processes. In this part, you'll see a few parameters related to these processes. By default, the following parameters are shown:

PID: The Process ID of the process

USER: The user who started the process

PR: The priority of the process. The priority of any process is determined automatically, and the process with the highest priority is eligible to be serviced first from the queue of runnable processes. Some processes run with a real-time priority, which is indicated as RT. Processes with this priority can claim CPU cycles in real time, which means that they will always have highest priority.

NI: The nice value with which the process was started

VIRT: The amount of memory that was claimed by the process when it first started

RES: Stands for *resident memory*. This relates to the amount of memory that a process is really using. You will see that in some cases, this is considerably lower than the parameter mentioned in the VIRT column. This is because many process like to over-allocate. This means they claim more memory than they really need, just in case they'll need it at some point.

SHR: The amount of memory this process uses that is shared with another process

S: The status of a process

%CPU: Relates to the percentage of CPU time this process is using. You will normally see the process with the highest CPU utilization mentioned on top of this list.

%MEM: The percentage of memory that this process has claimed

TIME+: The total amount of time that this process has been using CPU cycles

COMMAND: The name of the command that relates to this process

Understanding Linux Memory Allocation

When analyzing Linux memory usage, you should know how Linux uses virtual and resident memory. Virtual memory on Linux is to be taken literally: it is a nonexisting amount of memory that the Linux kernel can be referred to. When looking at the contents of the /proc/meminfo file, you can see that the amount of virtual memory is set to approximately 35TB of RAM:

```
VmallocTotal:     34359738367 kB
VmallocUsed:            486380 kB
VmallocChunk:     34359160008 kB
```

Virtual memory is used by the Linux kernel to allow programs to make a memory reservation. After making this reservation, no other application can reserve the same memory. Making the reservation is a matter of setting pointers and nothing else. It doesn't mean that the memory reservation is also actually going to be used. When a program has to use the memory it has reserved, it is going to issue a malloc system call, which means that the memory is actually going to be allocated. At that moment, we're talking about resident memory.

That Linux uses virtual memory when reserving memory may cause trouble later on. A program that has reserved memory—even if it is virtual memory—would expect that it can also use that memory. But that is not the case, as virtual memory, in general, is much more than the amount of physical RAM + Swap that is available. This is known as memory over-commit or over-allocation, and in some cases, memory over-allocation can cause trouble. If a process has reserved virtual memory that cannot be mapped to physical memory, you may encounter an OOM (out of memory) situation. If that happens, processes will get killed. In the "Optimizing Performance" section, later in this chapter, you'll learn about some parameters that tell you how to prevent such situations.

Analyzing CPU Performance

The top utility offers a good starting point for performance tuning. However, if you really need to dig deep into a performance problem, top does not offer sufficient information, and more advanced tools will be required. In this section, you'll learn what you can do to find out more about CPU performance-related problems.

Most people tend to start analyzing a performance problem at the CPU, since they think CPU performance is the most important on a server. In most situations, this is not true. Assuming that you have a recent CPU, and not an old 486-based CPU, you will not often see a performance problem that really is related to the CPU. In most cases, a problem that appears to be CPU-related is likely caused by something else. For example, your CPU may just be waiting for data to be written to disk. Before getting into details, let's have a look at a brief exercise that teaches how CPU performance can be monitored.

EXERCISE 15-2. ANALYZING CPU PERFORMANCE

In this exercise, you'll run two different commands that will both analyze CPU performance. You'll notice a difference in the behavior of both commands.

1. Log in as root and open two terminal windows. In one of these windows, start top.

2. In the second window, run the command dd if=/dev/urandom of=/dev/null. You will see the usage percentage in the us column going up, as well as the usage in the sy column. Press 1 if you have a multi-core system. You'll notice that one CPU core is completely occupied by this task.

3. Stop the dd job and write a small script in the home directory of user root that has the following content:

```
[root@hnl ~]# cat wait
#!/bin/bash

COUNTER=0

while true
do
        dd if=/dev/urandom of=/root/file.$COUNTER bs=1M count=1
        COUNTER=$(( COUNTER + 1 ))
                [ COUNTER = 1000 ] && exit
done
```

4. Run the script. You'll notice that first, the sy parameter in top goes up, and after a while, the wa parameter goes up as well. This is because the I/O channel gets too busy, and the CPU has to wait for data to be committed to I/O. Based on the hardware you're using, you might not see immediate results. If that is the case, start the script a second time.

5. Make sure that both the script and the dd command have stopped, and close the root shells.

Understanding CPU Performance

To monitor what is happening on your CPU, you should know how the Linux kernel works with the CPU. A key component is the run queue. Before being served by the CPU, every process enters the run queue. There's a run queue for every CPU core in the system. Once a process is in the run queue, it can be runnable or blocked. A runnable process is a process that is competing for CPU time; a blocked process is just waiting.

The Linux scheduler decides which runnable process to run next, based on the current priority of the process. A blocked process doesn't compete for CPU time. The load average line in top gives a summary of the workload that results from all runnable and blocked processes combined. If you want to know how many of the processes are currently in either runnable or blocked state, use vmstat. The columns r and b show the amount of runnable and blocked processes. In Listing 15-4, you can see what this looks like on a system in which vmstat has polled the system five times, with a two-second interval.

Listing 15-4. Use vmstat to See How Many Processes Are in Runnable or Blocked State

```
[root@lab ~]# vmstat 2 5
procs -----------memory----------- --swap-- ----io---- --system-- ------cpu-----
 r  b   swpd   free   buff cache    si  so  bi  bo   in   cs  us sy id wa st
 0  0      0 1412260   3956 3571532   0   0  39  62    0   71   3  1 97 0  0
 0  0      0 1412252   3956 3571564   0   0   0   0 1217 3478   2  1 97 0  0
 0  0      0 1412376   3956 3571564   0   0   0   0 1183 3448   2  1 97 0  0
 0  0      0 1412220   3956 3571564   0   0   0   0 1189 3388   2  1 97 0  0
 0  0      0 1412252   3956 3571564   0   0   0   0 1217 3425   2  1 97 0  0
```

Context Switches and Interrupts

A modern Linux system is always a multitasking system. This is true for every processor architecture that can be used, because the Linux kernel constantly switches between different process. In order to perform this switch, the CPU needs to save all the context information for the old process and retrieve the context information for the new process. The performance price of these context switches, therefore, is heavy.

In an ideal world, you have to make sure that the number of context switches is limited as much as possible. You may do this by using a multi-core CPU architecture or a server with multiple CPUs, or a combination of both, but if you do, you have to make sure that processes are locked to a dedicated CPU core, to prevent context switches.

Processes that are serviced by the kernel scheduler, however, are not the only cause of context switching. Another important reason for a context switch to occur is hardware interrupts. This is a piece of hardware demanding processor time. To see what it has been doing, you can look at the contents of the /proc/interrupts file (see Listing 15-5).

Listing 15-5. The /proc/interrupts File Shows You Exactly How Many of Each Interrupt Has Been Handled

```
[root@lab proc]# cat interrupts
            CPU0      CPU1      CPU2      CPU3
   0:         54         0         0         0  IR-IO-APIC-edge      timer
   8:          0         0         0         1  IR-IO-APIC-edge      rtc0
   9:          0         0         0         0  IR-IO-APIC-fasteoi   acpi
  23:          0         0        36         1  IR-IO-APIC-fasteoi   ehci_hcd:usb1
  56:          0         0         0         0  DMAR_MSI-edge        dmar0
  57:          0         0         0         0  DMAR_MSI-edge        dmar1
  58:      68468    113385     59982     38591  IR-PCI-MSI-edge      xhci_hcd
  59:         17   9185792        29         6  IR-PCI-MSI-edge      eno1
  60:     660908    640712    274180    280446  IR-PCI-MSI-edge      ahci
  61:     379094    149796    827403    152584  IR-PCI-MSI-edge      i915
```

```
62:         13           0           0           0  IR-PCI-MSI-edge      mei_me
63:        263           1           6           1  IR-PCI-MSI-edge      snd_hda_intel
64:       1770         506         106         516  IR-PCI-MSI-edge      snd_hda_intel
NMI:       967         983         762         745  Non-maskable interrupts
LOC:  32241233    32493830    20152850    20140483  Local timer interrupts
SPU:         0           0           0           0  Spurious interrupts
PMI:       967         983         762         745  Performance monitoring interrupts
IWI:    122505      122449      110316      112272  IRQ work interrupts
RTR:         0           0           0           0  APIC ICR read retries
RES:   2486212     2351025     1841935     1821599  Rescheduling interrupts
CAL:    483791      496810      318516      290537  Function call interrupts
TLB:    231573      234010      173163      171368  TLB shootdowns
TRM:         0           0           0           0  Thermal event interrupts
THR:         0           0           0           0  Threshold APIC interrupts
MCE:         0           0           0           0  Machine check exceptions
MCP:       512         512         512         512  Machine check polls
```

As mentioned, in a multi-core environment, context switches can cause a performance overhead. You can see if these occur often by using the top utility. It can provide information about the CPU that was last used by any process, but you have to switch this on. To do that, from the top utility, first press the f command and type j. (on some distributions, you'll have to scroll instead, to select the appropriate option). This will switch the option last used CPU (SMP) on for an SMP environment. In Listing 15-6, you can see the interface from which you can do this. Note that to make this setting permanent, you can use the W command from top. This causes all modifications to the top program to be written to the ~/.toprc file, so that they can be loaded again at restart of top.

Listing 15-6. After Pressing the F Key, You Can Switch Different Options On or Off in top

```
Fields Management for window 1:Def, whose current sort field is %CPU
   Navigate with Up/Dn, Right selects for move then <Enter> or Left commits,
    'd' or <Space> toggles display, 's' sets sort. Use 'q' or <Esc> to end!


* PID      = Process Id            TIME    = CPU Time
* USER     = Effective User Name    SWAP    = Swapped Size (KiB)
* PR       = Priority               CODE    = Code Size (KiB)
* NI       = Nice Value             DATA    = Data+Stack (KiB)
* VIRT     = Virtual Image (KiB)    nMaj    = Major Page Faults
* RES      = Resident Size (KiB)    nMin    = Minor Page Faults
* SHR      = Shared Memory (KiB)    nDRT    = Dirty Pages Count
* S        = Process Status         WCHAN   = Sleeping in Function
* %CPU     = CPU Usage              Flags   = Task Flags <sched.h>
* %MEM     = Memory Usage (RES)     CGROUPS = Control Groups
* TIME+    = CPU Time, hundredths   SUPGIDS = Supp Groups IDs
* COMMAND  = Command Name/Line      SUPGRPS = Supp Groups Names
  PPID     = Parent Process pid     TGID    = Thread Group Id
  UID      = Effective User Id      ENVIRON = Environment vars
  RUID     = Real User Id           vMj     = Major Faults delta
  RUSER    = Real User Name         vMn     = Minor Faults delta
  SUID     = Saved User Id          USED    = Res+Swap Size (KiB)
  SUSER    = Saved User Name        nsIPC   = IPC namespace Inode
  GID      = Group Id               nsMNT   = MNT namespace Inode
  GROUP    = Group Name             nsNET   = NET namespace Inode
```

```
PGRP     = Process Group Id      nsPID   = PID namespace Inode
TTY      = Controlling Tty       nsUSER  = USER namespace Inode
TPGID    = Tty Process Grp Id    nsUTS   = UTS namespace Inode
SID      = Session Id
nTH      = Number of Threads
P        = Last Used Cpu (SMP)
```

After switching the last used CPU option on, you will see the column P in top that displays the number of the CPU that was last used by a process.

Using vmstat

To monitor CPU utilization, top offers a very good starting point. If that doesn't offer you enough, you may prefer the vmstat utility. With vmstat, you can get a nice, detailed view of what is happening on your server. Of special interest is the CPU section, which contains the five most important parameters on CPU usage:

cs: The amount of context switches

us: The percentage of time the CPU has spent in user space

sy: The percentage of time the CPU has spent in system space

id: The percentage of CPU utilization in the idle loop

wa: The percentage of utilization the CPU was waiting for I/O

When working with vmstat, you should know that there are two ways to use it. Probably the most useful way to run it is in the so-called sample mode. In this mode, a sample is taken every n seconds. Specify the amount of seconds for the sample as an option when starting vmstat. Running performance monitoring utilities in this way is always good, because it will show your progress over a given amount of time. You may find it useful, as well, to run vmstat for a given amount of time only.

Another useful way to run vmstat is with the option -s. In this mode, vmstat shows you the statistics since the system has booted. As you can see in Listing 15-7, apart from the CPU-related options, vmstat shows information about processors, memory, swap, io, and system as well. These options are covered later in this chapter.

Listing 15-7. Using vmstat -s

```
[root@lab ~]# vmstat -s
    16196548 K total memory
    14783440 K used memory
    11201308 K active memory
     3031324 K inactive memory
     1413108 K free memory
        3956 K buffer memory
     3571580 K swap cache
     4194300 K total swap
           0 K used swap
     4194300 K free swap
     1562406 non-nice user cpu ticks
        1411 nice user cpu ticks
      294539 system cpu ticks
    57856573 idle cpu ticks
       22608 IO-wait cpu ticks
          12 IRQ cpu ticks
```

```
      5622 softirq cpu ticks
         0 stolen cpu ticks
  23019937 pages paged in
  37008693 pages paged out
       842 pages swapped in
      3393 pages swapped out
 129706133 interrupts
 344528651 CPU context switches
1408204254 boot time
    132661 forks
```

Analyzing Memory Usage

Memory is probably the most important component of your server, from a performance perspective. The CPU can only work smoothly if processes are ready in memory and can be offered from there. If this is not the case, the server has to get its data from the I/O channel, which is about 1,000 times slower to access than memory. From the processor's point of view, even system RAM is relatively slow. Therefore, modern server processors have large amounts of cache, which is even faster than memory.

You have read how to interpret basic memory statistics, as provided by top earlier in this chapter; therefore, I will not cover them again. In this section, you can read about some more advanced memory-related information.

Page Size

A basic concept in memory handling is the memory page size. On an x86_64 system, typically 4KB pages are used. This means that everything that happens, happens in chunks of 4KB. Nothing wrong with that, if you have a server handling large amounts of small files. If, however, your server handles huge files, it is highly inefficient if only these small 4KB pages are used. For that purpose, your server can use huge pages with a default size of 2MB per page. Later in this chapter, you'll learn how to configure huge pages.

A server can run out of memory. In that event, it uses swapping. Swap memory is emulated RAM on the server's hard drive. Because in swap the hard disk is involved, you should avoid it, if possible. Access times to a hard drive are about 1,000 times slower than access times to RAM. To monitor current swap use, you can use free -m, which will show you the amount of swap that is currently being used. See Listing 15-8 for an example.

Listing 15-8. free -m Provides Information About Swap Usage

```
[root@lab ~]# free   -m
                 total       used       free     shared    buffers     cached
Mem:             15816      14438       1378        475          3       3487
-/+buffers/cache:            10946       4870
Swap:             4095          0       4095
```

As you can see in the preceding listing, on the server where this sample comes from, nothing is wrong; there is no swap usage at all, and that is good.

If, on the other hand, you see that your server is swapping, the next thing you must know is how actively it is swapping. To provide information about this, the vmstat utility provides useful information. This utility provides swap information in the si (swap in) and so (swap out) columns.

If swap space is used, you should also have a look at the /proc/meminfo file, to relate the use of swap to the amount of inactive anon memory pages. If the amount of swap that is used is larger than the amount of anon memory pages that you observe in /proc/meminfo, it means that active memory is being swapped. That is bad news for performance, and if that happens, you must install more RAM. If the amount of swap that is in use is smaller than the amount of inactive anon memory pages in /proc/meminfo, there's no problem, and you're good. If, however, you have more memory in swap than the amount of inactive anonymous pages, you're probably in trouble, because active memory is being swapped. That means that there's too much I/O traffic, which will slow down your system.

Kernel Memory

When analyzing memory usage, you should also take into account the memory that is used by the kernel itself. This is called slab memory. You can see in the /proc/meminfo file the amount of slab currently in use. Normally, the amount of kernel memory that is in use is relatively small. To get more information about it, you can use the slabtop utility.

This utility provides information about the different parts (referred to as objects) of the kernel and what exactly they are doing. For normal performance analysis purposes, the SIZE and NAME columns are the most interesting ones. The other columns are of interest mainly to programmers and kernel developers and, therefore, are not described in this chapter. In Listing 15-9, you can see an example of information provided by slabtop.

Listing 15-9. The slabtop Utility Provides Information About Kernel Memory Usage

```
Active / Total Objects (% used)    : 1859018 / 2294038 (81.0%)
Active / Total Slabs (% used)      : 56547 / 56547 (100.0%)
Active / Total Caches (% used)     : 75 / 109 (68.8%)
Active / Total Size (% used)       : 275964.30K / 327113.79K (84.4%)
Minimum / Average / Maximum Object : 0.01K / 0.14K / 15.69K

 OBJS    ACTIVE  USE   OBJ    SIZE   SLABS      OBJ/SLAB CACHE SIZE NAME
1202526  786196  65%   0.10K  30834   39        123336K buffer_head
 166912  166697  99%   0.03K   1304  128        5216K kmalloc-32
 134232  134106  99%   0.19K   6392   21        25568K dentry
 122196  121732  99%   0.08K   2396   51        9584K selinux_inode_security
 115940  115940 100%   0.02K    682  170        2728K fsnotify_event_holder
  99456   98536  99%   0.06K   1554   64        6216K kmalloc-64
  79360   79360 100%   0.01K    155  512        620K kmalloc-8
  70296   70296 100%   0.64K   2929   24        46864K proc_inode_cache
  64512   63218  97%   0.02K    252  256        1008K kmalloc-16
  38248   26376  68%   0.57K   1366   28        21856K radix_tree_node
  29232   29232 100%   1.00K   1827   16        29232K xfs_inode
  28332   28332 100%   0.11K    787   36        3148K sysfs_dir_cache
  28242   27919  98%   0.21K   1569   18        6276K vm_area_struct
  18117   17926  98%   0.58K    671   27        10736K inode_cache
  14992   14150  94%   0.25K    937   16        3748K kmalloc-256
  10752   10752 100%   0.06K    168   64        672K anon_vma
   9376    8206  87%   0.12K    293   32        1172K kmalloc-128
   8058    8058 100%   0.04K     79  102        316K Acpi-Namespace
   7308    7027  96%   0.09K    174   42        696K kmalloc-96
   4788    4788 100%   0.38K    228   21        1824K blkdev_requests
   4704    4704 100%   0.07K     84   56        336K Acpi-ParseExt
```

The most interesting information a system administrator would receive from slabtop is the amount of memory a particular slab (part of the kernel) is using. If, for instance, you've recently performed some tasks on the file system, you may find that the inode_cache is relatively high. If that is just for a short period of time, it's no problem. The Linux kernel wakes up routines when they are needed, while they can be closed fast when they're no longer needed. If, however, you see that one part of the routine that is started continuously uses high amounts of memory, that might be an indication that you have some optimization to do.

EXERCISE 15-3. ANALYZING KERNEL MEMORY

In this exercise, you'll cause a little bit of stress on your server, and you're going to use slabtop to find out which parts of the kernel are getting busy. As the Linux kernel is sophisticated and uses its resources as efficiently as possible, you won't see huge changes, but some subtle changes can be detected anyway.

1. Open two terminal windows in which you are root.

2. On one terminal window, type slabtop and have a look at what the different slabs are currently doing.

3. In the other terminal window, use ls -lR /. You should see the dentry cache increasing. This is the part of memory where the kernel caches directory entries.

4. Once the ls -lR command has finished, type dd if=/dev/sda of=/dev/null, to create some read activity. You'll see the buffer_head parameter increasing. These are the file system buffers that are used to cache information the dd command uses.

Using ps for Analyzing Memory

When tuning memory utilization, there is one more utility that you should never forget, and that is ps. The advantage of ps, is that it gives memory usage information on all processes on your server and it is easy to grep on its result to find information about particular processes. To monitor memory usage, the ps aux command is very useful. It provides memory information in the VSZ and the RSS columns. The VSZ (Virtual Size) parameter provides information about the virtual memory that is used. This relates to the total amount of memory that is claimed by a process. The RSS (Resident Size) parameter refers to the amount of memory that is really in use. Listing 15-10 gives an example of some lines of ps aux output.

Listing 15-10. ps aux Gives Memory Usage Information for Particular Processes

```
USER      PID %CPU %MEM    VSZ    RSS TTY     STAT START  TIME COMMAND
root        1  0.0  0.0  53500   7664 ?        Ss  Aug16  0:07 /usr/lib/systemd/systemd
                                                                --switched-root --system
                                                                --deserialize 23
root        2  0.0  0.0      0      0 ?     Z   S   Aug16  0:00 [kthreadd]
...
qemu    31274  2.0  2.5 1286920 407748 ?       Sl  11:16  4:56 /usr/libexec/qemu-kvm -name vm
root    31276  0.0  0.0      0      0 ?        S   11:16  0:00 [vhost-31274]
root    31280  0.0  0.0      0      0 ?        S   11:16  0:00 [kvm-pit/31274]
qemu    31301  2.0  2.5 1287656 412868 ?       Sl  11:16  4:58 /usr/libexec/qemu-kvm -name vm
root    31303  0.0  0.0      0      0 ?        S   11:16  0:00 [vhost-31301]
root    31307  0.0  0.0      0      0 ?        S   11:16  0:00 [kvm-pit/31301]
```

```
root     31314  0.0  0.0        0      0 ?        S    11:16   0:00 [kworker/u8:2]
qemu     31322  2.1  2.5  1284036 413216 ?        Sl   11:16   5:01 /usr/libexec/qemu-kvm -name vm
root     31324  0.0  0.0        0      0 ?        S    11:16   0:00 [vhost-31322]
root     31328  0.0  0.0        0      0 ?        S    11:16   0:00 [kvm-pit/31322]
qemu     31347  2.1  2.5  1284528 408636 ?        Sl   11:16   5:01 /usr/libexec/qemu-kvm -name vm
root     31350  0.0  0.0        0      0 ?        S    11:16   0:00 [vhost-31347]
root     31354  0.0  0.0        0      0 ?        S    11:16   0:00 [kvm-pit/31347]
```

When looking at the output of ps aux, you may notice that there are two different kinds of processes. The name of some are between square brackets; the names of others are not. If the name of a process is between square brackets, the process is part of the kernel. All other processes are "normal" processes.

If you need more information about a process and what exactly it is doing, there are two ways to get that information. First, you can check the /proc directory for the particular process, for example, /proc/5658 gives information for the process with PID 5658. In this directory, you'll find the maps file that gives some more insight into how memory is mapped for this process. As you can see in Listing 15-11, this information is rather detailed. It includes the exact memory addresses this process is using and even tells you about subroutines and libraries that are related to this process.

Listing 15-11. The /proc/PID/maps File Gives Detailed Information on Memory Utilization of Particular Processes

```
00400000-004dd000 r-xp 00000000 fd:01 134326347          /usr/bin/bash
006dc000-006dd000 r--p 000dc000 fd:01 134326347          /usr/bin/bash
006dd000-006e6000 rw-p 000dd000 fd:01 134326347          /usr/bin/bash
006e6000-006ec000 rw-p 00000000 00:00 0
014d0000-015d6000 rw-p 00000000 00:00 0                  [heap]
7fcae4779000-7fcaeaca0000 r--p 00000000 fd:01 201334187  /usr/lib/locale/locale-
                                                         archive
7fcaeaca0000-7fcaeacab000 r-xp 00000000 fd:01 201334158  /usr/lib64/libnss_
                                                         files-2.17.so
7fcaeacab000-7fcaeaeaa000 ---p 0000b000 fd:01 201334158  /usr/lib64/libnss_
                                                         files-2.17.so
7fcaeaeaa000-7fcaeaeab000 r--p 0000a000 fd:01 201334158  /usr/lib64/libnss_
                                                         files-2.17.so
7fcaeaeab000-7fcaeaeac000 rw-p 0000b000 fd:01 201334158  /usr/lib64/libnss_
                                                         files-2.17.so
7fcaeaeac000-7fcaeb062000 r-xp 00000000 fd:01 201334140  /usr/lib64/libc-2.17.so
7fcaeb062000-7fcaeb262000 ---p 001b6000 fd:01 201334140  /usr/lib64/libc-2.17.so
7fcaeb262000-7fcaeb266000 r--p 001b6000 fd:01 201334140  /usr/lib64/libc-2.17.so
7fcaeb266000-7fcaeb268000 rw-p 001ba000 fd:01 201334140  /usr/lib64/libc-2.17.so
7fcaeb268000-7fcaeb26d000 rw-p 00000000 00:00 0
```

The pmap command also shows what a process is doing. It gets its information from the /proc/PID/maps file. One of the advantages of the pmap command is that it gives detailed information about the order in which a process does its work. You can see calls to external libraries, as well as additional memory allocation (malloc) requests that the program is doing, as reflected in the lines that have [anon] at the end.

Monitoring Storage Performance

One of the hardest things to do properly is the monitoring of storage utilization. The reason is that the storage channel typically is at the end of the chain. Other elements in your server can have a positive as well as a negative influence on storage performance. For example, if your server is low on memory, that will be reflected in storage performance, because if you don't have enough memory, there can't be a lot of cache and buffers, and thus, your server has more work to do on the storage channel.

Likewise, a slow CPU can have a negative impact on storage performance, because the queue of runnable processes can't be cleared fast enough. Therefore, before jumping to the conclusion that you have bad performance on the storage channel, you should really try to take other factors into consideration as well.

It is generally hard to optimize storage performance on a server. The best behavior really depends on the kind of workload your server typically has. For instance, a server that has a lot of reads has other needs than a server that does mainly write. A server that is doing writes most of the time can benefit from a storage channel with many disks, because more controllers can work on clearing the write buffer cache from memory. If, however, your server is mainly reading data, the effect of having many disks is just the opposite. Because of the large amount of disks, seek times will increase, and therefore, performance will be negatively affected.

Following are some indicators of storage performance problems. Have a look and see if one of these is the case with your server, and if it is, go and analyze what is happening.

- Memory buffers and cache is heavily used while CPU utilization is low.

- There is high disk or controller utilization.

- Long network response times are occurring while network utilization is low.

- The wa parameter in top shows very high.

Understanding Disk Working

Before trying to understand storage performance, there is another factor that you should consider, and that is the way that storage activity typically takes place. First, a storage device, in general, handles large sequential transfers better than small random transfers. This is because, in memory, you can configure read ahead and write ahead, which means that the storage controller already goes to the next block it probably has to go to. If your server handles small files mostly, read ahead buffers will have no effect at all. On the contrary, they will only slow it down.

In addition, you should be aware that in modern environments, three different types of storage devices are used. If storage is handled by a Storage Area Network (SAN), it's often not possible to do much about storage optimization. If local storage is used, it makes a big difference if that is SSD-based storage or storage that uses rotating platters.

From the tools perspective, there are three tools that really count when doing disk performance analysis. The first tool to start your disk performance analysis is vmstat. This tool has a couple of options that help you see what is happening on a particular disk device, such as -d, which gives you statistics for individual disks, or -p, which gives partition performance statistics. As you have already seen, you can use vmstat with an interval parameter and a count parameter as well. In Listing 15-12, you can see the result of the command vmstat -d, which gives detailed information on storage utilization for all disk devices on your server.

Listing 15-12. To Understand Storage Usage, Start with vmstat

```
[root@lab ~]# vmstat -d
disk- ------------reads------------ ------------writes----------- -----IO------
        total merged  sectors     ms   total merged  sectors      ms   cur   sec
sda   932899 1821123 46129712 596065 938744 2512536 74210979 3953625    0   731
dm-0    1882       0   15056     537   3397       0    27160   86223     0     0
dm-1   17287       0 1226434   17917  62316       0 17270450 2186073     0    93
sdb      216     116    1686     182      0       0        0       0     0     0
dm-2   51387       0 2378598   16168  58063       0  3224216  130009     0    35
dm-3   51441       0 2402329   25443  55309       0  3250147  140122     0    40
```

In the output of this command, you can see detailed statistics about the reads and writes that have occurred on a disk. The following parameters are displayed when using vmstat -d:

> reads: total: The total number of reads that was requested

> reads: merged: The total number of adjacent locations that have been merged to improve performance. This is the result of the read ahead parameter. High numbers are good.
> A high number here means that within the same read request, a couple of adjacent blocks have been read as well.

> reads: sectors: The total number of disk sectors that has been read

> reads: ms: Total time spent reading from disk

> writes: total: The total number of writes

> writes: merged: The total number of writes to adjacent sectors

> writes: sectors: The total number of sectors that has been written

> writes: ms: The total time in milliseconds your system has spent writing data

> IO: cur: The total number of I/O requests currently in progress

> IO: sec: The total amount of time spent waiting for I/O to complete

Another way of monitoring disk performance with vmstat is by running it in sample mode. For example, the command vmstat 2 10 will run ten samples with a two-second interval. Listing 15-13 shows the result of this command.

Listing 15-13. In Sample Mode, You Can Get a Real-Time Impression of Disk Utilization

```
[root@lab ~]# vmstat 2 10
procs -----------memory---------- ---swap-- -----io---- -system-- ------cpu-----
 r  b   swpd    free   buff  cache   si   so   bi   bo   in   cs us sy id wa st
 0  0      0 1319012   3956 3574176    0    0   36   58   26    8  3  1 97  0  0
 0  0      0 1318532   3956 3574176    0    0    0    2 1212 3476  2  1 97  0  0
 0  0      0 1318540   3956 3574176    0    0    0    0 1189 3469  2  1 97  0  0
 0  0      0 1318788   3956 3574176    0    0    0    0 1250 3826  3  1 97  0  0
 0  0      0 1317852   3956 3574176    0    0    0    0 1245 3816  3  1 97  0  0
 0  0      0 1318044   3956 3574176    0    0    0    0 1208 3675  2  0 97  0  0
 1  0      0 1318044   3956 3574176    0    0    0    0 1193 3384  2  1 97  0  0
 0  0      0 1318044   3956 3574176    0    0    0    0 1212 3419  2  0 97  0  0
 0  0      0 1318044   3956 3574176    0    0    0    0 1229 3506  2  1 97  0  0
 3  0      0 1318028   3956 3574176    0    0    0    0 1227 3738  2  1 97  0  0
```

The columns that count in the preceding sample listing are the io: bi and io: bo columns, because they show the number of blocks that came in from the storage channel (bi) and the number of blocks that were written to the storage channel (bo).

Another tool to monitor performance on the storage channel, is iostat. It is not installed by default. Use zypper in sysstat, if you don't have it. It provides an overview per device of the amount of reads and writes. In the example in Listing 15-14, you can see the following device parameters being displayed:

tps: The number of transactions (read plus writes) that was handled per second

Blk_read/s: The number of blocks that was read per second

Blk_wrtn/s: The rate of disk blocks written per second

Blk_read: The total number of blocks that was read since startup

Blk_wrtn: The total number of blocks that was written since startup

Listing 15-14. The iostat Utility Provides Information About the Number of Blocks That Was Read and Written per Second

```
[root@hnl ~]# iostat
Linux 3.10.0-123.el7.x86_64 (lab.sandervanvugt.nl) 08/18/2014 _x86_64_ (4 CPU)

avg-cpu:  %user   %nice %system %iowait  %steal   %idle
           2.63    0.00    0.53    0.04    0.00   96.80

Device:            tps    kB_read/s    kB_wrtn/s    kB_read    kB_wrtn
sda              11.28       138.98       223.59   23064928   37106736
dm-0              0.03         0.05         0.08       7528      13580
dm-1              0.48         3.70        52.04     613289    8636472
sdb               0.00         0.01         0.00        843          0
dm-2              0.66         7.17         9.71    1189299    1612108
dm-3              0.64         7.24         9.79    1201164    1625073
dm-4              0.65         7.24         9.62    1201986    1596805
dm-5              0.65         7.38         9.62    1225284    1596418
dm-6              0.65         7.38         9.57    1224767    1588105
dm-7              0.65         7.31         9.53    1213582    1582201
```

If, when used in this way, iostat doesn't give you enough detail, you can use the -x option as well. This option gives much more information and, therefore, doesn't fit on the screen nicely, in most cases. In Listing 15-15, you can see an example.

Listing 15-15. `iostat -x` Gives You Much More Information About What Is Happening on the Storage Channel

```
[root@hnl ~]# iostat -x
Linux 3.10.0-123.el7.x86_64 (lab.sandervanvugt.nl) 08/18/2014 _x86_64_ (4 CPU)

avg-cpu:  %user   %nice %system %iowait  %steal   %idle
           2.63    0.00    0.53    0.04    0.00   96.80

Device:    rrqm/s   wrqm/s    r/s    w/s    rkB/s    wkB/s avgrq-sz avgqu-sz   await r_await w_await  svctm  %util
sda         10.97    15.13   5.62   5.66   138.94   223.52    64.29     0.03    2.43    0.64    4.21   0.39   0.44
dm-0         0.00     0.00   0.01   0.02     0.05     0.08     8.00     0.00   16.43    0.29   25.38   0.15   0.00
dm-1         0.00     0.00   0.10   0.38     3.69    52.02   231.77     0.01   27.61    1.04   34.96   1.18   0.06
sdb          0.00     0.00   0.00   0.00     0.01     0.00     7.81     0.00    0.84    0.84    0.00   0.82   0.00
```

When using the -x option, iostat gives you the following information:

> rrqm/s: Reads per second merged before issued to disk. Compare this to the information in the r/s column, to find out how much gain of efficiency you have because of read ahead.

> wrqm/s: Writes per second merged before issued to disk. Compare this to the w/s parameter, to see how much performance gain you have because of write ahead.

> r/s: The number of real reads per second

> w/s: The number of real reads per second

> rsec/s: The number of 512-byte sectors that was read per second

> wsec: The number of 51-byte sectors that was written per second

> avgrq-sz: The average size of disk requests in sectors. This parameter provides important information, as it shows you the size of the average files that were requested from disk. Based on the information that you receive from this parameter, you can optimize your file system.

> avgqu-sz: The average size of the disk request queue. This should be low at all times, because it gives the amount of pending disk requests. A high number here means that the performance of your storage channel cannot cope with the performance of your network.

> await: The average waiting time in milliseconds. This is the time the request has been waiting in the I/Oqueue plus the time that it actually took to service this request. This parameter should also be low in all cases.

> svctm: The average service time in milliseconds. This is the time it took before a request could be submitted to disk. If this parameter is below a couple of milliseconds (never more than ten), nothing is wrong with your server. If, however, this parameter is higher than ten, something is wrong, and you should consider doing some storage optimization.

> %util: The percentage of CPU utilization that was related to I/O

Finding Most Busy Processes with iotop

The most useful tool to analyze performance on a server is iotop. This tool also is not installed by default. Use zypper install iostat to install it. Running iotop is as easy as running top. Just start the utility, and you will see which process is causing you an I/O headache. The busiest process is listed on top, and you can also see details about the reads and writes that this process performs (see Listing 15-16).

Within iotop, you'll see two different kinds of processes. There are processes whose name is written between square brackets. These are kernel processes that aren't loaded as a separate binary but are a part of the kernel itself. All other processes listed are normal binaries.

Listing 15-16. Analyzing I/O Performance with iotop

```
[root@hnl ~]# iotop
Total DISK READ :        0.00 B/s | Total DISK WRITE :       0.00 B/s
Actual DISK READ:        0.00 B/s | Actual DISK WRITE:       0.00 B/s
  TID  PRIO  USER     DISK READ  DISK WRITE  SWAPIN      IO>    COMMAND
24960 be/4 root        0.00 B/s    0.00 B/s  0.00 %    0.01 % [kworker/1:2]
    1 be/4 root        0.00 B/s    0.00 B/s  0.00 %    0.00 % systemd --switche~ --deserialize 23
    2 be/4 root        0.00 B/s    0.00 B/s  0.00 %    0.00 % [kthreadd]
    3 be/4 root        0.00 B/s    0.00 B/s  0.00 %    0.00 % [ksoftirqd/0]
16388 be/4 qemu        0.00 B/s    0.00 B/s  0.00 %    0.00 % qemu-kvm -name vm~us=pci.0,addr=0x7
    5 be/0 root        0.00 B/s    0.00 B/s  0.00 %    0.00 % [kworker/0:0H]
16390 be/4 root        0.00 B/s    0.00 B/s  0.00 %    0.00 % [vhost-16388]
    7 rt/4 root        0.00 B/s    0.00 B/s  0.00 %    0.00 % [migration/0]
    8 be/4 root        0.00 B/s    0.00 B/s  0.00 %    0.00 % [rcu_bh]
    9 be/4 root        0.00 B/s    0.00 B/s  0.00 %    0.00 % [rcuob/0]
   10 be/4 root        0.00 B/s    0.00 B/s  0.00 %    0.00 % [rcuob/1]
   11 be/4 root        0.00 B/s    0.00 B/s  0.00 %    0.00 % [rcuob/2]
   12 be/4 root        0.00 B/s    0.00 B/s  0.00 %    0.00 % [rcuob/3]
```

Normally, you would start analyzing I/O performance because of an abnormality in the regular I/O load. For example, you may find a high wa indicator in top. In Exercise 15-4, you'll explore an I/O problem using this approach.

EXERCISE 15-4. EXPLORING I/O PERFORMANCE

In this exercise, you'll start a couple of I/O-intensive tasks. You'll first see abnormal behavior occurring in top, after which you'll use iotop to explore what is going on.

1. Open two root shells. In one shell, run top. In the second shell, start the command
    dd if=/dev/sda of=/dev/null. Run this command four times.

2. Observe what happens in top. You will notice that the wa parameter goes up. Press 1.
    If you're using a multi-core system, you should also see that the workload is evenly
    load-balanced between cores.

3. Start iotop. You will see that the four dd processes are listed on top, but you'll notice no
    other kernel processes that are significantly high in the list.

4. Use find / -exec xxd {} \; to create some read activity. In iotop, you should see the
    process itself listed above, but no further significant workload.

5. Create a script with the following content:

    ```
    #!/bin/bash

    while true
    do
    ```

```
cp -R / blah.tmp
rm -f /blah.tmp
sync
done
```

6. Run the script and observe the list of processes in iotop. You should occasionally see the flush process doing a lot of work. This is to synchronize the newly written files back from the buffer cache to disk.

Understanding Network Performance

On a typical server, network performance is as important as disk, memory, and CPU performance. After all, the data has to be delivered over the network to the end user. The problem, however, is that things aren't always as they seem. In some cases, a network problem can be caused by misconfiguration in server RAM. If, for example, packets get dropped on the network, the reason may very well be that your server just doesn't have enough buffers reserved for receiving packets, which may be because your server is low on memory. Again, everything is related, and it's your task to find the real cause of the troubles.

When considering network performance, you should always ask yourself what exactly you want to know. As you are aware, several layers of communication are used on the network. If you want to analyze a problem with your Samba server, that requires a completely different approach from analyzing a problem with dropped packets. A good network performance analysis always bottom-up. That means that you first have to check what is happening at the physical layer of the OSI model and then go up through the Ethernet, IP, TCP/UDP, and protocol layers.

When analyzing network performance, you should always start by checking the status of the network interface itself. Don't use ifconfig; it really is a deprecated utility. Use ip -s link instead (see Listing 15-17).

Listing 15-17. Use ip -s link to See What Is Happening on Your Network Board

```
[root@vm8 ~]# ip -s link
1: lo: <LOOPBACK,UP,LOWER_UP> mtu 65536 qdisc noqueue state UNKNOWN mode DEFAULT
    link/loopback 00:00:00:00:00:00 brd 00:00:00:00:00:00
    RX: bytes  packets  errors  dropped overrun mcast
    0          0        0       0       0       0
    TX: bytes  packets  errors  dropped carrier collsns
    0          0        0       0       0       0
2: eth0: <BROADCAST,MULTICAST,UP,LOWER_UP> mtu 1500 qdisc pfifo_fast state UP mode DEFAULT qlen 1000
    link/ether 52:54:00:30:3f:94 brd ff:ff:ff:ff:ff:ff
    RX: bytes  packets  errors  dropped overrun mcast
    2824323    53309    0       0       0       0
    TX: bytes  packets  errors  dropped carrier collsns
    8706       60       0       0       0       0
```

The most important information that is given by ip -s link is that about the number of packets that has been transmitted and received.

It's not especially the number of packets that is of interest here but, mainly, the number of erroneous packets. In fact, all of these parameters should be 0 at all times. If you see anything else, you should check what is going on. The following error indicators are displayed:

Errors: The amount of packets that had an error. Typically, this is due to bad cabling or a duplex mismatch. In modern networks, duplex settings are detected automatically, and most of the time, that goes quite well. So, if you see an increasing number here, it might be a good idea to replace the patch cable to your server.

Dropped: A packet gets dropped if on the server there has been no memory available to receive the packet. Dropped packets will also occur on a server that runs out of memory, so make sure that you have enough physical memory installed in your server.

Overruns: An overrun will occur if your NIC gets overwhelmed with packets. If you are using up-to-date hardware, overruns may indicate that someone is doing a denial of service attack on your server.

Carrier: The carrier is the electrical wave that is used for modulation of the signal. It really is the component that carries the data over your network. The error counter should be 0 at all times, and if it isn't, you probably have a physical problem with the network board, so it's time to replace the network board itself.

Collisions: You may see this error in Ethernet networks where a hub is used instead of a switch. Modern switches make packet collisions impossible, so you will probably never see this error anymore.

If you see a problem when using ip -s link, the next step should be to check your network board settings. Use ethtool to find out the settings you're currently using and make sure they match the settings of other network components, such as switches. (Note that this command does not work on many KVM virtual machines.) Listing 15-18 shows what you can expect.

Listing 15-18. Use ethtool to Check Settings of Your Network Board

```
[root@lab ~]# ethtool eno1
Settings for eno1:
        Supported ports: [ TP ]
        Supported link modes:   10baseT/Half 10baseT/Full
                                100baseT/Half 100baseT/Full
                                1000baseT/Full
        Supported pause frame use:   No
        Supports auto-negotiation:   Yes
        Advertised link modes:   10baseT/Half 10baseT/Full
                                 100baseT/Half 100baseT/Full
                                 1000baseT/Full
        Advertised pause frame use:  No
        Advertised auto-negotiation: Yes
        Speed: 1000Mb/s
        Duplex: Full
        Port: Twisted Pair
        PHYAD: 2
        Transceiver: internal
        Auto-negotiation: on
        MDI-X: off (auto)
        Supports Wake-on: pumbg
        Wake-on: g
        Current message level: 0x00000007 (7)
                               drv probe link
        Link detected: yes
```

Typically, there are just a few parameters from the ethtool output that are of interest, and these are the Speed and Duplex settings. They show you how your network board is talking to other nodes. If you see, for example, that your server is set to full duplex, whereas all other nodes in your network use half duplex, you've found your problem and know what you need to fix. Duplex setting misconfigurations are becoming more and more uncommon, however. A common error is that the supported link speed cannot be reached. If a network card supports gigabit, but only gives 100Mbit/s, that is often due to a hardware misconfiguration of one of the network devices that is involved.

Another good tool with which to monitor what is happening on the network is IPTraf-ng (start it by typing iptraf-ng). This useful tool, however, is not included in the default installation or SLES repositories. You can download the RPM from the Internet, after which it can be installed manually. This is a real-time monitoring tool that shows what is happening on the network from a text-user interface. After starting, it will show you a menu from which you can choose what you want to see. Different useful filtering options are offered. (See Figure 15-1.)

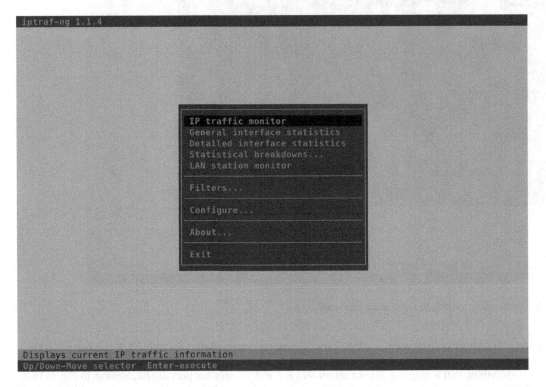

Figure 15-1. *IPTraf allows you to analyze network traffic from a menu*

Before starting IPTraf, use the configure option. From there, you can specify exactly what you want to see and how you want it to be displayed. For instance, a useful setting to change is the additional port range. By default, IPTraf shows activity on privileged TCP/UDP ports only. If you have a specific application that you want to monitor that doesn't use one of these privileged ports, select Additional ports from the configuration interface and specify additional ports that you want to monitor. (See Figure 15-2.)

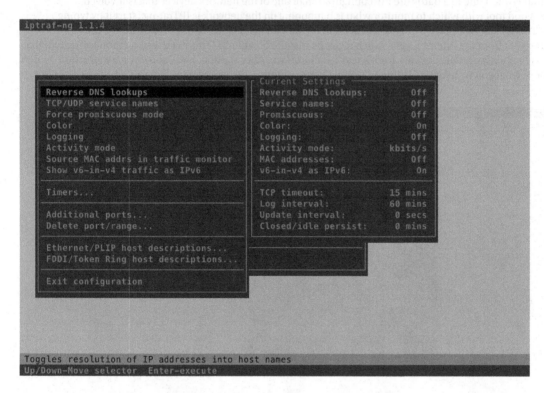

Figure 15-2. *Use the filter options to select what you want to see*

After telling IPTraf how to do its work, use the IP traffic monitor option to start the tool. Next, you can select the interface on which you want to listen, or just hit Enter to listen on all interfaces. This will start the IPTraf interface, which displays everything that is going on at your server and also exactly on what port it is happening. In Figure 15-3, you can see that the server that is monitored currently has two sessions enabled, and also you can see which are the IP addresses and ports involved in that session.

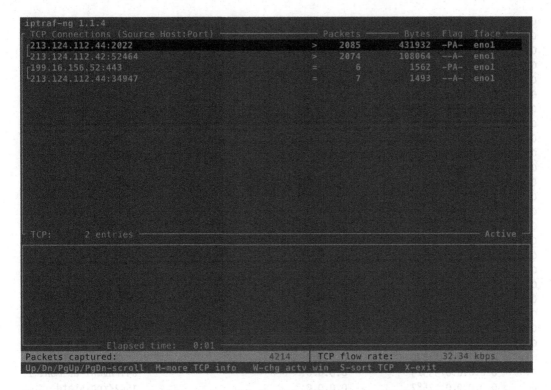

Figure 15-3. *IPtraf gives a quick overview of the kind of traffic sent on an interface*

If it's not so much the performance on the network board that you are interested in but more what is happening at the service level, netstat is a good basic network performance tool. It uses different parameters to show you what ports are open and on what ports your server sees activity. My personal favorite way of using netstat is by issuing the netstat -tulpn command. This gives an overview of all listening ports on the server and even tells you what other node is connected to a particular port. See Listing 15-19 for an overview.

Listing 15-19. With netstat, You Can See What Ports Are Listening on Your Server and Who Is Connected

```
[root@lab ~]# netstat -tulpn
Active Internet connections (only servers)
Proto Recv-Q Send-Q Local Address          Foreign Address        State          PID/Program name
tcp        0      0 127.0.0.1:5913         0.0.0.0:*              LISTEN         31322/qemu-kvm
tcp        0      0 127.0.0.1:25           0.0.0.0:*              LISTEN         1980/master
tcp        0      0 127.0.0.1:5914         0.0.0.0:*              LISTEN         31347/qemu-kvm
tcp        0      0 127.0.0.1:6010         0.0.0.0:*              LISTEN         28676/sshd: sander@
tcp        0      0 0.0.0.0:48702          0.0.0.0:*              LISTEN         1542/rpc.statd
tcp        0      0 0.0.0.0:2022           0.0.0.0:*              LISTEN         1509/sshd
tcp        0      0 127.0.0.1:5900         0.0.0.0:*              LISTEN         13719/qemu-kvm
tcp        0      0 127.0.0.1:5901         0.0.0.0:*              LISTEN         16388/qemu-kvm
tcp        0      0 127.0.0.1:5902         0.0.0.0:*              LISTEN         18513/qemu-kvm
tcp        0      0 127.0.0.1:5903         0.0.0.0:*              LISTEN         18540/qemu-kvm
tcp        0      0 0.0.0.0:111            0.0.0.0:*              LISTEN         1498/rpcbind
tcp        0      0 127.0.0.1:5904         0.0.0.0:*              LISTEN         18450/qemu-kvm
tcp        0      0 127.0.0.1:5905         0.0.0.0:*              LISTEN         18919/qemu-kvm
```

tcp	0	0 127.0.0.1:5906	0.0.0.0:*		LISTEN	19542/qemu-kvm
tcp	0	0 127.0.0.1:5907	0.0.0.0:*		LISTEN	19586/qemu-kvm
tcp	0	0 127.0.0.1:5908	0.0.0.0:*		LISTEN	19631/qemu-kvm
tcp	0	0 127.0.0.1:5909	0.0.0.0:*		LISTEN	24773/qemu-kvm
tcp	0	0 192.168.122.1:53	0.0.0.0:*		LISTEN	2939/dnsmasq
tcp	0	0 127.0.0.1:5910	0.0.0.0:*		LISTEN	31234/qemu-kvm
tcp	0	0 127.0.0.1:5911	0.0.0.0:*		LISTEN	31274/qemu-kvm
tcp	0	0 127.0.0.1:631	0.0.0.0:*		LISTEN	3228/cupsd
tcp	0	0 127.0.0.1:5912	0.0.0.0:*		LISTEN	31301/qemu-kvm
tcp6	0	0 ::1:25	:::*		LISTEN	1980/master
tcp6	0	0 ::1:6010	:::*		LISTEN	28676/sshd: sander@
tcp6	0	0 :::2022	:::*		LISTEN	1509/sshd
tcp6	0	0 :::111	:::*		LISTEN	1498/rpcbind
tcp6	0	0 :::58226	:::*		LISTEN	1542/rpc.statd
tcp6	0	0 :::21	:::*		LISTEN	25370/vsftpd
tcp6	0	0 fe80::fc54:ff:fe88:e:53	:::*		LISTEN	2939/dnsmasq
tcp6	0	0 ::1:631	:::*		LISTEN	3228/cupsd
udp	0	0 192.168.122.1:53	0.0.0.0:*			2939/dnsmasq
udp	0	0 0.0.0.0:67	0.0.0.0:*			2939/dnsmasq
udp	0	0 0.0.0.0:111	0.0.0.0:*			1498/rpcbind
udp	0	0 0.0.0.0:123	0.0.0.0:*			926/chronyd
udp	0	0 127.0.0.1:323	0.0.0.0:*			926/chronyd
udp	0	0 0.0.0.0:816	0.0.0.0:*			1498/rpcbind
udp	0	0 127.0.0.1:870	0.0.0.0:*			1542/rpc.statd
udp	0	0 0.0.0.0:35523	0.0.0.0:*			891/avahi-daemon: r
udp	0	0 0.0.0.0:52582	0.0.0.0:*			1542/rpc.statd
udp	0	0 0.0.0.0:5353	0.0.0.0:*			891/avahi-daemon: r

When using netstat, many options are available. Following, you'll find an overview of the most interesting ones:

- p: Shows the PID of the program that has opened a port
- c: Updates the display every second
- s: Shows statistics for IP, UDP, TCP, and ICMP
- t: Shows TCP sockets
- u: Shows UDP sockets
- w: Shows RAW sockets
- l: Shows listening ports
- n: Resolves addresses to names

There are many other tools to monitor the network as well, most of them fall beyond the scope of this chapter, because they are rather protocol- or service-specific and won't help you as much in finding performance problems on the network. There is, however, one very simple performance-testing method that I always use when analyzing a performance problem, which I will talk about at the end of this section.

In many cases, to judge network performance, you're only interested in knowing how fast data can be copied to and from your server. After all, that's the only parameter that you can change. To measure that, you can use a simple test. I like to create a big file (1GB, for example) and copy that over the network. To measure time, I use the time command, which gives a clear impression of how long it really took to copy the file. For example, time scp server:/bigfile /localdir will end with a summary of the total time it took to copy the file over. This is an excellent test, especially when you start optimizing performance, as it will show you immediately whether or not you've reached your goals.

Optimizing Performance

Now that you know what to look for in your server's performance, it's time to start optimizing. Optimizing performance is a complicated job, and you shouldn't have the impression that after reading the tips in this chapter you know everything about server performance optimization. Nevertheless, it's good to know about at least some of the basic approaches to make your server perform better.

You can look at performance optimization in two different ways. For some people, it involves just changing some parameters and seeing what happens. That is not the best approach. A much better approach is when you first start with performance monitoring. This will give you some clear ideas on what exactly is happening with performance on your server. Before optimizing anything, you should know what exactly to optimize. For example, if the network performs poorly, you should know if that is because of problems on the network, or just because you don't have enough memory allocated for the network. So make sure you know what to optimize. You've just read in the previous sections how you can do this.

Using /proc and sysctl

Once you know what to optimize, it comes down to doing it. In many situations, optimizing performance means writing a parameter to the /proc file system. This file system is created by the kernel when your server comes up and normally contains the settings that your kernel is working with. Under /proc/sys, you'll find many system parameters that can be changed. The easy way to do this is by just echoing the new value to the configuration file. For example, the /proc/sys/vm/swappiness file contains a value that indicates how willing your server is to swap. The range of this value is between 0 and 100, a low value means that your server will avoid a swap as long as possible; a high value means that your server is more willing to swap. The default value in this file is 60. If you think your server is too eager to swap, you could change it, using the following:

```
echo "30" > /proc/sys/vm/swappiness
```

This method works well, but there is a problem. As soon as the server restarts, you will lose this value. So the better solution is to store it in a configuration file and make sure that the configuration file is read when your server comes up again. A configuration file exists for this purpose, and the name of the file is /etc/sysctl.conf. When booting, your server starts the sysctl service that reads this configuration file and applies all settings in it. The sysctl file is always read when your server starts to apply the settings it contains.

In /etc/sysctl.conf, you refer to files that exist in the /proc/sys hierarchy. So the name of the file you are referring to is relative to this directory. Also, instead of using a slash as the separator between directory, subdirectories, and files, it is common to use a dot (even if the slash is accepted as well). That means that to apply the change to the swappiness parameter as explained above, you would include the following line in /etc/sysctl.conf:

```
vm.swappiness=30
```

This setting would be applied the next time that your server reboots. Instead of just writing it to the configuration file, you can apply it to the current sysctl settings as well. To do that, use the sysctl command. The following command can be used to apply this setting immediately:

```
sysctl -w vm.swappiness=30
```

Using sysctl -w is exactly the same as using the echo "30" > /proc/sys/vm/swappiness command—it does not also write the setting to the sysctl.conf file. The most practical way of applying these settings is to write them to /etc/sysctl.conf first and then activate them using sysctl -p /etc/sysctl.conf. Once activated in this way, you can also get an overview of all current sysctl settings, using sysctl -a. In Listing 15-20, you can see a part of the output of this command.

Listing 15-20. sysctl -a Shows All Current sysctl Settings

```
vm.min_free_kbytes = 67584
vm.min_slab_ratio = 5
vm.min_unmapped_ratio = 1
vm.mmap_min_addr = 4096
vm.nr_hugepages = 0
vm.nr_hugepages_mempolicy = 0
vm.nr_overcommit_hugepages = 0
vm.nr_pdflush_threads = 0
vm.numa_zonelist_order = default
vm.oom_dump_tasks = 1
vm.oom_kill_allocating_task = 0
vm.overcommit_kbytes = 0
vm.overcommit_memory = 0
vm.overcommit_ratio = 50
vm.page-cluster = 3
vm.panic_on_oom = 0
vm.percpu_pagelist_fraction = 0
vm.scan_unevictable_pages = 0
vm.stat_interval = 1
vm.swappiness = 60
vm.user_reserve_kbytes = 131072
vm.vfs_cache_pressure = 100
vm.zone_reclaim_mode = 0
```

The output of sysctl -a is overwhelming, as all the kernel tunables are shown, and there are hundreds of them. I recommend that you use it in combination with grep, to find the information you need. For example, sysctl -a | grep huge would only show you lines that have the text huge in their output.

Using a Simple Performance Optimization Test

Although sysctl and its configuration file sysctl.conf are very useful tools to change performance-related settings, you shouldn't use them immediately. Before writing a parameter to the system, make sure this really is the parameter you need. The big question, though, is how to know that for sure. There's only one answer to that: testing. Before starting any test, be aware that tests always have their limitations. The test proposed here is far from perfect, and you shouldn't use this test alone to draw definitive conclusions about the performance optimization of your server. Nevertheless, it gives a good impression especially of the write performance on your server.

The test consists of creating a 1GB file, using the following:

```
dd if=/dev/zero of=/root/1GBfile bs=1M count=1024
```

By copying this file around and measuring the time it takes to copy it, you can get a decent idea of the effect of some of the parameters. Many tasks you perform on your Linux server are I/O-related, so this simple test can give you an impression of whether or not there is any improvement. To measure the time it takes to copy this file, use the time command, followed by cp, as in time cp /root/1GBfile /tmp. In Listing 15-21, you can see what this looks like when doing it on your server.

Listing 15-21. Timing How Long It Takes to Copy a Large File Around, to Get an Idea of the Current Performance of Your Server

```
[root@hnl ~]# dd if=/dev/zero of=/1Gfile bs=1M count=1024
1024+0 records in
1024+0 records out
1073741824 bytes (1.1 GB) copied, 16.0352 s, 67.0 MB/s
[root@hnl ~]# time cp /1Gfile /tmp

real    0m20.469s
user    0m0.005s
sys     0m7.568s
```

The time command gives you three different indicators: the real time, the user time, and the sys (system) time it took to complete the command. Real time is the time from initiation to completion of the command. User time is the time the kernel spent in user space, and sys time is the time the kernel spent in system space. When doing a test such as this, it is important to interpret it in the right way. Consider, for example, Listing 15-22, in which the same command is repeated a few seconds later.

Listing 15-22. The Same Test, Ten Seconds Later

```
[root@hnl ~]# time cp /1Gfile /tmp

real    0m33.511s
user    0m0.003s
sys     0m7.436s
```

As you can see, the command now performs slower than the first time it was used. This is only in real time, however, and not in sys time. Is this the result of a performance parameter that I've changed in between? No, but let's have a look at the result of free -m, as in Listing 15-23.

Listing 15-23. Take Other Factors into Consideration

```
root@hnl:~# free -m
             total     used     free   shared   buffers   cached
Mem:          3987     2246     1741        0        17     2108
-/+buffers/cache:        119     3867
Swap:         2047        0     2047
```

Any idea what has happened here? The entire 1GB file was put in cache when the command was first executed. As you can see, free -m shows almost 2GB of data in cache, which wasn't there before and that has an influence on the time it takes to copy a large file around.

So what lesson is there to learn? Performance optimization is complex. You have to take into account multiple factors that all have an influence on the performance of your server. Only when this is done the right way will you truly see how your server performs and whether or not you have succeeded in improving its performance. When not looking properly, you may miss things and think you have improved performance, while in reality, you have worsened it. So, it is important to develop reliable procedures for performance testing and stick to them.

CPU Tuning

In this section, you'll learn what you can do to optimize the performance of your server's CPU. First you'll learn about some aspects of the working of the CPU that are important when trying to optimize performance parameters for the CPU, then you'll read about some common techniques to optimize CPU utilization.

Understanding CPU Performance

To be able to tune the CPU, you should know what is important with regard to this part of your system. To understand the CPU, you should know about the thread scheduler. This part of the kernel makes sure that all process threads get an equal amount of CPU cycles. Because most processes will do some I/O as well, it's not really bad that the scheduler puts process threads on hold for a given moment. While not being served by the CPU, the process thread can handle its I/O. The scheduler operates by using fairness, meaning that all threads are moving forward in an even manner. By using fairness, the scheduler makes sure there is not too much latency.

The scheduling process is pretty simple in a single CPU / core environment. If, however, multiple cores are used, it becomes more complicated. To work in a multi-CPU or multi-core environment, your server will use a specialized symmetric multiprocessing (SMP) kernel. If needed, this kernel is installed automatically. In an SMP environment, the scheduler should make sure that some kind of load balancing is used. This means that process threads are spread over the available CPU cores. Some programs are written to be used in an SMP environment and are able to use multiple CPUs by themselves. Most programs can't do that and for this depend on the capabilities of the kernel.

A specific worry in a multi-CPU environment is that the scheduler should prevent processes and threads from being moved to other CPU cores. Moving a process means that the information the process has written in the CPU cache has to be moved as well, and that is a relatively expensive process.

You may think that a server will always benefit from installing multiple CPU cores, but that is not true. When working on multiple cores, chances increase that processes swap around between cores, taking their cached information with them, and that slows down performance in a multiprocessing environment. When using multi-core systems, you should always optimize your system for that.

Optimizing CPU Performance

CPU performance optimization really is just about two things: priority and optimization of the SMP environment. Every process gets a static priority from the scheduler. The scheduler can differentiate between real time (RT) processes and normal processes, but if a process falls in one of these categories, it will be equal to all other processes in the same category. Be aware, however, that some real-time processes (most are part of the Linux kernel) will run with the highest priority, whereas the rest of available CPU cycles must be divided among the other processes. In that procedure, it's all about fairness: the longer a process is waiting, the higher its priority will be. You have already learned how to use the nice command to tune process priority.

If you are working in an SMP environment, a good utility to improve performance is the taskset command. You can use taskset to set CPU affinity for a process to one or more CPUs. The result is that your process is less likely to be moved to another CPU. The taskset command uses a hexadecimal bitmask to specify which CPU to use. In this bitmap, the value 0x1 refers to CPU0, 0x2 refers to CPU1, 0x4 to CPU2, 0x8 to CPU3, and so on. Note that these numbers do combine, so use 0x3 to refer to CPUs 0 and 1.

So, if you have a command that you would like to bind to CPUs 2 and 3, you would use the following command:

```
taskset 0x12 somecommand
```

You can also use taskset on running processes, by using the -p option. With this option, you can refer to the PID of a processes, for instance,

```
taskset -p 0x3 7034
```

would set the affinity of the process using PID 7034 to CPUs 0 and 1.

You can specify CPU affinity for IRQs as well. To do this, you can use the same bitmask that you use with taskset. Every interrupt has a subdirectory in /proc/irq/, and in that subdirectory, there is a file with the name smp_affinity. So, if, for example, your IRQ 5 is producing a very high workload (check /proc/interrupts to see if this is the case), and, therefore, you want that IRQ to work on CPU1, use the following command:

```
echo 2 > /proc/irq/3/smp_affinity
```

Another approach to optimize CPU performance is by using cgroups. Cgroups provide a new way to optimize all aspects of performance, including CPU, memory, I/O, and more. At the end of this chapter, you'll read about using cgroups.

Apart from the generic settings discussed here, there are some more specific ways of optimizing CPU performance. Most of them relate to the working of the scheduler. You can find these settings in /proc/sys/kernel. All files with a name that begins with sched relate to CPU optimization. One example of these is the sched_latency_ns, which defines the latency of the scheduler in nanoseconds. You could consider decreasing the latency that you find here, to get better CPU performance. However, you should realize that optimizing the CPU brings benefits only in very specific environments. For most environments, it doesn't make that much sense, and you can get much better results by improving performance of important system parts, such as memory and disk.

Tuning Memory

System memory is a very important part of a computer. It functions as a buffer between CPU and I/O, and by tuning memory, you can really get the best out of it. Linux works with the concept of virtual memory, which is the total of all memory available on a server. You can tune the working of virtual memory by writing to the /proc/sys/vm directory. This directory contains lots of parameters that help you to tune the way your server's memory is used. As always when tuning the performance of a server, there are no solutions that work in all cases. Use the parameters in /proc/sys/vm with caution, and use them one by one. Only by tuning each parameter individually, will you be able to determine if it gave the desired result.

Understanding Memory Performance

In a Linux system, the virtual memory is used for many purposes. First, there are processes that claim their amount of memory. When tuning for processes, it helps to know how these processes allocate memory, for instance, a database server that allocates large amounts of system memory when starting up has different needs than a mail server that works with small files only. Also, each process has its own memory space, which may not be addressed by other processes. The kernel takes care that this never occurs.

When a process is created, using the fork() system call (which basically creates a child process from the parent), the kernel creates a virtual address space for the process. The kernel part that takes care of that is known as the dynamic linker. The virtual address space that is used by a process is made up of pages. On a 64-bit server, you can choose between 4, 8, 16, 32, and 64KB pages, but the default pages' size is set to 4KB and is rarely changed. For applications that require lots of memory, you can optimize memory by configuring huge pages.

Another important aspect of memory usage is caching. In your system, there is a read cache and a write cache, and it may not surprise you that a server that handles read requests most of the time is tuned in another way than a server that handles write requests.

Configuring Huge Pages

If your server is a heavily used application server, it may benefit from using large pages, also referred to as *huge pages*. A huge page, by default, is a 2MB page, and it may be useful to improve performance in high-performance computing and with memory-intensive applications. By default, no huge pages are allocated, as they would be a waste on a server that doesn't need them—memory that is used for huge pages cannot be used for anything else. Typically, you set huge pages from the Grub boot loader when starting your server. In Exercise 15-5, you'll learn how to set huge pages.

EXERCISE 15-5. CONFIGURING HUGE PAGES

In this exercise, you'll configure huge pages. You'll set them as a kernel argument and then you'll verify their availability. Note that in this procedure, you'll specify the amount of huge pages as a boot argument to the kernel. You can also set it from the /proc file system, as explained later.

1. Using an editor, open the Grub menu configuration file in /etc/default.grub.

2. Find the section that starts your kernel and add hugepages=64 to the kernel line.

3. Save your settings and reboot your server to activate them.

4. Use cat /proc/sys/vm/nr_hugepages to confirm that there are 64 huge pages set on your system. Note that all memory that is allocated in huge pages is not available for other purposes.

Be careful, however, when allocating huge pages. All memory pages that are allocated as huge pages are no longer available for other purposes, and if your server needs a heavy read or write cache, you will suffer from allocating too many huge pages immediately. If you find that this is the case, you can change the amount of huge pages currently in use by writing to the /proc/sys/vm/nr_hugepages parameter. Your server will pick up this new amount of huge pages immediately.

Optimizing Write Cache

The next couple of parameters all relate to the buffer cache. As discussed earlier, your server maintains a write cache. By putting data in that write cache, the server can delay writing data. This is useful for more than one reason. Imagine that just after committing the write request to the server, another write request is made. It will be easier for the server to handle that write request, if the data is not yet written to disk but still in memory. You may also want to tune the write cache to balance between the amount of memory reserved for reading and the amount that is reserved for writing data.

The first relevant parameter is in /proc/sys/vm/dirty_ratio. This parameter is used to define the percentage of memory that is maximally used for the write cache. When the percentage of buffer cache in use comes above this parameter, your server will write memory from the buffer cache to disk as soon as possible. The default of 10 percent works fine for an average server, but in some situations, you may want to increase or decrease the amount of memory used here.

Related to dirty_ration are the dirty_expire_centisecs and dirty_writeback_centisecs parameters, also in /proc/sys/vm. These parameters determine when data in the write cache expires and have to be written to disk, even if the write cache hasn't reached the threshold, as defined in dirty_ratio, yet. By using these parameters, you reduce the chances of losing data when a power outage occurs on your server. On the contrary, if you want to use power more efficiently, it is useful to give both these parameters the value of 0, which actually disables them and keeps data as long as possible in the write cache. This is useful for laptop computers, because your hard disk has to spin up in order to write these data, and that takes a lot of power.

The last parameter that is related to writing data, is `nr_pdflush_threads`. This parameter helps in determining the amount of threads the kernel launches for writing data from the buffer cache. Understanding it is easy; more of these means faster write back. So, if you have the idea that buffer cache on your server is not cleared fast enough, increase the amount of `pdflush_threads`, using the following command by echoing a 4 to the file `/proc/sys/vm/nr_pdflush_threads`.

When using this option, do respect its limitations. By default, the minimal amount of `pdflush_threads` is set to 2, and there is a maximum of 8, so that the kernel still has a dynamic range to determine what exactly it has to do.

Overcommitting Memory

Next, there is the issue of overcommitting memory. By default, every process tends to claim more memory than it really needs. This is good, because it makes the process faster. If the process already has some spare memory available, it can access it much faster when it needs it, because it doesn't have to ask the kernel if it has some more memory available. To tune the behavior of overcommitting memory, you can write to the `/proc/sys/vm/overcommit_memory` parameter. This parameter can have some values. The default value is 0, which means that the kernel checks if it still has memory available before granting it. If that doesn't give you the performance you need, you can consider changing it to 1, which means that the system thinks there is enough memory in all cases. This is good for performance of memory-intensive tasks but may result in processes getting killed automatically. You can also use the value of 2, which means that the kernel fails the memory request if there is not enough memory available.

This minimal amount of memory that is available is specified in the `/proc/sys/vm/overcommit_ratio` parameter, which by default is set to 50. This means that the kernel can allocate 50 percent more than the total amount of memory that is available in RAM + swap. So, on a 4GB system that has 2GB swap, the total amount of addressable memory would be set to 9GB when using the value 50 in `overcommit_ration`.

Another useful parameter is the `/proc/sys/vm/swappiness` parameter. This indicates how eager the process is to start swapping out memory pages. A high value means that your server will swap very fast; a low value means that the server will wait some more before starting to swap. The default value of 60 does well in most situations. If you still think your server starts swapping too fast, set it to a somewhat lower value, like 40.

Optimizing Inter Process Communication

The last relevant parameters that relate to memory are the parameters that relate to shared memory. Shared memory is a method that the Linux kernel or Linux applications can use to make communication between processes (also known as Inter Process Communication or IPC) as fast as possible. In database environments, it often makes sense to optimize shared memory. The cool thing about shared memory is that the kernel is not involved in the communication between the processes using it. Data doesn't even have to be copied, because the memory areas can be addressed directly. To get an idea of shared memory–related settings your server is currently using, use the `ipcs -lm` command, as shown in Listing 15-24.

Listing 15-24. Use the `ipcs -lm` Command to Get an Idea of Shared Memory Settings

```
[root@lab ~]# ipcs -lm

------ Shared Memory Limits --------
max number of segments = 4096
max seg size (kbytes) = 4194303
max total shared memory (kbytes) = 1073741824
min seg size (bytes) = 1
```

When your applications are written to use shared memory, you can benefit from tuning some of their parameters. If, on the contrary, your applications don't know how to handle it, it doesn't make a difference if you change the shared memory–related parameters. To find out if shared memory is used on your server, and, if so, in what amount it is used, apply the ipcs -m command. In Listing 15-25, you can see an example of its output on a server on which only one shared memory segment is used.

Listing 15-25. Use ipcs -m to Find Out If Your Server Is Using Shared Memory Segments

```
[root@lab ~]# ipcs -m
```

```
------ Shared Memory Segments --------
key        shmid    owner   perms   bytes      nattch   status
0x00000000 65536    root    600     4194304    2        dest
0x00000000 163841   root    600     4194304    2        dest
0x00000000 557058   root    600     4194304    2        dest
0x00000000 294915   root    600     393216     2        dest
0x00000000 458756   root    600     2097152    2        dest
0x00000000 425989   root    600     1048576    2        dest
0x00000000 5865478  root    777     3145728    1
0x00000000 622599   root    600     16777216   2        dest
0x00000000 1048584  root    600     33554432   2        dest
0x00000000 6029321  root    777     3145728    1
0x00000000 6127626  root    777     3145728    1
0x00000000 6193163  root    777     3145728    1
0x00000000 6258700  root    777     3145728    1
```

The first /proc parameter that is related to shared memory is shmmax. This defines the maximum size in bytes of a single shared-memory segment that a Linux process can allocate. You can see the current setting in the configuration file /proc/sys/kernel/shmmax, as follows:

```
root@hnl:~# cat /proc/sys/kernel/shmmax
33554432
```

This sample was taken from a system that has 4GB of RAM. The shmmax setting was automatically created to allow processes to allocate up to about 3.3GB of RAM. It doesn't make sense to tune the parameter to use all available RAM, because RAM has to be used for other purposes as well.

The second parameter that is related to shared memory is shmmni, which is not, as you might think, the minimal size of shared memory segments but the maximum size of the shared memory segments that your kernel can allocate. You can get the default value from /proc/sys/kernel/shmmni; it should be set to 4096. If you have an application that relies heavily on the use of shared memory, you may benefit from increasing this parameter, for example:

```
sysctl -w kernel.shmmni=8192
```

The last parameter related to shared memory is shmall. It is set in /proc/sys/kernel/shmall and defines the total amount of shared memory pages that can be used system-wide. Normally, the value should be set to the value of shmmax, divided by the current page size your server is using. On a 32-bit processor, finding the page size is easy; it is always set to 4096. On a 64-bit computer, you can use the getconf command to determine the current page size:

```
[root@hnl ~]# getconf PAGE_SIZE

4096
```

If the shmall parameter doesn't contain a value that is big enough for your application, change it, as needed. For instance, use the following command:

```
sysctl -w kernel.shmall=2097152
```

Tuning Storage Performance

The third element in the chain of Linux performance is the storage channel. Performance optimization on this channel can be divided in two: journal optimization and I/O buffer performance. Apart from that, there are some other file system parameters that can be tunes to optimize performance.

Understanding Storage Performance

To determine what happens with I/O on your server, Linux uses the I/O scheduler. This kernel component sits between the block layer that communicates directly with the file systems and the device drivers. The block layer generates I/O requests for the file systems and passes those requests to the I/O scheduler. This scheduler, in turn, transforms the request and passes it to the low-level drivers. The drivers, in turn, next forward the request to the actual storage devices. Optimizing storage performance begins with optimizing the I/O scheduler.

Optimizing the I/O Scheduler

Working with an I/O scheduler makes your computer more flexible. The I/O scheduler can prioritize I/O requests and reduce times for searching data on the hard disk. Also, the I/O scheduler makes sure that a request is handled before it times out. An important goal of the I/O scheduler is to make hard disk seek times more efficient. The scheduler does this by collecting requests before really committing them to disk. Because of this approach, the scheduler can do its work more efficiently. For example, it may choose to order requests before committing them to disk, which makes hard disk seeks more efficient.

When optimizing the performance of the I/O scheduler, there is a dilemma: you can optimize read performance or write performance but not both at the same time. Optimizing read performance means that write performance will be not as good, whereas optimizing write performance means you have to pay a price in read performance. So before starting to optimize the I/O scheduler, you should really analyze what type of workload is generated by your server.

There are four different ways in which the I/O scheduler does its work.

- *Complete fair queueing (cfq)*: When choosing this approach, the I/O scheduler tries to allocate I/O bandwidth fairly. This approach offers a good solution for machines with mixed workloads and offers the best compromise between latency, which is relevant for reading data, and throughput, which is relevant in an environment in which there are a lot of file writes.

- *NOOP*: The NOOP scheduler performs only minimal merging functions on your data. There is no sorting, and therefore, this scheduler has minimal overhead. This scheduler was developed for non-disk-based block devices, such as memory devices. It also does well on storage media that have extensive caching.

- *Deadline*: The deadline scheduler works with five different I/O queues and, therefore, is very capable of making a difference between read requests and write requests. When using this scheduler, read requests will get a higher priority. Write requests do not have a deadline, and, therefore, data to be written can remain in cache for a longer period. This scheduler does well in environments in which a good read performance, as well as a good write performance, is required, but shows some more priority for reads. This scheduler does particularly well in database environments.

- *Anticipatory*: The anticipatory scheduler tries to reduce read response times. It does so by introducing a controlled delay in all read requests. This increases the possibility that another read request can be handled in the same I/O request and therefore makes reads more efficient.

■ **Note**   The results of switching between I/O schedulers heavily depend on the nature of the workload of the specific server. The preceding summary is only a guideline, and before changing the I/O scheduler, you should test intensively to find out if it really leads to the desired results.

There are two ways to change the current I/O scheduler. You can echo a new value to the /sys/block/<YOURDEVICE>/queue/scheduler file. Alternatively, you can set it as a boot parameter, using elevator=yourscheduler on the Grub prompt or in the grub menu. The choices are noop, anticipatory, deadline, and cfq.

Optimizing Storage for Reads

Another way to optimize the way your server works is by tuning read requests. This is something that you can do on a per-disk basis. First, there is read_ahead, which can be tuned in /sys/block/<YOURDEVICE>/queue/read_ahead_kb. On a default Linux installation, this parameter is set to 128KB. If you have fast disks, you can optimize your read performance by using a higher value; 512, for instance, is a starting point, but make sure always to test before making a new setting final. Also, you can tune the number of outstanding read requests by using /sys/block/<YOURDEVICE>/queue/nr_requests. The default value for this parameter also is set to 128, but a higher value may optimize your server in a significant way. Try 512, or even 1024, to get the best read performance, but do always observe that it doesn't introduce too much latency while writing files.

■ **Note**   Optimizing read performance works well, but be aware that while making read performance better, you'll also introduce latency on writes. In general, there is nothing against that, but if your server loses power, all data that is still in memory buffers and hasn't been written yet will get lost.

```
EXERCISE 15-6. CHANGING SCHEDULER PARAMETERS
```

In this exercise, you'll change scheduler parameters and try to see a difference. Note that, normally, complex workloads will show differences better, so don't be surprised if, with the simple tests proposed in this exercise, you don't detect much of a difference.

1. Open a root shell. Use the command cat /sys/block/sda/queue/scheduler to find out what the scheduler is currently set to. If it's a default SLES installation, it will be set to cfq.

2. Use the command dd if=/dev/urandom of=/dev/null to start some background workload. The idea is to start a process that is intense on reads but doesn't write a lot.

3. Write a script with the name reads that read the contents of all files in /etc, as follows:

```
cd /etc
for i in *
do
        cat $i
done
```

4. Run the script using time reads and note the time it takes for the script to complete.

5. Run the command time dd if=/dev/zero of=/1Gfile bs=1M count=1000 and note the time it takes for the command to complete.

6. Change the I/O scheduler setting to noop, anticipatory, and deadline and repeat steps 4 and 5. To change the current I/O-scheduler setting, use echo noop > /sys/block/sda/queue/scheduler. You now know which settings work best for this simple test environment.

7. Use killall dd to make sure all dd jobs are terminated.

Changing Journal Options

By default, all modern file systems on Linux use journaling. On some specific workloads, the default journaling mode will cause you a lot of problems. You will determine if this is the case for your server by using iotop. If you see that kjournald is high on the list, you have a journaling issue that you must optimize.

There are three different journaling options, which you can set by using the data=journaloption mount option.

- data=writeback: This options guarantees internal file system integrity, but it doesn't guarantee that new files have been committed to disk. In many cases, it is the fastest, but also the most insecure, journaling option.

- data=ordered: This is the default mode. It forces all data to be written to the file system before the metadata is written to the journal.

- data=journaled: This is the most secure journaling option, in which all data blocks are journaled as well. The performance price for using this option is high, but it does offer the best security for your files that you can imagine.

Network Tuning

Among the most difficult items to tune is network performance. This is because in networking, multiple layers of communication are involved, and each is handled separately on Linux. First, there are buffers on the network card itself that deal with physical packets. Next, there is the TCP/IP protocol stack, and then there is also the application stack. All work together, and tuning one will have its consequences on the other layer. While tuning the network, always work upward in the protocol stack. That is, start by tuning the packets themselves, then tune the TCP/IP stack, and after that, have a look at the service stacks that are in use on your server.

Tuning Network-Related Kernel Parameters

While it initializes, the kernel sets some parameters automatically, based on the amount of memory that is available on your server. So, the good news is that in many situations, there is no work to be done. Some parameters, by default, are not set in the most optimal way, so, in some cases, there is some performance to gain there.

For every network connection, the kernel allocates a socket. The socket is the end-to-end line of communication. Each socket has a receive buffer and a send buffer, also known as the read (receive) and write (send) buffers. These buffers are very important. If they are full, no more data can be processed, so data will be dropped. This will have important consequences for the performance of your server, because if data is dropped, it has to be sent and processed again.

The basis of all reserved sockets on the network comes from two /proc tunables:

```
/proc/sys/net/core/wmem_default
/proc/sys/net/core/rmem_default
```

All kernel-based sockets are reserved from these sockets. If, however, a socket is TCP-based, the settings in here are overwritten by TCP specific parameters, in particular the tcp_rmem and tcp_wmem parameters. In the next section, you can get more details on how to optimize those.

The values of the wmem_default and rmem_default are set automatically when your server boots. If you have dropped packets on the network interface, you may benefit from increasing them. For some workloads, the values that are used by default are rather low. To set them, tune the following parameters in /etc/sysctl.conf.

```
net.core.wmem_default
net.core.rmem_default
```

Especially if you have dropped packets, try doubling them, to find out if the dropped packets go away by doing so.

Related to the default read and write buffer size is the maximum read and write buffer size: rmem_max and wmem_max. These are also calculated automatically when your server comes up but, for many situations, are far too low. For example, on a server that has 4GB of RAM, the sizes of these are set to 128KB only! You may benefit from changing their values to something that is much larger, like 8MB.

```
sysctl -w net.core.rmem_max=8388608
sysctl -w net.core.wmem_max=8388608
```

When increasing the read and write buffer size, you also have to increase the maximum amount of incoming packets that can be queued. This is set in netdev_max_backlog. The default value is set to 1000, which is not enough for very busy servers. Try increasing it to a much higher value, like 8000, especially if you have long latency times on your network or if there are lots of dropped packets.

```
sysctl -w net.core.netdev_max_backlog=8000
```

Apart from the maximum number of incoming packets that your server can queue, there is also a maximum amount of incoming connections that can be accepted. You can set them from the somaxconn file in /proc.

```
sysctl -w net.core.somaxconn=512
```

By tuning this parameter, you will limit the amount of new connections dropped.

Optimizing TCP/IP

Up to now, you have tuned kernel buffers for network sockets only. These are generic parameters. If you are working with TCP, some specific tunables are available as well. Some TCP tunables, by default, have a value that is too low; many are self-tunable and adjust their values automatically, if that is needed. Chances are that you can gain a lot by increasing them. All relevant options are in /proc/sys/net/ipv4.

To start with, there is a read buffer size and a write buffer size that you can set for TCP. They are written to tcp_rmem and tcp_wmem. Here also, the kernel tries to allocate the best possible values when it boots, but in some cases, it doesn't work out that well. If that happens, you can change the minimum size, the default size, and the maximum size of these buffers. Note that each of these two parameters contains three values at the same time, for minimal, default, and maximal size. In general, there is no need to tune the minimal size. It can be interesting, though, to tune the default size. This is the buffer size that will be available when your server boots. Tuning the maximum size is also important, as it defines the upper threshold above which packets will get dropped. In Listing 15-26, you can see the default settings for those parameters on my server that have 4GB of RAM.

Listing 15-26. Default Settings for TCP Read and Write Buffers

```
[root@hnl ~]# cat /proc/sys/net/ipv4/tcp_rmem
4096     87380    3985408
[root@hnl ~]# cat /proc/sys/net/ipv4/tcp_wmem
4096     16384    3985408
```

In this example, the maximum size is quite good; almost 4MB are available as the maximum size for read as well as write buffers. The default write buffer size is limited. Imagine that you want to tune these parameters in a way that the default write buffer size is as big as the default read buffer size, and the maximum for both parameters is set to 8MB. You could do that by using the following two commands:

```
sysctl -w net.ipv4.tcp_rmem="4096 87380 8388608"
sysctl -w net.ipv4.tcp_wmem="4096 87380 8388608"
```

Before tuning options like these, you should always check the availability of memory on your server. All memory that is allocated for TCP read and write buffers can't be used for other purposes anymore, so you may cause problems in other areas while tuning these. It's an important rule in tuning that you should always make sure the parameters are well-balanced.

Another useful set of parameters is related to the acknowledged nature of TCP. Let's have a look at an example to understand how this works. Imagine that the sender in a TCP connection sends a series of packets, numbered 1,2,3,4,5,6,7,8,9,10. Now imagine that the receiver receives all of them, with the exception of packet 5. In the default setting, the receiver would acknowledge receiving up to packet 4, in which case, the sender would send packets 5,6,7,8,9,10 again. This is a waste of bandwidth, because packets 6,7,8,9,10 have been received correctly already.

To handle this acknowledgment traffic in a more efficient way, the setting /proc/sys/net/ipv4/tcp_sack is enabled (having the value of 1). That means, in such cases as the above, only missing packets have to be sent again, and not the complete packet stream. For your network bandwidth, that is fine, as only those packets that really need to be retransmitted are retransmitted. So, if your bandwidth is low, you should always leave it on. If, however, you are on a fast network, there is a downside. When using this parameter, packets may come in out of order. That means that you need larger TCP receive buffers to keep all the packets until they can be defragmented and put in the right order. That means that using this parameter involves more memory to be reserved, and from that perspective, on fast network connections, you had better switch it off. To do that, use the following:

```
sysctl -w net.ipv4.tcp_sack=0
```

When disabling TCP selective acknowledgments, as described previously, you should also disable two related parameters: tcp_dsack and tcp_fack. These parameters enable selective acknowledgments for specific packet types. To enable them, use the following two commands:

```
sysctl -w net.ipv4.tcp_dsack=0
sysctl -w net.ipv4.tcp_fack=0
```

In case you would prefer to work with selective acknowledgments, you can also tune the amount of memory that is reserved to buffer incoming packets that have to be put in the right order. Two parameters relate to this. First, there is `ipfrag_low_tresh`, and then there is `ipfrag_high_tresh`. When the amount that is specified in `ipfrag_high_tresh` is reached, new packets to be defragmented are dropped until the server reaches `ipfrag_low_tresh`. Make sure the value of both of these is set high enough at all times, if your server uses selective acknowledgments. The following values are reasonable for most servers:

```
sysctl -w net.ipv4.ipfrag_low_thresh=393216
sysctl -w net.ipv4.ipfrag_high_thresh=524288
```

Next, there is the length of the TCP Syn queue that is created for each port. The idea is that all incoming connections are queued until they can be serviced. As you can probably guess, when the queue is full, connections get dropped. The situation is that the `tcp_max_syn_backlog` that manages these per-port queues has a default value that is too low, as only 1024 bytes are reserved for each port. For good performance, better allocate 8192 bytes per port, using the following:

```
sysctl -w net.ipv4.tcp_max_syn_backlog=8192
```

Also, there are some options that relate to the time an established connection is maintained. The idea is that every connection that your server has to keep alive uses resources. If your server is a very busy server, at a given moment, it will be out of resources and tell new incoming clients that no resources are available. Because, for a client, in most cases, it is easy enough to reestablish a connection, you probably want to tune your server in such a way that it detects failing connections as soon as possible.

The first parameter that relates to maintaining connections is `tcp_synack_retries`. This parameter defines the number of times the kernel will send a response to an incoming new connection request. The default value is 5. Given the current quality of network connections, 3 is probably enough, and it is better for busy servers, because it makes a connection available sooner. So use the following to change it:

```
sysctl -w net.ipv4.tcp_synack_retries=3
```

Next, there is the `tcp_retries2` option. This relates to the amount of times the server tries to resend data to a remote host that has an established session. Because it is inconvenient for a client computer if a connection is dropped, the default value is with 15 a lot higher than the default value for the `tcp_synack_retries`. However, retrying it 15 times means that during all that time, your server can't use its resources for something else. Therefore, it is better to decrease this parameter to a more reasonable value of 5, as in the following:

```
sysctl -w net.ipv4.tcp_retries2=5
```

The parameters just mentioned relate to sessions that appear to be gone. Another area in which you can do some optimization is in the maintenance of inactive sessions. By default, a TCP session can remain idle forever. You probably don't want that, so use the `tcp_keepalive_time` option to determine how long an established inactive session will be maintained. By default, this will be 7200 seconds (2 hours). If your server tends to run out of resources because too many requests are coming in, limit it to a considerably shorter period of time.

```
sysctl -w net.ipv4.tcp_keepalive_time=900
```

Related to the `keepalive_time` is the amount of packets that your server sends before deciding a connection is dead. You can manage this by using the `tcp_keepalive_probes` parameter. By default, nine packets are sent before a server is considered dead. Change it to three, if you want to terminate dead connections faster.

```
sysctl -w net.ipv4.tcp_keepalive_probes=3
```

Related to the amount of keep alive probes is the interval you want to use to send these probes. By default, that happens every 75 seconds. So even with 3 proves, it still takes more than 3 minutes before your server can see that a connection has really failed. To bring this period back, give the tcp_keepalive_intvl parameter the value of 15.

```
sysctl -w net.ipv4.tcp_keepalive_intvl=15
```

To complete the story about maintaining connections, we need two more parameters. By default, the kernel waits a little before reusing a socket. If you run a busy server, performance will benefit from switching this off. To do this, use the following two commands:

```
sysctl -w net.ipv4.tcp_tw_reuse=1
sysctl -w net.ipv4.tcp_tw_recycle=1
```

Generic Network Performance Optimization Tips

Until now, we have discussed kernel parameters only. There are also some more generic hints for optimizing performance on the network. You probably already have applied all of them, but just to be sure, let's repeat some of the most important tips.

- Make sure you have the latest network driver modules.

- Use network card teaming to double performance of the network card in your server.

- Check Ethernet configuration settings, such as frame size, MTU, speed, and duplex mode on your network. Make sure all devices involved in network communications use the same settings.

- If supported by all devices in your network, use 9000-byte jumbo frames. This reduces the amount of packets sent over the network, and so, too, the overhead that is caused by sending all those packets, therefore speeding your network overall.

Optimizing Linux Performance Using Cgroups

Among the latest features for performance optimization that Linux has to offer, is cgroups (short for *control groups*), a technique that allows you to create groups of resources and allocate them to specific services. By using this solution, you can make sure that a fixed percentage of resources on your server is always available for those services that need it.

To start using cgroups, you first have to make sure the libcgroup RPM package is installed, so use zypper install libcgroup-tools to do that. Once its installation is confirmed, you have to start the cgconfig and cgred services. Make sure to put these in the runlevels of your server, using systemctl enable cgconfig and systemctl enable cgred on. Next, make sure to start these services. This will create a directory /cgroup with a couple of subdirectories in it. These subdirectories are referred to as controllers. The controllers refer to the system resources that you can limit using cgroups. Some of the most interesting include the following:

- blkio: Use this to limit the amount of IO that can be handled.

- cpu: This is used to limit CPU cycles.

- memory: Use this to limit the amount of memory that you can grant to processes.

There are some other controllers as well, but they are not as useful as the blkio, cpu, and memory controllers. Now let's assume that you're running an Oracle database on your server, and you want to make sure that it runs in a cgroup in which it has access to at least 75 percent of available memory and CPU cycles. The first step would be to create a cgroup that defines access to cpu and memory resources. The following command would create this cgroup with the name oracle: cgcreate -g cpu,memory oracle. After defining the cgroups this way, you'll see that in the /cgroups/cpu and /cgroups/memory directory, a subdirectory with the name oracle is created. In this subdirectory, different parameters are available to specify the resources that you want to make available to the cgroup. (See Listing 15-27.)

Listing 15-27. In the Subdirectory of Your Cgroup, You'll Find All Tunables

```
[root@hnl ~]# cd /cgroup/cpu/oracle/
[root@hnl oracle]# ls
cgroup.procs         cpu.rt_period_us       cpu.stat
cpu.cfs_period_us    cpu.rt_runtime_us      notify_on_release
cpu.cfs_quota_us     cpu.shares                   tasks
```

To specify the amount of CPU resources available for the newly created cgroup, you'll use the cpu.shares parameter. This is a relative parameter that only makes sense if everything is in cgroups, and it defines the amount of shares available in this cgroup. That means that to the amount of shares in the cgroup oracle, you'll assign the value 80, and for that in the cgroup other that contains all other processes, you'll assign the value of 20. Thus the oracle cgroup receives 80 percent of available CPU resources. To set the parameter, you can use the cgset command: cgset -r cpu.shares=80 oracle.

After setting the amount of CPU shares for this cgroup, you can put processes in it. The best way to do this is to start the process you want to put in the cgroup as an argument to the cgexec command. In this example, that would mean that you'd run cgexec -g cpu:/oracle /path/to/oracle. At this time, the oracle process itself, and all its child processes, will be visible in the /cgroups/cpu/oracle/tasks file, and you have assigned Oracle to its specific cgroup.

In this example, you've seen how to manually create cgroups, make resources available to the cgroup, and put a process in it. The disadvantage of this approach is that after a system restart, all settings will be lost. To make the cgroups permanent, you have to use the cgconfig service and the cgred service. The cgconfig service reads its configuration file /etc/cgconfig.conf, in which the cgroups are defined, including the definition of the resources you want to assign to that cgroup. Listing 15-28 shows what it would look like for the oracle example:

Listing 15-28. Sample cgconfig.conf file

```
group oracle {
        cpu {
                cpu.shares=80
        }
        memory {
        }
}
```

Next, you have to create the file cgrules.conf, which specifies the processes that have to be put in a specific cgroup automatically. This file is read when the cgred service is starting. For the Oracle group, it would have the following contents:

```
*:oracle   cpu,memory   /oracle
```

If you have ensured that both the cgconfig service and the cgred service are starting from the runlevels, your services will be started automatically in the appropriate cgroup.

Summary

In this chapter, you've learned how to tune and optimize performance on your server. You've read that for both the tuning part and the optimization part, you'll always have to look at four different categories: CPU, memory, I/O, and network. For each of these, several tools are available to optimize performance.

Often, performance optimization is done by tuning parameters in the /proc file system. In addition to that, there are different options, which can be very diverse, depending on the optimization you're trying to get. An important new instrument to optimize performance are control groups (cgroups), which allow you to limit resources for services on your server in a very specific way.

■■■

## CHAPTER 16

Creating a Cluster on SUSE Linux Enterprise Server

In addition to SUSE Linux Enterprise Server, the High Availability Extension (HAE) can be used to create a high-availability cluster. In this chapter, you will read how to set up such a cluster. The following topics are discussed:

- Why Cluster?
- Architecture of the Pacemaker Stack
- Configuring Shared Storage
- Creating the Base Cluster
- Using STONITH
- Setting Up Resources
- Use Cases

The Need for High-Availability Clustering

Many companies run important services on their servers. If one of these services stops, business can stop as well. High-availability clustering can help you make sure that business goes on after a failure in the network.

In high-availability (HA) clustering, cluster software is installed on the different nodes in the cluster. This software monitors the availability of other nodes and the critical services that are monitored by the cluster. If one of the nodes goes down, or if one of the monitored services goes down, the cluster reacts and makes sure the monitored service is started somewhere else.

Some administrators think that they don't need HA clustering, because they are using a virtualization solution that already includes HA. This is wrong, however. HA on the virtualization layer only protects virtual machines and not the services running in the virtual machine. If you set up virtualization HA to protect your virtual servers that are running your web shop, the virtualization HA layer will react when a virtual machine goes down. It won't, however, react if the web application running in those virtual machines goes down. That's why you need high-availability clustering, if you want to make sure that business-critical resources stay up and running no matter what.

Architecture of the Pacemaker Stack

To create a high-availability solution, two layers have to be installed. The lower layer is referred to as the membership layer. On SUSE Linux Enterprise Server, this layer is implemented by using the OpenAIS/Corosync software. On this layer, the totem protocol is used to monitor availability of nodes.

On top of the membership layer, the Pacemaker layer is used. The most important component of this layer is the Cluster Resource Manager (CRM), which decides on which nodes cluster resources have to be started. Information about resources and their current state is stored in the Cluster Information Base (CIB). The CIB is replicated in real time between the nodes that are members of the cluster, so that every node has an accurate view on the current state of the cluster.

Two additional components that play a role are the Local Resource Manager (LRM) and STONITH. After the CRM has decided that a specific resource has to be placed on a specific node, it gives instructions to the LRM to load the resource. So, the LRM can be considered the glue between the cluster and the local operating system.

Another important part of the architecture is STONITH (Shoot The Other Node In The Head). STONITH is used to guarantee the integrity of the cluster. To avoid corruption on shared resources such as file systems, the cluster must be sure that a node really is down.

Imagine a situation in a two-node cluster, in which both nodes don't see each other anymore. If misconfigured, both nodes could think that they are the only node remaining in the cluster and start servicing a shared file system. If this were a normal stand-alone file system, such as Btrfs or Ext4, and both nodes began writing to the file system simultaneously, the file system would become corrupted. That is why STONITH is a mandatory component of every cluster. Before migrating over the resource to the other node, STONITH makes sure the other node really is terminated.

Typically, STONITH is a hardware solution, where the STONITH agent in the cluster sends an instruction to a hardware device to terminate the failing node. In many cases, management boards, such as Dell DRAC or HP ILO, or the IPMI Management standard are used for this kind of STONITH. Other solutions are available as well, such as hypervisor STONITH. This makes sense if the cluster nodes are virtual machines that are running on the same hypervisor platform, in which case, the hypervisor could be instructed to bring down the node. Further on in this chapter, you can read more about different STONITH options and how to set them up.

Before Starting

Before you do anything else in the cluster, there are some critical tasks that you must accomplish. Make sure to take care of these tasks before you do anything else, because the cluster just won't work properly otherwise, and you will encounter lots of different problems. The following are the tasks you must perform:

- Set up hostname resolution.
- Configure Secure Shell (SSH).
- Make sure time is synchronized.
- Consider if shared storage is needed.

Hostname Resolution

Nodes in a cluster communicate with one another based on hostname. Typically, the kernel hostname is used for that. This is the hostname as returned by the uname -n command. For your cluster to work properly, you have to make sure that this hostname can be resolved on all levels. That means, not only by using DNS or an /etc/hosts file within the nodes, but also that you must make sure the names of the host correspond to the names that are used on the hypervisor level, if your hosts are running on top of a virtualization platform.

Configure SSH

Although not a strict requirement, it is rather convenient to set up Secure Shell (SSH) key exchange before starting configuration of the cluster. Make sure the root user has a pair of SSH keys, and copy the public key from each of the nodes to each of the other nodes. This helps you to copy over configuration files smoothly.

Time Synchronization

In the cluster, events are occurring, and these events are often time-stamped. A small deviation in time will be tolerated, but if the time is too different between nodes, you won't be able to exchange cluster information properly. So, make sure all nodes in the cluster are connected to a Network Time Protocol (NTP) time server, so that time will never be the reason why the cluster doesn't work.

Configuring Shared Storage

Shared storage is an important part of any high-availability (HA) cluster. You need shared storage, so that no matter where your clustered service is running, it can at all times have access to the same configuration and data files.

The typical solution for setting up shared storage is a Storage Area Network (SAN). Basically, this is a collection of disks that are configured in a redundant way and accessible over a dedicated storage network. On the SAN, different storage volumes are created. These are referred to as LUNs (logical unit numbers). Typically, cluster nodes would connect over the storage network to these LUNs. The result is that they would see these LUNs as additional disks.

Currently, there are two techniques dominating the market for storage: iSCSI and Fiber Channel SANs. Fiber Channel is the original storage solution, in which a dedicated infrastructure for accessing the SAN is offered by the Fiber Channel vendor. In the cluster nodes, a Host Bus Adapter (HBA) is installed, and this HBA typically has redundant connections to redundant switches in the Fiber Channel infrastructure. These switches normally are connected to redundant controllers, to give access to the shared LUNs.

The SAN access method in an iSCSI SAN is not much different, but instead of a dedicated infrastructure, iSCSI commands are encapsulated in IP packets and sent to the SAN. Because in iSCSI SANs the SAN access layer uses common network technologies, setting up an iSCSI SAN is typically a lot cheaper. This gives iSCSI the reputation of being a poor man's SAN. That's not the case, however. iSCSI SANs can be set up with a performance that is as good as Fiber Channel performance. The way it is accessed is just different. In this chapter, you'll learn how to set up an iSCSI SAN, because it is a SAN solution that is included in Linux.

Setting Up an iSCSI Target

Setting up an iSCSI Target is easily done from YaST. Roughly, it consists of two steps: first you set up some storage devices that you want to offer on the Storage Area Network (SAN). LVM Logical Volumes would be a good solution for that. After setting up the underlying storage layer, you can launch the YaST iSCSI Target module, to mark them as iSCSI volumes and export them.

1. From the YaST iSCSI Target module, select the Service tab and click When Booting, to start the service automatically when your server boots.

2. Activate the Targets tab and click Add, to add a new target.

3. The target will get a default name (the so called IQN), with an Identifier that is based on a UUID. For sanity, you might want to change the identifier name to something that makes sense.

4. Next, click Add to add an LUN. You'll do this for each disk device you want to share on the SAN. Every LUN receives a unique LUN number and requires a path. This path refers to the underlying storage device the SAN is going to export (see Figure 16-1). After creating the LUN, click OK, to write the configuration to the SAN.

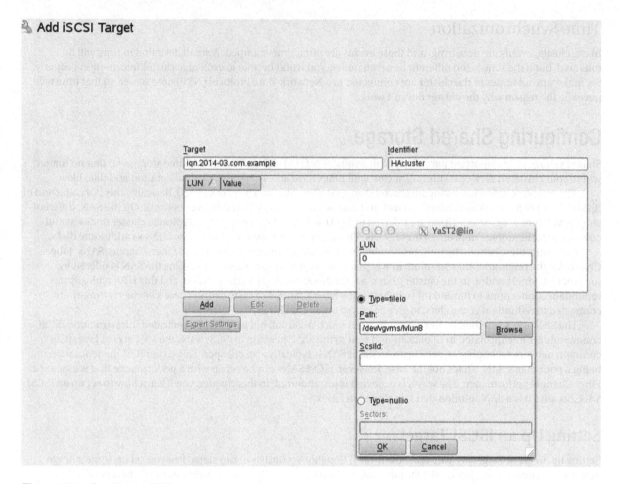

Figure 16-1. *Creating an LUN*

5. Now, click Next, which brings you to the Authentication window. On this window, select No Authentication and click Next. This adds the new LUN to your SAN configuration. Click Yes to make the new configuration available.

Connecting to the iSCSI Target

Now that the Storage Area Network (SAN) is ready, it's time to connect the cluster nodes to the SAN. This is something you have to do on every node that requires access to the SAN. There is also a YaST module to do this, but you might as well use the iscsiadm command. The procedure below explains how to connect to the SAN, using the iscsiadm command.

1. The first step is to discover all iSCSI storage that is available. To do this, use the following command:

```
iscsiadm --mode discoverydb --type sendtargets --portal 192.168.1.125 --discover
```

2. As a result, you will see the name of the iSCSI target. You need this name to connect, using the `iscsiadm --mode node` command

```
iscsiadm --mode node targetname iqn.2014-01.com.example:kiabi --portal 192.168.1.125
--login
```

At this point, you'll have a connection to the iSCSI SAN. You can verify this using the `iscsiadm --mode session -P1` command. Listing 16-1 shows the output of this command.

Listing 16-1. Showing Current iSCSI Session Information

```
node1:~ # iscsiadm --mode session -P 1
Target: iqn.2014-01.com.example:kiabi
        Current Portal: 192.168.1.125:3260,1
        Persistent Portal: 192.168.1.125:3260,1
                *********
                Interface:
                *********
                Iface Name: default
                Iface Transport: tcp
                Iface Initiatorname: iqn.1996-04.de.suse:01:2b3ab8c4c8c8
                Iface IPaddress: 192.168.1.145
                Iface HWaddress: <empty>
                Iface Netdev: <empty>
                SID: 1
                iSCSI Connection State: LOGGED IN
                iSCSI Session State: LOGGED_IN
                Internal iscsid Session State: NO CHANGE
```

Now that you have established connection to the storage, you can go on and start configuring the base cluster.

■ **Note** There's much more to connecting nodes to storage in complex data-center environments. Learn more about it by reading my book *The Definitive Guide to Linux HA Clustering (Apress, 2014)*.

Setting Up the Base Components

To start the installation of the cluster, you must acquire and install the High Availability Add-on disk, using the YaST2 Add-on Products module. Using this approach, you will conveniently install all packages related to high availability (HA). You can also install individual packages. To begin installation of the membership layer of the cluster, the `corosync.rpm` package is required. In this section, I won't rely on YaST for cluster configuration, but you will learn how to manipulate the cluster manually.

1. On each node, install `corosync.rpm`.

2. Copy the file `/etc/corosync/corosync.conf.example` to `corosync.conf`. Open the file `/etc/corosync/corosync.conf` in your favorite text editor.

3. Locate the `bindnetaddr` parameter. This parameter should have as its value the network address that is used to send the cluster packets on (so, use 192.168.1.0, not 192.168.1.1). Next, change the `nodeid` parameter. This is the unique ID for this node that is going to be used on the cluster. To avoid any conflicts with auto-generated node IDs, it's better to manually change the node ID. The last byte of the IP address of this node could be a good choice for the `nodeid`.

4. Find the `mcastaddr` address. By default, the multicast address 239.255.1.1 is used, and that is fine, as it is an address from the private multicast address range that is not used by any hardware device. All nodes in the same cluster need the same multicast address here. If you have several clusters, every cluster needs a unique multicast address.

5. Close the configuration file and write the changes. Now, start the openais service, using `service openais start`. Also, make sure that the service will automatically restart on reboot of the node, using `chkconfig openais on`.

6. At this point, you have a one-node cluster. As root, run the `crm_mon` command to verify that the cluster is operational. (See Listing 16-2.)

   Listing 16-2. Verifying Cluster Operation with `crm_mon`

   ```
   Last updated: Tue Feb  4 08:42:18 2014
   Last change: Tue Feb  4 07:41:00 2014 by hacluster via crmd on node2
   Stack: classic openais (with plugin)
   Current DC: node2 - partition WITHOUT quorum
   Version: 1.1.9-2db99f1
   1 Nodes configured, 2 expected votes
   0 Resources configured.

   Online: [ node2 ]
   ```

7. At this point, you have a one-node cluster. You now have to get the configuration to the other side as well. To do this, use the command `scp /etc/corosync/corosync.conf node1` (in which you need to change the name node1 by the name of your other node).

8. Open the file `/etc/corosync/corosync.conf` on the second node and change the `nodeid` parameter. Make sure a unique node ID is used.

9. Start and enable the openais service and run `crm_mon`. You should now see that there are two nodes in the cluster.

Networks Without Multicast Support

On some networks, multicast is not supported. If that is the case for your network, the procedure that was described in the previous section did not work. You'll have to create a configuration that is based on the UDPU protocol configuration, to get it working. The most relevant differences with the configuration that was described previously are the following:

- In the interface section, you have to include the addresses of all nodes that are allowed as members on the cluster.

- You no longer need a multicast address.

In the current SLES release, there is an example configuration file with the name
/etc/corosync/corosync.conf.example.udpu. Don't create your configuration based on this file, because
some important elements are missing. To create a working configuration file, you can easily create it by using
yast2 cluster. In the Communication Channels section, make sure the udpu transport mechanism is used, and
include the addresses of all nodes that are allowed as members in this cluster (see Figure 16-2).

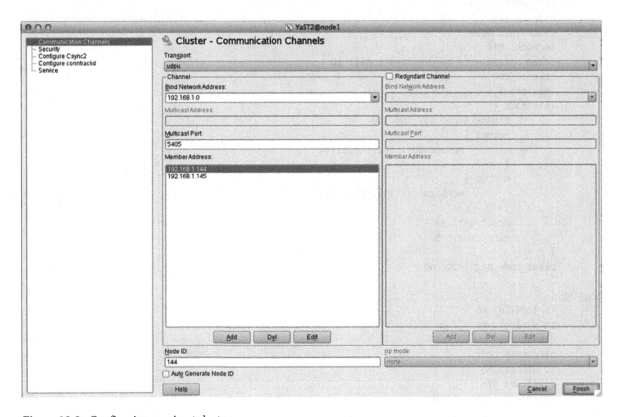

Figure 16-2. *Configuring a unicast cluster*

Listing 16-3 gives an example of a complete and working corosync.conf configuration that is based on unicast
communications.

Listing 16-3. Unicast Cluster Configuration

```
aisexec {
        group: root
        user: root
}
service {
        use_mgmtd: yes
        use_logd: yes
        ver: 0
        name: pacemaker
}
```

```
totem {
        rrp_mode: none
        join: 60
        max_messages: 20
        vsftype: none
        transport: udpu
        nodeid: 145
        consensus: 6000
        secauth: off
        token_retransmits_before_loss_const: 10
        token: 5000
        version: 2
        interface {
                bindnetaddr: 192.168.1.0
                member {
                        memberaddr: 192.168.1.144
                }
                member {
                        memberaddr: 192.168.1.145
                }
                mcastport: 5405
                ringnumber: 0
        }
        clear_node_high_bit: no
}
logging {
        to_logfile: no
        to_syslog: yes
        debug: off
        timestamp: off
        to_stderr: no
        fileline: off
        syslog_facility: daemon
}
amf {
        mode: disable
}
```

Understanding crm_mon Output

After creating your cluster, the crm_mon command provides a very good tool to monitor the basic state of your cluster. At this point, you only see the nodes that are currently known to the cluster and their actual status. At a later stage, you will see status information for resources as well.

The most important line in the crm_mon output is the line Current DC: node2 - partition with quorum. In the cluster, one node has to coordinate changes. This role is performed by the Designated Coordinator (DC). You normally don't have to do anything to appoint a DC, because it will be assigned automatically. However, you should be aware that changes are always synchronized from the DC. This means that if you want to manage the cluster, you better do it straight from the DC, to make synchronization easier.

In this same line, you can also see that the cluster has quorum. That means that a majority of nodes is present in the cluster. This is very important information. Only if a majority of nodes is available is the cluster in a reliable state.

In clusters that consist of three nodes or more, having quorum is a prerequisite, before the cluster can manage resources. This is to avoid getting in a split-brain situation.

Split brain is the situation in which communications in the cluster are lost. Without quorum, the result could be that there are two independent clusters that are each trying to run the resources. This can have catastrophic results. Therefore, only a cluster that has quorum is allowed to start resources.

Using the Cluster Management Tools

As cluster administrator, you have a choice of different management tools. This section provides a brief description of each.

CRM Shell

The most powerful management interface is the CRM shell. It is installed from the crmsh RPM package. CRM shell offers a specific shell interface, from which different management tasks can be performed. You can start it by launching the crm command.

CRM shell is a hierarchical environment, with different sub-environments. You can navigate down to a sub-environment by typing the name of the environment. Use end to go back up one level. In each environment, type help, to get a list of available commands.

Each of the sub-environments relates to a specific aspect of cluster configuration. A short description of the most important sections is given below. In the rest of this section, you'll find more specific examples of working with the CRM shell.

- cib: This option allows you to work on a different cluster information base. Instead of applying changes directly to the live cluster, you can work in a shadow CIB and apply changes offline. Type new, to create such a shadow CIB. Next, you can start applying changes. Once finished, use commit, to apply the shadow CIB to the live cluster.

- resource: This is the environment from which you manage the resources you've created in the cluster. It is probably the most important environment for day-to-day administration tasks.

- configure: This environment is used for meta-operations on the cluster. Different commands are available to manage the state of the cluster or apply changes directly to the cluster configuration.

- node: From here, an administrator can change the current state of nodes in the cluster. Some common management tasks are available as well, such as putting a node in maintenance mode or switching from an operational to a standby status.

- ra: This allows you to get information about resource agents—the scripts that are used to manage resources in the cluster.

Hawk

Apart from the versatile CRM shell environment, you can also use Hawk, the High Availability Web Konsole, to manage the cluster. Before using Hawk, you have to get through some configuration steps. These steps must be performed on each node on which you're planning to start the Hawk service.

1. Use the command passwd hacluster to set a password for the user account that is used for cluster administration.

2. Type usermod -A haclient hacluster to add the user hacluster to the haclient group. All users who are added to this group will be allowed to administer the cluster.

3. Start the Hawk service, using `service hawk start`. This will make Hawk available on its default port, 7630.

4. From a browser, access Hawk over HTTPS, as in `https://192.168.1.144:7630`. This gives you access to all aspects of cluster configuration. (See Figure 16-3.)

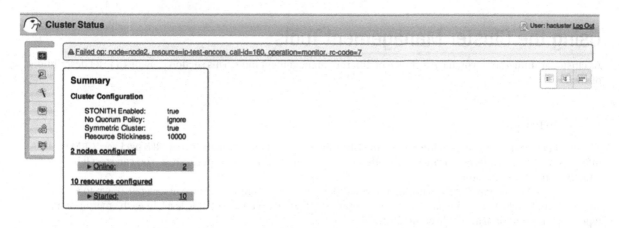

Figure 16-3. *Administering the cluster from the Hawk web interface*

Specifying Default Cluster Settings

Before creating anything in the cluster, you should take a minute to think about some cluster default settings. By default, the cluster is designed to work well without changing any of the cluster properties. Most of the default cluster settings only need to be changed in complex clusters. There are a few settings, however, that are important, including the following:

- `no-quorum-policy`
- `default-resource-stickiness`
- `stonith-action`

no-quorum-policy

The first generic cluster attribute to look at is the `no-quorum-policy`. This setting determines what the cluster should do if it loses quorum. There are two options that make sense: stop and ignore.

The `no-quorum-policy` stop is used as the default in clusters that consist of three or more nodes. It makes sense to use this in a three-node cluster, because in a split-brain situation, in which one node is running alone, it should really understand that it may never run any of the resources. That's exactly what the `no-quorum-policy` stop is doing: it stops all resources on a node that loses quorum, so that the other nodes in the cluster can safely take over the resources.

There is a special case, however, and that is the two-node cluster. If one node goes away in a two-node cluster, the remaining node won't have majority, because majority is half plus one. Therefore, a no-quorum-policy of stop in a two-node cluster would mean that no resources are moving over at all, and that is bad. Therefore, you should set no-quorum-policy to "ignore" in a two-node cluster.

1. Open a shell on one of the cluster nodes, either as root or as user hacluster.

2. Type crm configure edit. This brings you in a vim editing mode, in which you can change cluster parameters.

3. Locate the line that reads property $id="cib-bootstrap-options" and add the following line to the end: no-quorum-policy="ignore".

4. Note the use of slashes. All lines that are not the last line in this part of the configuration should end with a slash, as in the following:

```
property $id="cib-bootstrap-options" \
        dc-version="1.1.9-2db99f1" \
        cluster-infrastructure="classic openais (with plugin)" \
        expected-quorum-votes="2" \
        no-quorum-policy="ignore"
```

5. Write the changes and quit the editor interface. You have now successfully defined the required settings for a two-node cluster.

default-resource-stickiness

The default-resource-stickiness parameter can come in handy, if you want to influence where resources are placed. The default behavior is that resources will try to get back to the node that was originally servicing them. That means that after a failure, the resource will be moved over to another node in the cluster, and once the original node comes back, the resource will come back to the original node again. That is not ideal, as the user will experience a downtime twice. To prevent this from happening, you can set the default-resource-stickiness parameter.

This parameter takes a value between -1000000 and 1000000. A high negative value means that the cluster will always remove the resource from its current location after a change in the cluster topology, even if that means that the resource cannot be properly started (for which reason you should never use -1000000. A moderate negative value, such as -1000, means that the cluster will try to move the resource away, but it doesn't have to. The value of 0 normally means the resource will move back to its original location, and with a positive value, the resource will stay where it is. It is a good idea to use a moderate positive value here, such as 10000, which means that the cluster prefers leaving the resource where it is, preventing it from moving back to the original node with the downtime that is associated with that.

stonith-action

As you can read in the next section of this chapter, STONITH is what stops a node at the moment cluster communication to the node fails. By default, after a STONITH operation, the node will automatically be added to the cluster again. That might sound good, but if your node suffers from a serious problem, chances are that immediately after getting back in the cluster, it experiences the same problem and is restarted. To prevent this from happening, you might want to add stonith-action="poweroff" to the cluster configuration. That makes sure that after it has been killed by its peers, the node only comes back if it is manually restarted by the system administrator.

You can also configure the settings mentioned above from the Hawk web interface. In Hawk, select the Cluster Properties tab on the left. Next, under Cluster Configuration, use the drop-down list to set all properties you want to configure for your cluster (see Figure 16-4).

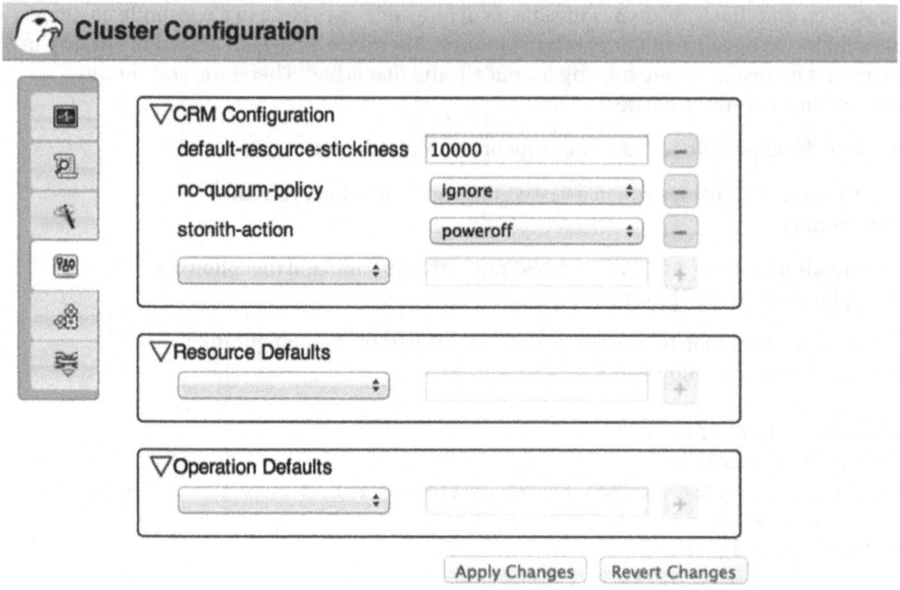

Figure 16-4. *Setting cluster properties from Hawk*

Setting Up STONITH

As discussed previously, STONITH is a mandatory mechanism that guarantees the integrity of the cluster before moving over resources. Even if it is technically possible, you should never disable STONITH, as unpredictable results may occur.

Different Solutions

The essence of STONITH is that one of the cluster nodes that is still in a stable state has to send a message to a failing node, so that it can be terminated. There's no need to bring it down in an orderly manner; just pulling the power plug is good enough. As you can imagine, a mechanism that is external to the operating system of the failing node is required for a good STONITH solution. Different approaches exist.

- Hardware-based
- Based on shared disk
- Hypervisor-based
- Test solutions

All of these solutions work well, with the exception of the test solution. However, it's always better to implement STONITH that is based on a test solution than no STONITH at all! In this section, I'll discuss three different solutions: a hardware solution that uses IPMI, the SBD shared disk-based solution, and a hypervisor-based solution.

Every STONITH solution consists of three parts:

- A stonithd process that is started when starting the cluster software. This stonithd process has to be running on all nodes. It normally doesn't require much additional configuration.

- A resource agent that can run as a program. You'll find these agents in the /usr/lib64/stonith/plugins directory, and you can get an overview of all installed agents by using the stonith -L command.

- Instructions in the cluster that tell the cluster how to execute STONITH operations.

The generic approach for setting up STONITH is that you first need to find out how exactly a specific STONITH agent should be used. A KVM-based STONITH agent, for example, requires a completely different approach than an IPMI-based STONITH agent. In the procedure descriptions that you'll read in the subsequent sections, you'll find specific instructions for three of the resource agents.

If you know how the STONITH agent works, you'll next have to run the agent without the cluster, to verify that you can operate STONITH actions from the command line. Once you've verified that part, you can integrate the STONITH configuration in the cluster.

Setting Up Hypervisor-Based STONITH

As a hypervisor-based STONITH solution is relatively easy to set up, I'll discuss this setup in detail. In this section, you'll learn about generic techniques that also apply to hardware and shared-disk-based STONITH. You'll also read how to set up STONITH for KVM virtual machines. This is a typical scenario that will be used in test environments in which multiple virtual machines are running on top of the same KVM hypervisor.

1. The first step in the configuration of every STONITH agent is to set up access for the STONITH agent to the device. If the device is an ILO board in an HP server, you need a username and password. In this case, the STONITH "device" is a KVM hypervisor, so you need a way of allowing the STONITH agent to communicate with the KVM hypervisor. For this specific STONITH agent, SSH keys are the most efficient solution. The following steps help you to set up SSK key-based authentication.

   - Make sure that hostname resolving is set up properly, so that all cluster nodes and the KVM host can find one another based on their names.

   - As root on the first cluster node, use ssh-keygen -t dsa. Press Enter to accept the default answers for all questions.

   - Still on the first cluster node, use ssh-copy-id ~/.ssh/id_dsa.pub kvmhost to copy the SSH public key to the kvmhost. Replace "kvmhost" with the actual name of the KVM host.

   - Repeat these commands on all other cluster nodes.

2. The libvirt STONITH agent that you are going to use to send STONITH commands to KVM virtual machines needs the libvirt package installed on all virtual machines. Use zypper in libvirt on all KVM virtual machines in the cluster now, to accomplish this.

3. At this point, you should have met all prerequisites, and it's time for the first test. To start with, you should now request the parameters this STONITH agent requires. To do this, use stonith -t external/libvirt -n. The command shows you that the STONITH agent needs a hostlist, a hypervisor_uri, and a reboot_method. To use all these in the appropriate command, you can now run the following command:

```
stonith -t external/libvirt hostlist="node1,node2"
hypervisor_uri="qemu+ssh://lin/system" -T reset node1
```

In this command, numerous arguments are used. First, following -t, the name of the STONITH agent is referred to. This name must be the same as something you've seen in the output of the stonith -L command. Next, the hostlist parameter is used to give a comma-separated list of nodes that can be managed by this STONITH agent. Next, there is the hypervisor_uri. The URI starts with the access mechanism, which in this case is qemu+ssh (which means you're sending a command to the qemu layer using ssh). Next in the URI is the name of the KVM host, followed by /system. Following that is the STONITH action, which is defined with the option -T reset, and as the last parameter, you have the name of the node to be STONITHed.

If the manual STONITH worked, you're ready to proceed. If it did not, you should check naming, which is the most common error with this STONITH agent. The names of the hosts you are addressing have to be recognized by the KVM hypervisor (run virsh list on the hypervisor to find out), and they also have to be the kernel names that are used on the nodes (use uname -n to find out).

At this point, you're ready to put all the required parameters in the cluster. You can, of course, take the easy approach and use the Hawk web interface, from which you can select all available options from drop-down list. You can also add the resource directly into the cluster, using the CRM shell interface. To be able to add the resource from the shell, you have to find out which parameters are supported by the resource you want to add. These are the parameters you've previously found with the stonith -t external/libvirt -n command. Next, the only thing you have to do is to put them in the cluster, using the right syntax. The procedure below describes how to do this.

1. On one of the cluster nodes (preferably the DC), as root or the user hacluster, enter the command crm. This takes you into the CRM shell.

2. Type configure. You are now in the configuration environment. Type help, to see a list of all commands that are available. Now type edit, to open the cluster editor. At this point, you should see something similar to Listing 16-4.

Listing 16-4. Editing the Cluster Configuration

```
node node1
node node2
property $id="cib-bootstrap-options" \
        dc-version="1.1.9-2db99f1" \
        cluster-infrastructure="classic openais (with plugin)" \
        expected-quorum-votes="2"
#vim:set syntax=pcmk
~
~
~
~
~
~
~
~
~
~
~
~
~
~
~
~
~
~
"/tmp/tmpFYbDVV.pcmk" 7L, 197C
```

3. As you are in a vim interface, you can use your normal editor skills to add the following block at the end of the file:

```
primitive stonith-libvirt stonith:external/libvirt \
       params hostlist="node1,node2" hypervisor_uri="qemu+ssh://lin/system" \
       op monitor interval="60" timeout="20" \
       meta target-role="Started"
```

4. At this point, type commit, to write the changes to the cluster, and type exit, to quit the CRM shell. You can now verify that the STONITH agent is running somewhere in the cluster, using crm_mon.

5. Before STONITH can become truly operational, you must now restart both nodes in the cluster. After that, you can run a STONITH test on either of the nodes, for instance, by removing the IP address from one of the nodes. That should put the node in an unreachable state and issue a STONITH action on the node.

Setting Up Shared Disk-Based STONITH

A convenient method for setting up STONITH is by using the Split Brain Detector (SBD). This STONITH method needs access to a shared disk device, so you can only use it if a Storage Area Network (SAN) disk is available. On the SAN disk, you have to create a small partition (8MB is sufficient) to store the SBD STONITH information.

SBD Stonith is based on the principle of a poison pill. If a node has to be terminated, a poison pill is written for that node in the SBD partition. Eating the poison pill is mandatory, which means that as long as the SBD process on the failing node is still available, it will process the poison pill and destroy itself.

In the following procedure, you'll learn how to set up SBD-based STONITH.

1. Make sure a shared device is available and create a small 8MB partition on the device. Do **NOT** put a file system on the partition; just an unformatted partition is enough!

2. From one of the nodes connected to the shared device, you have to initialize the shared device. To do this, use sbd -d /dev/sdc1 create. (Read carefully: the command is sbd, not sdb!)

3. Verify that the SBD metadata are written to the device, using sbd -d /dev/sdc1 dump. This should reveal something like Listing 16-5.

Listing 16-5. Verifying SBD Metadata

```
node2:~ # sbd -d /dev/sdc1 dump
==Dumping header on disk /dev/sdc1
Header version      : 2.1
UUID                : aaa1b226-8c0c-45ac-9f88-8fe5571f8fc7
Number of slots     : 255
Sector size         : 512
Timeout (watchdog)  : 5
Timeout (allocate)  : 2
Timeout (loop)      : 1
Timeout (msgwait)   : 10
==Header on disk /dev/sdc1 is dumped
```

4. To protect your configuration from a system hang (in which stonithd can no longer be addressed to crash the failing node), it is a good idea to load a watchdog module in the kernel. Some hardware has a specific watchdog. If your hardware doesn't, you can load the software based watchdog "softdog". To make sure this module is loaded on a system start, open /etc/init.d/boot.local with an editor and put the line modprobe softdog in this file.

5. To use SBD STONITH, you also have to make sure the sbd daemon is started with the cluster. This process is started from the openais cluster load script, but it needs a configuration file, /etc/sysconfig/sbd, that has the following contents:

```
SBD_DEVICE="/dev/sdc1"
SBD_OPTS="-W"
```

Note that making an error here has severe consequences. If the SBD device is not available, the cluster will not start. At this point, it's a good idea to restart the nodes in the cluster.

6. After restart, you can use the sbd -d /dev/sdc1 list command. This gives an overview of nodes that have the sbd daemon started and are currently using the SBD STONITH device.

```
node1:~ # sbd -d /dev/sdc1 list
0       node2      clear
1       node1      clear
```

7. At this point, it's time for a first test. Use the following command to effectuate a STONITH operation from the command line: stonith -t external/sbd sbd_device=/dev/sdc1 -T reset node2. This should crash the node.

8. If the previous test worked well, you can perform a second test also and see if the watchdog is doing its work. On one of the nodes, use echo c > /proc/sysrq-trigger to crash the node. If the watchdog is doing its work properly, the node will be STONITHed.

9. If your previous tests have all succeeded, you can now add the resource agent to the cluster. Use crm configure edit and add the following lines to the cluster configuration:

```
primitive sbd-stonith stonith:external/sbd \
        params sbd_device="/dev/sdc" \
        op monitor interval="3600" timeout="20" \
        op start interval="0" timeout="20" \
        op stop interval="0" timeout="15" \
        meta target-role="Started"
```

10. You can now use crm_mon to verify the current cluster configuration and check that the STONITH agent has properly loaded.

Clustering Resources

The purpose of high availability (HA) is to make sure your vital resources will be available at all times. To accomplish this goal, you have to make sure that the resources are not started by the node itself but are managed from the cluster. The way you will be doing that really depends on what you need to accomplish with your cluster. A simple cluster can just start a service without any further dependencies. A more complex cluster will take care of clustered file systems as well. And in really complex clusters, multiple dependency relations between resources may have to be defined. In this section, we'll work on some examples.

Clustering an Apache File Server

In this first example on creating a clustered resource, you'll learn how to cluster a typical Apache web service. This section, however, is not really only about clustering Apache; it's about clustering a simple service, so it may apply to other services, such as Samba, NFS, SQL databases, and many other services.

Understanding Resource Agents

To configure Apache in a cluster, you have to make sure that the Apache service can be reached no matter where it is running. That means that just clustering the Apache web service is not enough, because no matter where it runs, the web service has to be accessible by the same IP address, and it must be able to access the same files in its document root. Typically, that means that you'll have to create three resources: an IP address, a file system, and a web service. Next, you have to configure a group that is going to keep all these resources together, no matter where in the cluster they are activated.

To create resources, you need resource agents (RAs). A resource agent is like a service script, but a service script that contains cluster parameters as well. The resource agents are installed with the cluster, and they are subdivided in different classes.

- lsb: LSB (Linux Standard Base) resource agents are system V init scripts that can be started from the cluster. When browsing these, you'll see only a list of all the scripts in the /etc/init.d directory. They don't contain any cluster information and should, therefore, only be used if no real cluster resource agents are available.

- ocf: OCF (Open Cluster Framework) scripts look a lot like LSB scripts, but they have specific parameters that relate to the cluster. You'll notice that service properties can be managed by these resource agents as well. If you can choose between an OCF and an LSB resource agent, you should always use the OCF resource agent. OCF scripts come from different sources, and, therefore, you will find that there is a subdivision of the OCF RAs. Most of the important RAs are in the Heartbeat and Pacemaker subcategories.

- service: These resource agents are used to manage systemd service scripts from the cluster. Like LSB scripts, you better avoid using them.

- stonith: These are the resource agents for STONITH, as previously discussed.

Creating Resources

When adding resources to the cluster, it may be challenging to use the correct parameters. In the procedure below, you will learn how to discover parameters from the CRM shell and how to add resources to the cluster, based on the parameters you've found. After creating the individual resources, you'll next learn how they can be joined together in a group. Before proceeding, make sure that Apache is installed and a file system is created on the shared storage device.

1. Log in to one of the cluster nodes, either as user root or as user hacluster.

2. Type the crm command and, next, ra. From there, type list ocf, to display a list of all OCF resource agents. Browse through the list and verify that you see the IPaddr2, Filesystem, and apache resource agents.

3. Still from the crm ra environment, type meta IPaddr2, to show a list of parameters that can be used by the IPaddr resource agents. In this procedure, we are going to use the following parameters. Read through the explanation of how to use these resource agents:

    - ip: The IP address that is going to be used for the resource you're adding to the cluster

    - cidr_netmask: The cidr netmask that is used in your IP network. That is, 24 and not 255.255.255.0

4. You now have to find out the attributes for the file system. Still from the `crm ra` environment, type `meta Filesystem` and read the help that is provided. To create a resource for the file system on the shared storage device, you'll have to use the following parameters:

   - `device`: This is the name of the block device you want to mount. Make sure to choose a persistent name. A device name such as `/dev/sdb` is dynamically generated and may change. Better use a name that is based on device properties that won't change, like the names that are created in the `/dev/disk` directory.

   - `directory`: This is the directory in which you want to mount the shared storage device. In the case of an Apache web server, it makes sense to use the `DocumentRoot` (`/srv/www/htdocs`) as the directory.

   - `fstype`: This is the file system type that you've formatted the shared storage device with.

5. Next, you have to find the properties that are going to be assigned to the Apache OCF resource. If you use `meta ocf:apache` to display a list of parameters, you'll notice that there are no mandatory parameters for this resource. You'll also notice that many parameters can be managed by the cluster, like the Apache configuration file. This is useful, if you want to take out certain parameters from the regular location and store it on the shared storage device.

6. Based on the information you've gained in the previous three steps, you can now add the resources and their configuration to the cluster. So, enter the command `crm configure edit` and add the following lines to the end of the configuration file:

```
primitive ip-apache ocf:heartbeat:IPaddr2 \
        params cidr_netmask="24" ip="192.168.1.30" \
        op stop interval="0" timeout="20s" \
        op start interval="0" timeout="20s" \
        op monitor interval="10s" timeout="20s"
primitive fs-apache ocf:heartbeat:Filesystem \
        params fstype="ext3" device="/dev/disk/by-path/ip-192.168.1.125:3260-
        iscsi-iqn.2014-01.com.example:kiabi-lun-0-part1"
        directory="/srv/www/htdocs" \
        op stop interval="0" timeout="60" \
        op start interval="0" timeout="60" \
        op monitor interval="20" timeout="40"
primitive ip-apache ocf:heartbeat:apache \
        op stop interval="0" timeout="60" \
        op start interval="0" timeout="60" \
        op monitor interval="20" timeout="40" \
```

7. After adding the configuration to the cluster, type `crm_mon`, to verify that the resource is properly activated.

In the sample code from the previous procedure, you can see that a resource definition consists of several lines. The first line defines the name of the resources and the resource agent that has to be used. After that comes a line that defines the parameters of the resource, such as the `cidr_netmask` and the `ip` address parameters for the IP address. Following that are three lines that define the operations that this resource should use. These define how the resource should be stopped, started, and monitored.

Defining Operations

When adding a resource to the cluster, it is important to properly define how the resource should be started, stopped, and monitored. If a resource normally takes time to come up, you have to give it the appropriate time in the cluster as well. This is done by defining a time-out for stopping and starting the resource. The following two lines give a resource 60 seconds to start and 60 seconds to stop.

```
op stop interval="0" timeout="60" \
op start interval="0" timeout="60" \
```

If the resource cannot start within the start time-out interval, the cluster will draw the conclusion that the resource doesn't run on this node and try to start it somewhere else. And if the resource doesn't stop within the time-out of 60 seconds, the cluster will force it to a halt, with all possible negative consequences that are associated. Therefore, it is very important to measure the time it takes to start and stop the resource by starting it outside of the cluster as a stand-alone application. Next, make sure that your cluster has more than enough time to respect these time-out values!

Another important operation is the monitor operation. This defines how often the cluster should check if the resource is still available. The time-out defines the period of time the cluster should wait before attempting the first monitoring action. The interval defines once every however many seconds (or minutes or hours) the cluster should check if the resource is still available. If you need your cluster to be responsive, make sure to use low-interval values.

Grouping Resources

If resources should always be together, you have to tell the cluster. If you don't tell the cluster anything, it will load-balance the resources. That means that it will evenly distribute the resources among the nodes in the cluster. In the previous procedure, you added resources for an IP address, a file system, and an Apache web service. Now let's have a look at what their current state could look like:

```
Last updated: Tue Feb  4 13:03:02 2014
Last change: Tue Feb  4 13:02:57 2014 by root via cibadmin on node2
Stack: classic openais (with plugin)
Current DC: node1 - partition with quorum
Version: 1.1.9-2db99f1
2 Nodes configured, 2 expected votes
4 Resources configured.

Online: [ node1 node2 ]

stonith-libvirt  (stonith:external/libvirt):     Started node1
ip-apache        (ocf::heartbeat:IPaddr2):       Started node2
ocfs-apache      (ocf::heartbeat:Filesystem):    Started node1
service-apache-1 (ocf::heartbeat:apache):        Started node1

Failed actions:
    service-apache-1_start_0 (node=node2, call=26, rc=5, status=complete): not installed
```

As you can see, the IP address is hosted by node1, whereas the file system and the Apache service are hosted by node2. That means that all connections come in on an IP address that doesn't have an Apache service behind it.

There are two solutions that ensure that resources are always together. The easiest and recommended solution is to work with groups. Resources in a group are always kept together on the same node, and they will also be started in the order in which they are listed in the group. In the case of our Apache web service, this is also important, because the IP address and the file system have to be available at the moment the Apache service itself is starting. Creating a group is relatively easy; you only have to add one line into the cluster configuration:

1. Make sure you are logged in as root or user hacluster on one of the cluster nodes.

2. Type crm configure edit and add the following line:

    group apache-group ip-apache fs-apache service-apache

3. Close the editor, to save and apply the changes, and use crm_mon to verify that the resources are now started from a resource group.

Testing the Configuration

At this point, it's time to subject the configuration to a test. If the node that is currently hosting the Apache group goes down, the other node should automatically take over, and the failing node should be terminated by a STONITH operation.

1. Make sure you can see the console of both nodes and find out where the apache-group is currently running. Log in as root on the other node and start the command crm_mon here.

2. On the node that currently hosts the apache-group, use the command ifdown eth0. Watch what is happening in crm_mon. You should see that the resources are migrated over to the other node.

3. At the moment the failing node comes back, you will see it appearing in the cluster, and you'll notice that the resource group automatically fails back to the original node.

Normally, your cluster should work fine at the moment. If it doesn't, read the "Managing Resources," section, where you will find some important troubleshooting tips.

Using a Cluster File System

In some cases, it makes sense to use a cluster-aware file system. The default cluster-aware file system on SUSE Linux Enterprise Server is OCFS2. The purpose of a cluster-aware file system is to allow multiple nodes to write to the file system simultaneously. OCFS2 is doing this by synchronizing caches between the nodes that have the OCFS2 file system immediately, which means that every node always has the actual state of what exactly is happening on the file system.

To create a cluster-aware file system, you need two supporting services. The first of these is the distributed lock manager, dlm. The second is o2cb, which takes care of the communication of the OCFS2 file system with the cluster. As with the OCFS2 file system itself, these resources have to be started on all nodes that require access to the file system. Pacemaker provides the clone resort for this purpose. Clone resorts can be applied for any resources that need to be activated on multiple nodes simultaneously.

The procedure of creating an OCFS2 file system in a Pacemaker cluster is roughly as follows:

1. Create a group containing the dlm and o2cb resources.

2. Put this group in a clone resource.

3. Start the resource on all nodes that need to use the cluster file system.

4. Use mkfs.ocfs2 to format the OCFS2 file system.

5. Create a clone resource that mounts the OCFS2 file system as well.

The detailed procedure is described below:

1. Type crm configure edit and add the following primitives:

```
primitive dlm ocf:pacemaker:controld \
        op start interval="0" timeout="90" \
        op stop interval="0" timeout="100" \
        op monitor interval="10" timeout="20" start-delay="0"
primitive o2cb ocf:ocfs2:o2cb \
        op stop interval="0" timeout="100" \
        op start interval="0" timeout="90" \
        op monitor interval="20" timeout="20"
```

2. Create a group that contains the two primitives you've just added, by adding the following line as well:

```
group ocfs2-base-group dlm o2cb
```

3. At this point you can create a clone that contains the group and makes sure the primitives in the group are started on all nodes. To do this, also add the following lines:

```
clone ocfs2-base-clone ocfs2-base-group \
        meta ordered="true" clone-max="2" clone-node-max="1"
```

4. Write the changes and close the editor. This activates the cloned group immediately.

5. Type crm_mon to verify that the group has been started. The result should look as follows:

```
Last updated: Tue Feb  4 15:43:15 2014
Last change: Tue Feb  4 15:40:24 2014 by root via cibadmin on node1
Stack: classic openais (with plugin)
Current DC: node2 - partition with quorum
Version: 1.1.9-2db99f1
2 Nodes configured, 2 expected votes
8 Resources configured.

Online: [ node1 node2 ]

stonith-libvirt (stonith:external/libvirt):     Started node1
  Resource Group: apache-group
      ip-apache  (ocf::heartbeat:IPaddr2):       Started node1
      fs-apache  (ocf::heartbeat:Filesystem):    Started node1
      service-apache (ocf::heartbeat:apache):    Started node1
  Clone Set: ocfs2-base-clone [ocfs2-base-group]
      Started: [ node1 node2 ]
```

6. As the components that are required to create an OCFS2 file system are operational, you can now proceed and create the OCFS2 file system. Identify the shared SAN disk on which you want to create the file system. On this disk, use the mkfs.ocfs2 command: mkfs.ocfs2 /dev/sdb.

7. Mount the file system on both nodes and write a file on both nodes. You'll see that the file immediately becomes visible on the other node as well.

8. Unmount the file system on both nodes before proceeding. Also, on both nodes, create a mount point: `mkdir /shared`.

9. Use `crm configure edit` to add a primitive for the OCFS2 file system to the cluster:

```
primitive ocfs-fs ocf:heartbeat:Filesystem \
        params fstype="ocfs2" device="/dev/disk/by-path/ip-192.168.1.125:3260-iscsi-
        iqn.2014-01.com.example:kiabi" directory="/shared" \
        op stop interval="0" timeout="60" \
        op start interval="0" timeout="60" \
        op monitor interval="20" timeout="40"
```

10. Put the primitive you've just created in a clone, by adding the following lines to the configuration:

```
clone ocfs-fs-clone ocfs-fs \
        meta clone-max="2" clone-node-max=1
```

11. To tell the cluster that the `ocfs2-fs-clone` should only be started once the `ocfs2-base-clone` has successfully been started, you also have to add an order constraint (explained in more detail in the next section), as follows:

```
order ocfs2-fs-after-ocfs-base 1000: ocfs2-base-clone ocfs-fs-clone
```

12. Save the changes and quit editing mode. The cloned file system is added to the cluster, and you can now start running active-active resources on top of it.

LVM in Cluster Environments

The Logical Volume Manager (LVM) offers some advantages to working with storage. In clustered environments, LVM can be used as well, but you'll have to use Clustered LVM to make sure that the state of volume groups and logical volumes is synchronized properly on the cluster. In this section, you'll learn how to set up cLVM.

To use cLVM, you need a few supporting resources. The first of these is `dlm`, which you've also used to configure an OCFS2 file system. Apart from that, you need `clvmd`, the cluster volume manager daemon. This daemon is used to synchronize LVM metadata in the cluster. These modules have to be available on all nodes that are going to provide access to file systems on LVM volumes that are managed by the cluster. As they must be loaded on multiple nodes simultaneously, you have to configure clone resources for them.

Once the supporting modules are available, you can create a clustered LVM volume group. After that, you have to create an LVM logical volume as well. After creating these at the LVM level, you can create a cluster resource that manages the volume group. You only need this resource for the volume group, as it is the volume group that is responsible for managing cluster access to its logical volumes. When creating the volume group, you can also decide whether or not to configure it for exclusive access. By default, all nodes in the cluster can access the clustered volume group. If it is configured for exclusive access, it will be locked for all other nodes when it is in use. The procedure below describes how to create a cLVM setup.

1. Type crm configure edit and add the following code to the cluster configuration to add primitives for clvmd and dlm. Note that you only have to add the dlm primitive, if you haven't done that already in the preceding section.

```
primitive clvm-base ocf:lvm2:clvmd \
        op start interval="0" timeout="90" \
        op stop interval="0" timeout="100" \
        op monitor interval="20" timeout="20"
primitive dlm ocf:pacemaker:controld \
        op start interval="0" timeout="90" \
        op stop interval="0" timeout="100" \
        op monitor interval="10" timeout="20" start-delay="0"
```

2. As the resources have to be configured as clones, you have to add the clones as well (if you haven't already done that in the previous exercise).

```
clone dlm-clone dlm \
        meta target-role="Started" clone-node-max="1" \
                clone-max="2"
clone clvm-clone clvm-base \
        meta target-role="Started" clone-node-max="1" \
                clone-max="2"
```

3. Write and commit the changes to the cluster.

4. Type crm resource start dlm-clone; crm resource start clvm-clone. This should start both clones in the cluster. Don't proceed before you have confirmed that the clones have indeed been started.

```
Last updated: Fri Feb  7 13:47:26 2014
Last change: Fri Feb  7 07:37:53 2014 by hacluster via crmd on node1
Stack: classic openais (with plugin)
Current DC: node2 - partition with quorum
Version: 1.1.9-2db99f1
2 Nodes configured, 2 expected votes
15 Resources configured.

Online: [ node1 node2 ]

ip-test (ocf::heartbeat:IPaddr2): Started node1
ip-test-encore  (ocf::heartbeat:IPaddr2): Started node2
sbd-stonith     (stonith:external/sbd): Started node1
 Resource Group: apache-group
     ip-apache  (ocf::heartbeat:IPaddr2): Started node2
     fs-apache  (ocf::heartbeat:Filesystem): Started node2
     service-apache (ocf::heartbeat:apache): Started node2
 Clone Set: dlm-clone [dlm]
     Started: [ node1 node2 ]
 Clone Set: ocfs2-clone [ocfs2-group]
     Started: [ node1 node2 ]
```

5. At this point, you can create the LVM volume group with the cluster property enabled. The only requirement to do this is that shared storage has to be available. Assuming that the shared disk device is available on both nodes as /dev/sdd, use the following command to create the clustered volume group:

vgcreate -c y vgcluster /dev/sdd

With this command, you create a volume group with the name vgcluster that is based on the /dev/sdd shared disk device.

6. At this point, you can create the LVM logical volume. To create an LVM volume that consumes all disk space that is available in the volume group, use the following command:

lvcreate -n lvcluster -l 100%FREE vgcluster

7. Type lvs to verify that the volume group and the LVM logical volume have been created:

```
node2:~ # lvs
  LV        VG        Attr      LSize    Pool Origin Data% Move Log Copy% Convert
  lvcluster vgcluster -wi-a---- 508.00m
```

8. You now have to define a cluster resource that is going to manage access to the volume group. Use crm configure edit vgcluster and enter the following lines:

```
primitive vgcluster ocf:heartbeat:LVM \
        params volgrpname="vgcluster" \
        op start interval="0" timeout="30" \
        op stop interval="0" timeout="30" \
        op monitor interval="10" timeout="30"
```

9. As the primitive that manages access to the clustered volume group needs to be available on all nodes where the logical volumes can be accessed, you have to put it in a clone before starting it. To do this, type crm configure edit vgcluster-clone and add the following lines:

```
clone vgcluster-clone vgcluster \
        meta target-role="Started" clone-node-max="1" clone-max="2"
```

10. Write and quit the cluster editor, which automatically commits the new volume group resource to the cluster. Type crm resource status vgcluster-clone to verify the current status of the newly created resource. If all went well, you'll see that it has been started on both nodes.

11. Type lvs on both nodes to verify the availability of the logical volumes. You should see them listed on both nodes.

In many cases, the procedure described above will work fine. Sometimes it won't (see the following code listing).

```
Clone Set: vgcluster-clone [vgcluster]
    Started: [ node2 ]
    Stopped: [ vgcluster:1 ]
```

Failed actions:

vgcluster_start_0 (node=node1, call=68, rc=1, status=complete): unknown error

Before starting to dive in the log files (which often are huge), it's a good idea to stop the clone, clean up its status, and start it again. The following procedure describes how you can do that:

1. Type crm resource stop vgcluster-clone.

2. Type crm resource cleanup vgcluster-clone, to remove the current status attributes. This will remove the memory of the resource, which allows it to try to start on all nodes again, without having the memory that it was unsuccessful in starting on some of them.

3. Use crm start vgcluster-clone to start the resource again.

4. Type crm resource status vgcluster-clone to verify the status of the resource. You should see it running on all of its nodes now.

    node2:~ # crm resource status vgcluster-clone
    resource vgcluster-clone is running on: node2
    resource vgcluster-clone is running on: node1

At this point, you will have working resources. You can start creating file systems on the LVM volumes in the clustered volume group. However, when you reboot a node, starting these resources may fail. This is because nothing has been defined about the startup order.

In the previous section, you learned that you can create a group to keep resources together and have them started in the right order. In some cases, however, you cannot put resources in a group, and constraints are needed to define how resources should be started.

Imagine that you have an OCFS2 file system that is configured directly on top of shared storage, as discussed in the previous section. Imagine that apart from the OCFS2 file system, in the same cluster, you need access to clustered logical volumes as well. Both OCFS2 and cLVM need controld to be running on the nodes. Unfortunately, you cannot put the same primitive in multiple groups. You also cannot create multiple primitives and run them multiple times on the same node. You have to create a clone that starts controld and two groups: one for the cLVM resources and one for the OCFS2 resources. Next, you need a rule that defines that controld has to be started first and that the groups can be started next. You need an order constraint to do this. In the next section, you'll read how to configure constraints.

Fine-Tuning the Cluster with Constraints

Constraints are rules that define how resources should be started in the cluster. There are three different types of constraints:

-   location: Forces resources to run on specific nodes in the cluster

-   colocation: Forces resources to stay together, or to never be together

-   order: Forces constraints to be loaded in a specific order

-   ticket: Used in multisite clusters only, to determine which site can run which node (not covered here)

A location constraint is used to tell a resource on which host it should be started. Using location constraints is useful in clusters that consist of multiple nodes, because you can determine preferences for where to run resources in the cluster. That means that you can create a constraint in which the resource first tries to start on node1 and next tries to start on node2 and, only if that works, tries to start on some other node.

To define the willingness of a resource to start on a particular node in the cluster, you'll define a score for each of the resources. This score is indicated with a value that goes from -1000000 (which is also referred to as -infinity) to 0, to indicate a negative willingness. The bigger the number, the stronger the statement. That means that a score of -1000 tries not to run a resource on a specific node, but if it cannot be avoided, the resource will start on that node anyway. A score of -inf, however, is equivalent to "never." A resource that has a location constraint with a score of -inf will never run on the specific node, not even if it's the only option that's left. Likewise, you can use positive values from 0 up to 1000000 (inf).

In the listing following, we'll explore an example in which a resource is started by preference on node1. If that doesn't work, it will have a preference for node2 or node3, whereas it doesn't pronounce a specific preference for any of the other nodes. Because setting up constraints with complex scores is complicated, we'll use the Hawk web interface to avoid errors in syntax.

1. Start a browser and log in to the Hawk interface, using https://yourhawkserver:7630. Log in as the hacluster user with the password you've set for this user.

2. Click the Constraints button and, next, select to add a location constraint, by clicking the + sign (see Figure 16-5).

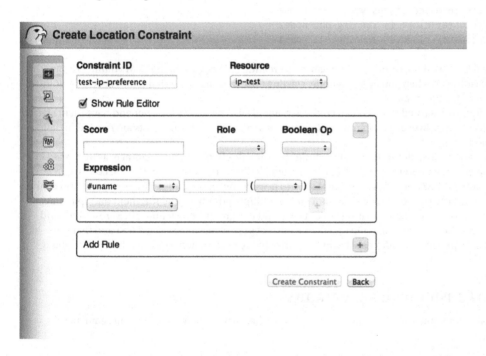

Figure 16-5. *Creating constraints from Hawk*

3. Enter a constraint ID and select a resource for which you want to create the constraint. Next, click the Show Rule Editor box, which shows you the advanced rule editor.

4. In the score field, enter the score 10000, to pronounce a strong preference. Next, select the expression #uname = node1.

5. Click Add Rule to add another rule to this constraint. At this time, enter the score 1000 and specify the expression #uname = node2. Under Boolean Op, select or and add another expression, #uname = node3.

6. At this point, click Create Constraint, to write and apply the constraint. The constraint has now been written to the CRM, where the following code has been added:

```
location ip-location ip-test-encore \
        rule $id="ip-location-rule" 10000: #uname eq node1 \
        rule $id="ip-location-rule-0" 1000: #uname eq node2 or #uname eq node3
```

As you can see, location constraints can get rather complicated. But this is also what makes Pacemaker cluster so versatile. You should take extreme caution when working with constraints, however. Especially when you're creating complex constraints, it is easy to create constraints that counter speak one another, which makes it impossible for the resource to load.

A colocation constraint can be useful if resources have to be together, or if on the contrary, they may never be together. The most common method to create a colocation constraint is by simply putting the resources in the same group. On some occasions, that is not feasible, for example, if a resource A is needed by both resources B and C, where resource B and C should not be together. Also, colocation constraints come in handy, if you want to make sure that resources will never be started on the same server. Imagine a multiple node cluster in which multiple instances of a database are started from multiple MySQL processes. In such a scenario, it could be very bad if multiple instances are started on the same node, and therefore, a colocation constraint with a negative score of -inf may be useful.

The last constraint type is the order constraint. As ordering is also implicit in groups, you can use groups in many cases, to specify the order that should be respected when starting resources. In cases where resources cannot be joined in groups, creating order constraints might be a good alternative. In the previous section, you read about an example in which this is the case: the dlm clone resource is needed by both cLVM volumes, as OCFS2 file systems in the cluster. If you're only using OCFS2 on top of cLVM, you can put them in the same group. If, however, you need them separately, it makes more sense to create a dlm clone, an OCFS2 group, and a cLVM group and then order constraints to make sure that the OCFS2 and cLVM groups are only started once the cLVM clone has been started.

Managing Resources

Normally, the cluster makes sure that failing resources are restarted somewhere else, thus providing high availability. In some cases, as an administrator, you may have to perform some management tasks as well. Some of the most common management tasks are discussed in this section.

Resource Cleanup

If the cluster tries to start a resource on a node, it may encounter problems that make it impossible to start the resource on that node. If that happens, the cluster remembers, which prevents it from trying to restart in vain a few moments later. This, however, can lead to a situation in which a resource still thinks it cannot be started somewhere else, whereas the problem may very well have been fixed. If that happens, you have to clean up the resources. By applying a cleanup action on a node, resource, or resource group, it will clear its memory and once more try to do what the cluster wants it to. Using resource cleanup is a very common action, after fixing problems in the cluster. The following procedure shows how to do it:

1. Open a CRM shell.

2. Type resource, to access the resource management interface.

3. Type list, to show a list of the resources that are currently active.

4. Type cleanup resourcename (replace "resourcename" with the name of the actual resource) to clean up resource properties.

5. Wait a few seconds, and the resource should automatically switch back to the state it should be in.

Resource Migration

High-availability clusters will take action when a node in the cluster is failing. The cluster can also be used to migrate resources away in preparation for scheduled node downtime. By migrating a resource or resource group, you will actually put a location constraint on the resource, preventing the resource from automatically moving back to its original location. Because of this constraint, you should also always un-migrate the resource, or remove the location constraint manually. The next procedure shows how to migrate the apache-group resource towards node1.

1. Open a CRM shell.

2. Type resource, to access the resource management interface.

3. Type status, to show a list of resources and their current status. Notice that this doesn't show you the actual node a resource is running on. The crm_mon command will do that, if you need to know.

4. Type migrate apache-group node1, to migrate apache-group to node1.

5. Exit the CRM shell and type crm_mon, to verify that the migration was successful.

6. Type crm configure edit, to display the contents of the current cluster configuration. Notice that a location constraint was added to the cluster, as follows:

```
location cli-prefer-apache-group apache-group \
        rule $id="cli-prefer-rule-apache-group" inf: #uname eq node1
```

7. Close the editor interface and type crm resource unmigrate apache-group. This removes the location constraint and, depending on the current resource stickiness configuration, might move the resource back to its original location.

Starting and Stopping Resources

Apart from migrating resources, you can also start and stop resources. Starting and stopping resources is easy: from the crm resource interface, just use start resourcename or stop resourcename to start or stop a resource. The result will be a meta target-role="Started" that is added to the cluster configuration. This meta target role defines the default state the resource should be in. Even after a complete restart of the cluster, this meta target role will stay. So, if you have stopped a resource manually, you will need to either remove this meta target role or start the resource again.

Using Unmanaged State for Maintenance

On some occasions, you will have to upgrade the cluster software. If an upgrade requires a restart of the cluster software, you will temporarily lose the resources that are managed by the cluster. Before restarting vital cluster components, resources are moved over to another node in the cluster. To avoid that, you can temporarily unmanage a resource. By doing this, you'll temporarily run the resource outside of the cluster, as if it would have been started locally. Once the cluster software is available again, you can manage the resource, so that the cluster can take control again. The following procedure shows how to do this.

1. Type crm to open the CRM shell.

2. Type resource, followed by status, to see the current state of your resources.

3. Type unmanage apache-group, to put the resources in the apache-group in a temporary unmanaged state.

4. Type status again, you'll see the resources being marked as unmanaged.

5. Enter the command `service openais stop`. You'll notice that the node is not STONITHed.

6. Type `ps aux | grep http`. You see that the Apache processes are still running.

7. Put the cluster resource back in a managed state by using the commands `service openais start`, followed by `crm resource manage apache-group`.

Use Case: Creating an Open Source SAN with Pacemaker

Storage Area Network (SAN) appliances are for sale for large amounts of money. In some cases, it just doesn't make sense to spend lots of money on a proprietary SAN appliance, and you might as well create an open source SAN solution. The creation of an open source SAN involves roughly two steps: first, you have to configure a Distributed Replicated Block Device (DRBD) device and have it managed by the cluster. After that, you'll have to configure an iSCSI target and have the master DRBD device. On the following pages, you'll learn how to do this.

Configuring RAID 1 over the Network with DRBD

If you want to create an environment in which multiple nodes can access your data simultaneously, the DRBD is an excellent choice. This is particularly true if you want to set up a two-node cluster, in which one node must be able to take over the exact state of the other node as quickly as possible.

Basically, DRBD is RAID 1 over the network. In the setup that is described in this section, one node behaves as the active node, whereas the other node is standby, but is fully synchronized at all times. This means that in case the active node goes down, the standby node can take over immediately. To accomplish this, it is necessary to create a cluster that manages the DRBD resource, as it is the cluster that takes care of the circumstance of one node knowing about the other node having gone away.

One of the good aspects of DRBD is that when using DRBD, you don't need an expensive SAN solution. That is because, basically, DRBD is your SAN. The basic function of a SAN is to provide a shared device on which access is provided at block level, and that is exactly what DRBD is doing for you. You can even build a further solution on top of DRBD, where an iSCSI target is installed on top of DRBD, to implement a mirrored SAN solution. This is not very hard to do, just add an iSCSI target resource in your Pacemaker cluster that follows the DRBD master as described in this chapter.

Precautionary Measures

The purpose of setting up a DRBD device is to create a device that is synchronized over the network. To accomplish this goal, you need two servers, and on both servers, you need a storage device, if possible of the same size on both nodes. There are many solutions to provide for this shared storage device, such as making a dedicated disk available or creating a partition or logical volume for this purpose. For maximal flexibility, installation of a dedicated disk is recommended. In this section, we'll assume that you have such a device, which can be reached under the name /dev/vdb. After making this device available, you'll also have to make sure that the DRBD software is installed.

■ **Important** The DRBD device is likely to synchronize large amounts of data. If this synchronization happens over the same network interface that is used for the cluster traffic, you may hit totem time-outs, with the result that the cluster starts thinking that other nodes are not available. To prevent this from happening, it is very important to separate DRBD synchronization traffic from totem traffic. The best approach is to use a dedicated network for DRBD. If that is not feasible, at least you have to make sure that the totem traffic is using another network interface. Especially in test environments, in which all is happening on one network interface, it happens too often that cluster time-outs are no longer respected, and nodes are receiving a STONITH because of that!

Creating the Configuration

After installing the software, you can create the DRBD configuration.

To start with, we'll assume that you're using two different servers that have the names node1 and node2, and on those servers, a dedicated hard disk /dev/vdb is available as the DRBD device. Also, you'll have to make sure that the default DRBD port 7780 is open on the firewall, and you'll be ready to get going.

1. The name of the default DRBD configuration file is /etc/drbd.conf. This file serves as a starting point to find the additional configuration, and to accomplish this goal, you'll have to include two lines that ensure that these configuration files can be found. To do this, make sure the following two lines are in the drbd.conf file:

    ```
    include "drbd.d/global_common.conf";
    include "drbd.d/*.res";
    ```

2. Now you have to make sure that the real configuration is defined in the /etc/drbd.d/global_common.conf file. Make sure it includes the following generic settings for smooth operation:

    ```
    global {
        minor-count  5;
        dialog-refresh  1;
    }
    common {
    }
    ```

3. As the next part of the configuration, you'll have to define the DRBD resource itself. This is done by creating several configuration files—one for each resource. Just make sure that this resource-specific configuration file is using the extension .res to have it included in the configuration, as indicated in the /etc/drbd.conf file. Below, you can see what the configuration file would look like for a DRBD resource with the name drbd0. Note that the handlers section only needs to be used if you're integrating DRBD with a Pacemaker cluster.

    ```
    resource drbd0 {
        protocol    C;
        disk {
            on-io-error        pass_on;
            fencing resource-only;
        }
        handlers {
            fence-peer "/usr/lib/drbd/crm-fence-peer.sh";
            after-resync-target "/usr/lib/drbd/crm-unfence-peer.sh";
        }
        on node2 {
            disk       /dev/vdb;
            device     /dev/drbd0;
            address    192.168.1.144:7676;
            meta-disk internal;
        }
    ```

```
    on node1 {
        disk    /dev/vdb;
        device  /dev/drbd0;
        address 192.168.1.145:7676;
        meta-disk internal;
    }
    syncer {
        rate 7M;
    }
}
```

As the first part of this file, the name of the resource is defined. In this case, we're using drbd0, but you're completely free to choose any name you like. Next, the name of the device node as it will occur in the /dev directory is specified, including the minor number that is used for this device. Make sure that you select a unique resource name as well as device name; otherwise, the kernel won't be able to distinguish between different DRBD devices that you might be using.

Next, you'll specify which local device is going to be replicated between nodes. Typically, this is an empty device, but it is possible to put a device with an existing file system on it in a DRBD configuration and synchronize the contents of that file system to the other device in the DRBD pair. Following the name of the device, you'll include the configuration for the different nodes. The node names must be equal to the kernel names as returned by the uname command. As the last part, you'll set the synchronization speed. Don't set this too high, if you don't have a dedicated network connection for DRBD; otherwise, you might be using all bandwidth, and you risk other traffic not getting through anymore, which may result in cluster nodes being STONITHed.

4. After creating the initial configuration files on one node, it's a good idea to verify the configuration. To do this, use the command drbdadm dump all. If this command shows the contents of all of the configuration files (instead of complaining about missing parts of the configuration), everything is okay, and you can proceed with the next step.

5. After verifying the configuration on the first node, you can transfer it to the second node. Make sure that you can perform the transfer using the node name of the other node. If nodes cannot reach each other by node name, your DRBD device is going to fail. So, if necessary, configure your /etc/hosts or DNS before moving on.

```
scp /etc/drbd.conf node2:/etc/
scp /etc/drbd.d/* node2:/etc/drbd.d/
```

6. Now it's time to create the DRBD metadata on both nodes. First, use the drbdadm command, as in the example below, and next, you can start the DRBD service.

```
#drbdadm -- --ignore-sanity-checks create-md drbd0
Writing meta data...
initializing activity log
NOT initialized bitmap
New drbd meta data block successfully created.
#service drbd start
```

7. At this point, you can use the service drbd status command to verify the current status of the DRBD device. You'll see at this point that both devices have the status connected but also that both are set as secondary devices and that they're inconsistent. That is because you haven't started the synchronization yet, which you're about to do now, using the following command:

```
drbdadm -- --overwrite-data-of-peer primary drbd0
```

If you now use the `service drbd status` command again to monitor the current synchronization status, you'll see that the status is set to synchronized (`sync'ed`) and that you have established a primary/secondary relationship. You'll now have to wait until the status on both nodes is UpToDate.

Working with the DRBD Device

Once the devices have been fully synchronized (this can take a long time!), you can assign a primary node and create a file system on that node. To do this, you can use the following commands:

```
drbdadm primary drbd0
mkfs.ext3 /dev/drbd0
mount /dev/drbd0 /mnt
```

If all goes well, the device will now be mounted on the primary node on the directory /mnt. If you now create files in that directory, they will immediately be synchronized to the other node. Because you are using a primary/secondary setup, however, it's not possible to access these files directly on the other node.

If all was successful until now, you can perform a test, in which you'll make the other node primary. To do this, use the following procedure:

1. Unmount the DRBD device on node node1.

2. Use the following command to make node node1 the secondary:
   `drbdadm secondary drbd0`.

3. Now go to node node2 and promote the DRBD device to primary, using the command
   `drbdadm primary drbd0`.

4. On node node2, use the command `service drbd status`, to verify that all went well.
   If this is the case, your DRBD device is now fully operational, and it's time to move on to
   the next step and integrate it in Pacemaker.

Troubleshooting the Disconnect State

If after a change of status both nodes in the DRBD setup return to a stand-alone state, your DRBD setup is in a split-brain situation, in which there is no way to verify which node contains the primary data set. To fix such a situation, you must manually intervene by selecting one node whose modifications will be discarded (this node is referred to as the *split-brain victim*). This intervention is made with the following commands:

```
drbdadm secondary resource
drbdadm -- --discard-my-data connect resource
```

On the other node (the *split-brain survivor*), if its connection state is also StandAlone, you would enter:

```
drbdadm connect resource
```

Working with Dual Primary Mode

To use an active-active configuration, in which two nodes are both primary, you have to enter some additional configuration. First, in the resource definition, you'll have to include a net section that allows the use of two primaries and sets the correct synchronization protocol. Also, you'll have a startup section that automatically switches to the primary role on both nodes on startup. The following lines will do this for you:

```
resource drbd0
        net {
                protocol C;
                allow-two-primaries yes;
        }
        startup {
                become-primary-on-both;
        }
        ...
}
```

If you're working in a dual primary configuration, you must also adjust the cluster configuration. Dual primary requires a clone resource and not a master-slave resource, as described in the following section.

Integrating DRBD in Pacemaker Clusters

Using the drbdadm command, you can manually determine which node is going to be primary and which will be secondary. In a real high-availability (HA) environment, you'll have to integrate the DRBD device in the Pacemaker cluster software. Doing this assumes that the cluster will manage DRBD and not the local nodes.

Before adding the resources to the cluster, you'll have to take some precautionary measures in the drbd resource file as well. By including the following lines, you'll ensure that if the DRBD replication link becomes disconnected, the crm-fence-peer.sh script contacts the cluster manager and determines the Pacemaker master-slave resource that is associated with this DRBD resource. Next, it will make sure that the master-slave resource in Pacemaker no longer gets promoted on any other node than the currently active one. This ensures that you don't get in a situation in which you'll have two nodes both thinking that they're master, which will lead to a split-brain situation. To accomplish this, include the following in the resource configuration file:

```
resource drbd0 {
        disk {
                fencing resource-only;
                ...
        }
        handlers {
                fence-peer "/usr/lib/drbd/crm-fence-peer.sh";
                after-resync-target "/usr/lib/drbd/crm-unfence-peer.sh"
        ...
        }
        ...
}
```

The next steps describe how to add a resource that manages DRBD in Pacemaker. This procedure assumes that you already have an operational Pacemaker cluster.

1. Start Hawk and log in as user hacluster.

2. Add a primitive for the DRBD resource. Select class OCF, the Provider Linbit, and the type drbd.

3. Set the drbd_resource parameter to the name of the DRBD resource that you've created. This is the name of the resource as defined in the drbd0.res file and not the name of the device, so enter drbd0 and not /dev/drbd0.

4. From the parameter's drop-down list, select the drbdconf parameter and provide the value of the drbd.conf file, which would be /etc/drbd.conf. Also add the resource name, which should be the same as the name of the resource as defined in the DRBD resource file. Next, click Create Resource, to add the resource to your configuration.

5. At this point, get back to the Create Resources tab and add a master-slave resource. Give it the name drbd-ms, and as the child resource, select the DRBD resource you've just created.

6. Under Meta-Attributes, set the target role to Started and click Create Master/Slave, to add the master-slave resource to the configuration.

```
primitive drbd ocf:linbit:drbd \
        params drbdconf="/etc/drbd.conf" drbd_resource="drbd0" \
        op start interval="0" timeout="240" \
        op monitor interval="20" role="Slave" timeout="20" \
        op monitor interval="10" role="Master" timeout="20" \
        op stop interval="0" timeout="100" \
        meta target-role="Started"
ms drbd-ms drbd \
        meta master-max="1" master-node-max="1" clone-max="2" \
        clone-node-max="1" notify="true" \
        meta target-role="Started"
```

Testing

Before you continue using your setup, it's a good idea to reboot both nodes in the cluster and make sure that the cluster is indeed managing the DRBD resource and not the local DRBD service. After the restart, verify that the DRBD resource is indeed started on both nodes and that one of the nodes is primary and the other is secondary. It's also a good idea to check the cluster configuration itself. As this is a two-node cluster, make sure the no-quorum policy is set to ignore. Also, make sure that STONITH is operational. If this is the case, you can perform a test and switch off the primary node. The secondary node should now automatically take over.

Adding an iSCSI Target to the Open Source SAN

Once your DRBD device is operational and managed by the cluster, you have to add an iSCSI target to it. In Chapter 2, you read how to set up storage, and the iSCSI target in particular. In this section, you'll read how to set up the iSCSI target to provide access to the active DRBD device and have it managed by the cluster.

There are different approaches to set this up. In a simplified architecture, you can set up a DRBD device on top of shared storage (as described in the previous section). On top of that, you can configure an iSCSI target and a dedicated IP address. Even if this option works, it won't offer you much flexibility at the storage layer, because you will need a new DRBD device for every additional iSCSI logical unit number (LUN) that will be added. This is why it is much more flexible to create the Logical Volume Manager (LVM) layer on top of the DRBD device.

In this configuration, lots of components need to work together.

1. A DRBD device

2. The DRBD master that is managed from the cluster

3. An LVM configuration with a Physical Volume, Volume group, and Logical Volume on top of the DRBD device

4. An iSCSI target

5. An iSCSI Logical Unit that replaces the definition of the LUN in the iSCSI target configuration file

6. An IP address that allows nodes to connect to the configuration

In the previous section, you learned how to set up the DRBD device and the DRBD master in a cluster environment. In Chapter 2, you learned how to set up an iSCSI target, based on the configuration file in /etc/ietd.conf. In this section, you'll learn how to set up a clusterized iSCSI target and iSCSI Logical Unit and an IP address on top of that. You will also learn how to set up the LVM configuration in a way that works in clustered environments.

Setting Up the LVM Environment

To start with, you need to create an LVM physical volume on top of the DRBD device. Next, access to the LVM volume group has to be set up as managed by the cluster. To create this configuration, take the following steps:

1. Make sure that the DRBD device is scanned by LVM for LVM metadata. To do this, you have to change the contents of the /etc/lvm/lvm.conf file to include the DRBD devices. This following example will only consider DRBD devices and ignore everything else:

   ```
   filter = [ "a|/dev/drbd.*|", "r|.*|" ]
   ```

2. Now, you have to disable LVM cache on both nodes. Do this by also including the following line in /etc/lvm/lvm.conf:

   ```
   write_cache_state = 0
   ```

Also make sure to remove the current cache that might exist: rm -rf /etc/lvm/.cache.

3. Before continuing, use the command vgscan to update LVM metadata.

4. Assuming the name of the DRBD device is drbd0, use pvcreate /dev/drbd0 to mark the DRBD device as a physical volume.

5. Now you can create the LVM stack, consisting of a PV, a VG, and an LV. The following three commands will create the volume group, and a GB logical volume as well. Issue them on the node that currently has the primary DRBD device (!).

   ```
   pvcreate /dev/drbd0
   vgcreate vgdrbd /dev/drbd/by-res/drbd0
   lvcreate -L 1G -n lvlun0 vgdrbd
   ```

6. At this point, you can put the LVM configuration in the cluster. Type `crm configure edit` and add the following lines to the cluster configuration (this configuration might give a warning about `timeout` values, which you can safely ignore):

```
primitive lvm-drbdvol ocf:heartbeat:LVM \
        params volgrpname="vgdrbd" \
        op monitor interval="10s" timeout="30s" depth="0"
```

7. Verify that the volume group resource is running in the cluster before continuing.

Setting Up the iSCSI Target in the Cluster

Now that you've added the DRBD and LVM resources in the cluster, you can continue and configure iSCSI. What you need at this point is an iSCSI target. The configuration related to the iSCSI target consists of three different parts:

- The iSCSI target process that has to be started by the cluster

- The iSCSILogicalUnit resource, which manages the LUNs that are presented by the iSCSI target

- A cluster IP address that will be used to access the iSCSI target

To create this configuration, take the following steps:

1. Make sure the iSCSI target software is installed on your computer by using `zypper install tgt`. Notice that this installs the `tgt` target software and not the `ietd` that is used by default on SUSE Linux. The `tgt` software offers more advanced ways to define node restrictions, and therefore, I like it more for complex environments.

2. Remove the software from the default startup procedure by using either `chkconfig tgtd off` or `sysctl disable tgtd`.

3. Add the service to the cluster by using `crm configure edit` and adding the following (note that you initially don't start the iSCSI target, because it needs additional configuration):

```
primitive iscsitarget-drbd ocf:heartbeat:iSCSITarget \
        params iqn="iqn.2014-02.com.example:drbdsan" tid="1" \
                implementation="tgt" \
        op monitor interval="10s" timeout="20s" \
        meta target-role="Stopped"
```

4. Add the following:

```
primitive drbdvol-lun0 ocf:heartbeat:iSCSILogicalUnit \
        params target_iqn="iqn.2014-02.com.example:drbdsan" lun="1" \
        path="/dev/vgdrbd/lvlun0" \
        op monitor interval="10"
```

At this point, your open source SAN is operational. You can start testing it now, by connecting to it from an iSCSI client interface. Even if the node currently hosting the SAN disk fails, the other node will take over, and you won't experience too many problems from the clients.

Summary

In this chapter, you've learned all you need to know to set up a high-availability cluster on SUSE Linux Enterprise Server 12. You've read about cluster base requirements, and you've learned how to connect the cluster to shared storage. Finally, you've learned about the different types of resources that you can create in the cluster.

CHAPTER 17

■ ■ ■

Creating a SLES 12 Installation Server

If you have to install only a few SUSE servers, there's nothing wrong with inserting the installation disk in the machine and performing a manual installation. If you have multiple installations to perform, a more automated method is preferable. In this chapter, you'll learn how to configure SLES 12 as an installation server, to perform fully or partially automated installations over the network.

Understanding the Components

In an installation server, different parts are used. The first part is an online repository. The online repository provides access to the files that have to be installed. To get access to these files, the server that has to be installed must start an installation image. This installation image can be on a DVD, but it can also be a small boot image that is provided through a PXE boot server. In that scenario, the PXE boot server delivers the boot image, and from the boot image, the installation server to be used is specified. To automate this process even further, AutoYaST can play a role. In AutoYaST, installation profiles containing all settings that have to be configured on the installable server are provided.

When setting up an installation environment, you can configure a complete environment, in which all these elements are used and working together. It is also possible to take elements of the complete environment and combine these, to facilitate an installation process that can be performed more smoothly.

Configuring an Online Repository

To configure an online repository, the YaST Installation Server module, which is in the miscellaneous section, is used. This module allows administrators to set up an installation server as an HTTP, FTP, or NFS repository (see Figure 17-1).

```
YaST2 - instserver @ linux-3kk5

Initial Setup -- Initial Setup




                (x) Configure as HTTP Repository
                ( ) Configure as FTP Repository
                ( ) Configure as NFS Repository

                [ ] Do Not Configure Any Network Services
                Directory to Contain Repositories:
                /srv/install▓▓▓▓▓▓▓▓▓▓▓▓▓▓▓▓▓▓▓[Select Directory]




 [Help]                    [Back]                    [Abort]                    [Next]

 F1 Help  F8 Back  F9 Abort  F10 Next
```

Figure 17-1. *The YaST Installation Server module provides different options*

While setting up an installation server, different protocols can be used. For optimal speed, HTTP is probably the best option, so if you don't have a specific reason to use one of the other protocols, select Configure as HTTP Repository, to set up the online repository. (In fact, what YaST calls an installation server isn't much more than an online repository).

In the screen shown in Figure 17-1, there's also a Do Not Configure Any Network Services option. Select this if the service that you want to use for the installation server is already operational on your server. You'll also have to specify the directory in which you want to put the installable files. By default, this is the /srv/install directory.

You'll now see a screen from which you can define a Directory Alias and Firewall settings. After selecting what you want to do, you'll see the screen that is shown in Figure 17-2. From this screen, you must install the installation sources.

```
YaST2 - instserver @ linux-3kk5

 Installation Server

 ┌Configuration│Product──────────────────────────────────────────────────────┐
 │                                                                             │
 │                                                                             │
 │                                                                             │
 │                                                                             │
 │                                                                             │
 │                                                                             │
 │                                                                             │
 │                                                                             │
 │                                                                             │
 │                                                                             │
 └─────────────────────────────────────────────────────────────────────────┘
 ┌─────────────────────────────────────────────────────────────────────────┐
 │                                                                             │
 └─────────────────────────────────────────────────────────────────────────┘
 [Add][Edit][Delete]                              [Server Configuration...]

 F1 Help  F3 Add  F9 Abort  F10 Finish
```

Figure 17-2. *Adding files to the repository*

After pressing Add from the screen depicted in Figure 17-2, you'll gain access to the Repository Configuration screen (see Figure 17-3). Here, you must specify the name of the repository that you want to create. It's a good idea to use the name of the SLES version that you want to install as the repository. Optionally, you can select to announce the repository as an installation service with the Service Location Protocol (SLP). When this option is selected, clients can search the network for available installation servers, which makes installing these servers a lot easier.

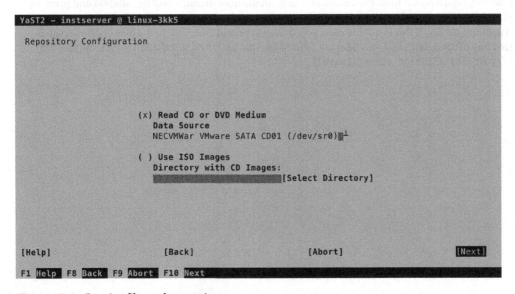

```
YaST2 - instserver @ linux-3kk5

  Repository Configuration




               Repository Name:
               sles12rc3

               [x] Announce as Installation Service with SLP









  [Help]              [Back]              [Abort]              [Next]
F1 Help  F8 Back  F9 Abort  F10 Next
```

Figure 17-3. Configuring the repository

After specifying the repository name, you'll have to copy files to the repository. To do this, the installation medium is required. You can copy files from either the physical installation disk or an ISO image. In either case, you must make sure that the installation files are available. From the screen shown in Figure 17-4, select the installation medium that you want to use and click Next to proceed.

```
YaST2 - instserver @ linux-3kk5

  Repository Configuration





               (x) Read CD or DVD Medium
                   Data Source
                   NECVMWar VMware SATA CD01 (/dev/sr0)

               ( ) Use ISO Images
                   Directory with CD Images:
                                        [Select Directory]




  [Help]              [Back]              [Abort]              [Next]
F1 Help  F8 Back  F9 Abort  F10 Next
```

Figure 17-4. Copying files to the repository

Once the files are copied to the repository, you're asked for the next CD. In general, it's safe to skip this. (Don't use Cancel, as it will cancel everything you've done so far!) At this point, the installation server is complete, and you'll see the screen shown in Figure 17-5. You can now press F10 to finalize the procedure.

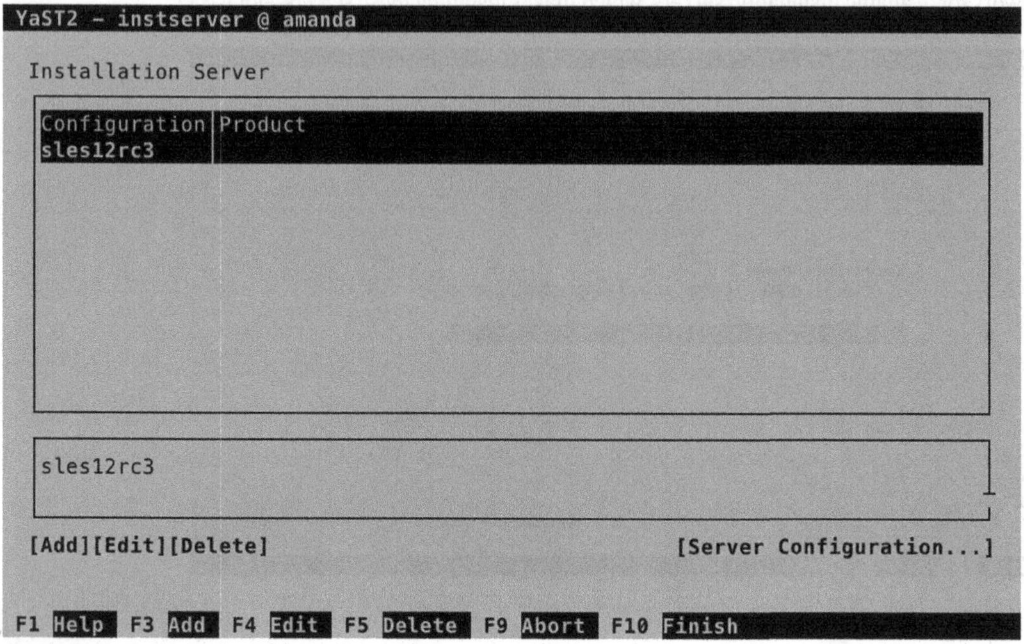

```
 YaST2 - instserver @ amanda

  Installation Server

  Configuration Product
  sles12rc3





  sles12rc3


  [Add][Edit][Delete]                           [Server Configuration...]


 F1 Help  F3 Add  F4 Edit  F5 Delete  F9 Abort  F10 Finish
```

Figure 17-5. *The repository has now been added to the installation server*

Before proceeding and creating the PXE boot server, it's a good idea to test whether what you've done so far is really working. To do this, boot a server from the installation disk. In the boot menu, select Installation and press F4 to select the installation source (see Figure 17-6). If you've set up the installation server with SLP, you can use the SLP option to find it automatically. If this is not the case, you'll have to provide the URL to the files on the server. If you haven't changed any of the details, and you have configured an Apache-based installation server, the files are available at http://your-installation-server/install.

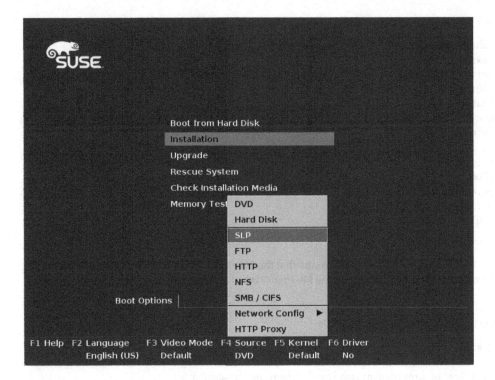

Figure 17-6. *Testing the installation server*

Creating the PXE Boot Configuration

Most modern network cards have an option that allows users to boot from the network card. This is known as a PXE boot, in which PXE stands for Preboot eXecution Environment. In this scenario, a boot image is delivered over the network. For this to work, you'll have to provide two elements: a DHCP server that is configured to hand out IP addresses to the servers you want to install and a TFTP server that is configured to hand out the boot image. In this section, you'll learn how to set up such an environment. This section focuses on the PXE-specific parts of the DHCP server. Read Chapter 11 for more details on setting up a DHCP server.

After configuring the DHCP server, you must include the following three additional elements in the subnet declaration:

- next-server: This is the server that the DHCP client should contact to get the PXE boot image.

- server-name: This optional parameter informs the client of the name of the server from which it is booting.

- filename: This specifies the name of the file that the TFTP server has to offer to the client.

With these parameters, the dhcpd.conf file should now look as in Listing 17-1.

Listing 17-1. dhcpd.conf with PXE Boot Parameters

```
amanda:~ # cat /etc/dhcpd.conf
option domain-name "example.com";
option domain-name-servers 192.168.4.2;
option routers 192.168.4.2;
default-lease-time 14400;
ddns-update-style none;
subnet 192.168.4.0 netmask 255.255.255.0 {
  range 192.168.4.100 192.168.4.110;
  default-lease-time 14400;
  max-lease-time 172800;
  next-server 192.168.4.210;
  server-name "amanda.example.com";
  filename "pxelinux.0";
}
```

After configuring the DHCP server, you have to make sure that the tftp and syslinux packages are installed. Use zypper in tftp syslinux to install them. This creates the file /etc/xinetd.d/tftp, which has the content that you can see in Listing 17-2.

Listing 17-2. The /etc/xinetd.d/tftp Configuration File

```
amanda:/etc/xinetd.d # cat tftp
# default: off
# description: tftp service is provided primarily for booting or when a \
#       router need an upgrade. Most sites run this only on machines acting as \
#       "boot servers".
#       The tftp protocol is often used to boot diskless \
#       workstations, download configuration files to network-aware printers, \
#       and to start the installation process for some operating systems.
service tftp
{
    socket_type  = dgram
    protocol     = udp
    wait         = yes
    flags        = IPv6 IPv4
    user         = root
    server       = /usr/sbin/in.tftpd
    server_args  = -u tftp -s /srv/tftpboot
#   per_source   = 11
#   cps          = 100 2
    disable      = no
}
```

Make sure that in this file, the parameter disable is set to no, which enables the tftp service the next time the xinetd service is restarted. Also, type systemctl enable xinetd, to make sure the xinetd service is started at next reboot.

You can now create the pxelinux configuration directory. To do this, type mkdir -p /srv/tftpboot/pxelinux.cfg. Next, use the following command: cp /usr/share/syslinux/pxelinux.0 /srv/tftpboot.

In the TFTP server document root, you need some additional files as well: at least, the kernel and installation image of the distribution that you want to install using the PXE boot server. You'll find them in the repository you've just created. If the name of the repository is sles12, and you are using an HTTP installation server, the directory to copy the linux and initrd files from is /srv/install/sles12/CD1/boot/x86_64/loader. From that directory, use cp linux initrd /srv/tftpboot to copy these files.

As a next step, you must create the file /srv/tftpboot/pxelinux.cfg/default. This file is used as a boot menu for PXE boot clients, and it makes sure that the PXE client knows what to install. Give this file a contents that looks like the following:

```
default SLES12
label SLES12
        kernel linux
        append initrd=initrd ramdisk_size=65536 \    install=http://yourinstallserver/install
```

After creating these configurations, use systemctl start xinetd; systemctl start dhcpd; systemctl enable xinetd; systemctl enable dhcpd to start everything. You can now try to PXE-boot a server you want to install, and you should receive a boot image that automatically starts the installation.

Using AutoYaST

After setting up an online repository and a PXE server, you'll still have to provide input as to how you want the server to be installed. This can be automated as well, by using AutoYaST. With AutoYaST, you can provide an answer file, containing all the answers that are needed for successful installation. Such an answer file is created on every server that has been installed, and you can find it under the name autoinst.xml, in the home directory of user root. To use the AutoYaST file, it suffices to add the following line to the PXE default file: autoyast=http://your-server/install/autoyast.xml. You can also pass this line as an argument on the boot prompt, while performing an installation.

The autoinst.xml file is an XML file, and it can be manually changed. This, however, is not the easiest approach, as the file is long, and it's hard to get an overview of everything it offers. As an alternative, you can use the autoyast module that is available in YaST. Using this interface allows you to specify everything that should be happening while installing. Figure 17-7 shows the interface that can be used to create an AutoYaST file.

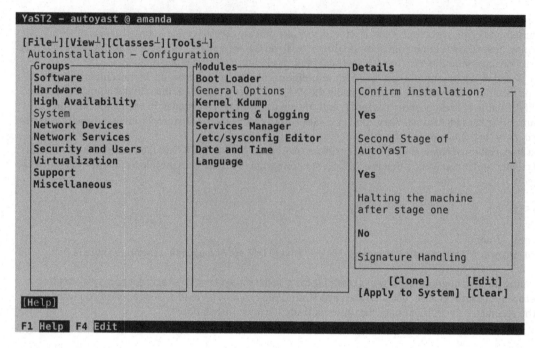

Figure 17-7. Creating an AutoYaST file from YaST

From the YaST AutoYaST module, you'll just walk through the different installation settings and provide the answers you want to use while installing. It's also possible to leave answers open, in which case, the installation procedure will still prompt you for input while installing.

Summary

In this chapter, you've learned how to set up an installation server. You've read how to create the repository containing the RPMs you want to use on installation, as well as a PXE boot environment. You've also read how to use AutoYaST to provide all installation parameters automatically.

CHAPTER 18

■ ■ ■

Managing SUSE Linux

SUSE offers two options for managing SUSE Linux. SUSE Manager is available as an additional purchase and allows you to deploy systems, manage software, and monitor systems. A Subscription Management Tool (SMT) server allows you to manage updates centrally on your network. SUSE Manager is the perfect solution for administrators who want a complete and well-integrated solution for managing SUSE Linux Servers. In this chapter, you'll learn how to configure and use it. The following topics are discussed:

- Preparing SUSE Manager Installation
- Installing SUSE Manager
- Creating the Base Configuration
- Registering SUSE Manager Clients
- Managing Software Channels in SUSE Manager
- Patching and Updating Systems
- Managing Configuration with SUSE Manager
- Auto-installation of Systems
- Using SUSE Manager Monitoring
- Using SUSE Manager Proxy
- Using Organizations

Preparing SUSE Manager Installation

To start with, go to the SUSE Customer Center and make sure you have access to registration keys for SUSE Manager and SUSE Linux Enterprise Server. You also need the SUSE Manager mirror credentials. If you are not yet entitled to use SUSE Manager, you can request a 60-day evaluation license and use that for installation. Make sure that you also have (evaluation) licenses available for the SUSE Servers you want to manage with SUSE Manager. Note that the SUSE Manager registration key must be assigned to the same account as the account that has the keys to use SUSE Linux Enterprise Server (see Figure 18-1).

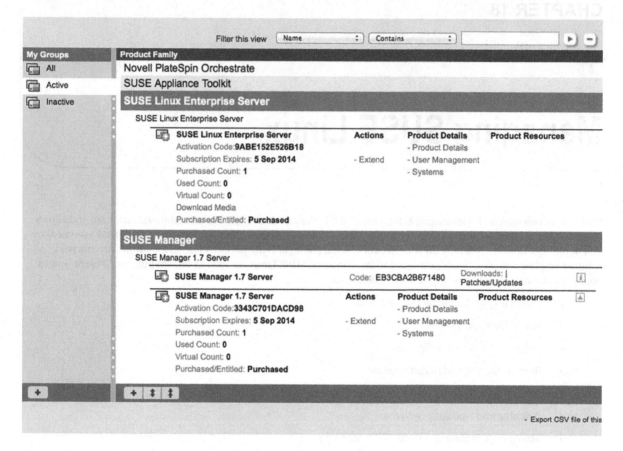

Figure 18-1. *Before you continue, make sure to get the registration codes for SUSE Manager as well as SLES*

Go to https://scc.suse.com and log in with your SUSE account settings. You'll get an overview of the products that are registered with your account. If you don't see your product listed here, check www.novell.com/center. At the time this was written, the SUSE Customer Datacenter was not completely synchronized with the Novell Customer Datacenter database, and it could be that information was available on one of the databases and not on the other.

Next, download the SUSE Manager 2.1 installation ISO from the SUSE web site (www.suse.com). Ensure that the physical or virtual computer on which you want to install meets at least the following hardware specifications:

- 4GB RAM

- 100GB hard disk

- 2 core or better

Installing SUSE Manager

At this point, you can boot from the SUSE Manager installation disk. From the menu, select Install/Restore SUSE-Manager-Server. The installer guides you through the steps of the installation. As SUSE Manager is an appliance that requires access to your entire hard disk, on the first screen, you are asked if you want to destroy all data on /dev/sda. Answer Yes, to start the installation and load the SUSE Manager Server software.

You are now guided through the remaining steps of the installation, which are summarized as follows:

1. Enter the language and keyboard settings you want to use.

2. Agree to the License Agreement.

3. Enter a password for the root user on the SUSE Manager Server.

4. Change the network configuration. Note that you must activate the Change button to get access to the options that allow you to change the address configuration for the network card on your server (see Figure 18-2). Also, make sure to change routing and DNS information according to the needs in your network.

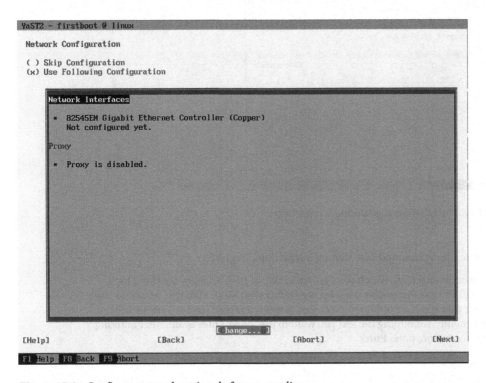

Figure 18-2. *Configure network settings before proceeding*

5. Enter your time zone information.

6. Set NTP time synchronization. It's also a good idea to enter the name or address of the server you want to synchronize with and test whether the server is responding. (If it is, you have confirmation that your network is working properly; if it's not, you know you have some fixing to do before moving on. As there is no back option, it is probably easiest just to reboot your installer and start all over).

7. You'll now get to the Novell Customer Center Configuration screen (see Figure 18-3). Unless you want to fetch patches from a Subscription Management Tool (SMT) server (described later in this chapter), registration at this point is mandatory. Note that after clicking Next, the installation module has to contact the registration server, and this might be slow.

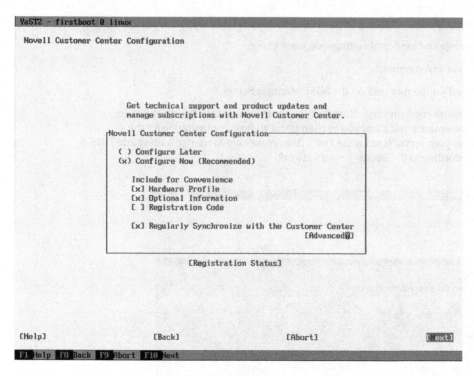

Figure 18-3. To proceed with installation, registration is mandatory

8. Select Continue when prompted that Manual Interaction is required.

9. When the text browser screen, which you can see in Figure 18-4, appears, you have to enter the e-mail address that you've used for registering with SUSE Manager, as well as the activation code that you have obtained. Note that to enter text, you have to select a field and press Enter. After submitting the text you want to use, press Enter again. After entering all required information, press Enter.

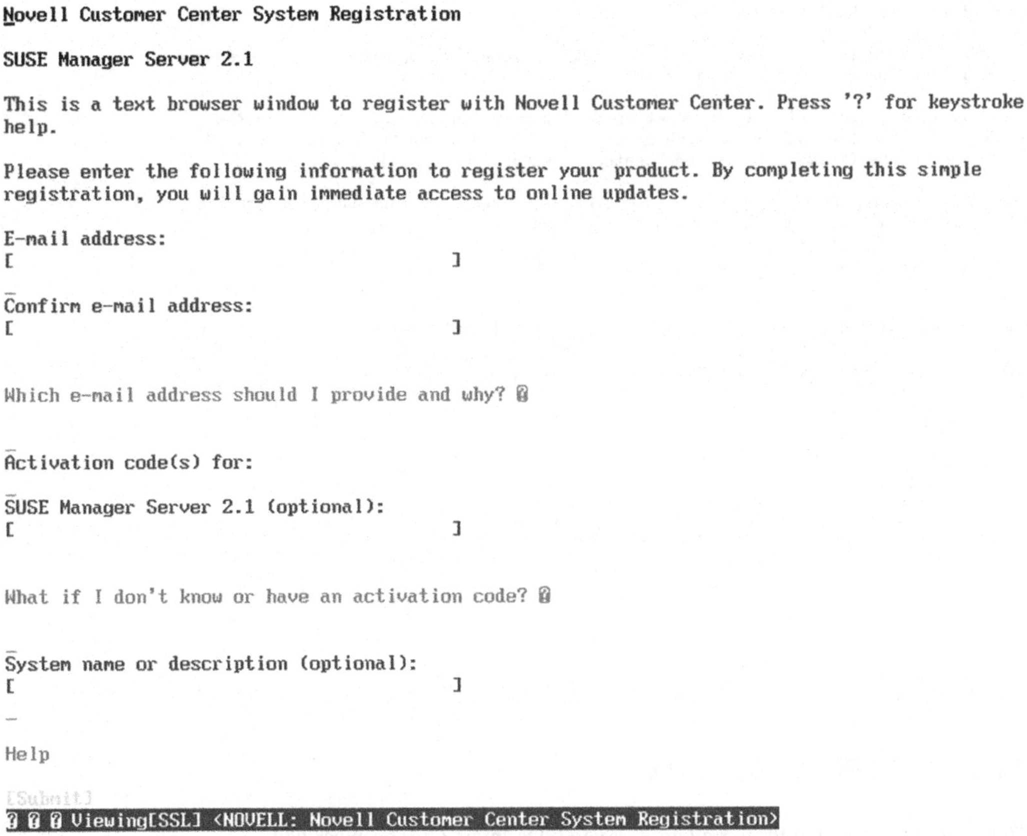

Novell Customer Center System Registration

SUSE Manager Server 2.1

This is a text browser window to register with Novell Customer Center. Press '?' for keystroke help.

Please enter the following information to register your product. By completing this simple registration, you will gain immediate access to online updates.

E-mail address:
[   ]

Confirm e-mail address:
[   ]

Which e-mail address should I provide and why? ⍰

Activation code(s) for:

SUSE Manager Server 2.1 (optional):
[   ]

What if I don't know or have an activation code? ⍰

System name or description (optional):
[   ]
—

Help

[Submit]

⍰ ⍰ ⍰ Viewing[SSL] <NOVELL: Novell Customer Center System Registration>

Figure 18-4. *Enter here the e-mail address associated with your account*

10. If you've entered the correct e-mail address, you will now see the screen shown in Figure 18-5. From this screen, press Q to quit and Y to confirm. Update repositories are now configured, and the installation is finalized. You will see another screen mentioning that the configuration was successful, which means that the registration key you've entered has been accepted also.

If at this point the registration fails, you can complete the installation and perform a manual registration. To register manually, use the command suse_register -n --no-hw-data -a regcode-sles=<YOURCODE> -a regcode-sms=<YOUR-SMGR-REGCODE> -a email=yourmail@example.com -L /root/suse_register.log.

```
Novell Customer Center System Registration

To complete the process of registering this system and getting access to online updates, you need
to finish the registration process. To proceed, click the Continue button.

To change the registration or subscription information for this system, you can log in to the
Novell Customer Center at any time using the same credentials that you use to log in to your Novell
Login account. You can access the Novell Customer Center at http://www.novell.com/center.

If you do not yet have a Novell Login account, please create one and make sure that you use the
same e-mail address that you used when registering this system.

To create the Novell Login account, access the Novell web site at http://www.novell.com/
createaccount.

For your convenience, you will be sent a follow up e-mail with this information.

To close this window, type Q and then Y to continue.
*




                                                                                                │




  0 0 0 Viewing[SSL] <NOVELL: Registration Completed>
```

Figure 18-5. *This is what you see after the e-mail address you have entered has been verified*

11. The primary phase of the installation is now complete, and you'll get access to a login prompt. Log in as user root with the password that you've provided earlier in the setup procedure. Make sure that the hostname of your SUSE Manager Server is in the Domain Name System (DNS), and if it is not, add it in /etc/hosts. Next, you can enter yast2 susemanager_setup, to start the second phase of the setup process.

12. From the first screen, you can select to setup an SUSE Manager from scratch. Alternatively, the configuration module offers to migrate from a Spacewalk or Satellite server.

13. Now enter the e-mail address for the administrator. This address is used for notification messages, and it is associated with the SSL certificate that is created in the next step. If there is an SLP server in your network, you may choose to register SUSE Manager with SLP (currently SLP registration by clients is not supported).

    When asked for credentials, the country code must be a valid code. If you're in the United Kingdom, the valid country code is GB, not UK. The installer will fail when entering the wrong country code here.

14. Now, an SSL certificate is created. The certificate is used if you want to configure access to a proxy and for establishing secure management connections from a browser. The certificate will, by default, be self-signed, as it is for internal use only. You have to provide all information that is requested before you can proceed.

15. You now have to configure database access (see Figure 18-6). The default selection is set to using an embedded database. For setting up an embedded database, enter the name of a database user, as well as a password. Notice that the password has to be secure. It needs a minimum of seven characters, cannot contain any special characters, and may not be based on a dictionary word. If you want to use either an external postgres database, or an Oracle database, enter the database SID, hostname, port, and protocol required to access the database. In our example, we'll be demonstrating connection to a local database only.

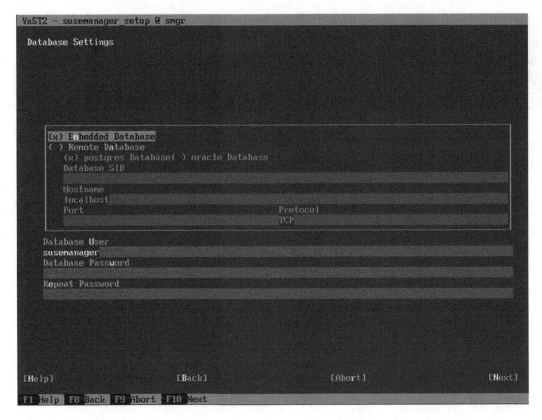

Figure 18-6. *Setting up database access*

16. After configuring database access, you have to enter your NCC mirror credentials. This is the username and password that you've looked up before starting the installation and configuration (on NCC, select My Products, Mirror Credentials). Enter your mirror credentials user name, the associated password, as well as the e-mail address associated with your account. The base SUSE Manager system will now be set up. This will take a few minutes (count on approximately five minutes).

17. Once the base system has been installed, you'll see a setup completed window. On this window, you see two important pieces of information: first is the command mgr-ncc-sync that you now need to run in order to start the synchronization. The second part is the URL to the SUSE Manager management interface, on which you can log in to begin administering SUSE Manager.

18. After completing the base installation, type mgr-ncc-sync, to start synchronizing repository information.

Creating the Base Configuration

Once the base setup is complete, you can now start the base configuration. To do this, establish an HTTPS session to the SUSE Manager Server. You'll now be prompted to create an admin user. Enter the desired login name, as well as the password you want to use, and click Create Login. After creating the administrator user, you'll get access to the SUSE Manager web interface. On this interface (see Figure 18-7), you're prompted to run the Setup Wizard. Click the Setup Wizard link to complete all of the base requirements.

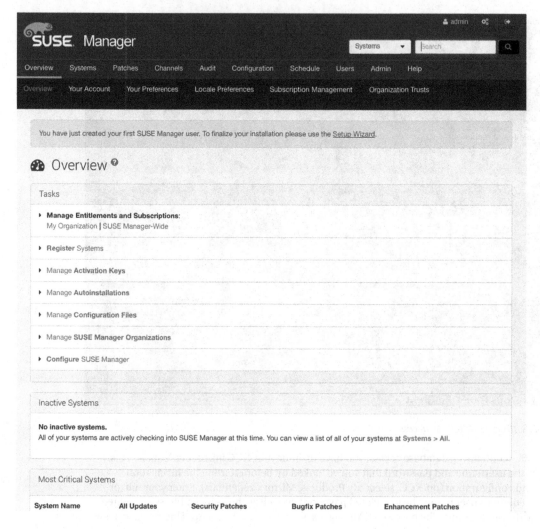

Figure 18-7. *First login to the web management interface*

Using the Setup Wizard from the Web Console

In the Setup Wizard that you get access to now, you'll first be able to enter the URL to a proxy and the username and password that are required to log in to the proxy. You just have to enter this information if you have to go through a proxy to fetch patches. If this is not the case, click Next to proceed to the next screen. On the following screen, you'll get access to the SUSE Manager mirror credentials. You'll see the mirror credentials that you've used while setting up

SUSE Manager, and you'll have occasion to enter additional mirror credentials here. Note that this is only useful if you're using multiple sets of mirror credentials to gain access to all the SUSE products that you're entitled to.

In the third screen of the initial Setup Wizard, you'll get access to the list of SUSE products that you're entitled to. You'll see those products that you're entitled to, depending on your current mirror credentials. If products are missing, check the customer center to ensure that you're entitled to using these products. If some products are associated with another SUSE account, enter the mirror credentials for that account also. From this screen, you can also initiate the synchronization of available channels, by clicking the + sign to the right of the channel (see Figure 18-8).

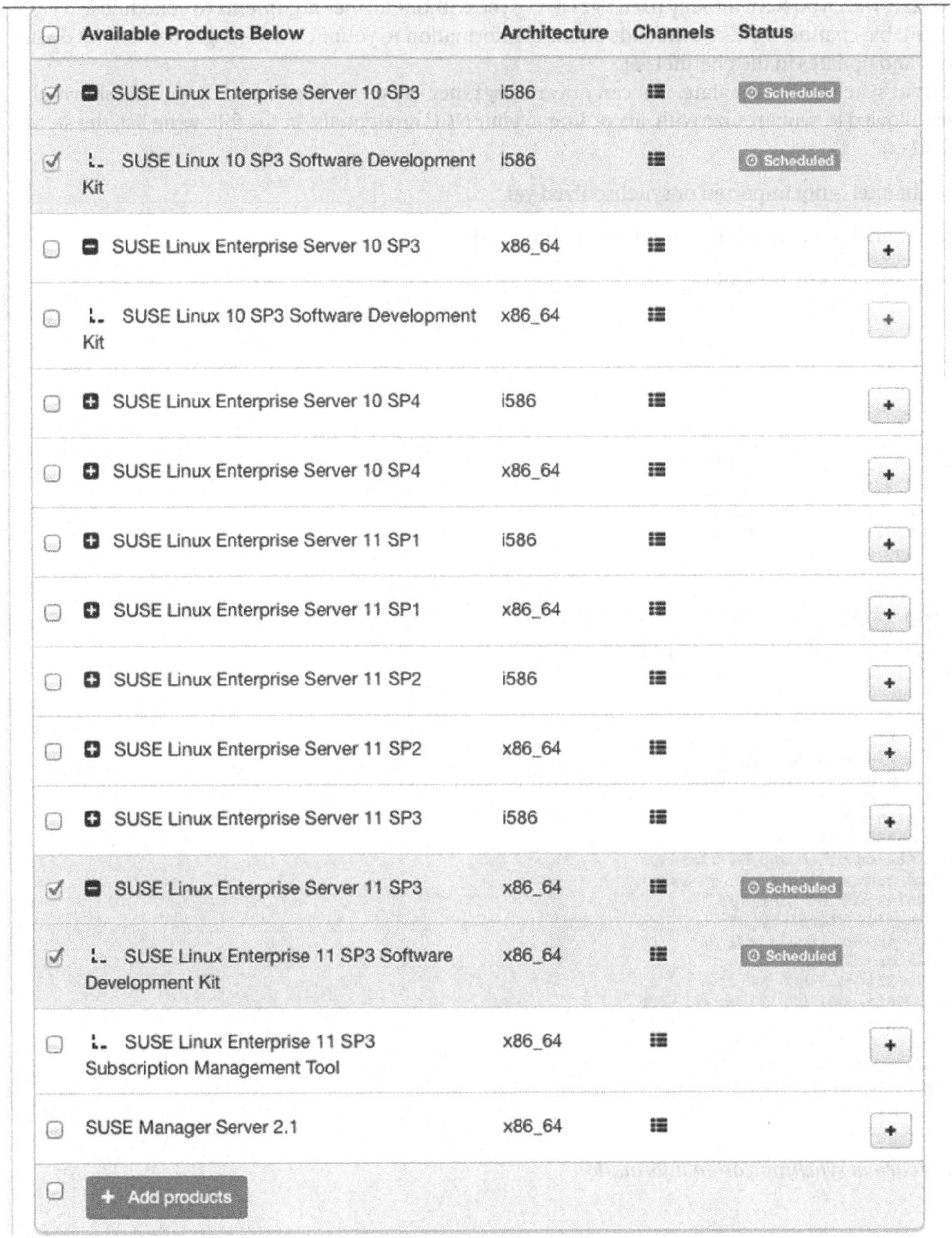

	Available Products Below	Architecture	Channels	Status	
☑	▬ SUSE Linux Enterprise Server 10 SP3	i586	▦	⊘ Scheduled	
☑	⌐ SUSE Linux 10 SP3 Software Development Kit	i586	▦	⊘ Scheduled	
☐	▬ SUSE Linux Enterprise Server 10 SP3	x86_64	▦		+
☐	⌐ SUSE Linux 10 SP3 Software Development Kit	x86_64	▦		+
☐	⊞ SUSE Linux Enterprise Server 10 SP4	i586	▦		+
☐	⊞ SUSE Linux Enterprise Server 10 SP4	x86_64	▦		+
☐	⊞ SUSE Linux Enterprise Server 11 SP1	i586	▦		+
☐	⊞ SUSE Linux Enterprise Server 11 SP1	x86_64	▦		+
☐	⊞ SUSE Linux Enterprise Server 11 SP2	i586	▦		+
☐	⊞ SUSE Linux Enterprise Server 11 SP2	x86_64	▦		+
☐	⊞ SUSE Linux Enterprise Server 11 SP3	i586	▦		+
☑	▬ SUSE Linux Enterprise Server 11 SP3	x86_64	▦	⊘ Scheduled	
☑	⌐ SUSE Linux Enterprise 11 SP3 Software Development Kit	x86_64	▦	⊘ Scheduled	
☐	⌐ SUSE Linux Enterprise 11 SP3 Subscription Management Tool	x86_64	▦		+
☐	SUSE Manager Server 2.1	x86_64	▦		+
☐	+ Add products				

Figure 18-8. Initializing channel synchronization

After initializing the channel synchronization from the SUSE Manager interface, it's a good idea to verify the current synchronization status from the SUSE Manager console.

Managing Package Synchronization

On the console of the SUSE Manager Server, many command-line utilities are available. Among the most important utilities is mgr-ncc-sync, which is used to synchronize channels and download patches and updates to your computer. To start with, you have already used mgr-ncc-sync without further arguments to schedule a synchronization of available channels. This downloads channel information to your SUSE Manager Server, but do not download the patches and updates in the channel yet.

To check the current synchronization state, you can now run mgr-ncc-sync -l (see Figure 18-9). This shows all channels that you are allowed to synchronize with, according to your NCC credentials. In the following list, the status of each channel is marked:

- [.]: The channel is not imported or synchronized yet.

- [P]: The channel is previously imported or synchronized.

- [X]: The channel is not available.

```
[.] sles10-sp4-pool-x86_64
[.] sles11-sp1-pool-i586
[.] sles11-sp1-pool-x86_64
[.] sles11-sp3-pool-i586
[P] sles11-sp3-pool-x86_64
    [.] sle11-sdk-sp1-pool-x86_64-sdk-sp3
    [.] sle11-sdk-sp1-updates-x86_64-sdk-sp3
    [.] sle11-sdk-sp2-core-x86_64-sdk-sp3
    [.] sle11-sdk-sp2-updates-x86_64-sdk-sp3
    [P] sle11-sdk-sp3-pool-x86_64
    [P] sle11-sdk-sp3-updates-x86_64
    [.] sle11-security-module-x86_64
    [.] sle11-smt-sp3-pool-x86_64
    [.] sle11-smt-sp3-updates-x86_64
    [.] sle11-sp1-debuginfo-pool-x86_64-sles-sp3
    [.] sle11-sp1-debuginfo-updates-x86_64-sles-sp3
    [.] sle11-sp2-debuginfo-core-x86_64-sles-sp3
    [.] sle11-sp2-debuginfo-updates-x86_64-sles-sp3
    [.] sle11-sp3-debuginfo-pool-x86_64
    [.] sle11-sp3-debuginfo-updates-x86_64
    [.] sles11-extras-x86_64-sles-sp3
    [.] sles11-sp1-pool-x86_64-sles-sp3
    [.] sles11-sp1-updates-x86_64-sles-sp3
    [.] sles11-sp2-core-x86_64-sles-sp3
    [.] sles11-sp2-extension-store-x86_64-sles-sp3
    [.] sles11-sp2-suse-manager-tools-x86_64-sp3
    [.] sles11-sp2-updates-x86_64-sles-sp3
    [.] sles11-sp3-extension-store-x86_64
    [P] sles11-sp3-suse-manager-tools-x86_64
    [P] sles11-sp3-updates-x86_64
[P] suse-manager-server-2.1-pool-x86_64
    [.] sle11-sp3-debuginfo-pool-x86_64-server-2.1
    [.] sle11-sp3-debuginfo-updates-x86_64-server-2.1
    [.] sles11-sp3-pool-x86_64-server-2.1
    [.] sles11-sp3-updates-x86_64-server-2.1
    [.] suse-manager-server-2.1-updates-x86_64
smgr:~ # _
```

Figure 18-9. Showing current synchronization information

If a channel has not been imported yet, you can either schedule a synchronization from the web interface or use `mgr-ncc-sync -c`, followed by the name of the channel to schedule a full synchronization. Use, for instance, `mgr-ncc-sync -c suse-manager-server-2.1-pool-x86_64` to start an immediate synchronization with the mentioned channel.

When working with channels, you should note that they are organized in a parent-child relationship. You'll first have to import the parent channel, using `mgr-ncc-sync -c`, which will make the information about child channels available. As, normally, not all of the child channels within a parent channel will be required, you'll next have to run `mgr-ncc-sync -c` on every child channel you want to import. Note that once a channel is imported, it cannot be deleted! Only custom channels can be deleted!

Be aware, too, that package import from the channels is a slow process. The best way to keep track of the current status of synchronization is by accessing the Channels tab on the SUSE Manager web interface (see Figure 18-10). If you've just started package synchronization, you'll see that one channel only has packages. Refresh the link, to verify that the channel is still working on downloading packages. The initial update process will take a long time, as many gigabytes of data have to be downloaded.

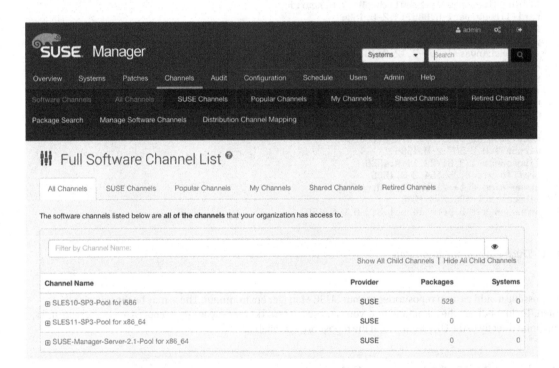

Figure 18-10. *To get information about current channel synchronization, consult the SUSE Manager web page*

To get more details about current package synchronization status, you can also monitor the `spacewalk-repo-sync` process on your SUSE Manager Server. This process downloads packages to the package database, and you can trace what it is doing by opening its log file. The log file is in the directory `/var/log/rhn/reposync` and has the same name as the name of the channel that you're synchronizing. In the log, you can see the total amount of packages going to be downloaded for this channel and the current state of the synchronization process (see Figure 18-11).

```
750/2296 : mono-data-1.2.2-12.27-0.i586
751/2296 : libibumad-devel-1.1.7-0.3-0.i586
752/2296 : aalib-devel-1.4.0-305.2-0.i586
753/2296 : perl-IO-Tty-1.02-305.4-0.i586
754/2296 : libicu-doc-3.4-16.10-0.i586
755/2296 : quagga-0.99.9-14.5-0.i586
756/2296 : Mesa7-7.0.4-0.6.31-0.i586
757/2296 : sax2-libsax-python-7.1-125.62.11-0.i586
758/2296 : yast2-mail-2.13.8-0.13.46-0.noarch
759/2296 : libibcm-1.0.4-6.5.15-0.i586
760/2296 : dbus-1-mono-0.60-33.25-0.i586
761/2296 : mozilla-xulrunner191-gnomevfs-1.9.1.2-3.5.9-0.i586
762/2296 : translation-update-en_GB-10.0.0-0.20.16-0.noarch
763/2296 : yast2-iscsi-client-2.14.47-0.4.9-0.noarch
764/2296 : limal-ca-mgm-perl-1.1.75-0.3-0.i586
765/2296 : lprng-3.8.28-21.15-0.i586
766/2296 : sles-startup_zh_TW-10.1-0.10-0.noarch
767/2296 : libol-0.3.16-14.2-0.i586
768/2296 : ttf-arphic-bsmi00lp-20001125-603.2-0.noarch
769/2296 : perl-libwww-perl-5.805-12.2-0.i586
770/2296 : kde3-i18n-pt_BR-3.5.1-8.6-0.noarch
771/2296 : permissions-2007.2.15-0.7-0.i586
772/2296 : libgnomecanvas-devel-2.12.0-19.2-0.i586
773/2296 : kde3-i18n-ja-3.5.1-8.6-0.noarch
774/2296 : pptpd-1.2.3-12.2-0.i586
775/2296 : ifnteuro-1.2.1-209.2-0.noarch
776/2296 : mozilla-xulrunner191-1.9.1.2-3.5.9-0.i586
777/2296 : oracleasm-kmp-xenpae-2.0.5_2.6.16.60_0.54.5-7.4.50-0.i586
778/2296 : libgnome-2.12.0.1-26.6-0.i586
779/2296 : kde3-i18n-en_GB-3.5.1-8.6-0.noarch
780/2296 : varmon-1.0.2-587.2-0.i586
781/2296 : libgnomedb-1.3.91-23.14-0.i586
782/2296 : traffic-vis-0.35-154.2-0.i586
783/2296 : gnome-mine-data-2.4.2-22.2-0.noarch
784/2296 : libmcal-0.7-136.2-0.i586
785/2296 : openwbem-smash-providers-1.0.9-0.9-0.i586
-
```

Figure 18-11. Tracing synchronization state

It's also possible to add custom repositories to your SUSE Manager environment. These may be repositories that you've created. To do this, from the command line, you can use spacewalk-repo-sync -c <repo_name> -u <repo_url>, in which you point directly to the URL from which the repository is available.

Registering SUSE Manager Clients

To register clients at SUSE Manager, there are two requirements. First, you need an activation key. After creating the activation key, you can create a bootstrap script that is going to be executed from the client to register the client.

Creating Activation Keys

Multiple activation keys can be created, and each activation key tells a client to what exactly he or she is entitled. If you have multiple platforms in your organization, it's useful to have multiple activation keys (but no longer required in SUSE Manager 2.1). It is also possible to create a system-wide default activation key, which can be created by selecting Systems ➤ Activation Keys from the SUSE Manager web interface (see Figure 18-12).

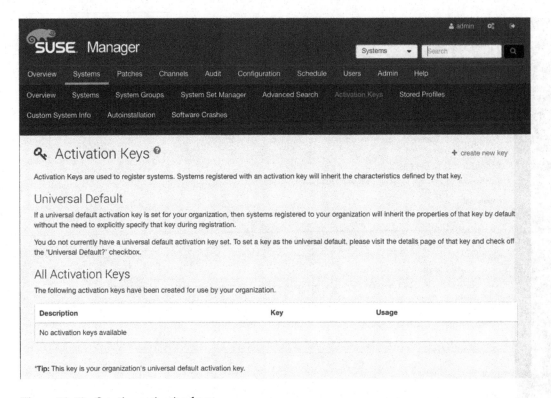

Figure 18-12. *Creating activation keys*

On the Activation Keys tab, click Create new key. You'll now enter a window on which you can enter all the activation key details (see Figure 18-13). On this window, you must enter the following properties:

- `Description`: This is a description that makes identification of this key easier.

- Key: An identifier for this key. Leave this empty, if you want the key to be automatically generated.

- `Usage`: Enter the number of clients who can use this key, or leave it empty for unlimited usage.

- `Base Channels`: Leave this to SUSE Manager Default. This allows the client to register on the channel that is compatible with his or her operating system version. It's recommended that you not change this setting.

- `Add-On entitlements`: By default, all SUSE Manager clients will be able to update software against SUSE Manager. Add-on entitlements are available for additional purchase. These allow customers to use monitoring, provisioning, or virtualization services as well. If applicable, select here the additional channels that clients are entitled to.

- `Contact Method`: Specifies how the client is going to communicate with SUSE Manager. In the Pull method, clients will fetch all they need for themselves. Push is available as well, but it requires additional SSH setup.

- `Universal Default`: Use this property to set this key as the default key for your organization.

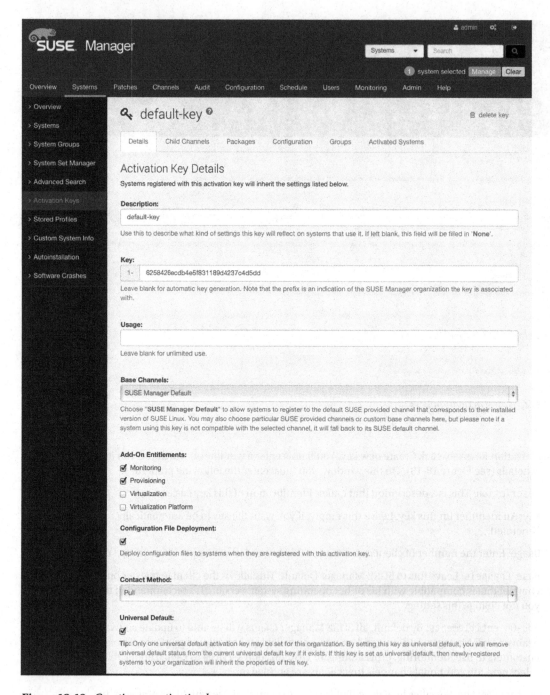

Figure 18-13. *Creating an activation key*

After creating the key, you'll see some tabs showing the child channels, groups, and activated systems associated with this key. If this is the default key, it doesn't make much sense to change these, but if this is a custom key that you've created for a specific use, you can manage either of these tabs, to configure what should be available to clients.

Using Activation Keys, it is also possible to install Software Packages. To do this, you must first select the Provisioning module in Add-On Entitlements. Note that this functionality is not included in the base package but requires an additional purchase. You also have to register a system to use this functionality; it doesn't show by default. Next, under Configuration File Deployment, select Deploy configuration files to systems. You can now access the Packages tab and specify a list of packages that you want to install to all systems that are using this key. To enable Push installation via jabberd and the osad agent on the server, make sure that the following packages are added using this method:

```
rhncfg
rhncfg-actions
rhncdg-client
osad
rhnmd
```

The Bootstrap Script

The bootstrap script is what is used to automatically configure each client for its role in the SUSE Manager environment. It can be used to perform multiple tasks, such as importing custom GPG keys, installation of SSL certificates, and performing post-configuration activities.

No default bootstrap script exists. The script is generated according to the needs for your specific environment. Before generating it, you should modify the contents of the file /srv/www/htdocs/pub/bootstrap/client-config-overrides.txt. This file, which you can see in Figure 18-14, contains all the settings that your clients need for successful registration with the SUSE Manager Server.

```
# RHN Client (rhn_register/up2date) config-overrides file v4.0
#
# To be used only in conjuction with client_config_update.py
#
# This file was autogenerated.
#
# The simple rules:
#        - a setting explicitly overwrites the setting in
#          /etc/syconfig/rhn/{rhn_register,up2date} on the client system.
#        - if a setting is removed, the client's state for that setting remains
#          unchanged.

enableProxy=0
enableProxyAuth=0
httpProxy=
noSSLServerURL=http://smgr.example.com/XMLRPC
proxyPassword=
proxyUser=
serverURL=https://smgr.example.com/XMLRPC
sslCACert=/usr/share/rhn/RHN-ORG-TRUSTED-SSL-CERT
useGPG=1
~
~
~
~
~
~
~
~
~
~
~
~
~
~
"/srv/www/htdocs/pub/bootstrap/client-config-overrides.txt" 21L, 621C          1,1          All
```

Figure 18-14. *The* `client-config-overrides.txt` *file contains specific settings for your environment*

As an alternative to a manual modification of the bootstrap script, a SUSE Manager administrator can apply modifications from the web console as well. To do this, select Admin ➤ SUSE Manager Configuration and select Bootstrap Script. This shows a screen on which you can enter properties of the bootstrap script and click Update to generate a new script.

After modifying the contents of the overrides file, you have to run the `mgr-bootstrap` utility, to create a bootstrap script for your specific SUSE Manager Server. This will write a bootstrap script with default contents to the file `/srv/www/htdocs/pub/bootstrap/bootstrap.sh`, which makes it available via the web server that is running on your SUSE Manager Server. It's a good idea to keep the original `bootstrap.sh` file and copy the file to a specific file, in which the purpose of the bootstrap script is reflected (such as `bootstrap-baseos.sh`).

Before using it, you have to apply some mandatory changes to the bootstrap script. First, you'll also find some other parameters, such as the option `FULLY_UPDATE_THIS_BOX`, which performs a full update of the registered server after it has been successfully registered, and the `ACTIVATION_KEYS` line that has to contain the activation key that is associated with this bootstrap script. Note that without any reference to the activation key, the clients will not be able to register! So make sure to go to the Systems ➤ Activation Keys tab; fetch the activation key; and add it to the `bootstrap.sh` file. Next, look for the line `exit 1` in the bootstrap script and put a comment sign in front of it.

After preparing the bootstrap script, you can run in from a client. On the server you want to register, use the following to do this:

```
wget https://yoursusemanager.example.com/pub/bootstrap/bootstrap.sh
chmod +x bootstrap.sh
./bootstrap.sh
```

This will execute a few tasks on the client, which results in a registered system. (Note that registration can complete successfully only if the channel that is needed for the client platform has been completely synchronized. Also, make sure that time is set correctly. Without proper time synchronization, this procedure will fail.) After registration, you'll be able to see the system on the Systems tab in the SUSE Manager interface (see Figure 18-15). In addition, you should verify that the `rhncfg-actions` software package has been installed successfully.

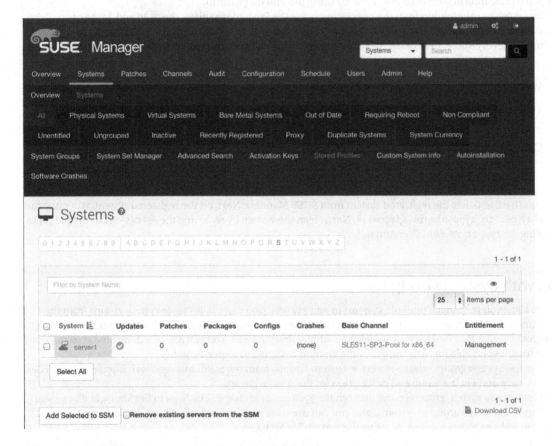

Figure 18-15. *Verifying system registration in the web interface*

For each registered system, you can get detailed information by clicking the system in the SUSE Manager Systems interface. For every registered server, you'll find a detailed overview of its configuration, software that is installed on the system, system groups it belongs to, and different events that are pending for this system or that have been executed on this system.

Based on the OS platform that is used on the client, you'll also find it in the channel that is relevant to the client. By registering the client, it will also add repositories that refer to the channels on the SUSE Manager Server. As a result, all software that will be installed on the clients will now be installed from the SUSE Manager repositories.

Troubleshooting and Unregistering Registered Systems

Normally, registration works well. On some occasions, it does not. If that is the case, there are different things that you can do. To start with, from the registered system, run the command rhn_check -vvv, to get information about the current communication with the database. Next, you may change the interval in /etc/sysconfig/rhn/rhnsd on the client. This interval, by default, tells the client to synchronize every 240 seconds. It may help to decrease it, if the client is configured to receive information from the server by using the Pull mechanism.

If the client receives information from the user by means of the Push mechanism, the osad and jabberd processes are used. To use these properly, it is important that hostname resolving is set up correctly and that FQDN hostnames are used everywhere. In general, the following three tips will help fix errors that are related to osad and jabberd:

- Verify that DNS is set up correctly (all hostnames involved can be resolved via /etc/hosts).

- Verify time synchronization. The osad process will not authenticate if time differs more than 120 seconds.

- Clean up the jabber database. Use service jabberd stop; cd /var/lib/jabberd/db/; rm -f db*; service jabberd start.

If nothing helps, you may have to unregister a registered system. To do this, a couple of steps must be performed. To start with, you have to delete the registered system from SUSE Manager. Next, on the registered system, you must run the command zypper rm zypp-plugin-spacewalk. Next, clean the system by removing the /etc/sysconfig/rhn file and by executing the zypper rm rhnlib command.

Working with System Groups

System groups allow you to manage multiple systems in an easy way. You can easily create system groups from the web interface and update activation keys that are associated through a system group. Another advantage of working with system groups is that they make it easy to delegate administration tasks. You can assign a dedicated system group administrator to be responsible for managing only the systems assigned to a specific group.

To create a new system group, select Systems ➤ System Groups from the SUSE Manager web interface. Next, click Create System Group and enter a name and description for the system group.

Adding systems to a system group is done through the System Set Manager. The System Set Manager allows you to apply settings to a selected group of systems, and you can use it for many more tasks. The following procedure describes how to add systems to a group, by using the System Set Manager.

1. From the list of systems, select All. Next, click System Set Manager (see Figure 18-16).

Figure 18-16. *After selecting the systems, click System Set Manager*

2. From the System Set Manager tab, click Groups (see Figure 18-17). This shows a list of system groups that have been defined on your computer. At the group you want to add the systems to, select Add. Next click Alter Membership and click Confirm, to finalize this step.

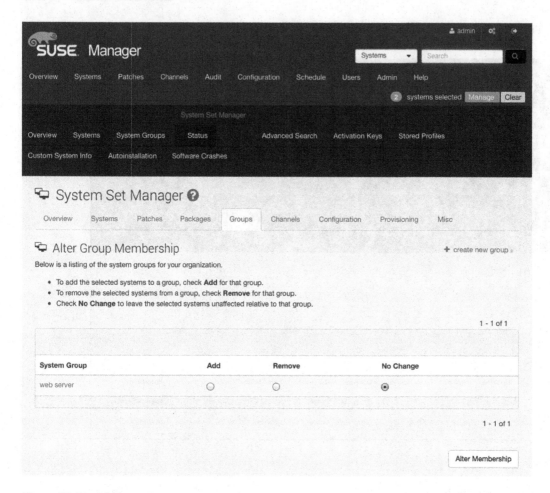

Figure 18-17. *Adding systems to a group*

3.   At this point, you can select the system Groups tab. It will list the system group(s) you have created and the systems that are a member of each group. In addition, you'll easily see if updates are available for systems in a specific system group.

After creating a system group, you can apply updates to the system group through the activation keys. This scenario applies if you have modified the settings in an activation key. To apply the changes you have made to the key, on the key management tab, select Groups ➤ Join. Select the system group that you want to join to the key and click Join Selected Groups.

Managing Software Channels in SUSE Manager

Software channels are a core element in SUSE Manager. When installing a SUSE Manager Server, all channels that you are entitled to appear in SUSE Manager. You have read how to use the mgr-ncc-sync command with different options to start downloading packages to the local channels on the SUSE Manager Server from the servers at SUSE. These channels are known as the Customer Center Channels, and they are the foundation for all software management and distribution tasks that you will want to perform with SUSE Manager.

In Customer Center Channels, you'll get base channels that contain a complete category of software. A base channel, for example, is the SLES11-SP3-Pool for x86_64, which contains everything required to manage SLES11 Servers. Within the base channel, different child channels are available. The hierarchy between base channels and child channels shows easily from the SUSE Manager web interface (see Figure 18-18). Apart from these default SUSE channels, an administrator can create custom channels, containing specific third-party packages.

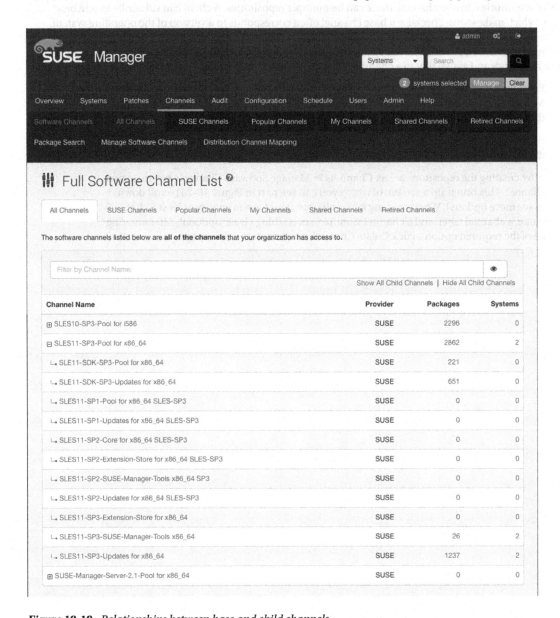

Figure 18-18. *Relationships between base and child channels*

An important task for an administrator is to ensure that channels can be cloned. This is useful in a software staging process. Cloning a channel freezes the state of a channel and guarantees that a specific version of packages is used on the clients. After cloning a channel, it becomes a custom channel. Custom channels can be removed, using the spacewalk-remove-channel command. SUSE channels cannot be removed.

When working with channels, administrators must be aware of a few basic rules. The channel is a pointer to a collection of repositories. In one channel, there can be multiple repositories. A client can subscribe to one base channel only, which makes sense, because a base channel often corresponds to a version of the operating system. Within a base channel, a client can subscribe to multiple child channels.

Managing channels begins with the management of repositories. The procedure described below shows how to create a new repository and assign that to a channel.

1. From the SUSE Manager web interface, select Channels ➤ Manage Software Channels ➤ Manage Repositories. Next, click Create Repository, to create a new repository. This shows the window that you see in Figure 18-19.

2. Enter a label for the repository, as well as a repository URL. All other options are discretionary. Next, click Create Repository, to create it.

3. After creating the repository, select Channels ➤ Manage Software Channels ➤ Create new channel. This brings up a screen, of which you can see part in Figure 18-20 (scroll down to see more options). When creating a new channel, you have to specify at least a channel name, a channel label, and a channel summary; everything else is optional. After entering all of the required options, click Create Channel, on the bottom of the page.

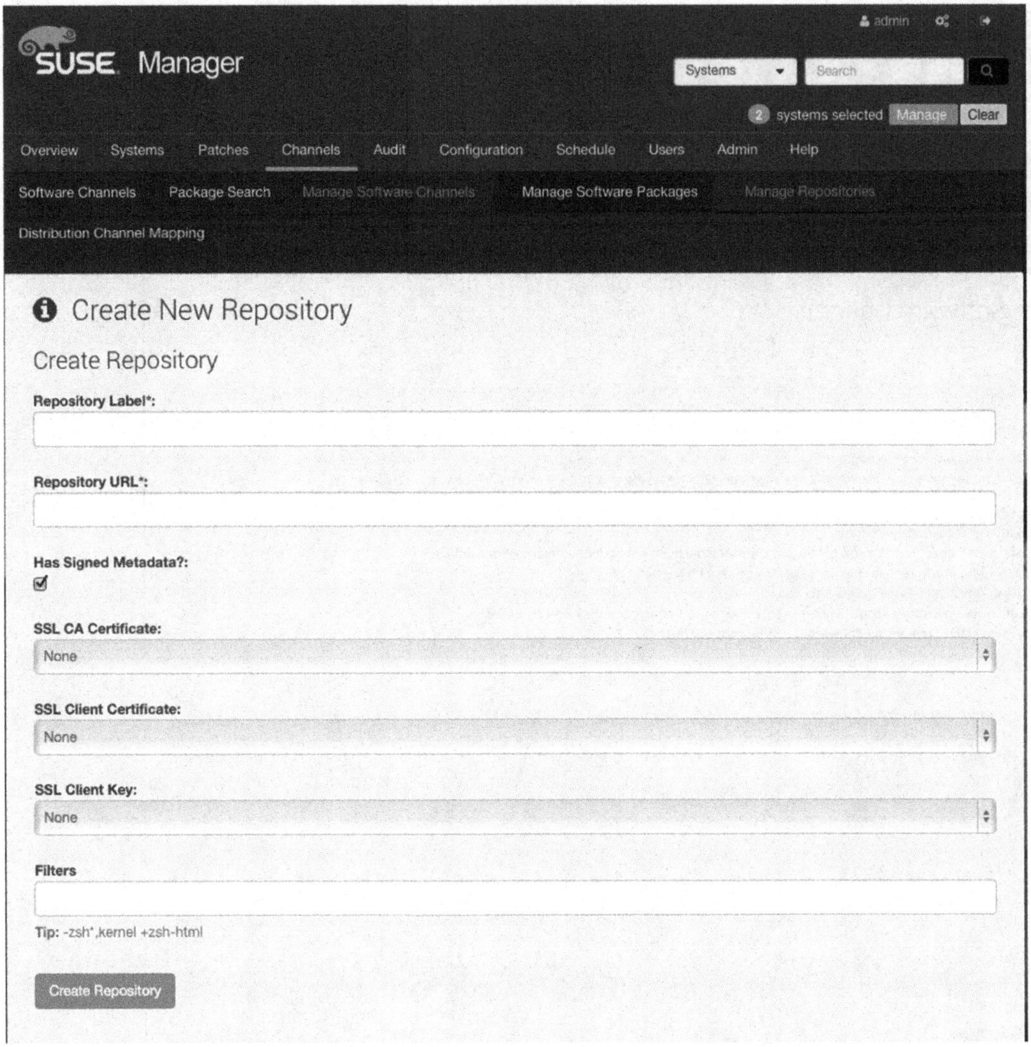

Figure 18-19. *Creating a repository*

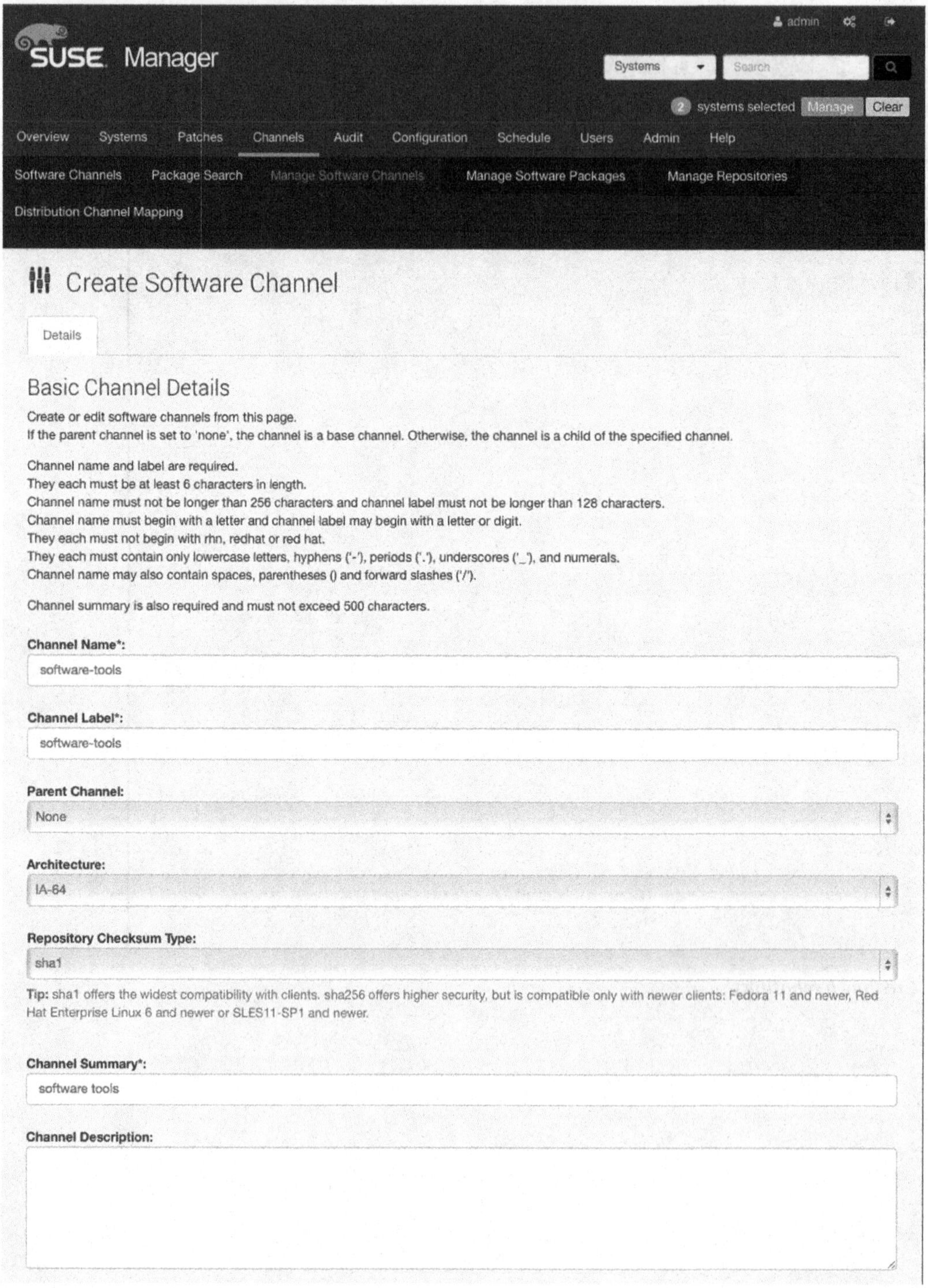

SUSE Manager

admin

Systems

Search

2 systems selected Manage Clear

Overview   Systems   Patches   Channels   Audit   Configuration   Schedule   Users   Admin   Help

Software Channels   Package Search   Manage Software Channels   Manage Software Packages   Manage Repositories

Distribution Channel Mapping

▌▌▌ Create Software Channel

| Details |

Basic Channel Details

Create or edit software channels from this page.
If the parent channel is set to 'none', the channel is a base channel. Otherwise, the channel is a child of the specified channel.

Channel name and label are required.
They each must be at least 6 characters in length.
Channel name must not be longer than 256 characters and channel label must not be longer than 128 characters.
Channel name must begin with a letter and channel label may begin with a letter or digit.
They each must not begin with rhn, redhat or red hat.
They each must contain only lowercase letters, hyphens ('-'), periods ('.'), underscores ('_'), and numerals.
Channel name may also contain spaces, parentheses () and forward slashes ('/').

Channel summary is also required and must not exceed 500 characters.

Channel Name*:

    software-tools

Channel Label*:

    software-tools

Parent Channel:

    None

Architecture:

    IA-64

Repository Checksum Type:

    sha1

Tip: sha1 offers the widest compatibility with clients. sha256 offers higher security, but is compatible only with newer clients: Fedora 11 and newer, Red Hat Enterprise Linux 6 and newer or SLES11-SP1 and newer.

Channel Summary*:

    software tools

Channel Description:

Figure 18-20. *Creating a software channel*

4. Continuing from the Manage Software Channels tab, click Repositories. This offers a list of all repositories existing on your system. Select the repository or repositories that you want to add to the channel and click Update Repositories, to confirm.

5. After adding a repository to the channel, you can now sync its contents and specify the synchronization frequency. This is the frequency at which updates are pushed to the subscribed clients. For an initial update, click Sync Now, which will start an immediate synchronization. You should notice that depending on the update mechanism you are using, it can take up to four hours before clients receive updates.

After a default registration of clients, they will use pull updates. That means that at four-hour intervals, the clients go to the SUSE Manager Server to fetch updates. If you want the clients to be more reactive, you should use osad (which is a Jabber client) and jabberd. The purpose is to keep clients updated in near real time. If these have been enabled, Manager will use the Jabber messaging protocol to send updates to the client. After receiving information about available updates, the client will use rhn_check, which fetches updates from the server. Using osad and jabberd makes your environment more reactive and is particularly recommended if you don't just want to install software packages and updates with SUSE Manager. It does, however, impose additional requirements to the network setup; you'll have to make sure that all of the ports these components require are open on the firewall.

After adding a channel, you can assign it to a system group, to make it available as a repository to the registered clients. To do this, apply the following procedure:

1. From the SUSE Manager interface, select Systems ➤ System Groups, and click the system group(s) you want to assign the channel(s) to.

2. After selecting the system group(s), click Work with Union. This opens the System Set Manager (see Figure 18-21).

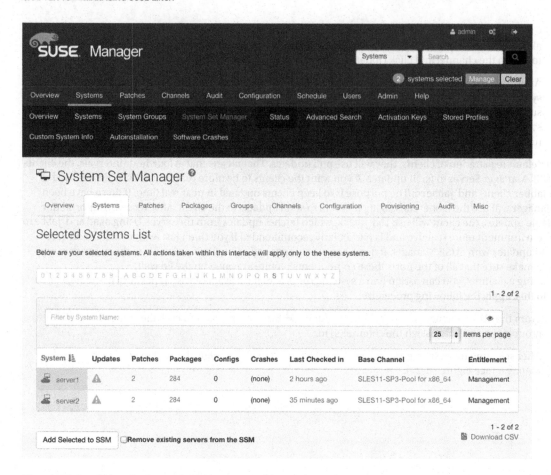

Figure 18-21. *Using the System Set Manager to add new channels to a system group*

3. From the System Set Manager, select Channels ➤ Child Channels and subscribe to the desired channels.

As an alternative method, you can add a software channel to an activation key. To do this, select Systems ➤ Activation Keys and click the activation key you want to assign the channel to. From here, you'll see a list of available channels. Ctrl+Click your selection of channels, to assign to the key.

As an alternative, you can add software channels to SUSE Manager from the command line. To do this, use the spacewalk-repo-sync -c <repo-name> -u <repo-url> command.

Understanding Software Staging

Staging is the process that can be used to ensure that only a specific state of software is installed. As an administrator of a large environment, you'll probably want to use staging, because it allows you to test software packages before installing them. In staging of software channels, typically, you would use four different channel states.

- *Vendor Software Channel*: The software as provided by the vendor

- *Development*: A frozen vendor channel from which changes can be applied

- *Testing*: A frozen development channel from which changes can be applied and fed back to the development cycle

- *Production*: A frozen testing channel

When using staging, it's a good idea to stick to the default naming that is used by SUSE, which consists of `<osrelease>-<type>-<arch>`. As, based on that, you would create stages for different system groups, it makes sense to add the system group name and the stage name to the channel name, which would bring names such as `sless11-sp3-updates-x86_64-web-01development`.

In staged channels, you can work with two different package types. A patch is an update that can apply to several packages at once. Patches are unique for each stage and contain the modifications in a specific stage. They don't have to be cloned through all the stages but merely contain differences between stages. A package is a complete state of a package in the way you want to have it in a specific stage. Managing patches can make managing staged channels easier, as it contains only the modifications in a package, as compared to the upper layer stage. When using complete packages, you could end up with a different version of a package in every single stage, which makes managing it more difficult, especially if you have many packages.

To implement staging in SUSE Manager, you can work with cloned channels. All cloned channels are created as custom channels, which means that there are more management options for them. When creating clones of a channel, three approaches are possible.

- Clone the current state of a channel.

- Clone the original state of a channel.

- Select patches only.

To clone a channel, you can use the Manage Software Channels tab in the web interface. From there, click Clone channel. This opens the window that you see in Figure 18-22. From that window, in the Clone From drop-down list, select the channel that you want to clone. Next, select which type of clone you want to create. This opens the Edit Software Channel window, which is the same window that you have seen when creating a new channel. As a minimum requirement, on this window, you have to enter a unique channel name and label. Next, click Create channel, to create the cloned channel.

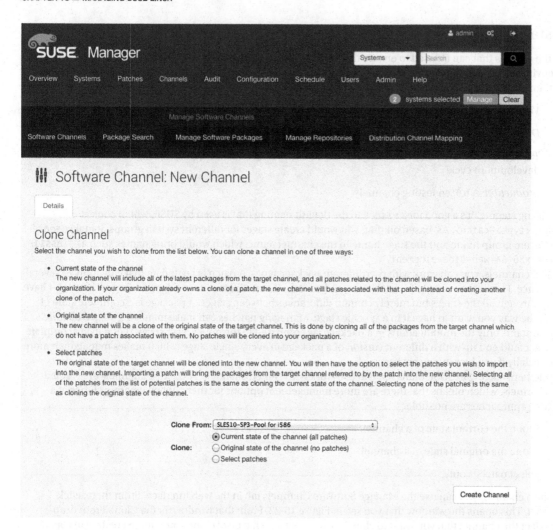

Figure 18-22. Cloning a software channel

You can also create a cloned channel by using the spacewalk-clone-by-date tool. This tool is available in the spacewalk-utils package, so use zypper in spacewalk-utils to install this package first. Next, you can use this tool to clone a channel up to the date it had on a specific date. This will include all patches up to that date, as well as the dependencies of those patches.

To clone a channel as it is on a specific date, you can use this `spacewalk-clone-by-date` command, as follows: `spacewalk-clone-by-date --username=admin --password=secret --server=smgr.example.com --channels=sles11-sp3-updates-x86_64 my-sles-clone --to_date=2014-08-08`. You can also be much more specific and, for example, only clone security data, while excluding the kernel package as well as `vsftp`, by using the command that follows: `spacewalk-clone-by-date --username=admin --password=secret --server=smgr.example.com --channels=sles11-sp3-updates-x86_64 my-sles-clone --to_date=2014-08-08 --security_only --background --blacklist=kernel,vsftpd --assumeyes`.

Patching and Updating Systems

When all channels are in place, you can start the real work and apply patches and updates with SUSE Manager. SUSE Manager also allows you to push packages for installation to systems. In this section, you'll read how this works.

Using OSA Dispatcher

To push software to registered servers, you need the OSA Dispatcher. This service is used to send messages via `jabberd` on the server to the `osad` instances that have to be installed with the `osa-dispatcher` package on clients. Once installed, you can run the `service osa-dispatcher start` command to make the service available on clients.

Once the `osad` service is running on your clients' servers, you can push install packages to them. To do this, you have to select the registered system to which you want to push the package from the SUSE Manager web interface. Next select Software ➤ Packages ➤ Install (see Figure 18-23), and from the list of packages that are available in the repositories, select the package or packages you want to install. Next, select Install Selected Packages.

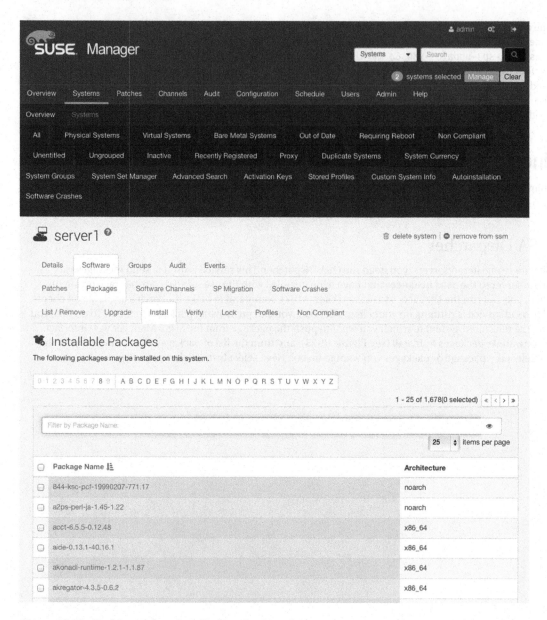

Figure 18-23. *Pushing package installation to registered servers*

You'll now see a window from which you can schedule package installation. Here, you can either specify a date and time when package installation may begin or select the option Add to Action Chain, which allows you to schedule installation when a specific event occurs (see Figure 18-24).

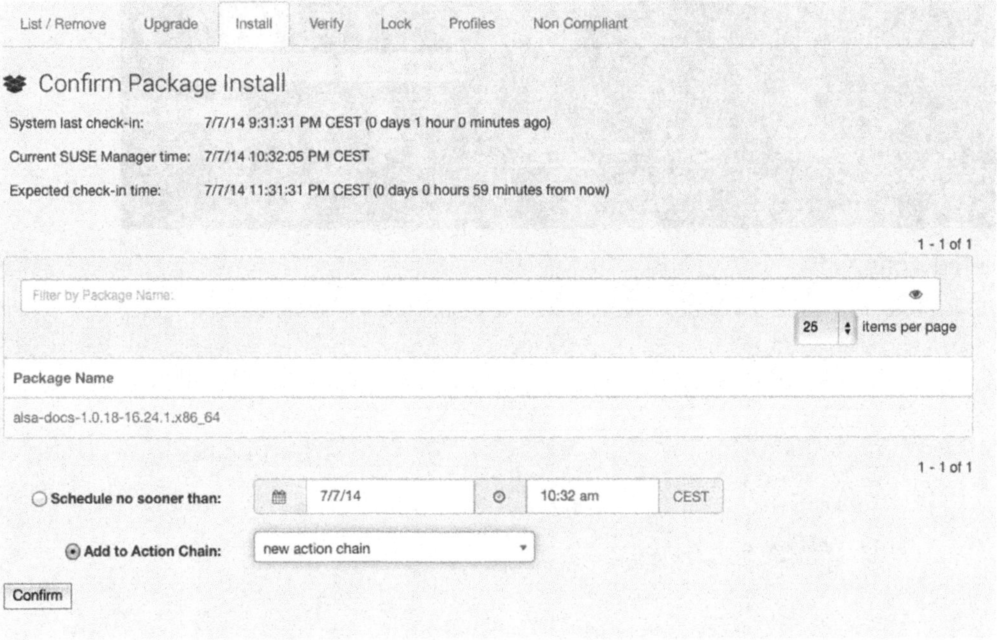

List / Remove   Upgrade   Install   Verify   Lock   Profiles   Non Compliant

🦋 Confirm Package Install

System last check-in: 7/7/14 9:31:31 PM CEST (0 days 1 hour 0 minutes ago)

Current SUSE Manager time: 7/7/14 10:32:05 PM CEST

Expected check-in time: 7/7/14 11:31:31 PM CEST (0 days 0 hours 59 minutes from now)

1 - 1 of 1

Filter by Package Name:	👁

25 ⬍ items per page

Package Name

alsa-docs-1.0.18-16.24.1.x86_64

1 - 1 of 1

○ **Schedule no sooner than:**   📅 7/7/14   🕐 10:32 am   CEST

◉ **Add to Action Chain:**   new action chain ▼

Confirm

Figure 18-24. *Specifying when to install the package*

Instead of pushing packages to an individual server, you can also install packages to a system group, using the System Set Manager. To do this, from the Systems tab, select System Set Manager. Next, select Packages ➤ Install. This shows the channels that are available to systems in this systems group. Select the channel and, next, click the package(s) you want to push to systems in that system group and click Install Packages. You'll now see a window from which you can select the schedule you want to apply and confirm package installation.

To confirm that a package has been successfully installed, from the web interface, select Schedule ➤ Completed Actions. Here, you should see the status of the action that has been executed, as in Figure 18-25.

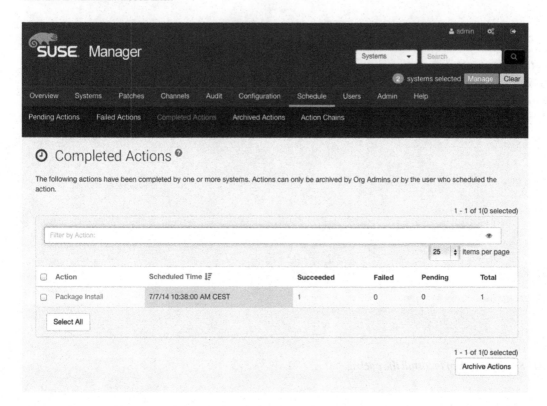

Figure 18-25. *Verifying successful package installation*

In the previous section, you read how to install packages on selected systems. To install patches, you can follow a similar approach. The only difference is that after selecting the system or System Set Manager, you will now select Software ➤ Patches and select the patches you want to install.

Managing Configuration with SUSE Manager

By using configuration management, you can run remote operations on registered servers. This allows you to do a few useful things.

- Deploy a configuration file on the system
- Upload a file from the system
- Compare what is currently managed on a system with what is available
- Run remote commands

When working with centrally managed configuration channels and files, you can make sure that changes to a single file are copied to all systems. To do this, systems need a provisioning entitlement and a local configuration channel. Even if configuration files are centrally managed, you can still use local management of configuration files, by employing individual system profiles. These will always override centrally managed configuration files on particular systems. To prepare systems for configuration file channels, make sure that the following `rhncfg` packages are installed:

- `rhncfg`
- `rhncfg-actions`
- `rhncfg-client`
- `rhncfg-management`

In addition, make sure to enable configuration file deployment in the activation key. Don't forget to click Update Key after selecting the Configuration File Deployment option. Without this option, you won't be able to add the channel to selected systems.

To create a configuration channel in the web interface, select Configuration ➤ Configuration Channels. Next, click Create new config channel, to add the channel. As with normal channels, you now must enter a name and a label for the configuration channel, as well as a description. Then click Create Config Channel, to add the channel to your configuration.

After creating the channel, you can add configuration files. The easiest way to do that is to upload a file from the computer on which you're running the web interface. Alternatively, you can also import files from other machines or use Create File, to create your own files. When working with configuration files, you can specify all properties of the files in the window shown in Figure 18-26.

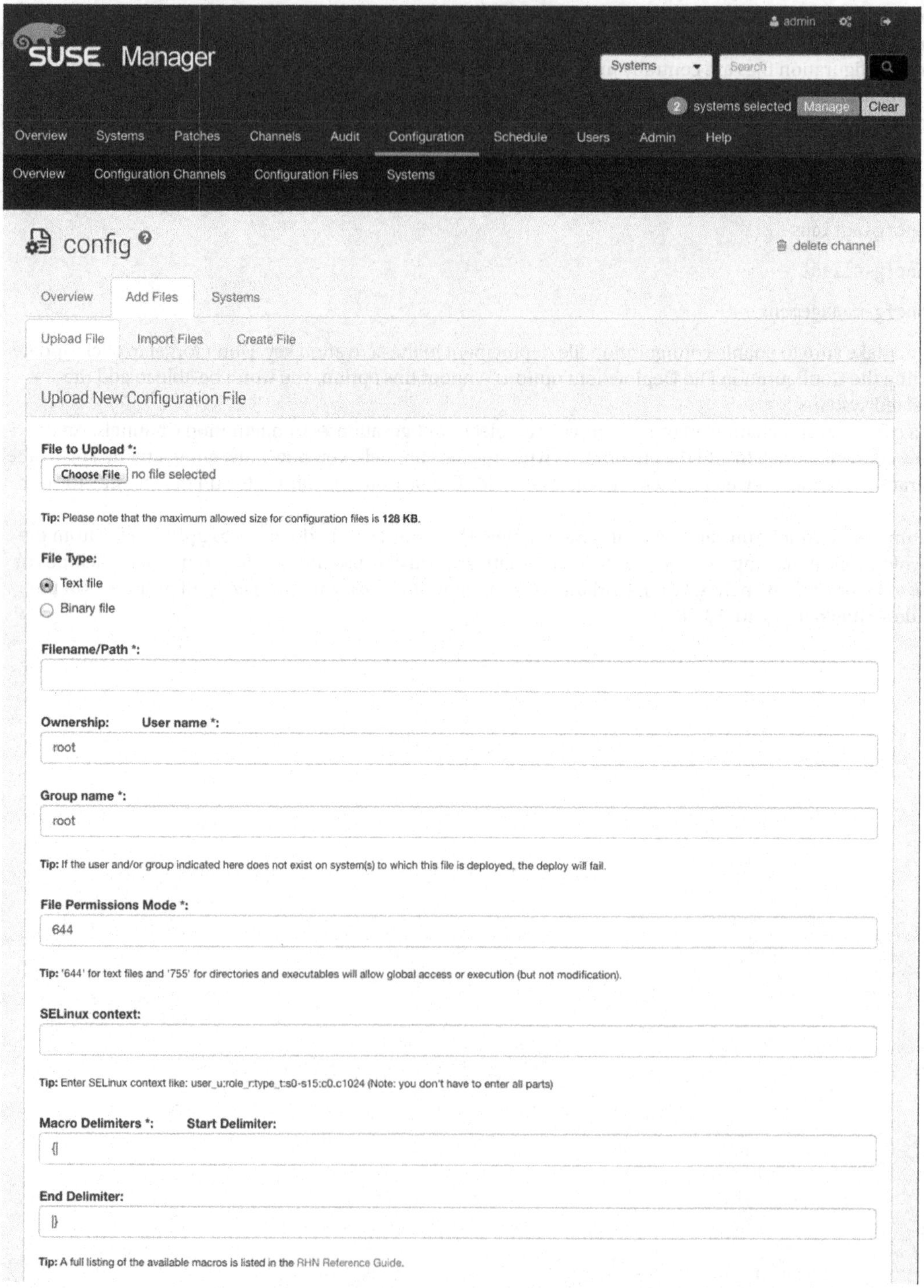

Figure 18-26. Adding a configuration file

After adding a file to the channel, you can manage its properties as well as its version. Among other options, this allows you to manage revisions of the configuration file, which makes it easy to roll back to a previous state (see Figure 18-27).

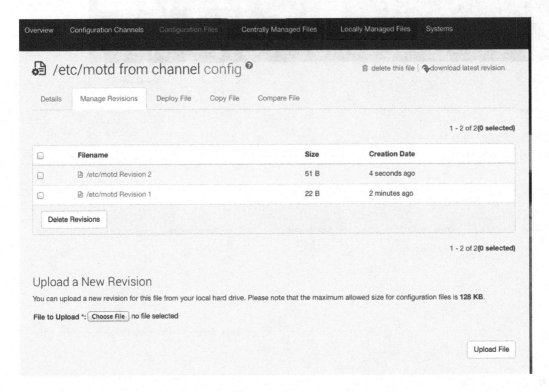

Figure 18-27. *Working with configuration file revisions*

To subscribe systems to configuration channels, you can use the System Set Manager. From the web interface, select Systems ➤ System Set Manager ➤ Configuration ➤ Subscribe to Channels. From here, select the configuration channel you want systems to subscribe to. This brings you to an interface from which you can see all configuration channels currently associated to the system set. From this interface, you can rank channels, A channel that is listed higher has higher priority and will overwrite files from channels that are listed lower.

Instead of connecting the configuration channel to individual systems or a systems group, you can also connect it to an activation key. Select Systems ➤ Activation Keys ➤ Configuration ➤ List/Unsubscribe from Channels and select the channel you want to subscribe this key to. If it takes too long for the systems to pick up the new configuration, you can re-register them by running the bootstrap script again. This will force them to refresh their configuration.

Once you have systems that are configured to use the configuration channel, you can deploy files on them. To do this, from the web management interface, select Configuration ➤ Configuration channels and select your configuration channel. On the window shown in Figure 18-28, click Deploy Files. Next, you can make a selection of files you want to deploy or just click Deploy All Files, to deploy all files to the selected systems.

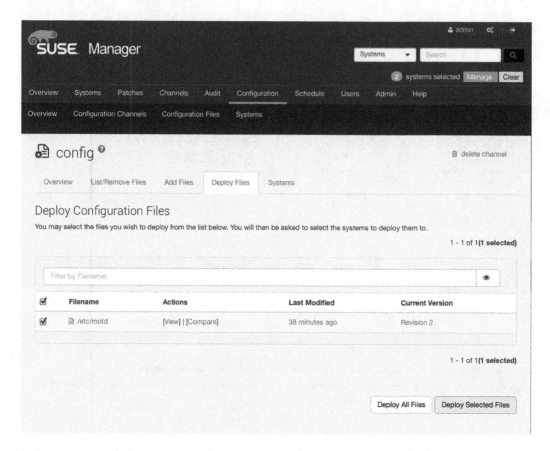

Figure 18-28. *Deploying files*

Auto-Installation of Systems

You can use SUSE Manager perfectly well to manage existing systems. You can also use it to install new systems. To do this, you must make sure that the installation files are available in SUSE Manager and that a boot image can be provided, as well as an `autoyast` file that provides the settings that are to be used during the installation.

The first step in preparing your SUSE Manager for auto-installation is to make the installation ISO of the distribution you want to install available on the SUSE Manager Server. To do this, copy it to a location on the SUSE Manager Server and next, use `mkdir /install`, to create a directory on which you can mount it. Next, type `mount -o loop /sles11sp3.iso /install` to loop mount it and make all files on it available.

After making the installation ISO available, you can create an auto-installable distribution in SUSE Manager. To do this, select Systems ➤ Autoinstallation ➤ Distributions and select Create new distribution, in the upper-right corner. You'll now see the window that you see in Figure 18-29. Here, enter the following information:

- *Distribution Label*: SLES11-SP3-x86_64 (This is an identifier for the distribution you want to install).

- *Tree Path*: This is the directory in which the installation media is mounted—`/install`, in the case of this example.

- *Base Channel*: This is the base channel that contains all packages as downloaded from SCC and which you have created earlier in this chapter. Select it from the drop-down list.

- *Installer Generation*: Select the operating system you want to install from the drop-down list.

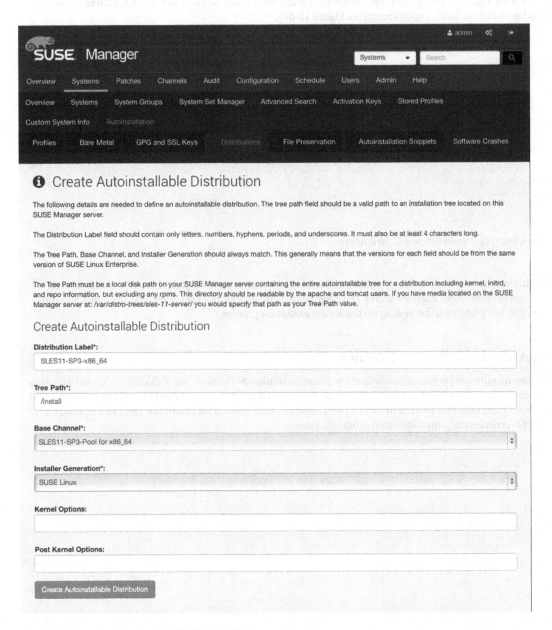

Figure 18-29. *Create Autoinstallable Distribution settings*

After filling these mandatory fields, click Create Autoinstallable Distribution. In the confirmation, you will see whether or not the distribution has been created as a valid distribution.

When the distribution is created, the kernel options will have been modified to include an installation path. By default, this path uses the DNS name of the SUSE Manager Server. This will only work if DNS has been configured correctly. If this is not the case, you should replace the DNS name with the IP address of the SUSE Manager Server. Next, click Update Autoinstallable Distribution (see Figure 18-30).

Installer Generation*:

SUSE Linux

Kernel Options:

install=http://192.168.4.180/ks/dist/SLES11-SP3-x86_64

Post Kernel Options:

Update Autoinstallable Distribution

Figure 18-30. *Updating Autoinstallable Distribution*

At this point, you have created an auto-installable distribution. That is not sufficient, however. You must still create a DHCP Server that works together with a TFTP Server, to provide PXE boot services. You also need an auto-installation profile. Let's first focus on setting up the auto-installation profiles.

Creating Auto-Installation Profiles

To create an auto-installation profile, select Systems ➤ Autoinstallation ➤ Upload New Kickstart/AutoYaST file. This option allows you to import an existing AutoYaST file that contains all the settings required to perform an automated installation. From the screen that you see in Figure 18-31, enter a label, select a Kickstartable Tree, and upload an AutoYaST file. This creates the autoinstallation profile for you.

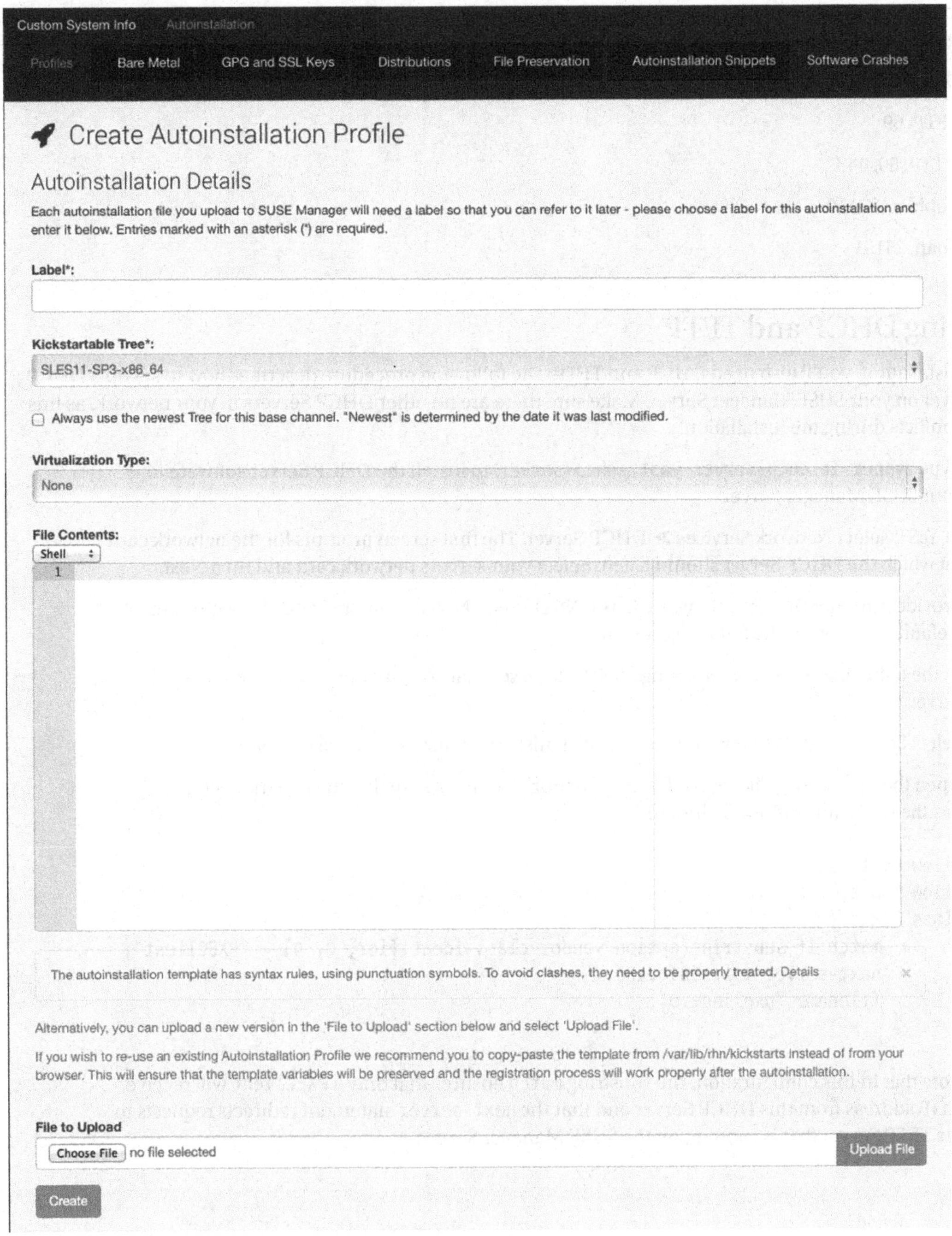

Profiles   Bare Metal   GPG and SSL Keys   Distributions   File Preservation   Autoinstallation Snippets   Software Crashes

🚀 Create Autoinstallation Profile

Autoinstallation Details

Each autoinstallation file you upload to SUSE Manager will need a label so that you can refer to it later - please choose a label for this autoinstallation and enter it below. Entries marked with an asterisk (*) are required.

Label*:

Kickstartable Tree*:

SLES11-SP3-x86_64

☐ Always use the newest Tree for this base channel. "Newest" is determined by the date it was last modified.

Virtualization Type:

None

File Contents:

Shell ▾

1

The autoinstallation template has syntax rules, using punctuation symbols. To avoid clashes, they need to be properly treated. Details   ✕

Alternatively, you can upload a new version in the 'File to Upload' section below and select 'Upload File'.

If you wish to re-use an existing Autoinstallation Profile we recommend you to copy-paste the template from /var/lib/rhn/kickstarts instead of from your browser. This will ensure that the template variables will be preserved and the registration process will work properly after the autoinstallation.

File to Upload

Choose File   no file selected   Upload File

Create

Figure 18-31. Creating an autoinstallation profile

Before continuing, make sure that all of the required ports in the firewall are open to use provisioning. The following ports are required:

- DHCP: 67
- TFTP: 69
- HTTP: 80, 443
- Cobbler: 25150
- Koan: 25151

Configuring DHCP and TFTP

To use auto-installation, you'll also need DHCP and TFTP. The following procedure describes how to set up a DHCP and TFTP Server on your SUSE Manager Server. Make sure there are no other DHCP Servers in your network, as this may lead to conflicts during the installation!

1. Type `zypper in dhcp-server yast2-dhcp-server`, to install the DHCP Server software to your SUSE Manager Server.

2. In YaST, select Network Services ➤ DHCP Server. The first screen prompts for the network card on which the DHCP Server should listen. Select your servers network card and then Next.

3. Provide minimal DHCP options, such as DNS Domain Name, Primary Name Server IP, and Default Gateway, in the following screen.

4. In the following screen, enter a range of IP addresses that you want to hand out with this server.

5. Select Service Start When Booting and click Finish, to finalize DHCP Server setup.

6. Open the file `/etc/dhcpd.conf` with an editor, and make sure that the generic section has the following options included:

```
allow booting;
allow bootp;
class "PXE" {
        match if substring(option vendor-class-identifier, 0, 9) = "PXEClient";
        next-server 192.168.4.180;
        filename "pxelinux.0";
}
```

Note that in this configuration, the substring `match` ensures that only a `PXEClient` will receive an IP address from this DHCP Server and that the `next-server` statement redirects requests to the TFTP Server that is running on the SUSE Manager Server.

7. TFTP is configured automatically, so you don't have to perform additional steps for that part of the configuration.

8. Use `service dhcpd start; insserv dhcpd`, to start and enable the DHCP Server.

9. Type `/usr/sbin/spacewalk-service stop`, followed by `/usr/sbin/spacewalk-service start`, to restart the SUSE Manager services.

At this point, all is ready, and you should be able to start the auto-installation of machines through SUSE Manager.

Using SUSE Manager Monitoring

If you've purchased a monitoring entitlement, you can monitor aspects of registered systems in SUSE Manager. In this section, you'll learn how to set up monitoring.

SUSE Manager Preparation

To set up monitoring, you'll have to enable it on the SUSE Manager Server first. To do this, from the SUSE Manager web interface, select Admin ➤ SUSE Manager Configuration ➤ General and click the Enable Monitoring option. Next, click Update, to write the settings to your system (see also Figure 18-32).

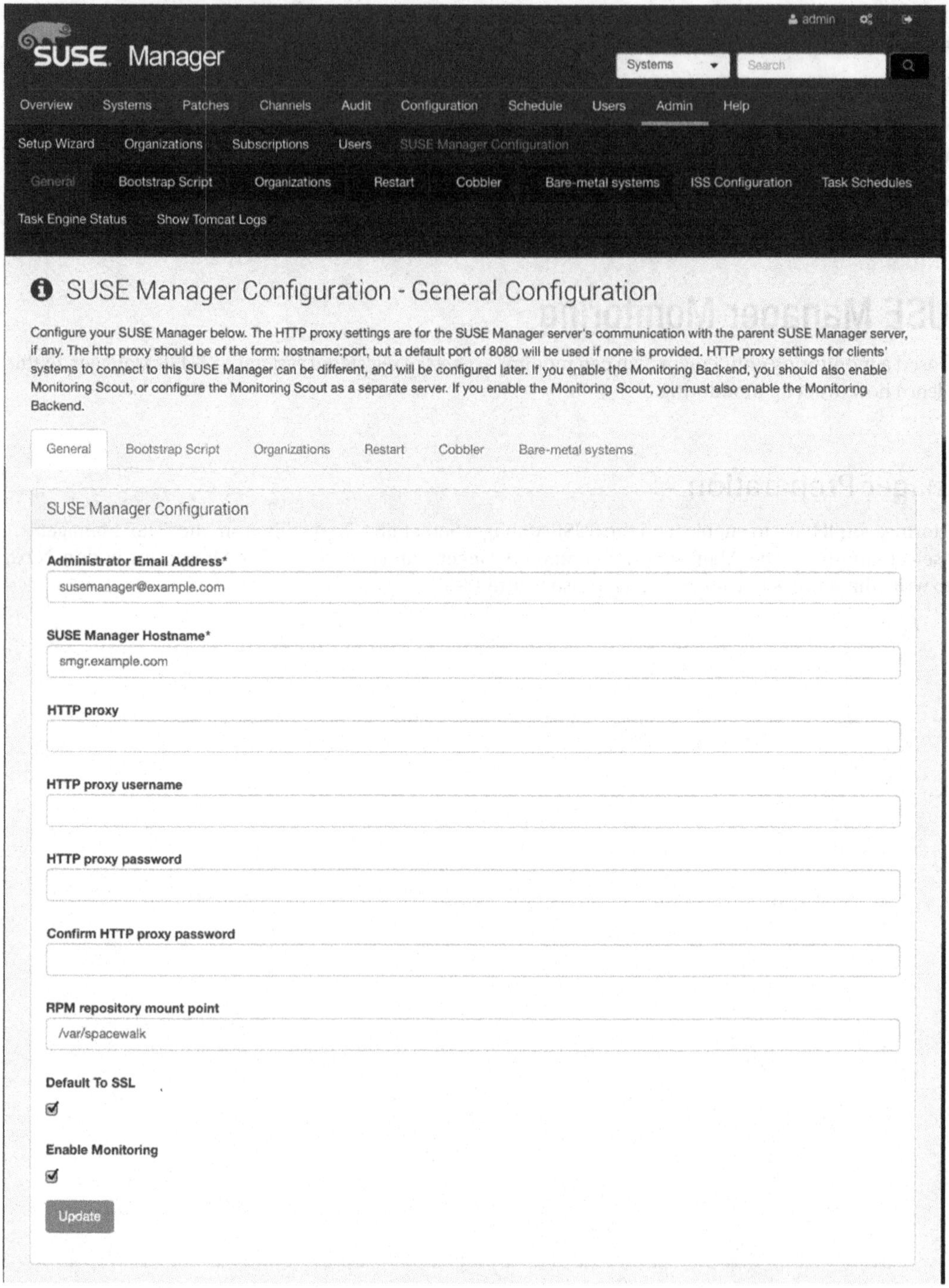

Figure 18-32. *Before using monitoring, you must enable it*

After enabling monitoring, you receive a message stating that SUSE Manager must be restarted to reflect these changes. At this point, restart. Next, you have to enable the monitoring scout. From the SUSE Manager web interface, select Admin ➤ SUSE Manager Configuration ➤ Monitoring. This opens the screen shown in Figure 18-33. Click Enable Monitoring Scout and specify all attributes you want to use for monitoring, such as the administrator e-mail address. Next, click Update Config to write the updated configuration to your system. This writes settings and enabled monitoring services.

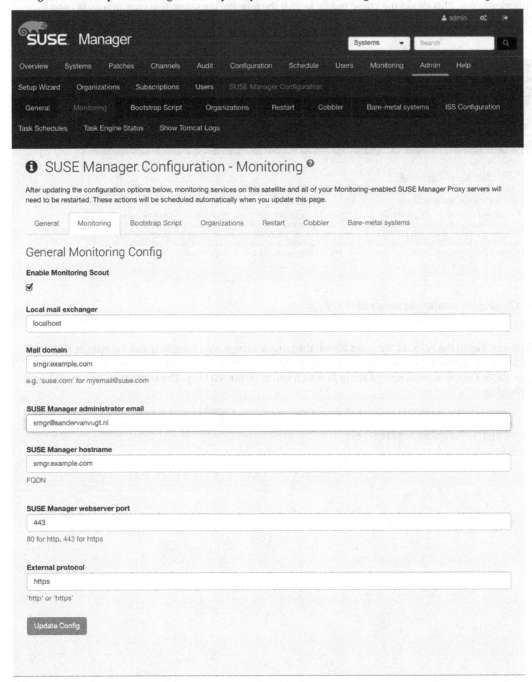

Figure 18-33. *Enabling the monitoring scout*

Preparing the Registered Servers for Monitoring

Now that on the SUSE Manager Server you have prepared all you need to perform monitoring operations, you have to prepare the registered servers as well. The first step consists of making the server available for monitoring. To do this, you have to copy SSH keys to the clients. To do this, select Monitoring ➤ Scout Config Push and select the SUSE Manager Monitoring Scout. This shows the rhnmd public key for the monitoring scout. Use your mouse to copy it (see Figure 18-34).

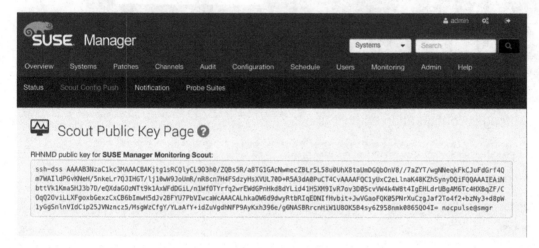

Figure 18-34. *Copying the monitoring scout public key*

To get the public key in the authorized_keys file on the remote system, you have to select the remote system from the SUSE Manager web interface. Next, select Details ➤ Remote Command, which brings you to the screen shown in Figure 18-35. On this screen, enter a script in which you copy the SSH key. The content of the script should look like the following:

```
#!/bin/sh
cat <<EOF >> ~nocpulse/.ssh/authorized_keys
COPY-THE-KEY-HERE
EOF
```

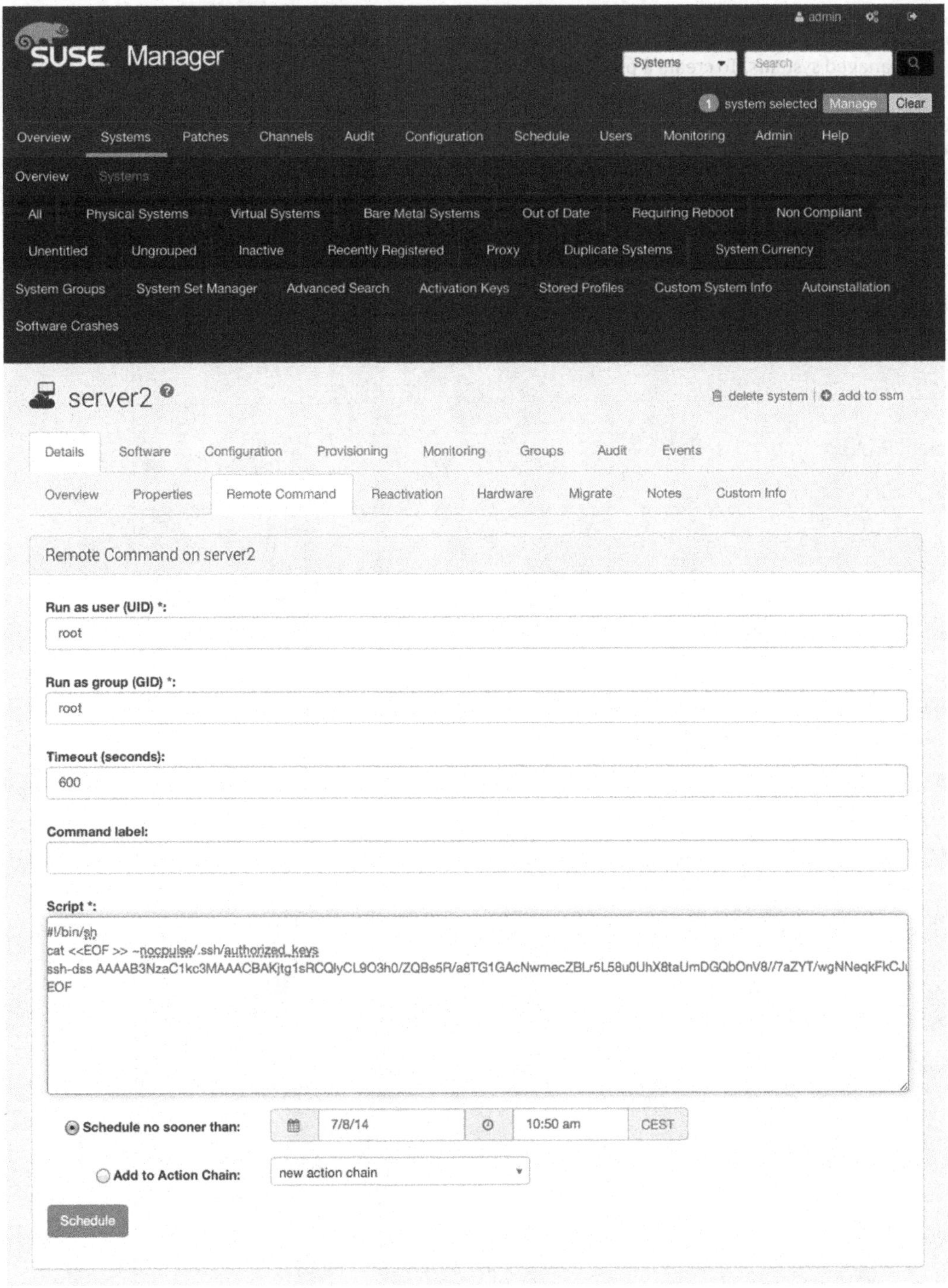

Figure 18-35. *Installing the SSH key by using a* remote command

Next, click Schedule, to schedule the script for execution on the remote server.

After copying the SSH key to the registered nodes, you can configure a probe. Probes define what exactly you want to do on the managed systems. To create a probe, select a system. On that system, select Monitoring and click Create probe. This brings up the window shown in Figure 18-36. This window provides access to a number of monitoring options. From the drop-down list, you'll first select the command group you want to use. Command groups are available for specific services (such as Apache, MySQL, and more), and you can select generic command groups, such as Linux or SUSE Manager. After selecting a command group, you have to select a specific command that is predefined in that particular command group. Next, scroll down the screen and specify monitoring parameters for that specific command.

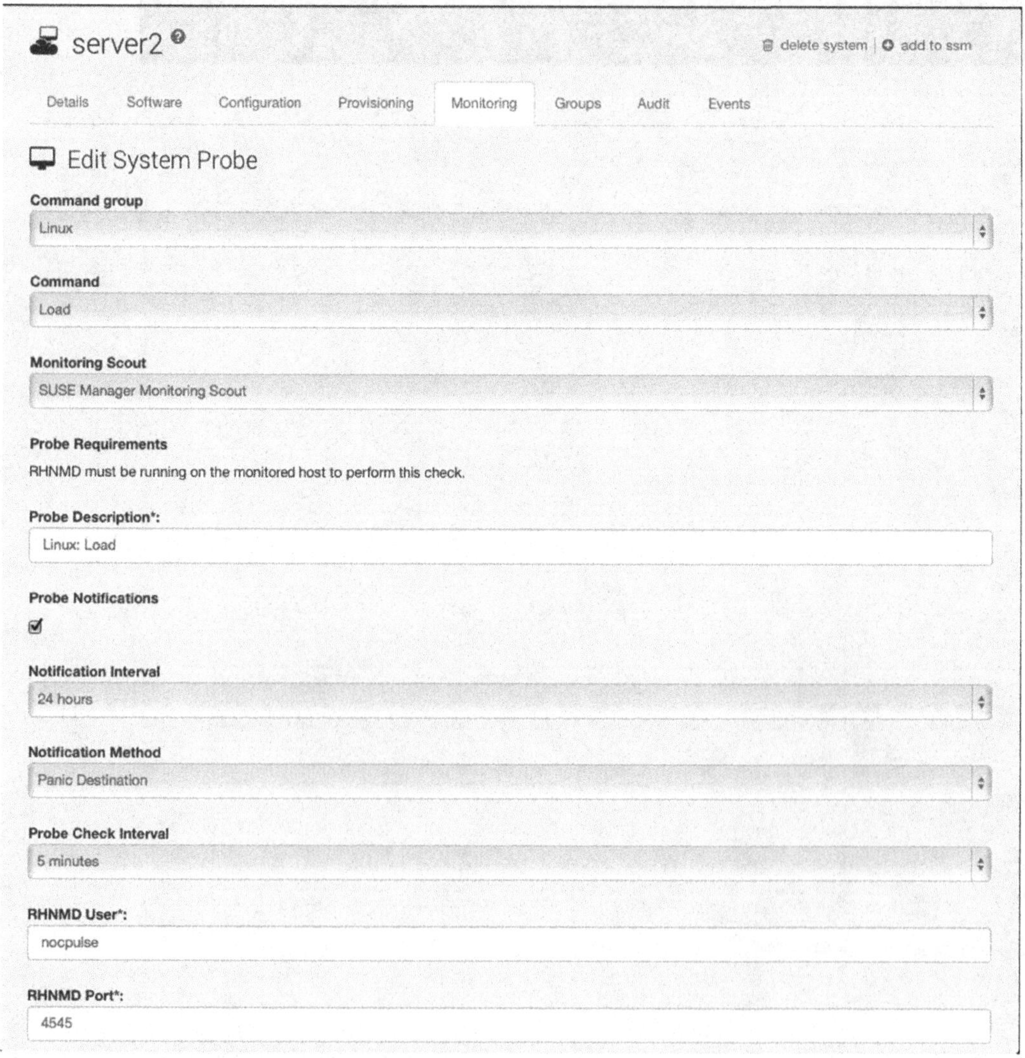

Figure 18-36. *Defining a probe*

When working with probes, you have the option to use probe notifications. Without these, you'll be able to monitor events from the SUSE Manager interface. With probe notifications, you can define how often and where you want notifications to be delivered. Even if it may sound tempting, you may want to think twice before configuring these, because configuring probe notifications wrongly may result in your being overwhelmed with monitoring messages. So, you probably don't want to use them. Don't forget to click Create Probe, after entering all probe parameters. This adds the probe to your configuration and makes it operational.

After creating the probe in SUSE Manager, you have to push it to the registered systems. To do this, select the Monitoring tab in the SUSE Manager web interface and click Scout Config Push. Select the scouts you want to distribute and click Push Scout Configs. This will use the SSH channel to push the probe to all registered systems (see Figure 18-37).

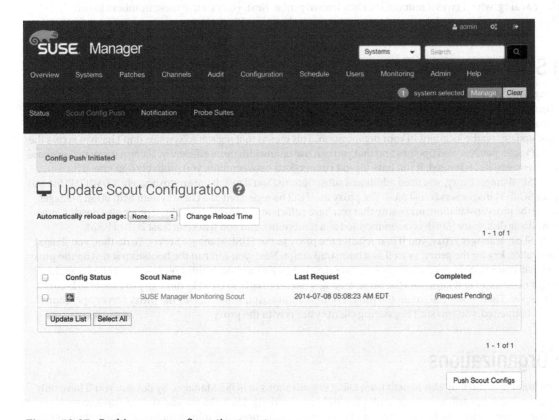

Figure 18-37. *Pushing scout configuration to systems*

Once the probe has been added, you can select it from the monitoring tab on a selected server. It will provide an update about its current status and offers the option to generate a report. From the probe report, you get easy access to the statistics related to this probe.

Analyzing Monitoring

To have monitoring working properly, there are a few settings that must be available on the client. First, this is the rhnmd process, so make sure that it is installed and running. If it is, you should also find a directory with the name /var/lib/nocpulse. This is the home directory for the monitoring user.

If the rhnmd process is running, the next step is to verify that it can be accessed. For access to the monitoring daemon, port 4545 must be accessible. On the SUSE Manager Server, you should find two parameters in the /etc/rhn/rhn.conf file. These are web.is_monitoring_scout = 1 and web.is_monitoring_backend = 1. If all these are available, monitoring should be operational.

If you're still experiencing problems, you can analyze the situation a bit more in depth on the server. Look in the /var/log/rhn/nocpulse file for errors. Also, to become the monitoring user, you can use su - nocpulse on the server and run rhn-catalog, which gives a number for each known probe. Next, you can use these numbers to run rhn-catalog --commandline --dump n to dump information about specific probes.

Using SUSE Manager Proxy

If you're using SUSE Manager in a multisite environment, there are basically two options. The first option is to create multiple organizations and use one organization per site. An organization is a more or less independent configuration of SUSE Manager. The other option is to use SUSE Manager Proxy. The purpose of using SUSE Manager Proxy is to cache packages and updates on the locations in your organization. This means that registered systems don't have to access the WAN to get packages, patches, and updates and that you can use bandwidth more efficiently. Using a proxy makes sense if bandwidth between sites is limited. If you have gigabit connections between sites, you probably don't need it.

To use SUSE Manager Proxy, you need additional subscriptions. You'll install the approximately 300MB ISO file and connect it to a SUSE Manager Server instance. The proxy itself will be registered as a client system with SUSE Manager. Before starting the proxy installation, make sure that you have sufficient resources. Typically, a proxy also needs a large amount of available disk space (50GB is recommended as a minimum), and you'll need at least 2GB of RAM.

To set up SUSE Manager Proxy, you'll first register the proxy to the SUSE Manager Server. To do that, you'll need a specific activation key for the proxy, as well as a bootstrap script. Next, you can run the bootstrap script on the proxy server, which will enter it in the registered systems overview in SUSE Manager. At this point, you can copy over the SUSE Manager certificates and keys from the SUSE Manager Server /root/ssl-build directory to /root/ssl-build on the proxy server. That allows you to run the proxy configuration script, which makes the proxy server operational. When that has happened, you can start registering client systems with the proxy.

Using Organizations

In a large environment, you may also benefit from using organizations in SUSE Manager. By default, you'll have only one organization, but it's possible to create multiple child organizations. The software and system entitlement for your company are assigned to the base organization, and the child organizations will inherit them. Administration of child organizations can be delegated to other users (who, of course, must be created from the SUSE Manager interface).

Creating an organization is not difficult. From the SUSE Manager web interface, under Admin ➤ Organizations, you'll create the organization. Next, you have to add SUSE Manager entitlements, as well as software entitlements, to the organization. Once this is done, you can create activation keys and corresponding bootstrap scripts, to start registering systems at the organization.

Summary

In this chapter, you have learned how to configure SUSE Manager. You have worked your way through the different kinds of functionality that are offered by SUSE Manager and have read how to use it to manage software, monitor systems, and much more.

Index

■ R

■ S

Get the eBook for only $10!

Now you can take the weightless companion with you anywhere, anytime. Your purchase of this book entitles you to 3 electronic versions for only $10.

This Apress title will prove so indispensible that you'll want to carry it with you everywhere, which is why we are offering the eBook in 3 formats for only $10 if you have already purchased the print book.

Convenient and fully searchable, the PDF version enables you to easily find and copy code—or perform examples by quickly toggling between instructions and applications. The MOBI format is ideal for your Kindle, while the ePUB can be utilized on a variety of mobile devices.

Go to www.apress.com/promo/tendollars to purchase your companion eBook.